CH00925756

Dubai

Residents' Guide

there's more to life...
ask**explorer**.com

Making
your mov
in tandem

Starting life in a new country with your significant other means sharing experiences. Spend more time creating meaningful memories and less time worrying about the move. Trust Allied Pickfords to make your move simpler, seamless and stress-free. Relax, we carry the load.

Call us now
+971.2.677.9765 (Abu Dhabi),
+971.4.818.0400 (Dubai)
www.alliedpickfords.ae

RESPECTED GLOBALLY PREFERED LOCALLY

MEDICLINIC MIDDLE EAST OPERATES:

- Mediclinic Welcare Hospital
- Mediclinic Dubai Mall
- Mediclinic Meadows
- Mediclinic Mirdif
- Mediclinic Beach Road
- Mediclinic Corniche
- Mediclinic City Hospital
- Mediclinic Ibn Battuta
- Mediclinic Arabian Ranches
- Mediclinic Al Qusais
- Mediclinic Al Sufouh
- Mediclinic Al Hili

EXPERTISE YOU CAN TRUST.

UAE • SOUTH AFRICA • NAMIBIA • SWITZERLAND
www.mediclinic.ae

ميديكلينيك
MEDICLINIC

نادي الجولف والرماية   GOLF & SHOOTING CLUB
الشارقة   SHARJAH

PRACTICE TARGET SHOOTING WITH REAL GUNS & REAL BULLETS

A COMPLETE
SHOOTING COURSE
WITH COURSE CERTIFICATE

INDOOR SHOOTING & ARCHARY RANGE - OUTDOOR AIR RIFLE SHOOTING RANGE - GARDEN ARCHERY RANGE

For more information, please call 050 524 8777

P.O. Box 12, Sharjah, UAE, Tel: +971 6 5487777, Fax: +971 6 5382305
Email: shooting@golfandshootingshj.com, URL:
www.golfandshootingshj.com

Dubai Duty Free

Stylish designer bags
Irresistible fragrances
Glamorous sunglasses
One way to have it all

TRAVEL LIGHT
Shop at Dubai Duty Free

www.dubaidutyfree.com

 Full of surprises.

YAS ISLAND YOUR TICKET TO A WORLD OF MAGIC

HABA®

Mircoscope tower

Building blocks

Scooters

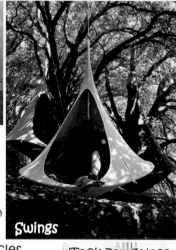

Swings

Sensory snail

Tricycles

Tack zap games

Creative sets

Ball track

Dolls & accessories

Sorting boxes

Puzzles

kidz inc.®

Shop Location: Al Quoz Industrial 1,
4B Street beside 'Lime Tree Cafe'
www.kidzincdubai.com
info@kidzincdubai.com
T +971 4 328 5775

AFRICAN + EASTERN STORES ARE ALL OVER TOWN!

And where there's African + Eastern, there's always an extensive portfolio of labels across ales, grape, malt and more from all over the world. Visit your nearest neighbourhood store for all the brands you love.

For more information call us on **800 CHEERS** (243377) or ask our staff in-store.

Al Wasl Road* · Arabian Ranches* · Bur Dubai* · Burj Views* · Deira* · Dubai Marina Mall*
Dubai Marina Walk* · Green Community** · Jumeirah* · Karama · Le Méridien Dubai** · Mirdif · TECOM*

*Stores also open on Fridays from 2:00pm - 9:00pm
**Stores open Saturday to Thursday from 2:00pm - 9:00pm

african eastern
INSPIRING GREAT BLENDS

an 'out of the world'
experience awaits...

For the latest updates   **Dreamland Aqua Park**
Umm Al Quwain, Etihad Road E11 through Mohammad Bin Zayed Road (E311)
or Emirates Road (E611), Exit 103, Tel: 06 7681888
Fridays and Public Holidays are reserved for families, pre-booked groups or special pass holders

www.dreamlanduae.com

Full Moon Desert Drumming

Come and join the amazing combined energy of drumming together under the full moon with friendly people and the earthy feel of the desert.

Join Dubai's Drumming crowd, connect with your inner rhythms and de-stress and "chillax!"

Corporate Team Building Events
Community Events
Staff Parties & Celebrations
Full Moon Desert Drumming
New Year Desert Drumming
Kidz Birthday Parties & Adult Parties
School & University Workshops
African Djembe Drum Classes
Summer Camp For Kids

Anchor your company's vision create synergy improve communications.

Leave a positive, lasting impression that people will talk about for months to come.

Corporate Team Building

UAE's first and foremost company for uniting teams and communities through rhythm based events for the past 13 years'

Contact: Dubai Drums 04 347 4790 / 056 744 2129
Dubai Drums, Al Qouz Industrial 4,
Street 17, Warehouse no. 2
P.O.Box 73102, Dubai
Email: fullmoon@dubaidrums.com
Website: www.dubaidrums.com

نحو مستقبل
مستدام لطائر الحبارى

TOWARDS A SUSTAINABLE
FUTURE FOR THE HOUBARA BUSTARD

INTERNATIONAL FUND FOR
HOUBARA CONSERVATION

www.houbarafund.org

VALUE SO EPIC YOU'LL NAME YOUR NEXT CHILD TOUAREG.

The new Touareg from AED 174,900.

Terms and conditions apply.

The new Touareg is here.

Newly designed, with features like 360° Area View, a large panoramic sunroof, keyless entry/start system and hands-free tailgate opening. All for a legendary price.

Take a deep breath because the new Touareg just got more epic.

German engineering for everyone.   **Das Auto.**

MEDECINS SANS FRONTIERES
DOCTORS WITHOUT BORDERS

DOCTORS
WITHOUT
HESITATION.

BUT NOT WITHOUT YOU.

EVERY DAY OUR TEAMS ON THE GROUND ARE WORKING TO SAVE LIVES IN POVERTY-STRICKEN,
WAR-TORN, AND DISEASE AFFECTED AREAS.THE CONDITIONS ARE ALWAYS CHALLENGING,
SOMETIMES DANGEROUS, BUT THANKS TO THE GENEROSITY OF OUR SUPPORTERS, WE CONTINUE TO
OFFER MEDICAL AID TO THOSE WHO NEED IT MOST, REGARDLESS OF RACE, RELIGION OR
POLITICAL AFFILIATION.

WWW.MSF-ME.ORG

Giving children back their childhood

GET INVOLVED

Each year the Christina Noble Children's Foundation supports thousands of vulnerable children and their families in Vietnam and Mongolia. Focusing on health, education and community support, the Foundation seeks to maximize the potential of each child. We believe that every child has the right to a childhood free of risk, exploitation and poverty.

None of this would be possible without your support and there are plenty of ways get involved, for example:

SPONSOR A CHILD

For the price of a daily cup of coffee you can give a child an education that can take them from Primary School to University and help break the cycle of poverty.

GIVE A GER

$3,500 is all it takes to provide a family in Mongolia with a traditional home. This not only provides a roof, but offers security and relief allowing parents to focus on their children's well being.

CHALLENGE YOURSELF

We are proud of our partnership with Gulf 4 Good and encourage you to take part in one of their life changing challenges.

CORPORATE SUPPORT

If your company has a dedicated CSR programme or nominates a 'Charity of the Year' we would love to talk to you about supporting the Foundation and the value it can bring to your employees and stakeholders.

To get involved and for more ideas visit www.cncf.org or contact tammy.urwin@cncf.org

Dubai Residents' Guide 2015/19th Edition
First Published 1996
2nd Edition 1997
3rd Edition 1998
4th Edition 2000
5th Edition 2001
6th Edition 2002
7th Edition 2003
8th Edition 2004
9th Edition 2005
10th Edition 2006
11th Edition 2007
12th Edition 2008
13th Edition 2009
14th Edition 2010
15th Edition 2011
16th Edition 2012
17th Edition 2013
18th Edition 2014
19th Edition 2015   ISBN 978-9948-22-525-6

Front Cover Photograph – Burj Khalifa – Pete Maloney

Explorer Publishing & Distribution
PO Box 34275, Dubai
United Arab Emirates
Phone   +971 (0)4 340 8805
Fax   +971 (0)4 340 8806
Email   info@askexplorer.com
Web   askexplorer.com

To buy additional copies of this or any other of Explorer's award-winning titles visit askexplorer.com. Special discounts are available for quantity purchases.

Welcome...

...to the new look Dubai Residents' Guide. This 19th anniversary edition gets straight to the crucial information you need to know about moving to, living in and enjoying life in this fascinating emirate. From red-tape procedures to schools, restaurants and things to see and do, it's all covered here.

Dubai is a modern, thriving metropolis – one that is constantly growing and changing. We can only fit so much exhaustive information onto these pages, so to keep abreast of the latest news, as well as reviews on the newest restaurants, information on upcoming events and updates to UAE laws, make askexplorer.com your online companion while in Dubai.

Finally, don't forget that Explorer publishes hundreds of maps and activity guides that help you to extract the most from life in the UAE. Discover more at askexplorer.com/shop.

In your hands, in the glovebox, in your rucksack; on your laptop, tablet or smartphone. Wherever you're going and whatever you're doing, be sure to take us with you.

There's more to life...
The Explorer Team

We'd love to hear from you, whether you make a great insider discovery or want to share your views about this or any of our products. Fill in our reader survey at askexplorer.com/feedback – and get 20% off your next online purchase.

      /ask**explorer**

CONTENTS

CONTENTS

CONTENTS

Open doors. Open minds.
Sheikh Mohammed bin Rashid Centre
for Cultural Understanding

الأبواب مفتوحة. العقول متفتحة.
مركز الشيخ محمد بن راشد آل مكتوم
للتواصل الحضاري

The SMCCU strives to remove barriers between people of different nationalities and raise awareness of the UAE's local culture, customs and religion. Located in a traditional wind tower house in the heart of Al Fahidi Historic District, the SMCCU regularly conducts various activities that aim to improve cross- cultural understanding and communication between locals and guests across the UAE.

Jumeirah Mosque Visit
The Jumeirah Mosque has become renowned as the focal point of SMCCU's "Open doors. Open minds." programme. Till recently, it was the only mosque in Dubai open to the public and dedicated to receiving non-Muslim guests. Every Saturday through Thursday at 10am. (closed Friday). Modest dress is preferred; traditional attire can also be borrowed from the mosque. AED 10 pp.
Duration 75 minutes No reservations required.

Cultural Meals
The most popular offering of the SMCCU is its Cultural Meals programme where guests can indulge in traditional and authentic Emirati cuisine in a relaxed and friendly ambience while a knowledgeable Emirati host chats to them about the local customs and traditions.
Breakfast: Every Mon & Wed at 10am, AED 80 pp.
Lunch: Every Sunday & Tuesday at 1pm, AED 90 pp.
Brunch: Every Saturday at 10:30am, AED 100 pp.
Dinner: Every Tuesday at 7pm, AED 100 pp.
Duration 90 minutes, Reservations are essential.

Heritage Tour
Enjoy a guided walk through the Al Fahidi Historic District and a visit and talk inside the Diwan Masjid (Mosque) followed by a Question & Answer session at the SMCCU house with freshly brewed Arabic coffee and dates.
Heritage Tour: Saturday at 9am & every
Sunday, Tuesday and Thursday at 10:30am, AED 65 pp.
Duration 90 minutes, Reservations are essential.

To find out more and book online, visit us at www.cultures.ae or call 9714 353 - 6666
@SMCCUDubai

THE UAE

THE UAE

From the rugged northern mountains, to the vast interior deserts, the UAE has an astounding amount of cultural and physical diversity across its seven emirates.

Marsa Dubai with its iconic skyscrapers

The United Arab Emirates (UAE) comprises seven emirates: Abu Dhabi, Ajman, Dubai, Fujairah, Ras Al Khaimah, Sharjah and Umm Al Quwain. Located in the heart of the Middle East, its rise from a quiet strategic trading destination to a regional and global economic powerhouse is nothing short of remarkable – and makes it one of the most exciting places to live.

The UAE Today

While its culture is still rooted in Islamic tradition, the UAE is also one of the most cosmopolitan countries in the Middle East.

The country has a bold vision for its future and is working towards becoming a first-choice destination for tourism, finance, industry and trade. This makes it a vibrant and opportunity-filled place to live in and work. Trade and commerce are still the cornerstones of the economy, with the traditional manufacturing and distribution industries now joined by finance, construction, media, IT and telecom businesses. With so many world-class hotels, and leisure and entertainment options, the UAE is becoming a popular tourist destination too. Similarly, people from over 150 nations now call the UAE home as they bring their skills and manpower to help in the country's plan; and many expats find the country so welcoming that it becomes difficult to leave.

Sunshine and tax-free salaries may be why expats come, but what keeps them here is the ability to mix with other cultures, live in a liberal Middle Eastern country, and enjoy the sort of lifestyle they would be hard-pressed to find at home.

COUNTRY PROFILE

If you're looking to move to the UAE, live here already or are just visiting, there are a number of things that are useful to know. This section highlights some of those facts and figures that can help you make your way in the UAE, or, at the very least, arm you with some good ammunition for a quiz night.

Capital

The capital city of the UAE is Abu Dhabi, a large part of which is actually an island linked to the mainland by bridges. The city is part of the largest emirate and is continuing to grow at a significant rate. To the east of the main Abu Dhabi island, an area of land between Khalifa City and Shakhbout City has been designated as Zayed City, or the Capital District. While still largely a huge patch of sand, the key initiative is for the Capital District to become the seat of power and government for the whole of the UAE. It will accommodate federal ministries as well as foreign embassies and help to reinforce the cultural diversity of the UAE. More details can be found in the Abu Dhabi Vision 2030 Plan, which outlines the city's plans to grow and diversify over the next 15 or so years.

Be Happy

Good news for UAE residents. A 2013 report by UN Sustainable Development Solutions Network ranked the country as the 14th happiest country in the world, higher than the USA, the UK, Germany and Japan. The World Happiness Report also rates the UAE as the happiest Arab country in the world.

Population

The UAE population has grown rapidly in recent years as expat arrivals, robust economic expansion and high birth rates have continued to push up the total number. According to the World Bank, the UAE's population was just 322,439, a year after the country was formed, in 1972.

By 2002, 30 years later, that had ballooned by 10 times to just over 3.2 million. After 40 years, population has now grown by over 28 times the 1972 figure, currently recorded at around 9.2 million. Compared to just 10 years previously, that's a 185% increase.

Unsurprisingly the vast majority of this growth has come from foreign workers moving to the country form all over the world, resulting in a diverse population. However, aside from the huge number of Indians settling in the UAE, Emirati nationals still make up the largest ethnic group and have considerable influence.

Area

The total land area of the UAE is approximately 83,600sq km, with around 1,318km of coastline. Dubai accounts for a huge 4,114sq km of that total. While not particularly mountainous, the highest named point is Jebel Yibir at 1,572m, 'jebel' meaning mountain or hill in Arabic. The UAE's coordinates are 24°00'North 54°00'East.

Flag

The UAE flag incorporates the Pan-Arab colours of green, white, black and red, symbolising Arabian unity. It was adopted on 2 December 1971 as the official flag of the country. Interestingly, each of the seven emirates aside from Fujairah also has its own flag, all of which use just red and white.

Currency

The monetary unit is the dirham (Dhs.), which is divided into 100 fils. The currency is also referred to as AED (Arab Emirate Dirham). On notes, all denominations are marked in both Arabic and English, although coin values are shown only in Arabic. Notes come in denominations of Dhs.5 (brown), Dhs.10 (green), Dhs.20 (light blue), Dhs.50 (purple), Dhs.100 (pink), Dhs.200 (yellowy-brown), Dhs.500 (blue) and Dhs.1,000 (browny-purple). Watch your Dhs.200 notes though, they can be mistaken for a Dhs.5 note if you're in a hurry.

All coins are silver in colour, with a total of six in circulation, but you typically only come across the three largest denominations: Dhs.1, 50 fils and 25 fils. The dirham has been pegged to the US dollar since 1980, at a mid-rate of $1 to Dhs.3.6725.

Time Zone

The UAE is four hours ahead of the UTC (Universal Coordinated Time, formerly known as GMT). Clocks are not altered for daylight saving in the summer, so when Europe and North America gain an hour in spring, the time in the UAE stays the same resulting in a shorter three hours time difference. Time differences between the UAE and some cities around the world (not allowing for any daylight savings in those cities) are: Bangkok +3; Hong Kong +4; London -4; Los Angeles -12; Moscow -1; New York -9; Sydney +6; and Tokyo +5.

Country Code

The international dialling code for the UAE is +971. Each city also has its own dialling code, which is the first digit (or two digits in some cases) that you dial when calling. These are: 2, Abu Dhabi; 6, Ajman; 3, Al Ain; 58, Aweer; 6, Dhayd; 9, Dibba; 4, Dubai; 6, Falaj-Al-Moalla; 9, Fujairah; 48, Khawaneej; 7, Ras Al Khaimah; 6, Sharjah; 88, Tarif; 6, Umm Al Quwain.

Business Hours

The UAE working week is from Sunday to Thursday. Friday is the Islamic holy day and therefore a universal day off for offices and schools, so the two-day weekend spans Friday and Saturday. Some companies still require a six-day working week from their staff, while others operate on a five-and-a-half-day system. Consumer demand means that the hospitality and retail industries are open seven days a week.

Larger shops and shopping centres are generally open throughout the day and into the evening until around 10pm or midnight. Traditional shops and street retailers often operate under split shift timings, closing for three or four hours in the afternoon. Some food outlets and petrol stations are open for 24 hours a day.

Ramadan Hours

According to UAE labour laws, all companies are obliged to shorten the working day by two hours during the holy month of Ramadan. This is to assist Muslim employees who are fasting but the law also technically applies to non-Muslims. In reality, many international companies don't follow this principle, so it's a bonus if an expat is allowed to work Ramadan hours. Many schools, shops and businesses do change their hours during Ramadan, often opening later in the day and staying open until midnight or even 1am. The city's shisha cafes and some restaurants stay open until the early hours.

If you're working in the UAE, 8am to 5pm or 9am to 6pm with an hour for lunch are normal shifts in the private sector. It is common for working hours in the UAE to be longer than in other countries when working for a private company.

Most government offices are open from 7.30am to 2.30pm, Sunday to Thursday. Embassies and consulates operate similar hours, but may designate specific times and days for certain tasks (such as passport applications), so it's best to call before you go. All will have an emergency number on their answering service, website or on their office door during times they are closed.

GEOGRAPHY

Located in the heart of the Middle East, the UAE borders Saudi Arabia and the Sultanate of Oman, with coastlines on both the Arabian Gulf and the Gulf of Oman. The country comprises seven emirates: Abu Dhabi, Ajman, Dubai, Fujairah, Ras Al Khaimah, Sharjah and Umm Al Quwain. Abu Dhabi is by far the largest emirate, occupying over 80% of the country; the emirate of Dubai is second largest, although Abu Dhabi and Dubai have similar population sizes.

The country is perhaps best known for the modern, rapidly expanding metropolises of Abu Dhabi and Dubai, but visitors may be surprised by the variety of landscapes beyond the cities. The coast is littered with coral reefs and more than 200 islands, most of which are uninhabited. The interior of the country is characterised by *sabkha* (salt flats), stretches of gravel plain, and vast areas of sand desert. To the east rise the Hajar Mountains ('*hajar*' is Arabic for 'rock') which, lying close to the Gulf of Oman, form a backbone through the country, from the Musandam Peninsula in the north, through the eastern UAE and into Oman.

Weather

The UAE only really experiences two seasons: hot and hotter. Without a doubt the best time to live, and visit, the country is from October to April, when it's mostly blue skies and temperatures of 10°C (50°F) to 24°C (75°F). Every day in the winter is a sunny reminder of why you chose to live here – tepid sea water to swim in, cloudless skies to sunbathe under, and warm, comfortable evenings for alfresco dining.

However, during the summer months (between June and September), be prepared for triple-digit temperatures and high humidity levels. Thermometers range from 41°C (106°F) up to a scorching 48°C (118°) in August. Yes, it's undeniably hot, but the UAE is well and truly geared up for it with AC in every mall, restaurant, office and even bus shelters, to keep sweaty brows at bay.

HOME OF WORLD RECORDS

There's barely a week goes by when something from the UAE doesn't claim to be the world's biggest, tallest, fastest or most expensive; and even then you can be sure there are plans to go bigger, taller, faster or even more costly. While it may look like showy extravagance, it's actually a smart way to get this relatively new country on the map and make it a must-visit destination for tourists and a more attractive proposition to foreign companies looking to invest. For residents though, the 100 and more entries by the UAE in the Guinness World Records 2014 mean a seemingly endless list of things to see or do while living in the country.

Fastest rollercoaster made from steel – Formula Rossa, Ferrari World, Abu Dhabi
Most environmentally friendly city – Masdar City, Abu Dhabi
Tallest man-made structure on land – Burj Khalifa, Dubai
Largest shopping centre – The Dubai Mall, Dubai
Longest driverless metro – Dubai Metro, Dubai
Tallest residential building – Princess Tower, Dubai
Furthest leaning man-made tower – Hyatt Capital Gate, Abu Dhabi
Largest automated car park – Emirates Financial Towers, Dubai
Largest firework display – New Year's Eve 2013, Palm Jumeirah and The World, Dubai

Humidity is usually between 50% and 60%, and, when combined with high summer temperatures, can be a little uncomfortable to endure. Many expats escape the suffocating heat during the summer and head home for an extended holiday.

Leave those umbrellas and wellies at home, as rainfall is almost non-existent – just 25 days per year – and when it does fall it is rarely for long periods. So, there's more than enough good weather to brag about to those back home.

HISTORY

As a country, the UAE is still young having only formed in 1971 when unifying the different emirates was seen as a progressive move to enhance security and influence in the area. However, the region has a long history before that.

Much of the early existence is closely linked to the arrival and development of Islam in the greater Middle East. Islam developed in modern-day Saudi Arabia at the beginning of the seventh century AD with the revelations of the Quran being received by the Prophet Muhammad. Military conquests of the Middle East and North Africa enabled the Arab empire to spread the teachings of Islam from Mecca and Medina to the local Bedouin tribes inhabiting the surrounding areas.

Periods of dominance from other empires followed over the centuries, with the Turks, Mongols and Ottomans exerting their influence over the region. In the early 19th century the British and Portuguese dipped their oars into Arabian waters, attracted by the area's strategic position between Europe and India and the desire to quash the rise of piracy in the local waters. By 1820, the British had flexed their naval muscle in the region and a general treaty was agreed by the local rulers, denouncing piracy. The following years witnessed a series of maritime truces, with the emirates accepting British protection in 1892. In Europe, the area became known as the Trucial Coast, a name it retained until the departure of the British in 1971, the same year the UAE was established.

British Withdrawal
When Britain announced plans for its withdrawal in 1968, the ruling sheikhs of Bahrain, Qatar and the Trucial Coast realised that they would have a stronger voice in the Middle East by uniting forces as a single state. Negotiations collapsed when Bahrain and Qatar chose independence; however, in 1971, the federation of the United Arab Emirates was born from the Trucial Coast, with Ras Al Khaimah joining in 1972 to establish the UAE we know today.

Under the agreement, the individual emirates retained a certain amount of autonomy, with Abu Dhabi and Dubai providing the most input into the federation. The leaders of the new federation elected the ruler of Abu Dhabi, His Highness Sheikh Zayed bin Sultan Al Nahyan, to be the president of the newly founded country. The well-liked and highly respected Sheikh held the position until he passed on 2 November 2004. The eponymous Sheikh Zayed Grand Mosque in Abu Dhabi was his final place of rest, his mausoleum complete when the mosque opened in 2007. The mosque itself was his great vision and was intended to unite not just the UAE but the wider Arab populace. His eldest son, His Highness Sheikh Khalifa bin Zayed Al Nahyan, was elected to take over the presidency and oversaw the final few years of the mosque's fantastic construction.

In 1958, huge oil reserves were discovered in Abu Dhabi. The discovery dramatically transformed the emirate. In 1966, oil was also found in Dubai, by then already a relatively wealthy trading centre. Dubai's ruler at the time, the late Sheikh Rashid bin Saeed Al Maktoum, ensured that the emirate's oil revenues were used to develop an economic and social infrastructure to secure the emirate's future, which is the basis of today's modern society. His forward-thinking work was continued through the reign of his son and successor, Sheikh Maktoum bin Rashid Al Maktoum and by the present ruler, Sheikh Mohammed bin Rashid Al Maktoum.

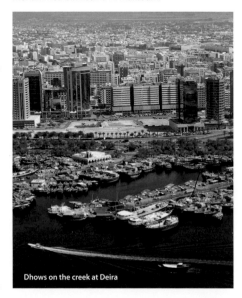
Dhows on the creek at Deira

UAE TIMELINE

The UAE's history is both rich and colourful, from the arrival and development of Islam in the greater Middle East region to the radical changes resulting from the discovery of oil to the formation of the federation of the United Arab Emirates.

Stone Age	Modern human settlement in the UAE dates back to ca. 7,000BC
Bronze Age	Archaeological evidence of human settlements; the domestication of the camel boosts trade
Iron Age	The invention of *falaj*, an irrigation technology, takes place somewhere between 1,300-300BC
630	Envoys from the Prophet Muhammad arrive, heralding the conversion of local people to Islam
761	The Baniyas tribe discovers fresh water in Abu Dhabi and settles on the island; leading to the construction of Qasr Al Hosn
1790s	The pearl trade is booming off the coast of Abu Dhabi
1835	Maritime Truce signed between the Trucial States and Britain
1930s	The first oil concession in Abu Dhabi is granted to Trucial Coast Oil Development Company
1950s	Oil is discovered in the UAE, exports begin in 1962
1966	Sheikh Zayed bin Sultan Al Nahyan becomes ruler of Abu Dhabi
1971	Britain withdraws from the Gulf and the UAE is established, with Sheikh Zayed bin Sultan Al Nahyan of Abu Dhabi as the leader; the UAE joins the Arab League
1972	Ras Al Khaimah joins the UAE
1973	The UAE launches a single currency, the UAE dirham
1981	The Gulf Cooperation Council (GCC) is formed, with the UAE as a founding member
1985	Emirates Airline is founded
1999	The doors of the Burj Al Arab, the tallest hotel in the world, open for the first time in Dubai
2001	Construction starts on Dubai's Palm Jumeirah
2003	Etihad Airways is founded
2004	Sheikh Zayed bin Sultan Al Nahyan dies and is succeeded as leader of the UAE by his son, Sheikh Khalifa bin Zayed Al Nahyan
2005	Emirates Palace, billed as the world's most expensive hotel, opens to the public
2007	Sheikh Zayed Mosque, the eighth largest mosque in the world, opens during Ramadan. Work also begins on Yas Island and Saadiyat Island
2008	In the wake of a global economic crisis, much of the UAE's property market crashes
2009	Abu Dhabi hosts its inaugural Formula 1 Grand Prix at Yas Marina Circuit; the Sheikh Khalifa Bridge opens, linking the new areas of Abu Dhabi directly to the corniche; Dubai Metro, the region's first public mass-transit system, is launched
2010	The tallest building in the world, the Burj Khalifa, opens in Dubai; Ferrari World Abu Dhabi, the world's largest indoor theme park, opens
2011	The first hotels on Saadiyat Island open their doors to the public; Capital Gate, the world's 'most leaning' tower also opens in Abu Dhabi
2012	Yas Waterworld is completed
2013	Dubai wins the bid to host the World Expo 2020
2014	Abu Dhabi Ports Company's Zayed Port unveils plans for a new cruise terminal, which is due to open in 2016; Dubai's Canal project progresses

GOVERNMENT

The UAE is a federation of seven emirates, each with its own ruler, rules and regulations. The Supreme Council of Rulers – made up of the hereditary rulers of the emirates – is the top policy-making body in the UAE, responsible for laws governing education, defence, foreign affairs, communications and development, and for ratifying federal rules.

The current President of the UAE is the ruler of Abu Dhabi, Sheikh Khalifa bin Zayed Al Nahyan, who took over the post In November 2004 from his late father, Sheikh Zayed bin Sultan Al Nahyan. The Vice President of the UAE is Sheikh Mohammed bin Rashid Al Maktoum, ruler of Dubai. Both members are elected by the Supreme Council for a five-year term, and are often re-elected time after time.

The UAE's Prime Minister, currently Sheikh Mohammed bin Rashid Al Maktoum, is appointed by the President and chairs the Council of Ministers, which meets once a week in Abu Dhabi to oversee the development and implementation of federal policy across all portfolios of government.

The Federal National Council (FNC) is a consultative assembly of 40 representatives, half of whom are elected. The Council monitors and debates government policy but has no power of veto. The last election was in 2011, and one-fifth of its members are currently women.

Key Government Figures

His Highness Sheikh Khalifa bin Zayed Al Nahyan, the President of the UAE and ruler of Abu Dhabi, has guided the country, and especially Abu Dhabi, through a period of astonishing growth. With his focus on the continuing development of the country's infrastructure, economic health and cultural contributions, he has laid the foundations for a prosperous UAE.

Sheikh Khalifa has always been generous with Abu Dhabi's oil wealth, ensuring other emirates within the country aren't left behind. In 2009, Abu Dhabi gave a US$10 billion loan to Dubai at the height of the financial crisis. The Burj Khalifa in Dubai, the world's tallest building, is named after Sheikh Khalifa.

The Abu Dhabi ruler is well known for his philanthropic commitments, particularly through the Khalifa Bin Zayed Al Nahyan Foundation, which focuses on providing support to the health and education sectors on a domestic, regional and global scale.

Sheikh Mohammed bin Rashid Al Maktoum is the Prime Minister and Vice President of the United Arab Emirates, and ruler of Dubai and is often considered the driving force behind Dubai's exponential growth, pioneering Free Trade Zones, such as Dubai Media City, offering tax exemptions which have attracted foreign companies to set up in the emirate, helping Dubai's economy flourish and reducing its reliance on oil-based industries. He has overseen the development of numerous landmark projects in Dubai including Palm Jumeirah, the 'seven-star' Burj Al Arab hotel and the Burj Khalifa. Find Sheikh Mohammed on Facebook at Facebook.com/HHSheikhMohammed. His brother, Sheikh Hamdan bin Rashid Al Maktoum, is the UAE Minister of Finance and Industry.

Emirs Or Sheikhs?

While the term emirate comes from the ruling title of 'emir', the rulers of the UAE are called 'sheikhs'. You may associate terms like 'sultan' with the Middle East, but this is a title given to rulers of sultanates.

ECONOMY

The UAE is considered the second richest Arab country, after Qatar, on a GDP per capita basis. Globally that equates to being the eighth richest country in the world. With just under 10% of the world's proven oil reserves (most of it within Abu Dhabi emirate) and the seventh largest proven natural gas reserves, hydrocarbon exports still play a large part in the country's wealth.

Since the financial crisis of 2009, which hit Dubai particularly hard, the UAE's perceived safe haven status amid regional political and social unrest has supported growing economic confidence. At an estimated $284.4 billion in 2013, the UAE economy is the second largest in the Gulf, after Saudi Arabia. In the Where-To-Be-Born Index, 2013 (which highlights the countries where new babies could expect the highest quality of life) the UAE came a respectable 17th, the highest ranking Arab country and just behind the United States and Germany.

Heading into 2015, the UAE's economic outlook is more positive than ever, with development projects thriving across the country. Successful economic diversification means that the UAE's wealth is no longer solely reliant on oil revenue; just 25% of GDP is based on oil and gas output now. The push to double

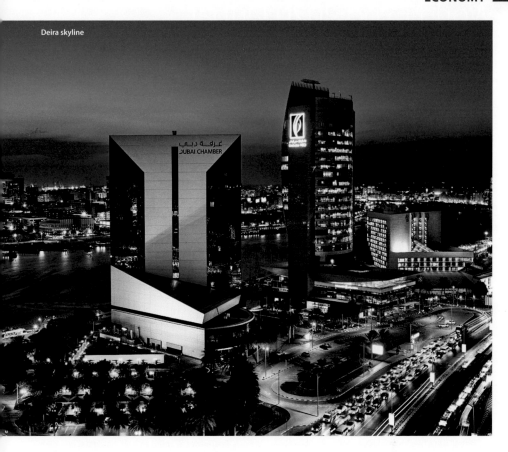

Deira skyline

tourist numbers by 2020, which includes increasing niche tourist markets, such as medical tourism, is also helping to expand the economy.

In June 2014, the Samba Economics Group forecast that Dubai's win to host the Expo 2020 had boosted the UAE's overall economy, forecasting that growth would remain at 4-5% in 2015. The UAE's non-oil sector is also predicted to accelerate, supported by a recovery in construction and real estate, as well as ongoing growth in tourism-orientated sectors.

Earning Potential

However, while the UAE GDP per capita income stands at around Dhs.183,000 ($49,800) this figure includes all sections of the community and the average labourer, of whom there are many, can expect to earn as little as Dhs.600 ($165) per month.

Even before the financial crisis, the salaries for most job types were dropping too. Aside from highly skilled professionals, the average expat coming to work in the UAE shouldn't expect to automatically be on a huge salary.

While the unemployment level of the national population in the UAE is lower than that of many other Arab states, there are still a significant number of Emiratis out of work (over 20% according to some reports). This is partly due to a preference for public sector work and partly because of qualifications not matching the skills required for the roles available in the private sector. However, the government is trying to reverse this scenario and reduce unemployment in the local sector with a 'Nationalisation' or 'Emiratisation' programme to encourage Emiratis to work.

Jobseekers searching for vacant positions and average salary details in Dubai are advised to do their research first via one of the many recruitment agencies based here. For an idea of what you can expect to earn (in a variety of roles) try charterhouseme.ae for further details.

World Expo 2020 Dubai

In November 2013, Dubai won the bid to host the World Expo 2020. Fireworks erupted from the Burj Khalifa and the ruler of Dubai promised that the city would 'astonish the world.'

What is the Expo?

Every five years and for a period of six months, World Expos attract millions of visitors. Also known as the World's Fair, it is an event that has been around for over 150 years. It is similar to the Olympic Games, except that instead of sports, it's about science, technology, culture and economics. The World Expo is effectively the largest mix of trade exhibitions or world fairs and is not by any means a new concept, with the first noted World Expo being hosted in London in 1851. Indeed, previous Expos have yielded legacies such as the Eiffel Tower, the telephone, ice cream and Heinz tomato ketchup.

Plans and development

While the majority of the design and construction of the Expo site is still in its infancy, organisers have reported that the site for the World Expo 2020 Dubai will be at Dubai Trade Center – Jabel Ali: a 438 hectare site on the south western edge of Dubai which is set to be one of the largest ever developed for a World Expo. Equidistant from the centres of Abu Dhabi and Dubai, the site is located next to the new Al Maktoum International Airport and also located in close proximity to Jebel Ali Port, the third busiest port in the world.

The theme for World Expo 2020 Dubai is Connecting Minds, Creating the Future – a nod to the importance of fostering partnerships and innovation to build a sustainable world today and in the future. Designed by architectural firm HOK, the sprawling new district features three main pavilions designed to symbolise opportunity, sustainability and mobility with 'innovation pods' and 'best practice areas' in each thematic zone. Different areas will be linked by walkways that are inspired by the layout of a traditional Arabic souk but their construction is set to be futuristic. A photovoltaic fabric structure is said to cover the walkways acting as a solar-powered sun shade capable of absorbing energy and supplying half the Expo's power requirements. At night, the fabric will act as a canvas for light displays and digital projections. At the core of the site there's said to be an open plaza called Al Wasl which is Arabic for

'the connection' – again in keeping with Dubai's Connecting Minds, Creating the Future theme – that will act as the central souk.

The plan for what to do with the site when the Expo closes is currently a hot topic for discussion. Recent news suggests that the organisers have agreed to combine the three major pavilions – the Welcome Pavilion, the Innovation Pavilion and the UAE's Pavilion – and transform them into one structure: the Museum of the Future.

The region's first

World Expo 2020 Dubai is the first to be held in the MENASA (Middle East, North Africa and South Asia) region. As the global community faces ever more complex and increasingly interconnected challenges, the links between people, societies and ideas have never been more important. The Expo promises to be a platform for connectivity to help pioneer new partnerships for growth and sustainability for the future. It was reported that the last Expo held in Shanghai in 2010 received over 73 million visitors from 250 countries. The site that showcased this phenomenon measured a massive 5.28sq km, and a new record attendance for a single day was set with more than 1.03 million people visiting the site. These numbers, by any standard, are hugely impressive, and an indicator of how important for the local economy the winning vote is to Dubai – especially when you consider the reported profits reached in excess of US$157 million for the Expo alone.

It is already predicted that there will be an influx to the region of 25 million visitors going through the turnstiles in Dubai. The knock-on effect is a predicted 277,000 jobs created for the region and a huge boost not only to the ensuing job market, but for the infrastructure of Dubai. With Al Maktoum International Airport's ambitious plans to overtake the likes of London Heathrow in the coming years, and its central location here in the Middle East, it is easy to see why this is the perfect platform and opportunity in which to raise the bar.

For updated information on news and events for the Expo, check out expo2020dubai.ae.

The Burj Al Arab hotel
celebrates the Expo 2020 win

Dubai

The pace of economic growth in Dubai over the last 20 years has been incredible. Trade alone has grown at more than 9% per annum over the past 10 years and the population has more than doubled since 1990.

Over the last decade, legislation and government institutions have been honed to reduce bureaucracy and create a constructive business environment. Free zones, such as Internet City, Media City and Healthcare City, offer financial incentives to encourage international business; they have flourished and multiplied and multi-billion dollar mega project proposals such as the three Palm Island projects, Dubai Sports City and Burj Khalifa, were the result of the government's active promotion of investment in Dubai.

According to the International Monetary Fund (IMF) the UAE's economy grew 4.8% in 2014 and is on track to grow 4.5% in 2015. Inflation increased to 3.37% in 2014 and is predicted to rise another 3% in 2015. The increased cost of living is mostly down to higher rent and food costs.

Really Tax Free?

Do taxes exist in the UAE? Yes and no. You don't pay income or sales tax, except when you purchase alcohol from a licensed liquor store – when you'll be hit with a steep 30% tax. The main tax that you will come across is the municipality tax of 5% on rent and 10% on food, beverages and rooms in hotels. The rest are hidden taxes in the form of 'fees', such as your car registration renewal, visa/permit fees and Dubai's Salik (road toll).

Bolstering feelings of confidence in economic recovery, many construction projects that had been put on hold are resuming, such as the Palm Deira along with several residential and commercial buildings.

On a less positive note for renters, the property market has been booming, with Dubai rents increasing 30% over the year from July 2012-2013 – but rental and sales prices did drop slightly towards the end of 2014.

All in all, the UAE is still one of the world's richest countries on a per capita basis. With its sizeable government-led projects and ongoing expansion plans, Dubai is well placed to continue growing as a global hub and tourist destination.

Trade

Strategically the UAE has always been well-placed geographically, but with a trade policy based on economic openness and liberalisation the country continues to flourish. With flexible and investor-friendly laws, availability of raw materials and funds, tax exemptions and low tariffs, the climate in the UAE is an ideal one for foreign investment. Non-oil exports have grown significantly with a particular emphasis on re-exports. In 2014, results published by the World Trade Organisation ranked the UAE 17th in its International Trade Statistics 2013 report, an increase of 16% compared to 2011. When it comes to exporting goods, the UAE surpasses India, Sweden and South Africa and claims almost a 2% of the world's total exports.

Roughly 60% of exports are manufactured goods, fuels and mining products; India, Iran, Iraq, Switzerland and the European Union (EU) being the main recipients. Meanwhile over $200 billion of merchandise is imported into the country every year, mainly coming from the EU, India, China, USA and Japan. Main imports include: pearls and other precious metals and stones, machinery, vehicles, base metals and chemicals.

Tourism

The UAE is well ahead of many other countries in the Middle East in terms of travel and tourism. Boosting tourism plays a central part in the government's economic diversification plan and is a major force behind the array of record-breaking infrastructure and hospitality developments of recent times. Dubai is perhaps the most famous tourist destination in the UAE, with over 580 hotels and attractions such as the man-made Palm Jumeirah island, the Burj Al Arab hotel and an ever-growing marina area. Meanwhile, in the Downtown area records are set: the Burj Khalifa,

Dubai Marina

the world's tallest building, towers over the world's largest dancing fountain and nearby is the world's largest mall, The Dubai Mall. Inside, visitors can even visit the world's largest sweet shop.

The development of these high-end tourist amenities and visitor attractions, in conjunction with an aggressive overseas marketing campaign, means that Dubai's popularity as a holiday destination continues to increase. It is striving to reach its target of 20 million visitors a year by 2020 – a goal that will surely be boosted following the emirate's winning bid to host the 2020 World Expo.

Visitor numbers to Dubai increased by 10.6% in 2013, with the city welcoming more than 11 million visitors over a one year period for the first time in its history. In 2014, the online statistics portal Statista estimated that Dubai welcomed 11.9 million visitors.

Passengers through Dubai International Airport – now ranked the world's second busiest in terms of international traffic – reached 63,977,063 in 2014 to November, up 5.9% from 2013. The 2013 passenger traffic exceeded Dubai Airports' forecast at the start of the year by more than 1 million passengers. Passenger numbers are projected to reach 78.4 million in 2015 and 103.5 million by 2020. Dubai World Central – Al Maktoum International Airport opened in 2010, in the south of Dubai, near to the Jabel Ali industrial area. It opened for passenger services in the second half of 2013, and will eventually become the world's largest airport, with a capacity of 160 million passengers and 12 million tonnes of cargo per year.

International Relations

The UAE remains open in its foreign relations and firmly supports Arab unity. Sheikh Khalifa bin Zayed Al Nahyan is very generous with the country's wealth when it comes to helping Arab nations and communities that are in need of aid.

The UAE became a member of the United Nations and the Arab League in 1971. It is a member of the International Monetary Fund (IMF), the Organisation of Petroleum Exporting Countries (OPEC), the World Trade Organisation (WTO) and other international Arab organisations. It is also a member of the Arab Gulf Cooperation Council (AGCC, also known as the GCC), whose members are Bahrain, Kuwait, Oman, Qatar and Saudi Arabia.

All major embassies and consulates are represented either in Abu Dhabi or in Dubai, or both. For many expats all their bureaucratic dealings (passport renewals, birth registration and the like) will be met via a trip to their home-country consulate. Most of the main consulates are located in the same area, off Al Seef Road, in Bur Dubai, beside Dubai Creek.

ENVIRONMENT

The UAE has environmental issues that can't be ignored thanks to a hot climate, a scarcity of natural drinking water and a growing population. Being a relatively wealthy country with high demands means that the average person in the UAE is consuming more than the country can produce on its own. The ecological footprint in the UAE, according to the WWF's Living Planet Report 2012, is 8.44 global hectares (gha). Meanwhile the capacity of the land to produce useful biological material and absorb waste created by humans is just 0.64gha. Globally, the UAE has the third largest deficit between these two figures, meaning a continued reliance on imports which could lead to problems in the future.

Couple that to being one of the largest consumers of water on the planet with a large population of expats, who are less likely to invest time into conservation than locals or long-term residents, and the situation needs addressing. Fortunately the government is conscious of this and has agencies set up across the emirates to help tackle the issues.

Flora & Fauna

The region has about 3,500 native plants, and the most famous is, of course, the date palm. In mountainous regions, flat-topped acacia trees and wild grasses create scenery similar to that of an African savannah. The deserts are unexpectedly green in places, even during the dry summer months, but it takes an experienced botanist to get the most out of the area.

Indigenous fauna include the Arabian leopard and the Arabian oryx, but sightings are extremely rare. Realistically, the only large animals you will see are camels and goats (often roaming dangerously close to the roads). Other desert life includes sand cats, sand foxes, desert hares, gerbils, hedgehogs, geckos and snakes. Studies have shown that the number of bird species is rising each year, due in part to concentrated greening efforts. This is most apparent in parks, especially in spring and autumn, as the country is on the migratory route between central Asia and east Africa. There's a big effort to preserve the local Houbara Bustard, whose numbers have declined due to urbanisation, poaching and unregulated hunting. For more information see houbarafund.org.

Off the coast of the UAE, the seas contain a rich abundance of marine life, including tropical fish, jellyfish, coral, dugong ('sea cows') and sharks. Eight species of whale and seven species of dolphin have been recorded in UAE waters. Various breeds of turtle, including loggerhead, green and hawksbill, are also indigenous with sightings off the east coast by Snoopy Island and Khor Kalba not uncommon.

Wildlife

A number of indigenous animals have been hunted to the edge of extinction in the past, including the Arabian oryx (a large antelope) and houbara bustard (a large bird and popular quarry for falconers). Meanwhile, others have found their habitats disappearing. The survival or continued protection of these animals has been mainly thanks to government activities. Even back in 1968, the late Sheikh Zayed ordered the capture of the four remaining Arabian oryx in the wild to initiate a captive breeding programme at Al Ain Zoo. After the development of Sir Bani Yas Island, he also started another captive breeding programme for the oryx, where they are today flourishing. In 2007 a release programme began for the Arabian oryx in the emirate of Abu Dhabi, with 100 animals being released into the wild.

Al Ain Zoo continues to be instrumental in conserving species, while the Breeding Centre for Endangered Arabian Wildlife at Sharjah Desert Park, has been particularly successful breeding the endangered Arabian leopard. The International Fund for Houbara Conservation (IFHC) has also become a world authority on understanding and protecting the bird so integrated in the UAE's cultural past.

Similarly agencies like the Environmental Agency Abu Dhabi (ead.ae) and Emirates Wildlife Society, a national environmental NGO that operates in association with the WWF, work tirelessly to ensure the conservation of native and migrating animals and their habitats. Projects on Saadiyat Island in Abu Dhabi have helped protect nests of rare hawksbill turtles.

Meanwhile, tagging of passing dugong have helped to keep their migratory routes safe, and specific protection has been given to breeding colonies of the rare Socotra cormorant on the islands of Marawah and Al Yasat. Internationally, the UAE-based Mohammed bin Zayed Species Conservation Fund has donated over Dhs.33 million to help safeguard the threatened flora and fauna of the world.

My Environment, My Country

In 2013 the UAE re-launched its My environment, My country initiative in schools. Following success in the previous year, it aims to inspire children to protect the natural world, focussing on the concepts and challenges faced by the UAE.

Dubai's Emirates Marine Environmental Group (EMEG), the Environmental Agency Abu Dhabi (ead.ae) and Emirates Wildlife Society, a national environmental NGO that operates in association with the WWF, work tirelessly to ensure the conservation of native and migrating animals, as well as their environments. Meanwhile, the Dubai Turtle Rehabilitation Project is dedicated to protecting the critically endangered native hawksbill turtle. Vulnerable turtles are brought to Dubai's Wildlife Protection Office and rehabilitated at the Burj Al Arab Aquarium; the project was established by the Jumeirah Group, who tag and monitor the turtles online at seaturtle.org.

Sustainability

From the outside, the UAE looks totally unsustainable. Huge petrol use, massive energy consumption (for all that air conditioning) and seemingly unending generation of waste; it all looks like an environmental headache. Rapid growth has probably necessitated much of this but the UAE government is keen to spread the message of sustainability. In fact, the late president of the UAE, Sheikh Zayed, was a passionate environmentalist and much of what happens now is part of his legacy. There is a realisation about the energy and water issues in the UAE; generating energy requires water, and producing water (through desalination) requires energy. The government is active in finding ways to use less of both through increased efficiency. As part of the continuing work to solve the issues, the International Water Summit is taking place in Abu Dhabi this year during the Abu Dhabi Sustainability Week.

In Abu Dhabi, Masdar City is a leading light, aiming to become a zero carbon, zero waste city by 2025. The first phase is already complete, with the eco-friendly buildings using 65% less energy than the average building in the city. Masdar also opened the world's largest solar thermal energy plant in 2013. The Abu Dhabi project creates 10% of the world's solar thermal energy (where mirrors heat a boiler full of steam which then generates turbines), enough to power 20,000 homes in the UAE.

Dubai's Expo Legacy

Meanwhile, as sustainability – lasting sources of energy and water – is one of the three themes of the World Expo 2020 Dubai (the other two being mobility and opportunity), the emirate can expect some noticeable changes during the next six years in the build-up to the event. Green plans for the future include solar-powered street lamps in parks, more green building codes and conversion efforts to shift to an efficient lighting system.

Heroes Of The UAE

This environmentally friendly initiative, jointly developed by The Emirates Wildlife Society in association with the Worldwide Fund for Nature (EWS-WWF) and The Environment Agency-Abu Dhabi, provides a go-to resource for individuals, schools and businesses to find out how to save energy and water, and reduce the UAE's carbon footprint – which currently has the highest per capita ecological footprint on earth – with virtual calculators, tips and information. As part of its commitment to the Heroes of the UAE campaign, the Abu Dhabi government has launched a programme to fit Watersavers in every tap, in every single home and place of work in the emirate.

Solar Heaters A Must-Have

Although the UAE still has a long way to go to reduce its ecological footprint, it's refreshing to see that measures are being taken. Since 2012, any developer submitting plans for a new build has to integrate solar water heaters that provide for at least 75% of the building's hot water needs and 50% of any swimming pool heating, or Dubai Municipality will refuse to grant a building licence.

Recycling

Recycling is a relatively new concept in the UAE, with just over 20% of all non-hazardous waste being recycled. While the importance of reducing waste through the three 'R's (reduce, reuse, recycle) is being taught throughout the country, different emirates are finding different solutions. In Abu Dhabi, the Centre of Waste Management has already taken many initiatives. Just a few years ago around 60% of waste from construction was going to landfill, roughly 3.5 million tonnes. This is now re-used in road construction, footpaths, playgrounds and sports areas.

Domestically, there can be some confusion about recycling. Even amongst expats, what seems obviously recyclable might be quite different in the UAE compared to your home country. However, UAE residents are becoming more proactive. The Emirates Environmental Group has reported a large increase in recycling drives from schools, corporate and community groups, which collect paper, plastic, glass, aluminium and toner cartridges. Mobile phones, broken computers and all kinds of electronic equipment can be recycled through Enviroserve (enviroserve.ae) or at your nearest Plug-ins store (800 758 4467).

A few of Dubai's residential areas now have an official recycling collection service for glass, paper, cans and plastic bottles (800 732 9253, zenath.com). If your area doesn't have a recycling scheme, it can involve rather a lot of administrative wrangling with the developer or community management company, but it's worth bringing the issue to the attention of your residents' committee to build support and put pressure on the developers.

In the meantime, there are now a lot of recycling bins dotted around Dubai. The municipality has installed recycling bins for paper, glass and plastic at petrol stations and bus stops, while you'll find recycling bins for everything from plastic bottles to shoes and clothing outside the UAE's bigger supermarkets. In addition, large cages for collecting recyclable materials have been installed on Al Wasl Road near Safa Park, at Mirdif Recycling Centre and on the service road near to the Shangri-La on Sheikh Zayed Road. Keep your eyes peeled – your nearest bins won't be far away.

In line with many countries, plastic bags have been phased out across supermarkets and stores in the UAE. Early 2013 statistics show that residents were using a whopping 11 billion plastic bags annually – but that figure is slowly dropping, thankfully. While Abu Dhabi's Environment Agency recently introduced an app to teach youngsters in the UAE about biodiversity and protecting their environment, another app has been designed in Dubai to promote and prioritise recycling. A new smartphone introduced by Union Paper Mills aims to ease recycling for residents. The app called 'Reyoutilizer' allows households and small companies to book the collection of recyclables such as paper, plastic and aluminium cans from their premises. The app can be downloaded for free by iPhone and Android users.

Recycling bins

CULTURE & LIFESTYLE

The UAE manages what some Arab countries fail to achieve; a healthy balance between western influences and eastern traditions. It is still a country very much rooted in Islamic culture; however, the country's effort to become modern and cosmopolitan is highlighted by an open-minded and liberal outlook.

Culture

Islam is an integral part of UAE life and to followers it is more than just a religion; it's a way of life that governs even everyday events, from what to wear to what to eat and drink. However, the UAE is progressively tolerant and welcoming; foreigners are free to practise their own religion, alcohol is served in hotels and the dress code is fairly liberal. Women face little discrimination and, contrary to the policies of neighbouring Saudi Arabia, are able to drive and walk around uncovered and unescorted.

The UAE has changed dramatically over the last 30 years, fuelled by economic prosperity that has made mega malls, towering skyscrapers and expensive 4WDs the norm. Yet the country is also keen to safeguard its heritage, with active promotion of cultural and sporting events that represent their traditions, such as falconry, camel racing and traditional dhow sailing. Arabic culture in poetry, dancing, songs, art and craftsmanship is encouraged too. Traditional virtues of courtesy and hospitality are also highly prized, although you may not always find this extended to the highways.

The Sheikh Mohammed Centre for Cultural Understanding (cultures.ae) near Dubai Creek actively promotes awareness of the local culture through various events and talks. Its motto, Open Doors, Open Minds, signifies a free and safe space to discuss sensitive topics openly and honestly. You can share a traditional meal with the hosts, learn about Muslim culture and ask questions that perhaps you were too nervous to ask before.

Language

Arabic is the official language of the UAE. However English is so widely used in all areas of life, including in business, that you might live here for years without needing to learn a single word of Arabic. Most road signs, shop signs and restaurant menus display both English and Arabic. That's not to say that learning a few words or phrases isn't a good idea, though. Arabic isn't the easiest language to pick up, or to pronounce, but if you can throw in a couple of words here and there, you're more likely to receive a warmer welcome or at least a smile – even if your pronunciation is terrible. Expats make up the vast majority of the UAE (around 80%, with the majority from India, Pakistan and Bangladesh) so you can expect to hear languages like Hindi, Malayalam and Urdu.

Religion

Islam is the official religion of the UAE, and is widely practised throughout the country. The Islamic holy day is Friday. The basis of Islam is the belief that there is only one God and that the Prophet Muhammad is his messenger. The faith shares a common ancestry with Christianity and many of the prophets before Muhammad can be found in Christian as well as Muslim writings. There are five pillars of Islam that all Muslims must follow: the Profession of Faith, Prayer, Charity, Fasting and Pilgrimage. Every Muslim is expected, at least once in his or her lifetime, to make the pilgrimage (Hajj) to the holy city of Mecca (also spelt Makkah) in Saudi Arabia.

Arabic Family Names

Arabic names have a formal structure that traditionally indicates the person's family and tribe. Names are usually taken from an important person in the Quran or from the tribe. This is followed by the word *bin* (son of) for a boy or *bint* (daughter of) for a girl, and then the name of the child's father. The last name indicates the person's tribe or family. For prominent families, this has *Al*, the Arabic word for 'the', immediately before it. For instance, the President of the UAE is His Highness Sheikh Khalifa bin Zayed Al Nahyan. When women get married, they do not change their name.

Muslims are required to pray five times a day (facing Mecca), and times vary according to the sun. Most people pray at a mosque, but it's not unusual to see people kneeling by the side of the road if they are not near a place of worship. It is considered impolite to stare at people praying or to walk over prayer mats. The modern-day call to prayer, transmitted through loudspeakers on the minarets, ensures that everyone knows it's time to pray.

Islam is the principle religion, but the UAE is tolerant of other denominations; the ruling family has, in the past, donated land for the building of churches. There is a vibrant Christian community in Dubai and there is even a Hindu temple.

BASIC ARABIC

General

Yes	na'am
No	la
Please	min fadlak (m) min fadlik (f)
Thank you	shukran
Please (in offering)	tafaddal (m) tafaddali (f)
Praise be to God	al-hamdu l-illah
God willing	in shaa'a l-laah

Greetings

Greeting (peace be upon you)	as-salaamu alaykom
Greeting (in reply)	wa alaykom is salaam
Good morning	sabah il-khayr
Good morning (in reply)	sabah in-nuwr
Good evening	masa il-khayr
Good evening (in reply)	masa in-nuwr
Hello	marhaba
Hello (in reply)	marhabtayn
How are you?	kayf haalak (m)/kayf haalik (f)
Fine, thank you	zayn, shukran (m) zayna, shukran (f)
Welcome	ahlan wa sahlan
Welcome (in reply)	ahlan fiyk (m)/ahlan fiyki (f)
Goodbye	ma is-salaama

Introductions

My name is...	ismiy...
What is your name?	shuw ismak (m)/shuw ismik (f)
Where are you from?	min wayn inta (m)/min wayn inti (f)
I am from...	anaa min...
America	ameriki
Britain	braitani
Europe	oropi
India	hindi

Questions

How many/much?	kam?
Where?	wayn?
When?	mataa?
Which?	ayy?
How?	kayf?
What?	shuw?
Why?	laysh?
Who?	miyn?
To/for	ila
In/at	fee
From	min
And	wa
Also	kamaan
There isn't	maa fee

Driving

Is this the road to...?	hadaa al tariyq ila...
Stop	kuf
Right	yamiyn
Left	yassar
Straight ahead	siydaa
North	shamaal
South	januwb
East	sharq
West	garb
Turning	mafraq
First	awwal
Second	thaaniy
Road	tariyq
Street	shaaria
Roundabout	duwwaar
Traffic light signal	ishaara
Close to	qarib min
Petrol station	mahattat betrol
Sea/beach	il bahar
Mountain/s	jabal/jibaal
Desert	al sahraa
Airport	mataar
Hotel	funduq
Restaurant	mata'am
Slow down	schway schway

Accidents & Emergencies

Police	al shurtaa
Permit/licence	rukhsaa
Accident	haadith
Papers	waraq
Insurance	ta'miyn
Sorry	aasif (m)/aasifa (f)

Numbers

Zero	sifr
One	waahad
Two	ithnayn
Three	thalatha
Four	arba'a
Five	khamsa
Six	sitta
Seven	saba'a
Eight	thamaanya
Nine	tiss'a
Ten	ashara
Hundred	miya
Thousand	alf
Million	million

National Dress

Emiratis generally wear traditional dress in public, although many will dress in more western clothes if travelling abroad. For men, traditional dress means a *dishdasha* or *khandura*; a white, full length shirt dress, which is worn with a white or red checked headdress, known as *gutra* or *sifrah*. This is secured with a black chord (*agal*). Sheikhs and important businessmen may also wear a thin black or brown robe (known as a *bisht*), over their *dishdasha* at important events, which is equivalent to a dinner jacket in western culture. In public, women wear the black *abaya*; a long, loose black robe that covers their normal clothes, plus a headscarf called a *sheyla*.

The abaya is often of sheer, flowing fabric and may be open at the front. Some women also wear a thin black veil hiding their face, and gloves. Older women sometimes still wear a leather mask, known as a *burkha*, which covers the nose, brow and cheekbones. Underneath, women traditionally wear a long tunic over loose, flowing trousers (*sirwal*), which are often heavily embroidered and fitted at wrists and ankles. However, these are used more by the older generation and modern women will often wear the latest fashions under their *abayas*. At the beach, it's not unusual to see Muslim women in special bathing costumes that keep their legs, arms, bodies and heads covered, with only their faces, hands and feet on show.

Food & Drink

The cultural diversity of the population is reflected in the vast range of culinary delights available in the country. Anything from Mexican and Asian fusion to an English roast dinner is available. Most of the popular restaurants are in hotels, where alcoholic drinks are also served. Some of the tastiest food can be found in the small streetside cafeterias, where two people can often feast on less than Dhs.50. Fast food fans searching for the familiar will also find McDonalds, Burger King, KFC and Subway – the latter three all offering home delivery.

When it comes to food shopping, there are a number of supermarkets that stock many international brands. French chain Carrefour is one of the largest with a huge selection, while LuLu Hypermarket and Co-op stores offer similar choice and are popular with those on a budget. Spinneys, Abela and Waitrose are more expensive but sell an excellent range of British, South African and American food.

Eat Like The Locals

While modern Arabic cuisine comes from a blend of Moroccan, Tunisian, Iranian and Egyptian cooking styles, the term invariably refers to Lebanese food.

Aside from mezze, it's fairly reliant on meat, often lamb, beef or fish cooked over a charcoal grill. Meals generally end with nutty Lebanese sweets and are accompanied by a variety of fresh fruit juices.

Shawarma: lamb or chicken sliced from a spit and served in a pita bread with salad and tahina

Falafel: mashed chickpeas and sesame seeds, rolled into balls and deep fried

Mezze: a selection of dishes served with Arabic bread, a green salad and pickles

Hummus: a creamy dip made from ground chickpeas, tahina, olive oil and garlic

Tabouleh: finely chopped parsley, mint and cracked wheat salad

Fatoush: lettuce and tomato with small pieces of fried Arabic bread

Fattayer: small pastries filled with cottage cheese and spinach

Khouzi: whole lamb served on a bed of rice, mixed with nuts, a popular Ramadan feast

Kibbeh: deep fried mince, pine nuts and bulgur

Baklava: filo pastry layered with honey and pistachio nuts

Umm Ali: a dessert with layers of milk, bread, raisins and nuts

Emirati Specialities

Camel is eaten, but as they are highly prized for their milk and load-carrying ability, camel meat is usually saved for special occasions. You can however pick up a pint of camel milk in most supermarkets, and the odd bar of camel-milk chocolate.

Dates are more of a staple having been cultivated in the region for around 5,000 years, and it's said that in some countries the Bedouin way of life was sustained primarily by dates and camel milk up until as recently as the mid-20th century. Dates are also a bit of a super food, high in energy but low in fat, so make a great cheap and healthy snack. Just five dates per day provide enough nutrition for one recommended daily portion of fruit or vegetables.

Pork

Pork is taboo in Islam. Muslims should not eat, prepare or even serve pork. In order for a restaurant to serve pork on its menu, it should have a separate fridge, preparation equipment and cooking area. It also needs a specific licence. In restaurants where bacon appears on a menu, you will usually be served beef or veal bacon. Supermarkets that sell pork are also required to do so from a separate area clearly labelled for 'non-Muslims'. These are more common in areas with high expat concentrations. Outlets of Spinneys, Choithrams and Park n Shop all have pork sections within their stores. As pork is not locally produced you

MAPPING SOLUTIONS

Real estate

Aviation

Tourism

Transportation

From our best-selling products to our innovative and fully client-integrated custom mapping solutions, we deliver maps of the highest quality that meet the exact needs of our customers, our clients, and their customers.

ask**explorer**.com

 askexplorer

will find that it's more expensive than other meats. All meat products for Muslim consumption have to be halal, which refers to the method of slaughter.

Alcohol

Alcohol is widely available in hotels plus a few leisure clubs, such as golf clubs and sports clubs, and the very occasional non-hotel bar/restaurant. During Ramadan, alcohol is only served after sunset, and there are 'dry' nights before certain public holidays. Officially you need a liquor licence to buy, transport or even consume alcohol, whether at home or at a hotel; you must also be a non-Muslim resident. Alcohol is sold at specially-licensed stores across the UAE. Sharjah is the only dry state in the UAE, and alcohol is not sold or served in any hotels there. If drinking, always be mindful that you are in a Muslim country; drunken behaviour is not tolerated, neither is drink-driving. See also the Living In and Shopping chapters.

Shisha

Also known as hookah pipes, hubbly bubbly or nagile, smoking the traditional shisha (water pipe) is a popular pastime throughout the Middle East. Shisha pipes can be smoked with a variety of flavours, such as strawberry, grape, mint or apple. Unlike a normal cigarette or cigar, the smoke is softened by the water, although it still causes smoking-related health problems (1g of shisha smoke has 100 times the tar content of a cigarette). Smoking shisha is an enjoyable experience but it's wise not to make it a habit. During Ramadan, when Iftar tents are erected throughout cities, shisha smoking is particularly popular.

Shisha pipes

CRIME

While crime figures aren't officially released, the UAE is known for having a low crime rate. Serious crimes like rape and murder are infrequent and unlikely to affect the quality of life of the average expat. The most common reason for expats getting on the wrong side of the law is often alcohol. In the UAE there is a zero-tolerance policy on drinking and driving; if you are arrested for this, the usual penalty is a minimum 30 days in prison. Being drunk and disorderly in public is also something that can land you in trouble.

Some stories about expats finding themselves on the wrong side of the law have gained international news coverage, and their seemingly harsh punishments do very little to appease concerned foreigners looking to relocate to the country. However, so long as you respect the UAE's laws, religion and cultural differences and act like a civilised human being, you'll be unlikely to land yourself in any kind of trouble.

Laws To Know

Get a liquor licence If you buy alcohol outside of a hotel you're required to have a liquor licence.
Don't live as an unmarried couple Unrelated men and women in a physical relationship cannot live together. You'd be unlucky to be pulled up on this law though.
Don't get pregnant out of wedlock At some point any hospital will ask to see your marriage certificate during the nine months up to birth. If you're unmarried and pregnant you may have issues registering the birth and may also be in hot water for non-marital sex.
Don't have one for the road The UAE has a zero tolerance approach to drink driving. There is no safe limit.
Illegal meds Some over-the-counter medicines from your home country may be illegal here. The Ministry of Health's website moh.gov.ae has a list of approved drugs.
Respect Ramadan Eating, drinking, smoking and even chewing gum in public during the daylight hours of Ramadan is illegal. You need to wait until *Iftar* (breaking of the fast) to eat, drink or smoke in public.
Don't phone while driving It's completely illegal to use your phone without a hands-free device, despite being one of the most flouted laws in history.
Get your Resident ID All expats must have a national identity card. Visit eida.gov.ae for details.
Don't bounce cheques Passing bad cheques is taken seriously in the UAE, resulting in fines or imprisonment.
Look before lighting up Smoking is illegal in many public areas such as shopping malls.

Dos & Don'ts

You'll find that, in general, people in the UAE are patient when it comes to cultural etiquette and are keen to explain their customs to you. However, there are a few cultural dos and don'ts that you should be aware of to avoid causing offence or landing yourself in trouble with the law.

PDAs
Public displays of affection are a no-no in the UAE and anything more than an innocent peck on the cheek will at best earn you disapproving looks from passers-by.

Appropriate attire
Beach wear on the beach is fine, but in public, dress should be more conservative. Covering shoulders and knees is a safe bet if you are unsure. It's wise for women to carry a pashmina so they can cover up when necessary. That said, pretty much anything goes when out at bars and clubs.

Arabic coffee
If you're offered traditional Arabic coffee (*kahwa*) during a meeting, it is polite to drink some. Cups should be taken in the right hand, and if there is a waiter there to replenish your cup, the signal to say you have had enough is to gently shake the cup from side to side.

Business etiquette
Introductions and small talk usually start a business meeting, with exchanging of business cards. Treat a received card with respect, like it's an extension of the person who gave it. Being late for a meeting is considered bad manners, but punctuality doesn't mean it will start at the appointed time or be uninterrupted.

Home values
When visiting an Emirati house, it is customary to remove your shoes. Traditionally men and women dine separately and meals are eaten sat on floor cushions. Be careful when sitting not to point your feet at anyone or show the soles of your feet. Try everything offered at the meal, but if not sure you'll like something, just take a small amount. If you invite a Muslim to your home, offering pork or alcohol may cause offence.

Meeting people
While warm greetings and long handshakes are common, if you are meeting someone of the opposite sex a handshake may not always be welcome. It's best to wait until they first offer their hand. It's polite to send greetings to a person's family, but can be considered rude to enquire directly about someone's wife, sister or daughter. The customary nose kiss greeting used between men in the Gulf region shouldn't be attempted either.

Photography
Like anywhere in the Arab world, it is courteous to ask permission before photographing people, particularly women. Photographs of government and military buildings shouldn't be taken, especially if there are 'no photography' signs. Unwitting tourists have found themselves in deep trouble for this before.

Out on the town
Dubai has a good variety of nightlife and alcohol is widely available in the city's hotel bars, pubs and clubs (see Going Out section). Remember, however, that you're in a Muslim country and drunken or lewd behaviour in not only disrespectful but can lead to arrest and detention.

Tipping
Tipping is not compulsory, but tipping for good service is common, normally around 10% of your bill. For valet-parking at hotels a Dhs.5 tip is average. Taxi fares are often rounded up to include a tip, but not if the driving standards were poor. Many restaurants include a 10% service charge although it's unclear how much will find its way into your waiter's pocket, so some people add a little extra.

The Legal System

The legal system in the UAE is a mix of Shariah (Islamic) and conventional laws, implemented by the Federal Judiciary. In comparison to Saudi Arabia and other Arab nations, the laws in the UAE are more liberal, but it is a Muslim country and so more conservative than some western countries. All emirates have Courts of First Instance and Courts of Appeal, either federal or local, in addition to the Shariah Courts which mainly deal with matters of personal status involving Muslims, such as marriage, divorce and inheritance.

Keep Calm

It pays to keep your calm if involved in any altercation; obscene gestures or profane language, even on the phone, are bad news. Physically or verbally abuse anyone so that it causes them harm, and you may end up in prison, unless the victim chooses to drop the charges.

Police

Dubai Police are generally calm and helpful – if you stay on the right side of the law. The police have a visible presence in the city, albeit not as prominent as in other large cities; you can recognise the police by their green army-style uniform and green and white saloon cars or 4WDs. You are most likely to be stopped for a traffic offence; you must always carry your driving licence and vehicle registration – failure to do so could result in a fine. If you are stopped by the police, it is important to appear helpful and co-operative at all times. Even if you are positive you are in the right, arguing your case aggressively or being impolite could land you in further trouble. If you are being charged with a very serious offence it is advisable to contact your embassy for more advice.

In an effort to better serve Dubai's visitors, the Dubai Police has launched the Department for Tourist Security. It acts as a liaison between you and Dubai Police, although in general police officers are extremely helpful. Its website (dubaipolice.gov.ae) is easy to navigate, helpful and has extensive information on policies and procedures. For assistance, call the toll free number (800 4438). This is a non-emergency number that you can call for information about the Dubai Police, its services and the locations of stations.

There is a hotline for people suffering problems at the beach such as sexual harassment (04 266 1228). However, for other emergency services call 999 for the police or ambulance and 997 for the fire department.

If You're Arrested

You'll first be taken to a police station and, if applicable, a court date will be set. Get arrested on a Thursday evening though and you'll be in the cell all weekend until the courts reopen; if it's a holiday (such as Eid) you could be there for longer. If the offence is a minor one, you may get bail; the police will keep your passport and often the passport of another UAE resident who is willing to vouch for you. If you don't get bail you'll be held in the police cell until the hearing.

All court proceedings are in Arabic so you'll need to hire a translator. If sentenced, you'll go straight from court to jail.

If you're in trouble with the law it's advisable to contact your embassy as soon as possible. They won't be able to pay your legal fees, secure bail, act as lawyers or get you released, but they can liaise with family, offer advice on procedures and provide you with a list of translators and lawyers.

Victim Support

Women and children who are victims of domestic violence can contact the Family Development Foundation (fdf.ae) for counselling and advice. The UAE Red Crescent runs women's shelters in Dubai, victims of sexual abuse can contact the National Committee to Combat Human Trafficking (nccht.gov.ae) for information on support services in the UAE, and Dubai Police (dubaipolice.gov.ae) also offers support for child victims of abuse.

Naif Police Station

LOCAL MEDIA

Media is one particular area that has boomed in the UAE. Expats from around the world have been recruited to voice the radio, write the newspapers and magazines, and film the TV shows. The idea is that their knowledge from more established media markets can be passed on to Emiratis and help local media to flourish further. The upshot of this is that there are many decent local media products available in the UAE now.

Censorship

International magazines are available in bookshops and supermarkets, at inflated prices. All titles are examined and, where necessary, censored to ensure that they don't offend the country's moral codes. You'll find much the same is true of the many international films and TV shows available in the UAE.

Internet

Around 85% of the UAE's population is online, reflecting how easy it is to get connected in the larger cities. Internet offerings might not be quite as quick as in areas like the US or Europe, but the UAE still ranks near the top for connectivity.

There are some things that expats need to remember though, particularly the despised proxy that blocks access to any site deemed offensive. What is or isn't offensive is up to the Telecommunication Regulatory Authority (TRA) which supposedly applies the same rules to both Etisalat and du subscribers, the two main providers.

Living in a Muslim community that means sites containing pornography (or explicit images) or dubious religious content will be blocked. Sites that offer online dating, gambling or drugs, and, oddly, some photo-sharing websites are also out of bounds. Of course, you can access these sites with the help of a proxy blocker (VPN), but then you're technically breaking the law.

Internet Entertainment

While satellite and digital TV or local radio were the only options to expats missing programmes from home, the internet now makes viewing and listening to favourites easy. Radio stations aren't blocked online, but you may need a VPN to access sources like Netflix. If you're using a tablet like an iPad, then cables can be bought to link it to your TV so you can even view it on a larger screen.

Similarly, despite VoIP (Voice over Internet Protocol) access having been blocked for a long time, regulators finally authorised it in 2010, but only to the four existing licence-holders; Etisalat, du and the satellite firms Yahsat and Thuraya. That meant making international calls through the internet was still effectively banned as authorised VoIP services weren't available from these companies. In 2013, both Etisalat and du lifted the ban on downloading the popular Skype service though, perhaps realising that the loss in revenue from calls could be made up by increased data use from customers.

It is shrouded in some confusion though, as Skype calls to mobile or landline phones still don't tend to work without a proxy blocker (such as VPN mentioned above). However, Skype or Google Chat can both be used well when communicating from computer to computer. The growth and popularity of the smartphone market here has also opened up a whole new world of communications for people and there are range of messaging apps enabling you to keep in touch with friends and family back home.

USEFUL APPS

Food On Click	Order takeaway from a selection of hundreds of eateries
The Dubai Mall	GPS app to help you find your way around the world's largest mall
Salik	Keep up-to-date on your Salik toll charges (the Dubai road toll system)
UAE Business	Guide to registration, licensing and costs for free zones and the mainland across UAE
UAE Off-Road	Choose from a selection of off-road routes and follow the interactive GPS coordinates
Abu Dhabi Map	A handy interactive map that offers detailed descriptions for POI and landmarks
Dubai Map	Navigate the city like a local with this handy and interactive map app

Radio

The UAE has a number of commercial radio stations that broadcast in a wide range of languages. The leading English stations operate 24 hours a day.

Your digital or satellite TV may offer various radio channels as well as music television like MTV and VH1. Internet radio is the other and possibly most comprehensive option, with most of your favourite channels from home available on the web.

BBC World Service: MW at 1413 and 639 kHz, bbc.co.uk/worldserviceradio
Channel 4 104.8FM: contemporary music for a younger audience, 104.8FM Shk Khalifa Bin Zayed St, Ajman, 06 06 746 1 444, *channel4FM.com*
Coast 103.2FM: middle of the road tunes and classic hits throughout the day, 103.2FM Nr Al Nasr Cinema, Zabeel Rd, Ajman, 06 600 55 1622, 1032thecoast.com
Dubai 92: music, competitions and popular DJs on 92.00FM, BS16 Bldg, Dubai, 04 391 2000, *dubai92.com*
Dubai Eye 103.8: quality talk radio, 103.8FM. BS16 Bldg, Dubai, 04 435 4700, *dubaieye1038.com*
Radio 1: hit music broadcast across the country, 104.1FM Gulf News, Dubai, 04 406 2677, *myradio1.ae*
Radio 2: contemporary music for the UAE, 99.3FM Gulf News, Dubai, 04 406 2677, *myradio2.ae*
Virgin Radio 104.4: hit music along the lines of Virgin Radio in other cities, 104.4FM Dubai, 04 391 2000, *virginradiodubai.com*

Newspapers

There's no shortage of reading material for expats, with a number of daily English language broadsheets. Abu Dhabi's The National is very popular, being one of the first to deliver real journalism in the region, but Gulf News, Khaleej Times and Gulf Today are all readily available. Most supermarkets will also have some foreign newspapers if you're missing a tabloid from home. Around Dubai you can also find 7Days daily tabloid newspaper and various magazines with events and news of the city. The UAE also has its own versions of many popular international magazines, like Esquire, Ok!, Hello, Grazia, Good Housekeeping, Men's Fitness and Stuff. Keep an eye out for expat titles like Connector, as well as for listings magazines like Time Out and What's On.

Television

Satellite or cable TV is a staple in most expat homes – although a bit hit and miss compared to international standards. Some shows are aired just a few days later than they are in the US or UK, while others are delayed by a few months. OSN (osn.com) offers a range of TV packages, although the free-to-air channels such as Dubai One, Fox Movies and MBC are improving year on year. If you have digital or satellite TV then you probably have internet access, which is another route to take for watching your favourite programmes.

USEFUL WEBSITES

Dubai	7days.ae	Free and popular national daily newspaper
	definitelydubai.com	UAE Government official tourism site
	dha.gov.ae	Dubai Health Authority: numbers and e-services
	dm.gov.ae	Dubai Municipality
	dubaipolice.gov.ae	Dubai Police Headquarters
	dubaitourism.ae	Department of Tourism & Commerce Marketing
	dubizzle.com	Dubai's largest website for classifieds and community
UAE Information	ameinfo.com	Middle East business news
	expatwoman.com	Living in UAE from a woman's perspective
	government.ae	UAE government website
	gulfnews.com	Local newspaper
	khaleejtimes.com	Local newspaper
	propertyfinder.ae	Rental and sales property portal
	sheikhmohammed.co.ae	Info on Sheikh Mohammed bin Rashid Al Maktoum
	sheikhzayed.com	Dedicated to the life of the late UAE President
	thenational.ae	National newspaper
	uae4kidz.biz	Great site for kids' info
	uaeinteract.com	UAE National Media Council

UAE NATIONAL DAY

Every 2 December, the country turns green, black, red and white all over. In fact, the flag becomes as ubiquitous as traffic jams as residents throughout the emirates celebrate the birth of the UAE. Cars, trucks and taxis are decorated with flags and pictures of the country's rulers to show their patriotism. And, especially along the Beach Road, in public parks, bands and folklore exhibitions entertain the crowds. The National Day Downtown Dubai Parade features floats, balloons, performers, horses, camels and music groups. It wouldn't be a celebration without spectacular fireworks and, as the city is illuminated, it's almost impossible not to feel patriotic.

Traditional Arabic dhows

UAE CALENDAR

The Islamic calendar starts from the year 622AD, the year of the Prophet Muhammad's migration (*Hijra*) from Mecca to Al Madinah. Hence the Islamic year is called the *Hijra* year and dates are followed by AH (AH stands from *Anno Hegirae*, meaning 'after the year of the *Hijra*').

Public Holidays

During the year there are holidays on set dates, such as National Day every December 2nd. Other Islamic holidays are based on the sighting of the moon and therefore the dates vary. Often this can mean confirmation of a holiday less the 24 hours before it is due, something most companies will inform employees about via email when it is announced.

The main Muslim festivals during the year are *Eid Al Fitr* (the festival of the breaking of the fast, which marks the end of Ramadan) and *Eid Al Adha* (the festival of sacrifice, which marks the end of the pilgrimage to Mecca). *Mawlid Al Nabee* is the holiday celebrating the Prophet Muhammad's birthday, and *Lailat Al Mi'raj* celebrates the Prophet's ascension into heaven. See below for holiday dates for your diary.

2015-2016

The list below of public holidays applies mainly to the public sector; if you work in the private sector you may get fewer days holiday per year as the days called off will be at your company's discretion. National Day, which celebrates the foundation of the federation of the United Arab Emirates in 1971, is one day for private sector workers but two days for the public sector. The day is a huge day of patriotic celebration throughout the UAE with plenty of flag flying and many buildings are adorned in the flag's vibrant colours.

New Year	1 Jan 2015 (fixed)
Mawlid Al Nabee	3 Jan 2015 (moon)
Lailat Al Mi'raj	16 May 2015 (moon)
Eid Al Fitr (3 days)	17 July 2015 (moon)
Arafat Day	22 Sept 2015 (moon)
Eid Al Adha (3 days)	23 Sept 2015 (moon)
Islamic New Year	15 Oct 2015 (moon)
UAE National Day (1 or 2 days)	2 Dec 2015 (fixed)
New Year	1 Jan 2016 (fixed)
Mawlid Al Nabee	11 Dec 2016 (moon)
Lailat Al Mi'raj	5 May 2016 (moon)

Events & Exhibitions

Dubai Shopping Festival   January-February
600 555 559
mydsf.ae
Established in 1996, the Dubai Shopping Festival is a great time to be in the city, with bargains galore for shoppers as well as many activities organised in malls across the city. Film festivals, special events for youngsters, impressive street displays, night fireworks, and international fashion shows, provide some of the cultural and entertainment programmes on offer. The prize draws held in participating malls are popular.

Omega Dubai Desert Classic   January-February
Emirates Golf Club Al Sufouh 2 **04 380 2112**
dubaidesertclassic.com
Map **1 M6** Metro **Nakheel**
This longstanding PGA European Tour fixture has been won in the past by golfing legends such as Ernie Els and Tiger Woods, and is a popular event among Dubai's golfing community.

Standard Chartered Dubai Marathon   January
Umm Suqeim Rd 04 433 5669
dubaimarathon.org
Map **1 R6** Metro **Mall of the Emirates**
This event attracts all types of runners, from those aiming to fundraise or work off that festive tummy in the 10km road race or 3km charity run, to dedicated pavement pounders and several of the biggest names in long distance running who tackle the full 42km.

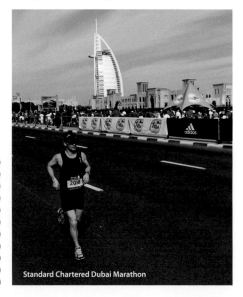
Standard Chartered Dubai Marathon

Dubai Duty Free Tennis
Championships
February-March

Dubai Tennis Stadium Al Garhoud **04 417 2415**
dubaidutyfreetennischampionships.com
Map **2 M8** Metro **GGICO**
Firmly established on the ATP and WTP circuit, the $2 million tournament attracts the world's top men's and women's seeds. Tickets for the semis and finals sell out in advance, but you can often buy tickets to the opening matches just days before at reasonable prices.

Dubai Polo Gold Cup
January-March

Dubai Polo & Equestrian Club Al Hebiah 2
050 256 9791
dubaipologoldcup.com
Map **1 N13** Metro **Dubai Internet City**
Some of the world's best polo teams and players compete for the Silver Cup and Gold Cup in this prestigious and international week-long tournament.

Emirates Airline Dubai
Jazz Festival
February

Media City Amphitheatre Al Sufouh 2 **04 391 1196**
dubaijazzfest.com
Map **2 M10** Metro **Nakheel**
The Jazz Festival, which celebrated its 12th year in 2014, attracts artists from all around the world. Courtney Pine, John Legend, James Blunt and David Gray have all performed previously.

Wild Wadi's Swim Burj Al Arab
February

Burj Al Arab Umm Suqeim 3 **04 348 4444**
jumeirah.com
Map **1 S4** Metro **First Gulf Bank**
A charity swimming race on an 800m route around the island on which the spectacular Burj Al Arab hotel sits. Both competitive swimmers and fundraisers can take part. All proceeds go to Medecins Sans Frontieres. There is also a non-competitive social swim. At the time of writing the 2015 date had not been confirmed.

Abu Dhabi Desert Challenge
March

Empty Quarter Liwa
abudhabidesertchallenge.com
Prestigious annual international event, running for five days around Liwa, in the vast Rub al Khali desert. It's the season-opening round of the FIA Cross Country Rally World Cup and the FIM Cross Country Rallies World Championship.

Art Dubai
March

Madinat Jumeirah Al Sufouh 1 **04 384 2000**
artdubai.ae
Map **1 R5** Metro **Mall of the Emirates**
An international art exhibition that sees visits from dozens of international galleries. Running alongside it is the Global Art Forum lecture and discussion board

Dubai World Cup

programme, plus art prizes including a people's choice award and the $1 million Abraaj Capital Art Prize.

Dubai International Boat Show
March

Dubai International Marine Club Marsa Dubai
04 308 6430
boatshowdubai.com
Map **1 M5** Metro **Nakheel**
You don't need to have big bucks to enjoy the Boat Show. The largest marine industry exhibition in the Middle East showcases yachts and boats from both local and international builders, together with the latest innovations in marine equipment and accessories.

Dubai World Cup
March

Meydan Racecourse Nadd Al Shiba 1 **04 327 0077**
dubaiworldcup.com
Map **2 E10** Metro **Business Bay**
The world's richest horse race takes place at the state-of-the-art Meydan race course. The huge prize fund (last year's was over $27 million), a buzzing, vibrant atmosphere, and the star-studded entertainment line-up ensure that the Dubai World Cup is one of the year's big social occasions.

Emirates Airline Festival
of Literature
March

InterContinental Dubai Festival City **04 353 4002**
emirateslitfest.com
Map **2 L9** Metro **Emirates**
This event draws a host of celebrated literary greats to take part in lectures, debates and panels. Past speakers have included Kate Adie, Alexander McCall

Smith, Carol Ann Duffy, Michael Palin and Margaret Atwood. Join the festival reading group to swot up on the latest releases by speakers.

Dubai Festival City Dragon Boat Festival
April

Al Kheeran **050 763 4008**
dubaidragonboat.com
Map **2 M9** Metro **Emirates**
Open to social, school and corporate groups, this is a fun, competitive and sociable team building event.

International Property Show
March-April

Dubai World Trade Centre Trade Center 2
04 392 3232
internationalpropertyshow.ae
Map **2 H6** Metro **World Trade Centre**
Featuring everything to do with buying international property, this show is particularly popular among expats who are looking to invest overseas.

Terry Fox Run
April

Atlantis The Palm Nakhlat Jumeira
dubaiterryfoxrun.org
Map **1 N1** Metro **Nakheel**
Each year, thousands of individuals run, jog, walk, cycle and rollerblade their way around an 8.5km course to raise funds for cancer research programmes at approved institutions around the world. At the time of writing, the 2015 date had not been confirmed. Another Terry Fox event is usually held in Ras Al Khaimah in March.

Dubai Summer Surprises
June-July

600 555 559
dubaievents.ae
Held in shopping malls around the city, with fun-packed, family-orientated activities and big shopping discounts, this is a popular event with Dubai residents and visitors looking to escape the summer heat.

Camel Racing
October-April

Camel Race Track Al Marmoom (and various location)
04 832 6526
This popular local sport is serious business, with racing camels changing hands for as much as Dhs.10 million. Races run October to March and admission is free.

GITEX Technology Week
October

Dubai World Trade Centre
Trade Center 2
gitex.com
Map **2 H6** Metro **World Trade Centre**
Part of this five-day event is the renowned Gitex Shopper, where the public can snap up some great deals on the latest technology and gadgets, which are newly released at the exhibition.

Gulf Bike Week

Gulf Bike Week
October

Dubai Media City Ampitheatre Al Sufouh 2
04 435 6101
gulfbikeweek.com
Map **2 M5** Metro **Nakheel**
Thousands of visitors attended last year's event, enjoying stunt shows in the live action arena, motorbike displays, test rides and rock concerts, with previous acts including Nickelback, N.E.R.D and Megadeth. At the time of writing, the 2015 date had not been confirmed.

DP World Tour Championship
November

Jumeirah Golf Estates Me'aisem 1
europeantour.com
Map **1 H9** Metro **Nakheel**
The world's best golfers congregate in Dubai for the final fixture of the PGA European Golf Tour and a shot at a share of the $8 million prize fund. One of Dubai's great spectator events attracting many of the world's top golfers, such as Henrik Stenson, 2013 champion.

Dubai Airshow
November

Dubai World Central Madinat Al Mataar **04 603 3300**
dubaiairshow.aero
Metro **Jebel Ali**
A five-day biennial event that has been attracting visitors for more than two decades. It began as the Arab Air Show in 1986 and today is a huge draw for all those interested in the aerospace sector, with more than 130 planes on display and spectacular aerial flybys. For the first time in 2013, the airshow moved to a new venue at Dubai World Central.

Dubai World Game Expo   November
**Dubai International Convention & Exhibition
Centre** Trade Center 2 **04 362 4717**
gameexpo.ae
Map **2 H6** Metro **World Trade Centre**
A must for all gaming fans desperate to try out the
latest software and hardware; the expo also plays host
to the Dubai World Game Championship.

Emirates Dubai
Rugby Sevens   November-December
The Sevens Al Marmoom **04 321 0008**
dubairugby7s.com
This is one of Dubai's biggest and most popular events,
as over 130,000 spectators descend on The Sevens
Stadium to watch top international teams compete for
the coveted 7s trophy, as Gulf teams contest the local
competitions. With friendly rivalry between competing
nations and prizes for the best fancy dress, the party
atmosphere carries on until the small hours.

Formula 1 Etihad Airways
Abu Dhabi Grand Prix   November
Yas Marina Circuit Abu Dhabi **02 659 9999**
yasmarinacircuit.com
Abu Dhabi always puts on a great show. As well as the
on-track action, live music has been served up by the
likes of Kanye West, Prince and Kings Of Leon, while
free concerts, exhibitions and competitions are held
for the public across the capital.

Powerboat Racing   November-Ferburary
Dubai International Marine Club Marsa Dubai
Dubai **04 399 5777**
dimc.ae
Map **1 M5** Metro **DAMAC**
The UAE is very well established on the world
championship powerboat racing circuit – in Dubai,
DIMC have a busy annual calendar of both traditional
dhow and full-throttle powerboat races. At the time of
writing, the 2015 date had not been confirmed.

UAE Horseracing   November-March
04 327 0077
emiratesracing.com
All horseracing in Dubai has moved to the impressive
Meydan City. Racing takes place at night under
floodlights (see the website for race dates) with the
winning horses, jockeys and trainers taking home
prizes or cash. The season ends with the spectacular
Dubai World Cup in March.

Whatever Floats Your Boat   November
Festival Marina Al Kheeran **04 701 1059**
Map **2 L9** Metro **Creek**
Schools and businesses build boats from recycled
materials to raise awareness of recycling and take

part in a fun day on the water. For more info, and
confirmation of date, email axelle.bouquet@ichdfc.ae.

Dubai International Film Festival   December
04 363 3456
dubaifilmfest.com
A hotly anticipated annual event showcasing
Hollywood and international arthouse films, as well
as work from the Middle East region. Premieres are
generally held at Madinat Jumeirah, while screenings
take place in cinemas across the city. The red-carpet
opening gala event has attracted Hollywood stars
such as Cate Blanchett and Kevin Spacey. It's a great
opportunity to catch non-mainstream films and do a
bit of celeb spotting.

Mother, Baby & Child Show   December
**Dubai International Convention & Exhibition
Centre** Trade Center 2
motherbabyandchild.com
Map **2 J6** Metro **World Trade Centre**
Mums and kids will love this show, featuring exhibits
by child-friendly companies and lots of entertainment
for the little ones, plus endless samples and giveaways.

Sharmila Dance Extravaganza   December
Centrepoint Theatre, DUCTAC Mall of The Emirates,
Dubai
Map **1 R6** Metro **Mall of the Emirates**
Over 160 renowned dancers perform Latino, Soul,
Indian and hip-hop. The Stuttgart Ballet and talented
local dance companies have performed here. At the
time of writing, the 2015 date had not been confirmed.

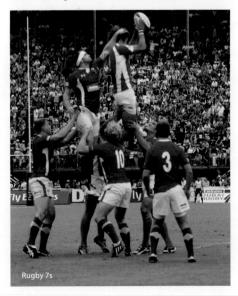
Rugby 7s

"You think it, we'll Make it"

LIVING IN DUBAI

LIVING IN DUBAI

Deciding to move to Dubai is the first step, now discover all you need to know to start a new life in the sun.

Marsa Dubai

Dubai is for most people a wonderful place to live, with excellent career opportunities, a network of social contacts, unique activities and, apart from a few sweaty months in summer, brilliant weather. Most expats tell you their standard of living is better than it was back home, they travel more, spend more time with family, enjoy outdoor living and make more friends.

Erasing The Myths

Dubai does have a reputation for being bold and brash – it likes to have the biggest and best of everything – but there's far more to the city than that. Think of Dubai's showy attitude as the persona it likes to reveal to the rest of the world, while on the inside it can actually be quite down to earth. You just have

to take time to get to know the city's personality. Yes, there are plenty of glitzy clubs and outrageously expensive restaurants, and people do dress up to the extreme, but there are also loads of low-key hidden corners, eclectic nightlife options and bars to satisfy the grungiest hippy.

The art and culture scene is growing, with new theatres, galleries and even Dubai's answer to jam sessions for aspiring musicians, as well as indie movie nights and artist groups. Life here is not just about showing off; it's not obligatory to get a flash 4WD and a Rolex, live on the Palm, and to dine in the Burj Khalifa every weekend.

Hopefully, this book, and this chapter in particular, will provide you with useful information about how to get settled in Dubai, deal with the paperwork, and eventually meet like-minded people.

CITY PROFILE

There are certain descriptions of Dubai that are frequently used: pearl of the Gulf, sleepy fishing village transformed into modern metropolis, tax-free expat haven, headquarters of luxury living, and so on. There's more than a grain of truth in these cliches, but Dubai offers so much more.

On The Up

Living in Dubai got a tad more expensive in 2014, according to the 2014 Worldwide Cost Of Living survey. The emirate is ranked number 94 in the index – published by the Economist Intelligence Unit (EIU) – climbing two places since 2013.

City Of Dreams

This chapter can help you, whether you are making the decision to move, if you've just arrived and don't know where to start, or if you find yourself faced with an overwhelming amount of red tape. Procedures and laws do change regularly, often in quite major ways. Changes are generally announced in newspapers, but they are often implemented quickly so it's a good idea to be prepared for the unexpected.

If you're still trying to make up your mind if Dubai is for you, then think about the sunny days, great shopping, outdoor living and tax-free salaries.

Economically, you'll probably find yourself slightly better off than back home, which is the draw for most expats. Prices have begun to climb again – especially rent – and salaries haven't climbed as much, but it's still affordable to live here, and if you're careful, you can also save some money each month.

The best way to make the move is to contact potential employers prior to your first visit and set up interviews and appointments to coincide with a short trip. Then head over and get a feel for the place whilst knocking a few job interviews on the head in the process. Dubai is an expensive city to live without a job, so finding the right job should be your first priority. Plus, your employer is usually the one who sponsors you and thus gets you a residence visa – you can't live in Dubai long term without this visa.

Now that Dubai will be hosting the Expo 2020, new projects are popping up all over the city, and more tourists are being tempted to visit – by the year of the Expo, Dubai hopes to host 20 million visitors annually.

BEFORE YOU ARRIVE

There are several things you can do before arriving in Dubai to help you get prepared. Be sure to run through this checklist a few weeks ahead of your planned trip:

Checklist

- Qualification certificates and important documents attested (see below)
- Inform banks, building societies and the tax office about your move to Dubai
- Speak to your pension company to see if moving to Dubai affects your pension plan
- Research schools for children well in advance and get your child's name on the waiting list
- Get information about different neighbourhoods you might want to live in
- If accommodation is not provided by your employer, arrange temporary accommodation for when you arrive
- Bring at least 10 passport-sized photos with you for the visa applications
- Organise a shipping company to move your goods over, and bear in mind it can take two-three months

Attesting Certificates

To be accepted by the authorities here, your education certificates must be verified by a solicitor or public notary in your home country, then by your foreign office to verify the solicitor as bona fide, and finally by the UAE embassy. It's a good idea to have this done before you come to Dubai. There are private attestation companies in Dubai offering a verification service, but this is likely to take a minimum two weeks.

Customs

Before you fly into Dubai, be aware that several prescription medications are banned, especially anything containing codeine or temazepam. The UAE maintains a zero-tolerance policy on recreational drugs, and even microscopic amounts could land you in jail. Your bags will be scanned on arrival to ensure you have no offending magazines or DVDs. Each passenger is allowed to bring in 400 cigarettes, 50 cigars, or 500 grams of tobacco. Non-Muslims are also allowed five bottles of wine, four bottles of liquor or 24 cans of beer and there is a value limit of Dhs.3,000 on gifts being brought into Dubai by travellers. See dubaicustoms.gov.ae for more information.

WHEN YOU ARRIVE

As you would expect during an international move to any new city, you're very likely to find a long 'to do' list waiting for you when you arrive in Dubai. You'll be doing a lot of driving around, form filling, and waiting in queues in government departments. Just keep your sense of humour handy, bear in mind that language barriers can sometimes delay things, and soon all the boring red tape will be a distant memory.

Helping You Move

Allied Pickfords (04 818 0400, alliedpickfords.ae) are an expert relocation company. They offer: total move management, transport options, purpose-built packing materials to offer maximum protection, full house, part loads and small consignments service, transit protection programme, and storage facilities all over the world.

Checklist

To get you started, here's a checklist of everything you need to do to become 'legal' in Dubai – and read on to find out exactly what to do to achieve each of the points below. Easy!

- Apply for a residence visa through your employer: you cannot live or work in Dubai without one
- Sponsor any family members who are not working for a residence visa: they also cannot live in Dubai without one
- Go for a medical test
- Apply for a Resident Identity Card: this is compulsory as part of the residence visa process
- Get a UAE driving licence: this is compulsory once you have a residence visa (if you want to drive)
- Apply for a liquor licence: this is compulsory if you plan to drink alcohol in Dubai
- Open a bank account

Arrive In Style

For a hassle-free arrival into Dubai you can book the Marhaba Meet & Greet Service (marhabaservices.com). You'll be met at arrivals before immigration, assisted through airport clearance and escorted with your baggage to the exit. A Gold package offers priority buggy car transfer, and the Family service is ideal for mothers travelling alone with children.

Visit Visa

Everyone entering the UAE needs a visit visa (also known as an entry permit) except for citizens of GCC countries; this must then be transferred to a residence visa if you plan to live and work here. The procedures for obtaining a visit visa vary depending on your nationality. Always check the regulations before travelling as details can change.

GCC citizens do not require a visa, while nationalities from 46 other countries can obtain a 30 day visa on arrival at no cost. The 30 day visa can be renewed for a further 30 days at a cost of Dhs.625, but it works out a lot cheaper to do a 'visa run' to the border of Oman, where you leave the country and re-enter on a new visit visa.

All other nationalities can apply for a visit visa in advance, sponsored by a hotel, tour operator, or a Dubai resident. The fee is Dhs.620 for a 30 day visa, and Dhs.1,120 for 90 days. Also, a Dhs.1,000 deposit should be paid by a local sponsor and can be reimbursed after the visitor has left the country.

Expats resident in other GCC countries, who do not belong to one of the 46 visa-on-arrival nationalities, but who do meet certain criteria (professions such as managers, doctors and engineers), can get a non-renewable 30 day visa on arrival – check with your airline before flying.

All visitors to the UAE must have an eye scan upon arrival at immigration, except citizens of the GCC and anyone from the countries listed below.

Visa On Arrival

Citizens of these countries receive an automatic visa on arrival: Andorra, Australia, Austria, Belgium, Brunei, Bulgaria, Canada, Croatia, Cyprus, Czech Republic, Denmark, Estonia, Finland, France, Germany, Greece, Hong Kong, Hungary, Iceland, Ireland, Italy, Japan, Latvia, Liechtenstein, Lithuania, Luxembourg, Malaysia, Malta, Monaco, Poland, The Netherlands, New Zealand, Norway, Portugal, Romania, San Marino, Singapore, Slovakia, Slovenia, South Korea, Spain, Sweden, Switzerland, United Kingdom, United States of America and Vatican City.

Business travellers can get multiple entry visas, which are issued by the General Directorate of Residency and Foreigners Affairs, the UAE's Consular offices abroad, or applied for after arrival on a visit visa. The visa is valid for 14 days, for six months from the date of issue and costs Dhs.2,100. For an additional Dhs.200, a multiple-entry visa holder is eligible to use the airport e-Gates. Cruise tourists and property investors can also apply for a multi-entry permit; conditions apply and see the government website, dnrd.ae, for details.

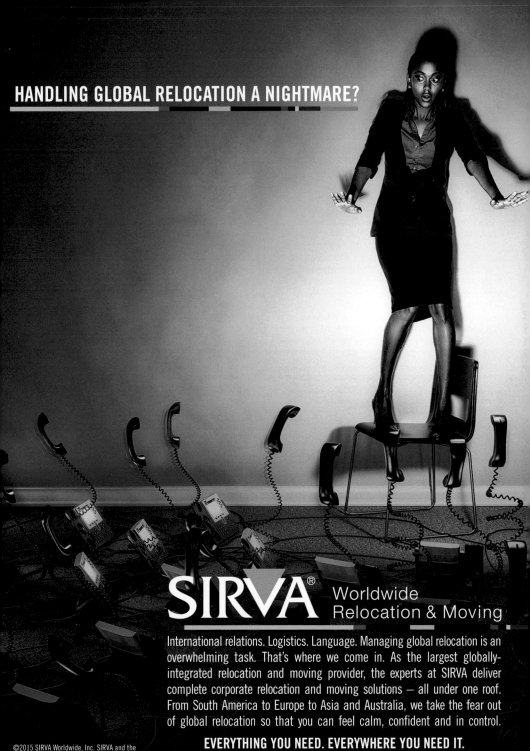

HANDLING GLOBAL RELOCATION A NIGHTMARE?

SIRVA® Worldwide Relocation & Moving

International relations. Logistics. Language. Managing global relocation is an overwhelming task. That's where we come in. As the largest globally-integrated relocation and moving provider, the experts at SIRVA deliver complete corporate relocation and moving solutions — all under one roof. From South America to Europe to Asia and Australia, we take the fear out of global relocation so that you can feel calm, confident and in control.

EVERYTHING YOU NEED. EVERYWHERE YOU NEED IT.

Call +971 2 677 9765 (Abu Dhabi) +971 4 818 0400 (Dubai) or visit SIRVA.com to learn more

There are numerous companies that will arrange visas for you for a fee of up to Dhs.50. For further advice on visas, contact the government's toll free AMER service on 800 5111.

The General Directorate of Residency and Foreigners Affairs (GDRFA) has launched technology that enables visitors to apply for, cancel and renew tourist visas through smartphones. More info: mobile@moi.gov.ae.

Residence Visas

To live in Dubai, you need a residence visa, and there are three main types: employment, family and domestic worker. You either need to have a job in the UAE and be sponsored by an employer, or be married to, or related to (son/daughter) someone who has a job here and they will sponsor you. As part of any residence visa process you will need to take a medical test and apply for your Resident Identity Card (formerly known as the Emirates ID). Once you have your visa – and this process can be completed in less than a month if your employer is on the ball – you can legally live and work in the UAE. Well, for two years at least (or three years if working in some free zones and government jobs).

Once you initially enter the UAE, you have 60 days to complete the visa application process – but it's unlikely to take that long. While your visa is being processed you should be able to leave the country as long as you have the visit visa that was stamped in your passport when you first entered. Citizens of the visa on arrival countries may need to do a 'visa run' to get a new visit visa after 30 days.

The residence visa permits you to live anywhere in the UAE, and you can live and work in different emirates. It is valid for two or three years (depending on where you work), after which you'll need to re-apply.

To renew your visa you'll need another medical, and the rest is usually looked after by your employer's PRO (Public Relations Officer). If you're out of the country for over six months, your residence visa will be cancelled.

See Explorer's *Dubai How-To* guide and visit askexplorer.com for detailed step by step procedures for all residency applications, renewals and transfers.

Interactive Kiosks

New smart kiosks currently being installed in Dubai's malls, public areas and government buildings, will allow residents to easily attend to many bureaucratic procedures. The kiosks let you pay fines, renew visas and access all the Ministry of Interior's services. They will even print maps of the nearest police station or hospital. In addition, new police kiosks will offer more than 20 smart services including printing certificates of good conduct and fine payment.

Employment Visa

To work in the UAE you need be under 65 years of age and pass the medical test. For those being sponsored by an employer for their residence visa, the majority of the legwork will be done by the company or their Public Relations Officer (PRO). Your company PRO will submit your medical certificate, passport, Resident ID application form, and attested education certificates to the General Directorate of Residency and Foreigners Affairs (GDRFA), and pay the required fees. At the same time, they will also apply for your labour card (which is now electronic since summer 2014) or free zone ID; the Ministry of Labour website (mol.gov.ae) has a facility to check the status of your labour card application online. Your employer will typically start the visa application process during your probation period. They will also be responsible for renewing the card when needed.

Your residence visa will be valid for two or three years, and to renew it you will need to complete another medical and re-apply for both the visa and your Resident ID at the same time; once again your PRO will help with this.

Free Zones

If you are an employee of a company in a free zone, the free zone authority will process your residence visa directly through the GDRFA without having to get employment approval from the Ministry of Labour. This speeds up the process significantly, and visas can sometimes be granted in a matter of hours.

Electronic Labour Card

If you are sponsored by your employer, the company will apply for your labour card (or free zone ID); technically a work permit. The card is no longer a physical card, and the process is all done electronically. If you are on a family sponsorship and decide to work, your employer and not your visa sponsor, has to apply for a labour card. You'll need to give your employer a No Objection Certificate (NOC) from your sponsor, your passport with residence visa, attested education certificates, passport photos, and a copy of your sponsor's passport. All labour cards must be renewed every two or three years in line with your residence visa; eventually, the Resident ID will replace this card.

PROs & NOCs

A PRO (Public Relations Officer) is the person in your company who liaises with government departments and carries out admin procedures: visa, residency, health card, and labour card applications.

An NOC (No Objection Certificate) is a letter stating that the person in question permits you to carry out a procedure. You'll need one of these in a variety of situations: your employer allowing you to switch jobs, or your own NOC permitting a family member to work.

10 REASONS TO LIVE HERE

Dubai is – simply put – a great place to live. Have a look at our top 10 reasons to live here.

1. **It's ready-made for outside living** Sunshine all year. There are more than 850 hectares of parks and in excess of 22,500 hectares of conservation areas. Seven Blue Flag beaches to lounge on.
2. **High standard of living** Spacious villa/apartment lifestyle, with private/shared pool in the garden. Live-in nanny or maid an affordable option. Access to world-class restaurants, attractions and hotels.
3. **It's all about the money, money, money** Competitive, tax-free salaries. Expat packages including housing, education and health allowances, if you're lucky. Cheap-as-chips fuel.
4. **Very low crime rate** It's a safe place to live and raise a family.
5. **It's a melting pot of old and new** Middle Eastern traditions are well and truly alive in the local food, architecture, dress and museums. Where else can you watch camel racing and the international golf and tennis in one weekend?
6. **Access to world-class education** Highly rated public schools and universities.
7. **Developing arts and cultural centre** The region will be home to the Dubai Modern Art Museum and Opera House District – it doesn't get artier than that. International superstars, the likes of Bruno Mars, The Killers and Florence and the Machine, come to town – and you can get tickets!
8. **Meet and work with many nationalities** Explore new cuisines and learn about different cultures.
9. **You're at the centre of everything – literally** It's only a 30 minute drive at most to any attraction, restaurant or beach from home. Dubai airports are less than a five-hour flight away from Goa, the Seychelles, parts of Africa and Europe, and the Maldives. Depending on the traffic, it's a one-hour drive to Abu Dhabi.
10. **It's the future** Forward-thinking companies. Fast-developing landscape. Growing economy.

Cost Of Living

Most expats find they enjoy a higher quality of living in Dubai than back home, but it's worth calculating how far that salary can take you.

Housing

Property prices and rents are on the increase, but you should still be able to keep the cost of your accommodation to a maximum of a third of your income. If you want to rent, as most expats initially do, spend a couple of months searching because you have to sift through some less desirable properties and prices before you find what you want. You'll need to search for newly advertised abodes on a daily basis to find the best deals because they get snapped up the same day (especially if you're looking to rent a room in a shared house). Be aware that many landlords ask for quarterly, half-yearly or annual rent up front – so you'll need some savings to get started. For a more detailed breakdown of property prices see the Housing section.

Transport costs

The good news is that taxis are dirt cheap and readily available. A 15 minute journey comes in at around Dhs.25. Likewise, the metro and buses are also affordable and you can expect to pay in the range of Dhs.2 and Dhs.7 for a single journey, depending on the distance travelled and the type of card purchased.

Special Deals

Residents soon learn that there are many ways to get discounts on everything from restaurant meals, to beauty treatments and holidays. There are several online companies offering special deals, such as groupon.ae and cobone.com as well as The Entertainer books full of vouchers, available to buy at most supermarkets and bookshops.

Food and drink

Depending on your tastes, eating out can be cheap as chips if you visit some of the authentic Indian eateries in Bur Dubai, or you can pay top dollar for a Michelin-star meal at a number of the city's poshest restaurants. Every weekend, many restaurants offer all you can eat and drink brunch for a fixed price, which is a good way to dine out cheaply as the best-priced deals begin at Dhs.150 per person. See the Going Out section for our pick of budget eateries.

As with restaurants, supermarkets also vary – the most affordable include stores such as Choithrams and LuLu, and the more upscale stores are Spinneys and Waitrose. Much of the fruit and veg have to be imported and so costs slightly more than back home, but other groceries are comparable in price what you are used to. A family of four will need about Dhs.2,400 to buy monthly groceries.

As alcohol is taxed it's advisable to set a budget for your social tipples because otherwise those nights on the town can end up putting a big hole in your pocket. Girls should look out for special 'ladies nights' where females get free or discounted drinks, while everyone should check which bar is holding a happy hour. Full price, it can cost as much as Dhs.50 for a pint of beer.

Petrol

An added bonus is that fuel is extremely affordable and it generally costs no more than Dhs.100 for a full tank in a mid-range family car. A Jeep Liberty 4WD costs about Dh.120 to fill up, a Mazda 2 hatchback about Dhs.60 – and don't forget to tip the petrol pump attendant.

Renting a car

Many new arrivals choose to rent a car, and it's worth haggling over prices as rental companies will negotiate. For an older saloon-type car you can find deals starting at Dhs.1,300 per month if you commit to six months or more. Renting a new family sized saloon will set you back about Dhs.1,800 monthly. Make sure you opt for the best insurance package you can to help put your mind at ease when you find new dents along the side from inconsiderate door-openers in neighbouring parking spaces.

Buying a car

If you've always dreamed of owning an expensive sports car or 4WD, living in the UAE might be your opportunity. Many expats find the cost of cars is much lower in the UAE than in their home country. Try test driving one of the latest sports models or 4WDs at one of the dealers or in the city centre. You'll also find good-quality second-hand cars with low mileage being sold by expats who are packing up and moving on. Visit a dealer or check out the used vehicles for sale on websites such as dubizzle.com.

Maids and nannies

A maid may cost Dhs.1,600 to Dhs.3,000 a month plus a food, clothes and toiletries allowance. You'll also need to cover their flight home at least every two years, their annual visa costs and basic health insurance.

Education

For a good school you can expect to pay Dhs.25,000 plus per year for the nursery years, Dhs.30,000 and up for the middle primary years, and as much as Dhs.80,000 per year for secondary school. Ouch! On top of this you will usually need to pay around Dhs.500 to put your child's name on a school's waiting list, and a registration fee (around Dhs.2,000), which comes off the fees.

Health insurance

By 2016, all employers must provide employees with basic health insurance. However, you may want to pay extra for more comprehensive health insurance, with extra cover for dental, maternity etc. This can cost about Dhs.180 a month. Without insurance, a medical consultation will cost you around Dhs.150-300, a dental check-up Dhs.250, and a hip replacement Dhs.50,000.

Additional costs

Consider also the expense of travelling on your annual holidays and back home to visit family and friends. Most employers provide one flight per year back home for expat employees, but the whole family is not always covered. The good news is that Dubai is surrounded by countries where you can enjoy very cheap holidays, such as India, Sri Lanka or SE Asia.

Average Prices

Cappuccino (regular)	Dhs.15
Water (small bottle)	Dhs.1
Milk (regular, 1 litre)	Dhs.5.50
Glass of wine	Dhs.40
Pint of beer	Dhs.35
Eggs (12)	Dhs.9
Average monthly utility bills for one-bed apartment	Dhs.500
Taxi (5km trip)	Dhs.10
Monthly internet bill	Dhs.250
Monthly gym membership	Dhs.300
Cinema ticket	Dhs.40
Fuel	Dhs.1.72 per litre

Dubai Marina

Family Visa

If you have a UAE residence visa (employment) you should be able to sponsor your family members (wife, husband, children), allowing them to stay in the country as long as you are here. If the family member is already in the country on a visit visa you can still apply for their residency. You'll need to pay Dhs.680 to have the visa swapped. If the family member ends up getting a job, they don't need to change to employer sponsorship, but the company will need to apply for a labour card for them.

You will need a minimum monthly salary of Dhs.3,000 plus accommodation, or a minimum all-inclusive salary of Dhs.4,000. Only what is printed on your labour contract will be accepted as proof of your earnings, so make sure you're happy with this before starting the job.

Visa Procedures

Everything related to your visa is handled at the General Directorate of Residency and Foreigners Affairs (GDRFA), also known as the Department of Naturalisation and Residency Dubai – DNRD (dnrd.ae/en). There are GDRFA branches across Dubai in Umm Suqeim, Deira, Karama and Dubai International Airport (T3), and the HQ is in Al Jafiliya.

If that's all in place, you'll need to take your passport, the passports of the family member(s), their Resident ID application form certified by the EIDA, your labour contract, attested marriage and/or birth certificates for spouse/child, and their medical test results if over 18. You will also need copies of your Ejari-registered tenancy contract – see the Renting section in this chapter for further information – and a copy of a DEWA utilities bill (which covers your gas, electricity and water) in the sponsor's name. Take all documents to the Family Entry Permit counter at the General Directorate of Residency and Foreigners Affairs (GDRFA). Your company PRO may help, but in most cases you will need to do it (and pay for it) on your own.

The family member's passport with residence visa stamp can be collected within three to five days, or you can pay Dhs.15 to have it couriered to you. You will be responsible for renewing their visas; they will be valid for two or three years in line with your employment visa. If switching jobs, and therefore sponsorship, you can avoid having to cancel your spouse and/or children's visas by paying Dhs.5,000 to the GDRFA; this will be refunded once your new visa is issued.

Renewing a visa is a relatively simple process that requires another medical test. Expat residents in Dubai are now required to renew and show their Resident

Identity Card for residence visa renewal. For further information on all procedures related to visas, see Explorer's *Dubai How-To* guide.

Sponsoring Your Husband

A working woman can sponsor her husband if she meets the minimum salary requirements; in this scenario, the spouse's visa must be renewed annually. If a husband sponsors his wife, the visa need only be renewed every two or three years, depending on whether he works in the private or public sector.

Older Children

For parents sponsoring children, difficulties arise when sons (not daughters) turn 18. Unless they are enrolled in full-time education at a recognised institution in the UAE, they must transfer their visa to an employer. Or, the parents can pay a one-off Dhs.5,000 deposit and apply for an annual visa, which must be renewed yearly and is valid until the son turns 21. Daughters can stay on their father's sponsorship until they marry.

Property Owners

Property owners and investors (and sometimes their family) can apply for a six-month multiple-entry permit, which is renewable for Dhs.2,000 provided the owner leaves and then re-enters the country. This is a permit, and doesn't give the holder as many rights as residency, such as being able to apply for a UAE driving licence, bank account etc. The property value must be a minimum of Dhs.1 million.

Sponsoring Your Parents

There are constraints when Dubai residents want to sponsor their parents – a new ruling at the end of 2013 states that individuals must earn a minimum monthly salary of Dhs.20,000 or Dhs.19,000 and live in a two-bedroom accommodation before they can sponsor their parents. The tenancy contract must be Ejari-registered, as must the proof of salary certificate (by the Ministry of Labour).

Upon applying to sponsor a parent a Dhs.2,000 deposit per parent is charged. In addition, you also need a letter stating that your parents are dependent on you and have no one at home to look after them, and this letter must be verified by the embassy in your home country. Contact the GDRFA for more information (dnrd.ae).

Domestic Worker Visa

It's not unusual in Dubai to have a live-in maid or nanny. If you have one, you will need to organise and pay for her immigration, labour and health documents. She

must be a national of Bangladesh, India, Ethiopia or Sri Lanka, and be under 58 years. In 2014, Indonesia and the Philippines stopped sending maids to the UAE.

To sponsor a domestic worker (maid/nanny) you must have a salary above Dhs.6,000 per month, and be able to provide the maid with housing and benefits, including an airfare home at least once every two years. The process is similar to sponsoring a family member, although you'll also be asked to sign a contract stating the domestic worker's salary (typically around Dhs1,600-2,500 per month). You will need copies of your Ejari-registered tenancy contract and a DEWA utilities bill. You will also need to apply for her entry permit, Resident ID card, labour card and government health card (unless you choose to pay for private healthcare). The residence visa is then valid for one year, and allows a maid/nanny to legally live and work in Dubai. From 2016, all employers have to provide private health insurance under the new government scheme – Insurance System for Advancing Healthcare in Dubai (ISAHD – 'bringing happiness' in Arabic).

There are additional costs involved – you have to pay a 'maid tax' of around Dhs.5,080 per year (to the GDRFA), as well as a refundable deposit of Dhs.3,000. The maid/nanny will need to pass a medical test, as well as be tested for pregnancy. Additionally, there's a one-off Dhs.50 fee for a compulsory Hepatitis B vaccination. There will also be a small typing fee and Dhs.130 payment to have the employment contract attested if the maid is a private sector employee outside of a free zone.

See Explorer's *Dubai How-To* guide for a step-by-step guide to renewing, cancelling and transferring a domestic worker visa.

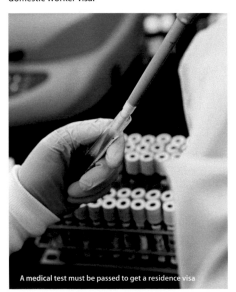
A medical test must be passed to get a residence visa

Medical Test

Any expat over the age of 18 must pass a medical test in order to get any type of residence visa. You will be tested for communicable diseases such as tuberculosis and HIV; if your tests are positive you will be deported to your home country. You will also need to have a chest x-ray to test for TB.

If you are sponsored by your employer, your PRO will arrange for you to take the medical test. Otherwise, it's up to you to get yourself to a Dubai Health Authority medical fitness centre with the following: test form completed in Arabic (there are typing offices near the medical centres that can do this for you for around Dhs.20), passport and visit visa, proof that your Resident ID Card application is underway, and the test fee of Dhs.250.

Once you have taken the required tests (expect to wait for around one to three hours, although you can pay Dhs.500 for a VIP/same-day service) you will be given a receipt, which will tell you when to collect your medical certificate (usually three days later).

See Dubai Health Authority (dha.gov.ae) for a full list of medical centres; some offer complete medical tests for all applicants, others are dedicated to female, executive employees or domestic workers. They also offer varying services: normal, 24 or 48 hours, and VIP. Free zones including JAFZA and DIFC have their own medical centres, as does Emirates airline.

Executive Medical Test

If you want to avoid the queues and are happy to splash that extra cash for convenience, visit Al Safa Health Centre. Arrive at 8am with your documents at the ready and there are hardly any queues. You'll be fast-tracked through the medical process and will be able to collect your medical forms that same afternoon. The executive medical test costs Dhs.690.

As with nannies and maids, all female domestic workers must also take a pregnancy test as part of the medical exam. Those working at nurseries, salons and health clubs, must also complete a course of Hepatitis B vaccinations, which costs Dhs.50; this is then valid for 10 years, so keep the certificate as proof.

You will need to take a medical test every two or three years depending on when you need to renew your residence visa; domestic workers must take the test annually in line with their visa.

You may find the government testing centres chaotic, which can be a little bit scary if this is your first experience of Dubai's healthcare system. Rest assured that, despite appearances, medical hygiene standards are followed and test results are processed efficiently. A good tip is to go wearing a plain, pale-coloured

T-shirt: this way you should not have to remove your clothes and wear a hospital gown (which may have been used by someone else before you) for your x-ray.

Online Applications

You can complete the necessary paperwork, submit required documents and pay the fees online at dha.gov.ae – a big time saver. To apply online you'll need a health card number; you can apply for a temporary one at dha.gov.ae if you don't already have one. After attending the DHA centre you will receive your test results via SMS, and then you just need to collect the test certificate. Once you have the results you will be able to proceed with the residence visa procedure.

Health Card

Once you have passed your medical test and obtained your residence visa, you are able to get a DHA health card. If you are not covered by a company or private medical insurance, it is advisable to apply for a health card as it entitles residents to low cost medical treatment at public hospitals and clinics. See Health, later in this chapter. The health card must be renewed each year (this can be done online at dha.gov.ae), but you only need to take a new medical test when your visa is up for renewal.

Digital Age

The Department of Health & Medical Services is embracing the digital age; online booking is now available at government health clinics and health cards can be renewed using the Express HC service. Register at dha.gov.ae to use these services.

Resident Identity Card

All expats living in Dubai need to register with the Emirates Identity Authority (EIDA) for a Resident Identity Card (previously called Emirates ID) before applying for their residence visa. Without a card you won't be able to complete the medical tests required for the visa. Additionally, if you fail to sign up you'll also face daily fines of Dhs.20, up to a total of Dhs.1,000.

Each card contains the holder's address, photo, date of birth and fingerprints, and is now an official source of identification in the UAE. It will eventually replace all other cards, such as health cards and labour cards, and can already be used at the e-Gate service at Dubai International Airport if the user pays the Dhs.150 activation fee (renewable every two years for Dhs.150). Great for frequent flyers!

UAE nationals must pay Dhs.100 for their ID cards; expat residents pay Dhs.100 per year of validity on their residence visa (two years on the visa equals Dhs.200), plus a small delivery fee. Children under the age of 15 also need one, but the fee is halved.

To register for your card, take your passport with your visit or residence visa, ID fee and a typing fee of Dhs.30 to an authorised typing centre, where your application will be filled in and translated into Arabic. Then, take the completed form to a registration centre, with your fee receipt, where you'll be fingerprinted and have your photo taken. You will then need your Resident ID application form, certified by the EIDA, to process your residence visa. Once your residence visa is approved and stamped you will receive a confirmation SMS that your Resident ID card is ready for collection; alternatively, it can be delivered to you (for an additional fee of Dhs.20). A fast-track service at the Al Barsha centre sees Resident IDs ready within 24 hours. See id.gov.ae for those who are exempt from fees when applying for the Resident Identity Card.

For new residents this process is wrapped up in the visa application process and your company PRO will look after the whole process. If you're already a resident and need to apply, a list of registration centres and further details can be found at id.gov.ae. If you're registering yourself you'll need to take your passport to an authorised typing centre to get the forms processed. You'll then receive a SMS confirmation of your appointment to get your fingerprints and photograph taken (a step everyone must go through), then receive your ID card a few weeks later.

Apply Online

You can apply online at id.gov.ae and pay by credit card for first-time registration, renewals and replacement ID cards. This not only speeds up the process, it saves the need to visit a typing centre. If applying for a new card, you'll then be able to reserve an appointment to visit a Resident ID registration centre where your fingerprints and a photograph will be taken. Once it's time to renew your ID, you should be able to complete the entire process online. A list of authorised typing and registration centres, plus up-to-date information, can be found at id.gov.ae.

For a step-by-step guide to applying for or renewing a Resident ID, see Explorer's *Dubai How-To* guide.

Bank On It

Plans are in the pipeline for the Resident ID to be used as a bank card. Results of the pilot phase with UAE Central Bank in 2014 are still being assessed. If the project is deemed successful, bank cards will be integrated with ID cards, meaning that you can use them at ATMs. This service is optional for all Resident ID card holders.

Driving Licence

If you're in Dubai on a visit visa you can drive a rental car so long as you have a valid driving licence from your home country or an International Driving Permit (IDP). Once you have your residence visa, however, you must apply for a UAE driving licence (apart from GCC nationals who are allowed to drive on their existing GCC licences). This licence is then valid for 10 years. Countries listed below are given the option of an automatic licence transfer. If you are not eligible, you will have to re-sit a theory and practical driving test. It is the same procedure for obtaining a motorcycle licence.

If you are a resident with a UAE driving licence and you cancel your visa and leave Dubai, and then return later on another visa, your UAE driving licence will still be valid (as long as it hasn't reached the expiry date on the licence). If you do need to renew your licence, you can now do so at one of the RTA's 16 smart kiosks across the city (see rta.ae).

Traffic Police

Traffic Police HQ: Al Quds St, Al Twar 1 (04 269 4444)
Bur Dubai Police Station: Nr Trade Centre Roundabout, Al Jafiliya (04 398 1111)
Bur Dubai Traffic Department: Al Qouz Industrial 3 (04 347 2222)

Automatic Licence Transfer

Citizens with licences from the following countries are eligible for automatic driving licence transfers: Australia, Austria, Bahrain, Belgium, Canada, Denmark, Finland, France, Germany, Greece, Ireland, Italy, Japan, Kuwait, the Netherlands, New Zealand, Norway, Oman, Poland, Portugal, Qatar, Romania, Saudi Arabia, South Africa, South Korea, Spain, Sweden, Switzerland, Turkey, United Kingdom, United States.

Licence holders from some countries require translation or consulate letters: Canada, Greece, Cyprus, Poland, Turkey, Japan and South Korea.

You can read about the exact procedure to follow to get your UAE driving licence in Explorer's step-by-step *Dubai How-To* guide. In short, you need to take an eye test and submit the following documents to the Roads and Transport Authority (RTA): existing foreign licence, passport with residence visa, resident ID, No Objection Certificate (NOC) from your sponsor or employer, and Dhs.410. The licence is produced within minutes and is valid for 10 years.

Eye Test

To get a UAE driving licence, you'll need to take an eye test at an RTA/government-approved opticians. Just go to an optician and tell them you need the driving licence eye test; most will do it there and then for around Dhs.100. You'll need two passport photos. Once passed, you'll receive a stamped form that can be used in your licence application.

Online services

These opticians are approved to upload eye test results electronically to the RTA and renew driver licences: Barakat Optical, Grand Optics, Magrabi Optical, Yateem Optician and Al Jaber. Driving fines and fees can also be paid online, through RTA call centres, or at an RTA office.

Liquor Licence

Dubai has a relatively liberal attitude towards alcohol. You can't buy alcohol in supermarkets, but you can buy it from licensed liquor shops for home consumption if you have a liquor licence. Independent restaurants cannot serve alcohol, but hotels, sports clubs and areas with special dispensation (Festival City and Wafi, for example) are permitted to serve alcoholic drinks in their bars and restaurants.

There's some confusion about what the legal situation really is, so let's clear a few things up. To drink in a bar or restaurant you need to be 21 or older. Visitors do not require a licence to drink alcohol, but they will not be able to buy it from licensed stores.

You need a liquor licence to buy alcohol from a liquor store in Dubai or Abu Dhabi. Residents can travel to other emirates and purchase alcohol without a liquor licence from licensed booze shops such as Barracuda Beach Resort in Umm Al Quwain or Al Hamra Cellar in Ras Al Khaimah, and can also purchase a limited amount at the airport Duty Free when passing through. However, you are legally required to have a licence in order to transport alcohol or consume it outside of licensed premises, such as at home. The reality is that it's very rare for people to be stopped and searched, and as long as you're driving carefully you should be OK. Have an accident though and it's likely to be a very different story.

The law states that UAE residents (i.e. anyone who has a visa) should be in possession of a liquor licence when drinking in licensed premises, such as bars, restaurants and clubs. In reality, it's unheard of for the police to enter a bar or sports event and check.

At home, as long as you're not throwing raucous parties and causing a drunken disturbance, it's unlikely that the police will call on you to justify that glass of red you sip with your dinner at the weekend.

Liquor Stores

There are two licensed liquor chains operating in Dubai: African + Eastern (africaneastern.com) and MMI (mmidubai.com), and you do need a licence to buy from these. They have branches throughout the city (MMI also has a branch in Al Hamra, Ras Al Khaimah,

NEW TO DUBAI?

(handwritten notes) School admissions · Internet connections · who? · how? · Driving Licence · NATIONAL ID · House hunting · Bank Accounts · Navigating The City · ? · where? · Phone and TV packages · who?

GET OFF TO AN EASY START BY APPLYING FOR YOUR BEVERAGE LICENCE WITH US!

Whether you are applying for a new beverage licence or renewing your existing one, African + Eastern helps you get it done in **3 easy, hassle free steps!** Visit any one of our stores conveniently located all over Dubai to pick up an application form, get expert advice and have all your questions answered. **It's as EASY as that!**

If you have any queries, please ask our staff in-store or call **800 CHEERS** (243377)

Al Wasl Road* · Arabian Ranches* · Bur Dubai* · Burj Views* · Deira* · Dubai Marina Mall*
Dubai Marina Walk* · Green Community** · Jumeirah* · Karama · Le Méridien Dubai** · Mirdif · TECOM*

*Stores also open on Fridays from 2:00pm - 9:00pm
**Green Community and Le Méridien Dubai stores open Saturday to Thursday from 2:00pm - 9:00pm

african eastern

07 244 7403) and, once you have your licence, you can buy alcohol from any branch. They can work out expensive thanks to a 30% tax but the range and service is excellent. And they're extremely convenient. Plus, it's always better to be safe than sorry. You can also take advantage of special offers and events run by the liquor stores and even join the wine club.

Getting Your Licence

Applying for a liquor licence is straightforward, as long as you are non-Muslim and a resident of Dubai. The whole process can be carried out online at africaneastern.com or in any branch of MMI or African & Eastern. You must be 21 or older, in possession of a resident's visa, and earn more than Dhs.3,000 per month. You'll need to get the application form stamped by your employer, and then submit it along with a passport photo, copy of your passport with residence visa, copy of your Ejari-attested tenancy contract, (or a letter from your employer if you're in company accommodation), plus copies of your official Ministry of Labour contract in both Arabic and English, or salary certificate if you work in a free zone. The application costs Dhs.160, which the store typically gives you back in vouchers or credit.

If you want your spouse to use your liquor licence, you will need their photo, and a copy of their passport and residence visa.

The liquor licence, an easily identifiable red card, should be ready in around 10 days.

Using The Red Card

With your licence you get a monthly allowance, which is based on your salary and will be enough to keep one person in drinks for the month. However, you can't save up an unused allowance and use it the following month; so, for big parties, start to stock up a few months in advance. Alternatively, pay a visit to Barracuda or Al Hamra where you can buy in bulk.

Temporary Accommodation

When you first arrive in Dubai for work, usually your employer will have arranged accommodation for you for a week or more. If you find that you need more time to search for a home, then you may want to consider staying in a cheap hotel once you move out of the digs your company has paid for. Or perhaps you're just heading to Dubai for a look-see and need a good-value room to lay your head.

Al Bustan Residence Hotel Apartments Al Qusais 1, 04 263 0000, *al-bustan.com*
Al Waleed Palace Hotel Apartments Nr Lamcy Plaza, Oud Metha, 04 336 0004, *alwaleedhotels.com*
Arjaan By Rotana Dubai Media City Nr MBC,

Media City, Al Sufouh 2, 04 436 0000, *rotana.com*
Ascott Park Place Dubai Shk Zayed Rd, Trade Center 1, 04 310 8555, *the-ascott.com*
Chelsea Tower Hotel Apartments Shk Zayed Rd, Trade Center 1, 04 343 4347, *chelseatowerdubai.com*
Dusit Residence Dubai Marina Marsa Dubai, 04 425 9999, *dusit.com*
Gloria Hotel Al Sufouh 2, 04 399 6666, *gloriahoteldubai.com*
Golden Sands Hotel Apartments > p.67 Bur Dubai, Al Mankhool, 04 355 5553, *goldensandsdubai.com*
Grand Hyatt Residence Shk Rashid Rd, Umm Hurair 2, 04 317 1234, *dubai.grand.hyatt.com*
JA Oasis Beach Tower Al Mamsha St, Jumeirah Beach Residence, Marsa Dubai, 04 8145 700, *jaresortshotels.com*
Lotus Hotel Apartments & Spa Marina Nr Trident Waterfront, Marsa Dubai, 04 440 2888, *lotus-hospitality.com*

Budget Hotels

Aside from the fancy hotels Dubai is famed for, there are plenty of alternative options where visitors can rest their heads. Radisson Blu (radissonblu.com), Rotana (rotana.com) and Holiday Inn (holidayinn. com) all have several outlets in Dubai. Al Barsha is home to a number of decent, less spectacular but well-priced hotels, while in Bur Dubai and Deira you'll find a number of places that offer good facilities and a central location, such as the Grand Excelsior Hotel (grandexcelsiorburdubai.com) and Park Regis Kris Kin Hotel (parkregishotels.com).

Guest houses are also becoming more popular in Dubai. While smaller in size, B&Bs offer a homely feel and are ideal for guests who want to see more of the 'real Dubai'. Located in residential areas, they won't have access to private beaches, but there is no shortage of good public beaches to enjoy. Some will have their own pool and benefit from intimate surroundings, while owners will be only too happy to give personal recommendations on what to see and do. Villa 47 (04 286 8239, villa47.com) has only two guest rooms, but is located close to the airport in Garhoud.

You can also find a good selection of properties and rooms to rent through the website airbnb. com. Just register on the site to be able to contact individual property owners.

Hotels & Serviced Apartments

Hotel apartments are expensive, but ideal if you need temporary, furnished accommodation. There's a large concentration in Bur Dubai, but more and more are cropping up around town, especially in Al Barsha. They can be rented on a daily, weekly, monthly or yearly basis. Water and electricity are also included in the rent.

SHAKEN AND STIRRED

Without a liquor licence you could be both,
DON'T TAKE THE RISK!

The process couldn't be simpler, just follow these 3 easy steps.

STEP 1	STEP 2	STEP 3
Complete the Application Form and get it stamped by your employer.	Attach copies of the required documents.	Visit any MMI shop to submit your Application Form and documents.

For more information please contact our Liquor Licence team on
04 304 0331/0332 or e-mail lipsadmin@mmi.ae

 mmidubai.com   /mmidubai   @mmi_dubai   MMIDubai

SETTLING IN

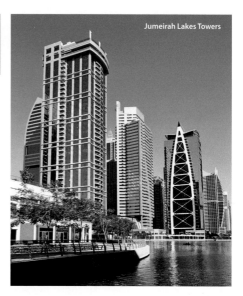
Jumeirah Lakes Towers

Relocating to a new country is a major upheaval, especially if your support network of family and friends is left behind. It's important to meet new people as soon as possible – start looking online for groups that share your interests before you arrive, and that way you can schedule to meet people as soon as you get here. Your new friends will be an invaluable source of information regarding the best restaurants, hairdressers, schools and more, and as they've already made the move themselves, they'll totally understand how it feels to be new in town. Dubai is a transient society, but consequently those who are here are more open and friendly. You'll find it easy to meet new people, and most likely many of them will end up as life-long friends.

National Groups

Dubai presents numerous opportunities to meet people from all over the world, but it's also important to have a network of friends from your own country. Sharing banter with someone from home is a good tonic for culture shock and will help you adapt quicker to your new environment. There are several groups formed by individual nationalities, where members enjoy reminiscing about home. Below are just a few of the nationality-based groups in Dubai:

Anza UAE: Australians and New Zealanders' social and community group with regular events. *anzauae.org*
BilgiDubai: A large, sociable network for the Turkish community, with regular activities and meet-ups. *bilgidubai.com*
Dubai Caledonian Society: A social network for Scottish expats with several annual events including the St Andrew's Ball in November and the Chieftain's Ball in May. *scotsindubai.com*
Dubai Toastmasters Club: The Dubai branch of this worldwide, non-profit organisation provides a supportive environment that promotes self-confidence and personal growth. *7492. toastmastersclubs.org*
Dubai St George's Society: Serving the British expat community, the DSGS focuses mainly on fun and social activities, but also raises money for various charities. *dsgs.org*
South African Women's Association: SAWA is dedicated to bringing together South African women in Dubai through various networking and social events. *sawa-uae.org*

Social Networks

These social networking groups are great for meeting like-minded people in a friendly, social setting.

Ranches Ladies: A multinational ladies group which organises coffee mornings, social nights, activities and fundraising events. *arabianranchesladies.com*
Social Circles UAE: A well-organised social community that focuses on meeting new people and networking for business or pleasure. *socialcircles.me*
Speak Dating: Foreign language speakers can find 'language exchange' partners who help you practise your foreign language in return for you helping them to learn your native tongue. *shelter.ae*

Online forums

abudhabiwoman.com and expatwoman.com are great places for women to meet through forums. You'll also find job opportunities, group days out and advice. Expatwoman.com is like a permanent virtual coffee morning for women to chat about issues ranging from irritating husbands and cookery tips, to more serious problems. They also hold real life coffee mornings too.

meetup.com is a popular forum for finding friends with similar hobbies where you can arrange times for sessions in an easy-going manner, rather than having to stick to a rigid routine.

In the UAE there are stricter guidelines for using social sites such as facebook: no hate speech (not even a re-post); nothing showing violence or nudity; and no tagging of others' photos without their consent. See tra.gov.ae/index.php for more details.

Places Of Worship

The UAE has a fairly liberal and welcoming attitude to other religions and, as a result, various places of worship also act as good community hubs, even if you're not a regular worshiper. In addition to the churches below, there is a Hindu temple complex in Bur Dubai, near Dubai Museum.

Christ Church Jebel Ali, *christchurchjebelali.com*
Dubai Evangelical Church Centre, *deccc.com*
Emirates Baptist Church International, *ebci.org*
Fellowship Of The Emirates, *fellowshipoftheemirates.org*
Holy Trinity Church Dubai, *holytrinitychurchdubai.org*
New Covenant Church Dubai, *nccuae.org*
St Francis of Assisi Church, *stfrancisjebelali.ae*
St Mary's Catholic Church Dubai, *saintmarysdubai.com*
Well Of Life Church Dubai, *wolhome.com*

BEFORE YOU LEAVE

If your time in Dubai has come to a close, there are a few things you should see to before leaving. To begin, get your electricity, water and other utilities disconnected. Most providers (DEWA, Etisalat, du) will need at least two days' notice to take a final reading and return any security deposits you have paid. You'll need to settle the final bill before you get your deposit, and make sure you keep hold of the original deposit receipt to smooth the process.

You'll also need to close any bank accounts you have here. Banks have been known to freeze an individual's account once they have been informed by the sponsor of a visa cancellation, or continue to charge you a monthly fee once you stop paying your salary into the account – bad news if you ever plan to return to the UAE.

Settle your debts – you can get into serious trouble if you try to leave the country without paying off all your loans and outstanding bills. You should also cancel all credit cards before you leave.

If you are leaving rented accommodation, make sure the place is spick and span so that you can reclaim your security deposit. The landlord may also require a clearance certificate from DEWA to prove you've paid all your bills, so leave enough time for the administration involved. If you own a property you may choose to either sell or rent out your home – see dubai.ae for more information.

Sell your car – but be prepared to take a financial knock if you need to offload it quickly with a dealer. Make sure you transfer ownership to the new owner and keep a copy of their new registration card; fail to do this and you will remain liable for any fines on the vehicle. It's also a good idea to cancel your Salik, although you won't be able to claim a refund on any credit not used.

Organise shipping: give as much notice as possible to the shipping company. Sell the stuff you're not taking with you. Have a garage sale, list your items on dubizzle.com or expatwoman.com, or put photos up on supermarket noticeboards. Dubai Flea Market is a good option for last-minute clearouts. Also, takemyjunkuae.com will collect everything you can't get rid of.

If you're taking pets with you, you will need to make sure their vaccinations are up to date, particularly rabies. There are other procedures to be followed when exporting pets, and ideally you need around six months to prepare. If you can't take your pets with you, find them a new family home, ask friends and family, or advertise online – Dubai has a dreadful problem with abandoned pets.

Feeling overwhelmed? Allied Pickfords (alliedpickfords.ae) can assist with relocating.

Cancelling Visas

Different visa types require slightly different cancellation procedures. If your residence visa was sponsored by your employer, then they will be responsible for cancelling it once you cease to work for them. It's a simple process – you'll have to submit your passport and sometimes sign a document saying you've received all monies owed to you. You will also need to hand in your Resident ID.

The visa should only take about five days to be cancelled (longer during Ramadan), and your employer can pay to have the process fast-tracked if you need your passport back in a hurry.

Once the visa is cancelled you have 30 days before you have to leave the country – if you stay after this, you'll be fined at a rate of Dhs.25 per day for the first six months, Dhs.50 per day for the next six months, and Dhs.100 after that.

If you are in Dubai on a spousal visa and have separated, or need to leave, your husband or wife will need to help with the visa cancellation. If your spouse's company completed the paperwork, they will need your husband or wife to sign the cancellation papers.

You will also need to cancel your maid's visa, in which case, you must also arrange for her flight home. Alternatively, if she finds another employer in the emirate you can transfer the visa to her new sponsor. There is no notice period and you can cancel her visa at any time within the 12 month contract.

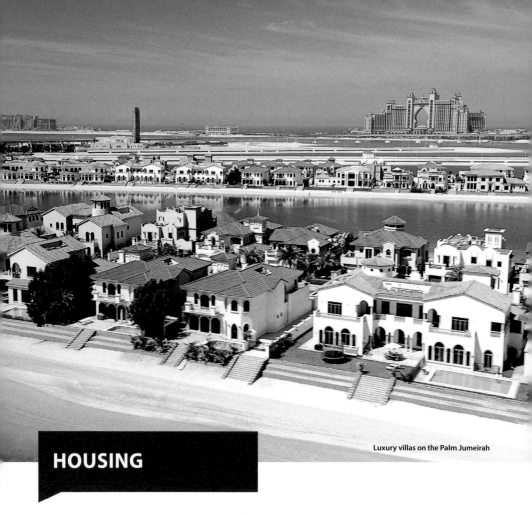
Luxury villas on the Palm Jumeirah

HOUSING

Housing is one of the great challenges about setting up in Dubai. Expat packages either include housing or an allowance to cover at least part of your accommodation costs, although the amounts are much smaller than in the boom days so it's likely that you'll need to top up from your own pocket to cover the rent or mortgage.

The first question to answer is: to rent or to buy? Most expats opt for renting as it gives you more flexibility, particularly when you first arrive in Dubai and are unsure of the best location to live in. Also, you need to have lived in Dubai for a minimum of six months before you can apply for a mortgage with a UAE bank, so your first year at least is likely to be in rented accommodation.

However, an increasing number of expats living in Dubai are now choosing to buy rather than rent property as they plan to put down longer term roots.

Unfortunately, the days of getting a 90% mortgage are over and at the end of 2013, Central Bank announced a new ruling to cap mortgages. As restrictive as it sounds, the good news for those wanting to buy a home is banks have dropped interest rates to attract borrowers.

Property Search

All your property questions are answered in this section, from which utilities you need to set up to some of the legalities regarding housing in the UAE. Like any major city, there is a varying scale of property: from labour camps for lower-paid workers and maid's rooms for domestic workers to modern high-rise apartments and spacious villas in affluent or up-and-coming areas across the emirate. And, whether you're single or moving here with a family in tow; whether you're living on a budget or have cash to splash, there is a place for you to call home.

ACCOMMODATION

When You Arrive

Apart from securing your new job, getting your accommodation satisfactorily sorted out is probably the most crucial factor in making your move to Dubai a success. Most expats will rent at first, although there are selected areas around the city where expats can buy property; this section covers the procedures and practicalities involved in both the rental and ownership markets.

Companies are legally obliged to provide employees with either accommodation or an accommodation allowance. This really varies as there are no official guidelines as to how much this should be. Some large organisations have complexes for employees, other companies have arrangements with particular developments and reserve a percentage of their properties for workers. It's worth checking your job offer though as often the housing allowance is included in your salary, so you won't get any additional help; your actual salary will only be a percentage of your monthly pay packet. You can use your housing allowance on either rent or a mortgage; if your company gives you the option of accommodation they may let you have the money to find your own place instead.

In previous years, Dubai has been home for many people working in Abu Dhabi; since 2013, however, public sector employees working in Abu Dhabi are now required by law to also live in the emirate, or forfeit their housing allowance.

Apartments

Apartments in Dubai are generally quite spacious, with everything from studios to seven bedrooms available. Master bedrooms in new builds can even come with an en-suite bathroom, walk-in wardrobe and lounge space. Newer apartments usually have central air conditioning, while older buildings can have noisier air-conditioning units built into the walls. Some are linked up to district cooling, a system where all buildings in an area receive cold water from a central cooling plant. In this scenario, residents sign an agreement with the cooling company and pay monthly instalments. In winter, you won't need air conditioning much, so make sure it's possible to turn it off. Chilled water costs can creep up in the hotter months too.

Top of the range apartments generally come with white goods, have 24 hour security, covered parking (check if you get a space), a gym and a pool. Expats from some parts of the world tend to prefer villas to apartments, especially when they have families, but some of the facilities in the larger apartment complexes make for fun, comfortable and safe family living.

No Place To Park

Many apartments charge an additional rental fee for covered or underground parking. In some areas, this is essential, as finding parking outside your apartment can be nearly impossible, particularly if you live in the city centre, JBR or Marsa Dubai.

Villas

The villa lifestyle doesn't come cheap, and smart villas are snapped up pretty quickly. The good news is that if you look hard enough and use the grapevine, you might find the perfect villa that won't break the budget. Depending on the location, size and age of the property, it may be cheaper than some apartments, even if air-conditioning costs will be higher. Villas differ greatly in quality and facilities. Independent ones often have bigger gardens, while compound villas are usually newer and most have shared facilities like a pool or gym.

One Villa, One Family

Dubai bylaws prevent more than one family sharing a villa, although there are no restrictions on the number of members of the same family sharing. Children under 18 and maids are not included. The aim is to stop illegal villa sharing that can see dangerous overcrowding, as unauthorised partition walls turn a villa meant for a family to one housing up to 60 people in some cases.

Home Address

Traditionally, addresses in Dubai have not been as straightforward as you might be used to at home. Often your house would have two numbers, there's no postcode, and streets have only been labelled with numbers or letters – resulting in many streets of the exact same 'name', such as Street 1B.

However, Dubai is introducing a new integrated address system, and the city has been divided into several districts, with each district further sub-divided into communities. Communities include Burj Khalifa (including Downtown); Al Thanyah Third (including The Greens and The Gardens); and Marsa Dubai, which is the new name for Dubai Marina. The project will see more than 22,000 Dubai streets renamed over the next five years, so that each address will have a building number, street name and sector. Many streets in Jumeira and Umm Suqeim have already been renamed.

Many names used for Dubai roads reflect the heritage and culture; for example, Jumeira will have street names reflecting the marine environment like the names of fish, traditional boats and ships as well as other elements of the sea. Similarly, street names in the Financial District reflect various currencies.

In terms of giving directions to your abode, it's best to note nearby landmarks. When receiving post, many people rent a PO Box or use their company's address and PO Box, though this is slowly changing as the post office rolls out new services (see Postal Services).

RERA

When buying or selling a property, it is important to check that the real estate agent is registered with the government's Real Estate Regulatory Agency (RERA), which is there to safeguard and protect your rights.

An arm of the Dubai Land Department, the agency's responsibilities include the following: licensing all real estate activities; regulating and registering rental agreements, owners' associations, and real estate advertisements in the media; regulating and licensing real estate exhibitions; and publishing official research and studies for the sector.

Any potential property dispute can be taken to RERA; there are comprehensive rules on issues such as payments, escrow accounts and more. For more information, visit dubailand.gov.ae.

Real Estate Agents

ARENCO Real Estate *> p.67* Arenco Tower, Al Sufouh 2, 04 440 1144, *arencore.com*
Better Homes Jumeira 1, 600 522 212, *bhomes.com*
Chestertons *> p.55* Emaar Square, Downtown Dubai, 04 381 0200, *chesterton-mena.com*
Déjà Vu Real Estate Brokers Sheikh Zayed Road, Al Barsha 1, 04 399 6487, *dejavuproperties.com*
Deyaar Al Barsha 1, 04 395 7700, *deyaar.ae*
Pacific Ventures Bayswater Tower, Business Bay, 04 451 9771, *pacificventures.co*
Premier Habitat Smart Heights Tower TECOM, Al Thanyah 1, 04 435 7433, *premierhabitat.com*
Smith & Ken Real Estate Al Thanyah 5, Jabal Ali, 04 439 4300, *smithandken.com*
Union Properties *> p.57* Green Community, Dubai Investment Park 1, 04 422 0888, *up.ae*

Renting A Home

Paying for rental accommodation in Dubai may be very different to what you're used to. Most landlords demand one cheque, and if you manage to negotiate two or three cheques, expect to pay a slightly higher rent. Some landlords accept post-dated cheques that are cashed on their due date, while some employers will arrange to pay your rent payments directly from your salary, which can save a lot of hassle. Rental contracts are typically one year, and 90 days' notice must be given if you or the landlord want to cancel the contract rather than renew it. There is usually a fine of two months' rent if you break the lease early.

With a UAE residence visa you can rent a home in any emirate; the rapid increase in Dubai rents during 2013 has led to many expats seeking cheaper accommodation in the neighbouring emirate of Sharjah, although the downside to this are the hellish traffic jams if you commute.

Finding A Rental Home

Using a real estate agent is the easiest and often best option, although they will charge you for their services, usually around 5% of the annual rent, Dhs.5,000 or whichever is higher. Only ever deal with a RERA-registered broker or agent (see dubailand.gov.ae for full list). All registered agents are given a Broker's Register card, with photo ID, which verifies that their office is licensed by RERA to manage, rent and sell real estate. If you do not use a registered agent, you will not be covered by the housing watchdog, RERA, or the Dubai Municipality's Rent Committee.

Alternatively, check out classified adverts in local newspapers or websites like dubizzle.com. It can also be useful to drive around the areas you fancy living in. Often there will be 'To Let' signs on vacant villas; if you like a certain complex, ask the security guard if they know of any that are available.

Once you find a property, ask for proof of ownership of the property being rented out; a licensed agent will be able to present the owner's documents (including a copy of the landlord's passport and title deed). Also, always demand a receipt for any payments made by cash or cheque.

Rental Costs

Extra costs to be considered when renting a home are:
- Water and electricity deposit (Dhs.4,100 for villas, Dhs.2,100 for apartments) paid directly to Dubai Electricity & Water Authority (DEWA) and fully refundable on cancellation of the lease
- If your accommodation is in an area that uses district cooling, you will need to pay a deposit to the cooling company (usually Palm District Cooling, palmutilities.com). The deposit amount varies depending on the size and location of the property.

INTERNATIONAL PAPERWORK OUT OF CONTROL?

SIRVA® Worldwide Relocation & Moving

Applications. Background checks. Legal documents. Managing global relocation is a daunting task. That's where we come in. As the largest globally-integrated relocation and moving provider, the experts at SIRVA deliver complete corporate relocation and moving solutions – all under one roof. From North America to the Middle East to Africa, we take the fear out of global relocation so that you can feel calm, confident and in control.

EVERYTHING YOU NEED. EVERYWHERE YOU NEED IT.

Call +971.2.677.9765 (Abu Dhabi), +971.4.818.0400 (Dubai) or visit SIRVA.com to learn more.

- Real estate commission is around 5% of annual rent and is a one-off payment
- Maintenance charges vary, but could be around 5% of annual rent, and are sometimes included
- A housing fee of 5% of your yearly rent is charged through your DEWA bill, spread across 12 months

If you're renting a villa, don't forget that you may have to maintain a garden and pay for extra water. It's worth asking the landlord what the average DEWA bills are for a particular property.

Renting A Room

When you first arrive, if you're alone, it works out cheaper just to rent a room because the rental payments are usually monthly (as opposed to quarterly, half-yearly or annually if you get your own place). In this scenario though, there is no guarantee that you will get a rental contract, which means that you can't get a liquor licence. The advantage is that you can usually leave your room with just one month's notice, so it gives you more flexibility. Also, the price will probably include all bills, so you can budget more easily knowing that your living costs are fixed.

Sharing

Let's clarify the issue of unrelated singles of the opposite sex sharing accommodation. There have been stories of people being evicted, but Dubai Municipality stated in the press at the time that the evictions were done to avoid overcrowding. Officially, under UAE law, it is illegal for unmarried or unrelated people of the opposite sex to live together if they are in a relationship. In reality, the police don't investigate

who is living with whom unless they have need to visit you in relation to an official complaint. Do bear in mind that you are more likely to be frowned upon for sharing with someone of the opposite sex (who you are not married to or related to) if you're living in a family designated area such as Al Barsha or Jumeira where there is a high concentration of local families. Many expats share accommodation, but the issue should always be approached with caution.

Ejari

Meaning 'my rent' in Arabic, Ejari is an online system set up by RERA to oversee the rental market and its procedures. Its main purpose is to legalise the relationship between landlord and tenant, and all rental contracts must be registered with RERA, through Ejari.

Tenancy Contract

So, once you have found a property, you'll need to sign a tenancy contract and pay the 5% deposit required to secure the property; an official RERA template can be downloaded at ejari.ae, although your agent or landlord is ultimately responsible for this. Only a Dubai resident can sign a tenancy contract, so you cannot rent a property if you are still on a visit visa; however, by this stage you should have your residence visa stamped.

All tenancy/rental contracts must be registered through RERA's online Ejari service; this is required by law to safeguard the rights of both the tenant and the landlord. You will need an Ejari-registered contract in case you need to dispute a rent increase, eviction etc. For a lease to be registered with Ejari, the landlord must have an official title deed for the property – so always check this before handing over your deposit.

Once you have the keys to the property you can register the tenancy contract. Visit any Ejari typing centre with your tenancy contract (see ejari.ae for locations), Resident ID or passport copy for landlord, a copy of the security deposit receipt, and your Resident ID and passport. Pay the fee of Dhs.195 and your Ejari-registered contract (called a Tenancy Contract Registration Certificate) will be ready for collection within three days.

Your rental contract will cover the financial terms, the length of the rental and who is responsible for maintenance; since payments are usually made through post-dated cheques, make sure that payment terms are clearly stated. Before signing on the dotted line, you should also check the following:

- **Maintenance:** Some rents might be fully inclusive of all maintenance and repairs, while you could negotiate a much cheaper rent (particularly on older properties) if you agree to carry out any maintenance work

Many expats share villas

- **Utilities:** While not common, some landlords will include DEWA/utility expenses in the rent
- **Security deposit:** This can sometimes be negotiated, but Dhs.5,000 to Dhs.10,000 is standard
- **Parking:** Landlords do not have to provide parking, so check first if there is an additional fee for underground or covered parking
- **Home improvements:** Is DIY and decorating allowed in the property?
- **Pets:** Are they permitted and are there any restrictions on the type of pet? In some apartments, cats are permitted but dogs are not; there are seldom such restrictions in villas
- **Gardens:** If in a villa, are you responsible for the maintenance? This can become costly due to the amount of water needed. A well and pump can be installed for between Dhs.1,500 and Dhs.3,000, which may be more cost effective in the long run

Once you have your tenancy contract, and only then, you will be able to apply for services, such as DEWA water and gas utilities, internet, and TV.

Renewals & Rent Rises

Rental contracts are valid for one year, after which they can be renewed for another year or terminated. A tenancy contract does not terminate automatically. Instead, it renews on the same terms until you or the landlord agree to change the terms or end it. If the landlord wants to evict you or increase the rent, he must give you 90 days' notice before the end of the contract; likewise, if you want to move out of the property you must give 90 days' notice. You re-register your lease with Ejari when you renew your contract.

There are four circumstances under which a landlord can serve a notice for eviction on expiry of the tenancy contract: to demolish or add to the premises, making it unlivable; for repair or maintenance; to recover the premises for personal use or for a next of kin; or to sell the property.

Landlords can raise rents annually based on prevailing market conditions since the government removed the 5% rent cap at the end of 2013; landlords are able to increase rents by up to 20%, which overrides the previous 5% rental cap. There are restrictions though: the maximum increase is 10% if the property falls 21-30% below market rates and 15% if the property is 31-40% under average rents. Check the rent cap calculator at dubailand.gov.ae to see the increase cap and average rental for your area and unit.

At the end of 2013 a rental dispute settlement centre (800 4488) was established to replace the rent committee, which was where tenants and landlords previously took their arguments about rental contracts.

This new centre functions more like a proper court with a fully integrated judicial system, a judge and the chance of appeal for those who don't agree with the judge's final ruling.

Buying A Home

The property market in Dubai grew at the fastest pace in the world in the year up to the end of June 2013, financed primarily by cash buyers. Mortgage lending is increasing though, and so buying a home is a viable option for well-paid expats planning to stay long-term or for those wanting to buy to let and make a return on their investment – especially as rents are rising each quarter. Interest rates on mortgages have dropped since 2010 from 9% to 4.5% per year, and banks are also offering incentives to would-be homeowners, such as discounts on processing and valuation fees, and reduced interest rates during the first year. Talk of another property bubble has been rejected by those in real estate, and the recent mortgage cap is an attempt to stabilise the market.

To buy a property in Dubai you need to have a UAE bank account, and have a 25% down payment/deposit (or 15% of the property value). Typically, you need to be salaried or self-employed with a minimum monthly salary of Dhs.15,000, and aged 21 or over. Mortgages are available to both UAE and non-UAE residents.

For an in-depth, step-by-step guide, see Explorer's *Dubai How-To* guide to buying and selling property in the UAE.

Freehold Or Leasehold?

Most property in Dubai available for purchase by expats is freehold. Maintenance fees are payable by the property owner and cover the cost to the developer of maintaining all the shared facilities. Fees are typically paid annually, though some developers will accept quarterly payments. If you buy leasehold your lease will stipulate who is responsible for maintenance and repairs, and any other conditions you should meet. There is also a small, annual ground rent fee payable to the owner of the land (the freeholder). Check that the seller is up to date on ground rent payments before you take over the contract.

House Hunting

The list of real estate agents earlier in this section is a great place to start, but it's often better to trawl through the property listings in *Gulf News* (gnads4u. com) or on dubizzle.com to find out which properties are listed with which agent. Always deal with a RERA-registered agent or broker. In general, expect to pay a flat fee of around 2-5% of the purchase price to the agent upon completion of sale.

One key point is that non-UAE nationals can only buy in specially designated areas for expatriate freehold or leasehold (typically 99 years) sales. Property in some areas is only available for purchase by Emiratis or GCC nationals; such areas include Jumeira, Umm Suqeim, Al Barsha and most parts of Old Dubai.

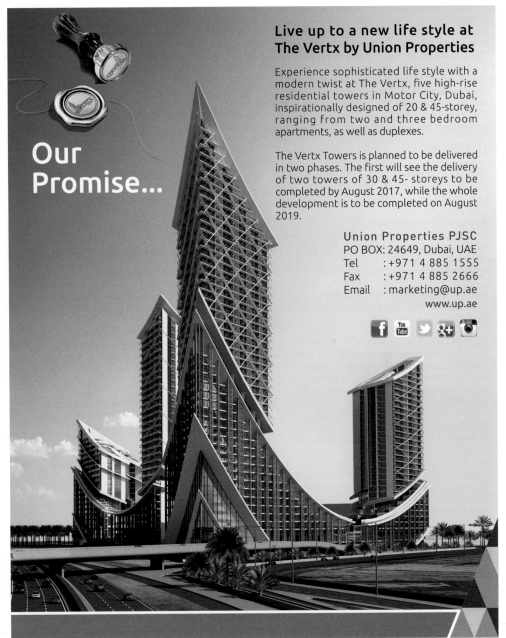

Our Promise...

Live up to a new life style at The Vertx by Union Properties

Experience sophisticated life style with a modern twist at The Vertx, five high-rise residential towers in Motor City, Dubai, inspirationally designed of 20 & 45-storey, ranging from two and three bedroom apartments, as well as duplexes.

The Vertx Towers is planned to be delivered in two phases. The first will see the delivery of two towers of 30 & 45- storeys to be completed by August 2017, while the whole development is to be completed on August 2019.

Union Properties PJSC
PO BOX: 24649, Dubai, UAE
Tel   : +971 4 885 1555
Fax   : +971 4 885 2666
Email   : marketing@up.ae
www.up.ae

If you're buying a new development in an apartment building in Marsa Dubai, Jumeirah Lakes Towers (JLT) or Business Bay, be aware that many are built by sub-contractors and consequently the finished standard and management capability will vary. For peace of mind, stick with reputable companies.

You can choose to buy off-plan – though few UAE banks provide mortgages for this. This option means you get a good price for your property, but you have to be prepared for the possibility that the construction could be delayed, so check regularly on progress.

Likewise if you buy a completed property, the handover could be subject to delays due to rent or mortgage issues, which could delay your moving-in date. When buying or selling a property, always check that the real estate agent is registered with RERA, which is there to safeguard and protect your rights.

Developers

DAMAC Properties
Executive Heights Bldg TECOM, Al Thanyah 1
04 373 1000
damacproperties.com
Map **1 N6** Metro **Dubai Internet City**
Develops apartment buildings and commercial office towers, including Ocean Heights, Marina Terrace and The Waves in Marsa Dubai, Palm Islands, and Lake View and Lake Terrace in Jumeirah Lakes Towers.

Emaar Properties > p.271, 273, 289
Emaar Square Bldg 3 Downtown Dubai
04 367 3333
emaar.com
Map **2 F6** Metro **Burj Khalifa**
Emaar's flagship property is Burj Khalifa; its portfolio of freehold real estate projects includes: Marsa Dubai, Arabian Ranches, Emirates Living, Emaar Towers and Downtown Dubai (Burj Khalifa, Burj Residence, Burj Views, Old Town, South Ridge).

Nakheel Properties
Al Sufouh St Nakhlat Jumeira **04 390 3333**
nakheel.com
Map **1 N5** Metro **Dubai Internet City**
Builds, sells and is responsible for maintaining several large developments, including: Palm Jumeirah, Jumeirah Islands, International City, Discovery Gardens, Jumeirah Village, Palm Jebel Ali, Palm Deira, The World and Al Furjan Community.

Meraas Holding
Emaar Square Bldg 1 Downtown Dubai **04 511 4500**
meraas.com
Map **2 F6** Metro **Burj Khalifa/Dubai Mall**
Meraas has numerous projects in Dubai, including the hugely popular, low-rise Wasl Square development,

which is made up of apartments and townhouses and is within walking distance of Safa Park. There's actually a waiting list to be able to rent a Wasl Square apartment.

Pacific Ventures
Bayswater Tower 21st Floor, Office No. 2106
04 4519 771
pacificventures.co
Map **2 E6** Metro **Business Bay**
A developer focused on creating communities and providing facilities for comfortable lifestyles. Their properties are luxurious and located in picturesque areas in prime locations. Their projects include Burj Pacific, Pacific Edmonton Elm and Pacific Residencia.

Union Properties > p.57
Green Community Dubai Investment Park 1
04 885 1555
up.ae
Map **1 F10** Metro **Energy**
Union Properties is a property investment developer, established for 25 years, whose portfolio includes Green Community, MotorCity and Uptown Mirdiff. They also offer property management services.

Real Estate Law

The Real Estate Regulatory Authority (RERA) is a government organisation that, aside from setting the rental index, regulates the real estate market and aims to maintain healthy property investment in Dubai.

The agency's responsibilities include the following: licensing all real estate activities; regulating and registering owners' associations, and real estate advertisements in the media; regulating and licensing real estate exhibitions; and publishing official research and studies for the sector.

Any potential property dispute can be taken to RERA; there are comprehensive rules on issues such as payments, escrow accounts and more. To find out more about RERA, visit dubailand.gov.ae or call 04 222 1112.

Homeowners' Associations
Dubai Strata Law, better known locally as the Jointly Owned Property (JOP) Law, was implemented by RERA in Dubai in April 2007. This recognised Homeowners' Associations as democratic authorities, which enable people who own units in a development to decide the financial governance and service levels provided to the community's occupants. Dubai Strata Law is designed to remove ambiguities about who is responsible for common property management. It helps settle disputes over issues such as parking, pets that disturb neighbours, privacy and maintenance of common areas. There are numerous such associations registered with RERA, mostly in 'new' areas such as

Marsa Dubai, Jumeirah Lakes Towers and the Palm Jumeirah. If you are thinking of buying property in Dubai, it's worth checking whether your chosen development offers a Homeowners' Association; it can provide you with an extra level of security.

Check out the government's official website for information on laws, fees and general facts related to property purchases in the emirate: dubailand.gov.ae (Dubai Land Department).

Mortgages

Before you go house hunting, it's advisable to get a mortgage in place, or pre-approval, so you're in a position to make an offer should you find the place of your dreams. A 10% deposit is required to secure a property and this could be money wasted should you then find nobody is willing to lend to you.

At the end of 2013, the UAE Central Bank announced a new ruling to cap mortgages (also known as home loans here). For properties valued at less than Dhs.5 million, expat first-time buyers can get a mortgage of 75%. For properties valued above Dhs.5 million, expats can only get a mortgage of 65%. Expats taking out a 'home loan' for a second, third, fourth or subsequent property will be able to get a 60% mortgage. Financing for off-plan property is restricted to 50%, regardless of the value of the property or the nationality of the applicant.

A mortgage can be calculated on more than one salary, providing they are listed as co-borrowers in the loan contract. Central Bank rules also state that your monthly mortgage instalments and other debts should not consume more than 50% of your income. Expats may also find it more difficult to get a mortgage if they are single and have been here less than six months. If you have a family, a stable job and been in the country for a few years then they presume you are committed to the country and are happier to lend you money.

The amount financed by the lender also varies and depends on whether the property is a villa or an apartment, where they are and who built them. It's also worth noting that some banks and lenders will only provide mortgages for select developments. Additionally, they may also have different acceptance criteria and mortgage processes, which change frequently, so it's advisable to do your homework.

There are international names such as HSBC, Barclays, Standard Chartered and Citibank alongside local financial houses in Dubai, including Emirates NBD and Mashreq.

Fortunately, interest rates are currently much lower than the 9% highs of the pre-financial crisis era, with fixed rate deals available at around 3.99-4.99% depending on the term.

To help you get started, try some of the new price-compare websites such as Souqalmal.com or Moneycamel.com. Here you can compare rates from various national banks as well as international banks with UAE branches.

Lenders will only provide mortgages on a select number of developments, which varies from institution to institution. You'll probably be expected to take out a life insurance policy to cover the amount of the loan, and this should be done well in advance of the transfer date in order to avoid delays getting the mortgage though. Equity release and mortgage transfers have recently been introduced to the market, offering investors the opportunity to release equity and secure better rates. To combat price sensitive customers moving their loans, most banks have introduced exit fees but there are still completely flexible mortgages available. More recent innovations also include international mortgages, which offer loans in currency denominations other than dirhams. This offers clients the ability to structure their loan in a preferred currency, with the ability to switch if they choose to.

Islamic Mortgages

Shariah-compliant or Islamic mortgages are alternative financing options available to non-Muslims. The term 'home finance' is used as opposed to mortgage. Complying with Islamic beliefs, the bank purchases the asset on behalf of the buyer, who then effectively leases it back from the institution at a marked-up price, but with zero interest. The bank owns the title deeds of the purchased property until the full amount is repaid.

Mortgage Application

The first step towards getting a mortgage is to get a pre-approval before beginning your property search – that way you can find out how much the banks are willing to lend you. The documents needed for this process are: the original and copies of your passport, six months of bank statements, salary confirmation from your employer and six months of salary slips.

The 'approval in principle' should come through in four working days. Generally, employed applicants will be able to borrow a higher percentage of their income than the self-employed. The amount is approximately 50% of disposable monthly income – and the calculations will take into account all your financial commitments. If you're able to pay a large deposit the terms are likely to improve. Mortgages are usually granted for 25 years and lenders will generally finance individuals up to 65 years of age.

The next step is for the lender to provide an unconditional approval on the basis that any conditions noted in the pre-approval are satisfied.

Purchase Costs

Make sure you budget for the additional costs associated with buying a house, as they can add up. The obligatory amounts equate to around 6% of the purchase price, not including any cash deposit.

Solicitor fees: By law there is no requirement to have a solicitor act for you when buying property in Dubai, but you may wish to employ legal help to see you through the process. Legal costs will vary depending on whose services you use

Real estate agent/broker's fee: The flat fee to the agent is usually 2-5% of the purchase price, upon completion of sale

Mortgage broker fee: Often 0.5% of the purchase price or a pre-determined flat fee

Arrangement fee: Dhs.3,000, but can often be offset against the processing fee

Processing fee: Often around 1.5% of purchase fee, but minimum amounts of around Dhs.3,000 are common

Valuation fee: Expect to pay around Dhs.3,000

Life and household insurance: Life insurance to the value of the property is mandatory for a mortgage. Shop around for the best deal

Land registry: Payable to the Dubai Land Department (600 666 556, dubailand.gov.ae). The fee is 4% of the property value, plus a Dhs.10 surcharge, and establishes legal ownership of the property. The buyer also pays Dhs.250 fees (plus Dhs.10 surcharge) for the title deed and a Dhs.100 map issuance fee (plus Dhs.10 surcharge)

Buying Process

Once your offer has been accepted, a Sales & Purchase Agreement (SPA) will be drawn up by the real estate agency, which defines all the terms and conditions for the transfer of property. If you require a mortgage, the lender will issue an unconditional offer letter, which states the terms and conditions of the mortgage.

To process the mortgage, you need your passport plus copies, six months of bank statements, salary confirmation from your employer and six months of salary slips. Once the paperwork is signed and sent back to the lender, the settlement process begins. This is when the lender transfers the mortgage payment to either the seller or to the existing lender who has the first charge over the property. This usually occurs on the day of the transfer. Equal instalments are then taken from your bank every month. For the full transfer of ownership to take place, you will need to register the property and your mortgage with the Dubai Land Department. And then? Collect your keys and call the removal van.

Sales & Purchase Agreement

When you buy a property, a Sales & Purchase Agreement (SPA) will be drawn up by the real estate agency, which defines all the terms and conditions for the transfer or property. It is advisable to consult a lawyer so that you make sure you understand all the terms. When selling a property, you will need to provide this agreement, along with the title deeds, floorplans, location map and liability letter from the bank you have the mortgage with.

Land Registry

When you buy a property, in order for the full transfer of ownership to take place, you will need to register the property with the Dubai Land Department – the central agency for all transactional processes related to freehold and leasehold purchases.

This establishes legal ownership of the land or property, thus safeguarding the owner from future dispute, and provides the owner with the title deeds to their property or land. Fees levied by the Dubai Land Department are dependent on whether the property purchase is covered by a conventional mortgage, an Islamic (Shariah-compliant) mortgage or a cash purchase. All fees are payable by the buyer.

Fast-track service

Sign up to the e-Smart Travel Estate Pack (E-STEP) and the department will come to you, register your transaction and even issue the title deed – all in less than one hour. This service costs Dhs.4,000, and both the buyer and the seller need to be present at the same time.

Selling A Home

Selling a property in the UAE can be a simple process, but takes around six weeks to complete. Before putting up the 'For Sale' sign, sort out any maintenance issues and redecorate if needed. Then, you should market the property across a range of property websites. Most real estate agents can assist you with this by drawing floorplans, arranging viewings and giving you a free valuation based on market trends; you may also want to advertise the property on sites such as dubizzle.com.

Property transactions in Dubai can be viewed at their actual selling value on the Real Estate Regulatory Agency's (RERA) site, dubailand.gov.ae. Finding a good agent to help you sell your home is important, as private property sales here are rare. Agents can charge up to 2% of the property price to cover the costs of marketing your property. It shouldn't take long to find a buyer – Dubai's real estate market consistently ranks towards the top of numerous indices, which measure the world's best-performing markets.

Rental & Property Prices

The price of renting and the cost of buying are hot topics for expats seeking a home in Dubai. It's no secret that the real estate sector is booming. Here's a look at the figures from the past year.

Levelling out

Dubai's economy is the subject of global speculation, having plunged into economic crisis in 2008, and rocketed again in 2013 as the country was awarded the right to host the world fair, Expo 2020.

After its ups and downs, Dubai's property market now looks to be maturing. The second half of 2014 was a period of stabilisation, with rents remaining fairly flat, according to global commercial real estate advisor CBRE Middle East.

Year-on-year, average rental rates increased by 7%, much less drastic than the 24% rise witnessed during 2013.

Demand remains very strong from both occupiers and investors, and developers continue to increase their stock across this vibrant city.

Transport links

Proximity to metro stations and the recently opened tram affects the popularity of neighbourhoods among residents. Dubai Tram now connects to Dubai Metro in Marsa Dubai and runs along Al Sufouh Road and Jumeirah Beach Road to provide a much-needed link for residents on the Palm Jumeirah and JBR.

What you'll pay

If you're single and looking to rent a one-bedroom apartment in a central location such as Marsa Dubai, prices start at about Dhs.90,000 per year for an unfurnished place. To rent a three-bedroom villa, prices start at around Dhs.200,000 annually for an unfurnished property somewhere a little further out such as Arabian Ranches.

The cost of renting a room in a central area or near the beach (in JBR for example) starts at around Dhs.5,000 per month for a furnished room with an en-suite bathroom.

Going down

In Q3 2014, sales prices dropped marginally for the first time since 2012, according to property management firm Atesco. Villa prices were down 4% on the previous quarter and apartments 1%, although prices remained an average of 17% and 31%, respectively, higher than Q3 2013. Apartment prices in Marsa Dubai fell the furthest by 8%, and villas in Jumeirah Islands and Victory Heights also declined by 8%.

Booming sales

The Expo 2020 win is driving a rise in asking prices for both plots and villas/apartments in developments close to the Expo site and Jabal Ali area; rents have already increased.

Buying an apartment in Dubai's prime neighbourhoods, such as Marsa Dubai, Downtown Dubai and the Palm Jumeirah, costs on average Dhs.1,900,000 for a one-bedroom apartment, according to classified ads website Dubizzle. However, if you search further away from the seafront, prices are lower and a villa at Dubailand on the outskirts of the city will cost an average of Dhs.530,000.

Popular Places

Marsa Dubai is consistently the most searched-for neighbourhood, according to propertyfinder.ae website, followed by the Palm Jumeirah and Downtown Dubai. The most affordable areas have been identified as International City, with annual rents from Dhs.42,000; Discovery Gardens; Dubai Silicon Oasis; Dubai Investment Park and Dubailand.

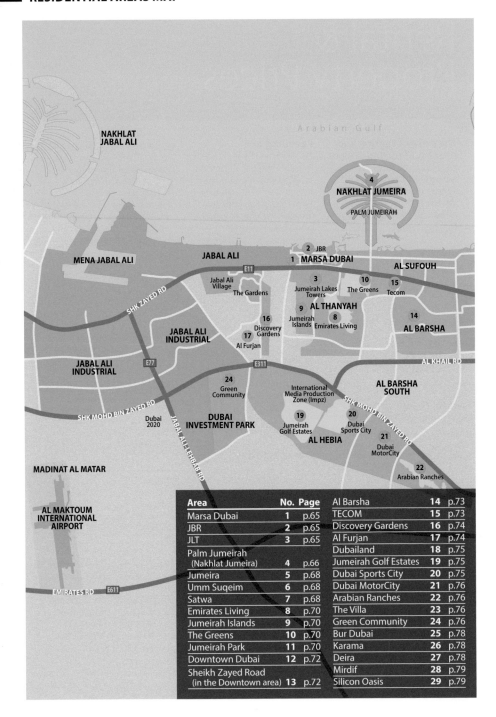

LIVING IN DUBAI
RESIDENTIAL AREAS MAP

Arabian Gulf

NAKHLAT JABAL ALI

4 NAKHLAT JUMEIRA

PALM JUMEIRAH

MENA JABAL ALI

JABAL ALI

2 JBR
1 MARSA DUBAI

AL SUFOUH

Jabal Ali Village
The Gardens

3 Jumeirah Lakes Towers
10 The Greens
15 Tecom

16 Discovery Gardens
9 Jumeirah Islands
AL THANYAH
8 Emirates Living
14 AL BARSHA

17 Al Furjan

JABAL ALI INDUSTRIAL

JABAL ALI INDUSTRIAL

24 Green Community

International Media Production Zone (Impz)

AL BARSHA SOUTH

Dubai 2020

DUBAI INVESTMENT PARK

19 Jumeirah Golf Estates
20 Dubai Sports City
AL HEBIA
21 Dubai MotorCity

MADINAT AL MATAR

AL MAKTOUM INTERNATIONAL AIRPORT

22 Arabian Ranches

SHK ZAYED RD
SHK MOHD BIN ZAYED RD
AL KHAIL RD
EMIRATES RD E611

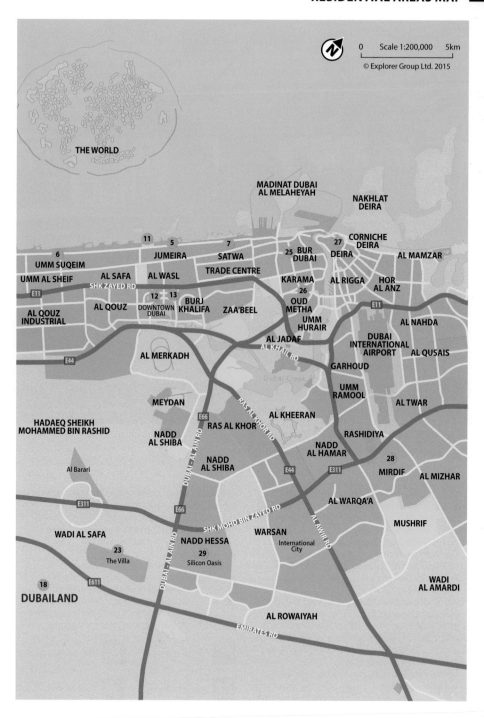

0   Scale 1:200,000   5km

© Explorer Group Ltd. 2015

THE WORLD

MADINAT DUBAI
AL MELAHEYAH

NAKHLAT
DEIRA

11   5   7   27   CORNICHE
DEIRA

6   JUMEIRA   SATWA   25 BUR   DEIRA   AL MAMZAR
UMM SUQEIM   DUBAI

UMM AL SHEIF   AL SAFA   AL WASL   TRADE CENTRE   KARAMA   AL RIGGA   HOR
AL ANZ
SHK ZAYED RD
E11   12   13   26
AL QOUZ   BURJ   OUD   AL NAHDA
AL QOUZ   DOWNTOWN   KHALIFA   ZAA'BEEL   METHA
INDUSTRIAL   DUBAI   UMM   DUBAI
HURAIR   INTERNATIONAL
AL JADAF   AIRPORT   AL QUSAIS
E44   AL MERKADH   AL KHAIL RD   GARHOUD

Dubai Creek   UMM
RAMOOL   AL TWAR
MEYDAN   AL KHEERAN

HADAEQ SHEIKH   E66   RAS AL KHOR   RASHIDIYA
MOHAMMED BIN RASHID   NADD   NADD
AL SHIBA   AL HAMAR   28
Al Barari   NADD   MIRDIF   AL MIZHAR
AL SHIBA   E44   E311
E311   AL WARQA'A   MUSHRIF
SHK MOHD BIN ZAYED RD
WADI AL SAFA   E66   NADD HESSA   WARSAN
23   29   International
The Villa   Silicon Oasis   City   WADI
AL AMARDI
18   E611
DUBAILAND   AL ROWAIYAH

EMIRATES RD

Lakeside villas at Jumeirah Islands

RESIDENTIAL AREAS

Dubai has plenty of residential areas to choose from, ranging from family villas to snazzy high-rise apartments. More developments are springing up all the time and each, when finished, will have its own shops and restaurants, and usually, access to a school.

Some areas are more popular with local families, such as Al Warqa (south of Mirdif) or Al Sufouh (near Umm Suqeim), while others are so well established that it's challenging to even find available accommodation, as is the case in Garhoud – although it benefits from being very near the airport and having a metro stop. The Gardens near Ibn Battuta Mall has virtually nothing available – the low-rise buildings here are set in an oasis of green and were snapped up long ago.

Select areas that appeal to you from our guide and then spend a few days driving to each place you are interested in – so you can see if the development is well established or still under construction, what facilities there are and what the traffic is like.

We've provided a price guide, with prices being for unfurnished properties – if you want to rent a furnished place, anticipate adding Dhs.10,000 or more a year to the rental price.

You'll find these icons (below) throughout the following section. They're a handy way to understand at a glance the main differences between housing developments in the same areas, or to quickly compare the dominant housing type in different areas of the city. Also see the Residential Areas Map for locations.

 By the beach

 Family friendly

 High-rise living

 On a budget

Marsa Dubai & JBR

Map **1 K5** Metro **DAMAC**

The high-rise apartment towers of Marsa Dubai and Jumeirah Beach Residence (JBR) are a popular choice for expats. The many hotels are home to numerous restaurants and bars and The Walk at JBR is packed every evening with people socialising and strolling, as is the new shopping and dining area The Beach. Roads in and out do get congested due to the dense population and the area's popularity as a leisure destination and cruising ground for showing off expensive cars.

Much of the neighbourhood is walkable with easy access to amenities. If you have a car, check if the property you want comes with a parking space.

Schools

None, but the Wellington International School and the International School of Choueifat in Al Sufouh are both just five minutes' drive away. There are a few nurseries in the marina.

Healthcare

Medcare Hospital near Al Safa Park has the closest emergency room. The Cedars Jebel Ali International Hospital offers 24 hour care. JBR has a medical centre and Al Sufouh and Knowledge Village also house medical and dental clinics.

Shops

Dubai Marina Mall – not huge, but has Waitrose and a number of high-street shops. Marina Walk has a Spinneys supermarket, a pharmacy, a bookshop, a florist and a liquor store, plus numerous ATMs. The Walk along JBR has clothing boutiques and furniture stores and The Beach is an open air mall bang on the beach, with more than 70 shops and restaurants and a cinema. Mall of the Emirates and Ibn Battuta Mall are a short drive or metro ride away.

Bars & Restaurants

The Walk below JBR is teeming with places to eat to suit all tastes and budgets. Many are open until the early hours, adding to the buzzing atmosphere. Marina Walk also has a number of popular restaurants. The hotels along the beach all have bars and restaurants too, including the popular Mai Tai bar and Frankie's Italian restaurant at Oasis Beach Tower. The new The Beach development is packed with cafes and restaurants with outdoor terraces, highlights include Aprons & Hammers and The Cheesecake Factory.

Attractions

Sandy beach and marina. There is yoga on the beach and an outdoor market in the grounds of the Beach mall. Currently under construction on a manmade spit of land out to sea – the world's largest Ferris wheel.

Marsa Dubai

Apartments here vary in quality. Most have a pool and amenities in the pedestrianised Marina Walk are a stone's throw away.
Annual rental prices: One-bedroom from Dhs.90,000. Three-bedroom from Dhs.210,000.

JBR

JBR consists of several identical towers of around 40 storeys high, with communal pools, grassed areas and amenities. Most buildings are owned by expats.
Annual rental prices: One-bedroom from Dhs.100,000. Three-bedroom from Dhs.180,000.

Neighbouring Community: JLT

Jumeirah Lakes Towers (JLT) is comprised of 79 towers across Sheikh Zayed Road from the marina. There are lakes flanked by a promenade with cafes, shops and a park. Access to the area by car can be quite tedious due to the one-way system, but there are two adjacent metro stations and the Dubai Tram passes through. Build quality is similar to Marsa Dubai.
Annual rental prices: One-bedroom from Dhs.90,000. Three-bedroom from Dhs.150,000.

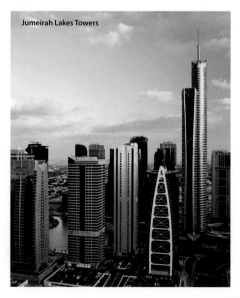
Jumeirah Lakes Towers

Palm Jumeirah

Map **1 N1** Metro **Nakheel**

The Palm Jumeirah (also referred to by its Arabic name of Nakhlat Jumeira) is synonymous with Dubai's extravagance, and the rental prices on the man-made island match its reputation. In a recent survey, local estate agents said The Palm is one of the most sought-after areas for families due to its wide range of facilities and the fact it's away from the hustle and bustle. Its proximity to the beach is also a plus.

A monorail system links areas on The Palm and also now connects to Dubai Tram, which opened in 2014. The tram joins Dubai Metro at Marsa Dubai's DAMAC Metro station (formerly known as Marina Metro).

Schools
Al Sufouh is 10-15 minutes' drive and has several popular expat schools.

Healthcare
Medical centres at JBR and Al Sufouh are within a 15 minute drive.

Shops
Construction is due to start on a huge mall, The Pointe, which is due to be completed by 2016. Dubai Marina Mall is a 15 minute drive.

Bars & Restaurants
Several high-class hotels are now open on the Palm including Sofitel The Palm, Atlantis and Rixos The Palm, all offering an array of superb restaurants and bars. There are also a few licensed restaurants and bars in the Shoreline Apartments on the trunk – The Palm is becoming a high-class hub for dining and partying. Also, the marina and Madinat Jumeirah are five minutes away by car.

Attractions
The Atlantis hotel houses several attractions including a waterpark and dolphinarium. This is also the home of live music events, including the hugely popular Sandance festival, which sees world famous rock and dance groups perform on the adjacent beach.

The Palm has its own yacht marina, and the calm waters make it excellent for hiring watersports gear from the area's hotels – Stand-Up Paddleboarding (SUP) is becoming more and more popular here.

Palm Jumeirah
The trunk of the island is made up of large one to four-bedroom apartments, and the fronds are covered in nearly identical three to six-bedroom villas. Traffic onto the island isn't a problem (unless there's a large event) and there is plenty of parking underneath the apartment buildings and next to the villas.

Despite the Palm's obviously engineered shape when viewed from above, once you've got your feet planted on it, it doesn't appear quite so symmetrical.
Annual rental prices: One-bedroom from Dhs.130,000. Three-bedroom townhouse from Dhs.350,000.

Palm Jumeirah

ARENCO
REAL ESTATE

Make Golden Sands Apartments your home during your stay in the dazzling emirates of Dubai and Sharjah. Arenco, as an established icon in Real Estate will make sure you enjoy best amenities and facilities. Choose from three key locations including Bur Dubai and Al Barsha in Dubai, and Al Nahda in Sharjah.

From affordable to luxurious, our apartments suit all individuals, from Executives to large Families. Our Apartments are of fine finishing and provide all premium facilities, a place to call Home.

Studios, 1, 2, 3 & 4 Bedrooms

+971 4 352 8666   leasing@goldensands.ae   www.arencore.com

Jumeira

Map **2 G4** Metro **Business Bay**
The actual area of Jumeira occupies a prime nine-kilometre strip of coastline stretching south-west from the port area, but the name has been hijacked to such an extent that new residential and commercial developments bearing the Jumeira tag are cropping up for miles around. Even the Palm Jumeira doesn't connect with Jumeira, but actually extends from the area of Al Sufouh. Jumeira itself is characterised by quiet streets lined with sophisticated villas, golden beaches, and good access to lots of shopping. Traffic and parking on the back streets is never a problem, but Al Wasl Road and Jumeira Road can get clogged during peak hours.

Within the same stretch of land between the beach and Sheikh Zayed Road are the areas of Al Wasl, Al Safa and Umm Suqeim. All these areas contain mostly villas and share the same facilities. Al Wasl and Al Safa are further from the beach, between Al Wasl Road and Sheikh Zayed Road.

Jumeirah or Jumeira?

According to the 'official' spelling used by Dubai Municipality, it's Jumeira, so that's what we use when referring to this area. However, many hotels, parks, clubs, schools, and residential developments have added an 'h' to the end, so don't be surprised if you see the two different spellings side by side throughout the book.

Schools

There are several schools including Jumeirah English Speaking School, Horizon School, Jumeirah College and GEMS Jumeirah Primary School, as well as an assortment of nurseries that includes Jumeirah International Nursery School and Blossom Village. The proximity to Sheikh Zayed Road makes GEMS Wellington International School a popular choice. The largest secondary school in Umm Suqeim is Emirates International School and the area is home to two Raffles International campuses.

Healthcare

Al Wasl Road and nearby Jumeira Road (also known as Beach Road or Jumeira Street) have plenty of private medical centres, specialist doctors and dentists. The private Medcare Hospital near Safa Park has an emergency room, and the excellent value Iranian Hospital is just down Al Wasl Road towards Satwa.

Shops

Jumeira Road (Beach Road) is home to art and fashion boutiques. For groceries, there are two Spinneys, a Union Co-op, two Choithrams and other supermarkets. There is also the popular Mercato Mall on Jumeira Road, along with several smaller shopping centres. Wasl Square, next to Safa Park, is a new retail hotspot with a variety of shops and eateries.

Bars & Restaurants

Jumeira Road hosts several independent restaurants, takeaways and fast food joints. The Jumeirah Beach Hotel and Madinat Jumeirah both have impressive licensed restaurants and bars, and the restaurant-filled hotels on Sheikh Zayed Road are nearby.

Attractions

The city's most popular beaches are within walking distance of Jumeira and Umm Suqeim. There are also parks, but Jumeirah Beach Park and parts of Jumeirah Open Beach and Safa Park are closed while construction of a canal takes place. By 2016 Dubai Canal will be a waterway lined with shops and pedestrian zones, that will pass through Safa Park, Jumeirah Beach Park and into the sea.

Jumeira

Jumeira villas have high rents. There's a mixture of huge 'palaces', independent villas, and villas in compounds with shared facilities. You can pick up a cheaper rental if you are prepared to take care of the maintenance.
Annual rental prices: Three-bedroom villa from Dhs.200,000.

Neighbouring Community: Satwa

Despite having large sections demolished for the now-on-hold Jumeirah Garden City project, Satwa is still a desirable place to live. The main 2nd December Street buzzes with pedestrians and is home to several popular Arabic restaurants and fast food venues. There are a number of low-rise apartment blocks on 2nd December Street and Al Hudeiba Street (Plant Street), popular with singles looking for a vibrant area. There are also villas on the outskirts of the area, in Al Bada'a. Chelsea Plaza and Jumeirah Rotana have long been nightlife hubs and there are several three-star hotels in the area that are home to intimate licensed restaurants and bars.

2nd December Street and Plant Street are full of local stores, and supermarkets include two Carrefour Expresses and a Westzone. Traffic can be bad at rush hour and street parking is hard to come by, but it's an easy neighbourhood to walk around. Residents have easy access to the facilities in the Jumeira area.
Annual rental prices: Two-bedroom apartment from Dhs.130,000. Three-bedroom villa from Dhs.170,000.

THINKING RELOCATION?
THINK SANTA FE.

We make it easy

SANTA FE
RELOCATION SERVICES

Relocation | Storage | Moving | Immigration

Santa Fe Relocation Services
T: +971 (4) 454 2724
T: 800 32800
F: +971 (4) 454 2726
Email: UAE@santaferelo.com
www.santaferelo.com

PROUDLY
PART OF **SANTA FE**
GROUP

Emirates Living

Map **1 L6** Metro **Nakheel**

Rated by property experts as one of the top five neighbourhoods to raise a family in Dubai, Emirates Living is a desirable address with a range of villa-style houses in The Springs, The Lakes, The Meadows and the exclusive Emirates Hills. Tree-lined streets and pathways, attractively landscaped lakes, gardens and recreation areas make it perfect for those who want to enjoy the peace and quiet of suburbia. Located between Sheikh Zayed Road and Al Khail Road, each individual zone of Emirates Living (for example Springs 6, Meadows 5) has its own gated security entrance. The gated-community feel runs throughout each neighbourhood, as kids play in the streets and parks, while adults jog the pavements. Traffic within each community is not a problem, though intersections near the highways can get busy at rush hour.

Of a similar style is the adjacent Jumeirah Islands community. There's a well-established community there (see Jumeirah Islands page on Facebook) and good health and leisure facilities.

The nearby apartments at The Greens are convenient for those working in Media or Internet City, as there is a flyover connecting the two sides of Sheikh Zayed Road.

Schools

Waiting lists for a place in the most sought-after schools and nurseries are long, and it is best to sign up well in advance. Schools include Emirates International School in The Meadows, Dubai British School, Dubai International Academy in The Springs, and Dubai American Academy at the Emirates Living entrance near The Lakes. As for nurseries, Raffles International School (04 427 1200) operates several nurseries in The Springs, Springs Town Centre, Emirates Hills and The Lakes.

Healthcare

The Rosary Medical Centre is located at Springs Town Centre in Springs 7, while nearby facilities include a private medical centre in Al Barsha, Medical Specialist Centre (04 340 9495), the Cedars Jebel Ali International Hospital, and Mediclinic Al Sufouh in Knowledge Village (04 366 1030). There's also the Saudi German Hospital, close to The Greens.

Shops

There are supermarkets within the various compounds. There's a Choithrams at The Springs end, a large Spinneys at Springs Town Centre and a Spinneys Market in the Meadows. The Greens has a Choithrams and a small shopping centre. There are also beauty salons, pharmacies and ATMs. Both Ibn Battuta and Mall of the Emirates are only 10 minutes away.

Bars & Restaurants

Fitness First in The Lakes has a licensed restaurant and bar, The Reform Club, and the Mongomerie Golf Club also has a licensed restaurant. Other than that, you'll have to venture to the marina or Al Barsha for a better selection of dining venues.

Attractions

The Montgomerie Golf Club, and three Fitness Firsts with outdoor pools at the Lakes, Springs and Meadows.

Emirates Living

Generally, the style and quality of all houses in Emirates Living is good. The smallest villas available are located in The Springs, the larger properties are in The Meadows and Emirates Hills.

Annual rental prices: Two-bedroom townhouse from Dhs.130,000. Six-bedroom mansion from Dhs.350,000.

Neighbouring Community: Jumeirah Islands

Jumeirah Islands is made up of small artificial islands, each home to 16 villas, sitting in a man-made lake.

Annual rental prices: Four-bedroom villa is from Dhs.330,000.

Neighbouring Community: The Greens

The Greens offers a range of one to four-bedroom apartments, which are well appointed but a bit small for the money. There are small lakes and pathways lined with trees and flowers.

Annual rental prices: One-bedroom apartment from Dhs.80,000. Three-bedroom from Dhs.140,000.

Neighbouring Community: Jumeirah Park

Its prime location – next to Meadows, Lakes and Springs – is a draw. The three-, four- and five-bedroom villas are great for families. There's a children's daycare centre, play area, and kindergarten through to secondary school, as well as shops and restaurants.

Annual rental prices: Three-bedroom villa from Dhs.200,000.

Emirates Hills

View of JLT from Jumeirah Islands

Emirates Hills

Downtown Dubai

Map **2 F6** Metro **Burj Khalifa/Dubai Mall**
Downtown has a community feel: children's play areas, cafes and restaurants, souks and swimming pools. The wide promenades, Arabian passageways and palm-lined streets that link the different residential quarters encourage residents to get around on foot.

The adjacent Sheikh Zayed Road is Dubai's busiest motorway, but if traffic doesn't bother you, the strip between Trade Centre Roundabout and Interchange One is home to some of Dubai's biggest towers.

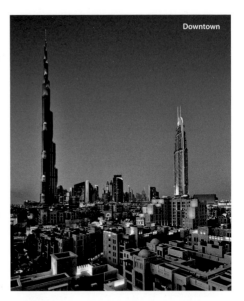
Downtown

Schools

There are nurseries (Old Town Nursery, Kangaroo Kids' and Cello Kids Club) but no schools in Downtown Dubai, although those in Jumeira and Al Qouz are close.

Healthcare

Apart from pharmacies dotted round the Old Town, The Dubai Mall and the Residences, there is the large Mediclinic Dubai Mall. The closest hospitals are Medcare Hospital (04 407 9100) in Al Safa and the Iranian Hospital (04 344 0250) on Al Wasl Road in Satwa. On Sheikh Zayed Road is also Al Zahra Medical Centre (04 331 5000) in Al Safa Tower.

Shops

Downtown Dubai is a shopper's dream with both The Dubai Mall and Souk Al Bahar within walking distance. The Dubai Mall has a Waitrose and there are Spinneys stores and Al Maya outlets scattered around. Several banks are on the ground floor of the Dubai Mall, along with pharmacies, money exchanges and opticians. Next to the mall, Souk Al Bahar houses boutique shops.

Sheikh Zayed Road also has Mazaya Centre and the supermarkets of Jumeira nearby. Both sides of Sheikh Zayed Road have pharmacies and smaller shops.

Bars & Restaurants

Souk Al Bahar is a nightlife hub with several licensed bars and restaurants. The Dubai Mall has a few unlicensed restaurants along with two huge foodcourts. Also, there's the two Address hotels, home to Neos sky bar on the 63rd floor of the Downtown hotel, and Cabana, the funky pool bar at The Dubai Mall hotel.

Sheikh Zayed Road has plenty of takeaway restaurants and the strip is full of nightlife in the Shangri-La, Fairmont, Crowne Plaza and Towers Rotana.

Attractions

The Burj Khalifa is on your doorstep, as is Dubai Mall (with its aquarium) and the dancing fountains.

Downtown Dubai

The massive Downtown Dubai development is made up of high and low-rise residential units, with landmark buildings – The Address (Dubai Mall and Downtown), The Palace Hotel, Emaar Square and the Burj Khalifa – as the cornerstones. At one end, near to the Burj, are the Burj Residence towers, The Lofts and 8 Boulevard Walk, while at the opposite end, on the border with the Business Bay development, are the South Ridge and Burj Views high-rises. In between is the Arabian architecture of Old Town. There is plenty of parking within each of the residential complexes, and the Burj Khalifa/Dubai Mall Metro stop is walking distance from some apartments and a short feeder bus ride from the others.

Options range from tiny studios to expansive four-bedroom townhouses, and the finishing in most buildings is of a high spec. Most residential towers come with facilities including games rooms, libraries, barbecue areas, gyms, pools and sports courts.

Annual rental prices: One-bedroom from Dhs.100,000 in Old Town or Dhs.160,000 in Burj Khalifa.

Neighbouring Community: Sheikh Zayed Road

On the high-rise strip along Sheikh Zayed Road you'll find a mix of residential and commercial buildings alongside impressive hotels. It's a popular area.
Annual rental prices: One-bedroom from Dhs.85,000. Three-bedroom from Dhs.150,000.

Al Barsha

Map **1 Q6** Metro **Mall of the Emirates**
Al Barsha has two distinct zones. The main area offers large villas with big gardens popular with local families. Some of the older apartment blocks offer competitively priced options, while the new apartment blocks, closer to Mall of the Emirates, are popular with Media and Internet City workers.

New villas are being built on the other side of Al Khail Road (called Al Barsha South).

Schools
The Dubai American Academy and Al Mawakeb are located in Al Barsha, and Wellington International School, Dubai College and Jumeirah English Speaking School are nearby.

Healthcare
There is a GP and paediatrician at the Medical Specialist Centre (04 340 9495), in the Khoury Building near Sheikh Zayed Road, but the nearest emergency room is in the Medcare Hospital in Al Safa.

Shops
The nearby Mall of the Emirates has a Carrefour supermarket, high-street shops and designer fashion.

Bars & Restaurants
The Kempinski and Pullman hotels at Mall of the Emirates have licensed restaurants and bars, as do a handful of other business hotels nearby. Good-quality independent eateries are aplenty and Al Barsha is a short drive from Madinat Jumeirah and the marina.

Attractions
Mall of the Emirates with cinema and indoor ski slope.

Al Barsha
Mainly including fairly new, three to five-bedroom villas, around 75% of the houses are locally owned and inhabited. Al Barsha 1, near Mall of the Emirates has apartments, such as Golden Sands hotel apartments, which offer long-term rentals.
Annual rental prices: Three-bedroom villa from Dhs.170,000.

Neighbouring Community: TECOM
TECOM is made up primarily of residential towers. There is still a lot of construction going on, and although the roads have all been finished, there are no pedestrian pavements. So, rents tend to be a bit cheaper than in neighbouring Al Barsha or The Greens. The quality of apartments varies, and traffic can get busy during peak hours. There is a metro stop in front of the area, which is useful for anyone working on Sheikh Zayed Road, and there are small Geant and Park n Shop supermarkets, with the Choithrams and other amenities in The Greens just a stone's throw away. Nightlife destinations such as the marina and Al Sufouh are just across Sheikh Zayed Road and the Media Rotana in TECOM is home to local pub Nelson's.
Annual rental prices: Two-bedroom apartment from Dhs.90,000.

Up & Coming Areas
When buildings in brand new developments are completed, shops and services, and the gym and pool within the building, tend to follow a few steps behind. Until amenities are in place, prices are cheaper, and so while you may have to travel further for shops, chemists, schools and clinics, and you may regularly find your balcony inch-deep in construction dust, a brand new apartment can be a bargain.

Some up and coming areas include: Business Bay (particularly Executive Towers), Dubai Studio City, and The Crescent in International Media Production Zone. For a bargain new villa try The Plantation, Equestrian & Polo Club in Dubailand or one of Meydan City's developments, due to be completed in 2015. If you don't mind living on a building site with few facilities, you can pick up a bargain at the Mediterranean-themed Jumeirah Village Circle. A one-bedroom apartment here starts at Dhs.55,000 (unfurnished).

Villa in Al Barsha

Discovery Gardens

Map **1 H7** Metro **Nakheel Harbour and Towers**
Made up of clusters of Mediterranean style low-rise apartment blocks, Discovery Gardens is surprisingly green. Traffic bottlenecks can be a problem during rush hours, but there is plenty of parking around the buildings. The metro is not easy to walk to; a bus or taxi is the best option. There is also a metro stop outside Ibn Battuta; you need to take the F43 feeder bus to access it. The neighbouring development Al Furjan is designed with families in mind.

Schools
Al Furjan has two schools. Jebel Ali Primary School and the Winchester School are both in the Jabal Ali vicinity approximately 15-20 minutes' drive away.

Healthcare
Discovery Gardens has the Aster Medical Centre. The Cedars Jebel Ali International Hospital is near to both Discovery Gardens and Al Furjan.

Shops
Although there aren't any major shops within the Discovery Gardens development, Ibn Battuta Mall is conveniently close and contains a large Geant hypermarket. Al Furjan has the Village Centre with several shops and supermarkets.

Bars & Restaurants
Heading to Marsa Dubai and Al Barsha for a drink or a nice dinner isn't much of a hassle, and the Movenpick Ibn Battuta Gate Hotel is a welcome addition to the immediate area's dining and bar scene. Ibn Battuta Mall houses a cinema and several restaurants.

Attractions
Al Furjan has 50 hectares of park and outdoor spaces as well as cycling and jogging tracks.

Discovery Gardens
Rents tend to be lower here and apartments easy to come by. The buildings only contain studios and one-bedroom apartments. It's one of the few places where landlords will still accept quarterly rental payments as opposed to six months or a year upfront.
Annual rental prices: One-bedroom apartment from Dhs.60,000.

Neighbouring Community: Al Furjan
Al Furjan is a low-rise development with four communities of apartments, three- to six-bedroom villas and three-bedroom terraced houses. The whole area is designed to promote outdoor living.
It's a peaceful and pleasant area, but a little out of town and so is better for families and those seeking a peaceful existence.
Annual rental prices: Three-bedroom villa from Dhs.150,000.

Discovery Gardens

Dubailand

Dubailand is a vast development encompassing several varied communities within it. It stretches along Sheikh Mohammad bin Zayed Road (formerly known as the Emirates Road) and will include sporting attractions as well as entertainment facilities, retail outlets and residential areas of villas and apartment blocks. Developments that are already built, or under construction are detailed below, but there are many more still to come.

Schools

Both Jumeirah English Speaking School Arabian Ranches (jess.sch.ae) and the giant GEMS World Academy (04 373 6373) are a stone's throw away. There are further options in Al Barsha and Emirates Living. Greenfield Community School and the International School of Choueifat are both in the nearby Dubai Investment Park, and Building Blocks Nursery in MotorCity takes infants and toddlers.

Healthcare

There's a Medicentre clinic (04 360 8866) in Uptown MotorCity, along with a couple of pharmacies. The Mediclinic Arabian Ranches (04 453 4020) offers general practice and a range of medical specialities. The nearest emergency room is Cedars Jebel Ali International Hospital.

Shops

MotorCity has a nice strip of cafes and shops, and Arabian Ranches has the Village Community Centre, which houses Le Marche supermarket, a chemist, liquor store and several cafes, restaurants and takeaways.

Bars & Restaurants

The Arabian Ranches Golf Course is home to a restaurant and bar. The licensed Dubai Polo & Equestrian Club are just a couple of minutes away from Arabian Ranches.

Attractions

Arabian Ranches Golf Course, The Els Club and Dubai Polo Club are all close at hand, plus it's just 20 minutes to Mall of the Emirates, Marsa Dubai and Madinat Jumeirah.

Jumeirah Golf Estates

Lots of people dream of living on a golf course. But now you can put on your Callaways, step out your front door and you're ready to sneak in a quick nine holes before dinner. Anyone looking to garner a slice of the residential golfing lifestyle could do a lot worse than moving into one of the villas at Jumeirah Golf Estates, home to the DP World Tour Championship.

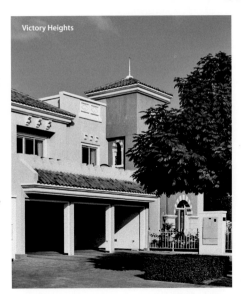
Victory Heights

There are many things to love about living on a golf course: the stunning vistas, an expanse of manicured grass fairways, and unlimited access to first-class golf courses designed by the pros. There's a range of villa types, from four-bedrooms upwards, all oozing style and luxury. At the heart of this exclusive development is the Norman Country Club, with a leisure centre, bar and restaurants (including one by Jamie Oliver), tennis academy, lap pool and leisure lagoon.
Annual rental prices: Four-bedroom villa from Dhs.290,000.

Dubai Sports City

The world's first integrated sports city is not quite completed, but there are now a handful of occupied towers. The prices are competitive when you consider that facilities in each tower include underground parking, a gym, barbecue area, Jacuzzi, steam room and sauna, and free internet.
Annual rental prices: Two-bedroom apartment from Dhs.80,000. Four-bedroom townhouse from Dhs.250,000.

The area also includes the Victory Heights development – Spanish-style villas and townhouses all within a stone's throw of the Els Golf Club, and use of the same facilities as Dubai Sports City.

Dubai MotorCity

Built around the Dubai Autodrome, MotorCity has access to first-class race car action. The development is completed and consists of pretty, medium-rise apartments finished to a high standard with cobbled streets and a pleasing amount of greenery around.

The buildings have English-sounding names in the vein of 'Dickens Circus' and 'Sherlock House', which adds to the quaint feel of this community. A good array of services make it an attractive place to live for couples and singles after a slice of suburbia.

You may be able to hear the sound of cars racing around the Autodrome circuit if the wind is blowing towards the residential area though.

Annual rental prices: One-bedroom apartments from Dhs.65,000.

Arabian Ranches

The quiet, curving, grass-lined lanes of the Arabian Ranches development are home to several swimming pools, basketball and tennis courts, barbecue pits and grassy areas.

This is an all-villa project set among lush greenery, lakes and the Arabian Ranches Golf Course, with a range of luxury facilities that all add up to some pretty fine suburban living. It was one of the first freehold residential areas to be completed and there is certainly a homely and mature neighbourhood feel to the place. Most of the people who bought villas in the development still live in them, so finding one that suits your needs can be difficult.

Annual rental prices: Two-bedroom villa from Dhs.145,000.

The Villa

The Villa offers residents spacious villas – many with pools – meaning luxury living at an affordable price. Due to its location further out in Dubailand, and the lack of facilities as yet, most people who move here are large families looking for luxury and space. Prices are competitive, but be prepared to foot the bill for landscaping if you are the first to move in. For shops, schools and other amenities, Dubai Silicon Oasis, Dubai Autodrome, International Media Production Zone and Arabian Ranches are all only a short drive away.

Annual rental prices: Five-bedroom villa from Dhs.230,000.

Neighbouring Development: Green Community

An oasis of green in the desert, this modern and established development is good for families, and homes are hard to come by. The area is made up of high-quality villas with gardens, as well as spacious, low-rise apartment blocks set among small lakes and green parks. There's plenty of room for kids to play in and the place has quietly developed a strong community feel. It's a bit out of the city, but a good choice for people working in the Jebel Ali Free Zone. Its location away from the rest of Dubai means that taxis can be expensive for nights when the car needs to be left at home. However, the development of the site for the Expo 2020 is nearby and so access and facilities in the area are bound to improve over the coming years.

The original Green Community was so well received that the developer built a new phase – Green Community West – and another Green Community at MotorCity. Both are in the same style, with villas surrounded by greenery with meandering cobbled streets.

Schools: The Children's Garden (04 885 3484) offers a primary bilingual curriculum in English/German or English/French, and there are various primary and secondary schools in Emirates Living and Jabal Ali.

Healthcare: The private GMC Green Community (04 885 3225) is upstairs in The Market, while the nearest government-run clinic is at Jabal Ali. For emergencies, the Cedars Jebel Ali International Hospital is nearest. For government A&E care, it's quite a trip to Rashid Hospital.

Shops: The area is serviced by The Market shopping centre, which houses a large Choithrams supermarket, as well as a jewellers, clothes shops, and home furnishing outlets. There's also a pharmacy, a florist, a dry cleaners, an optician, and a branch of ACE Hardware. Ibn Battuta Mall is not far away either.

Bars & restaurants: There are a few good licensed restaurants within the Courtyard by Marriott, and The Market is home to a number of coffee shops and good unlicensed restaurants. For a better selection, Marsa Dubai is about 15 minutes by car.

Attractions: The golf course at Jumeirah Golf Estates is nearby.

Annual rental prices: One-bedroom apartment from Dhs.75,000. Four-bedroom villa from Dhs.230,000.

The Villa

Arabian Ranches

Green Community

Old Dubai

Encompassing Bur Dubai, Deira and Karama, this older, traffic-laden area is a concrete jungle, with mid-size apartment blocks and virtually no green spaces. The area is well connected with both the red and green metro lines. Newer apartments have excellent facilities, and the area is always humming with activity. The dense population means traffic and parking can be a problem, and it also means the streets are full of people. Women may get stared at in the street at night – but it's not dangerous.

Schools

There's a wide choice of nurseries, and plenty of choice for schools nearby including the Dubai English Speaking School (DESS) in Oud Metha.

Healthcare

Bur Dubai and Karama have small medical centres. The emergency room at Rashid Hospital is near, as is the private American Hospital. Healthcare City, which has two hospitals and more than 100 outpatient medical centres, is a few minutes' drive.

Shops

The area has corner shops, supermarkets, banks and more, as well as BurJuman Mall. Bur Dubai's souks and the markets in Karama are good for picking up funky gifts. Close to the bus station, there's the fish and fruit and vegetable markets. Karama Market sells imitation handbags and a wide range of goods.

Bars & Restaurants

There are great 'dive bars' around Khalid bin Al Waleed Road and for cheap eats, also check Al Rigga Street.

Attractions

There are some pleasant walking areas by the creek and along the corniche. Al Fahidi Historical Neighbourhood (formerly called Bastakiya), is the original old heart of Dubai with cafes and art galleries. Stroll around Zabeel Park in Karama with its lake and landscaped gardens, or Creek Park in Bur Dubai. BurJuman Mall is currently undergoing renovations and by the end of 2014 will feature a 14 screen VOX cinema and a Carrefour hypermarket.

Bur Dubai

The area is dominated by apartments in a mix of new and old medium-rise buildings. Golden Sands apartments offer reasonably priced rentals here.
Annual rental prices: Two-bedroom apartment from Dhs.70,000.

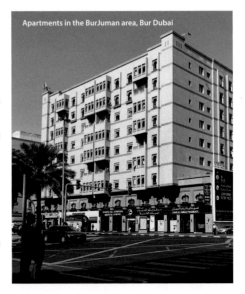
Apartments in the BurJuman area, Bur Dubai

Deira

Deira is not very popular with expats in higher income brackets; the centre is densely built up with old apartments, but nearer the creek there are more modern apartments, many with spectacular views across the water. Rents are relatively low in some of the more built-up areas, while the creekside dwellings cost more. Not so good for cars, but easy to walk around.
Annual rental prices: Two-bedroom apartment from Dhs.60,000.

Karama

Mostly low-rise blocks with apartments ranging from studios to three-bedrooms. Karama has large Filipino and Indian communities, which means a great selection of affordable Eastern eateries on your doorstep.
Annual rental prices: Two-bedroom apartment from Dhs.80,000.

Falling Out Of Favour

Some areas are no longer as popular with expats. They are far from the centre, have a reputation for shoddy maintenance, or are looking a little jaded. International City, Qusais and districts neighbouring Bur Dubai tend to be eschewed by expats these days.

Mirdif

Map **2 Q 12** Metro **Rashidiya**
Mirdif is perceived to be a bit out in the sticks, but airport workers find it ideal. The development includes villas and newer buildings, such as the Uptown Mirdiff complex, the upmarket Shorooq community villas and the low-cost Ghoroob apartments. There's everything you need within the area.

Schools

There is a choice of nurseries in Mirdif including Small Steps (04 288 3347), Super Kids and Emirates British Nursery. Uptown Primary is recommended. Other new schools include Star International School in Mirdif, the Sharjah American International School (04 280 1111) in Al Warqa, Royal Dubai School in Muhaisanah, and the American Academy in Al Mizhar.

Healthcare

Mediclinic Mirdif (04 288 1302) is in Uptown Mirdiff, as well as Drs Nicolas & Asp Dental Clinic (04 255 9977).

Shops

The Mirdif City Centre mall offers a central point for residents to shop. Small convenience stores are also scattered throughout the area along with all the other facilities you could need.

Bars & Restaurants

Though there are no licensed bars in the area (Festival City provides the nearest watering holes), there are plenty of dining options without booze.

Attractions

The massive Mirdif City Centre houses a cinema and Playnation, so there's plenty for the little ones. Further down Airport Road is the smaller Arabian Centre shopping mall which has a World Mart and a Cinecity cinema.

Mirdif

It's a great area for families and has developed into a bustling community with a well-established feel. Take your time with your search as the quality of the buildings varies greatly, and some areas are under the flight path to the airport.
Annual rental prices: One-bedroom apartment from Dhs.60,000. Three-bedroom villas from Dhs.115,000.

Out On A Limb

Silicon Oasis, off the Academic City Road, is a development containing hundreds of high-standard villas with gardens and apartment blocks. People say it's far out of town, although it is just a 10 minute drive from Mirdif. As new facilities open, it's starting to develop an identity and community feel.

The Outlet Mall is just a quick trip over the other side of the Dubai-Al Ain Road too. If you work locally, or are happy with a longer commute, you can find some bargains here, with two-bed apartments available for Dhs.70,000. For more information, see siliconoasis.org.

Mirdif

A furnished apartment in Dubai

SETTING UP HOME

Keys in hand and foot through the door; now the fun really begins. There's a fantastic selection of places that can supply furnishings for your new place and expats often find some unusual styles to try out that they can't get back home. However, there are familiar companies like IKEA, as well as many other furniture stores that can give that modern feel to your new apartment or villa. See the Shopping chapter for more.

First Things First

For all the joy of moving in, there's also an array of phone calls to make and services to set up. Rarely does anything happen quickly or easily when it comes to this sort of thing, but being armed with the right information and approaching it all with a calm attitude can certainly help.

Don't forget that once you've moved in, the regular utility bills will need to be paid on time or you risk

being cut off. No notice is given, you'll simply find your internet has stopped working or there's no water coming from the taps. Often you can get these reconnected quite quickly, but it can depend on the provider. Direct debits are only just starting to be employed in the country, so it can sometimes mean a one-off monthly payment and even a trip to a counter to pay the bill in person.

However, there isn't much else that you should be too worried about, aside from the slowness at which things can take to get done. For everything else, this chapter should point you in the right direction. Once you're settled in you'll find domestic life in Dubai is likely to be remarkably similar to the one that you left back at home. The dining, nightlife, sunshine and vast array of activities you'll be enjoying may be different, but you'll probably still find time to slouch on the sofa and catch up with your favourite TV shows.

Moving Services

If you're arriving with more than a suitcase, you'll need to send your belongings by air or by sea. Air freight is faster but more expensive. Sea freight takes longer but it's cheaper, and containers can hold a huge amount.

Most relocation companies will take care of the paperwork for you and also deal with the procedures at customs and so you don't need to be present when your goods arrive. Just be sure that you have booked and paid for a 'door-to-door' service and your boxes will be brought directly to your new home. Many companies specify that the quote they provide only covers your move to the first floor – the likelihood is in Dubai you could be on a much higher floor, but if there's elevator access then you shouldn't be charged any extra. Advise your security guard and check for any parking restrictions. One popular relocation company is Al Futtaim Logistics, who are specialists in international removals, with more than 80 years' experience.

Relocation Expertise

It is important to consider a moving company's certifications and experience, as well as their quote, to find a team that you trust to look after your precious belongings. Allied Pickfords is a global moving company operating across the Middle East, which offers total move management across air, road and sea. Selected by numerous Global 500 companies to relocate their employees, the business can advise on all aspects of the move and will provide purpose-built packing materials and use expert techniques to maximise protection of your goods in transit. See the listing to the right for their contact details.

If you have only paid for delivery of your belongings as far as Dubai Customs, then you'll need to go to Cargo Village in Garhoud to collect air freight, or Jebel Ali Port to pick up sea freight. Take a copy of the inventory so you know what is in each box. And be patient.

Once at Cargo Village, head to the warehouse, fill out the customs information, and pay any applicable fees. You'll then have to go across to customs where you'll pay any duty, plus a processing fee. Once this has been done, you can go back to the warehouse and collect your shipment. Before you can leave, you'll have to head back over to customs to have your goods x-rayed.

The process for sea freight is a little longer. Once your sea freight is ready for collection (you'll get a call or letter), go to the agent's office and pay the administration and handling charges. Keep these documents. The Bill of Lading number must be marked on all paperwork and entered into the customs computer system. Then go to Dubai Customs House, on Al Mina Road.

The staff are helpful and the procedure is straightforward. Ignore the touts outside. When the papers have been stamped and the port clearance received (there are fees), head to Jebel Ali Port.

Relocation & Removal Companies

Acorn Movers 04 323 6920, *acornmovers.com*
AGS Movers Jumeirah Business Centre, Al Thanyah 5, 04 454 1531, *agsmovers.com*
Al Futtaim Logistics Mena Jabal Ali, 04 881 8288, *aflogistics.com*
Allied Pickfords *> p.ii, iii, 35, 53, 83*
One Business Bay, Business Bay, 04 818 0400, *alliedpickfords.com*
Crown Relocations Dutco House, Al Itihad Rd, Port Saeed, 04 230 5300, *crownrelo.com*
Inchcape Shipping Services Office Court Bldg, Oud Metha, 04 303 8500, *iss-shipping.com*
Interem *> p.73* Nr Lipton R/A 13, Mena Jabal Ali, 04 807 0584, *interem.ae*
Santa Fe Relocations *> p.69* Warsan Bldg, Al Thanyah 1, 04 454 2724, *santaferelo.com*
SIRVA *> p.35, 53, 83* One Business Bay, Business Bay, 04 818 0400, *sirva.com*
STORALL Jabal Ali Ind. 1, 04 880 3644, *storall.ae*

Smooth Moves

- Get more than one quote – some companies will match lower quotes to get the job
- Make sure all items are covered by insurance
- Ensure you have a copy of the inventory and that each item is listed
- Don't be shy about requesting packers to repack items if you are not satisfied
- Take photos of the packing process to use for evidence if you need to make a claim
- Carry customs-restricted goods (DVDs, books) with you; it's easier to open a suitcase at the airport than empty a box outside in the sun

Local Move

If you are moving within Dubai and have valuable possessions, you can hire an insured company to do the packing and moving for you. If not, you may benefit from packing your belongings yourself and hiring an uninsured 'man with a van'. There are several trucks-for-hire companies in the city. Make sure the driver is clear about where you are heading to.

Otherwise, go to large furniture places such as Dragon Mart or IKEA where these unlicensed movers often congregate. A quick drive through an industrial area such as Al Qouz will also turn up some results. The trucks will usually have a mobile number written on the side of the door. Call the number and try to negotiate a good price (usually around Dhs.60 an hour) for the truck, driver and moving labour.

Storage

Whether you're making the move to Dubai and haven't yet found the perfect home for all that furniture you've had shipped over, you've downsized a little and have possessions that simply won't fit between your current four walls, or you're moving on for a few months but don't want to take all your worldly goods with you quite yet, storage can be an excellent option. STORALL (storall.ae) based in Jabal Ali, for example, is a good facility with space rentable on a monthly basis and accessible seven days a week. Sentinel Storage (sentinelme.com) is another option, while the bigger removal and delivery firms may also be able to offer storage services.

Furnishing Accommodation

Most properties, including rentals (unless you're renting a room), come unfurnished, and don't even have basic white goods such as a cooker or fridge. Not all villas have fitted cupboards and wardrobes, although most apartments do. Dubai is home to a wide range of furniture shops offering different types of furnishings, from Swedish simplicity at IKEA and modern design at Home Centre and Dogtas (dogtasuae.com) to rich Indian teak at Marina Gulf Trading. Alternatively, head to one of the carpentry workshops on Naif Road or in Satwa.

Second-hand furniture is easy to come by thanks to the transitory nature of Dubai's population. You'll find small shops in Karama, Naif Road and Satwa and online classifieds should turn up good results. Visit

dubizzle.com, expatwoman.com or websouq.com and try supermarket noticeboards, or Dubai Flea Market (dubai-fleamarket.com). It's even possible to furnish an entire apartment in one fell swoop if you're lucky enough to find someone who is leaving in a hurry and selling everything they own – you could get everything from the cooker and fridge to the bedroom furniture at once.

See the Buyers' Guide for more information on where to buy furniture and white goods.

Renting furniture is an option worth considering. Indigo Living (indigo-living.com) provides rentals on a short and long-term basis – perfect for new arrivals and those who are in town on a short working contract.

Curtains & Blinds

Finding the right blinds or curtains can add a finishing touch to your room, ensure privacy if the house is overlooked, or stop you waking up with the sun. Some properties have windows built to standard sizes, which means you can buy ready-made options from shops such as IKEA and THE One. If these don't measure up, there are several companies that will tailor and install curtains and blinds to fit your property. Curtain specialist Dubai Blinds can bring swatches to your home to help you ensure the curtains or blinds match your decor, and they'll also take measurements for tailor-made finishes.

Swanky new curtains don't always come cheap though, so if you're looking for something more affordable, try your regular tailor, or look on community noticeboards for second-hand blinds or curtains that were made to fit the strange window sizes found in many freehold developments.

Interior Design

When you get your first place in Dubai, starting with an empty apartment can be a great opportunity to create a home from scratch. Whether you need help with choosing colours for the walls, decorative art to hang on them, or the furnishings throughout, there are an increasing number of specialists just a phone call away. A good interior designer will pick options that suit your lifestyle best, so it can be a good option to help you get settled, especially if you're busy with that new job.

3 Square 04 346 3872, *3squareinteriors.com*
Avenue Interiors 04 341 2505, *avenueinteriors.ae*
Cecilia Clason 04 362 6261, *ceciliaclason.com*
Elan Interiors 04 338 7417, *elaninteriorsdubai.com*
Emirates Decor & Furniture Directory 04 267 4274, *emiratesdecor.com*
Indigo Living 04 339 7705, *indigo-living.com*
Jadis Interiors 04 347 4233, *jadisuae.com*
OX Interior Design 04 257 3330, *oxinterior.com*
WA International 04 266 3050, *wa-international.com*

Interior designers can add style

INTERNATIONAL PAPERWORK OUT OF CONTROL?

SIRVA®
Worldwide
Relocation & Moving

Applications. Background checks. Legal documents. Managing global relocation is a daunting task. That's where we come in. As the largest globally-integrated relocation and moving provider, the experts at SIRVA deliver complete corporate relocation and moving solutions — all under one roof. From North America to the Middle East to Africa, we take the fear out of global relocation so that you can feel calm, confident and in control.

EVERYTHING YOU NEED. EVERYWHERE YOU NEED IT.

Call +971.2.677.9765 (Abu Dhabi), +971.4.818.0400 (Dubai) or visit SIRVA.com to learn more.

Utilities & Services

Electricity & Water >p.85

Dubai Electricity and Water Authority (DEWA) provides electricity and water products and services for the entire emirate of Dubai. You can easily sign up for a new connection at one of the 15 conveniently located DEWA customer care centres, or online at dewa.gov.ae. A deposit (calculated based on supplied load) is required, which will be refundable when you close your account and leave the property.

Standard DEWA charges are applicable as per its slab system with a fixed rate (fils per kWh and fils per gallon) in each slab, and rates will change based on your consumption. There will be an additional variable fuel surcharge of fils per kWh and fils per gallon, which will be added to the bill. For more information, visit dewa.gov.ae/tariff/newtariff.aspx.

Electricity

The electricity supply in Dubai is 220/240 volts and 50 cycles. The socket type is identical to the three-point UK system but most appliances here are sold with two-pin plugs. Adaptors can be bought from any grocery or hardware shop.

DEWA has an active campaign to reduce greenhouse gas emissions by encouraging everyone to moderate their use of electricity and water (which will also help you save on bills). You'll find helpful advice and tips on the website, as well as a range of online services; for example, use the consumption calculator to help you manage and conserve your consumption. Customers with special needs are catered for through a video chat service, called Ash'ir, meaning 'to signal' in Arabic. Once you register, it's easy to pay your bills through one of DEWA's 20 payment methods. All DEWA customers are to receive only electronic bills from 2015. Your DEWA bill also includes a housing charge from Dubai Municipality; this adds up to approximately 5% of the rental value of your property divided over the course of 12 months.

Failing to pay your DEWA bill by its due date will most likely result in the disconnection of your home's electricity and water services, often without warning. You will then have to pay a reconnection fee.

Clearance Certificate

In order to prove to your landlord that you have settled your DEWA account before moving out – or if you are looking to sell your own property – you need to obtain a clearance certificate from DEWA. This procedure is fairly simple and hassle-free, and you can obtain it the same day you disconnect your service.

Drinking Water

Bottled water is cheap, but most people end up buying a water cooler or pump (available from most large supermarkets), or leasing one from a water supplier and using the four or five-gallon bottles of purified water to drink at home. Prices vary per company; some charge a deposit of around Dhs.50 for each re-useable bottle, and then Dhs.7 per refill, while Masafi recycles its bottles rather than re-using them and charges Dhs.12 per new bottle. Companies will deliver the bottles straight to your door, and then collect your empties.

Al Shalal 800 4342, *alshalalwaters.com*
Culligan International 12th St, Al Qouz Ind. 1, 800 4945, *culligan.ae*
Desert Springs 800 6650, *desertspringswateruae.com*
Falcon Spring Drinking Water 04 396 6072, *falconspringwater.com*
Masafi Nr Dubai Garden Centre, Al Qouz Ind. 3, 04 3465 959, *masafi.com*
Nestle Waters Management & Technology Nr Wafi City, Healthcare City, Umm Hurair 2, 04 324 0800, *nestle-waters.com*
Oasis Water 600 522 261, *oasiscome2life.com*

Gas

There's no mains gas in Dubai, and individual gas canisters need to be purchased and attached to cookers. There are gas suppliers that will deliver the canisters and connect up the supply. Supply companies tend to slip stickers or flyers under doors on a regular basis and they're all essentially the same in terms of service and price. A few of the largest companies include Al Fahidi Gas (04 351 6452), Oasis Gas (04 396 1812) and New City Gas (04 351 8282).

Gas bottles come in three sizes: most houses use the medium size, the small are better in apartments and the large are really only for industrial use – they are enormous. The canisters initially cost about Dhs.350 and refills are usually Dhs.75 (keep your receipt so that you can get some of your deposit back). There is usually a gas van operating around each area at all times; chances are that if you run out of gas in the middle of cooking your chips, one call to your local gas man and he can be with you in less than 20 minutes.

Sewerage

Much of Dubai now has mains sewers but there are areas where houses and apartment buildings are still serviced by septic tanks. These are emptied by municipality contractors, but should you have a problem, contact your landlord or local municipality office. All sewage has to be treated, hence the charges on the DEWA bill even for houses not on the main sewer network.

GOVERNMENT OF DUBAI

هيئة كهرباء ومياه دبي
Dubai Electricity & Water Authority

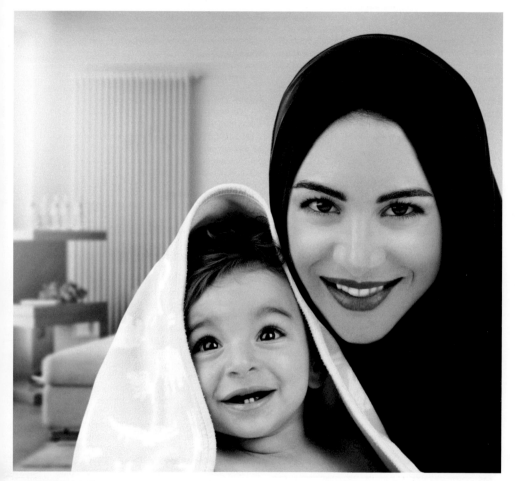

YOUR SMILE
DEFINES OUR SUCCESS

For years we have always been part of your life.

That is why no matter what time, day or night, we are always there to serve you better for generations to come.

For generations to come

DEWA SMART WORLD

DEWA_OFFICIAL

DEWAOFFICIAL

DEWAOFFICIAL

You Tube DEWAVIDEOGALLERY

CALL US 04 6019999

www.dewa.gov.ae

EXPO 2020

DUBAI, UNITED ARAB EMIRATES

Rubbish Disposal

Dubai's per capita domestic waste rate is extremely high, with some estimates saying that each household generates over 1,000kg of rubbish per year – one of the worst offenders in the world. Fortunately, rubbish disposal is efficient, with municipality trucks driving around each area and emptying skips daily. Just empty your household bins into the skips (there is usually one on every street). If you don't have a skip on your street, then contact the municipality on 800 900 to request one. Certain areas, such as Emirates Living, have wheelie bins outside each house, where waste is regularly collected from. Recycling efforts are poor but slowly improving.

Telecommunications

There are two home phone providers in the UAE, Etisalat and du. Both are government-owned. The majority of homes in Dubai will have an Etisalat landline, but several new developments will have du, and du also provides services to many business and residential Emaar and Nakheel properties (such as Marsa Dubai, Arabian Ranches, Emirates Living, the Greens/Springs/Lakes, and International City). Villas and apartments in these areas are equipped with multiple sockets for telephone, internet and TV signals. You can subscribe to du's call packages and internet services if you have an Etisalat landline (and vice versa), but you still have to pay the du (or Etisalat) line rental charge. Etisalat offers two landlines per property; installation of the second landline is free, you just pay the extra rental charges. du offers an unlimited number of landlines and extensions; each additional landline comes with a new subscription, a new phone number and a new handset. Additional extensions are added onto your existing landline subscription. Both Etisalat's Home Landline packages and du's Homephone packages include free local calls.

Additional Services

Etisalat's Najma 7 Services in 1 bundle includes call waiting, barring and forwarding and costs Dhs.50 installation, and Dhs.25 per month rental. du offers call barring for Dhs.50 (activation fee) plus Dhs.10 per month (rental).

Installing A Landline

To install a landline with Etisalat or du you must apply directly with a completed application form, the original and a copy of your passport and residence visa, and your Resident ID. Etisalat charges Dhs.180 for installation and Dhs.39 per month for line rental. du charges Dhs.200 for installation and Dhs.15 per month for line rental, as well as a Panasonic handset. (Anyone with an Etisalat landline can sign up to du's Homephone calls package, which costs Dhs.50 to activate). You will then be charged monthly for all calls to international and any mobile numbers. When applying, taking the number of the landline closest to your house can help pinpoint your location. The tariffs for international calls vary by country but there is some variation in peak timings, depending on country. For more information see etisalat.ae or du.ae.

Closing A Landline

A landline may be cancelled at any time, but it must be done in person at either an Etisalat or du office. You will be charged an early termination fee of Dhs.100 if you cancel within the first month.

Codes & prefixes

Abu Dhabi	02	Ajman	06
Al Ain	03	Dubai	04
Fujairah	09	Ras Al Khaimah	07
Sharjah	06	Umm Al Quwain	06
UAE Country Code	971		

Pre-paid Mobile

Mobile phone users can choose between du (prefix 055 and 052) and Etisalat (prefixes 050 or 056). Both providers offer monthly or pay-as-you-go packages.

Anyone visiting or living in Dubai, and above the age of 18, can apply for a pre-paid mobile phone account – you just need to buy a SIM card and then you can pay as you go by purchasing phone cards or topping up online. Newcomers to Dubai and short-term visitors often opt for a pre-paid service: there are no monthly bills, you don't sign a contract, you can cancel at any time, and you do not need a residence visa. Etisalat's pre-paid Wasel card and du's Pay As You Go cards can be topped up with credit to use on calls, SMS and 4G internet. Recharge cards are available in denominations ranging from Dhs.20-500 from fuel stations, supermarkets and electrical stores. You do not need to renew the line as long as you keep using it, and for du you get lifetime validity if you recharge the phone more than 20 times in four months.

Post-paid Mobile

Both companies also offer monthly post-paid services. To sign up for a post-paid plan through du or Etisalat, you will need to bring your passport and residence visa as well as either a UAE credit card, a recent utility bill with your physical address, your tenancy agreement, or a salary certificate that shows a minimum salary of Dhs.2,500 per month.

A new du post-paid line costs from Dhs.25 monthly plus a Dhs.125 connection fee, while an Etisalat line costs from Dhs.50 per month plus a Dhs.125 connection fee (covered by a Dhs.125 welcome credit).

You can complete the application form online at shop.du.ae/en/mobilePlans or at etisalat.ae, or visit any phone outlet.

That's My Number

All mobile phone customers now have to register their SIM card with Etisalat or du. Wait until you receive an SMS asking you to register, then take along your Resident ID or a passport with your residency visa to the nearest service provider outlet. You have three months to register your details, after which any unregistered SIM cards will be cancelled. Registration is free and once only.

Mobile Services

Lost your mobile? For Etisalat, call 101, or for du call customer care on 055 567 8155 to temporarily disconnect your number (you will need to know your passport number for security). Your SIM card can be replaced and you can keep the same number, but you'll lose the numbers you had saved in your phone's memory. To replace a lost SIM card, du charges a flat rate of Dhs.55. Etisalat charges Dhs.25 to replace a lost SIM. You can also cancel your number permanently by simply filling out and submitting a cancellation form.

Etisalat and du launched a mobile phone number portability service at the end of 2013, which allows customers to switch between the two network operators while retaining their phone number. Enquiries about switching to du can be made on 800 242 643, and for Etisalat on 800 99.

Internet

Internet services in the UAE are provided by either Etisalat or du. You should note, however, that all internet usage, is regulated by the Telecommunications Regulatory Authority (TRA). This means that any sites that are deemed to be offensive, either religiously, culturally or politically, are blocked and can't be accessed.

Etisalat is the main Internet Service Provider (ISP), but du primarily serves the newly developed areas and free zones in the emirate. Currently, residents don't get to choose their service provider; rather you must go with whoever your home is pre-wired to, although there are plans to broaden the network to each ISP. Etisalat services range from a basic Al Shamil broadband connection to an eLife bundle that includes internet, TV and landline. For a 1mbps broadband connection with unlimited usage you pay a Dhs.199 installation fee plus Dhs.259 per month. Or, you can opt for an eLife landline, TV and internet bundle, which starts from Dhs.359 per month for 10mpbs plus Dhs.199 installation fee.

du services range from the Talk & Surf internet and landline packages, which start at Dhs.275, to Talk, Surf and Watch packages, which also include digital TV. Talk, Surf and Watch packages range from 8mbps (Dhs.335 per month) to 100mbps (Dhs.810 per month). There is a Dhs.200 installation fee.

Visit any Etisalat or du store to sign up and arrange for home installation. The whole process takes at least one week.

Skype

Downloading voice over internet protocol (VoIP) services such as Skype can be difficult within the UAE due to the sites being blocked here. However, if you have downloaded it in a different country, or within an area where the restriction is lifted, such as in some free zones, it will work when calling another computer, but not when calling landlines or mobiles.

Wi-fi

When out and about, look out for Etisalat's wi-fi hotspots to get online. These are located all over town at various malls, cafes and restaurants and you can connect by purchasing a pre-paid card at the venue. See izone.ae for listings. Existing broadband customers can get a period of free time in these hotspots, depending on their package.

Postal Services

Previously, there was no postal delivery service to home addresses, and everyone had their mail delivered to a PO Box. In January 2012, Empost rolled out a new system that more closely resembles the traditional postal services in western countries. If you live in a villa, you can sign up to the My Home service which will see post delivered direct to your home three times a week – or six for an additional payment. My Building is the option for apartment residents, with post delivered to a PO Box in the lobby or basement. My Box sees your mail delivered to a PO Box at a post office, and finally there's My Zone, where post is delivered to local shelters that contain a large number of boxes, with the idea that you get a box close to your place of work or home. Visit empostuae.com for more details and rates. Alternatively, many people have personal mail delivered to their company's PO Box; this traditional method still works and, for many, may be the best option.

Letters and packages do occasionally go missing and, if the item has not been registered, there's little that you can do apart from wait – some turn up months after they are expected, although this happens less and less frequently.

Empost offers a courier service, while registered mail is a relatively inexpensive alternative and can be tracked via a reference number. The major international courier services also deliver and have a presence in Dubai, including DHL (04 299 5333), FedEx (04 218 3860), UPS (800 4774) and Aramex (600 544 000). If you're expecting a package, ensure the person sending it has included your phone number, as that is often the only way for the courier to find your location.

Television

There are a number of free television channels, but non-Arabic language channels are limited. Most expats opt for paid TV from one of the satellite services like Orbit Showtime Network (OSN), but if you don't fancy a satellite dish or your rental terms don't allow one, then Etisalat and du offer digital TV. Digital TV providers can also provide your broadband and landline phone services, with bundles offering various levels of broadband speed, call time and channel choice. It can get expensive for the best of each.

High Definition (HD) channels are now commonplace and there are plenty of the 'on demand' options available that many expats are used to. For example, OSN customers can purchase a Showbox (a recordable digital receiver) that allows them to pause live television and record favourite shows. They can also watch movies and series online through OSN Play, which is free to subscribers. Digital TV subscribers also get the benefits of recording and pausing live television. Etisalat has launched its eLife TV iPad App to let subscribers watch on their tablet via wi-fi or Etisalat's super-fast mobile internet.

Football Fans

If you're after English Premier League, Spanish La Liga, French Ligue 1, Italian Serie A or the UEFA Champion's League then you'll need to subscribe to BeIN Sports package with access to channels +1 to +10. If you're an existing Etisalat or du subscriber you can do this through them for Dhs.78 or Dhs.53 respectively.

Free To View

Local free-to-air English language channels in Dubai include:
Dubai One: 24 hour entertainment specialising in various US series
MBC 4: primarily US series targeted at women
MBC Action: US action series, targeted at men
MBC Max: latest Hollywood films
MBC 2: mainly Western movies
City 7 TV: independent Dubai-based broadcaster. News, business, lifestyle, drama and comedy shows
Fox HD: a mixture of English and Arabic – mainly US comedy and Arabic drama series

Maids & Cleaners
Domestic Help

Domestic help is readily available in Dubai, both full and part-time. Legally, a live-in or out maid can only be employed by the individual who sponsors her and organises her residence visa.

To avoid exploitation, the Gulf countries have agreed on conditions for domestic workers, limiting working hours to eight, with a maximum of two hours overtime. The contract provisions state the employer must provide quality accommodation and flights home, and enshrines the employee's right to freedom and days off, banning an employer from keeping the employee's passport.

Many maids take on extra cleaning or babysitting for other families, but if you are caught you face a hefty fine and the maid may be deported. If you are looking for someone part-time, but want to stay within the law, there are many companies in Dubai that provide cleaners and maids on an hourly basis, and for around Dhs.35 per hour they'll take care of all your sweeping, mopping, dusting, washing, and ironing. Most companies stipulate a minimum number of hours, usually two or three per visit.

City Sky Maid Services Al Tayer Bldg, Al Wasl, 04 332 4600, *cityskymaid.com*
Dubai Carpet Cleaning G1 Deira Tower, Al Rigga, 04 221 9800, *dubai-carpet-cleaning.com*
Ecomaid Middle East Nr Mazaya Shopping Centre, Al Wasl, 04 388 1292, *ecomaidme.com*
Home Help Emirates Islamic Bank Bldg, Al Mankhool, 04 380 5111, *homehelp.ae*
Housekeeping Co 800 57827, *housekeepingco.com*
Howdra 04 238 0088, *howdra.ae*
Molly Maid Al Qouz 3, 04 339 7799, *mollymaidme.com*
Ready Maids Nasser Lootah Bldg, Umm Hurair 1, 04 396 6779, *readymaids.ae*

Laundry Services

Wall-to-wall carpets are rare in this part of the world, but many homes do sport loose rugs and carpets. When they're looking a bit grubby, the companies listed below can pay you a visit, give you a quote, and take the rugs away to be cleaned, returning them a couple of days later.

Alpha Cleaning Services 055 608 8393, *alphaserves.com*
Churchill Business Bay, 800 7076, *churchill-gulf.com*
Dubai Maids Jabal Ali Ind. 1, 04 880 4670, *dubai-maids.com*
Modern Cleaning Methods Nr Al Amani Spare Parts, Al Rashidiya, 04 285 1668, *modernmethodsco.com*

There are no self-service launderettes, but laundry shops are everywhere. Some of the largest chains in the city include Butler's (04 885 6616) and Champion Cleaners (04 344 9727). As well as dry cleaning and laundry, they all offer ironing services. If you have specific instructions, make sure these are noted when you drop off your laundry – creases in trousers are standard, so if you don't want them, speak up.

Compensation policies for lost or damaged items vary, but losses are rare, even in the places that look most disorganised. Large chains normally have a free pick-up and delivery service.

As a guide to prices, you can expect to pay around Dhs.19 for a shirt, Dhs.60 for a suit and Dhs.27 for a double quilt cover.

Home Improvements

Builders

Exact regulations are constantly changing when it comes to making alterations to your property, but so far they have always been extremely restrictive. In Nakheel and Emaar developments, for example, you are not allowed to build any higher than your perimeter wall.

To build an extension, you need to apply for permission via your master developer, and you then need to wait while they approve the plans. Following that, you have to pay a deposit of Dhs.5,000.

Once the works have begun, an inspector will make a site visit, and on completion of the building,

Apartments near Downtown

a final assessment will be carried out. After this, your deposit will be returned if you have met all the guidelines. These guidelines are very stringent as developers seek to protect the look and feel of communities. They can determine the colour of the paint you may use on the exterior of your property and also the particular design and style of any doors, gates or decorative iron fencing.

All this may change though as the Planning & Engineering Department of Dubai Municipality is currently working to centralise all structural work carried out on residential buildings in Dubai, effectively taking the responsibility out of the hands of the developers. The anticipation is that when the new laws are passed, rules on extension plans and designs will be more lenient. See login.dm.gov.ae for more information.

If you are intending to make some structural changes to your property, you should always use a licensed and experienced contractor. There are a number of options, including Kalandoor Contracting (04 884 9426), Al Baraha Land Building Contracting and General Maintenance (04 272 2999), and Danube Buildmart (04 297 7020).

Interior Decorating

Once you own your property, you are free to paint the inside in any style you choose. If you rent, the likelihood is that your landlord will not mind on the basis that he has your deposit, and will be happy to keep hold of it should you not leave the villa or apartment in its original state. Many Dubai landlords do not need much of a reason to hold back security deposits though, so it's worth checking and getting something in writing before you get the roller out.

An excellent range of paints can be found at Jotun Paints and ACE Hardware (04 206 6690). Companies like Alpha Services (055 608 8393) offer painting services, and artists such as MacKenzie Art (mackenzieart.com, 04 341 9803) can be commissioned for children's murals and original artwork. The cost of internally painting a whole villa can vary between Dhs.3,000 and Dhs.8,000, depending on size.

Maintenance

Whether you're a homeowner or live in rental property, somebody must be responsible for your property's general maintenance, whether that's you, your landlord or an assigned company – check your tenancy contract if you're renting. Housing in Dubai requires constant maintenance due to the climate. Air-conditioning units can be temperamental and need regular servicing, plumbing problems aren't uncommon, electrics can go haywire and creepy crawlies like to pay a visit.

Most homeowners and tenants employ the services of a maintenance company. Annual contracts don't come cheap, but the benefit is it will cover you for most of your maintenance needs. The contract should include regular scheduled servicing of air-conditioning units and boilers, seasonal pest control protection, basic masonry works and 24 hour emergency call-out services, while extra paid services include swimming pool maintenance and gardening.

Contracts ideal for tenants that cover emergency call-outs only can start from Dhs.59 per month, or for more comprehensive cover, prices increase to Dhs.250 per month and up. Companies that offer maintenance services include Emrill (covering Emaar Properties, emrill.com), Howdra (howdra.ae), and Hitches & Glitches (hitchesandglitches.com); Green Facilities Management (green-fms.com) which prides itself on its environmental credentials, offers a 24/7 emergency call-out service, will assess your home for energy efficiency, and sources environmentally sound maintenance products. You'll also hear adverts on local radio stations for maintenance companies – as there are so many, prices should be competitive.

For more specialist services, try Under One Roof (04 323 2722, underoneroof.ae); Floorworld (800 35667, floorworld.ae) and Alomi Real Wood Flooring (04 884 8462, alomirealwoodflooringllc.ae).

Whichever community you live in, your developer will have standard rules and regulations relating to noise, parking and general upkeep of your property. These will be detailed on the developer's website and local security guards perform regular checks. If you live in a villa, a dirty or messy garage may be frowned upon, and you could be fined for parking on the street rather than in a designated bay. It's worth being aware of what is required of you as a tenant or homeowner.

Gardens

For a city on the edge of the desert, Dubai boasts a surprising amount of lush greenery – but, with very little annual rainfall and rapidly diminishing groundwater, plenty of artificial hydration is required if you want to create your very own garden oasis. Gardens need watering twice a day ideally – as green can turn to brown within just a matter of days. You can install a timed irrigation system or employ the services of a gardener, while boring a well in your garden to access natural water supplies is also an option. For houses further in from the coast, you'll need to drill down approximately 25 metres before you hit groundwater, whereas houses in areas near to the coast will access water after just a couple of metres. The level of salt in the water can vary considerably, and it is possible to pump the water into a mixed tank to desalinate it for your domestic use. The cost for drilling and finding should start from approximately Dhs.1,800 if you secure the expertise of any of the landscaping companies found in the Plant Street area of Satwa. Alternatively, opt for AstroTurf – all you need to do is hose it down every few weeks. You can buy AstroTurf in ACE Hardware (800 275 223), while Clearview (clearview.ae) and Cape Reed (capereed. com) both install fake lawns. Another option is to go for block paving or decking. You can purchase various qualities of decking in ACE Hardware.

Landscaping

To buy pot plants, trees and shrubs head to the Dubai Municipality Nursery in the Jadaf area, next

Al Barsha villas

to Business Bay Crossing. Prices are reasonable and discounts based on quantity will be given.

Dubai Garden Centre (04 340 0006) sells pretty much everything you could ever need for your outdoor space; prices here are often at the higher end of the spectrum, but you can expect excellent service and expertise, as well as delivery for large orders. Plant Street in Satwa has a number of basic nurseries, but choice here can be limited.

Larger retailers such as Spinneys, Carrefour and IKEA sell plants, pots and smaller sized gardening implements, while ACE Hardware is a one-stop-shop for the outdoor enthusiast, selling everything from flora to furniture, tools to trees and plants to pergolas.

If you are buying a brand new house, the developers may have left you with no more than a sandpit plot, so you will need to start your garden from scratch, which can be somewhat challenging. Equally, landlords are not obliged to landscape the gardens of new villas before they rent them to you, so don't assume that the 'work in progress' you see upon viewing a property will be an outdoor oasis by the time you move in.

If the green-fingered DIY is not for you, Dubai Garden Centre offers a full landscaping service.

Plant Street is a great place to start for cheap labour and materials, while Terraverde (terraverde.ae), Toscana Landscaping & Pools (toscanalandscaping. com) and Bespoke Concept (bespokeconcept.com) all offer full service design and installation for gardens.

For more information on where to buy garden furniture see Shopping.

Swimming Pools

A lot of properties in Dubai have private pools or access to a shared pool. If you don't have one in your villa, you can always pay to have one installed – but it doesn't come cheap.

One option is to have a custom-made, free-form fibre glass and ceramic tiled pool fitted. As tough and durable as a concrete version, these are effectively portable. Delivery takes about four weeks, with an onsite installation period of approximately 10 days. Prices for such a pool start at about Dhs.110,000 including labour, pumps and filtration. Try Pools by Design (poolsdesign.net).

Aside from cleaning, your pool will also need the water to be changed and chemical levels balanced on a regular basis. MAK Pools (makpools.com) offers a full range of swimming pool cleaning and maintenance services. Those Pool Guys (thosepoolguys. com), Al Wasel Swimming Pools Maintenance (alwaselswimmingpools.com) and Pools r Us (poolsrusdubai.com) are also well established in Dubai.

If you have a young family, then take a look at Aqua-Net (aquanet.ae), which creates custom safety netting that quickly and easily covers your pool.

Home Insurance

Crime and natural disasters are not generally a big concern for Dubai's residents – though the minor earth tremors of April 2013 did shake people up a bit, there was no substantial damage to property.

However, insuring your household goods against theft or damage is still wise. To create a policy, the insurance provider will need your home address, a list of household items and valuation, and invoices for anything worth more than Dhs.2,500. Cover usually includes theft, fire and storm damage. You can also insure personal items outside the home.

As a guideline you can expect to pay about Dhs.1,500 per 1.2 sq m for building insurance, Dhs.250 for up to Dhs.60,000 worth of home contents and Dhs.850 for up to Dhs.60,000 worth of personal possessions.

Established in 2001, Greenshield Insurance (greenshield.ae, 04 388 2200) offers some good insurance packages for your home (as well as medical, life, motor and travel insurance and more), and has a good reputation and high client retention rates of 98%. You can visit their website and submit an online query, or find their offices in Bur Dubai.

Animal lovers will also need to insure their pet(s). It's best to do so while he or she is still young and healthy, as prices can rise steeply over a certain age.

For peace of mind, register your home in the Dubai Police Home Security Programme, a free service that provides round-the-clock protection for houses while residents are away. Register at any Dubai Police station.

AFIA Insurance Brokerage Services LLC Kanoo Group Bldg, Al Karama, 04 337 9987, *afia.ae*
AXA Insurance (Gulf) > *p.105* Umm Hurair 2, 04 324 3434, *axa-gulf.com*
Emirates Insurance Company Al Ittihad St, Port Saeed, 04 294 2949, *eminsco.com*
Greenshield Insurance Brokers > *p.107, 119* Boulevard Plaza Tower 1, Burj Khalifa, 04 388 2200, *greenshield.ae*
National General Insurance Co Al Ittihad Rd, Port Saeed, 04 211 5800, *ngi.ae*
Nexus Insurance Emaar Square, Burj Khalifa, 04 323 1111, *nexusadvice.com*
RSA Insurance Office Court Bldg, Oud Metha, 04 302 9800, *rsadirect.ae*
Zurich Insurance 04 376 5700, *zurich.ae*

Additional Insurance

Insurance companies cover more than just your home – AXA, for example, also provides health insurance. Companies providing pet insurance include Pet Secure, 04 252 2570, petsecure.ae.

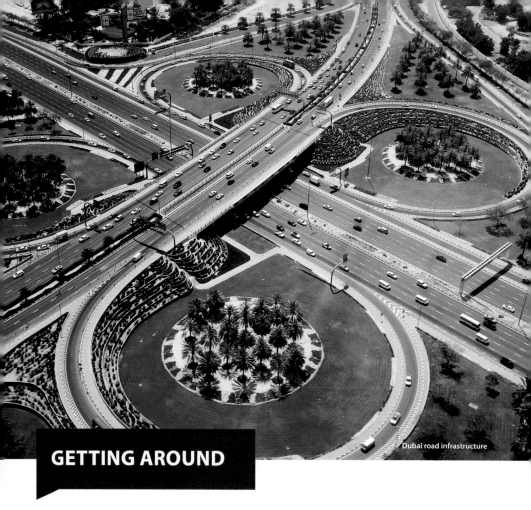
Dubai road infrastructure

GETTING AROUND

Dubai is a city geared up for cars, and has a good and continuously improving infrastructure. With a grid-like street system it shouldn't take you too long to find your way around either. However, if you're planning on using satellite navigation systems they won't help you much due to a lack of official addresses in the city at the moment; so you'll have to get your Explorer map out if you get lost.

There are some good public transport options, but most people travel by car, whether that's driving themselves or using the generally excellent and inexpensive taxi service. Getting behind the wheel of a car is probably the best way to get the measure of the city's numerous districts though.

Traffic during rush hours can get heavy, especially if there's even a minor accident, but you'll soon learn where the hotspots are and either avoid or leave for your destination at an appropriate time. There

are other idiosyncrasies you'll find too; traffic lights spring up everywhere and you can find yourself sat at a red light in an empty building site for ages. You'll also encounter plenty of speed bumps, that even the largest 4WDs will take at crawling pace.

Other sights you may find unusual at first are the number of cars that pull over and stop on the hard shoulders of the highways. This is particularly obvious at sunset when some drivers will stop to answer the call to prayer by the side of the road. And once it's dark, watch out for workers who loiter by the side of roads waiting for lifts back to their camp. Sometimes they can be quite close to the road and difficult to spot. People sometimes try to cross highways on foot too.

While there are government guidelines on driving, don't count on other road users being aware of them or choosing to obey them. Cautious driving is the best approach to stay incident free.

Dubai Road Network

When you arrive, the extensive, expanding network of roads can be intimidating, but once you find your bearings things become easier. The creek divides Bur Dubai (to the south) and Deira (to the north), and has five main crossing points: Shindagha Tunnel, Maktoum Bridge, Garhoud Bridge, Business Bay Bridge and the Floating Bridge. The Floating Bridge is due to be replaced by 12 lane Al Ittihad Bridge in early 2018.

The main thoroughfare through the city is Sheikh Zayed Road, which runs from Sharjah, parallel to the sea, all the way to Abu Dhabi. Three bypass roads have been constructed inland towards the desert to ease the city's congestion problems. All run parallel to the coast and Sheikh Zayed Road.

Al Khail Road (E44) is the closest bypass to the coast and runs from Sports City to Ras Al Khor, where it turns east and heads towards Hatta and Oman. Sheikh Mohammed bin Zayed Road (E311), formerly Emirates Road, is the next furthest from the coast and connects Abu Dhabi directly to Sharjah and the northern emirates.

The Outer Ring Road (E611) sits outside of the E311 and runs roughly from the southern border of Dubai all the way to the Sharjah-Umm Al Quwain border, although it is still being expanded. There are also a few main east-west roads, including Umm Suqeim Road (D63), the Dubai-Al Ain Road (E66), Financial Centre Road (D71), and Muscat Street (D69). Despite all the road expansions, traffic is still a problem in Dubai, especially at the creek crossings.

Within the city, the roads in older parts of town, such as Bur Dubai and Deira, are smaller and more congested, while the road networks in newer developments such as Downtown Dubai tend to accommodate greater traffic flow.

Address System

As part of Dubai's new District Addressing project, which will cover the entire city by 2016, the city has been divided into several districts, and each district further sub-divided into communities. The project will see more than 22,000 streets renamed to better reflect the local culture and history of the surrounding area. Addresses will include building number, street name, community and district. This replaces the rather confusing system of street numbers.

New districts to be aware of include Marsa Dubai, which is the new name for Dubai Marina; and Nakhlat Jumeira, which is the new name for Palm Jumeirah. 'Marsa' is Arabic for 'marina' and 'nakhlat' is Arabic for 'palm'. Another new district is Burj Khalifa, which includes the Downtown community (and of course, the Burj Khalifa building); and the old district Al Souk Al Kabeer, which includes Al Fahidi Historical Neighbourhood (formerly known as Bastakiya).

Although all roads in the city have an official name or number, several roads are referred to by a different moniker. For instance, Jumeira Road is often known as Beach Road, and Interchange One, on Sheikh Zayed Road, is invariably called Defence Roundabout. Dubai Municipality has started a more formal road-naming process to help eliminate confusion, and many of the city's main roads have been given the names of prominent Arab cities, such as Marrakech Road. Street signs now also include the direction of travel, so you know whether you are travelling north or south. This lack of consistency makes locating an address difficult. This is set to change with the implementation of the Makani satellite address system in 2015. Dubai Municipality will add location coordinate plates to 120,000 buildings in Dubai that are accurate down to a metre, with the different entrances visible on smartphones and GPS devices. Installation will be done over the year.

Finding Your Way Around

When you start driving it's pretty much a given that you'll need to schedule an extra 20 minutes for getting lost. Dubai is famed for its U-turns, which are used instead of allowing cars to turn across oncoming traffic. Many times you'll see the building you are aiming for, but will have to navigate a spaghetti-like tangle of roads to get to it – or drive for some distance in the opposite direction before you can link to the road that takes you to your destination. Once you get the hang of the thinking behind the road system it gets much easier, and once you have done a journey for the first time, repeating it is simple. Taxi drivers quite often get confused too – usually if they are new – so it's a good idea to have some specific directions or a simple map with you if you aren't sure how to get to your destination. When giving instructions to a taxi driver, remember that a traffic light is commonly referred to as a 'signal'.

Maps

With new roads popping up on a weekly basis, finding your way around Dubai can be difficult. Explorer produces several of the most up-to-date street maps available, including the fully indexed *Dubai Street Atlas* and the pocket-sized *Dubai Mini Map*. Newly released is the Dubai Map app, one of a series of GCC map apps.

Road Signs

Signposting in Dubai is generally good once you understand the system. Blue or green signs indicate the roads, exits or locations out of the city, and brown signs show heritage sites, places of interest and hospitals. Dubai's new signage system relies more heavily on street names and compass directions, compared to the older system which featured local area names. If the signage gets confusing, remember that Abu Dhabi is south of Dubai, Sharjah is north, the beach is to the west and the desert is to the east.

Driving in Dubai

While the infrastructure is superb, the general standard of driving is not. You'll see drivers displaying all manner of dangerous driving habits and, as a result, you must take extra care when driving. Once you're behind the wheel, it isn't as scary as it looks, and you'll soon learn to drive defensively and safely.

You drive on the right side of the road in Dubai, and you should overtake on the left – people often ignore this rule but if you are caught you could receive a fine. Speed limits are usually 60 to 80kph in town, while on main roads and roads to other emirates they are 100 to 120kph. The limit is clearly indicated on signs. Both fixed and movable radar traps, and Dubai Traffic Police, are there to catch the unwary violator. Be warned – you can be fined for gesticulating at another driver, and using the offensive middle finger can mean jail.

Automatic Licence Transfer

Citizens with licences from the following countries are eligible for automatic driving licence transfers: Australia, Austria, Belgium, Canada, Denmark, Finland, France, Germany, Greece, Ireland, Italy, Japan, Netherlands, New Zealand, Norway, Poland, South Africa, South Korea, Sweden, Switzerland, Turkey, United Kingdom and United States. Citizens of GCC countries do not need to apply for a licence transfer.

Roads & Transport Authority (RTA)

The RTA was launched by the government in 2005 and has taken over the responsibility for most procedures described in this chapter. Among other things the RTA deals with all transport and traffic projects in Dubai and enforcing transport legislation. The RTA is also a great source of information on Dubai's driving and licensing laws. Visit rta.ae for up-to-date information and all the latest traffic news.

Licence To Drive

Tourists can drive hire cars on their domestic licence or International Driving Permit. If you have a residence visa then you must have a UAE driving licence – it is illegal to drive without one. Some nationals qualify for an automatic licence transfer, so long as their original licence has not expired. See Getting Started. Always keep your driving licence in the vehicle, along with the vehicle registration card – you could be fined if stopped by the police otherwise.

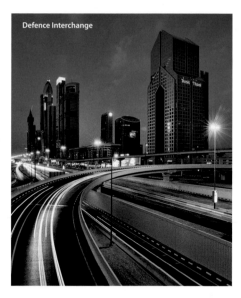

Defence Interchange

Parking

Most street parking in Dubai is now governed by parking meters. After feeding your coins into the machine, you get a ticket to display on your dashboard. The minimum fare is Dhs.2 for one hour. The price increases steeply the longer you park in a spot, so you'll pay Dhs.4 or Dhs.5 for two hours, Dhs.8 for three hours, and Dhs.11 for four hours (the maximum). Parking is free from 1pm to 4pm and 9pm to 8am daily, and on Fridays and public holidays.

Several areas support the mParking system (mpark.rta.ae), which allows drivers to pay parking tolls through SMS (non-Dubai registered vehicles must register online first). Areas where mParking is supported have an orange sign displaying the parking code and a guide on how to use the system. To use mParking, send an SMS to PARK (7275) with your car licence plate number (including the first letter), a space, the area parking code listed on the sign, a space, and the number of hours you wish to pay for (one to four). The system will then send you a confirmation SMS, and the parking fee plus a 30 fils service charge will be deducted from your Etisalat or du phone credit. Ten minutes before your time has expired, the system will send an SMS reminder and ask if you'd like to add more time. Commuters can also use their Nol Metro card to pay for parking at many machines, with the appropriate fee being deducted from the card's credit.

Parking at Dubai's shopping malls used to be mostly free, but since the opening of the metro several shopping centres that are adjacent or near to metro stations have introduced parking charges for stays over a certain length of time.

RTA are currently in the pilot stages of installing parking sensors on Sheikh Zayed Road over a section stretching from Crowne Plaza Hotel to Shangri-La Hotel. A mobile app will provide instant data on the location of parking spaces in the area. The project is likely to extend to multi-storey car parks and shopping malls.

Disabled spaces do exist, though are sometimes taken by drivers who don't need the facility. Police monitor these spaces and hand out fines.

Pre-paid Parking

Pre-paid parking cards are divided into two sections A and B. An A-card holder has the right to park in all car parks. A B-card holder has the right to park only in B-marked car parks. Just take a copy of your car registration card to Al Twar Centre, Dubai Municipality – Al Karama branch, or the Dubai Roads and Transport Authority HQ, and pay the required fee – from Dhs.450 for three months. The card is not valid in car parks at Dubai International Airport, Dubai Media City and Dubai Internet City.

Road Tolls

Salik is an automated toll system for Dubai's roads. There are currently six gates: one at Garhoud Bridge, another on the Sheikh Zayed Road after Mall of the Emirates, one at Safa Park on Sheikh Zayed Road (between interchanges one and two), another on Maktoum Bridge, one on Al Ittihad Road and another near Dubai Airport Tunnel.

The Maktoum Bridge crossing is free between 10pm and 6am Saturday to Thursday, and 10pm and 9am on Fridays, when the Floating Bridge is closed. There are no booths, and no need to stop as you drive through. Instead, drivers stick a tag to their windscreen, which is read by radio frequency as they pass through.

Salik Tag

Drivers must initially buy a 'welcome pack' costing Dhs.100: Dhs.50 for the tag and Dhs.50 credit. The kit can be bought from Emarat, EPPCO, ENOC, and ADNOC petrol stations, Dubai Islamic Bank and Emirates NBD.

It costs Dhs.4 each time you pass a toll gate (rental car drivers can be charged Dhs.5), but if you travel between the Al Barsha toll gate and the Al Safa toll gate during one trip (and in the space of an hour) you will only be charged once. If your Salik card is out of credit you will be fined Dhs.50 for each gate you pass through, regardless of whether your vehicle is registered in Dubai or another emirate.

The Salik system will send you an SMS when your account balance runs low or when you pass through a gate without any balance. Top up is now quick and easy, with e-vouchers available at 3,000 stores across the country. For more information, visit the Salik website, salik.gov.ae, or call 800 72545 (800 SALIK).

Traffic Offences

In an effort to help combat bad driving, the Dubai Police initiated a black points system to go along with the existing fines system. You are issued a certain number of black points against your licence according to the particular violation. For example, the fine for allowing a child under 10 years of age to sit in the front of a car is Dhs.400 and the driver will be given four black points. If you get 24 points you will lose your licence for a year, but any points you acquire will expire 12 months after they are issued.

The white points system came into operation in 2013, and it 'rewards' law-abiding drivers with one white point every month; motorists will be given incentives to collect white points, ranging from raffle prizes to exemption from traffic fines.

Check Online For Fines

You can check whether you have any outstanding traffic fines against your vehicle by entering your registration plate number at dubaipolice.gov.ae. There is no time limit to pay your fines – but you will have to pay them at the end of each year in order to re-register and insure your vehicle. Hire car details may not always appear online.

Bad drivers can choose to eradicate some of their black points by electing to take a driving course costing Dhs.200 per session (there are three sessions in a course). They can also cancel out black points by gaining white points in some cases.

Fines

Parking fines start at Dhs.200, and speeding fines start at Dhs.400 for driving up to 10kph over the speed limit and go up from there. Driving in a reckless manner or racing will earn you six points, as will parking in a handicapped zone or in front of a fire hydrant.

There are numerous speed cameras on Dubai's roads; drivers caught racing can face a fine of up to Dhs.2,000 as well as 12 black points and confiscation of their licence for 30 days. To see all the possible penalties for bad driving go to dubaitrafficfines.org or check dubaipolice.gov.ae for more information.

Be careful to avoid driving in the dedicated bus and taxi lanes, which have recently been added to some major roads. The lanes are clearly marked, and you are liable to a fine of Dhs.600 if you enter one without authorisation. The only exception is if you need to cross the lane to enter or exit the thoroughfare.

Average-speed and stopping-distance traps have recently been introduced to try to catch speeding drivers who only slow down when they see speed cameras, and to discourage tailgating. On-the-spot traffic fines for certain offences have been introduced, but in most cases you won't know you've received a fine until you check on the Dubai Police website or renew your vehicle registration.

Most fines can be paid with your annual car registration renewal. However, tickets that appear on your windscreen must be paid within a week, or the fine increases.

Blood Money

By law, the family of a pedestrian killed in a road accident is entitled to Dhs.200,000 *diya* (blood) money. The money is usually paid by the insurance company unless there's any whiff of the driver having been under the influence of alcohol. However, an amendment to the law is being considered to put a stop to the terrible trend among desperate lower-income workers of killing themselves to provide for their family. This will mean blood money is not automatically due if the victim was walking across a road not intended for use by pedestrians, such as Sheikh Zayed Road.

Drinking & Driving

Dubai Police exercises a strict zero-tolerance policy on drinking and driving. If you get into an accident, whether it is your fault or not, and you fail a blood-alcohol test, you could find yourself spending a night in a cell before a trial in Dubai Courts, after which you'll most likely be jailed. In addition, your insurance is automatically void. Police have increased the number of random drink-driving checks.

Breakdowns

In the event of your vehicle breaking down, you will usually find that passing police cars will stop to help, or at least to check your documents. It's important that you keep water in your car at all times so you don't get dehydrated while waiting, especially during the hotter months. Dubai Traffic officers recommend, if possible, that you pull your car over to a safe spot. If you are on the hard shoulder of a highway you should pull your car as far away from the yellow line as possible and step away from the road until help arrives.

Make sure you've got a red warning triangle and reflective jacket stored in your car for use in case you have to stop by the side of the road.

Recovery Services

The Arabian Automobile Association – the AAA – (04 266 9989 or 800 4900, aaauae.com) offers a 24 hour roadside breakdown service for an annual charge. This includes help in minor mechanical repairs, battery boosting, or help if you run out of petrol, have a flat tyre or lock yourself out. Mashreq Bank Visa card holders receive free AAA membership. The more advanced service includes off-road recovery, vehicle registration and a rent-a-car service. Other breakdown services that will be able to help you out without membership include AAA Service Centre (aaadubai.com), Dubai Auto Towing Services (04 359 4424) and AKT Recovery (04 263 6217). Some dealers and insurance companies offer a free breakdown and recovery service for the first few years after buying a new car. Ask the dealership about this option when purchasing a new car.

Traffic Accidents

If you are involved in an accident, call 999. If the accident is minor and no one has been hurt you need to agree with the other driver where the blame lies and move your cars to the side of the road to avoid obstructing the flow of traffic. You can be fined Dhs.200 for failing to do so even if the accident wasn't your fault. If blame has been clearly decided and the accident is minor, the 999 dispatcher may ask you to drive yourself to the nearest Traffic Police station to fill out the necessary paperwork. The Dubai Police Information Line (800 7777, Arabic and English) gives the numbers of police stations around the emirate.

If blame cannot be decided without police intervention, an officer will be dispatched to assess the accident and apportion blame. The officer will then give you a copy of the accident report; if it is green then you are not at fault, and if it is pink then you are to blame for the accident and you will receive a Dhs.200 fine from the attending officer. You will need to submit the accident report to the insurance company in order to process the claim, or to the garage for repairs. Keep in mind that garages rarely repair vehicles without a police report.

Stray animals are something to avoid on desert roads. If the animal hits your vehicle and causes damage or injury, the animal's owner should pay compensation, but if you are found to have been speeding, you must compensate the animal's owner.

Be sure to keep your licence on you at all times. If you are pulled over by the police or are involved in an accident you'll need to show your driving licence or risk being fined. You will be given a grace period in which to present your licence at the police station; if you fail to do so, you risk having your car impounded and facing a court appearance.

Petrol Stations

Petrol is subsidised in the UAE and generally inexpensive. Within Dubai, you will find Emarat, ENOC and EPPCO stations, and the price of unleaded petrol (around Dhs.1.75 per litre) is the same at all of them. The octane rating of unleaded petrol in the UAE is high – 'Special' is rated at 95 octane and 'Super' at 98 octane. Many of the stations have convenience stores and some have small cafes or fast food restaurants attached to them; Tim Hortons and Costa have opened at several fuel stations across the emirate.

Every station is manned by attendants who will pump your petrol for you, and often clean your windscreen too; it's commonplace to give them a Dhs.5 tip. Most petrol stations offer other services such as car washes, oil changes and even tyre replacement.

Some petrol stations only accept cash, though there is usually an ATM if you are caught short.

Learning To Drive

Emirates Driving Institute (EDI) is one choice of driving school. You complete 40 lessons, each for 30 minutes in two blocks of two hours per week. So it should only take 10 weeks to complete your practical training.

You'll also need to attend eight one-hour lectures – the first two must be attended before you can begin your practical lessons – to prepare for the theory test. After 20 lessons there's also a parking test. After 36 lessons, you will have an assessment test which you

need to pass before you can register for your final practical test. The final four lessons include highway training on Al Khail Road.

The final driving test should last around 20 minutes. There could be two or three passengers in the car – other students taking their tests too. After you've each had a turn behind the wheel, the instructor will take you all back to the centre and reveal who has passed.

Women learning to drive will be given a female instructor unless they specifically request a male, which they can do on the condition that they produce an NOC and pay a Dhs.10 fee. Regardless of the instructor you have for your 40 lessons, women will have a female instructor for their parking, assessment and final tests.

If you fail the test, you'll have to take another set of lessons before you can take the test again.

Pre-booked Driving Lessons

Some driving schools insist that you pay for a set of pre-booked lessons. The package can include 40 lessons and cost up to Dhs.3,000, although the cost can be paid in instalments. Lessons usually last 30 minutes and must be taken on consecutive days.
Al Ahli Driving Center Nr Atlas Marine Services, Al Qouz Ind. 4, 04 341 1500, *alahlidubai.ae*
Belhasa Driving Center Nr Latifa Hospital, Sama Al Jadaf, Al Jadaf, 04 324 3535, *bdc.ae*
Dubai Driving Center Nr Dry Docks, Madinat Dubai Al Melaheyah, 04 345 5855, *dubaidrivingcenter.net*
Emirates Driving Institute >*p.101* Nr Al Bustan Centre, Al Qusais 1, 04 263 1100, *edi-uae.com*
Galadari Motor Driving Center Amman St, Al Qusais Ind. 4, 04 267 6166, *gmdc.ae*

Hiring A Car

New arrivals to Dubai often find that they have no other option than to hire a vehicle until their residence visa goes though. Most leasing companies include the following in their rates: registration, maintenance, replacement, 24 hour assistance and insurance. All the main car rental companies, plus a few extra, can be found in Dubai.

It is best to shop around as the rates vary considerably. The larger, reputable firms, such as Dollar Rent A Car, generally have more reliable vehicles and a greater capacity to help in an emergency (an important factor when dealing with the aftermath of an accident). Find out which car hire agent your company uses, as you might qualify for a corporate rate. Most rental companies will keep track of how many times you pass through Salik gates and charge you at the end of the month, along with a Salik service charge.

Leasing is generally weekly, monthly or yearly. Monthly lease prices start at around Dhs.1,800 for

Driving centre

a small vehicle such as a Toyota Yaris, and go up from there. As the lease period increases, the price decreases, so if you're considering keeping the car for a long period, it may not work out that much more expensive than buying.

Before you take possession of your leased car, check for any dents or bumps. To hire any vehicle you will need to provide a passport copy, credit card and a valid driving licence. Those with a residence visa must have a UAE driving licence to drive a hired car, while those on a visit visa can use a licence from their home country as long as it is at least one year old. Comprehensive insurance is essential; make sure that it includes personal accident coverage, and perhaps Oman cover if you're planning on exploring.

Car Hire Companies

Autolease Rent A Car Nr Garhoud Private Hospital, Al Garhoud, 04 282 6565, *autolease-uae.com*
Avis Al Maktoum Rd, Al Rigga, 04 295 7121, *avisuae.ae*
Bettercar Rentals Damascus Rd, Al Qusais Ind. 1, 04 258 6331, *bettercardubai.com*
Budget Car & Van Rental UAE Lehbab Rd, Dubai Investment Park 2, 800 2722, *budget-uae.com*
Diamondlease Car Rental Kharbash Bldg, Trade Center 1, 04 343 4330, *diamondlease.com*
Dollar Rent A Car > *p.99* Arenco Bldg, Zabeel Road, 04 336 5065, *dollaruae.com*
Dubai Exotic Limo Nr Chili's Restaurant, Al Garhoud, 04 286 8635, *dubaiexoticlimo.com*
Euroline Rent A Car 052 999 5555, *euroline-rent.com*
EuroStar Rent A Car Al Wuheida Rd, Hor Al Anz East, 04 266 1117, *eurostarrental.com*
Green Car Rental Dubai World Trade Centre, Trade Center 1, 04 358 8488, *greencardubai.com*
Hertz UAE Airport Rd, Umm Ramool, 04 202 0206, *hertzuae.com*
Thrifty Rent A Car > *p.xi* Dubai International Airport, 04 224 5404, *thrifty.com*

Buying A Car

Aside from the horrendous traffic, the UAE is a motorist's dream. Petrol is cheap, big engines are considered cool and the wide motorways stretching across the country are perfect for weekend drives.

Most of the major car makes are available through franchised dealerships in Dubai, especially big Japanese and American brands. New vehicles are surprisingly affordable too. A new BMW 3-series in Dubai is likely to cost around 20% less than the same car in the UK.

There is a large second-hand car market in the UAE. Dealers are scattered around town but good areas to start are Sheikh Zayed Road and Warsan, behind Ras Al Khor. Expect to pay a premium of between Dhs.5,000 and Dhs.10,000 for buying through a dealer (as opposed to buying from a private seller), since they also offer a limited warranty, insurance, finance and vehicle registration.

The Al Awir complex houses several smaller used-car dealers and it's easy to spend a whole day walking around the lots speaking with salesmen. Al Awir is also the location for Golden Bell Auctions (goldenbellauctions.com), with sales held each Wednesday evening. All cars up for auction have to undergo a test at the nearby Eppco Tasjeel garage, and all outstanding fines will have been cleared. There's a Traffic Department office on the site so buyers can register their new vehicles on the spot.

For private sales, check the classifieds in *Gulf News* and *Khaleej Times* and supermarket noticeboards. Online sites such as dubizzle.com and expat forums such as expatwoman.com are also useful.

Tinted Windows

Currently, the government allows you to avoid the sun somewhat by tinting your vehicle's windows up to 30%. Some areas have facilities where you can get your car windows tinted but don't get carried away – remember to stick to the limit. Random checks take place and fines are handed out to those caught in the dark. Tinting in Sharjah is allowed for a fee of Dhs.100 and Ajman residents may tint for Dhs.200 per annum, but only if they are women. Company cars are banned from having tinted windows.

Second-hand Sales

As well as getting the vehicle tested, check that the engine plate number on the car corresponds with that given on the vehicle registration card. Also, check with the Dubai Traffic Police that the vehicle is neither stolen nor has any fines; visit dubaipolice.gov.ae.

After you have purchased the vehicle, you will need to insure it, then transfer ownership/vehicle registration, and purchase a Salik tag, if required.

Transferring Ownership

If you buy a second-hand vehicle, you will need to transfer ownership to your name. If you fail to do this, you are liable to pay a Dhs.3,000 fine by Dubai Police. You will need to collect an application form from the Traffic Police and submit it, along with a no objection certificate from the finance company (if using one), the original licence plates, the previous owner's valid registration card, your new insurance certificate, your UAE driving licence and Dhs.100 transfer fee. The previous owner must also be present to sign the form. The new registration card will then be issued within five to 10 minutes.

"NO REVERSE...
WE ARE ONLY GOING FORWARD"

"Your International car rental company"

MONTHLY RENTALS

YEARLY RENTALS

DAILY RENTALS

LOCATIONS & GPS

WEEKLY RENTALS

CORPORATE LEASING

Deira: 04 2216089
Bur Dubai: 04 5013110
DIP: 04 8853266
Sheikh Zayed Road: 04 3327510
Jebel Ali Free Zone: 04 8857837
Media City: 04 4474930
Jumeirah Beach Residence: 04 4398895
World Trade Center: 04 3318623
Sharjah: 06 5722402

600 599909

Wide range of vehicles available throughout 24 locations across the UAE.
Dubai & Sharjah: 04 336 5065 / Abu Dhabi : 02 641 9055.
www.dollaruae.com

Importing A Car

It is possible to import or export your car, but be prepared for lots of paperwork. If you're keen to hang onto your chosen four wheels, contact Kanoo Shipping (kanooshipping.com) for help.

If you're buying a car within the UAE but from outside of Dubai you will need to complete export and import procedures. Both buyer and seller will need to be present at the traffic licensing department in the seller's emirate. The department will ask for copies of a passport and driving licence, the vehicle registration card, an insurance policy in the new owner's name (three day policies can be available at the site) and a technical inspection certificate. The seller may also need a no objection letter from their bank if there is an outstanding loan amount. In all emirates aside from Dubai you will be issued with export plates to drive the car home on. You will then have to register it in Dubai. Midland Cars in Karama (04 396 7521, midlandcarsdubai.com) can help you import a vehicle to Dubai from another emirate.

Vehicle Finance

Many new and second-hand car dealers will be able to arrange finance for you, often through a deal with a preferred banking partner. Most official dealers and main financial establishments should be able to sort out monthly automatic payments for you too. Alternatively a personal loan can often have lower interest rates and better terms (plus it's difficult to get an auto loan on cars of a certain age) so it's worth checking. If you go with the bank that receives your salary, the application is often easier. Just make sure you can afford the payments as bad debt is not good news.

Second Opinion

When buying a used car it's well worth having it checked over by a garage or mechanic. Eppco Tasjeel, AAA and Max Garage offer a checking service. Alternatively, speak to the service department at the dealership where the car was originally bought. A thorough inspection will cost about Dhs.250.

New Car Dealers

Bentley Al Habtoor Motors, Port Saeed, 04 294 4492, emirates.bentleymotors.com
Bugatti Al Habtoor Motors, Port Saeed, 04 294 4492, bugatti.com
Cadillac Liberty Automobiles, Al Qouz Ind. 3, 04 341 9341, cadillacarabia.com
Chevrolet Al Ghandi Auto, Al Qouz Ind. 3, 04 231 0880, chevroletarabia.com
Chrysler Trading Enterprises, Al Qouz Ind. 3, 04 340 2445, mideast.chrysler.com

Dodge Trading Enterprises, Al Qouz Ind. 3, 04 340 2445, tradingenterprises.ae
Ferrari Al Tayer Motors, Al Qouz Ind. 1, 04 303 7878, dubai.ferraridealers.com
Ford Al Tayer Motors, Al Garhoud, 04 282 7825, me.ford.com
Honda Al Futtaim Motors, Al Qouz Ind. 1, 04 348 5988, honda.ae
Jaguar Al Tayer Motors, Al Garhoud, 800 668 677, jaguar.com
Jeep Trading Enterprises, Al Qouz Ind. 3, 04 340 2445, mideast.jeep.com
Land Rover Al Tayer Motors, Al Garhoud, 800 668 677, landrover.com
Lexus Al Futtaim Motors, Al Qouz Ind. 3, 04 507 6300, lexus.ae
Lincoln Al Tayer Motors, Al Qouz Ind. 1, 04 303 7777, me.lincoln.com
Maserati Al Tayer Motors, Al Qouz Ind. 1, 04 303 7878, maserati.com
McLaren Dubai The Lofts, Downtown Dubai, Burj Khalifa, 04 382 7500, dubai.mclarenretailers.com
Mercedes-Benz Gargash Enterprises, Al Khabaisi, 04 209 9777, gargash.mercedes-benz.com
Mitsubishi Motors Al Habtoor Motors, Port Saeed, 04 608 4000, mitsubishi-uae.com
Opel Liberty Automobiles, Al Qouz Ind. 3, 04 341 9341, opel-libertyautos.com
Peugeot Swaidan Trading, Al Qouz Ind. 3, 04 347 9000, swaidanpeugeot.com
Ram Trading Enterprises, Umm Ramoul, 04 206 6526, tradingenterprises.ae
Saab Gargash Motors, Al Khabaisi, 04 340 3333, gargashme.com
Toyota Al Futtaim Motors, Al Kheeran, 04 206 6000, toyota.ae
Volkswagen > p.xvii Al Naboodah Automobiles, Al Qouz Ind. 1, 04 705 3333, volkswagen-dubai.com
Volvo Trading Enterprises, Al Kheeran, 04 206 6400, volvocars.com

Used Car Dealers

4x4 Motors Al Aweer Auto Market Phase 1, Ras Al Khor Ind. 3, 04 333 2757, 4x4motors.com
Al Futtaim Automall Nr Times Square, Al Qouz Ind. 1, 04 340 8029, automalluae.com
Al Tayer Motors Al Ittihad Rd, Al Khabaisi, 800 668 677, altayermotors.com
Elite Cars 4th Street, Ind. 3, Al Quoz, 04 321 2290 elitemotorsdubai.com
House Of Cars Nr Mazaya Centre, Al Wasl, 04 343 5060, houseofcarsgroup.com
Liberty Automobiles Shk Zayed Rd, Al Qouz Ind. 3, 04 341 9341, libertyautos.com
Reem Automobiles Nr Mazaya Centre, Al Wasl, 04 343 6333, reemauto.ae

Insurance

Before you can register your car you must have car insurance. The insurers will need to know the usual details such as year of manufacture, and value, as well as the chassis number. If you got a real bargain of a car, make sure you instruct the insurance company to cover it at the market value.

Annual insurance policies last for 13 months (allowing a one-month grace period for when registration expires). It's best to get fully comprehensive cover with personal accident cover, and advisable to be covered for 'blood money'. Rates depend on age and model of your car and your previous insurance history, although no-claims bonuses accrued in your home country are rarely recognised. Expect to pay between 4-7% of the vehicle's value, or a flat rate of 5% for cars over five years old. If you feel your car is worth more than you paid for it, make sure the insurance company covers it at the market value. Insurers will need to see copies of your UAE driving licence, passport and vehicle registration form.

Most insurance agencies now let you request a quote online, and there's a multitude of choice out there from local companies such as AWNIC (awnic.com) to international favourites, AXA (axa-gulf.com), RSA (rsadirect.ae) and Zurich (zurich.ae). If you're driving to Oman you will need additional cover, which can be part of your annual insurance or purchased ad hoc. Also see the UAE's online car insurance comparison websites, which will save you time and are a good starting point; try insurancemarket.ae or insureme.ae.

Fully comprehensive cover with personal accident insurance is highly advisable, and you are strongly advised to make sure the policy covers you for 'blood money'. For more adventurous 4WD drivers, insurance for off-roading accidents is also recommended.

To Oman & Back

It is wise to check whether your insurance covers you for Oman as you may find yourself driving through small Oman enclaves when exploring the UAE (especially if you are off road, near Hatta, through Wadi Bih and in Dibba). Insurance for visit to Oman can be arranged in a short-term basis, usually for no extra cost.

Registering A Vehicle

All cars must be registered annually with the Dubai Police department; if you're buying new, then the dealer should do this for you. All cars over three years old must also have an annual vehicle inspection test, which is part of the registration process.

Vehicle registration, vehicle testing and the renewal of annual car insurance generally take place at the same time. To start the process, first check you have no outstanding traffic offence and fines against your car at dubaipolice.gov.ae as registration renewal can't be completed until they are cleared. Then, renew your insurance as you will be asked to show a valid 13 months certificate. With this done, take your vehicle to a Vehicle Licensing Department-approved service centre.

Pay the Dhs.120 test fee, wait for around 20-30 minutes for the test, and hopefully it should pass and you'll receive a test certificate. If your vehicle fails the inspection, have it repaired and retested within 30 days for no additional fee. Some insurance companies offer to collect your vehicle and handle the test and registration for you – often within a couple of hours.

Once passed and with test certificate in hand, go to a registration office and submit your insurance certificate, current registration card (or that of the previous owner if you are transferring ownership), UAE driving licence and Resident ID, plus the Dhs.100 fee. You'll receive a new registration card plus a new sticker for your vehicle's rear plate. Now you're all legal to drive the vehicle for another year.

You have one month's grace for renewal of your car registration, hence the 13 month insurance policy. This keeps you legal if it's inconvenient to get the car registration renewed at the specified time. After that month though, you will incur fines of Dhs.10 for each month you delay. If renewal hasn't happened for over a year, the charge for re-registration is Dhs.325.

Both EPPCO Tasjeel and Emarat Shamil offer VIP pick-up and drop-off registration services for an extra charge, usually around Dhs.200. Call 800 4258 to make an appointment with Tasjeel or 800 4559 for Shamil. The RTA also recently launched a service enabling owners to carry out vehicle registration online; to sign up to the service, visit rta.ae. Usually a dealer will take care of registering a new car for you.

Vehicle Repairs

By law, no vehicle can be accepted for major 'collision' repairs without an accident report from the Traffic Police, although very minor dents can be repaired without one. Your insurance company will usually have an agreement with a particular garage to which they will refer you. The garage will carry out the repair work and the insurance company will settle the claim. Generally, there is Dhs.500 deductible for all claims, but check your policy details.

If you purchase a new vehicle your insurance should cover you for 'agency repairs', that is, repairs at the workshop of the dealer selling the car, although this is not a guarantee and you may have to pay a

THE BEST 4X4 SERVICE X FAR

WE KNOW CARS, WE KNOW 4X4s, WE KNOW PEOPLE, AND WE KNOW SERVICE

FOR ALL YOUR VEHICLE SERVICE, REPAIRS AND MAINTENANCE NEEDS, CONTACT THE SPECIALISTS

For more than 35 years, AAA Service Center has been providing quality automotive services and repairs to customers, with timeliness and cost effectiveness in mind. Our qualified technicians and supervisors guarantee clear quotations, efficient service, and quick turnaround. No mess, no fuss, just honest quality work.

To book your service experience, please contact any of service centers:

AL RASHIDIYA SERVICE CENTER +971 4 285 8989
Workshop Supervisor, Benjamin Tyrrell – ben@aaadubai.com

AL QUOZ SERVICE CENTER +971 4 347 0400
Workshop Manager, Glenn Power – glenn@aaadubai.com

premium. It's worth it though as your car's warranty (two to three years) may become invalid if you have non-agency repairs done on it. Even if you buy a fairly new second-hand car (less than three years old) it may be beneficial to opt for agency repairs in order to protect the value of the car.

Besides accidents and bumps, you may also have to deal with the usual running repairs associated with any car. Common problems in this part of the world can include the air-conditioning malfunctioning, batteries suddenly giving up and tyres blowing out. With the air con, it may just be a case of having the system topped up, which is a fairly straightforward procedure. Car batteries don't tend to last too long in the hot conditions, and you may not get much warning (one day your car just won't start), so it's always handy to keep a set of jump leads in the boot.

If you do manage to get your car started then it's worth taking a trip to Satwa; before you know it, your car will be surrounded by people offering to fix anything. Haggle hard and you can get a bargain for simple repairs and spares – including a new battery.

When buying a used vehicle, many shoppers like to see a history of agency maintenance, especially for relatively new cars. It may seem ridiculous to have your oil changed at the dealership every 5,000km, but it often pays in the long run when selling your car.

4x4 Garage Nr Oasis Centre, Al Qouz 3, 04 323 2100, *4x4motors.com*
AAA Service Centre >*p.103* 4B Street, Al Qouz, 04 347 0400 *aaadubai.com*
Al Wataniya Workshop Nr ENOC Petrol Station, Al Qouz Ind. 1, 04 340 8546, *aww.ae*
Bosch Service Centre Al Quoz Ind 4, 04 338 6000, *cmeuae.ae*
Central Motors & Equipment Shk Zayed Rd, Al Qouz 3, 04 338 6000, *cmeuae.ae*
House Of Cars. Shk Zayed Rd, Al Qouz Ind 1, 04 339 3466, *houseofcarsgroup.com*
Icon Auto Garage 8th Street, Al Qouz 3, 04 338 2744, *icon-auto.com*
Max Garage Umm Suqeim Rd, Al Qouz Ind. 3, 04 340 8200, *maxgaragedubai.com*
Octane Al Qouz Ind. 1, 04 341 4511

Cycling

The RTA has often talked about the benefits of cycling in the city's most congested districts, and it is working to promote this form of transportation with its 850km Dubai Bicycle Master Plan. You cannot cycle on Dubai's highways and even riding within city neighbourhoods can be dangerous. Also, summer temperatures can reach 45°C, which makes riding to work a very sweaty option. There are, however, a number of places where

you can cycle safely for pleasure (See Activities and below). If you do decide to take to two wheels, you are required to wear a helmet and a high visibility jacket, or you could face a fine of Dhs.500.

The RTA has completed various cycling tracks in neighbourhoods across the emirate. There is a 23km long track along Jumeirah Street, 1.4km track along Street No 7 which links Jumeirah Street with Al Mankhool Street, and a 1.6km track at the Mall of the Emirates station. Also included in the project is the 67km track spanning Seih Assalam Road and Al Qudra Road as well as the 11km track at the centre of Bur Dubai covering Al Fahidi, Al Falah, Al Ghubaiba and Al Hisn Roads.

Future plans include tracks in Al Barsha, Al Khawaneej, Al Warqa, Al Qouz 3, Al Sufouh Street, Al Mamzar Park, Mushrif Park, and Hor Al Anz East.

Jumeirah Corniche

Joggers and cyclists have a new outdoor area to enjoy now that Jumeirah Corniche has been built. Linking six residential areas, the 14km long zone incorporates jogging and cycling tracks all the way from Dubai Marine Beach Resort down to the Burj Al Arab hotel.

Bike-sharing

For the cooler months, there are now public bike-sharing schemes available. In Downtown Dubai, the Emaar-sponsored bikes are available at docking stations in Mohammed bin Rashid Boulevard, The Dubai Mall/Burj Khalifa Metro station, Emaar Square, Burj Park, Burj Plaza, and next to The Dubai Mall. On the Palm Jumeirah, three are six locations: the Park, the Fairmont, the Shoreline side and three on the outer crescent at Atlantis, Zabeel Saray and Anantara.

Register online at bykystations.com and then use your mobile phone to retrieve your registration details once you arrive at a bike station. A computer voice will ask you for the number of the bike you want to rent and give you a code to unlock it. Bikes can be rented for any time from 30 minutes to 24 hours, with credit card payment. Bikes are also available in Marsa Dubai and Jumeira.

Walking

Cities in the UAE are generally very car-oriented and not designed to encourage walking. Additionally, searing summer temperatures are not conducive to spending any length of time outdoors – within minutes you'll be sweating buckets.

The winter months, however, make walking a pleasant way to get around and people can be found strolling through the streets, especially in the evenings. Most streets are lined with pavements and there are pedestrian paths either side of the creek, along the seafront in Deira and Jumeira, at The Walk at JBR, and around Marsa Dubai, as well as in the city's parks.

Despite the pavements, it's pretty common to end up with sandy shoes as many car parking spaces are on dusty vacant lots, so if you're off to an important business meeting, take a cloth to clean your shoes. There are also plans underway to build an extra 17 footbridges by 2016, at key locations including Emirates Towers and Al Khail Road. Police are cracking down on jaywalking, and you can be fined Dhs.200 for crossing the road in an undesignated area, so always use the pedestrian crossings available.

Creek Park
Nr Al Garhoud Bridge Umm Hurair 2 **04 336 7633**
dm.gov.ae
Map **2 L7** Metro **Dubai Healthcare City**
It may be in the heart of the city but Creek Park is a welcome slice of green with expansive gardens, fishing piers, jogging tracks, barbecue sites, children's play areas, restaurants and kiosks. Rest your legs and take the cable car that runs the 2.3km length of the park. Alternatively, four-wheel cycles can be hired from Gate 2 for Dhs.20 per hour. Admission costs Dhs.5.

Down By The Creek
Al Souk Al Kabeer
From the embassy area, stroll along the creek to take photos of the much-loved NBD building opposite. Explore Al Fahidi Historical Neighbourhood, where hidden alleyways, secret shops and tiny cafes abound. From here, walk towards the Majlis Gallery, stopping for a much needed juice at XVA Gallery. Continue past the Dubai Museum, through the textile souk and down towards the creek. Take an abra across the creek and you will find yourself at the entrance to the spice souk. You can then wander through the packed streets of Deira towards the gold souk. Fridays are the quietest, as are the early afternoons when stores often close for a break.

Downtown Dubai
Nr The Dubai Mall Downtown Dubai, Burj Khalifa
mydowntowndubai.com
Map **2 F6** Metro **Burj Khalifa/Dubai Mall**
Wander along wide promenades, linger by the lake or get lost in the narrow passageways of the Old Town. This is one of Dubai's trendiest residential communities and was designed for getting around on foot. With cafes, restaurants and coffee shops at every turn, there are plenty of pit-stop possibilities as well as interesting streets to explore. There's also a public bike-sharing scheme available in the area.

The Els Club
Shk Mohammed Bin Zayed Rd Sports City, Al Hebiah 4 **04 425 1000**
elsclubdubai.com
Map **1 L11**
Inspired by links golf, the beautiful Ernie Els Club golf course has an excellent 10km pedestrian path around its exterior. The Els Club golf course stretches almost 7,000 metres and incorporates natural dunes and plants native to the UAE.

Jumeira Open Beach Running Track
Jumeira 1
Map **2 H4**
An early morning walk on the beach got easier (and less sandy) when the 1.5km track on Jumeira Open Beach opened. With running and cycling lanes, distance markers and regular maintenance, it offers a fun and free way to get active while enjoying some people watching and sunshine. The track starts near Dubai Marine Resort and is open 24 hours.

The Beach (opposite JBR)
Marsa Dubai **04 431 0190**
thebeach.ae
Map **1 K4** Metro **DAMAC**
An evening stroll could quickly turn into a shopping spree at this new beachside development, with a running track alongside the sand and a tempting choice of shops and eateries, as well as a cinema. By evening, the adjacent road is where people bring their expensive, diamond-encrusted (we're not kidding) cars, to sit in a slow-moving traffic jam and rev their engines in the hope of impressing those strolling by.

Mirdif
Tripoli St Mirdif
Map **2 Q13** Metro **Rashidiya**
Mirdif residential area has two community parks with sprung walking tracks and swings for the kids. Uptown Mirdiff shopping centre also makes for a nice outdoor stroll.

Safa Park
Al Wasl St Al Wasl **04 349 2111**
dm.gov.ae
Map **2 D5** Metro **Business Bay**
This huge park is a great place to exercise and escape the hustle and bustle of the city, or simply to enjoy the boating lake, a multitude of play areas, the maze or The Archive library and cafe. Entry costs Dhs.3 (free for children under three years old). There's a great 3km spongy running track around the park's perimeter, not to mention the countless paths that criss-cross the grassy space. Sadly parts of the park are shut in 2015 due to the ongoing construction work of Dubai Canal, but there is still plenty to enjoy.

Mall Walkers

If outdoor activities aren't your thing, or if it's so hot you could fry an egg on the pavement, then combine window shopping at Mall of the Emirates with a brisk walk. To make sure you don't get distracted, the Mall Walkers group will guide you along. Register at the customer service desk on the ground floor near parking area A and turn up at Gate 1 on the ground floor at 8am daily (in suitable shoes).

Public Transport

In an effort to ease the city's congestion problems, the government's Roads & Transport Authority (rta. ae) has made a serious commitment to improving public transport. The metro is the centrepiece of its efforts since its opening in September 2009 – and in November 2014, Dubai Tram also took its first journey. Dubai's bus system has seen major improvements over the past few years. The RTA's fleet of water buses offers commuters and travellers an expanding network of routes along Dubai's waterways; alternatively, there is a more costly water taxi service – operating from Deira across to Jabal Ali.

Nol Card

Nol cards are used to pay for public transport and street car parking. They are rechargeable and can be used on the metro, tram, bus, and water buses, with fares calculated depending on how many zones your journey takes you through. Single journeys start at Dhs.1.80 for up to 3km, rising to Dhs.5.80 for travel across two or more zones. The red Nol card is a paper ticket aimed at tourists. It can be charged for up to 10 journeys, but is only valid on one type of transport – bus, metro or water bus. The silver Nol card costs Dhs.20, including Dhs.14 credit. It can be recharged up to Dhs.500 and can be used across all forms of transport and for street parking. The gold Nol card is identical to the silver, except that holders are charged first-class prices (usually double the standard fare) and can travel in the Gold Class cabins on the metro. RTA has just introduced weekly, quarterly and annual packages for both silver and gold classes. The packages offer up to 47% discount for regular commuters and 50% reduction for students, the elderly and people dependent on social aid. Nol cards can be purchased and topped up at metro and bus stations and at selected supermarkets including Carrefour and Spinneys. Information on the Nol fare structure and zones can be found at nol.ae.

Smartphone users can swipe in and out at metro stations, public bus and water bus stations if they have a NFC (Near Field Communication) enabled phone. You can buy NFC SIM cards from Etisalat and du business centres.

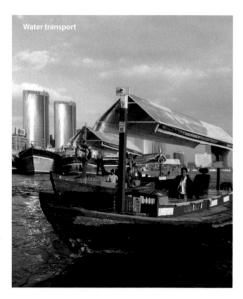
Water transport

Boat

Crossing Dubai Creek by abra is a common mode of transport for many people. The fare for a single journey across the creek is Dhs.1, and the abras run from 5am to midnight. There are four abra stations, two on the Deira side near the souks and two on the Bur Dubai side near the Ruler's Court. The RTA manages a fleet of air-conditioned water buses costing Dhs.4 per round trip. There are two routes across the creek and four stations. Route 2 between Al Sabkha Station and Dubai Old Souk Station operates 24 hours a day. A route opened in February 2013 between the Festival City Station and Ras Al Khor Wildlife Sanctuary.

Abra Ka Dabra

An abra is a wooden, single engine boat used to carry passengers across the creek. Abras have long been the primary method of crossing the creek. Each one can carry around 20 seated passengers. They tend to depart as soon as all of their seats have been filled.

There is also the Dubai ferry service – two excellent value sightseeing trips aimed at tourists. The first Dubai ferry makes the round trip from Al Ghubaiba station in Bur Dubai to Burj Al Arab and back and the second goes from Dubai Marina Mall and turns around near Atlantis The Palm. Each journey lasts around an hour and cost Dhs.50 for silver class and Dhs.75 for gold class, with four trips per day.

The RTA launched the first phase of a new water taxi project in mid-2010. An initial five luxury 10 seater boats shuttle passengers between 26 stops, stretching from JA Jebel Ali Golf Resort to Festival City. Fares range from Dhs.50 to travel one stop, up to a hefty Dhs.570 to travel the whole route. Water taxis are available between 10am and 10pm and some routes are available for families to book at a reduced price.

Tourists can also book a water taxi for an hour for Dhs.400; the number to call is 800 9090. For information about the stops that are open see rta.ae. The RTA has also announced future marine transport stations for the Palm Jumeirah and Dubai Marina – check the RTA website for up-to-date information.

Bus

There are currently around 88 bus routes servicing the main residential and commercial areas of Dubai. While all of the buses and most of the bus shelters are air conditioned and modern, they can be rather crowded during rush hour. Many of the buses from Dubai to Abu Dhabi, Sharjah and Fujairah also have free wi-fi – although there is talk of charging for the wi-fi in the future. There are also on-board catering services on the Bur Dubai to Abu Dhabi bus.

The main bus stations are near the Gold Souk in Deira and on Al Ghubaiba Road in Bur Dubai. Buses run at regular intervals, starting between 5am and 6am and running until midnight or so, and a handful of Nightliner buses operate from 11.30pm till 6am. The front three rows of seats are reserved for women and children only. Cash is not accepted so you need to purchase a Nol card before boarding. For a complete list of the RTA's inter-emirate routes, see rta.ae.

Metro

Dubai's driverless metro currently has two lines. The Red Line, which runs from Rashidiyah to Dubai International Airport, and down Sheikh Zayed Road – passing the financial district, Downtown, Al Barsha and Marsa Dubai – before terminating at Jabal Ali. The Green Line runs from Al Qusais on the Sharjah border to Jaddaf. Most of the stations along the existing lines are now open – you can check dubaimetro.eu for updates. Blue, Gold and Purple Lines are planned to be running by 2030 and the current Red and Green Lines will be further expanded.

Trains run from 5.50am to midnight Saturday to Wednesday; 5.50am to 1am on Thursdays; and 1pm to 1am on Fridays. The frequency is every 3.45 minutes during peak times, and every seven minutes during off-peak hours. Each train has a section for women and children only, and a first or Gold Class cabin. The fare structure operates as a pay-as-you-go system, in which you scan your pre-paid Nol card in and out of stations.

Commuters can also take advantage of du wi-fi at stations and on the trains themselves. Access cards are available for Dhs.20 per hour, or you can pay via credit card at a rate of Dhs.10 per hour.

There is a feeder bus system to transport passengers from stations to local destinations. Buses are free if boarded within 30 minutes of exiting metro.

Tram

After years of construction work, Dubai Tram finally set off on its first journey in November 2014. The first phase is now fully operational, with the tram running 10.6km on a loop around Marsa Dubai, and then along Al Sufouh Street to the final station at the Tram Depot, next to Dubai Police Academy. In total, there are 11 air-conditioned stations on the route in use.

Trams run from 6.30am to 1.30am Sunday to Thursday; and 9am to 1.30am on Fridays. The frequency is every 10 minutes during peak times and every 12 minutes during off-peak times. For the four stations in Marsa Dubai, a new service has increased frequency to every six minutes.

Fares are exclusively through Nol cards, which can be purchased at any station. Standard rides start at Dh.3 per ride and Gold Class (red tickets) start at Dhs.8. Phase 2 will see another 5km of track added, with stations at Madinat Jumeirah, Burj al Arab, and Mall of the Emirates. Completion is expected by 2020.

The tram has free wi-fi for passengers.

Plan Your Trip

The best way to work out your public transport options is to use the Roads & Transport Authority's (RTA) online journey planner (wojhati.rta.ae). For further assistance, call the RTA on 800 9090.

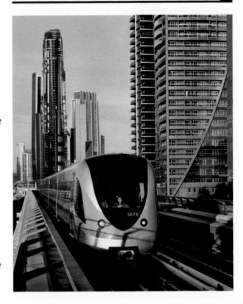

Taxi

If you don't have a car, taxis are still the most common way of getting around. There are nearly 7,000 metered taxis in Dubai with a fixed fare structure. The cars are beige with different coloured roofs. A fleet of 'ladies taxis' with pink roofs have female drivers and are meant for women or family groups only; In-Safe Hands caters to women, children, students, families and people with special needs; and there is a luxury VIP taxi fleet.

Another World Record

In February 2012, Dubai Metro entered the Guinness World Records Book as the longest driverless metro network in the world, spanning 74.69km.

Taxis can be flagged down by the side of the road or you can call 04 208 0808. If you make a booking, you will pay a slightly higher starting fare. The Dubai Taxi automated phone system stores your address after the first time you call. Each subsequent time you ring from that number, listen to the prompts, hit 1, and a taxi will be dispatched automatically, (or hit 2, then enter a later time using the phone's keypad). Unfortunately, the dispatch centre never gives waiting times, so the taxi could arrive in five minutes or 30. Waits are longer at weekends.

The minimum taxi fare is Dhs.12, and the pick-up fare ranges from Dhs.5 to Dhs.7, depending on the time of day, and whether or not you ordered by phone. The starting fare inside the airport area is Dhs.25. Specialist services charge higher rates. Taxis are no longer exempt from Salik tolls, and crossing the border into Sharjah adds another Dhs.20 to the fare. The rate for stoppage or waiting is 50 fils per minute, so don't be surprised when the meter keeps running in standstill traffic. Taxis can be hired for six hours for Dhs.500 or for 12 hours for Dhs.800.

Finding a taxi in congested areas can be difficult, and in their frustration, many people are using illegal cabs. Be warned though that unlicensed taxis haven't had to meet the same vehicle safety standards that legal cabs do. As these cabs are difficult to trace, there have also been cases where drivers have either been the victim of crimes or have perpetrated them.

The Dubai Taxi fleet also now includes several hybrid taxis – Toyota Camrys – that consume a third less fuel and produce a third less carbon. The fleet also has a few a few specially modified taxis for people with wheelchairs travelling from the airport and around town.

The Hala Taxi fleet is the newest fleet in Dubai. You can't flag them down as they only respond to telephone or online bookings. The cars are black or white, and equipped with wi-fi, Nol and NFC payment systems (for smartphones).

Chauffeur Service

A new app called Uber enables you to summon a chauffeur through your smartphone. Download and input your credit card details and a photo. When you call, the driver can see your location, and, you can track his progress through your phone. There's no need to call to give directions. The app shows your driver's name, type of car, estimated time of arrival and a rating. Once in the car, you will be offered water and a choice of music. The service costs almost double that of a taxi, but for pick-ups in remote or difficult to find areas, it makes sense.

Air Travel

Currently, about 107 airlines take advantage of Dubai's open skies policy, operating to and from over 220 destinations. Dubai International Airport's three terminals are a 15 to 30 minute taxi ride apart, depending on the traffic, and there's also a shuttle bus. All terminals offer car rental, hotel reservations and exchange services. Most of the better-known airlines use Terminal 1, while Terminal 2 is used primarily by flydubai and airlines serving former Soviet countries and central Asia. Terminal 3, which opened in 2008, is the newest and most luxurious of the three and exclusively dedicated to Emirates Airlines. By comparison, Terminal 2 has limited facilities and, invariably, extensive queues, while both Terminal 1 and Terminal 3 have a vast selection of drinking and dining venues, plus a large duty free shopping section. For up-to-date flight information from Dubai International Airport, call 04 216 6666. In addition, Dubai International Airport's Concourse D project is due to open in 2015.

All three terminals have both short and long-term parking facilities, as well as busy taxi ranks. There are metro stations at both Terminal 1 and Terminal 3. The stations are part of the Red Line, which runs throughout Deira, under the creek and along Sheikh Zayed Road all the way to Jabal Ali. Keep in mind that luggage larger than a large holdall or standard case is not permitted on the metro. Airport buses operate to and from the airport. Call 800 9090 or visit rta.ae.

Dubai World Central

A second airport, Dubai World Central – Al Maktoum International opened in 2011 for cargo flights. The airport, which is located at the Jabal Ali end of town, will eventually be the world's largest, with five runways handling passenger flights too. Phase 2 of the airport opened for passenger traffic in October 2013, prior to hosting the Dubai Air Show in December 2013. Budget airline Wizz Air was the first to take off from the airport, flying to various European destinations, with new carriers including Qatar airways added throughout 2014.

Airlines

There's an ever-increasing choice of budget airlines based in the UAE including Rotana Jet, flydubai and Air Arabia, each offering no-frills, cheap flights to a wide variety of international destinations. If you want a little more comfort, flydubai now offers business class seats that won't break the bank.

For those searching for the best airline deals between the UAE and destinations in Europe or North America, British Airways has recently introduced an option that allows you to hold a flight for up to 72 hours for as little as Dhs.30. Visit ba.com to make a booking online.

Other airlines include Etihad operating out of Abu Dhabi and low-cost carriers Air Arabia in Sharjah and flydubai in Dubai. Air Arabia offers a city terminal check-in at Lamcy Plaza. Rotana Jet, the UAE's first domestic airline, connects Abu Dhabi with Al Ain, Fujairah and Sir Bani Yas Island for a reasonable fee.

Abu Dhabi airport is a 90 minute drive from Dubai, and Sharjah airport is 45 minutes away. Etihad also runs its own private bus service, which is free for those with a boarding pass and makes the journey between Abu Dhabi International Airport and Dubai.

Air Arabia 06 558 0000, *airarabia.com*
Air France 800 23 823, *airfrance.ae*
Air India 04 227 6787, *airindia.com*
Air Mauritius 04 221 4455, *airmauritius.com*
Air Seychelles 04 286 8008, *airseychelles.com*
American Airlines 04 316 6116, *aa.com*
Austrian Airlines 04 211 2538, *austrian.com*
Bahrain Air 04 239 9921, *en.bahrainair.net*
British Airways 04 307 5555, *britishairways.com*
Cathay Pacific 04 204 2888, *cathaypacific.com*
China Airlines 04 286 8008, *china-airlines.com*
Cyprus Airways 04 221 4455, *cyprusair.com*
Delta Air Lines 04 397 0118, *delta.com*
Emirates 600 55 5555, *emirates.com*
Etihad Airways 04 407 2200, *etihad.com*
flydubai 04 231 1000, *flydubai.com*
Gulf Air 04 271 6207, *gulfair.com*
IranAir 04 224 0200, *iranair.com*
Japan Airlines 04 217 7501, *jal.com*
Jazeera Airways 04 224 4464, *jazeeraairways.com*
KLM Royal Dutch Airlines 800 556, *klm.com*
Kuwait Airways 04 228 5896, *kuwaitairways.com*
Lufthansa 04 373 9100, *lufthansa.com*
Malaysia Airlines 04 397 0250, *malaysiaairlines.com*
Middle East Airlines 04 223 7080, *mea.com.lb*
Oman Air 04 351 8080, *omanair.com*
Qantas 04 316 6652, *qantas.com*
Qatar Airways 04 231 9999, *qatarairways.com*
Rotana Jet 02 444 3366, *rotanajet.com*
Royal Air Maroc 04 286 9499, *royalairmaroc.com*
Royal Brunei Airlines 04 334 4884, *flyroyalbrunei.com*
Royal Jet 02 505 1777, *royaljetgroup.com*

Royal Jordanian 04 294 4288, *rj.com*
Saudi Arabian Airlines 04 221 4000, *saudiairlines.com*
Singapore Airlines 04 316 6888, *singaporeair.com*
South African Airways 04 397 0766, *flysaa.com*
SpiceJet 04 396 5186, *spicejet.com*
SriLankan Airlines 04 316 6711, *srilankan.aero*
Swiss International Air Lines 04 381 6100, *swiss.com*
Thai Airways 04 268 1701, *thaiair.com*
Tunisair 04 221 1176, *tunisair.com*
Turkish Airlines 04 444 0999, *turkishairlines.com*
United Airlines 800 0441 5492, *united.com*
Virgin Atlantic 04 406 0600, *virgin-atlantic.com*

e-Gate

Once you have your residence visa you can apply for a smart card to use at the airport e-Gates. Simply swipe the smart card and pass through the gates. Applications for a card are processed within minutes at Dubai International Airport, in the dnata buildings (one on Sheikh Zayed Road and one in Deira near Deira City Centre), or the GDRFA office on Sheikh Khalifa bin Zayed Road. You'll need your passport, with residence visa, and the process will involve being fingerprinted and photographed. The e-Gate card costs Dhs.200 and is valid for two years; however, you can now activate the e-Gate service on your Resident ID and pay just Dhs.150 for two years. Payment can be made by cash or credit card.

For further information, contact 04 316 6966 or see dubai.ae. Better still, you can now check in and out through passport control without having to apply for an e-Gate card. All holders of modern passports with barcodes, including children above the age of seven, can use the new e-Gate service, which has been rolled out across Dubai International Airport.

The Future

The UAE has big expansion plans for its public transport network. Etihad Rail is working on installing a rail network linking the emirates, and sections of the track are already in place and being utilised by freight trains. The overall plan will see a high-speed passenger rail connection linking Dubai and Abu Dhabi by 2017. Initially this will be aimed at freight transport, but a passenger service between Abu Dhabi and Dubai is likely by 2018. Etihad Rail also plans to extend train lines into other GCC countries and is even looking at expanding its reach as far as Turkey. Once the planned Blue, Gold and Purple metro lines are added to the network by 2030, it could eventually cover 421km with 197 stations – though the size of the expansion will be linked to the official population size. The plan will also see the metro connecting to the Etihad rail network across the Gulf countries.

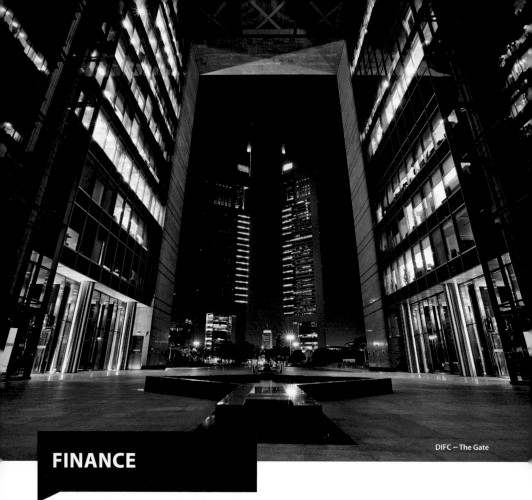

FINANCE

Money is a big reason for expats to be in Dubai; attracted by tax-free pay cheques. From setting up a bank account to credit cards and debt, this chapter will give you the information you need to know.

Main Banks

To open an account in most banks, you will need a residence visa or to have your residence visa application underway. To apply, you will need to submit your original passport, copies of your passport (personal details and visa pages) and an NOC from your sponsor. Some banks set a minimum account limit – this can be anything from Dhs.2,000 for a deposit account and as much as Dhs.10,000 for a current account.

This means at some point during each month your account balance must be over the minimum limit; but if your wages are paid into this account then for most expats that shouldn't be a problem.

There are plenty of ATMs (cash points) available in Dubai, and most cards are compatible with the Central Bank network, though you may pay a small fee if you have to use another bank's ATM. Even if you use your bank card from your home country, you shouldn't have too many issues using an ATM, although the exchange rate given may not always be favourable.

Banks are open from 8am to 1.30pm, Saturday to Wednesday, and 8am to noon on Thursday. Some branches, especially in the malls, stay open until later, even as late as 10pm. All banks are closed on Fridays.

There are also numerous money exchanges; try UAE Exchange (uaeexchange.com) if you want to buy or sell currency. UAE Exchange also offers convenient ways to pay bills and a unique pre-paid travel card for use on Dubai's public transport system.

Banks that operate internationally rarely have connections with their counterparts in other parts of the world, so you won't be able to manage accounts held in other countries through your Dubai account.

ABN AMRO Bank DIFC, Zaa'beel 2, 04 440 9400, *abnamroprivatebanking.com*
Barclays Emaar Square Bldg 6, Downtown Dubai, Burj Khalifa, 04 438 1038, *barclays.ae*
Citibank Nr BurJuman Centre, Al Mankhool, 04 311 4000, *citi.com*
Commercial Bank of Dubai Al Ittihad Rd, Port Saeed, 04 211 2700, *cbd.ae*
Emirates Islamic Bank Sunshine Bldg, Al Garhoud, 04 282 9778, *emiratesislamicbank.ae*
Dubai Islamic Bank MoE, Al Barsha 1, 04 405 1930, *dib.ae*
Emirates NBD Mena Jabal Ali, 600 540 000, *emiratesnbd.com*
FGB Al Yamamah Tower, Al Khabaisi, 600 525 500, *fgb.ae*
HSBC Bank Middle East 3A St, Al Souk Al Kabeer, 600 554 722, *hsbc.ae*
Mashreq Bank MoE, Al Barsha 1, 04 511 8601, *mashreqbank.com*
RAK Bank Better Homes Business Centre, Al Qouz 3, 04 213 0000, *rakbank.ae*
Standard Chartered Bank – Middle East Nr Majestic Hotel, Al Mankhool, 600 522 288, *standardchartered.ae*
Union National Bank Khalid Bin Waleed St, Al Mankhool, 600 566 665, *unb.co.ae*

Mobile Banking

Most banks now offer banking by SMS. You can access your account balance, see your last five transactions, or request a chequebook, simply by sending a text. You'll also get SMS messages to your phone whenever money is paid in or leaves your account.

Online Banking

Banks in the UAE offer online facilities where you can send a transfer, set daily withdrawal limits, check your balance and apply for a loan. It's easy to set up and usually works in conjunction with your mobile phone, in that any security codes required for online transactions will be sent to your mobile for you to then input online.

Credit Cards

It's quite easy to get a credit card and if you're eligible your bank will probably call you to offer you a Visa or MasterCard. For American Express visit americanexpress.ae or call 800 4013. Eligibility usually depends on a minimum salary, a salary certificate detailing your earnings (provided by your employer) and a copy of your passport with your residence visa and work permit. Once you have your card you'll find it's accepted at most shops, hotels and restaurants – though smaller retailers may not always have the facility for credit card payments, or they may charge 5% for processing, even though that is a contravention of the card company rules. However, if you are paying cash you may get a discount! Dubai is relatively safe but the same security measures apply regarding credit cards as anywhere: report lost or stolen cards to your bank immediately, and change your PIN frequently. There will be a limit to the amount of cash that you can withdraw in one day, but you should be able to change this either in your online settings or by contacting your bank.

Pre-paid Cards

Pre-paid cards are available from a number of national banks. These are great for under 18s, as they can shop safely online, can stop the card if it's lost which means they don't lose the money, and parents can track online what they've been spending money on. Using pre-paid cards can mean two for one deals in some eateries can be taken advantage of too.

Cheques

Previously post-dated cheques have mainly been used to secure finances and pay rent, with a year's rent being 'paid' up front in several cheques. The country's first direct debit system came into force in October 2013, with the aim of reducing the need for post-dated cheques in order to guarantee loans.

Bear in mind that if you do write a post-dated cheque, it is a criminal offence if the cheque bounces. More than four bounced cheques in one year will get you blacklisted by the UAE Central Bank, and your account may be closed. Remember too that a cheque cannot be cancelled unless it is lost or stolen, and so think ahead when writing post-dated cheques. In some cases you can be prosecuted, lose your visa or even face a few years in jail.

Financial Planning

Many expats are attracted to Dubai for the tax-free salary and the opportunity to put a something away for the future. However, Dubai's alluring lifestyle can quickly steer you away from your goal. It is often necessary for residents to get credit cards and bank loans to finance their life in Dubai and it is easy to slip further into debt – you'll find there is little or no support if you do. It is important to plan your finances and arrange a safeguard in case your finances take a turn for the worse.

When choosing a financial planner in Dubai, you should ensure that they are licensed by the Central Bank of the UAE (centralbank.ae), so that you have some recourse in the event of a dispute. You should also consider the company's international presence – you'll still want the same access to advice and your investments if you return home. It may be better to use an independent company or advisor who is not tied to a specific bank, and will objectively offer you the full range of savings products on the market.

Before leaving your home country you should contact the tax authorities to ensure that you are complying with the financial laws there. Most countries will consider you not liable for income tax once you prove you're a UAE resident (a contract of employment is normally a good starting point). However, you may still have to fulfil certain criteria, so do some research before you come (if you are already here, check with your embassy). You may be liable for tax on any income you receive from back home (for example if you are renting out your property).

If you have a pension scheme in your home country, it may not be worth continuing your contributions once you come to Dubai, but rather to set up a tax-free, offshore savings plan. It is always advisable to speak to your financial adviser about such matters before you make any big move.

Financial Advice

There seems to be an overabundance of financial advisors in the city who may contact you over the phone and advertise their services. Most advisors won't ask for money initially; however, they may ask you for contact details of your friends and family members so that they can continue to spread the word.

Pensions

The UAE's first pension scheme for expatriates was launched by the NBAD Trust Company (Jersey) Limited – a wholly owned subsidiary of the National Bank of Abu Dhabi (NBAD). The Wealth Builder Plan is a corporate trust solution that allows employers to offer expat staff greater rewards through corporate savings – the first service of its kinds to be offered by a UAE bank.

The Wealth Builder Plan is underpinned by a range of investment fund options that employees can choose based on their risk appetite. The schemes are tailored for each client, and regular investments can be made solely by the company or by both employer and employee.

Dubai has several international banks

Financial Advisors

These companies are experienced in providing financial advice to expats.

6 Sigma Financial Consultancy Liberty House, DIFC, Zaa'beel 2, 04 325 9159, *6sigmagrp.com*
Acuma 703 API World Tower, Trade Centre 1, 04 332 8582, *acuma.ae*
Ernst & Young Al Attar Business Tower, Trade Center 2, 04 332 4000, *ey.com*
Globaleye VIlla 801, Jumeira St, Umm Suqeim 3, 04 404 3700, *globaleye.com*
Guardian Wealth Management Mazaya Business Avenue, Al Thanyah 1, 04 436 2322, *guardianwealthmanagement.com*
Holborn Assets Al Shafar Tower, Al Thanyah 1, 04 457 3800, *holbornassets.com*
InvestME Financial Services LLC > *p.115*
608 Dusseldorf Business Point, Al Barsha 1, 04 453 4400, *investme.ae*
Nexus Insurance Emaar Square Bldg 1, Burj Khalifa, 04 323 1111, *nexusadvice.com*
PIC Middle East Marina Plaza, Marsa Dubai, 04 343 3470, *pic-uae.com*

Insurance Companies

Contact one of these companies for insurance advice.

Abu Dhabi National Takaful Company 04 210 8700, *takaful.ae*
Aetna Global Benefits (Middle East) 04 438 7500, *aetnainternational.com*

AFIA Insurance Brokerage Services 04 337 9987, *afia.ae*
Al Ain Ahlia Insurance Company 04 272 5500, *alaininsurance.com*
Al Khazna Insurance Company 04 217 3333, *alkhazna.com*
Alfred's Insurance Market 04 337 9987, *insurancemarket.ae*
Alliance Insurance 04 605 1111, *alliance-uae.com*
Allianz SE 04 702 6666, *allianz.com*
Arab Orient Insurance Company 04 253 1300, *insuranceuae.com*
AXA Insurance (Gulf) 04 324 3434, *axa-gulf.com*
Daman National Health Insurance Company 04 436 0222, *damanhealth.ae*
Emirates Insurance Company 04 294 2949, *eminsco.com*
Gargash Insurance 04 337 9800, *gargashinsurance.com*
Greenshield Insurance Broker 04 388 2200, *greenshield.ae*
Lifecare International 04 331 8688, *lifecareinternational.com*
MedNet UAE 800 4882, *mednet-uae.com*
MetLife Alico 04 415 4445, *metlifealico.ae*
Nasco 04 352 3133, *nascodubai.com*
National General Insurance Co (NGI) 04 211 5800, *ngi.ae*
Neuron 04 388 6374, *neuron.ae*
Nexus 04 323 1111, *nexusadvice.com*
Oman Insurance Company 04 233 7777, *tameen.ae*
Qatar General Insurance & Reinsurance Co 04 268 8688, *qgirco.com*
Qatar Insurance Company 04 222 4045, *qatarinsurance.com*
RSA 800 772, *rsagroup.ae*
Zurich International Life 04 363 4567, *zurich.com*

Debt
Despite the city's reliance on credit, harsh penalties are dealt for late or missed payments. It can be expensive to initially set up here and you may need sizeable loans to purchase a car or cover rent – but if you suddenly lose your job there's no safety net to cover your expenses. However, banks do generally require that you have received six salary payments into your account before they will grant you a loan.

Unlike some countries, where you will receive several reminders for missed payments, if you are late paying for basic household bills such as electricity or water, your services may be disconnected without much warning. Missed payments on credit cards bills will often incur fines or restrictions to services. There are no bankruptcy laws in the UAE and so if you fall into difficulties you are fully liable for your debt. If your bank files a complaint, you could face a visa ban or jail.

Tax
The UAE levies no personal income taxes or withholding taxes. The only noticeable taxes you pay as an expat are a 5% municipality tax on rental accommodation, a 30% tax on alcohol bought at Dubai liquor stores and 50% tax on tobacco (although cigarettes are still comparatively cheap). A municipality tax is included in your DEWA bill, and if you don't pay this your utilities will be cut off. This has resulted in some complaints – the tax is meant to cover refuse collection, street lighting and community road networks, but people renting freehold properties also pay maintenance to cover these things. There is also a 10% municipality tax and a 10% service charge in hotel food and beverage outlets, but you'll find that these are usually incorporated into the displayed price.

Taxing Issues
You may need to register your residency in the UAE with the government in your home country to avoid paying income tax or capital gains tax. It's best to check with your consulate for exact details. British expats can visit the Inland Revenue's website at hmrc. gov.uk/international/abroad.htm for comprehensive advice on tax and National Insurance payments. If you still spend time working in your home country, check with an accountant to see if you are still liable to pay tax at home.

Offshore Accounts
An offshore account works in the same way as a conventional account, but with additional flexibility. Money can be moved where it will produce the best rewards, and cash accessed whenever you need it, in your desired currency. Offshore accounts allow for management through the internet and over the phone, in a range of currencies (commonly in US dollars, euros or pounds sterling). If you are travelling outside the UAE, make sure your account comes with 24 hour banking, internationally recognised debit cards, and the ability to write cheques in your preferred currency.

To open an account, there is usually a minimum balance of around $10,000. Do some thorough research before opening an account, and check the potential tax implications in your home country. It is important to seek independent financial advice, and not just the opinion of the bank offering you an account. To open your account, you may have to produce certain reports or documents from your chosen country. However, for those willing to do the research and undertake the admin, offshore banking can prove to be a lucrative investment.

Welcome to

DUBAI

Living in Dubai is a wonderful experience. Navigating the bureaucracy though is frustrating especially when you are trying to buy a property, getting a mortgage, insurance or protecting your assets.

We are here to help you! We save you time, money and take all the pain away.

Simply call us now! **+971 (0) 4 453 4400**

propertyme.ae
insureme.ae
investme.ae

mortgageme.ae
Fxme.ae
willsme.ae

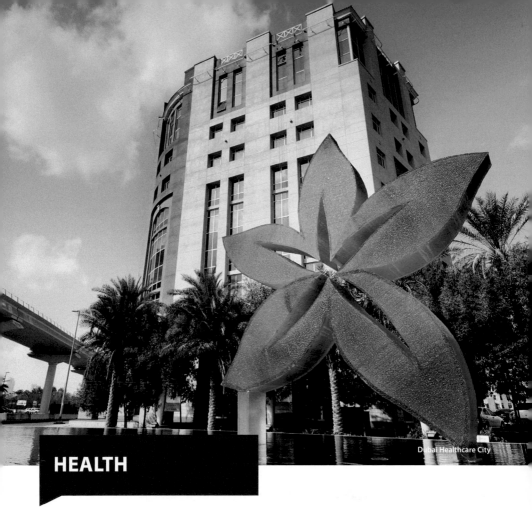
Dubai Healthcare City

HEALTH

Both private and public healthcare services are available in the UAE. General standards are high, with English speaking staff and internationally trained medical staff in most facilities, the main difference being personal service and dorm style rooms rather than private hotel-style rooms (and food!).

Historically, an employer in Dubai can choose to provide access to healthcare for its employees: either the employer pays for a private medical insurance policy, or it pays the cost of obtaining a health card for each employee, which can be used to receive healthcare at any government hospital.

Under a new law introduced in January 2014 (Insurance System for Advancing Healthcare in Dubai – ISAHD), Dubai companies with 1,000 or more employees must cover their staff with private health insurance before the end of October 2014; smaller companies with 100-999 employees will have until the end of July 2015, and companies below 100 employees

have until end of June 2016 to cover their employees. Health insurance packages, which must come from a government approved provider, cover all essential health services including emergency care, access to GPs, referral to specialists, tests and investigations, surgical procedures and maternity care.

The new legislation also states that employee's spouses and children must also have health cover – but this may be at the employee's own expense. It is also mandatory for sponsors to provide domestic workers – nannies and maids – with health insurance.

Healthcare in Dubai is managed by the Dubai Health Authority (DHA). As well as introducing compulsory health insurance in 2014, there are plans underway to expand the Rashid Hospital trauma centre, and introduce electronic medical records; all patients will be assigned a password and any doctor in Dubai – whether at a private or public hospital – will be able to access your medical records.

Government Healthcare

In Dubai, the Department of Health & Medical Services (dohms.gov.ae) runs Dubai, Rashid and Latifa hospitals. Dubai Hospital is renowned as one of the best medical centres in the Middle East, while Latifa is a specialised maternity and paediatric hospital. DOHMS also operates a number of outpatient clinics. Al Baraha Hospital is run by the Ministry of Health. The Iranian Hospital, while not a government hospital, provides healthcare subsidised by the Iranian Red Crescent Society. With the exception of emergency care, you will need a health card to access government health services.

Health Card

The Dubai Health Authority issues a health card, which entitles any UAE resident to receive healthcare at a government hospital or clinic. The card costs Dhs.500 and can be applied for at Rashid, Latifa or Dubai hospitals; you will need your residence visa, Resident ID, two passport photos and an application form typed in Arabic. You can also apply online at dha.gov.ae. Even if you already have access to private health insurance, it is perhaps sensible to have a health card as well, as not all policies will cover you for certain treatments and it may be cheaper to go to a government hospital or clinic.

Private Healthcare

If you have private health insurance, you will have access to a network of private hospitals and clinics. Levels of cover vary depending on the policy, so check what you're entitled to. Dental care, maternity and screening tests aren't usually covered as standard, and you may need to have been on the policy for a year before you can receive maternity cover.

Before making an appointment to see a healthcare professional, always check whether the clinic or hospital is part of your insurer's network to avoid being landed with the full costs yourself. Your insurer will also provide details about its payment policy; some companies offer direct billing, which means the insurer pays the hospital or clinic directly and you only pay a nominal fee each time you access medical services, while others require you to pay the cost of the consultation, treatment and medication up front and then file a claim to the insurer.

If your employer is paying for your medical insurance, your employment contract will state whether your spouse and dependants are included in the policy. If you plan to cover the cost of insuring your family yourself, you may need to purchase a separate policy for them as it's not always possible to extend existing policies.

Private hospitals, medical centres and specialist clinics are located across Dubai, and there are over 120 medical facilities in Healthcare City alone, including two hospitals.

Accidents & Emergencies

If you witness an accident or need an ambulance in an emergency situation, the number to call is 999. Anyone can receive emergency treatment in government hospitals but charges apply to anyone without a health card. Some private hospitals have accident and emergency (A&E) departments but unless you have private medical insurance, you'll be landed with a large bill. Your best bet is to check with your insurer that you are covered for treatment in a particular hospital before heading there.

Of the government hospitals, Rashid Hospital (04 219 1000) deals with most emergency cases as it has a well-equipped A&E department. Dubai Hospital also has an emergency unit. Latifa Hospital offers emergency services to children under the age of 12 and women with maternity or gynaecological emergencies; it does not deal with trauma cases. The Iranian Hospital has a busy A&E.

Who You Gonna Call?

Need a doctor urgently? du customers have access to Mobile Doctors, a round-the-clock medical helpline. Licensed and experienced physicians from Dubai Healthcare City are standing by day and night to advise you over the phone and help you make an appointment with leading hospitals, clinics, pharmacies and other health services across the UAE. To subscribe, SMS 'MD' to 2470. For more information and to subscribe online, visit mobiledoctors24-7.com or call 800 63247; there is a daily fee of Dhs.29, and monthly subscriptions are also available.

While finding a place to get emergency treatment is easy, Dubai's paramedic services are somewhat underdeveloped. Ambulance response times are below those in most western cities but in recent years, a large number of well-equipped response vehicles have been added and times have come down.

When you call 999 (which goes through to Dubai Police) an ambulance will be dispatched to take the patient to the relevant hospital depending on the type of medical treatment needed. Rashid Hospital receives all trauma patients; all other medical emergencies are transported to Dubai Hospital with the exception of cardiac, neurological and gastrointestinal patients, who are taken to Rashid or a speciality hospital.

General Medical Care

There are a few different options available for general, non-emergency medical care. Most hospitals have a walk-in clinic where you can simply turn up, present your health or insurance card, register and queue to see a general practitioner. It's commonplace to be seen by a triage nurse who will take down the details of your medical history and ailment before you see a doctor. These departments usually operate on a first-come, first-served basis. It's advisable to call the hospital prior to visiting to make sure that they have a walk-in service and when it's open. If you are on a private healthcare plan, check in advance that the hospital is on your insurer's network.

Doctor On Call

800 Doctor (800doctor.com, 800 362867) offers a 24/7 doctor on call service. Its team of certified doctors can visit your home, work or business, normally within an hour of your call. They can help with eye infections, sore throat, common viral infections, tonsillitis, asthma, bronchitis, vaccinations and more. A house call will cost Dhs.500 plus medications.

Many hospitals and smaller clinics offer family medicine as part of their outpatient services. You can usually call to make an appointment but there are no guarantees you'll get an appointment on the same day. If your usual family medicine department has no appointments available but you need immediate non-emergency medical care, they may admit you through the A&E department, but they will advise you of this when you call. American Hospital offers a fast-track service through its A&E department for people needing immediate medical attention.

While some people like the convenience of walk-in clinics, others prefer to register with a practice where they are familiar with the administrative procedures and can see the same doctor on return visits. There are countless clinics in Dubai which offer general practice and family medicine. Standards are generally high but it's worth asking friends, neighbours and colleagues for recommendations. Most parts of the city have a local medical centre, so if proximity to your home or office is important, you should be able to find something nearby.

A number of clinics and hospitals offer Well Man, Well Woman and Well Child packages. These care packages involve medical examinations, screenings for common diseases, and routine tests, and offer well-being advice. You can even get your holiday vaccinations topped up as part of some packages. The package that you opt for will depend on factors such as age, gender and medical history.

Al Diyafa Modern Medical Centre 2nd December St, Al Bada', 04 345 4945
Al Mousa Medical Centre Al Wasl Rd, Jumeira 1, 04 345 2999
Al Noor Polyclinic Saif Center, Naif, 04 223 3324, *alnoorpolyclinic.ae*
Amber Clinics Rigga Business Centre, Al Muraqqabat, 04 230 9100, *amber-clinics.com*
Aster Medical Centre Icon Towers, Al Thanyah 1, 04 453 4830, *astermedicalcentre.com*
Belgium Medical Services Ibn Sina Bldg, Healthcare City, Umm Hurair 2, 04 362 4711
Belhoul European Hospital Al Bada', 04 345 4000, *belhouleuropean.com*
Canadian Specialist Hospital Nr Abjar Grand Hotel, Hor Al Anz East, 04 707 2222, *csh.ae*
Crescent Cosmetic Medical Center Villa 39, Nr Mercato, Jumeira 1, 04 342 2288, *crescentmc.ae*
Drs Nicolas & Asp Villa 446, Jumeira St, Jumeira 3, 04 394 7777, *nicolasandasp.com*
Dubai London Specialty Hospital Jumeira St, Umm Suqeim 2, 800 352, *dubailondonclinic.com*
Family First Medical Center Al Wasl St, Umm Al Sheif, 04 380 5430, *familyfirst.ae*
General Medical Centre Nr Market Shopping Mall, Dubai Investment Park 1, 04 885 3225, *gmcclinics.com*
General Medical Centre Trade Centre Apartments, Trade Center 2, 04 331 3544, *gmcclinics.com*
Health Call Bldg 27, Healthcare City, Umm Hurair 2, 04 363 5343, *health-call.com*
JTS Medical Centre Jumeirah Terrace, Jumeira 1, 04 379 9954, *jtsmedicalcentre.com*
kidsFIRST Medical Center Villa 1171A, Al Wasl Rd, Umm Al Sheif, 04 348 5437, *kidsfirstmc.com*
Lifeline Medical Centre Dubai Marina Al Fattan Marine Tower 2, Marsa Dubai, 04 399 1119, *lifeline.ae*
Manchester Clinic Jumeira Rd, Jumeira 1, 04 344 0300, *manchester-clinic.com*
Medcare Medical Centre Al Barajeel Oasis Complex Bldg, Mirdif, 04 284 7199, *medcarehospital.com*
Mediclinic Dubai Mall > *p.iv, v* Dubai Mall, Downtown Dubai, Burj Khalifa, 04 449 5111, *mediclinic.ae*
Mercato Family Clinic Nr Mercato Shopping Centre, Jumeira 1, 04 344 8844
Thumbay Hospital Al Qusais, Dubai (opening March) 04 298 8805 *thumbayhospital.com*

Medical History

Be sure to give a copy of your medical history to your new clinic. Most insurance policies don't cover holiday vaccinations; you can save yourself a lot of money if you have a record of which jabs you've already had. Be aware though, that pre-existing conditions will probably not be covered by your new policy.

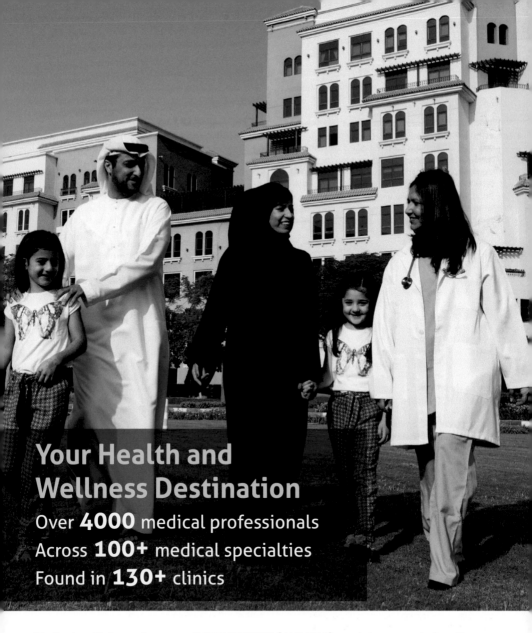

Your Health and Wellness Destination

Over **4000** medical professionals
Across **100+** medical specialties
Found in **130+** clinics

To find a clinic or doctor call **800 HEALTH (432584)** or visit our website **dhcc.ae**

Government Hospitals

There are four main government hospitals in Dubai that you may need to visit.

Al Baraha Hospital

Al Khaleej St Al Baraha **04 271 0000**
Map **2 P4** Metro **Palm Deira**
This government hospital is commonly referred to as the Kuwaiti Hospital and is one of Dubai's older medical centres. It is on the Deira side of the Shindagha Tunnel. You're unlikely to use this hospital for treatment, but you might need to come here for your blood test when processing your residence visa or for a birth or death certificate.

Dubai Hospital

Al Khaleej St Al Baraha **04 219 5000**
dohms.gov.ae
Map **2 P4** Metro **Palm Deira**
Dubai Hospital is one of the best government hospitals in the UAE. Having opened in 1983, it is one of the oldest, but it's clean and well maintained. The hospital offers a full range of medical, dentistry and general surgical services. It is large and usually busy but has a very efficient emergency department.

Latifa Hospital

Oud Metha St Sama Al Jadaf, Al Jadaf **04 219 3000**
dha.gov.ae
Map **2 K7** Metro **Al Jadaf**
The Latifa Hospital specialises in obstetrics, gynaecology and paediatric. Its emergency department provides 24 hour care seven days a week. It cares for children up to the age of 12 with medical, surgical and non-trauma cases, and women with serious problems relating to pregnancy and gynaecology. It's the only hospital to deal with emergency pregnancies and has a special unit for premature and sick neonates. Expat residents admitted in an emergency without a health card are charged Dhs.250 a day plus any medication costs.

Rashid Hospital

Nr Maktoum Bridge Umm Hurair 2 **04 219 1000**
dha.gov.ae
Map **2 L6** Metro **Oud Metha**
Rashid is the main government hospital for A&E, trauma, intensive care and paramedic services. It's likely that you'll be brought here if you have a road accident. It also offers diagnostics, surgery, maternity, paediatrics, physiotherapy and a social affairs unit. The standard of care is good, but it is busy, so seek non-emergency treatment in another government hospital. The hospital is currently undergoing a Dhs.3bn redevelopment; there will be state-of-the-art medical facilities, along with two hotels, residences and a lake.

Private Hospitals

In general private hospitals deliver high standards of care in Dubai. Most hospitals offer a comprehensive range of inpatient and outpatient facilities, so if you like a particular hospital but need to see a specific specialist, the chances are the hospital will be able to cater to your needs. Once you have registered with your chosen hospital it is easier and faster to return for further treatment.

For very specialist treatment you'll be referred to somewhere else in the city. Many of the services offered in hospitals are also offered in clinics and small practices, so if you have a hospital phobia, these might be a better option for non-emergency treatment. See Specialist Clinics & Practitioners. It is worth having a look around the main hospitals to see which one suits you – especially if you are intending to have a baby in Dubai. For more information on Having a Baby in Dubai see Family & Parenting.

Al Garhoud Private Hospital

Nr Millennium Hotel Al Garhoud **04 454 5000**
gph.ae
Map **2 N7** Metro **GGICO**
Almost all areas of medical care are offered at this 52 bed multi-speciality private hospital which offers emergency care, plus general surgery, and obstetrics and gynaecology. There is also an ENT department, plastic aesthetic surgery and physiotherapy.

Private Medical Insurance

Private medical cover in Dubai is available from several providers. Greenshield Insurance (greenshield.ae, 04 388 2200) offers comprehensive medical cover for expats. Their website contains a well-explained guide as to how their policies work. You'll need insurance cover when using private hospitals and clinics; otherwise you'll be landed with the entire bill for your treatment. Using an insurance provider such as Greenshield gives you peace of mind because medical treatment in Dubai can be expensive.

American Hospital Dubai > p.121

19th St Oud Metha **04 336 7777**
ahdubai.com
Map **2 L6** Metro **Oud Metha**
American Hospital is usually pretty busy with its excellent in and outpatient facilities and a fast-track A&E unit. The hospital has top-of-the-range diagnostic equipment and a number of dedicated units including a heart centre and cancer care centre. Its maternity unit is a popular choice, with packages for prenatal care and delivery and private rooms on the labour ward. It also has a good Pediatric Allergy and Asthma clinic.

RK41590

Delivering Better Health in the Middle East

The first hospital in the Middle East to be awarded Joint Commission International Accreditation (JCI)
The first private laboratory to be certified by the College of American Pathologists (CAP)

Scope of Services at American Hospital Dubai

- Ablation Therapy
- Anesthesia
- Audiology
- Cochlear Implant
- Cardiac Surgery
- Cardiac Catheterization
- Cardiology
- Cardiopulmonary
- Dermatology
- Diabetes / Endocrinology
- Dietary Counseling
- Endoscopy
- ENT Surgery

- Gastroenterology / Hepatology
- Hematology
- General Surgery
- Internal Medicine
- Medical Imaging
- Minimally Invasive Surgery
- Nephrology / Dialysis
- Neurology
- Neurosurgery
- Obstetrics / Gynecology
- Oncology / Chemotherapy
- Ophthalmology

- Orthopedics
- Pathology & Laboratory
- Palliative Medicine
- Pediatrics (Children)
- Pediatric Allergy and Asthma
- Pediatric Surgery
- Primary Care
- Rheumatology
- Sports Medicine and Physical Therapy
- Urology
- Vascular Surgery
- 24 Hour Emergency Service

Organization Accredited
by Joint Commission International

ahdubai.com

American Hospital Dubai accepts most major insurance plans 800 - 5500

Belhoul Speciality Hospital
Al Khaleej Rd Al Baraha **04 273 3333**
belhoulspeciality.com
Map **2 P4**
Belhoul Speciality Hospital's nephrology department offers state-of-the-art dialysis machines for kidney disorders. It also has advanced diagnostic technology and health check packages. It has an emergency room and a range of in and outpatient services. The service is efficient as is its customer service.

Cedars Jebel Ali International Hospital
Shk Zayed Rd Jabal Ali Port, Mena Jabal Ali
04 881 4000
cedars-jaih.com
Map **1 C5** Metro **Danube**
Cedars Jebel Ali International Hospital is a private healthcare centre near Jebel Ali Free Zone. Services include a 24 hour emergency clinic and dedicated ambulance (04 881 4000 and 04 881 8816). It specialises in trauma and occupational medicine. A hospital extension is currently under construction.

Healthcare City
Dubai Healthcare City is a centre of excellence dedicated to hospitals and healthcare facilities. There are more than 120 medical facilities and 4,000 doctors spanning all specialities. It's a hub for pioneering research and cutting edge technology. You can find everything from eye doctors to Ayurveda treatments. For more information see dhcc.ae.

Dubai London Specialty Hospital
Jumeira St Umm Suqeim 2 **800 352**
dubailondonclinic.com
Map **1 T4** Metro **Noor Bank**
The Dubai London Specialty Hospital is a part of Dubai London Clinic, a well-established clinic with fairly new medical and surgical premises in Umm Suqeim. Another branch is at Festival City (04 232 5751). The Dubai London Dental Centre is on Al Wasl Road. The hospital offers round-the-clock emergency services, inpatient surgery, cosmetic surgery and comprehensive outpatient care.

Emirates Hospital
Nr Jumeirah Beach Park Jumeira 2 **04 349 6666**
emirateshospital.ae
Map **2 D4** Metro **Business Bay**
This small private hospital on Jumeirah Road may not be the newest of Dubai's private medical facilities but it delivers a high standard of care. It is primarily a surgical hospital but it also runs outpatient services including a 24 hour walk-in clinic, though the number of doctors available at weekends is limited.

Iranian Hospital
Al Wasl St Al Bada' **04 344 0250**
ihd.ae
Map **2 H4** Metro **World Trade Centre**
This mosaic-fronted hospital is affiliated with the Red Crescent Society of Iran, so it isn't strictly a UAE government hospital. It offers its own health card and the fee is reasonable. The card, which costs Dhs.300, offers 20% discount on in and outpatient services, but even without a card, the prices are still affordable. In addition, some of the medicines which they prescribe are free. On the downside the hospital is rather busy, particularly at the walk-in clinic during peak hours.

Medcare Hospital
Nr Safa Park Al Safa 1 **04 407 9100**
medcarehospital.com
Map **2 C5** Metro **Business Bay**
Medcare Hospital is a modern 60 bed private hospital. It offers emergency services and advanced medical care with a particularly strong maternity department. A satellite clinic, Medcare Medical Centre, recently opened in Uptown Mirdiff and takes walk-ins. There is also a multi-speciality clinic on The Walk at JBR.

Medcare Medical Centre
Nr Umm Suqeim Municipality Umm Suqeim 1
04 395 3115
medcarehospital.com
Map **2 A4** Metro **Noor Bank**
Offering primary, secondary and tertiary medical services including surgery, dentistry, family medicine, rheumatology, diagnostics, psychiatry, endocrinology, urology and paediatrics. There are also branches at Mirdif, Mirdif City Centre and The Walk at JBR.

Medcare Orthopaedics & Spine Hospital
Shk Zayed Rd Al Safa 1 **04 376 8400**
medcareorthopaedics.com
Map **2 C6** Metro **Business Bay**
Medcare Orthopaedics & Spine Hospital, or MOSH, exclusively caters to orthopaedic and spine patients. It specialises in joint replacement, paediatric orthopaedic cases, foot and ankle ailments, sports-related injuries, and hand and spine ailments. It boasts one of the largest and most comprehensive associations of private orthopaedic surgeons in the emirate.

Mediclinic Al Sufouh > *p.iv, v*
Knowledge Village, Al Sufouh 2 **04 366 1030**
mediclinic.ae
Map **1 N5** Metro **Dubai Internet City**
Has everything from its own ambulance services to an operating theatre and 25 outpatient and speciality clinics including daycare surgery, gastroenterology, paediatrics and urgent care. Open 8am to 10.30pm, Saturday to Thursday, 11.30am to 8.30pm on Friday.

Mediclinic City Hospital > *p.iv, v*

Bldg 37 Healthcare City, Umm Hurair 2
04 435 9999
mediclinic.ae
Map **2 L7** Metro **Dubai Healthcare City**
Mediclinic City Hospital is a modern, multi-disciplinary hospital delivering world-class healthcare services with the most advanced equipment available. The 229 bed premium facility offers specialised treatment in areas such as cardiology, neurology and neurosurgery, obstetrics and gynaecology, paediatrics, general surgery and radiology. Patient care units provide sophisticated diagnosis and treatments in hand surgery, eye care, kidney stones and breast care. The maternity unit has a dedicated operating theatre for caesarean sections and a neonatal intensive care unit, which is one of the largest in the UAE.

Mediclinic Welcare Hospital > *p.iv, v*

2nd St Al Garhoud **04 282 7788**
mediclinic.ae
Map **2 N7** Metro **GGICO**
Welcare Hospital's special services include a contact lens clinic, diabetic clinic, holiday dialysis and home call consultations (specialist and GP). Its prenatal and delivery care is considered to be among the best in Dubai. Welcare offers postnatal packages for parents and newborns, which is a nice way for mums to meet. Welcare also operates primary healthcare clinics in Mirdif (04 288 1302) and Al Qusais (04 258 6466) and an ambulatory care unit in Knowledge Village (04 366 1030) that comes highly recommended. Appointments can be booked online.

Emirates Hospital

Neuro Spinal Hospital

Jumeira St Jumeira 2 **04 342 0000**
nshdubai.com
Map **2 D4** Metro **Business Bay**
The Neuro Spinal Hospital's emergency room is open around the clock and treats all kinds of spinal, neurosurgical and neurological emergencies. The hospital has 40 beds and a multinational team of specialists, doctors and nurses. As well as spinal treatment facilities, the hospital has a stroke centre for treatment of acute cerebro-vascular accidents and its own ambulance, which can be dispatched by calling 04 315 7777.

NMC Hospital

Al Quds St Hor Al Anz **04 268 9800**
nmc.ae
Map **2 Q6** Metro **Abu Hail**
NMC Private Hospital in Deira has a 24 hour walk-in general practice clinic so advance appointments are not necessary. The levels of service are high and the staff are generally efficient. The hospital has an emergency room and its own ambulance with attendant doctors. There is an NMC Specialty Hospital in Al Nahda (04 267 9999), with specialist clinics for allergies, reconstructive surgery, paediatrics and more. Other branches are located in Abu Dhabi and Sharjah.

Saudi German Hospital

Al Hessa St Al Barsha 3 **04 389 0000**
sghgroup.ae
Map **1 P6** Metro **Dubai Internet City**
SGH has numerous healthcare establishments located across the MENA region. The Dubai facility is an impressively state-of-the-art 300 bed speciality tertiary care hospital that is extremely convenient for many residents in new Dubai. It offers medical and surgical specialities and subspecialities including cardiac surgery, neurosurgery, oncology, maxillofacial surgery, orthopaedics, and vascular surgery.

Zulekha Hospital

Nr HCT-Dubai Women's College Al Nahda 2
04 267 8866
zulekhahospitals.com
Map **2 T7** Metro **Stadium**
Zulekha is a multi-speciality hospital offering care in fields from cardiology to urology, as well as 24 hour emergency services. The Zulekha Hospital also has a branch in Sharjah and a medical centre in Dubai. In 2012 it was awarded the coveted Dubai Quality Award. It offers health packages to assess your current well-being. Choose from Basic, Executive, Cardiac or Well Woman packages. An initial consultation, followed by blood and urine analysis, analysis of organ functionality and other tests are typically included in the various packages.

Specialist Hospitals & Clinics

Whatever your ailment, the chances are you'll find at least one relevant specialist in Dubai. You don't need a referral to be seen by a specialist so you are free to seek whatever medical advice is relevant to your condition. If you are not sure what is wrong with you, or which kind of specialist you should consult, ask your doctor or seek advice from a hospital. Most places will advise you over the phone to save you the hassle of trying to make an appointment. The majority of hospitals also offer a range of outpatient medical specialities, although many people prefer the more personalised environment of smaller practices for long-term medical care. In addition, many general practice clinics offer a range of medical services so it's worth checking at your local clinic before going elsewhere.

Al Borj Medical Center
Al Wasl **04 321 2220**
alborjclinicdubai.com
Map **2 F6** Metro **Business Bay**
Specialises in endocrinology, dermatology, plastic surgery, gynaecology, paediatrics and general surgery.

Al Shifa Al Khaleeji Medical Centre
Abu Baker Al Siddique St Port Saeed **04 294 0786**
alshifaalkhaleeji.com
Map **2 N6** Metro **Al Rigga**
This clinic offers paediatrics, gynaecology, dentistry, internal medicine and orthopaedic medical services.

Allied Diagnostics
2nd December St Al Satwa **04 332 8111**
allieddiagnostics.net
Map **2 J5** Metro **World Trade Centre**
Provides diagnostic services for clinics that do not have on-site facilities. You may be referred here for investigative procedures.

Amber Clinics
Rigga Business Centre Al Rigga **04 230 9100**
amber-clinics.com
Map **2 N5** Metro **Al Rigga**
One of a number of Amber establishments in Dubai, the Al Rigga clinic is a large, one-stop 'polyclinic' with numerous specialty departments and laboratories under one roof.

Atlas Star Medical Center
Khalid Bin Al Waleed St Al Raffa **04 359 6662**
atlasstar.co
Map **2 L4** Metro **Al Fahidi**
Offers general practice, general surgery, ENT, gynaecology and dental services.

British Medical Consulting Centre
Nr Mercato Jumeira 1 **04 344 2633**
bmccdubai.com
Map **2 F4** Metro **Financial Centre**
Western-trained medical staff specialising in cosmetic surgery, psychotherapy, psychology, dentistry, hair transplantation and marriage counselling. The initial consultation is usually free. Plus they offer psychological support for people with a fear of dentists and dental treatment.

The Diabetes & Endocrine Center
Building 64 Healthcare City, Umm Hurair 2 **04 375 2345**
Map **2 L7** Metro **Dubai Healthcare City**
Screening and treatment clinic for diabetes and thyroid problems.

Dr Kamil Al Rustom Skin & Laser Centre
Villa 8, Al Wasl St Al Bada' **04 308 4000**
alrustom-laser.com
Map **2 H4** Metro **Al Jafiliya**
A specialist dermatology clinic, offering a range of cancer services, laser surgery and cosmetic procedures.

Dr Mahaveer Mehta Skin Medical
Al Muraqqabat **04 221 9300**
skinlaserdubai.com
Map **2 N5** Metro **Baniyas Square**
A laser surgery clinic offering treatment for dermatological conditions and cosmetic procedures.

Dr Mohamed Al Zubaidy Clinic
Al Rigga St Al Muraqqabat **04 227 7533**
Map **2 N5** Metro **Union**
Dr Al Zubaidy offers dermatology and venereology investigations and treatments.

Dr Taher H Khalil Clinic
Shk Zayed Rd, Al Safa 1 04 268 7655
Map **2 C6** Metro **Business Bay**
A general medical clinic specialising in hormone therapy including treatment for low fertility, diabetes and thyroid irregularities.

Dubai London Specialty Hospital
Jumeira St Umm Suqeim 2 **800 352**
dubailondonclinic.com
Map **1 T4** Metro **Noor Bank**
This is a long-established clinic with a new medical and surgical premises in Umm Suqeim. Another branch is located at Festival City (04 232 5751) and Dubai London Dental Centre is on Al Wasl Road (see Dentists). The Umm Suqeim branch offers round-the-clock emergency services, inpatient surgery, cosmetic surgery and comprehensive outpatient care.

German Heart Centre Bremen
Al Faris Bldg Healthcare City, Umm Hurair 2
04 362 4797
german-heart-centre.com
Map **2 L7** Metro **Dubai Healthcare City**
Cardiac treatment, investigation and intervention services, and after treatment care from Germany's most renowned cardiology clinic.

German Medical Center
Ibn Sina Bldg Healthcare City, Umm Hurair 2
04 362 2929
gmcdhcc.com
Map **2 L7** Metro **Dubai Healthcare City**
Offering medical specialities including urology, andrology, infertility, gynaecology, obstetrics, internal medicine, general and orthopaedic surgeries and ENT.

Hear Life Clinic
Dubai Healthcare City, Building 64
Unit 4018 **04 457 3099**
hearlifeclinic.ae
Map **2 L7** Metro **Dubai Healthcare City**
Offers solutions to hearing loss, including cochlear implants, as well as other forms of implants.

iCARE Clinics
Oasis Centre Al Qouz 1 **04 384 7272**
icare-clinics.com
Map **2 C6** Metro **Noor Bank**
The first of 20 proposed iCARE Clinics is now open at the Oasis Centre on Sheikh Zayed Road. The clinics offer a wide range of medical services, including paediatrics, gynaecology, dental, radiology, pathology, family medicine, as well as general practitioner services.

Lifeline Hospital
Nr Jebel Ali Primary School Jabal Ali 1
04 884 5666
lifeline.ae
Map **1 F6** Metro **Ibn Battuta**
Run by the same company as the 800-Doctor initiative, this is hospital offers luxury healthcare with chauffeur-driven transfers and private suites. It also offers antenatal classes and has an excellent maternity wing. A second Lifeline Hospital is under construction, set to open in Mirdif in 2015 with 120 beds.

Mediclinic Al Qusais > *p.iv, v*
Dubai Residential Oasis Al Qusais Ind. 2 **04 258 6466**
mediclinic.ae
Map **2 T8** Metro **Dubai Airport Freezone**
This Al Qusais clinic offers patients a wide range of services, from a team of highly experienced staff, including inpatient treatment at the renowned Mediclinic Welcare hospital.

Mediclinic Al Sufouh > *p.iv, v*
Knowledge Village, Al Sufouh 2 **04 366 1030**
mediclinic.ae
Map **1 N5** Metro **Dubai Internet City**
Has everything from onsite ambulance services to an operation theatre and 25 outpatient and specialty clinics that include daycare surgery, gastroenterology, paediatrics and urgent care.

Mediclinic Arabian Ranches > *p.iv, v*
Nr Arabian Ranches Community Centre
Wadi Al Safa 6 **04 453 4020**
mediclinic.ae
Map **1 Q13**
An 'ambulatory care centre' with excellent facilities and services. General medicine and day surgery are provided along with specialities such as dentistry, gynaecology, ophthalmology and dermatology.

Mediclinic Beach Road > *p.iv, v*
Al Hudaiba Awards Bldg Madinat Dubai Al Melaheyah **04 379 7711**
mediclinic.ae
Map **2 J4** Metro **Al Jafiliya**
Located in Sheikh Hamdan Complex in Jumeira, this newly-opened medical centre offers a range of specialist services, with facilities including an observation unit and its own in-house laboratory.

Mediclinic Dubai Mall > *p.iv, v*
Dubai Mall Downtown Dubai, Burj Khalifa
04 449 5111
mediclinic.ae
Map **2 F6** Metro **Burj Khalifa/Dubai Mall**
Offering the full range of general and specialty medicine, from cardiology to urology, this is the region's largest outpatient facility and has the latest facilities to boot.

Mediclinic Ibn Battuta > *p.iv, v*
Ibn Battuta Jabal Ali 1 **04 440 9000**
mediclinic.ae
Map **1 G5** Metro **Ibn Battuta**
An ultra-modern, fully equipped multi-specialty clinic with its location in Ibn Battuta Mall, making it ideal for residents in the surrounding communities. Has support services like labs and x-rays.

Mediclinic Meadows > *p.iv, v*
Nr Emirates International School Emirates Hills, Al Thanyah 4 **04 453 4040**
mediclinic.ae
Map **1 K6** Metro **Jumeirah Lakes Towers**
Combines advanced medical equipment, an onsite laboratory and diagnostic imaging centre, and a vast range of specialist medical services, including paediatrics, obstetrics and gynaecology.

Mediclinic Mirdif > p.iv, v
Uptown Mirdiff Mirdif 04 288 1302
mediclinicl.ae
Map **2 Q13** Metro **Rashidiya**
Family healthcare clinic specialising in primary
medical care, and a wide range of specialised services.
Has a direct link to the Welcare Hospital and The
Mediclinic City Hospital.

Men's Health Clinic
Al Muhaisnah Medical Fitness Centre Muhaisanah 2
04 502 3939
dha.gov.ae
Map **2 T10** Metro **Etisalat**
The region's first men-only clinic specialises in male-
related diseases and health concerns such as heart
disease, infertility and prostate cancer. The Ministry of
Health is due to open more such clinics at its medical
centres across the emirate.

Neuro Spinal Centre
Jumeira St Jumeira 2 04 342 0000
nshdubai.com
Map **2 D4** Metro **Business Bay**
A 40 bed neurosurgical, neurological, spinal and
orthopaedic specialist facility offering superior
diagnostic, rehabilitative and curative services.
Located opposite Jumeirah Beach Park, the centre's
facilities include emergency room, operating suite and
radiology department.

Panacea Medical & Wellness Centre
Easa Saleh Al Gurg Bldg Al Karama 04 358 2020
panacea.ae
Map **2 L6** Metro **BurJuman**
A modern clinic that offers everything from the more
traditional internal medicine, paediatrics, obstetrics,
gynaecology, diagnostics and chiropractics to dietetics
and homeopathy. Even has a dentistry department
and an emergency department.

Prime Medical Center > p.127
Ibri House Bldg Al Qouz Ind. 1 04 349 4545
primehealth.ae
Map **2 A6** Metro **Noor Bank**
The Prime Healthcare Group runs six clinics throughout
Dubai, offering a wide range of outpatient services, as
well as a diagnostics centre in Deira (04 272 0720).

Wooridul Spine Centre
Shk Zayed Rd Al Safa 2 04 304 6767
wsc.ae
Map **2 A6** Metro **Noor Bank**
Provides patients with full spinal treatment
programmes, from radiological and lab investigations
to pain management, physiotherapy and complete
surgical plans.

Maternity

The standard of maternity care in Dubai is excellent.
Among expats, the most popular maternity hospitals
are Welcare, American and Latifa Hospitals (see
Hospitals). Latifa Hospital may lack some of the private
hospital frills but it has an excellent reputation for
maternity care and paediatrics.

Before you decide on a government hospital,
check its policy regarding husbands and family
members in the labour ward. Some hospitals may
not allow husbands in the labour ward (although
they can be present at delivery and often, if you are
persuasive and there are no local ladies admitted,
they will allow access).

All government hospitals now charge expats
for maternity services and delivery, and costs vary
depending on the package you choose. Private
hospitals will be more expensive, but if you shop
around you may be surprised to find that sometimes
the difference between government and private is
not as great as you expected. No matter which you
choose, if you have medical insurance check it covers
maternity costs. Some have a limitation clause which
means you need to have been with the insurer for at
least 12 months before conception, and some may not
cover any costs at all.

Private hospitals offer maternity packages that
include prenatal care, delivery and postnatal care
for you and the baby. But remember, the price you
are quoted by the hospital is usually for the most
basic 'best case scenario' delivery. Should you have
additional requirements, such as an epidural (when
the anaesthetist must be present) or an assisted
delivery (when the paediatrician must be present), you
will be charged extra.

If you give birth by caesarean section, for example,
the cost is usually significantly higher and the hospital
stay is notably longer (five days, compared to just
two days for a standard delivery). If you go to an
independent gynaecologist for your prenatal care,
you will usually be offered a choice of hospitals and
delivery packages, where your doctor can attend for
the birth. For more information on the practicalities of
having a baby in Dubai, see Family & Parenting.

Below is a list of hospitals offering maternity care.
For more information on each hospital see the main
Hospitals section of this chapter.

Al Zahra Private Medical Centre
Al Safa Tower, Shk Zayed Rd Trade Center 1
04 331 5000
alzahra.com
Map **2 H5** Metro **Financial Centre**
A large medical facility offering wellness packages,
maternity care and diagnostics in addition to a full
range of outpatient services.

American Hospital Dubai > p.121
19th St Oud Metha **04 336 7777**
ahdubai.com
Map **2 L6** Metro **Oud Metha**
This hospital's maternity unit is a popular choice, with packages for prenatal care and delivery and private rooms on the labour ward.

Fetal Medicine & Genetic Center
Bldg 39 Healthcare City, Umm Hurair 2 **04 360 4040**
fetalmedicine.ae
Map **2 L7** Metro **Dubai Healthcare City**
The Fetal Medicine & Genetic Center specialises in foetal care, offering first trimester screening tests, prenatal diagnostics, pregnancy assessment and patient care.

Health Bay Clinic
Villa 977, Al Wasl Rd Al Manara **04 348 7140**
healthbayclinic.com
Map **1 U5** Metro **Noor Bank**
This family clinic is known for its high standards of care in several fields including gynaecology and midwifery. Its western-trained physicians also specialise in internal medicine, gastroenterology, dermatology, podiatry and allergies.

Latifa Hospital
Oud Metha St Al Jadaf **04 219 3000**
dha.gov.ae
Map **2 K7** Metro **Dubai Healthcare City**
Latifa Hospital is a government facility specialising in obstetrics, gynaecology, paediatrics and paediatric surgery. It cares for women with serious problems relating to pregnancy and gynaecology. It is the only hospital in Dubai that deals with emergency pregnancies and has a special baby care unit for premature and sick neonates.

Medcare Hospital
Nr Safa Park Al Safa 1 **04 407 9100**
medcarehospital.com
Map **2 C5** Metro **Business Bay**
Medcare Hospital has a particularly strong maternity department, and staff are qualified to international standards.

Mediclinic City Hospital > p.iv, v
Building 37 Healthcare City, Umm Hurair 2
04 435 9999
mediclinic.ae
Map **2 L7** Metro **Dubai Healthcare City**
Mediclinic City Hospital is a modern, multi-disciplinary hospital. Its maternity unit has a dedicated operating theatre for caesarean sections and a neonatal intensive care unit, which is one of the largest in the UAE.

Mediclinic Welcare Hospital > p.iv, v
2nd St Al Garhoud **04 282 7788**
mediclinic.ae
Map **2 N7** Metro **GGICO**
Welcare Hospital's prenatal and delivery care is considered to be among the best in Dubai. Welcare offers postnatal packages for parents and newborns. Welcare also operates primary healthcare clinics in Mirdif (04 288 1302) and Al Qusais (04 258 6466) and an ambulatory care unit in Knowledge Village (04 366 1030) that comes highly recommended.

NMC Specialty Hospital
Nr HCT-Dubai Women's College Al Nahda 2
04 267 9999
nmc.ae
Map **2 S7** Metro **Stadium**
The NMC Specialty Hospital has a maternity ward, as well as other departments.

Rashid Hospital
Nr Maktoum Bridge Umm Hurair 2 **04 219 1000**
dha.gov.ae
Map **2 L6** Metro **Oud Metha**
Amongst other things, the government-run Rashid Hospital offers maternity care.

Obstetrics & Gynaecology

Most hospitals and general practice clinics in Dubai offer gynaecological and obstetrics medical services. In your home country you may be used to receiving reminders when you are due for a smear test or mammogram; in the UAE, you'll need to be more proactive, and while a gynaecologist can advise you on how frequently you should have check-ups, it will be up to you to remember when the time comes. If you are looking for a long-term gynaecologist, try Health Bay Clinic (04 348 7140), which has a gynaecology department. Many clinics offer well woman check-ups that can be done regularly (usually annually) and offer the chance to get all your checks done in one go, at the same time as a general health review. Latifa Hospital (04 219 3000) and Mediclinic City Hospital (04 435 9999) also have gynaecology departments.

Most contraceptives are available in Dubai (the morning after pill is not) and a gynaecologist can advise you on the most suitable form of contraception for you. If you take oral contraceptives, a variety of brands are available over the counter without prescription. Because of the risk of thrombosis, you should make a point of going to your doctor to have your blood pressure checked every six months, just to make sure everything is okay. Note that, while rarely enforced, the law is that you should be married in order to be prescribed or purchase contraceptives.

Bourn Hall Clinic

Al Hudaiba Awards Bldg Madinat Dubai
Al Melaheyah **04 705 5055**
bournhall-clinic.ae
Map **2 J4** Metro **Al Jafiliya**
A state-of-the-art IVF clinic equipped with the
latest technology and staffed by expert physicians,
nurses and scientists working in the field of Assisted
Reproductive Technology.

Dr Leila Soudah Clinic

Villa 467B, Jumeira Rd Jumeira 3 **04 395 5591**
Map **2 C4** Metro **Business Bay**
An independent gynaecology clinic offering pre- and
post-natal care. Dr Leila is affiliated with American
Hospital, so most of her patients deliver there.

Dubai Gynaecology & Fertility Centre

Building 64 Umm Hurair 2 **04 439 3800**
dgfc.ae
Map **2 L7** Metro **Oud Metha**
This clinic specialises in assisted reproductive
technology. It is one of the few facilities in Dubai
that offers IVF treatment. A range of gynaecological
services are also available.

Fakih IVF Fertility Centre

Villa 37, Al Wasl Rd Jumeira 1 **04 349 7600**
fakihivf.com
Map **2 G4** Metro **Burj Khalifa/Dubai Mall**
One of the leading fertility centres in the region,
it specialises in IVF and assisted reproductive
technology. Dr. Michael Fakih is a recognised leader in
the field of assisted reproduction and is responsible
for over 10,000 IVF deliveries. His clinic provides
infertility treatments as well as PGD for gender
selection, PGD for single gene disorders, preserving
fertility in cancer patients, and more.

German Clinic

Al Razi Bldg Healthcare City, Umm Hurair 2
04 429 8346
germanclinic-dubai.com
Map **2 L7** Metro **Dubai Healthcare City**
A specialist gynaecology, obstetrics and paediatrics
clinic designed to meet German standards of
healthcare, based in Dubai Healthcare City. Wellness,
fertility and antenatal packages are also available.

Mitera Clinic

Al Razi Bldg Healthcare City, Umm Hurair 2
04 363 5464
miteraclinic.com
Map **2 L7** Metro **Dubai Healthcare City**
Dr Rihab Awad has a number of long-term patients
who have followed her from American Hospital to
her new clinic. She is progressive in terms of stem

cell technology and also teaches breast examinations
when you have a check-up. If you're looking for a long-
term gynaecologist and obstetrician then it's worth
getting on her patient list.

Primavera Medical Centre

Al Razi Bldg Healthcare City, Umm Hurair 2
04 375 4669
primaveraclinic.com
Map **2 L7** Metro **Dubai Healthcare City**
This clinic is run by highly recommended obstetrician,
gynaecologist and fertility specialist Dr Rosalie Sant.

Orthopaedics

For orthopaedic treatment there are several places to
choose from, including Medcare Orthopaedics & Spine
Hospital (04 376 8400) in Al Safa, off Sheikh Zayed
Road; and the Prime Healthcare Group (042 720 720)
hospital in Deira has an orthopaedic unit.

Paediatrics

Most public and private hospitals and medical
centres in Dubai have full-time paediatricians on
staff, and a growing number have devoted paediatric
departments. American Hospital and Mediclinic
Welcare Hospital (both private) have teams of
specialist paediatric doctors, while Latifa Hospital
(government) has dedicated paediatric surgeons and
neurodevelopment therapists who care for children
with special needs and learning difficulties. Dr Anil
Gupta at American Hospital, Dr Zuhair Mahmandar
at Emirates Hospital and Dr Loubser at Infinity Clinic
(04 394 8994) are popular paediatricians among
expat parents. The GMC Clinic in Jumeira has friendly
paediatricians who will take the trauma out of doctor's
appointments for your child, and who specialise in
allergies (04 3494 880). Health Call sends doctors for
home visits 24 hours a day, seven days a week and
is a handy service if your child is too sick to take to a
surgery or hospital (04 363 5343, health-call.com).

Cooper Health Clinic

Nr Choithrams, Al Wasl St Umm Suqeim 2
04 348 6344
cooperhealthclinic.com
Map **1 T5** Metro **Noor Bank**
This family medicine clinic offers paediatric, obstetric
and gynaecology specialities including pioneering
procedures in laser vaginal rejuvenation – popular
with women who have given birth. There are also
antenatal classes, infant massage and a hypnobirthing
course to help pregnant women relax. Dr Khan at the
clinic is a popular paediatrician.

Isis The French Clinic

Al Razi Bldg Healthcare City, Umm Hurair 2
04 429 8450
isisclinicdubai.com
Map **2 L7** Metro **Oud Metha**
Located close to the Alliance Francaise and the Ecole
George Pompidou (04 337 4161) this practice offers
specialist paediatric pulmonary care in addition to
asthma, allergies, paediatric general practice and
neonatal clinics. Standards are monitored by Dubai
Healthcare City and the Harvard Medical School.

Keith Nicholl Medical Centre

Villa 610B, Jumeira St Umm Suqeim 1 **04 394 1000**
keithnicholl.com
Map **2 A4** Metro **Noor Bank**
A child-friendly practicc in Jumeira staffed by
a paediatrician, paediatric nurses and a parent
counsellor and educator. In addition to standard
paediatric services, there's also a Well Baby Clinic
that offers well baby check-ups, immunisations,
development checks, as well as first aid courses for
parents, nannies and other caregivers.

kidsFIRST Medical Center

Villa 1171A, Al Wasl St Umm Al Sheif **04 348 5437**
kidsfirstmc.com
Map **1 S5** Metro **Mall of the Emirates**
In addition to paediatric medicine, kidsFIRST
offers occupational therapy, speech therapy and
physiotherapy for kids. The kidsFIRST team serves
children across a full range of special needs, such as
autism, ADHD, cerebral palsy and dyslexia.

Medcare Hospital

Physiotherapy

Many Dubai residents lead an active lifestyle, working
hard and then playing harder. But accidents and
injuries do happen, so whether you get roughed up
playing rugby, pull something in the gym or put your
back out moving a wardrobe, you'll be pleased to
hear that the city has some excellent facilities with
specialists from all around the world to help you on
the road to recovery.

Popular with expats, Drs Nicolas & Asp offer sports
medicine and physiotherapy, as well as a range of
other exercises that can help prevent further injury.

Pilates is said to be the safest form of neuromuscular
reconditioning and back strengthening available and
is often provided by qualified physiotherapists. Classes
are offered by a number of gyms as part of their group
exercise schedules.

Blue Tree Clinics

Villa 967, Al Wasl St Al Manara **04 348 8262**
bluetreeclinics.com
Map **1 U5** Metro **Burj Khalifa/Dubai Mall**
This health clinic treats a range of health problems
and sports injuries including ADHD, headaches,
stress, scoliosis, neck pain, asthma and pain following
accidents. A number of physiotherapists and a
nutritionist are also based at the clinic.

California Chiropractic & Sports Medicine Center

Al Razi Bldg Healthcare City, Umm Hurair 2
04 429 8292
californiachiropracticcenter.com
Map **2 L7** Metro **Dubai Healthcare City**
Partnering a number of the UAE's major sports teams,
groups and events, this clinic is a real sports specialist
with experts who know their golf, running and cycling
every bit as well as they know their bones, tendons
and muscles.

Canadian Chiropractic & Natural Health Centre

Al Wasl St Jumeira 2 **04 342 0900**
Map **2 E5** Metro **Business Bay**
This clinic offers chiropractic treatments and
acupuncture as well as reflexology. They also treat
sports injuries and give advice for people with long
term back problems.

Dubai Bone & Joint Center

Al Razi Bldg Healthcare City, Umm Hurair 2
04 423 1400
dbaj.ae
Map **2 L7** Metro **Oud Metha**
Focuses on research into and treatment of musculoskeletal problems. Well-equipped with diagnostic

technologies, the centre offers rehabilitative services including physiotherapy and sports medicine, and has a very high standard of facilities for joint replacements, orthopaedic, and back and neck surgeries.

Dubai Physiotherapy & Family Medicine Clinic
Town Centre Jumeirah Jumeira 1 **04 349 6333**
dubaiphysio.com
Map **2 F4** Metro **Burj Khalifa/Dubai Mall**
Open since 1992, this is one of Dubai's most established clinics. Specialising in physiotherapy for musculoskeletal disorders and sports injuries, it also offers family medicine, sports therapy, osteopathy, acupuncture, nutrition, speech therapy, orthotics, podiatry and psychology.

Emirates European Medical Centre
Villa 119, Al Thanya St Umm Suqeim 2 **04 348 1166**
chiropracticdubai.com
Map **1 T5** Metro **First Gulf Bank**
Located in the Emirates European Medical Centre is Chiropractic Dubai, which has a team of experienced chiropractors and physiotherapists who can diagnose all manner of injuries and create a treatment plan to fit the individual's needs. Chiropractor Dr. Samuel Saukkonen is especially skilled in the treatment of lumbar disc herniation.

Orthosports Medical Center
Jumeira St Jumeira 1 **04 345 0601**
orthosp.com
Map **2 H4** Metro **Al Jafiliya**
Specialises in orthopaedics and sports medicine, offering physiotherapy, hydrotherapy and orthopaedic surgery to international standards. Sports therapy for fitness and injury rehabilitation and hydrotherapy for a range of conditions including obesity, arthritis, back pain and joint replacements are also available.

Osteopathic Health Centre
Al Wasl St Umm Suqeim 2 **04 348 7366**
osteopathydubai.com
Map **1 T5** Metro **Noor Bank**
The serene Osteopathic Health Centre has a number of therapists practising osteopathy in addition to physiotherapy, exercise, sports and massage therapy, chiropractic treatments, homeopathy and counselling.

Specialists at the centre have years' of experience helping clients develop a system of self-help, and giving support to people in pain. The effective, holistic approach of therapists can help reduce muscle tension and relieve pain rapidly and the therapists' bedside manner is sympathetic, friendly and understanding. Centres are also at: Uptown Mirdiff (04 288 8525) and Dubai Healthcare City (04 423 2096).

Up & Running Integrated Sports Medical Center
Al Wasl St Al Manara **04 328 4600**
upandrunningdubai.com
Map **1 U5** Metro **Noor Bank**
Another sports medicine and rehabilitation centre that you'll find teaming up with major events and local teams, staff here are mainly UK and Australia-trained with extensive backgrounds in treating sports and occupational injuries. Also offers VO2 max testing, sports massage and sessions such as clinical pilates.

Pharmacies

The UAE has a more relaxed policy on prescription drugs than many other countries and most can be bought over the counter, such as antibiotics (though it is best to seek a doctor's advice before taking antibiotics as over-use can result in a reduction in their ability to cure symptoms).

If you know what you need, it cuts out the hassle of having to see a doctor just to get a prescription. Pharmacists are willing to offer advice, but bear in mind that they don't know your medical history. Always tell the pharmacist if you have any pre-existing conditions and allergies or are taking other medication, and make sure that you understand the administration instructions in case these aren't available in English. You might find it frustrating that certain common medications from your home country are not available here (such as Gaviscon for infants and Pepto Bismol). But there are similar products (such as Infacol instead of infant Gaviscon). There are pharmacies all over the city with some open 24 hours a day, such as Life Pharmacy on Al Wasl Road in Jumeira (04 344 1122). Supermarkets and petrol station convenience stores sell basic medications and first aid equipment.

Medication

Certain medications do require a prescription, and there are some medications (such as codeine, diazepam and temazepam) that are actually banned here in the UAE, even though they are widely available on prescription in other countries. It is a crime to have these medicines in your possession or to take them, unless you can produce an official prescription from your doctor in your home country. The complete list of banned drugs can change regularly, so it is best to check with the Registration & Drug Control Department at the Ministry of Health (moh.gov.ae) before travelling with any medication.

If you have private cover, you'll find that most prescriptions are covered by your insurance, so always be sure to have your card with you as proof.

Dentists

Dentistry in Dubai is, like most other medical services, of a high standard with prices to match. Standard health insurance packages don't generally cover dentistry, unless it's for emergency treatment brought about by an accident. You may be able to pay an additional premium to cover dentistry, but the insurer may first want proof that you've had regular, six-monthly check-ups for the previous two or three years.

If you have insurance, you're entitled to basic dentistry at your assigned hospital, and if your hospital doesn't have a dental section, they'll refer you to a public hospital that does, such as Rashid Hospital. You will be charged Dhs.100 for the visit, as well as for any other services that are performed, such as cleaning and filling. Service is generally good, but the rates may not be any lower than at a private dental clinic.

For a standard filling you could be looking at paying anywhere between Dhs.100 and Dhs.1,000. If it is root canal treatment that you need, expect to part with anything from Dhs.600 to Dhs.3,000.

As well as routine and surgical dental treatment, cosmetic dentistry is also big business in Dubai, so if you're looking for a smile make-over, there is plenty of choice.

The clinics listed below are specialist dental clinics. Many primary healthcare clinics and hospitals also offer dental services. For a full listing of dental practices and surgeons in Dubai, visit askexplorer.com.

American Dental Clinic
Villa 54, Nr Dubai Zoo Jumeira 1 **04 344 0668**
americandentalclinic.com
Map **2 G4** Metro **Financial Centre**
The surgery has a wide range of cutting edge dental services available, and even offers virtual reality movie glasses so patients can watch a film during treatment – while seated in a massage chair!

British Dental Clinic
Nr Emirates NBD Jumeira 1 **04 342 1318**
britishdentalclinic.com
Map **2 F4** Metro **Financial Centre**
The clinic specialises in the most modern dental treatments, cosmetic dentistry, orthodontics, periodontics and implantology. Dentists are from Europe and Canada.

Charly Polyclinic
Shk Khalifa Bin Zayed St Al Karama **04 337 9191**
charlypolyclinic.com
Map **2 K5** Metro **Al Jafiliya**
This practice offers a range in dental services including cosmetic, laser, implant and general dentistry, orthodontics and oral surgery. They also have an ophthalmologist, gynaecologist and two homeopaths.

The Dental Center
Al Razi Bldg Healthcare City, Umm Hurair 2
04 375 2175
dentalhealthdubai.com
Map **2 L7** Metro **Dubai Healthcare City**
This bright and modern clinic in Healthcare City offers cutting edge dentistry. Routine dentistry and cosmetic procedures, including dental make-overs, are available.

The Dental SPA
Jumeira St Jumeira 3 **04 395 2005**
thedentalspa.org
Map **2 B4** Metro **Business Bay**
This clinic offers spa-like surroundings with calming mood music and aromatherapy pillows for your general or cosmetic dental treatment. You can also opt for foot and hand massages during your check-up.

The Dental Studio
Villa 61, Umm Al Sheif St Jumeira 3 **04 395 5095**
thedentalstudio.ae
Map **2 B5** Metro **Noor Bank**
This sleek, modern and Zen-like clinic is great to go to if you suffer from fear of the dentist as they are 'dental phobia certified' and will put you at ease. They offer a wide range of treatments, including child dentistry, bridal make-overs and speciality services.

Dr Michael's Dental Clinic
Villa 418 Jumeira 2 **04 349 5900**
drmichaels.com
Map **2 A5** Metro **Noor Bank**
This clinic prides itself on its personalised service, high safety standards, state-of-the-art dental equipment and an international team of dentists at its two branches in Jumeira and Umm Suqeim (04 394 9433).

Drs Nicolas & Asp
Villa 446, Jumeira St Jumeira 3
04 394 7777
nicolasandasp.com
Map **2 D4** Metro **Business Bay**
In addition to regular services, Drs Nicolas & Asp offers a state-of-the-art dental lab for creating implants, veneers and crowns on site. Additionally, cosmetic dentistry, advanced brace fitting and oral maxillofacial surgery are available at its various dental clinics.

Dubai London Clinic Dental Centre
Al Wasl St Jumeira 2 **04 378 2921**
dubailondonclinic.com
Map **2 E5** Metro **Burj Khalifa/Dubai Mall**
In addition to routine dental care and cosmetic treatment, the clinic has a periodontics specialist. One treatment available is 'clear braces' – a method of straightening teeth using clear aligner trays.

Dubai School of Dental Medicine

Bldg 34 Healthcare City, Umm Hurair 2
04 424 8777
dsdm.ac.ae
Map **2 L7** Metro **Dubai Healthcare City**
A specialist clinic offering a complete range of dental services including fillings, crowns and bridges, cosmetic dentistry, orthodontics, root canal treatment, oral surgery and periodontal treatment. There is also a paediatric dentistry department.

Dubai Sky Clinic

BurJuman Business Tower Al Mankhool **04 355 8808**
dubaiskyclinic.com
Map **2 L5** Metro **Al Fahidi**
Dubai Sky Clinic offers a full range of dental services from its high-tech clinic on the 21st floor of BurJuman Business Tower. Treatment rooms have floor-to-ceiling windows, and patients can watch DVDs or plug in their MP3 players.

GMC Clinics

Magrudy's Mall, Jumeira St Jumeira 1 **04 349 4880**
gmcclinics.com
Map **2 H4** Metro **Al Jafiliya**
There are several clinics around Dubai, and each houses a variety of specialists doctors as well as dentists. The clinics' philosophy is to care for the whole family, and they make an extra special effort to make children feel comfortable.

Park Dental Centre

Al Mardoof Bldg, Shk Zayed Rd Al Safa 1
04 346 6111
parkdentalcenter.ae
Map **2 C6** Metro **Business Bay**
Offers a comprehensive list of treatments including orthodontics, implantology, teeth whitening and oral surgery. The practice also offers the latest in root canal therapies and bridge and denture technology, as well as general and cosmetic dentistry.

Sansaya Clinic

Villa 795, Al Wasl St Al Safa 2 **04 394 0044**
sansayaclinic.com
Map **2 A5** Metro **Noor Bank**
Services include general, cosmetic and periodontal dentistry, as well as orthodontics and paediatric dental care. The practice also offers specialist restorative procedures, and anxiety-free dentistry.

Seven Dental Centre

Nr HSBC, Jumeira St Jumeira 3 **04 395 2177**
sevendentalcentre.com
Map **2 C4** Metro **Business Bay**
Dentists at this practice speak French, English and Arabic and offer a 'no pain' policy. Cosmetic

reconstruction, prosthetic and orthodontic procedures available plus routine and children's dentistry.

Swedish Dental Clinic

Al Reem Tower, Al Maktoum St Al Muraqqabat
04 223 1297
Map **2 N5** Metro **Baniyas Square**
This experienced practice, established in Deira back in 1985, offers dental and orthodontic care for patients of all ages. Dr. Nabil Mockbil qualified in Sweden.

Swiss Dental Clinic

Crowne Plaza Trade Center 1 **04 332 1444**
swissdentalclinic.com
Map **2 H5** Metro **Emirates Towers**
Dr Marco Fedele seeks to soothe a patient's anxieties by thoroughly explaining the procedure. General and aesthetic dentistry is available, as well as orthodontic treatments. He speaks English, French, German, Italian and Spanish.

Talass Orthodontic & Dental Center

Villa 114, Jumeira St Jumeira 1 **04 349 2220**
talass.com
Map **2 G4** Metro **Financial Centre**
Dr. M. F. Talass and his team of Western-educated, multilingual dental specialists offer family and general dentistry as well as cosmetic dentistry, orthodontics, root canal therapy and TMJ (jaw joint) treatments.

Tower Clinic

Ibn Sina Bldg Healthcare City, Umm Hurair 2
04 362 2939
towerclinic.com
Map **2 L7** Metro **Dubai Healthcare City**
Tower Clinic is one of the UAE's largest private dental clinics. It offers general dentistry and orthodontics plus oral surgery and Zoom!, a one-hour, in-office tooth whitening treatment.

Opticians

You're never far from an optician in Dubai, with most malls and shopping centres having at least one outlet.

The dry, dusty environment in Dubai can cause problems for eyes, even if you've had no trouble in the past. Natural tear or refresher eye drops can increase eye comfort and are available in most opticians and pharmacies. Spending lengthy periods in air-conditioned environments can cause problems for contact lens wearers. Opticians can advise on the most suitable lenses. Sunglasses are an essential accessory in Dubai and prescription lenses are widely available.

For eye problems requiring specialist treatment, many hospitals and clinics, including Moorfields Eye Hospital (moorfields.ae) and The American

Hospital Dubai (ahdubai.com), have well-equipped ophthalmology departments. If you want to ditch the glasses, a number of clinics and medical centres offer laser eye surgery. Prices start from around Dhs.4,000 per eye. All good laser surgery packages should include a complete year's follow-up care.

Even if you've never had an eye test in your life, you will need to undergo one in order to get a driving licence. This test can be carried out at most opticians for a minimal fee, sometimes free of charge.

Al Jaber Optical MoE, Al Barsha 1, 04 341 1322, *aljaberoptical.com*
Anna by Top Vision Optics Nr Dune Centre, Al Hudaiba, 04 398 4888, *annabytopvisionoptics.com*
Atlanta Vision Clinic Al Wasl St, Umm Al Sheif, 04 348 6233, *dubailasik.com*
Barakat Optical The Walk at JBR, Marsa Dubai, 04 427 0565, *barakatoptical.com*
Dubai Optical Ibn Battuta, Jabal Ali 1, 04 368 5540, *dubaioptical.com*
Eye Boutique. The Dubai Mall, Downtown Dubai, 04 325 3291 *eyeboutiqueme.com*
Grand Optics MoE, Al Barsha 1, 04 341 0350, *grandoptics.com*
Gulf Eye Center Fairmont, Trade Center 1, 04 329 1977, *gulfeyecenter.com*
Lunettes House of Quality Optics Jumeira 1, 04 349 2270
Lutfi Optical Centre Umm Hurair 2, 04 324 1865, *lutfioptical.com*
Magrabi Optical MoE, Al Barsha 1, 04 341 0445, *magrabioptical.com*
Moorfields Eye Hospital > *p.135* Al Razi Bldg, Healthcare City, Umm Hurair 2, 04 429 7888, *moorfields.ae*
Sharif Eye Center Ibn Sina Bldg, Healthcare City, Umm Hurair 2, 04 423 3664, *sharifeyecenter.com*
Vasan Eye Care Zabeel Plaza, Zabeel Rd, Dubai International Airport, 04 357 9444, *vasaneye.com*
Vision Express Ibn Battuta, 04 368 5926, *alshaya.com*
Yateem Optician Al Mizhar 1, 04 284 5505, *yateemgroup.com*

Alternative Therapies

The Ministry of Health grants licences to and administrates qualified practitioners of alternative medicine through its dedicated department for Traditional, Complementary & Alternative Medicine. Natural medicine can be very specialised, so when consulting with someone, do make sure that you ask questions and explain your needs and expectations. This will ensure that practitioners can indeed help with your situation. Prices vary greatly but are

generally comparable to western medicine, however most insurance companies will not cover the costs of alternative therapies. As always, word of mouth is the best way of establishing who might offer the most appropriate treatment. Yoga and pilates are available at a number of studios and health clubs. Fitness-focused, clinical and classic, meditative forms of yoga are available. There is also a range of clinics that provide 'well-being' services, such as U Concept, which combines personal fitness, a balanced nutrition plan and numerous relaxation techniques, in order to help you achieve the healthy lifestyle you're looking for.

Dubai Herbal & Treatment Centre (04 335 1200) in Oud Metha offers a range of treatments and diagnostic procedures from conventional and alternative medical schools of thought. You can get everything from a tailor-made detox plan, to ozone therapy and allergy testing, as well as massage and a myriad of other complimentary medicines. See dubaihtc.com for more information.

Talise Spa & Wellness Polyclinic at Madinat Jumeirah (jumeirah.com/mjtalise) is a haven of tranquillity that houses a bona fide medical centre, directed by the multilingual Dr Elizabeth Makk. Dr Makk is also qualified in homeopathy and nutrition and offers holistic treatments as well as focusing on disease prevention. Call 04 366 6810 for an appointment.

Cosmetic Treatment & Surgery

Dubai is becoming established as a luxury healthcare destination. Cosmetic surgery is at the heart of this growing industry and the city now boasts a mass of clinics that specialise in reducing, reshaping, removing and enlarging various parts of your anatomy. The clinics listed below are exclusively cosmetic practices, but many of the private hospitals and independent clinics offer cosmetic services including aesthetic and reconstructive surgery. As with all medical facilities, standards are generally high, but it's worth checking out a few different clinics before you go under the knife. If you want a bit of sprucing and don't fancy being sliced into, a lot of the cosmetic clinics will do Botox and other non-surgical treatments.

Aesthetica Clinic Bldg 39, Healthcare City, Umm Hurair 2, 04 429 8533, *aestheticaclinic.com*
American Academy of Cosmetic Surgery Hospital Bldg 73, Healthcare City, Umm Hurair 2, 04 423 7600, *aacsh.com*
Biolite Aesthetic Clinic Villa 57, Al Thanya St, Umm Suqeim 2, 04 346 6641, *biolitedubai.com*
CosmeSurge Nr Emirates Hospital, Jumeira 2, 04 344 5915, *cosmesurge.com*

www.moorfields.ae

Bringing over 200 years of British specialist eye care to the UAE.

Long recognised as one of the leading eye hospitals in the world we have replicated the exceptional standards of our London hospital here in the UAE. Our state-of-the-art facility in Dubai Healthcare City is fully equipped and staffed by highly qualified consultants.

Call 04 429 7888 or visit www.moorfields.ae today.

Moorfields
Eye Hospital Dubai
A BRANCH OF MOORFIELDS LONDON

EM59013/31/3/15

LASIK | CATARACT | COSMETIC | PAEDIATRIC | RETINA | CORNEA | GLAUCOMA | STRABISMUS

Dermalase Clinic Villa 4, Jumeira St, Jumeira 2, 04 349 7880, *dermalaseclinic.com*
Dubai Cosmetic Surgery Nr Choithrams, Al Wasl St, Al Manara, 04 348 5575, *dubaicosmeticsurgery.com*
Dubai Medical Village Nr Sunset Mall, Jumeira 3, 04 346 9999, *medicalvillage.ae*
EuroMed Clinic Villa 611, Jumeira St, Umm Suqeim 04 394 5422, *euromedclinicdubai.com*
General Medical Centre Trade Centre Apartments, Trade Center 2, 04 331 3544, *gmcclinics.com*
Gulf Speciality Hospital Hamarain Centre, Al Muraqqabat, 04 269 9717, *gshdubai.net*
Imperial Healthcare Institute Healthcare City, Umm Hurair 2, 04 439 3737, *imperialhealth.org*
Kaya Skin Clinic Mirdif, 04 283 9200, *kayaskinclinic.me*
London Centre For Aesthetic Surgery Healthcare City, Umm Hurair 2, 04 375 2393, *lcas.com*
Rebecca Treston Aesthetics At EuroMed Jumeira 3, 04 394 5422, *euromedclinicdubai.com*

Nutritionists & Slimming

Slimming clubs offer nutritional advice and hospitals can perform weight loss surgery. Dietary advice for diabetes, allergies, menopause, pregnancy and digestive disorders such as coeliac disease is on hand.

Mediclinic Welcare Hospital provides a dietary counselling service and unique diet plan. The American Hospital offers a food and nutrition service managed and provided by ADNH Compass. The hospital also runs a Diabetic Centre of Excellence. Emirates Hospital has a weight reduction programme that uses liquid supplements and a very low calorie diet. The hospital also has experts who specialise in medically supervised weight reduction, obesity in children, obesity in diabetic patients and patients with high blood pressure or cholesterol. It also offers gastric band fitting.

For a more holistic approach to nutrition, the Osteopathic Health Centre offers a complete nutritionist service. You'll find dieticians at Cooper Health Clinic, Dubai London Clinic Medical & Surgical Centre and Drs Nicolas & Asp. The Organic Foods and Cafe sells fresh organic and biodynamic food and supplements, and a nutritionist is on hand at all its stores to give tailor-made advice on supplements and vitamins, detox, weight loss and aromatherapy.

BiteRite
Lotus Apartments Marsa Dubai **04 292 8888**
biterite.ae
Map **1 J5** Metro **Nakheel**
Eat a nutritionally balanced meal in the cafe or use its tailor-made healthy eating service. Healthy meals are delivered to your door. The BiteRite Plan offers an online menu with over 100 varieties of meals.

BodySmart
Meadows Town Centre Al Thanyah 4 **04 363 8318**
bodysmart.ae
Map **1 K8** Metro **Nakheel**
Hypoxi combines cardiovascular exercise with applied pressure to increase blood flow to fatty problem areas. Improvements are within four weeks and goals achieved by week 12. You wear what feels like a wet suit and speed walk on a treadmill or cycle inside a vacuum pod. Results are felt in reduced inches (and each session the trainer will measure your chest, waist and hips). Weight loss can also occur. There's also a Hypoxi studio at the Aviation Club (04 282 4122, aviationclub.ae).

Eternel Clinic
Villa 397, Jumeira St Jumeira 2 **04 344 0008**
eternelclinic.com
Map **2 D4** Metro **Business Bay**
Offers mesotherapy for cellulite treatment, Botox, laser hair removal, slimming treatments as well as general wellness coaching. Mesotherapy involves administering microinjections of conventional or homeopathic medicines, vitamins, minerals or amino acids into the middle layer of skin.

Good Habits
04 344 9692
goodhabitsuae.com
Meetings focused on healthy eating are held every week across Dubai, and often include food tasting and cookery demos. Exercise classes are also organised and individual programmes are offered.

Health Factory
Warehouse 26 Al Qouz Ind. 3 **04 347 3808**
healthfactory.com
Map **1 T7** Metro **First Gulf Bank**
After a consultation you'll be sent three meals a day to help you lose weight or get healthy according to your needs. There's also a diet plan for mothers-to-be, a diabetic meal plan, and healthy eating for kids.

Live'ly
Villa 925, Al Wasl St Al Manara **04 348 1008**
lively.ae
Map **1 U5** Metro **Noor Bank**
This new centre specialises in nutritional, educational and catering services to help people to manage their weight and live healthier lives.

Perfect Figure
Aviation Club Al Garhoud **050 255 9402**
allbodysolutions.com
Map **2 M8** Metro **GGICO**
This studio creates personal weight loss and toning programmes, which combine exercise using Hypoxi and Vacunaut machines with nutritional advice.

Right Bite
Al Hudaiba Awards Bldg Madinat Dubai Al Melaheyah **04 338 8763**
right-bite.com
Map **2 J4** Metro **Al Jafiliya**
Right Bite offers a tailor-made healthy eating service. Tasty, low calorie, low fat and low cholesterol meals, devised by their own dieticians, are freshly prepared and delivered to your door.

Slim Spa
Al Attar Tower, Shk Zayed Rd Trade Center 2
04 321 3485
slimspa.ae
Map **2 G6** Metro **Financial Centre**
There's a wide range of non-invasive treatments for weight and inch-loss, cellulite reduction, body sculpting, anti-ageing and rejuvenation. Slim Spa also offers personalised programmes, four and eight-week packages, massages and facial treatments.

VLCC
Indigo Central 2 Al Safa 2 **04 338 7897**
vlccwellness.com
Map **1 V6** Metro **Noor Bank**
VLCC offers hair removal, beauty services and customised weight loss programmes which combine dietary advice, exercise and toning and detox therapies. There are women-only centres at Marsa Dubai (04 447 1488) and Uptown Mirdiff (04 288 4880).

Counselling & Therapy

Starting a new life in a different country can be a stressful process, and sometimes it can help just to talk through the emotional aspects. Mental health services in the UAE are not as developed as in some other countries; Al Amal is Dubai's only psychiatric hospital, and Rashid Hospital has a dedicated psychiatric ward.

There are however a number of well-regarded therapy centres offering services including counselling, psychodynamic therapy, family and couples' therapy, paediatric psychiatry, treatment of mental health disorders and learning difficulties support. Dubai Community Health Centre offers a range of counselling and psychiatric services and provides space for support group meetings; it comes highly recommended, as does the Counselling & Development Clinic. In addition to the clinics and centres listed, the British Medical Consulting Centre and Drs Nicolas & Asp have counsellors, family therapists and psychiatrists on staff. Dubai Herbal & Treatment Centre has a psychodynamic counsellor, a psychologist and a learning specialist, and is recommended for child counselling services.

In the neighbouring emirate of Sharjah, Al Tamimi Stables offers Animal Assisted Therapy to help provide people with a positive outlook (tamimistables.com).

Counselling & Development Clinic
Nr Jumeirah Beach Park Jumeira 3 **04 394 6122**
drmccarthypsychologyclinic.com
Map **2 D4** Metro **Business Bay**
This centre caters to adults and children. As well as assessing and treating psychological disorders, the clinic offers counselling, family therapy and couples' clinics. It is well regarded for the treatment and management of bipolar disorder (manic depression), obsessive-compulsive disorder and panic attacks.

Dubai Community Health Centre
Nr Al Nasr Leisureland Oud Metha **04 507 8000**
dubaicommunityhealthcentre.org
Map **2 L6** Metro **Oud Metha**
A private, non-profit facility with counselling, family and marriage therapy, psychology, speech therapy and parenting courses. It also offers occupational therapy, dietetics and special needs education.

Health Psychology UAE
Well Woman Clinic Al Satwa **04 332 7117**
healthpsychuae.com
Map **2 J5** Metro **World Trade Centre**
Dr Melanie C Schlatter is a health psychologist helping people to learn to manage the psychological impact of illnesses and medical conditions that they have. She also offers preventative health psychology in the form of stress management and coping with anxiety, phobias, depression, grief and anger. Her website covers some of the main questions people have about receiving psychological help.

Human Relations Institute & Clinics
Jumeirah Business Center 3 Al Thanyah 5 **04 365 8498**
hridubai.com
Map **1 L5** Metro **DAMAC**
The HRI's services include clinical, forensic, organisational, educational and domestic psychology. It offers counselling, life coaching, psychotherapy and workshops for conditions including anxiety, phobias, addiction, behavioural and eating disorders, stress, low self-confidence and depression.

LifeWorks
Villa 996 Al Wasl St Umm Suqeim 1 **04 394 2464**
counsellingdubai.com
Map **1 V5** Metro **Noor Bank**
Whether you need self-confidence, personal insight, Cognitive Behavioural Therapy, marriage counselling, help with phobias or would like to join a workshop, this centre can help. Therapists are experienced in treating people from diverse backgrounds.

Al Barsha Pond Park

FAMILY & PARENTING

Bringing your family out to Dubai, or starting one while you're here, can be a fantastic experience. There's plenty of help, great education facilities and a whole range of activities for the kids. This section covers much of that, but also takes a look at some of the more sobering topics like bereavement and divorce; issues that you may be faced with during your time here.

Marriage

When living in the UAE under Shariah law, marriage is the only legal bond for a man and a woman to establish a relationship and have children. It is illegal to live together as a couple if you are unmarried and you cannot have children out of wedlock.

If you're Christian or Catholic, you can marry in a church; if you'd prefer a non-religious marriage, you

may be able to tie the knot at your embassy. Muslim weddings take place before a Shariah court; the man must be a Muslim while the woman can be non-Muslim, and a Muslim woman cannot marry a non-Muslim man in the UAE. Whatever your nationality, you should contact your embassy to notify them of your intent to get married and find out the exact process and paperwork necessary. Once wed, you will need to register the marriage with your embassy to get it validated internationally.

The Big Day

This chapter outlines the basics to get you started organising your wedding and reception. For step-by-step procedures, including specifics on which documents to take where, see Explorer's *Dubai How-To* guide, which covers Christian, Catholic, Muslim and Hindu weddings.

The Ceremony
While the wedding must be conducted in either a church, court or at your embassy, you have a large choice of where to have a wedding blessing and the reception. Many couples choose to have a small church ceremony and then celebrate at one of the luxury hotels, on the beach or even aboard a yacht.

Anglican wedding ceremonies can take place at the Holy Trinity Church, Dubai at Christ Church in Jabal Ali, Dubai, St Andrew's Church in Abu Dhabi or St Martin's Church in Sharjah, all of which are recognised by the UAE government. Ministers from the Anglican Church can also marry people at other approved locations.

Roman Catholic marriages can take place at St Mary's Catholic Church in Dubai (saintmarysdubai.com). To marry in a Roman Catholic church, at least one of the partners must be Roman Catholic, and both of them must be resident in Dubai. Women must be at least 18, men must be over 21.

Hindu marriages are conducted by the maharaj at Dubai's Hindu Temple in Bur Dubai. The Hindu Temple is run in conjunction with the Indian consulate who solemnise the marriage. Both parties must be Hindi and at least one of the couple should be an Indian citizen with a Dubai residence visa; there should also be three witnesses who have a UAE residence visa.

People of other religions (Buddhist, Sikh or Bahai) may be able to get married at their embassies or consulates. A Muslim marrying another Muslim can apply at the marriage section of the Dubai Courts, next to Maktoum Bridge.

Fees for a church wedding are around Dhs.2,000 and you can get married on any day of the week if a minister/vicar is available. You will typically need two or three witnesses who are UAE residents.

There are certain conditions for a church wedding:
- At least one member of the couple has to have been baptised (or equivalent)
- At least one of the couple must have a UAE residence visa; expats on a visit visa cannot get married in the UAE
- Both people must be aged 18 or over

Depending on your faith and denomination, you may have to go for counselling sessions and regular church services. You will also need to register certain documents including birth and christening certificates, and written evidence that each is single and free to marry (divorce papers or a letter from your embassy). You will need a Banns certificate or certificate of no impediment, which takes up to three weeks to process and needs to be applied for at your home embassy. For example, the British embassy will display a notice of marriage for 21 days and, assuming no one objects, you are then free to tie the knot.

The Paperwork
In order to register the marriage, your wedding certificate has to be translated into Arabic by a court-approved legal translator. Take this, and the original, along with your essential documents to the Notary Public Office at the Dubai Courts. They will certify the documents for a fee of about Dhs.80. Next you will need to go to the Ministry of Justice (ejustice.gov.ae) to authenticate the signature and the Notary Public seal. Just when you think it's all over, you still have to go to the Ministry of Foreign Affairs (behind the distinctive Etisalat building in Deira) to authenticate the seal of the Ministry of Justice. Now you just need to pop back to your embassy for final legal verification.

In Preparation
Get organised! Visit the Dubai Bride Show (thebrideshow. com), held every April at the Dubai International Exhibition Centre; it covers everything you'll need for your big day.

The Reception
When it comes to your reception, any one of Dubai's stunning hotels would make the perfect venue and they will assist you with everything from the music and menus to floorplans and florists.

Arabian Ranches Golf Club
Shk Mohd Bin Zayed Rd Arabian Ranches, Wadi Al Safa 6 **04 366 3000**
arabianranchesgolfdubai.com
Map **1 Q13**
Choose between the spacious Baker-Finch indoor venue or one of the magnificent terraces featuring stunning views of the golf course. Packages start from Dhs.270 per person.

Atlantis The Palm > *p.275*
Crescent St Nakhlat Jumeira **04 426 0000**
atlantisthepalm.com
Map **1 N1** Metro **Nakheel**
Choose from various unique venues, from the private tent at Asateer, or the grand luxurious Atlantis Ballroom, or a personalised venue such as the idyllic Dolphin Bay Beach for a more unique touch, The Lost Chambers Aquarium, or even the picture perfect Palm Grove for an intimate setting.

Bateaux Dubai
Nr British Embassy Al Hamriya **04 814 5553**
bateauxdubai.com
Map **2 M5** Metro **Baniyas Square**
Opt for a unique and tasteful reception on the water, where the wedding planner will take care of every last detail from floral arrangements to signature menus.

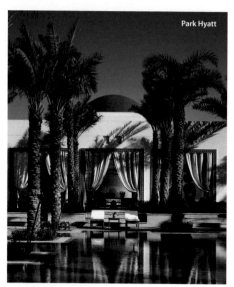
Park Hyatt

network; if this is the case, a wedding planner can provide invaluable assistance and ensure that the big day runs smoothly.

Try Fonoon (fonoon-uae.com), Aghareed (www.aghareed.com) or Couture Events (coutureevents.ae), who will help you every step of the way – from the paperwork to the seating plan. Upscale & Posh offers a tailored service for flowers and wedding reception decorations (upscaleandposh.com). Brides needn't worry about missing out on the princess treatment since most spas offer tailor-made services for them.

Try the following photographers for your big day: Blue Eye Picture (photographerdubai.ae) or Itsoura (www.itsoura.com).

Wedding Ideas

There are numerous resources available in Dubai to help you plan your wedding and provide inspirational ideas. Bride Club ME (brideclubme.com) is an online portal with a comprehensive list of vendors (offering everything from dresses, to food, to venues), as well as features, forums and photos of weddings they've helped organise. If you want to wow your guests with a stunning, otherworldly theatrical wedding venue design, check out Ali Bakhtiar Designs LLC (alibakhtiardesigns.com).

Park Hyatt Dubai
Nr Dubai Creek Golf & Yacht Club Port Saeed
04 602 1234
dubai.park.hyatt.com
Map **2 M7** Metro **GGICO**
Packages including catering, floral arrangements and special guest room rates are available in the ballroom and garden, for an indoor or outdoor day to remember.

The Westin Dubai Mina Seyahi Beach Resort & Marina
Al Sufouh St Marsa Dubai **04 399 4141**
westinminaseyahi.com
Map **1 M5** Metro **Nakheel**
The Serdaal Ballroom can accommodate up to 450 guests in gala dinner set-up style, while the outdoor Arabian Terrace offers breathtaking views of the Gulf and the Palm Jumeirah.

XVA Art Hotel
Al Fahidi Historical Neighbourhood Al Souk Al Kabeer **04 353 5383**
xvahotel.com
Map **2 M4** Metro **Al Fahidi**
This boutique hotel in the heart of the historical Al Fahidi neighbourhood makes for a stylish setting for a reception – the alfresco courtyard is relaxed, casual and stunning when candlelit at night.

All the Frills
One of the challenges of getting married outside your country of origin is being far away from your support

Family Law

All matters of family law, from divorce and child custody cases through to wills and inheritance, are generally dealt with under Shariah (Islamic) law or by the laws of your home country. In any instance it is best to contact your embassy for an approved list of law firms to assist you, and then deal with a company that is familiar with both the law in your home country and here in Dubai.

Afridi & Angell Emirates Towers, Trade Center 2, 04 330 3900, *afridi-angell.com*
Al Tamimi & Company DIFC, Zaa'beel 2, 04 364 1641, *tamimi.com*
Bayat Legal Services Al Moosa Tower 2, Trade Center 1, 04 355 4646, *ilsgroup.com*
The Rights Lawyers Building 8, Media City, Al Sufouh 2, 04 390 3646, *therightslawyers.com*
Trench & Associates Albwardy Bldg, Al Mankhool, 04 355 3146, *trenchlaw.com*

Wills
It is essential that you have a will in place, and it's especially important to seek legal advice if you become a property owner in Dubai. That's because, under Shariah law, the rules for who inherits property

after someone's death differ from those in other countries. For example, in the event of your death, it may be that your sons (or brother, if you don't have any sons) are first in line for inheritance and your wife could end up with nothing.

The UAE does claim to guarantee a woman's right to inherit property, but it's worth making your will watertight to this. Also, if a family member dies, the government can freeze his/her accounts until all liabilities of your husband are cleared such as loans, credit cards and business debts; this can happen very quickly but can easily be overturned if a UAE will is in place. Providing each other with a 'Power of Attorney' document in addition to a will is also recommended to prevent this.

A Dubai-based lawyer can assist you with a locally viable will (do check that they are authorised by the government to write wills), or contact The Wills Specialists (willsuae.com), or Just Wills (just-wills.net), part of a UK-based estate planning organisation with a UAE presence.

Making A Will

Firstly, make an appointment with a licensed estate planner, preferably one with knowledge of the law of your home country. You will need to take passport copies, contact details of executors and proof of assets. A will can be drawn up, and needs to be attested at your embassy or consulate. Have this attested document translated at an authorised typing centre, and then attested by a notary public in the emirate you live in.

Divorce

Divorce, like other matters of family law, is either governed by UAE law, Shariah law, or by the laws of the individuals' originating country. If the parties are from different countries, the applicable law is that from where the marriage was solemnised.

The first step in any divorce hearing is to look at reconciliation with the aid of the Family Guidance and Reformation Centre, which functions under the Department of Justice at Dubai Courts (04 334 7777). Anyone experiencing marital problems or family disputes can use this service, and you can file a complaint against your spouse by simply providing the centre with copies of your ID (passport or Resident Identity Card) and your marriage certificate.

If counsellors at the centre are unable to help a couple to reach an amicable settlement then the case may get referred to the Court of First Instance, Dubai Courts for legal proceedings to take place. This is when you need to seek legal advice. At this stage you will need the services of an expat law firm, who can advise you which 'jurisdiction' (either UAE or your home country) is the most appropriate for you in terms of cost, timescale and outcome.

If the case is straightforward and uncontested you may not even need to attend court, and you can expect to pay around Dhs.10,000, inclusive of all court fees and other expenses. The procedure is fairly standard for Christian, Roman Catholic and Hindu religions: the couple apply to the court for a decree nisi, stating their reasons for divorce, and if the judge finds the reasons to be convincing, the divorce will be granted.

In cases of child custody, the paramount concern of the court is the child's welfare. In Shariah law, the custody of a child classed as a minor, will be the mother's unless there are compelling reasons to decide otherwise.

Death

There's never a more tragic time than when a friend or relative dies. While there is a lot of bureaucracy surrounding a death here, there are companies who can take care of the practical matters and advise you on all aspects of the mourning process.

In the event of a death outside a hospital, notify the police by dialling 999. The police will then file a report and the body will be taken to Rashid Hospital where a doctor will determine the cause of death and produce a report; this usually takes three to seven days.

If the death occurs in a hospital, that hospital will be responsible for completing the initial death report and transferring the deceased to the mortuary.

The first administrative step is to get a death certificate, which is needed before you can arrange a local burial or cremation, or send the body home. Thereafter, the process for registering a death will vary depending on the deceased's religion and whether he or she was an expat or not.

It's best to get in touch with the relevant embassy for guidelines on what the next steps are. To help guide you through the process, contact the private company, Middle East Funeral Services (mefs.ae).

Helping Hand

Middle East Funeral Services (mefs.ae) has partnered up with a network of Worldwide Repatriation Specialists, and are able to manage the entire process, from the initial stages (including obtaining death certificates and registrations) until the deceased is at the funeral home of choice.

Death Certificate

On receipt of the doctor's report, the hospital will issue a death certificate declaration (not to be confused with the actual death certificate). Take this, along with the deceased's passport, to the nearest police department, which will issue a No Objection

Certificate (NOC) addressed to Al Baraha Hospital. You should also request NOCs addressed to the mortuary for embalming, the airport for transportation and the hospital for the release of the body. This letter, plus the death declaration certificate, original passport and copies should be taken to the Department of Preventative Medicine at Al Baraha Hospital, where the death certificate will be issued in Arabic. This must be translated into the appropriate language if the body is being sent home.

The certificate must then be attested for by the Ministry of Health, the Ministry of Foreign Affairs and registered at the General Directorate of Residency and Foreign Affairs (GDRFA). You will also need to cancel the deceased's visa at the GDRFA. Since Islam requires that the body be buried immediately, the death certificate and registration procedures for deceased Muslims can be performed after the burial.

You will also need to inform the embassy of the deceased's home country – the embassy will register the death, issue an embassy death certificate and cancel the passport. This can cost up to Dhs.1,000 depending on which country's embassy you are dealing with.

Local Burial Or Cremation

Before the deceased can be buried or cremated locally, you will need the following documentation: cancelled passport, death certificate, proof that the visa was cancelled and an NOC from the sponsor stating that all debts have been settled.

For a Hindu cremation, you must also provide written permission from the next of kin, as well as that person's passport. The procedure for local cremation and burial can be complicated and changes often, so you will need to contact the Dubai Municipality (04 221 5555, dm.gov.ae), the Christian Cemetery (04 337 0247), or the Hindu Temple in Bur Dubai (04 353 5334) for the latest information.

If you want to arrange a local burial it can be done at the Muslim or Christian cemeteries in Dubai. The cost of a burial is Dhs.1,100 for an adult and Dhs.350 for a child. You will need to get a coffin made, as well as organise transport to the burial site. Cremation is also possible, but the deceased must have had a valid Dubai residence visa, and a cremation permit must be obtained from the municipality, which costs Dhs.1,100. There's also a Dhs.2,500 fee for the cremation.

Transporting Ashes Back Home

If the deceased has been cremated in Dubai, you might want to send their ashes back to their home country. The best people to contact are at the dnata Export Office, Cargo Village. Call them on 04 211 1111. They can provide further assistance and information.

Returning The Deceased Home

To return the deceased to his or her country of origin, you will need to book your own ticket with the airline of your choosing (if you want to travel with the body) as well as make shipping arrangements through dnata (04 211 1111), which will handle the body at Cargo Village and process any required documentation.

The deceased will need to be embalmed before reaching Cargo Village, and you will need the original death certificates (both the local certificate and the embassy certificate), the NOC from Dubai Police, an NOC from the embassy of the deceased (which must be the same as the destination to which they are being sent), the cancelled passport and visa and a copy of the air tickets specifying flight details.

You will also need to purchase a coffin. Embalming can be arranged through the Dubai Health Authority and will cost around Dhs.1,000, which includes the embalming certificate. The body must be identified before and after embalming, after which it should be transferred to Cargo Village for shipping.

Cargo fees are calculated by the kilo and distance travelled. The total charge can be anywhere between Dhs.1,500 to Dhs.30,000. A coffin costs upwards of Dhs.1,200. When preparing the documentation, remember that dnata will require seven copies of each document and the translation.

You'll also need to arrange for a funeral company to receive the body when it reaches its destination. It is not obligatory for anyone to accompany the body during the flight home.

Having A Baby

The standard of maternity healthcare in Dubai, either private or government, is excellent. As long as you have insurance or the means to pay, there is no reason to return to your home country to give birth. It's also easier to get by with one income in Dubai, meaning that many mothers get to stay at home with their new babies rather than having to return to work. And, you will have access to cheap childcare and babysitting services here.

However, there are a few disadvantages to be aware of. Maternity leave is paltry: just 45 days paid leave, and no paternity leave. You can take another month unpaid, provided your employer agrees. If you need extra time for medical reasons, you can take up to 100 days, although this is only granted upon production of a medical certificate from your doctor. Plus, there's also the absence of the family support network you may have had back home. Fortunately, there are strong networks of other parents who meet up regularly and offer plenty of support to each other; for example, see dubaimums.com and expatwoman.com.

Registering Your New Baby

If you're planning to have a baby in Dubai, the following is an essential checklist to ensure your child is properly registered once born.

Get a UAE birth certificate

You have 30 days after the birth to get your newborn's UAE birth certificate, which is needed to apply for a passport and residence visa.

After the baby is born, the hospital will issue a notification of birth upon receipt of copies of both parents' passports, the attested marriage certificate, and a fee of Dhs.50.

To get the actual UAE birth certificate, take the birth notification and the above documents to the Mediexpress office (04 272 7190) at Al Baraha Hospital. For a fee of Dhs.490, they will issue the English birth certificate and the Arabic birth certificate, and have both attested by the Ministry of Health and the Ministry of Foreign Affairs.

Register the birth with your embassy

Once you have the UAE birth certificate, you can register the birth with your embassy. They will issue you with a registration of birth certificate that can be used to apply for the passport. (Note that this is not the birth certificate from your home country; that will need to be applied for separately). The fees and process will vary depending on nationality. Visit your embassy's website to download the application form and find out more about the procedure.

Apply for your baby's passport

Once the birth is registered with your embassy, you can apply for the passport. You'll need to provide the birth certificate (UAE or home nationality), the registration of birth certificate (issued by your embassy), one parent's birth certificate and two passport-sized photos of your child. The fees for the passport and courier service will vary depending on nationality. The procedure should take four to six weeks.

Apply for a birth certificate from your home country

Depending on your nationality, you may have to wait up to six months from registering the birth with your embassy to request a birth certificate, either at your embassy or in some cases, online. The certificate will then be couriered to you.

Get a residence visa for your baby

You have 120 days from the birth to get a UAE residence visa for your newborn or risk being fined Dhs.100 a day. To qualify, the parent (sponsor) must earn at least Dhs.4,000 (or Dhs.3,000 plus accommodation) per month. You'll need the following documents (originals and copies unless otherwise specified):

- Typed application form
- Baby's passport
- Baby's attested birth certificates (both in English and Arabic)
- Three passport-sized photos of the baby
- Attested marriage certificate
- Sponsor (parent)'s passport (copy)
- Mother's passport and visa page (copy)
- Sponsor's attested salary certificate (copy)
- Ejari tenancy contract
- Resident ID of the sponsor
- Last three months' bank statements (not printed online statements)
- Dhs.310 application fee and typing fee

Pick up an application form from a typing office and have them complete it for you. Then, visit the residency section of the General Directorate of Residency & Foreigners Affairs. Hand in the completed form and supporting documents at the Family Entry Permit counter. The residence visa will be sent to you through a courier service or can be collected.

Born Back Home

Babies born abroad to expat mums with UAE residency are required to have a residence visa or visit visa of their own to enter the UAE. The application should be filed by the father or family provider, along with the essential documents, a salary certificate and a copy of the newly born child's birth certificate.

Let's just clear up some of the misunderstandings and urban myths about having a baby in Dubai.

Here we go:
- Your baby will have an Arabic birth certificate
- He/she will not have UAE citizenship or a passport
- Breastfeeding is allowed in the UAE, just be discreet
- Home births are not permitted in the UAE
- You must be married before giving birth
- The husband is allowed to be present at the birth at most private hospitals

Overseas Births

If you have your baby back in your home country, you will need to organise their residence or visit visa before entering the UAE. The application should be filed by the father along with his passport and residence visa, salary certificate, and a copy of the birth certificate.

Pregnant Out Of Wedlock

If you fall pregnant but are not married then there is no reason to panic, but there are several decisions that you will need to make fairly quickly. It is illegal to have a baby out of wedlock while you are a resident in the UAE and if you deliver your baby at any hospital here, private or public, and can't produce a marriage certificate, you will most likely face a prison sentence. Therefore, as soon as you see the blue lines on the pregnancy test, you need to sort a few things out.

The easiest solution is to have a quick wedding, after which you can go on to have antenatal care in a government or private hospital without any fear of punishment. If this is not an option, you can stay in Dubai until a reasonable time before you are due to give birth, and even have your antenatal check-ups in a private hospital. But you will need to ensure that you return to your home country to actually deliver the baby. Once you have delivered you can return to Dubai with the baby: there are no rules against being a single mother here.

From Bump To Birth

As soon as you find out that you're going to have a baby, you need to choose where to go for your maternity care. Most expecting expat mothers opt for a private hospital rather than a government hospital, and as long as you have private health insurance this should be affordable, if not free. Bear in mind that some hospitals may charge extra for certain procedures, such as caesarean sections, costing around Dhs.20,000, and epidurals, which normally cost about Dhs.2,000. Having twins, triplets or more will cost you more, too. There are also additional costs for resuscitation after the birth, Neonatal Intensive Care Unit (NICU), your husband staying overnight in the room with you, and, in some hospitals, baby's nappies and wet wipes.

Unlike some other countries, in the UAE the delivery will be performed by the doctor who treats you throughout your pregnancy, rather than a midwife. Therefore, it's important to find a doctor that you are comfortable with from the beginning, as he or she will be with you 'from bump to birth'. You can choose to have all your antenatal care at a local clinic, as many obstetricians are then authorised to deliver at a certain hospital. It's also more than likely that you will be able to receive more frequent check-ups and scans in the run up to the birth as part of your care, including a 4D scan.

See the Health section for listings of maternity clinics; Mediclinic City Hospital, which has one of the largest Neonatal Intensive Care Units (NICU) in the UAE, and American Hospital are by far the most popular. There is also an NICU at the government-run Latifa Hospital; this is the largest NICU facility in the Middle East and provides treatment for babies from 24 weeks onwards.

Water Births

While water births are not available in Dubai, you can go to the Al Ain Cromwell Women and Children's Hospital (alaincromwell.com). However, you'll need to sign up to their whole delivery package which will cost you between Dhs.12,000 and Dhs.14,000 if you don't have insurance, or if your insurance won't cover it.

Healthy Pregnancy

To prepare you for parenthood why not sign up to an antenatal class. Health Bay Polyclinic in Umm Suqeim (healthbayclinic.com) runs classes costing Dhs.1,500 for four hour-long sessions; Mediclinic City Hospital has an antenatal programme (Dhs.1,725 for eight classes or Dhs.250 per class); and Cooper Clinic (cooperhealthclinic.com) offers one-day courses including an introduction to baby massage.

Compulsory Vaccinations

By law, parents are required to ensure that their baby's immunisation shots are up to date. While the first vaccines are given as soon as your baby is born, you will be required to return to your hospital or clinic every two months until the baby is one year old. At 18 months, babies receive three booster shots and then do not have any more until they are aged five.

The UAE's national immunisation programme includes Hepatitis A + B, polio, MMR (measles, mumps and German measles), chicken pox, Hib and whooping cough. Do bring copies of your child's vaccination records from your home country with you when moving to Dubai.

Adoption

While you can't adopt a UAE National baby, many couples in Dubai adopt children from Africa, Asia and Far Eastern countries. Adoption regulations vary according to which country the child comes from, but once you clear the requirements of that country, and complete the adoption process, you will have no problems bringing your new child into the UAE on your sponsorship. Check with your embassy about the procedure for applying for citizenship of your home country for your new child.

You are advised to go through the Hague Adoption Convention, an internationally recognised process. You'll be required to provide a file of essential documents, undergo a police check, and complete a 12 hour home-study programme – which involves psychological analysis and parental preparation. After a home visit and final interview, you will receive 'approval', and your home study file can be handed over to any international adoption agency recognised by the UAE, and your name added to their adoption list. It is then a matter of waiting for the phone to ring. If you are considering adopting a child, a good place to start is the Adoption Support Group Dubai. Join the Yahoo group (groups.yahoo.com/group/asgdubai), or email asgdubai@yahoogroups.com.

Single Parents

It is possible to live in Dubai and sponsor your children as a single parent, even if you are a woman. There will, however, be a number of extra requirements that you need to meet, including a minimum salary level and a letter of no objection from the other parent (or a death certificate, in the case of a deceased spouse). You may also need to show your divorce certificate, but it is best to visit the Immigration Department to find out the exact requirements, as these may change.

Being a working single parent in Dubai may seem daunting for a number of reasons. Firstly, as an expat, your support system may not be as great as back home, where friends and family can help out, and, secondly, in a country where marriage and family are so important you may feel a little like the 'odd one out'. However, once you get used to people enquiring where your husband is (if you have a child with you, people assume you're married), there are actually lots of advantages of living in Dubai as a working single parent. For one thing, there's the standard of childcare: the nurseries in Dubai are very good and a few offer full daycare; they are also generally much more affordable than in your home country. There is also the option of having a live-in nanny, which means that you can not only work as a single parent, but can enjoy an active social life too.

Mother & Baby Groups

Dubai is a great place for young families because it is safe, has great weather and close-knit expat communities. While you may not have the helpful hand of family close by, there are lots of mother and baby groups to keep you and your baby happy. The city's parks make great spots for mothers to meet, and many of them have walking tracks which are excellent for a bit of pram pushing exercise. As pavements are rare in Dubai, going for a stroll with your pushchair may be a challenge – malls are of course an option, The Walk at Jumeirah Beach Residence has nice wide walkways and Uptown Mirdiff's pedestrianised area provides traffic-free space, as does much of the Downtown Dubai area.

Dubai Mums Club
dubaimumsclub.com
This group operates via its online site and through meet-ups. Registered members have access to the club forum, as well as special discounts. Members can also consult an online paediatrician and fitness instructor.

Mirdif Mums Dubai
Mirdif **055 735 4759**
Metro **Rashidiya**
Mirdif has a strong family population, so it is fitting that the mums get together to share coffee mornings, afternoons in the park and activity days. The group also has some social outings without the kids, which is a great way to make new friends. The group is now primarily based on Facebook. Search 'Mirdif Mums'.

Mumcierge
050 640 8322
mumcierge.com
An online concierge club for busy parents wanting to set up activities for their children. The group has weekly coffee meetings at Lime Tree Cafe & Kitchen in Al Qouz.

Hiring A Nanny

Many families choose to hire live-in, full-time maids (nannies) to assist them with childcare and babysitting. It is a relatively simple process, detailed in Explorer's *Dubai How-To* guide, which explains all the documents you will need and procedures to follow to organise a domestic worker visa.

If both you and your spouse work full time then a live-in maid is really your best option as there is no official network of childminders. Your maid can also help with cleaning, washing, cooking and other household jobs.

Finding the right live-in person can certainly be a challenge. There are a number of registered agencies in Dubai, which organise everything from interviews through to airfares and the visa; they will charge an agency fee of around Dhs.3,500. It is preferable to recruit someone who is already in Dubai, and therefore your best bet would be to find an expat who is leaving the country and no longer needs their maid. Speak to other parents and check/put up notices on Spinneys and community noticeboards, as check the ads on expatwoman.com and dubizzle.com.

Residence Visa

If you employ a full-time live-in maid you will need to sponsor her for a residence visa. You can only sponsor a maid from the following countries: India, Sri Lanka, Philippines, Ethiopia, Bangladesh, and Indonesia. You must have a salary above Dhs.6,000 per month and be able to provide her with housing (many apartments and villas have a maid's room inside or outside), medical insurance and benefits, which include an airfare back to her home country at least once every two years, food, clothing and toiletries. Depending upon the nationality of your live-in maid (and whether or not you need to organise her entry permit into the UAE) you may have to visit their local embassy to get a contract drawn up before beginning the sponsorship process (see When You Arrive).

Can You Afford It?

Once you've made the decision to employ a nanny, you'll need to work out if you can actually afford to do so. The average monthly wage is around Dhs.2,000 although you should allow an extra Dhs.400 for things like phone credit, food, clothes and toiletries. One of the prerequisites is an airfare to her home country, which is likely to cost about Dhs.3,500. The residence visa is Dhs.5,080 a year and her annual medical will cost Dhs.325. You'll also need to make a few one-off payments: Dhs.600 for health insurance, Dhs.140 for a Resident ID card and a refundable residence visa deposit of Dhs.2,030.

First Aid Courses

Make sure that you and your maid are able to cope with minor medical emergencies and take a first aid course. The Perfect Help (theperfecthelp. com) run a number of training courses for maids, including first aid. Back To Basics also run courses in several languages (backtobasicsme.com).

Pros & Cons

There are plenty of advantages to having a live-in nanny. Not only is it relatively inexpensive, but having someone to look after your child means that you have reliable childcare support as and when you need it, and can enjoy the odd night out!

On the other hand, you should keep in mind that first aid and childcare qualifications are not legally required for your babysitters or childcare workers in the UAE, so it's worth doing your research to find someone with experience. Networking and word of mouth can pay dividends as many parents with young children will be in the same boat as you.

Babysitting

Domestic help agencies can provide part-time babysitters, although there is no guarantee that you will get the same babysitter every time.

Ask around your neighbourhood to see if any of the local maids or teenagers are available for ad hoc evening babysitting, or try your child's nursery, as classroom assistants are often up for a bit of extra work and they will already have a rapport with your children. If you do manage to find someone for part-time babysitting, the rate ranges from Dhs.30 to Dhs.40 per hour. Western childminders are most likely to charge more than this.

Activities For Kids

During the cooler months (October to May), kids can enjoy the parks and beaches around Dubai, which house playgrounds for varying ages, as well as tennis and basketball courts. Try the boating lake in Safa Park, the petting zoo in Mushrif Park, and the camel and pony rides in Creek Park. There are also water parks in and around the city; however, while swimming is obviously popular, there are few public pools. Mushrif Park has separate women's and men's pools but, outside the hotels and health clubs, the only other options are villa compound pools or the beach. See Things to See & Do for more information.

During the warmer months (June to September) the many amusement centres and kids' play areas keep your brood from getting bored. Fun Corner is a soft play centre with a few arcade games and small rides located in Bin Sougat Centre, Al Ghurair City, and the Spinneys Centre on Al Wasl Road. Fun City (funcity. ae) offers similar facilities, plus scheduled classes, and can be found in the Arabian Center, Oasis Centre, Reef Mall, Ibn Battuta, Mercato, Lamcy Plaza and Century Mall. Located near Dubai Garden Centre along Sheikh Zayed Road, Mini Monsters (minimonsters.ae) is the UAE's largest indoor soft play venue.

There are various sports and activity clubs that run after-school activities and summer camps, plus some great kids' attractions such as KidZania. The Activities chapter covers a range of hobbies for children. Visit uae4kidz.biz for up-to-date information on family events and activities.

Keep an eye on the local press too as, most months, there's something going on for families whether that's shows on the ice, exhibitions or one-off entertainment. Many malls have specific kiddie entertainment during Eid, DSF and other popular calendar events.

After-School Activities

Many schools will run ECAs (Extra Curricular Activities) from kindergarten upwards. Generally, the younger years only have one ECA a week for around 30-60 minutes directly after school, while the older years may have multiple classes at various times. School-run ECAs are often included in the school fees, however, independent companies also hold classes at schools during the afternoons and evenings and charge term fees (which are far from cheap), as well as at weekends and holidays.

Turning Pointe runs ballet classes for all ages in various schools around Dubai, as does Kids' Theatre Works, and Active Sports Academy has a range of sports classes. If your kids are sports players (or you want them to be) there are a number of academies that can develop their talents – would-be Federers should sign up with the Clark Francis Tennis Academy, budding Beckhams can hone their skills with the International Football Academy or UAE English Soccer School of Excellence, wanna-be Olympic gold medallists should dive in with Australian International Swim Schools and potential Bruce Lees can kick it with various clubs around Dubai (see Martial Arts). Many parents get together in the parks (in the winter) and play centres (in the summer) around Dubai for their own impromptu after-school activities, so new families shouldn't worry about long afternoons and bored kids.

Keep The Kids Happy

For a taste of the past, and guaranteed to get the little ones excited, flag down the Desert Chill icecream van. Complete with melodic tinkling tunes, this classic van travels around several communities in Dubai all week long. See desertchill.ae for the schedule or call 050 612 2108.

Indoor

From around May to September, having fun in air-conditioned venues like these is often the best option.

Aquaplay

Mirdif City Centre 04 231 6307
theplaymania.com
Map **2 P12** Metro **Rashidiya**
An indoor play centre dedicated to water fun, this gem in Mirdif City Centre boasts a swinging pirate ship, log flume ride, water guns and bumper boats.

It's a child-friendly change from the usual outdoor water parks and available at a fraction of the cost. Plus, the fact that it's indoors makes it perfect for the summer months.

Cheeky Monkeys Playland

Al Barsha Mall Al Barsha 2 **04 385 0875**
cheekymonkeys.ae
Map **1 Q7** Metro **Sharaf DG**
This hugely popular play centre is well suited to little ones, thanks to its toddler-friendly soft play areas as well as Art Garden, Sports Room and Princess Room. It's a great spot for hosting birthday parties, and there's a cafe selling snacks and freshly squeezed juices where mums and dads can relax while the kids play.

Children's City

Gate 1, Creek Park Umm Hurair 2 **04 334 0808**
childrencity.ae
Map **2 L7** Metro **Dubai Healthcare City**
An edutainment venue in Creek Park with hands-on interactive displays and learning zones where kids have fun and can swot up on subjects like science, geography and even astronomy at the planetarium. In addition to the permanent displays, there are regular events such as drum shows and light displays.

Favourite Things

Marsa Dubai 04 434 1984
favouritethings.com
Map **1 K5** Metro **Jumeirah Lakes Towers**
The perfect place to leave your kids happily playing for an hour or two, Favourite Things, in Dubai Marina Mall,

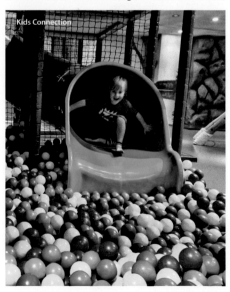
Kids Connection

has more than enough activities to keep the rug rats happy. There's everything from toddlers' soft play area to a mini race track, jungle gym and dressing up area. Parents can join in, watch from the comfort of the cafe, or even leave the tots in the centre's capable hands while they go shopping.

Kiddies Cafe
Lake Shore Tower Cluster Y, JLT **04 360 8571**
kiddiescafe.com
Map **1 L5** Metro **Jumeirah Lakes Towers**
With a two-storey play house, small jungle gym, and art and craft area, kids are entertained for hours in this new JLT-based play area. With a floor-to-ceiling window separating the play area and cafe, parents can enjoy a coffee with full view of their little ones playing.

Kids Connection
Wafi Umm Hurair 2 **04 327 9011**
Map **2 L7** Metro **Dubai Healthcare City**
Located on the first floor of Wafi Mall, this bright, colourful attraction brings the outside in with a variety of wooden park attractions in a very green, woodland inspired setting. Kids can climb, swing, seesaw and slide while mum and dad enjoy a coffee in the Cafe Court – or burn off some energy on the trampolines, bouncy castle and climbing wall. The soft play area with a ball pool is great for toddlers too. Prices range from Dhs.3 to Dhs.27.

Kidz Venture > *p.239*
Ibn Battuta Jabal Ali 1 **04 368 4130**
kidzventure.ae
Map **1 G5** Metro **Ibn Battuta**
Open seven days a week, from 7am to 10pm, Kidz Venture offers a variety of childcare options as and when you need them. From nursery and after-school programmes, to drop 'n' shop babysitting, birthday parties, and arts and crafts activities, there is always something to keep your little one amused.

Le Petit Palais
The Dubai Mall, Burj Khalifa **04 382 7333**
Map **2 F6** Metro **Burj Khalifa/Dubai Mall**
Located in the ever-sophisticated Galeries Lafayette in The Dubai Mall, the French-themed play centre is the perfect place for kids to have fun while parents shop. It's like a miniature city where children can play at being grown-ups, with a mini supermarket, salon and even a karaoke room, as well as other games and soft play areas to keep them entertained.

Little Explorers
Mirdif City Center Mirdif
Map **2 P12** Metro **Rashidiya**
Little Explorers at Playnation Mirdif City Centre is an edutainment centre for children from two to seven

years old. Focused on acquiring skills in a fun and safe environment, this venue is set out in five distinctly themed zones offering plenty of variety to keep kids interested; there's everything from seeing how fast you can run, to scientific experiments that investigate the natural environment. With games and activities spanning over 97 different exhibits that get the brain ticking and stimulate the senses, children can discover hidden talents and new skills. There are also a variety of birthday party packages available.

Magic Planet
Mall of the Emirates Al Barsha 1 **04 341 4444**
magicplanet.ae
Map **1 R6** Metro **Mall of the Emirates**
A blaring and boisterous play centre that's a huge hit with families, Magic Planet's many attractions include bowling lanes, bumper cars and video games. Play the arcade games and collect tickets to exchange for prizes or, for a more exhilarating game experience, check out the XD Theatre with its interactive 3D and 4D cinema effects.

Peekaboo Creative Play Centre
The Village Jumeira 1 **04 344 7122**
peekaboo.ae
Map **2 H4** Metro **Emirates Towers**
Here there's a packed schedule of organised activities, which aim to be fun while developing the children's creativity and providing an educational experience. Children aged zero to seven can join in with cooking, nursery rhymes, yoga, arts, crafts and more. Kids under three-and-a-half must be accompanied by an adult. The centre operates an hourly fee structure with memberships also available. Also at Mall of the Emirates and Ibn Battuta.

Skillz Youth Facility
Madinat Jumeirah Al Sufouh 1 **050 480 7670**
skillz.ae
Map **1 R5** Metro **Mall of the Emirates**
Dedicated children's gym with secure entry and specialised trainers who provide an environment for kids aged seven to 16 to exercise, while adults can use the extensive club facilities. Includes running machines, spinning bikes, cross trainers, fitness trampolines and rowing machines all tailored to the needs and interests of the younger gym-goer.

Zebra Crossing
Nr Noor Islamic Bank MS Al Qouz Ind. 1 **050 559 4903**
zebra-crossing.com
Map **2 A6** Metro **Noor Bank**
Join Ziggi the Zebra at this play centre, which boasts a host of soft play areas and bouncy castles. It's the perfect spot for a party, with activities ranging from arts and crafts and face painting to magic shows and

puppet shows. There's even the option to host a spa party at the Zebra Lounge, where little princesses can enjoy mini mani-pedis.

Classes

Keep the grey matter working and learn something new or perfect an existing skill with classes and courses from these clubs and service providers.

Apple Seeds

Gold & Diamond Park Al Qouz Ind. 3 **04 380 6064**
appleseedsdubai.com
Map **1 S6** Metro **Mall of the Emirates**
This New-York themed indoor playground has some innovative ideas and features an NYC taxi cab and apartment, yoga block skyscraper, shape sorter garden, deli with play foods, Lego table, magnet wall and even more. There are also classes covering everything from science to ballet, cooking to art – so lots to keep the little ones amused. They also have character and confidence building programmes for four to 13 year olds.

Creche Out

Wafi Umm Hurair 2 **056 293 0168**
crecheoutinternational.com
Map **2 L7** Metro **Dubai Healthcare City**
Established UK childcare company Creche Out has recently arrived in Dubai, offering fully supervised care within its facility in Wafi. There are a range of classes to attend with babies, toddlers, and young children, from music to dance. The facility also hosts parties, with a different packages available for every budget.

DuGym Gymnastics Club

050 553 6283
dugym.com
DuGym offers gymnastics and trampoline coaching to children of all ages and abilities. Established in 2000, the club now operates at 15 locations including Wellington International School, Jumeirah English Speaking School and Emirates International School. Classes are held from Sunday to Thursday. Contact Suzanne on the above number for more details.

Kids' Theatre Works

DUCTAC Al Barsha 1 **050 158 5653**
kidstheatreworks.com
Map **1 R6** Metro **Mall of the Emirates**
This club holds classes in creative drama, musical theatre, acting, dance, youth theatre, music and scene work for children aged three and over; if your kids are budding superstars, Kids' Theatre Works is a good start. It runs classes at DUCTAC (the theatre inside Mall of the Emirates), Uptown Mirdiff Primary, Jabal Ali, Gems Academies and the American School of Dubai.

Kidville

The Walk at JBR Marsa Dubai **04 440 1220**
mykidville.ae
Map **1 K4** Metro **Jumeirah Lakes Towers**
Based on an innovative concept pioneered in New York, Kidville offers newborns to six year olds a unique range of classes that include musical journeys on the Rockin' Railroad, building 3D art projects in Construction Junction, and exploring a variety of paints, dough, crayons, chalk and collage in My Big Messy Art Class. There's also the Kidville University, an alternative programme for pre-schoolers. Other branches include MotorCity (04 454 2760) and Uptown Mirdiff (04 236 3648).

My Gym UAE

Villa 520, Jumeira St Jumeira 3 **04 394 3962**
mygymuae.com
Map **2 B4** Metro **Noor Bank**
Offering a wide range of programmes for kids up to 13 years old, the expert staff-led classes that combine increases in strength, agility, coordination and flexibility with the development of social skills and self-esteem.

Tickles & Giggles

The Walk at JBR Marsa Dubai **04 432 8681**
ticklesandgiggles.com
Map **1 K4** Metro **Jumeirah Lakes Towers**
Tickles & Giggles has a kids' salon and spa, and offers unique classes such as baby yoga, etiquette classes, arts and crafts and nursery rhymes. It also hosts ultra-trendy parties for kids (no bears or tank engines in sight), and will match decorations and the menu to your chosen theme. You can become a member on the website, where you can order party supplies as well as make online bookings.

Scouts & Guides

Girls can join the Girl Guides, Brownies or Rainbows clubs in Dubai. Email girlguidingdubai@gmail.com for more information about meeting times and places. Scout groups operate too. Contact gasplampke@msn.com for information on Cub Scouts and hoytjk2@aol.com for information on Boy Scouts of America.

The majority of Scout and Guide groups in Dubai are held at schools, so check with your child's school. With each new group comes a need for adult volunteers. If you have experience with Scout or Guide groups, or your child was once a member, contact Mary Dunn (alistair@emirates.net.ae) to get involved.

British Guides In Foreign Countries

girlguidingdubai.wordpress.com
Groups for girls of various ages include Rainbows (five to seven years), Brownies (seven to 10), Guides (10 to 14), and Senior Section (14 to 25) with groups in Al

Safa, Jabal Ali, Dubai Investment Park, Mirdif, Silicon Oasis, Emirates Living and Arabian Ranches.

The Scouts Association (British Scouting Overseas)

britishscoutingoverseas.org.uk
The Scouts Association encourages the development of youngsters through weekly activities and outings for ages six to 18 and 18-25. Contact Steve Sutton (dc_middle-east@bsomail.org.uk) for more information.

Scouts Abroad

From April 2012, the existing Scout Areas of British Scouts in Western Europe (BSWE) and British Groups Abroad (BGA) were merged into a new Scout Area referred to as 'British Scouting Overseas' (BSO), which functions to support UK Scouting based outside the UK. The area is classed as an independent educational UK charity.

Summer Camps

Soaring temperatures that have everyone cooped up indoors can make summer a challenging time to entertain the kids. To help keep boredom at bay, various organisations throughout Dubai run summer camps during the hottest months, while several nurseries also offer summer daycare for young children.

While many activities will be inside air-conditioned buildings there are plenty that will have your little ones getting a good dose of fresh air. Most language schools run summer courses for kids (see Language Courses), or if you'd rather see them having fun over the holidays, many leisure clubs offer summer camps that focus on sports, arts and crafts. Alternatively, contact Active Sports Academy, which arranges sporty summer camps at various venues around the city.

Another option is to sign them up for sailing lessons – if there's a breeze, then being out on the water can be significantly cooler than on land, and that way, they're still getting some fresh air. Clubs such as Dubai Offshore Sailing Club (DOSC – dosc.ae) run dinghy sailing courses for kids.

Active Sports Academy

Al Rebat St Al Kheeran **050 559 7055**
activeuae.com
Map **2 M10** Metro **Emirates**
In operation for 14 years, Active Sports Academy organises various coaching classes in multiple venues around Dubai, including at campuses after school. It teaches tennis, soccer, cricket, basketball, swimming and gymnastics and runs various tournaments, as well as holiday camps through all school break periods, including spring, Eid, Christmas and summer.

Blossom Village Nursery

Villa 43, Al Ragay St Umm Suqeim 1 **04 394 8837**
theblossomnursery.com
Map **2 A5** Metro **Noor Bank**
This vibrant nursery will give your child plenty of stimulation as it emphasises creativity, play and personal development – and its summer camp, Passports, is no different. Based on the British Early Years Foundation Stage and aimed at children aged two and older, it's an imaginative summer adventure that includes arts and crafts, mini Olympics, swimming, baking and more. Flexible enrolment and pick up at 1pm, 3pm, 5pm or 6pm are available, making it a good choice if both parents work full time.

Dubai Holiday Camps

Grosvenor House Business Tower Al Thanyah 1 **04 420 3732**
dubaiholidaycamps.com
Map **1 P6** Metro **Dubai Internet City**
One of the longest established camps in the UAE, Dubai Holiday Camps provides a range of holiday activities for children aged three to 14 since its inception in 1998. Juniors take part in classroom-based fun like arts and crafts, storytelling, movie time and face painting, while older kids (those aged five to 14) can try their hands at a range of sports as well as talent shows, dance, drama and cooking classes. The experienced staff are English speakers with additional languages and trained to handle large groups of kids.

E-Sports

Al Garhoud **04 282 4540**
esportsuae.com
Map **2 M8** Metro **GGICO**
Each day follows a set structure at E-Sports Holiday Camps – there are around 20 activities to choose from that are rotated throughout the week with kids taking part in five activities a day. (Guaranteed to tire them out!) These range from sports like football, tennis and swimming to arts and crafts, and dodgeball. Led by professional, enthusiastic teachers and assistants, E-Sports camps are a firm favourite with youngsters and a popular choice for busy parents.

Gulf Star Sports

050 429 4860
gulfstarsports.com
These action-packed, multi-activity camps are targeted at children aged from two to 17. There's a strong focus on sports and children and teens can try their hands (and feet) at everything from football, cricket and basketball to martial arts, dance, and water polo, as well as drama and crafts. Professional, enthusiastic staff and top notch facilities make for an unforgettable experience. Staff are happy to meet with parents to discuss their children's needs.

PICKING A HOTEL FOR YOUR PET

Choosing a cattery or kennel for your pets while you're on holiday? You'll be pleased (or perhaps amused) to discover that Dubai offers something one step up from a simple kennel or cattery – pet hotels.

Many of us moved here with our furry friends in tow, or have since adopted a pet. If you have to travel and can't find anyone to care for your animals, here are some options.

Pet Accommodation

Kennels and catteries are of a high standard. Segregated spaces for dogs and cats are the norm, and well-established organisations, such as Dubai Kennels and Cattery (DKC) have their own clinic.

But what can your pet expect from his or her stay at a pet hotel? Luxury suites, landscaped gardens, play areas, doggie boot-camps and even swimming pools for the hotter months. We're serious. Some places even offer advanced ventilation and air-conditioning to minimise smells and maximise comfort.

Some rooms overlook gardens and fountains, and come with outdoor space for exercise, shaded green areas, pet gyms and treadmills. At the seven-star Urban Tail Pet Resort, rooms are equipped with plasma TVs so your hound can kick back and watch his favourite soaps, and webcams to monitor the animals, while some play soothing animal music to settle any nervous visitors.

In safe hands

While you're away, who will cuddle your pets and care for them as much as you? Well, fear not, as many of the well-established kennels in Dubai employ well-trained staff on a 24-hour a day pet watch, who know how to handle your homesick hounds and crabby kittens. If you're worried about the staff-to-pet ratio though, other boarding places even offer dedicated, one-to-one supervision.

Budget boarding

Before you blow your budget on your holiday, take into account how much it will cost to board your pets. Paying for your pet's luxury accommodation doesn't come cheap, especially if they have developed a taste for gourmet steak or salmon. Rates vary from Dhs.85 per night (off peak) up to Dhs.100.

All of Dubai's pet-boarding accommodation gets booked up well in advance. Plan ahead.

Pet Boarding

Dubai Kennels & Cattery > *p.153* Al Rebat St, Umm Ramoul, 04 211 4800, *dkc.ae*

Pet Palace
26th St, Al Quoz Industrial Area 4 04 323 6993, *petpalace.ae*

Paws Pet Planet
Nr Green Community, Dubai Investment Park 2, 04 884 8894 *pawspetplanet.com*

Posh Paws
The Desert Equestrian Club, Wadi Al Armadi, 050 273 0973 *poshpawsdubai.com*

Urban Tails Pet Resort > *p.157*
Nr Green Community, Dubai Investment Park 2, 04 884 8847 *urbantailsdubai.com*

PETS

Having a pet is always a comfort, and Dubai has no shortage of abandoned animals in need of homes. If you're not sure you can commit for the long term, there are also options to foster animals as cat and dog homes especially are overcrowded.

You should check with your landlord what the pet policy is before you move in. In many cases it is not permitted to keep a pet, particularly in apartments. Some landlords will be amenable if you negotiate, but it is advisable to get any permission in writing to avoid difficult situations further down the line.

Pets are banned from parks and beaches, and popular walkways such as The Walk at JBR are also off limits, so finding a place for a good long walk can be a challenge. Paws Pet Planet (pawspetplanet.com) has a 20,000 square feet outdoor and indoor dog park, where you can let your pooch run off the leash.

When walking your dog, keep it on a short leash. Remember that dogs are considered by many conservative Muslims as unclean and are traditionally only kept for guarding property, so just be mindful of these attitudes when you are out in public. Be sure to keep your pet indoors or within your garden to avoid contact with strays and to prevent any problems with frightened neighbours. Dubai has a significant problem with strays, although both Feline Friends (050 451 0058) and K9 Friends (04 887 8739) are hard-working animal charities that take in as many as they can. The Dubai Municipality is also helping to fix the stray problem.

In addition to having dogs kept on leads at all times when walking, certain dogs have to be muzzled in Dubai when walked in public (see dkc.ae for details). All cats and dogs must be registered, microchipped and vaccinated, or you could face fines and confiscation.

Hot Dogs

The summer heat in Dubai is a serious health risk for cats, dogs and other pets. They cannot sweat to regulate body temperature as humans can, and so are at risk from heat-related issues, which can be fatal. Never walk your dog in the summer sun – be prepared to get up at dawn to ensure your dog gets the exercise it needs in a bearable temperature. Remember too that hot pavements will burn your pooch's paws. If your dog is bred for colder climes, think very carefully before you subject your pet to desert heat. Keeping the animal penned up inside with the air conditioning on is not a healthy option either; a dog needs regular exercise.

While rare, there have been reports of dogs being stolen, either to be sold to unscrupulous pet shops or for dog fighting. Ensure your garden is secure and don't let your dog roam around on the street. If you witness animal abuse see dm.gov.ae for advice or call 04 289 1114.

Sleek Salukis

The saluki is the breed of dog most commonly associated with the region; they are used in traditional forms of hunting and resemble a greyhound in many ways. The Arabian Saluki Centre (02 575 5330) offers a wealth of information and care for these thoroughbred dogs and even welcomes visitors to learn about them.

Moving Your Pet

Pets may be brought into the UAE without quarantine as long as they are microchipped and vaccinated with verifying documentation, including a government health certificate from the country of origin; however, you'll also need an import permit. You cannot import cats and dogs under four months old and all pets must arrive as manifest cargo with a valid rabies vaccination more than 21 days before their arrival. Imports from some countries will also be subjected to a rabies test. For more information visit petimport.moew.gov.ae and create an account.

There are certain breeds of dog that are banned from being imported into the UAE: pit bull terriers, Argentinean and Brazilian mastiffs, Japanese tosa inu, American Staffordshire terriers, Rottweilers and any wolf hybrids; the UAE also bans any dogs crossed with any of the banned breeds listed. There are other breeds which, while not banned outright, have restrictions on them too. Make sure you check with the municipality before you embark on the process. Dubai Kennels & Cattery provides a detailed guide to importing and exporting pets.

The international removal company Allied Pickfords (alliedpickfords.ae, 04 818 0400) offers a pet relocation service and can provide useful information on how best to transport your pet.

Buying a Pet

If you want to buy a pet it makes sense to start by visiting some of the rescue centres in Dubai – there are many abandoned animals in need of a home. K9 Friends (04 887 8739) helps to rehome stray and injured dogs, many of which are abandoned family pets looking for a second chance. See k9friends.com for more information. Another useful website for

how can you save 100 homeless dogs?

easy... just spay one

We are a voluntary organisation that rescues and rehomes stray & abandoned dogs in the UAE. Our finances are solely dependent on fundraising and donations. Log on to our website to find out how you can help.

info@k9friends.com
www.k9friends.com

k9 friends
homes for life

pet owners in the Emirates is petdubai.com. Feline Friends (050 451 0058) is a non-profit organisation, aiming to improve the lives of cats by rescuing and rehoming stray cats and kittens. It has a 24 hour telephone answering service as well as a useful website, felinefriendsdubai.com. The saluki is a breed of dog most commonly associated with the region; they are used in traditional forms of hunting. The Arabian Saluki Center (02 575 5330) can provide information on all aspects of the care of these animals. Many 'desert dogs' descend from the saluki. If you'd like to adopt your own desert dog, contact K9 Friends (k9friends.com).

Vaccinations & Registration

You should inoculate dogs annually against rabies, distemper, canine hepatitis, leptospirosis, parainfluenza virus and parvovirus. There is an optional vaccination against kennel cough which is recommended for all dogs going to kennels, doggy daycare or dog-training in mixed classes. Cats have to be vaccinated against rabies, feline rhinotracheitis, calicivirus and panleukopnia. You must also register your pet with the Dubai Municipality (04 289 1114); this is an annual registration which requires all cats and dogs to have the above vaccinations. They are then microchipped and given a plastic neck tag (there's a different colour for each year), as well as normal ID tags. If the municipality picks up an animal without a tag and chip, it is treated as a stray and there is a strong chance it will be put down. Registration can all be done at any vets or at Dubai Municipality Veterinary Services, and costs approximately Dhs.1,000.

Taking Care Of Turtles

Turtles are native to the waters off Dubai, but with more construction, boats and pollution, they are having a tough time. Luckily, there are organisations doing their bit to help save the turtles. One such rehabilitation project is a collaboration between the Jumeirah Group and the Wildlife Protection Office, with veterinary support provided by Dubai Falcon Clinic & Central Veterinary Research Laboratory. To see how you can help, go to facebook.com/turtle.rehabilitation.

Taking Your Pet Home

To take your pet home contact the airline you will be using – the animal may be able to travel with you or as unaccompanied cargo. Many boarding kennels and vets offer an export service, including Dubai Kennels & Cattery and The Doghouse (dubaidoghouse.com).

Vets, Kennels & Boarding

Standards of care at Dubai's veterinary clinics are reasonably high. Prices do not vary dramatically, but the Deira Veterinary Clinic (04 258 1881) and Al Barsha Veterinary Clinic (04 340 8601) are a little cheaper than the rest. Dubai Municipality has a veterinary services department (04 289 1114) next to Mushrif Park that only vaccinates animals.

There are also several new seven-star pet resorts such as Urban Tails, with luxury suites, landscaped gardens, a pet gym with treadmills, a doggie bootcamp, an outdoor swimming pool and fountains. Paws Pet Planet is another posh pad for pooches (see Where To Walk Your Dog). The Nad Al Shiba Veterinary Hospital (04 323 4412) also treats more exotic animals and birds. Kennels are generally of a good standard, although spaces are limited during peak times (summer and Christmas) – try Dubai Kennels & Cattery (see below).

An alternative is to use an at-home pet-sitting service – someone will come into your house at least once a day to feed and exercise your pet for a reasonable fee (for a bit extra they might even water your plants). For further information on pet shops see Shopping. There are a number of firms that offer a variety of grooming treatments from the basic (shampooing, medicated baths and nail clipping) to the more indulgent, like fashion advice.

Below is our pick of just some of the many vets and boarding and training schools.

For more listings see askexplorer.com

Al Barsha Veterinary Clinic SS Lootah Bldg, Al Barsha 1, 04 340 8601, *abvc.ae*
Blue Oasis Veterinary Clinic *>p.159* Dubai Investment Park (Green Community), 04 884 8580, *blueoasisvetclinic.com*
Doggies Palace Nr Al Quoz Cemetery, Al Qouz 1, 04 339 3737, *doggiespalace.com*
Dubai Kennels & Cattery Pet Boarding *>p.153* Al Rebat St, Umm Ramoul, 04 211 4800, *dkc.ae*
Dubai Kennels & Cattery *>p.153* New vet clinic in MotorCity, 04 211 4800, *dkc.ae*
Energetic Panacea Wasl St, Jumeira 2, 04 344 7812
European Veterinary Centre Villa 63, Umm Al Sheif St, Jumeira 3, 04 380 4415, *evc.ae*
Jumeirah Veterinary Clinic Jumeira St, Jumeira 3, 04 394 2276
Modern Veterinary Clinic Al Wasl St, Umm Suqeim 1, 04 395 3131, *vetdubai.com*
Pampered Pets Dreams Tower 2, Marsa Dubai, 04 447 5330
Positive Paws Umm Suqeim St, Al Qouz Ind. 4, 04 379 0996, *positivepaws.ae*
Urban Tails Pet Resort *>p.157* Nr Green Community, Dubai Investments Park 2, 04 884 8847, *urbantailsdubai.com*

Where To Walk Your Dog

Dogs are not as widely accepted in Dubai as they are back home, and there are far more restrictions on dog-walking here. But we've sniffed out some places where your pet can stretch his paws.

Dogs are banned from many areas including Jumeirah Beach Residence (JBR) waterfront, and are frowned upon along Marina Walk and some areas on Palm Jumeirah. Walking a dog off-leash is not permitted and many beaches and parks have large signs up clearly stating these rules. Dubai Municipality will slap you with a Dhs.200 on-the-spot fine (per dog) if you flout the law. Fortunately, you do have a few options when it comes to pooch-friendly spots.

Doggy daycare

This safe, sociable dog park in Dubai, Paws Pet Planet (pawspetplanet.com) is ideal for letting your dog play with other dogs. A first of its kind in the Middle East, the park welcomes all sizes, ages and breeds of dogs and puppies; there are individual dog areas depending on size and the dog's nature. The 2,000 sq m indoor arena is climate-controlled with splash pools, bridges, tunnels and obstacles.

All dogs are supervised and if you are unable to be there, the park also runs a doggy daycare centre. To attend, all dogs must have a prior assessment and have up-to-date vaccinations (including kennel cough). Dogs must also pass a mandatory temperament assessment. See website for timetable and prices.

Desert and beach walks

As long as you're vigilant that a snake or scorpion doesn't bite your dog, you can walk your pet in the desert. For a long off-the-lead run, dog-owners get together to organise doggy play dates at various locations. Head out to the open desert behind Arabian Ranches, in Mirdif and Al Barsha 1 (behind the Mall of the Emirates).

In Nadd Al Shiba, there is also a popular area behind the camel market, which is safe, and far away from main roads. Meanwhile, in Al Warqa there is a large area for long walks, only a seven-minute drive from Mirdif.

In Jabal Ali, many people walk dogs on the beach next to the JA Jebel Ali Golf Resort & Spa, while other dog owners drive to Abu Dhabi where dogs are permitted in 'open water' beaches, away from the public and any shops. Also try Shahama Harbour and the beach club and bungalows at the Al Jazira Hotel near Ghantoot.

Dog-walking groups

Find fellow dog owners on the following websites: dubaidogclub.com, k9friends. com and petwatchdubai.com. Expatwoman.com is also a great forum for sharing local dog knowledge and news.

Dog-Friendly Cafes

Some cafes do welcome well-behaved dogs. The Lime Tree Café, on Jumeira Road and the new Tim Horton's and Coffeol cafes at Al Wasl Square don't seem to mind dogs passing through with their owners. There are even some trees close by for some much-needed shade in the summer months.

BLUE OASIS
VETERINARY CLINIC
HOSPITAL • PET STORE • GROOMING • RELOCATION

worm prevention and treatment   microchipping
dentistry intensive care and hospitalization
grooming radiology and ultrasound
vaccinations for dogs and cats   laboratory tests
petfood and accessories
surgery   boarding
dermatology   orthopedic surgery
other veterinary services

SOMETIMES THEY NEED MORE THAN JUST A MEDICINE

24/7 Emergency Service

800-PETCARE
04-8848580

Dubai Investments Park, Green Community Dubai

To keep up to date with the events and, of course special offers, visit us on our
website at www.blueoasisvetclinic.com or follow us on
http://www.facebook.com/BlueOasisVetClinic

 @BlueOasisVets

FITNESS

Gyms & Fitness Clubs

While the Dubai lifestyle can be conducive to inactivity and overindulgence, the good weather throughout most of the year means that it's a pretty good place to be active too. So, whether you need to shift that 'Dubai stone' or want to hit the beach bootcamp-style to ramp up your endurance, you'll find plenty of ways to get off your sofa and on your feet.

If it's a new sport you're after there's a wide variety of team sports to choose from (see also Activities & Hobbies). If you prefer to hit the treadmill or cross-trainer, you may be lucky to find accommodation with its own gym, particularly in apartment blocks and new housing complexes.

There are also plenty of gyms to join, and hotels offer health club memberships if your complex doesn't have facilities. Independent gyms usually offer day passes for Dhs.100, or monthly membership from Dhs.350-1,000. With 27 branches across the UAE, Fitness First is one of the leading gym brands in the region; standard membership costs Dhs.4,199 per year including all exercise classes and two free personal training sessions, after which you will receive a personalised programme.

Fitness 360 offers unusual fitness classes such as dancing in heels and partner yoga; U Concept is a boutique gym with DJ decks, art on the walls and a UFC cage in the basement; Engine offers a class-only package at Dhs.450 per month (including suspended yoga using a padded hammock); and Symmetry Gym offers personalised workouts in a small gym environment. The Circuit Factory (circuitfactory.ae) sets the four-week challenge of circuit sessions and a diet. So, there is plenty of choice and no excuse to fester on the sofa or in the bar!

The Aviation Club Al Rebat St, Al Garhoud, 04 230 8560, *jumeirah.com*

Bodylines Health & Fitness Centre Trade Center 1, 04 312 2556

Cleopatra's Spa & Wellness Umm Hurair 2, 04 324 7700, *cleopatrasspaandwellness.com*

Core Fit Dreams Tower 2, Marsa Dubai, 04 422 5338, *corefit.me*

Crowne Fitness Crowne Plaza, Trade Center 1, 04 305 6600, *crowneplaza.com*

Dubai Ladies Club Jumeira St, Jumeira 1, 04 349 9922, *dubailadiesclub.com*

Exhale Marsa Dubai, 04 424 3777, *exhaledubai.com*

Fidelity Fitness Club Almas Tower, Al Thanyah 5, 04 451 1133, *fidelityfitnessclub.com*

Fitness 360 J3 Mall, Al Wasl Road, 04 236 2111, *fitness360.me*

Fitness First DIFC, Zaa'beel 2, 04 363 7444, *fitnessfirstme.com*

Fitness O2 35A Street, Umm Suqeim, 04 379 2757, *fitness02.com*

Goal Attained 056 693 9258, *goalattained.com*

In Shape Ladies Fitness Club Al Joud Bldg, Al Qouz Ind 1, 04 395 5718, *inshapeme.com*

India Club Nr Indian High School, Oud Metha, 04 337 1112, *indiaclubdubai.com*

Insportz Club Nr Dubai Garden Centre, Al Qouz Ind. 3, 04 347 5833, *insportzclub.com*

Motion Fitness Center Villa 122, Jumeira St, Umm Suqeim 3, 04 328 2538, *motionfitnesscenter.com*

Original Fitness Fairmont, Trade Center 1, 04 311 6571, *originalfitnessco.com*

Optimal Fitness *> p.163* Commerical Building 3, Dubai Studio City, 04 457 2048, *optimalfitness.ae*

The Pavilion Marina & Sports Club Jumeira Beach Hotel, Umm Suqeim 3, 04 406 8800, *jumeirahbeachhotel.com*

Sharjah Wanderers Sports Club University City Rd, Sharjah, 06 566 2105, *sharjahwanderers.com*

ShuiQi Spa & Fitness Atlantis, Nakhlat Jumeira, 04 426 2000

Symmetry Gym Gold & Diamond Park, Al Qouz Industrial 3, 04 346 6479, *symmetrygymdubai.com*

Synergy Fitness Al Samrey Bldg, Al Barsha 1, 04 454 1471

Talise Fitness Trade Center 2, 04 319 8181, *jumeirah.com*

Talise Spa Madinat Jumeirah, Al Sufouh 1, 04 366 6821 *jumeirah.com*

U Energy Gate Village, DIFC, Zaa'beel 2, 04 422 8721, *uenergy.me*

Mother & Child

If you want to give your kid a mind, body and soul workout, then My Gym (mygym.com/dubai) is the place to go for gymnastics and Mommy & Me sessions. The Little Gym (thelittlegym.com) runs gym classes from four months to 12 years. Urban Energy runs prenatal fitness classes in the park using weights and gentle exercises. And for mums looking to get back into shape, Pure Fitness (purefitnessuae.com) offers BuggEfit Bootcamp and a baby-friendly, four-week Results programme.

Ladies Only

There are several ladies-only gyms and fitness clubs in Dubai including Fitness 360 at J3 Mall, the Dubai Ladies Club, and Curves, which is based around a circuit of machines, both cardio and toning, which, along with stretching, is completed twice in 30 minutes. Dance Fit is a ladies-only centre running classes in Zumba, hip-hop, tap-dancing and Bootylicious, as well as a six-week course in the flirty Burlesque.

Yoga & Pilates

If pumping iron or running a marathon isn't for you, the ancient art of yoga and the ever more popular pilates method are gentle yet effective alternatives to help you get and stay in shape. Pilates is said to be the safest form of neuromuscular reconditioning and back strengthening available and is often delivered by trained physiotherapists. The method can help you become stronger, fitter, more toned and more flexible – either as a means to treat a problem, or as an exercise regime in small groups or one-on-one sessions. Classes are offered by a number of gyms as part of their group exercise schedules.

Yoga is a low-impact (but deceptively challenging) form of holistic exercise which has been practised for thousands of years. It involves holding sequences of poses or 'asanas' that, combined with breathing exercises, gently but powerfully help your body become stronger and more flexible. Many health and fitness clubs offer yoga on their weekly schedule.

Club Stretch

Nr Mercure Hotel, Al Mina Rd Al Hudaiba **04 345 2131** clubstretch.ae
Map **2 J4** Metro **Al Jafiliya**
Club Stretch offers reformer pilates classes taught by highly qualified instructors who also teach Bikram yoga at the studio.

Exhale

Marsa Dubai **04 424 3777** exhaledubai.com
Map **1 K4** Metro **DAMAC**
This ladies-only centre specialises in pilates and yoga. Prices start at Dhs.80 for a single pilates reformer class. A set of 10 Exhale classes costs Dhs.750 and is valid for two months. Exhale has another studio in Dubai MotorCity (04 447 4220).

The Hundred Pilates Studio
53B St, Jumeira 1 **04 344 7333**
thehundred.ae
Map **2 G4** Metro **Financial Centre**
Personalised pilates sessions are available at this
studio in Jumeira 1, as well as small group classes with
a maximum four participants. Prices start at Dhs.90 for
a single class.

Real Pilates
Palm Strip Mall, Jumeira Rd, Jumeira 1 **04 345 3228**
real-pilates.com
Map **2 H4** Metro **Emirates Towers**
At its bright studio, Real Pilates focuses on STOTT
pilates (which focuses on maintaining the spine's
natural curve) and you can expect high-quality
equipment and well qualified instructors. Single
sessions start at Dhs.65 with block booking offers
available; mat and reformer pilates are on offer. The
company has a second studio, located at JLT (nearest
metro: DAMAC).

Zen Yoga
BBC Bldg Al Sufouh 2 **04 367 0435**
yoga.ae
Map **1 N5** Metro **DAMAC**
Mat and reformer pilates (using a machine to increase
intensity) are available, with yogilates also offered.
Expectant mums can join pre-natal pilates classes. A
trial lesson costs Dhs.90, with five classes for Dhs.450.
Emirates Living (04 422 4643), Dubai Media City
(04 367 0435), Town Centre Jumeirah (04 349 2933).

Desert Palm Gym

Personal Training

Whether your goal is a rippling six pack, to run
a marathon, or just to feel fitter, the support,
encouragement and expertise of a good personal
trainer might be just the shot.

A personal trainer will assess your fitness, design the
perfect regime for you – and motivate you to show up.
There are a number of indoor and outdoor personal
trainers in Dubai, some attached to gyms or health and
fitness centres, others employed by fitness companies,
and some working for themselves. Make sure your
trainer is properly qualified with an internationally
recognised certificate and registered with the
International Register of Exercise Professionals.

Quick Fix
Exercise will relax you, provide you with that vital mental
break from stress, and give you the physical strength to
power on when you don't feel like it. Research shows that
even if you only have time for 10-15 minutes activity at
a time, the benefits can still be significant. So even a 10
minute run on the beach after work is worth the effort.

Original Fitness
Fairmont Trade Center 1 **04 311 6571**
originalfitnessco.com
Map **2 H5** Metro **World Trade Centre**
All ages and fitness levels are catered for by the
trainers at Original Fitness. They also run bootcamps
on the beach for those who like to push themselves.

Regime Fitness
Marina Yacht Club Marsa Dubai **04 366 3234**
regime.ae
Map **1 K5** Metro **Jumeirah Lakes Towers**
Regime Fitness offer a free initial personal training
consultation, and also provide wellness programmes
for companies.

UAE Active
Abu Dhabi **055 348 6377**
uaeactive.com
With the philosophy that 'your body is your gym', UAE
Active trainers are a dab hand at helping you figure
out how to train in almost any environment – so even
if you can't get to the gym, or have no equipment at
home, they'll design a programme to suit you.

WPT Dubai Women Personal Training
04 452 0194
wptfitness.com
Personal trainers just for women, who are specialised
in women's needs. Several training programmes are
available including pre-natal and post-natal.

SHOULD YOU WORKOUT TODAY?

START

YES ← Do you want to improve your health? → **NO**

Do you want to lose weight? → **NO**

YES

Do you want to get stronger & more toned?

YES

NO → Do you want to meet new people & make new friends?

YES   **NO**

We'll be here when you change your mind!

GO TO optimalFITNESS

At optimal**FITNESS**, our mission is to have a positive impact on your life by creating a memorable health and fitness experience in a friendly, boutique club environment. We offer a personalized service and deliverThe optimal fitness, therapy and nutrition solutions through fun, challenging, and effective programs! Visit our gym, optimal**THERAPY**, and health food cafè, *Caporilli's* located in Dubai Studio City.

WHAT ARE YOU WAITING FOR?
opt to be FIT

Call us at 04-4572048 or email info@optimalfitness.ae for more information!
Dubai Studio City, Building 3, Ground Floor (Opposite Arabian Ranches)
www.optimalfitness.ae

Exercise Your Options

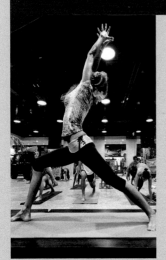

Getting fit in Dubai is easy. There are several types of exercise classes available.

Military style

If you like a good, hard workout in a gym or outdoors, then try bootcamp, a demanding regime of sprints, boxing, pushups, squats and bicep curls designed for military recruits. It will dramatically and quickly increase your strength and fitness levels, but be warned. You're going to be shouted at. A lot. Down a megaphone. At dawn. Original Fitness runs camps on the beach at JBR, in Safa Park and in Downtown Dubai – both early mornings and evenings.

Martial arts

Martial arts have been a form of self defence for thousands of years. The idea was to use physical and mental discipline to take control of your attacker without doing harm. Try Muay Thai boxing (dubaikarate. com), jiu jitsu and kickboxing (mmafitcenter.com), or capoeira (capoeiradubai.com), a Brazilian blend of martial arts, dance and acrobatics set to music.

Gym classes

A well air-conditioned gym is a lifesaver during the Dubai summer. Good gyms offer an array of classes with almost countless combinations of aerobics and floor exercises, weights, circuit training, and cycling, all set to a great sound track. They're a fun and effective way to burn fat, build muscle, lose weight, and improve heart health. Ask about joining discounts. In addition, many hotels offer memberships to their in-house gyms. They're

often more expensive but can be quieter and include access to the hotel spa. Some of the more popular ones are Le Meridien Mina Seyahi, the Grand Hyatt and JA Jebel Ali Golf Resort.

Dance

So you think you can't dance (or maybe you can)? Try Irish, tango, salsa, ballet, African or flamenco at a Dubai dance school (jamesandalex.com), gym, or even a meetup group. Other classes blend dance and aerobics such as Zumba, or Fitness First's Dance Mania. Xtend Barre borrows elements from ballet training (real-pilates.com).

Yoga & pilates

For a subtle yet powerful exercise try yoga, a holistic form of exercise in which holding a series of asanas, or poses, will make you stronger and more supple, as well as helping to balance emotions. Pilates classes are designed to build core strength, or try water aerobics. Bikram yoga takes yoga and adds a heated room to make things even tougher, which you can take part in at Raw Yoga (rawryoga.com). Real Pilates runs Xtend Barre classes, combining pilates with ballet.

Cross Fit

This is a really demanding workout that pushes the super fit to their physical limit and it's booming in Dubai. Check out Fitness First at Knowledge Village and Reebok CrossFit LifeSpark at Jumeirah Lakes Towers, if you think you're up to the challenge.

4-14 November 2015

Sharjah, United Arab Emirates

Books
are the
key of
knowledge

#SIBF15   sibf.com

مهرجان الشارقة للكتاب
SHARJAH
INTERNATIONAL
BOOK FAIR

SensAsia Urban Spa

WELL-BEING

Beauty Salons & Nail Bars

Beauty is big business in Dubai, and you're never far from a salon where you can pop in for a quick mani-pedi, massage or facial. You can expect to pay around Dhs.60 for a manicure and Dhs.80 for a pedicure. Fridays tend to be the busiest day for salons, with customers prepping for the weekend ahead, so book in advance. Keep an eye out for discounts for spas on websites such as groupon.ae, which can offer surprisingly big savings on a variety of treatments.

Branches of Mary Foot Spa, a pleasant, no-frills spa, are located throughout the city, where you can expect to be pampered by therapists who really know their stuff, within a calm, candlelit, soothing atmosphere.

Branches of N.Bar and Nail Lounges can be found pretty much all over Dubai and they're a popular spot for waxing, threading, massages and mani-pedis, and the chain of Tips & Toes offers everything from gelish

mani-pedis to Turkish and Moroccan hammams. Most nail salons now offer in the chair head, neck and shoulder massages too.

Unbelievably, there are also a number of spas specifically aimed at children, such as Hello Kitty Spa and Tickles & Giggles (800 82634). Increasingly, men's spas such as Urban Male Lounge are popping up in the city to provide metrosexual gents with some pampering too.

Many beauty salons and spas offer the traditional art of henna or mendhi, for special occasions or a fun experience for visitors. A design is drawn on your skin with henna paste that dries, flakes off, and leaves a stain that darkens, then fades after two or three weeks. Prices vary depending on the complexity of the design you choose. Try Rachna on Jumeira Rd (04 394 4489) that has designs from Dhs.100, or Aroushi on Oud Metha Rd (04 336 2794), with prices from Dhs.40.

Aroushi Beauty Salon Nr Lamcy Plaza, Oud Metha, 04 336 2794, *aroushibeautysalon.com*

Clarins Boutique Dubai Mall, Downtown Dubai, Burj Khalifa, 04 434 0522, *clarins.com*

Color Nail Beauty Lounge Al Qouz Ind. 1, 04 341 8848

Dermalogica Dubai Mall, Downtown Dubai, Burj Khalifa, 04 339 8250, *dermalogica.com*

Elyazia Beauty Center Nr Uptown Mirdiff, Mirdif, 04 288 8300, *elyaziabeautycenter.com*

Essentials Hair & Beauty Salon Nr Al Safa Centre, Jumeira 3, 04 395 5909, *essentialsdubai.com*

Hello Kitty Beauty Spa Jumeira 1, 04 344 9598, *hellokittybeautyspa.com*

Mary Foot Spa Al Mamsha St, JBR, Marsa Dubai, 04 440 4888, *maryfootspa.com*

N Bar Jumeira 1, 04 346 1100, *nbaruae.com*

Nail Moda Umm Hurair 2, 04 327 9088, *nailmoda.com*

The Nail Spa Dubai Mall, Downtown Dubai, Burj Khalifa, 04 339 9078, *thenailspa.com*

Nail Station Jumeira 1, 04 349 0123

Nail Zone Nr Jumeirah Beach Park, Jumeira 2, 04 344 6969

Nails At Home 04 298 0707, *nailsathome.ae*

Natalie Beauty Saloon JLT Gold Crest Views -1, JLT, Al Thanyah 5, 04 435 8077

NStyle Nail Lounge MoE, Al Barsha 1, 04 341 3300, *nstyleintl.com*

The Organic Glow Beauty Lounge Nr Safa Park, Al Wasl St, Jumeira 3, 04 380 4666

Pastels Nr Choithrams, Al Wasl Rd, Umm Suqeim 2, 04 388 3534, *pastels-salon.com*

Sisters Beauty Lounge Jumeira 1, 04 342 0787, *sistersbeautylounge.com*

Tilia & Finn Al Mamsha St, JBR, Marsa Dubai, 04 438 0636, *tiliaandfinn.ae*

Tips & Toes JBR, Marsa Dubai, 04 429 3477, *tipsandtoes.com*

Version Francaise Marina Heights Tower, Marsa Dubai, 04 360 5360, *version-francaise.com*

Organic

If you want to go organic, then try the Organic Glow Beauty Lounge, where they only use natural toxin-free ingredients.

The Organic Glow Beauty Lounge Nr Safa Park, Al Wasl Rd, Jumeira 3, 04 380 4666

Kids

Spas for children are growing ever-popular, particularly for birthday parties. Here tots to tweens can enjoy a manicure, pedicure, nail design, hair style, temporary hair colour, braiding, body sprays, body glitter, body tattoos, make-up and more. Tickles & Giggles at The Walk, JBR (04 432 8681) is a fun choice.

Hairdressers

In Dubai, you'll find ladies and gents hairdressers to suit every budget, from small salons where fellas could pay as little as Dhs.30 for a simple wet cut to larger, branded salons where prices start at around Dhs.165 (with a junior stylist). For higher quality styling and colouring prices start at Dhs.350. Straightening treatments can cost upwards of Dhs.1,000 and extensions will set you back from Dhs.500. Recommendations from friends and colleagues are a good way to find a stylist that you like; Salon Ink, Ted Morgan and Pastels are all popular spots with the city's expats. Men in search of something more than a simple barbershop should try male spas Man/Age or Urban Male Lounge.

Alain & Milad CNBC Bldg, Media City, Al Sufouh 2, 04 390 2815

Amaya Salon & Spa Oud Metha, 04 335 1101, *idm.ae*

Baré Gents Salon Ibn Battuta, Jabal Ali 1, 04 368 5111, *baresalongroup.com*

Bilal Le Salon Dubai Marine Beach Resort, Jumeira 1, 04 346 1111

Carla K Styling Nr Mazaya Centre, Al Wasl, 04 343 8544

Code Men's Salon Al Hudaiba Awards Bldg, Madinat Dubai Al Melaheyah, 04 386 9909

De La Mer Day Spa Jumeira St, Umm Suqeim 2, 04 328 2775, *delamerspa.com*

The Edge Hair & Beauty Salon Wafi Residence, Umm Hurair 2, 04 324 0024

Elyazia Beauty Center Nr Uptown Mirdiff, Mirdif, 04 288 8300, *elyaziabeautycenter.com*

Essentials Hair & Beauty Salon Nr Al Safa Centre, Jumeira 3, 04 395 5909, *essentialsdubai.com*

Franck Provost MoE, Al Barsha 1, 04 341 3245, *franckprovostdubai.com*

The Gold Salon Al Attar Tower, Shk Zayed Rd, Trade Center 2, 04 321 1423, *goldsalondubai.com*

The Hair Corridor Al Safa Centre, Al Wasl Rd, Al Safa 1, 04 394 5622, *thehaircorridor.com*

The Hair Shop Capitol, Madinat Dubai Al Melaheyah, 04 345 8566

Jen's Hair Studio White Crown Bldg, Trade Center 1, 04 331 1425

JetSet Grosvenor, Marsa Dubai, 04 399 5005

Juan Hair Salon Indigo Tower, JLT, Al Thanyah 5, 04 438 9570, *juansalon.com*

Maison de Joelle Kempinski Mall of the Emirates, Al Barsha 1, 04 323 6011, *maisondejoelle.com*

Maria Dowling Nr Capitol Hotel, Al Hudaiba, 04 345 4225, *mariadowling.com*

Pace e Luce Al Manzil Mall, Burj Khalifa, 04 420 1165, *paceeluce.com*

Pastels Nr Choithrams, Al Wasl Rd, Umm Suqeim 2, 04 388 3534, *pastels-salon.com*

Patsi Collins Hair Beauty Nails Nr RTA, Al Garhoud, 04 286 9923, *dubaibeautysalon.com*
Reflection Hair & Beauty Centre Umm Suqeim 1, 04 394 4595, *reflectionhairandbeautycentre.com*
Roots Salon Nr Jumeirah Beach Park, Jumeira 2, 04 344 4040, *rootssalons.com*
Saks Hair Salon Downtown Dubai, Burj Khalifa, 04 430 8572, *saksdubai.com*
Salon Ink Jumeira 2, 04 385 4402, *saloninkdubai.com*
ShuiQi Salon Atlantis, Nakhlat Jumeira, 04 426 1020, *atlantisthepalm.com*
Sisters Beauty Lounge Jumeira 1, 04 342 0787, *sistersbeautylounge.com*
SOS Beauty Salon Jumeira 1, 04 349 1144
Ted Morgan Hair Shoreline Apartments, Nakhlat Jumeira, 04 430 8190, *tedmorganhair.com*
Toni & Guy Gate Village, DIFC, Zaa'beel 2, 04 330 3345, *toniandguyuae.com*
Top Style Hair Salon Aviation Club, Al Garhoud, 04 282 9663, *topstylesalon.com*
Top Style Salon Nr Grand Millennium Hotel, Al Thanyah 1, 04 422 5633, *topstylesalon.com*
VOG Color Your Life Jumeira 3, 04 380 8960, *vog.ae*
Zouari Hair Salon Palace At One&Only Royal Mirage, Al Sufouh 2, 04 399 9999, *oneandonlyresorts.com*

Barbers & Male Salons

Caractere Gents Saloon Jumeira 3, 04 380 4188, *caracteresalongroup.com*
Chill Salon Loft Office 1, Media City, Al Sufouh 2, 04 446 2991, *chill-salon.com*
Julian Hairdressing Jumeira 1, 04 344 9006
Urban Male Lounge (UML) MoE, Al Barsha 1, 04 395 1103, *nstyleintl.com/uml*
Y12 Ritz-Carlton DIFC, Zaa'beel 2, 04 372 2712, *y12salons.com*

Kids

Caboodle Pamper & Play Dubai Mall, Downtown Dubai, Burj Khalifa, 04 325 3367, *caboodle.ae*
Fun City Jumeira 1, 04 349 9976, *funcity.ae*
Hello Kitty Beauty Spa Jumeira 1, 04 344 9598, *hellokittybeautyspa.com*
Kiddo Cuts Al Manara, 04 338 7299
Kids Cuts Marsa Dubai, 04 434 1984, *favouritethings.com*
Tickles & Giggles The Walk at JBR, Marsa Dubai, 04 432 8681, *ticklesandgiggles.com*

Spas

Whatever your pampering budget, you'll find a spa to suit you in Dubai. The city is blessed with world-class luxury spas within five-star hotels as well as small, independent establishments that offer fewer bells and whistles but better value for money. As well as the usual massages, body scrubs and wraps, you'll also find more unusual treatments such as the ancient practice of Ayurvedic massage, reflexology and traditional hammams. Budget and mid-range spas are perfect for regular indulgence, but if you want to splash your cash for a special occasion, there are some amazing treatments – think royal hammams and 24 carat gold facials – to leave you feeling like a million bucks. Expect to pay around Dhs.700 for a 90 minute treatment at a hotel spa or around Dhs.300 at smaller spas.

Relaxing Prices

Certain spas will offer special treatments at certain times of year such as Ramadan, as well as reductions on packages. If you're thinking about indulging yourself check out sites like groupon.com, which often has discounts on spa treatments. Also, get the Entertainer Body book or app and enjoy BOGOF deals year-round.

Budget

There are spas of all sizes and styles ready to rub, scrub and knead you into relaxation. And here are handful of the more independent places that offer better value for money, but you may have to forego some of the most luxurious facilities.

Kalm Beauty

Riva Beach Club Nakhlat Jumeira **04 451 9988**
kalmbeauty.com
Map **1 N3** Metro **Nakheel**
Located on the Shoreline of Palm Jumeirah, Kalm is a firm favourite among local residents wanting a soothing aromatherapy massage, relaxing mani-pedi or reviving facial, all of which are reasonably priced. Kalm also has monthly specials on discounted packages such as Keratin hair treatments and full body massages.

The Nail Spa

Dubai Mall Downtown Dubai, Burj Khalifa **04 339 9078**
thenailspa.com
Map **2 F6** Metro **Burj Khalifa/Dubai Mall**
With branches located throughout the UAE, the Nail Spa is the perfect spot for some reasonably priced pampering. Try the Minty Chocolate Sole Scrub or the Lavender Heel Peel as add-ons to your pedicure, and add a blissful shoulder massage.

SpaDunya Club

The Walk at JBR Marsa Dubai **04 439 3669**
spadunyaclub.com
Map **1 K4** Metro **Jumeirah Lakes Towers**
This wallet-friendly spa specialises in colour therapies that harmonise the body's energy levels. You'll find a

B/Attitude Spa

ShuiQi Spa & Fitness

Talise Ottoman Spa

range of treatments including face reflexology and a Body Harmonising Colour Treatment that includes a colour consultation, scrub, wrap and massage. There's also a hammam, steam room, sauna and beauty rooms.

Tips & Toes
209 Pinnacle Bldg Al Barsha 1 **04 399 0550**
tipsntoes.com
Map **1 Q6** Metro **Sharaf DG**
This popular salon and spa chain has branches across the UAE with a comprehensive treatment menu including manicures, pedicures, waxing, threading, massages and hair services. Visit the signature spa in Al Barsha and try the Turkish Hammam, a combination of being scrubbed, steamed and massaged that will leave you squeaky clean and relaxed.

Mid-range
Plenty of hotels and boutique spas dotted around Dubai have pitched mind and body treatments somewhere in the middle – affordable but with extra personal touches.

Amara Spa
Park Hyatt Port Saeed **04 602 1234**
Map **2 M7** Metro **GGICO**
Amara boasts amazing private treatment rooms with all the facilities of a changing room, as well as a relaxation corner. After your scrub or wrap, you can rinse off in the lovely private outdoor shower, then dry off and soak up some rays in the secluded relaxation area.

Tips & Toes

Cleopatra's Spa & Wellness
Pyramids at Wafi Umm Hurair 2 **04 324 7700**
cleopatrasspaandwellness.com
Map **2 K7** Metro **Dubai Healthcare City**
While the entrance and changing facilities may lack the opulence of some hotel spas, Cleopatra's plush relaxation area is a lovely ancient Egypt-themed affair with drapes, silk cushions and *majlis*-style seats. There is also a small plunge pool with a Jacuzzi and sauna. Enjoy facials, body wraps and anti-ageing miracles.

The Cure
Building 10 Media City, Al Sufouh 2 **04 391 6485**
thecure.ae
Map **1 N5** Metro **Nakheel**
A friendly haven in the heart of Media City, The Cure is the answer to whatever ails you, whether you're in need of a rejuvenating facial or a relaxing massage. The menu is extensive, the therapists are highly knowledgeable and well trained, and the quality of the treatments is exceptional given the reasonable prices.

Dreamworks Spa & Massage
Shoreline Apartments Nakhlat Jumeira **04 447 5511**
dreamworks.ae
Map **1 N4** Metro **Nakheel**
If it's a massage you're after, then you can't go wrong with a trip to Dreamworks Spa, which specialises in kneading out your knots. Let go of your daily stresses by treating yourself to some foot reflexology, a Balinese head massage or even an exquisite four hands massage. There's also a home service option, so you can get pampered in the comfort of your own place.

Perfect Shape Up Beauty Centre
Al Shafar Bldg, Al Wasl St Al Bada' **04 342 7722**
perfectshapeup.com
Map **2 F5** Metro **Noor Bank**
This spa bridges the gap between five-star luxury and a neighbourhood salon – the quality is just that little bit higher, the ambiance just that little bit more relaxing. Behind the doors of this unassuming villa you'll find a world of beauty services delivered by friendly and knowledgeable staff, including tanning, waxing, nails and hair care.

Hammam
The Oriental hammam is a traditional pampering experience in the Middle East, which shares similarities with Turkish baths. It involves being bathed, steamed, washed with black soap, scrubbed with a loofa and massaged on a hot marble table – an intense treatment that leaves your skin squeaky clean and glowing. Try the hammam at the One&Only Royal Mirage (04 315 2130, royalmirage.oneandonlyresorts.com) for a real treat.

Spaces Spa & Salon
Oasis Centre Al Qouz 1 **04 515 4400**
spacessalon.com
Map **2 C6** Metro **Noor Bank**
This small salon is split into gents' and ladies' quarters and offers massages that are just as good as a premium spa's, but without the exorbitant five-star hotel prices. Service is polite and exceptionally friendly. Offering a range of services from a deep tissue massage and facials to hair and nail treatments, Spaces is a nice, affordable option. And not breaking the bank makes it all the more relaxing.

Thai Elite Spa
Mercure Gold Madinat Dubai Al Melaheyah
04 345 9992 thaielitespa.com
Map **2 J4** Metro **Al Jafiliya**
This quaint spa on the upper level of the Gold Swiss-Belhotel may lack the facilities you'll find in some of the city's other spas, but its laid-back approach is refreshing. All the usual therapies are on offer, with the full-body scrub followed by a Thai oil massage a particularly relaxing and yet invigorating choice. Long opening hours and reasonable prices also make it attractive.

Luxury
These spas will customise every detail of your treatment for a blissful experience – and a massage or facial at one of these havens usually means you can wallow in Jacuzzis, saunas and steam rooms before and after your treatment – but you'll often pay top dollar.

Angsana Spa Arabian Ranches
Arabian Ranches, Al Hebiah 2 **04 361 8251**
angsanaspa.com
Map **1 N13**
Minimalist decor, exotic oils and soft music set the tone for relaxation at Angsana Spa. You can relax in peace and quiet with refreshments before and after your massage. The impeccably trained staff work wonders, turning tight muscles to putty and sending overworked minds to cloud nine. The massage menu includes Balinese, Hawaiian and Thai, and you get a heated massage table.

Armani/Spa
Armani Downtown Dubai, Burj Khalifa **04 888 3888**
dubai.armanihotels.com
Map **2 F6** Metro **Burj Khalifa/Dubai Mall**
Armani/Spa is modern, elegant and sleek. There are three categories of treatment – Stillness (relaxing), Freedom (rejuvenating) and Fluidity (detoxifying), encompassing massages, facials and body wraps. The pod-like treatment rooms create a feeling of being truly cocooned from the stress of the outside world.

Talise Spa (formerly Assawan Spa & Health Club)
Burj Al Arab Umm Suqeim 3 **04 301 7338**
jumeirah.com
Map **1 S4** Metro **First Gulf Bank**
Assawan is an elaborate affair. There are saunas, steam rooms, plunge pools and two relaxing infinity pools decorated in mosaic and gold leaf tiles – swim to the edge, put your nose to the window, and enjoy the amazing views of Dubai. For pure unadulterated indulgence, try the caviar body treatment.

B/Attitude Spa
Grosvenor House Dubai Marsa Dubai
04 399 8888 battitudespa-dubai.com
Map **1 L5** Metro **DAMAC**
An Asian-inspired spa with treatments ranging from Eastern massages to Ayurvedic facials, exotic body wraps and Swiss Bellefontaine treatments. The overall vibe is Oriental chic – think Tibetan relaxation techniques, sacred stones and Ayurveda, all delivered in treatment rooms that are named after the chakras.

Residence&Spa at One&Only Royal Mirage
Al Sufouh St Al Sufouh 2 **04 399 9999**
oneandonlyroyalmirage.com
Map **1 M4** Metro **Nakheel**
Understated decor, natural light and soft music create a serene effect in the treatment rooms of this spa. There are a variety of treatments including Swedish lymphatic drainage, slimming and sports massages, as well as an energy-balancing massage using warm and cool stones 'charged' in the moonlight and cleansed with salt. The hammam is not to be missed. Alternatively, opt for a peel, wrap or oil bath, exclusively with Espa products.

Rixos Royal Spa
Rixos The Palm Nakhlat Jumeira **04 457 5555**
rixos.com
Map **1 P3** Metro **Nakheel**
Treatments at this white and ice-blue spa vary from facials to traditional massages, and the signature packages offer a complete head-to-toe experience for extravagant pampering. The spa promises a relaxing experience from start to finish, with well-trained therapists who are friendly and attentive, and an indulgent fruit platter to give you an energy boost after your treatment.

Saray Spa
Marriott Harbour Marsa Dubai **04 319 4630**
marriott.com
Map **1 L5** Metro **DAMAC**
The treatments at the stunning Saray Spa are inspired by the ancient healing and beautifying rituals of the Arabic world, with the highlight of the menu undoubtedly being the Signature Dead Sea

Journey. This treatment is over two hours long and incorporates a salt scrub, mud mask wrap and a soothing soak in a heated flotation tank, salinated to imitate the Dead Sea itself.

Satori Spa
Bab Al Shams Mugatrah **04 809 6232**
meydanhotels.com
This spa makes the most of its desert location – the treatment rooms feature a window with a blind; unusual for spas in Dubai, which are usually cosseted away in the heart of a hotel. The sense of being close to the desert wilderness seeps into the gently lit room, and the quiet music empties your mind of everything but the rhythmic strokes of the therapist. Aromatherapy Associates is the oil of choice here, and a beguiling scent surrounds you as you are kneaded and massaged into a state of semi-conscious bliss.

ShuiQi Spa & Fitness
Atlantis Nakhlat Jumeira **04 426 1020**
Map **1 N1** Metro **Nakheel**
This spectacular spa has around 27 treatment rooms set over two floors, and offers a personal touch. Whether you choose a simple massage and facial to the intricate Japanese ritual Shiseido spa journey, you can expect the undivided attention of expertly trained therapists. Be sure to stock up on spa goodies in the boutique area at the entrance.

Softouch Spa
Kempinski Mall of the Emirates Al Barsha 1
04 409 5909
softouchspa.com
Map **1 R6** Metro **Mall of the Emirates**
You wouldn't expect to find such a sanctuary of calm in the midst of a mall, but the Softouch Spa is a true haven. Specialising in treatments based on Ayurveda, it's one of the few spas in the UAE with therapists that are fully trained in this tradition. It's also open 24 hours. Try the detoxifying warm Aromatic Moor Mud Wrap followed by a bliss-inducing massage with lavender essential oils.

The Spa At The Palace Downtown Dubai
The Palace Downtown Downtown Dubai, Burj Khalifa
04 428 7805
theaddress.com
Map **2 F6** Metro **Burj Khalifa/Dubai Mall**
This spa truly makes the most of its enviable location with its lakeside spa cabanas. These luxurious treatment beds directly overlook Burj Khalifa lake, providing gorgeous views of the world's tallest building and the Dubai Fountain, while ensuring the utmost privacy despite the glamorous outdoor setting. Attentive therapists ensure that your treatment is personalised to meet your needs.

Talise Ottoman Spa
Jumeirah Zabeel Saray Nakhlat Jumeira **04 453 0456**
jumeirah.com
Map **1 L3** Metro **Nakheel**
With 50 treatment rooms, mineral pools, *majlis* areas, saunas, ice chambers, couples' suites, gyms and stunning hammams, Talise Ottoman Spa is one of the biggest in the Middle East and amongst the largest in the world. Relax with an indulgent massage in a private outdoor cabana, or splash out on the authentic Turkish hammam for true top to toe pampering.

Talise Spa at Jumeirah Emirates Towers
The Boulevard Trade Center 2 **04 319 8181**
jumeirah.com
Map **2 H6** Metro **Financial Centre**
This compact spa is a suitably suave affair for the prestigious address in one of Dubai's most established five-star hotels. The menu features a handful of facials, but the real emphasis is on the body treatments. Massages range from Swedish to Hawaiian Lomi Lomi and reflexology; however, the real stars of the show are the signature spa rituals, many of which include flotation in the spa's fantastic salt water pool.

Waldorf Astoria Spa
The Palm Jumeirah Crescent East **04 818 2244**
waldorfastoria.com
Map **1 Q3** Metro **Nakheel**
An impressive, opulent and elegant spa. Treatments are tailored for ladies and gents in separate zones. The spa includes six treatment rooms, a nail care studio, a Spa boutique, thermal and water flotation lounges, an ice fountain, a herbal steam room and Himalayan salt stone saunas. For couples who really want a special treat, there are two private VIP Spa suites. Highly recommended is the signature 'Butterfly technique' of massage that the Waldorf Spa is famed for.

Day Spas
If you fancy more than a quick treatment, these places can help you make a day of it. Most spas will actually offer some kind of day-long service which generally involves use of pool areas, saunas and steam rooms.

De La Mer Day Spa
Jumeira St Umm Suqeim 2 **04 328 2775**
delamerspa.com
Map **1 T5** Metro **Noor Bank**
This spa is perfect for a day-long girly gathering with body wraps, facials, massages, manicures and pedicures. Soak up some sun in the secluded garden, which has a swimming pool and Jacuzzi. The spa is great for occasions such as hen parties, birthdays and baby showers – you can book the VIP suite and bring your own food, drink and decorations.

One&Only

ROYAL MIRAGE
Dubai

Oriental Hammam

The traditional Hammam, has long played a part in the cultural and social life of eastern
cities. An 'oasis of retreat' from daily stresses entering the Hammam is akin to a journey.

Located at Residence & Spa, One&Only Royal Mirage

Open daily 8.30am - 10pm
Ladies only 8.30am - 2pm, Gentlemen only 8pm - 10pm

Telephone +971 4 399 99 99 oneandonlyroyalmirage.com

Lime Spa
Desert Palm Warsan 2 **04 323 8888**
desertpalm.ae
More of a retreat than a spa; with any treatment
you get use of the facilities for the day. Six stunning
treatment rooms are all naturally lit by large windows
overlooking the polo fields. The couples' room has its
own plunge pool and private relaxation area.

Raffles Spa
Raffles Umm Hurair 2 **04 314 9870**
raffles.com
Map **2 K7** Metro **Dubai Healthcare City**
Raffles Spa is pure lavish indulgence. Try the Dubai
Decadence treatment – a full six hours of head-to-toe
pampering including a steam bath, body scrub, hot
stone massage, facial, manicure and pedicure. There's
also a gym, pool, sauna and steam room if you wish to
delay your departure even further.

Talise Spa Madinat Jumeirah
Madinat Jumeirah Al Sufouh 1 **04 366 6818**
madinatjumeirah.com
Map **1 R5** Metro **Mall of the Emirates**
This is a true destination spa, with a wonderful steam
room, sauna and plunge pools. Indoor sunbeds
provide lazing-around space, and there's even a
lounge with sofas to chill on. There's an extensive
range of therapies, with a strong focus on using
natural oils, and the expertly trained staff ensure that
your treatment is meticulously tailored to your needs.
Yoga, including the popular classes held under the
stars, is also available.

Kids' Spas
It's not just grown-ups that can be pampered. Other
spas may accommodate kids too, if asked nicely.

Caboodle Pamper & Play
Dubai Mall Downtown Dubai, Burj Khalifa
04 325 3367
caboodle.ae
Map **2 F7** Metro **Burj Khalifa/Dubai Mall**
A lovely spot for some mother-daughter pampering,
Caboodle Pamper & Play uses organic, chemical free
products. It's also a great place for kids' haircuts, as
little ones get DVDs, games and toys while they sit in
the styling chair.

Hello Kitty Beauty Spa
Town Centre Jumeira 1 **04 344 9598**
hellokittybeautyspa.com
Map **2 F4** Metro **Burj Khalifa/Dubai Mall**
Girls can get a 'kitty-cure' to match their mum's
manicure and have their nails painted with stars
and flowers. Facials use organic ingredients such as
oatmeal, honey and chocolate.

Tickles & Giggles
The Walk at JBR Marsa Dubai **04 432 8681**
ticklesandgiggles.com
Map **1 K4** Metro **Jumeirah Lakes Towers**
A salon and spa aimed at little ones, offering child-
friendly face masks using natural ingredients and
non-toxic, water-based polishes for mini mani-pedis.
There's more to this venue than pint-sized pampering
– it also hosts fun classes such as arts and craft as well
as ultra-trendy parties for mini stylistas.

Male Spas
Damaging sun, skin-drying air conditioning and usual
daily stresses can make the world of massages, facials
and spas start looking like a good idea, even for men.

1847
Grosvenor Marsa Dubai **04 399 8989**
1847uae.com
Map **1 L5** Metro **DAMAC**
Men are the centre of attention at 1847, which was
the first dedicated 'grooming lounge' for men in the
Middle East. Skilled therapists offer traditional shaves,
beard styling, facials, massages, manicures and
pedicures, and simple haircuts.

Kalm Grooming Lounge
Riva Beach Club Nakhlat Jumeira **04 451 9888**
kalmgrooming.com
Map **1 N3** Metro **Nakheel**
Located on Shoreline of Palm Jumeirah, above Riva
Beach Club, Kalm Grooming Lounge has a good range
of treatments on offer, from express manicures to
haircuts, waxing and massages. Try the unusual Hot
Lava Shell Massage, which uses warmed shells to melt
the tension from your muscles.

Man/Age
Arjaan by Rotana Media City, Al Sufouh 2
04 437 0868
managespa.com
Map **1 M5** Metro **Nakheel**
This luxury men's spa offers male grooming including
haircuts and shaving, manicures, massages and facials.
It also has a Moroccan bath. All the treatments on offer
are very reasonably priced and there are annual and
six month memberships.

Urban Male Lounge (UML)
Precinct Building 2 DIFC, Zaa'beel 2 **04 425 0350**
nstyleintl.com/uml
Map **2 G6** Metro **Financial Centre**
This award-winning male-centric spa offers a chic,
relaxed setting. With locations in the DIFC and the Mall
of the Emirates, Urban Male Lounge is the perfect spot
for gents to indulge in a massage or sharpen up their
look with a hip new cut.

SPOIL YOURSELF.
BECOME A MEMBER.

SNOW

ICE

crystal

For more information visit www.skidxb.com

 /SKIDXB   /SKIDXB   You Tube /SKIDUBAI   /SKIDXB

SKI DUBAI
سكي دبي
DO SOMETHING DIFFERENT

Bikers join the National Day parade

CLUBS & GROUPS

All the different cultures converging in Dubai bring a diverse range of activities with them. Everything from jumping out of an airplane to scrapbooking is covered in this section and, for every traditional pursuit such as tennis, running or football, there is the opportunity to try something you never even dreamed of doing back home, such as kitesurfing, sandboarding, yogilates or even caving. For the adventurous, the UAE's topography lends itself to outdoor pursuits including rock climbing, mountain biking, dune bashing, wadi driving and skydiving. Thanks to the miles of coastline, watersports are popular, with scuba diving, snorkelling, sailing, surfing and water-skiing all firm favourites. You need not leave behind those hobbies you enjoyed back home either. From dance classes to photography, there are like-minded people in the city who will be more than happy to hear from you. How these activities are organised varies from regular meetings and paid-for classes to forum or social media based groups. If one of your interests isn't catered for, there's nothing to stop you from starting your own group or club – and you're likely to find plenty of takers in this active city. Alternatively, a trip to Abu Dhabi can often help you find clubs and groups that aren't available in Dubai.

Team Spirit
More than 10,000 members are signed up for Duplays recreational sports leagues in the UAE – a phenomenal number given that the organisation was set up by expats in 2009. What better way to keep fit, meet new people and settle in to a new city. Players of all skill levels are welcome. Get stuck into five- or seven-a-side football, beach volleyball, kickball or badminton, to name a few. Individuals joining can be assigned a team. For details visit duplays.com.

Sport

American Football

The Emirates American Football League offers full-contact American football in the UAE for players of all skill levels, from beginner to experienced. There are adult and youth teams, as well as recreational flag league teams. Contact info@eafl.ae for info. To find out how to join the Duplays Mighty Eagle I flag football league, as an individual or a team, visit duplays.com.

Active Sports

A fun sports club for kids offering everything from swimming, football and tennis, to cheerleading, basketball and gymnastics. There are several venues across the city, which are detailed on the website (activeuae.com). Co-founder, Cees Valk has previously coached tennis stars, Stefan Edberg and Emile Sanchez.

Badminton

Badeemonz Badminton Club Dubai

facebook.com/
BadeemonzBadmintonClubUaeDubai
Founded in 2008, the club also organises tournaments. Check their Facebook page for more information.

Badmintown

Al Safa Sports Centre Al Wasl **050 770 6711**
Map **2 D5** Metro **Business Bay**
A group of badminton players who meet to play and take part in tournaments. They also offer coaching and discounted Yonex items.

Badminton Dubai

Bradenton Prep Academy, Sports City **055 370 3035**
badminton-dubai.com
Map **1 M12** Metro **Mall of the Emirates**
This Sports City based club runs a competitive Badminton League on a Wednesday and Friday, along with professional coaching for all ages and skill levels (ladies-only sessions available). There's also a Kids Clinic every Saturday morning for 5-7 years olds.

India Club

Nr Indian High School Oud Metha **04 337 1112**
indiaclubdubai.com
Map **2 L6** Metro **Oud Metha**
This members club has been in existence since 1964 and offers a range of sports and entertainment activities including badminton (four courts), basketball, squash, bowling, tennis, a gym and table tennis. Experienced coaches are on hand and the club hosts numerous tournaments throughout the year.

Baseball

Dubai Little League

Nr Al Qouz Pond Park, Al Khail Rd Al Qouz 2
050 293 3855
eteamz.com/DubaiLittleLeague
Map **2 D7** Metro **Business Bay**
Parent volunteers field more than 20 baseball teams for boys and girls aged five to 16. Beginners welcome. Dhs.1,200 registration includes season fees, team picture, uniform and year-end trophy.

Basketball

Dubai has a number of public basketball courts but getting a game on them in the evenings can be tricky because they're so popular. There are courts near the Canadian University of Dubai, at Hamriya Park in Abu Hail and on 2nd December Street in Satwa, next to Chelsea Plaza Hotel. You can also go to Safa Park and Al Barsha Pond Park and get regular pick-up games on Wednesday, Thursday and Sunday evenings. Air-conditioned indoor courts can be hired for Dhs.35 per person per hour at Chevrolet Insportz (insportzclub.com), behind Dubai Garden Centre in Al Qouz 3. Duplays organises men's and women's recreational and competitive leagues (duplays.com).

MPAC Sports Basketball Academy

Jumeirah Primary School 04 385 1777
mpacsports.com
Map **1 C5** Metro **Business Bay**
Founded in Chicago Illinois in 2002, MPAC Sports is now international – and children in Dubai can learn everything there is to know about basketball at the academy. The company's objective is to promote the game at grass roots level through quality instruction and structured competitions.

Boxing

Al Nasr Leisureland

Nr American Hospital Oud Metha **04 337 1234**
alnasrll.com
Map **2 L6** Metro **Oud Metha**
Boxing classes are Saturdays, Mondays and Wednesdays from 8.30pm to 10.30pm. A 12 lesson package costs Dhs.550. For more information on the different weight classes, contact the coach, Iraj Dortolouee, on the above number.

Colosseum Muay Thai Health & Fitness Club

Zaabeel St Al Karama **04 337 2755**
colosseumuae.com
Map **2 M5** Metro **BurJuman**
Gym specialising in boxing, Muay Thai (Thai boxing), kickboxing and street fighting. Group classes meet daily between 8.30pm to 10pm. Costs Dhs.75 per session.

Dubai Fight Academy
Dusseldorf Bldg Al Qouz Ind. 1 **04 420 7902**
fightacademy.ae
Map **1 U6** Metro **Noor Bank**
The academy offers Thai boxing lessons and holds tournaments. Membership is Dhs.1,500 for six months including use of gym and pool. Another branch is in Jumeira (050 650 1184).

Climbing
See Activities, Things To See & Do.

Cricket
On weekends you'll see informal cricket games springing up on scratchy patches of open space on the outskirts of the city. Zabeel and Safa parks are favourite spots if you prefer a little more green for your stumps. There are also several small-scale training centres, such as the Emirates Cricket Training Centre (050 497 3461). International matches are regularly hosted in the United Arab Emirates, particularly at the state-of-the-art cricket ground in Dubai Sports City (dubaisportscity.ae) where it's possible to see some of the world's best teams in action.

ICC Global Cricket Academy
Nr Autodrome Sports City, Al Hebiah 4 **04 448 1355**
iccglobalcricketacademy.com
Map **1 M11**
The ICC cricket Dubai Sports City offers cricket coaching for all ages with ICC-affiliated coaches and some of the most advanced facilities in the cricketing world.

Insportz Club
Nr Dubai Garden Centre Al Qouz Ind. 3 **04 347 5833**
insportzclub.com
Map **1 S6** Metro **First Gulf Bank**
Insportz has three main net courts with a scoreboard and one side court, available for social games as part of a league, or just for practice.

Last Man Stands
Al Kifaf
lastmanstands.com
Map **2 K6** Metro **Al Jafiliya**
Amateur T20 cricket league with several Dubai teams taking part. Registration fees are Dhs.640 per year. Matches are played at Zabeel Park.

Cycling & Mountain Biking
Dubai is not a particularly bicycle-friendly city, but there are pleasant areas where you can ride such as along both sides of the creek and Jumeira Road, and on the cycle tracks at Mamzar Park and Jumeirah Open Beach. Also, try out the Meydan Cycle Park, a converted camel racing track with varying distances (4km, 6km and

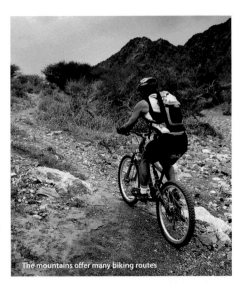
The mountains offer many biking routes

8km), and the Dubai Autodrome. Dubai Autodrome and Yas Marina Circuit in Abu Dhabi host weekly track cycling sessions. Check the CycleSafeDubai Facebook page discussion threads for the next event.

Wolfi's Bike Shop and Probike offer equipment, advice on technique and recommend weekly riding groups. For cycling as a mode of transport in Dubai, see Getting Around.

Away from the cities, the UAE has a lot to offer outdoor enthusiasts, especially mountain bikers. On a mountain bike it's possible to see the most remote and untouched places that are not even accessible in 4WDs. For hardcore, experienced bikers there is some good terrain, from super-technical rocky trails in areas like Fili and Siji, to mountain routes like Wadi Bih, which climb to over 1,000m and can be descended in minutes. The riding is mainly rocky, technical and challenging.

Even if you are experienced, always be sensible and go prepared – the sun is strong, you will need far more water than you think, and it's easy to get lost. Wide, knobbly tires work much better on the loose, sharp rocks. For further information on mountain biking in the UAE, including details of possible routes, refer to the *UAE Off-Road Explorer*.

The Cycle Hub
Dubai Autodrome MotorCity, Al Hebiah 1
04 425 6555
thecyclehub.com
Map **1 N12**
Organises numerous trails and weekly group rides for mountain bikers and also offers a rider development programme for beginners to elite. You can also get your bike serviced here and buy new bikes and spare parts.

Cycle Safe Dubai
050 680 4528

cyclesafedubai.com

A road biking club that organises races including the Spinneys Dubai 92 Cycle Challenge, Friday morning rides between 35km and 100km and the Saturday morning Bab Al Shams coffee ride. It is also the brains behind the Wednesday cycle nights at the Dubai Autodrome, where expert cyclists are on hand to teach beginners the basics. For Dhs.500 a year, you can join Team CSD and get a range of services and discounts (as well as a team jersey) but membership is not mandatory to join in the rides.

Dubai Mountain Bikers UAE
facebook.com/pages/Dubai-Mountain-Bikers-UAE-Dubikers

Also known as Dubikers, this mountain-biking club aims to encourage more people to the sport and is best for those who don't yet have elite technical riding experience. They regularly organise rides – see their facebook page for more information.

Dubai Roadsters
04 339 4453

dubairoadsters.com

Possibly the more serious of the organised road-biking groups and rides, the Friday ride offers options of 80km, 120km and, occasionally, 140km. Weekday rides range from 30km to 50km. There are also special events, from the epic twice-yearly 240km coast-to-coast ride to group training rides in the Hatta hills. The group's socials are a great place to meet like-minded people.

Hot-Cog Mountain Bike Club
056 170 8087

hot-cog.com

An active group of enthusiasts who organise weekend trips all over the country and midweek off-road mountain-biking night rides. They also camp, hike and barbecue, and new riders are always welcome.

Dragon Boat Racing
Training sessions in the ancient eastern sport of dragon boat racing are held most mornings and evenings at either Dubai Festival City or Le Meridien Mina Seyahi. There are several teams in Dubai which compete against each other and teams from Abu Dhabi. Most are more than happy to accept new members with little or no experience.

Dragon boats are low-lying vessels that are paddled along by hardworking teams (hence why the sport is also referred to as 'paddling').

The UAE Dragon Boat Association lists all of the country's teams. For details and a history of the sport visit dubaidragonboat.com.

Dubai Dawn Patrol
Barasti Beach Marsa Dubai **050 879 5645**

dubaidawnpatrol.org

Map **1 M4**

Dawn Patrol members make up a diverse group which started in 2008. They combine serious sporting dedication with a fun environment and general love of the water and the outdoors. Training takes place on Tuesday and Thursday mornings (5.45am to 7am) and Saturday evenings (4.30pm to 6pm) in the Dubai marina area. The first three sessions are free and then there's an annual membership fee of Dhs.1,000.

Dubai Diggers
Jumeirah Beach Hotel Umm Suqeim 3 **050 718 5104**

dubai-diggers.com

Map **1 S4** Metro **First Gulf Bank**

Dubai Diggers are coached by Nick Hando, who founded Australia's Bondi Diggers team. The Dubai Diggers train three times a week. Beginners can attend any session, although the sessions held from 7.30am to 9.30am on Friday mornings at Jumeirah Beach Hotel (which include circuit training) are recommended for a first taste of the sport. Other sessions are Mondays and Wednesdays between 6am and 7am.

Dubai Flying Dragons
Le Meridien Mina Seyahi Marsa Dubai **050 640 9017**

dubaidragonboat.com

Map **1 M4** Metro **Nakheel**

Holds training sessions at Le Meridien Mina Seyahi. Beginners' sessions are on Saturdays at 4pm – email info@dubaidragons.com for more information. The first Saturday of every month is 'social Saturday' where members can get to know each other better.

Dragon Warriors Dubai
056 174 0305

dragonwarriorsdubai.com

Dubai's first all-Filipino dragon-boat race team are very hardworking. They train on weekday evenings and weekend mornings and are aiming to compete in international events. New paddlers of any age or ability are welcome.

Dubai Sea Dragons
Le Meridien Mina Seyahi Marsa Dubai **050 354 9193**

dubaiseadragons.net

Map **1 M4** Metro **Nakheel**

An independent dragon boating club, affiliated with the International Dragon Boat Federation and DBA Federation. The Sea Dragons participate in local and international competitions. Newcomers are welcome. The one-hour training sessions take place Mondays and Wednesdays (8am and 5pm), and Saturday mornings at 8am. All are on the beach at Mina Seyahi and cost Dhs.50 per session.

Fencing

MK Fencing Academy
Umm Suqeim 3 **050 794 4190**
mkfencingacademy.com
Map **1 S5** Metro **First Gulf Bank**
Offers individual (Dhs.200) and group (Dhs.55) training
in épée (épée is French for sword) and foil for all levels.
Fencers receive masks, gloves and weapons, with
three fencing paths. Electrical scoring and weapons
are available for advanced levels.

UAE Fencing Federation
Al Quds St Hor Al Anz East **04 269 9866**
dubaifencingclub.com
Map **1 D5** Metro **Al Fahidi**
This body organises and supervises fencing in the UAE
and has affiliations with local competition organisers
and the UAE national team.

Fishing
The Dubai government has introduced regulations to
protect fish stocks but you can still fish as long as you
have the right permit or you charter a licensed tour
guide. The best fishing is from September to April,
although it is still possible to catch sailfish and queen
fish in the summer.

Fish commonly caught in the region include king
mackerel, tuna, trevally, bonito, kingfish, cobia and
dorado. Beach or surf fishing is popular along the
coast and, in season, you can even catch barracuda
from the shore. The local hammour, however, is being
over-fished, and so anglers are advised not to pluck
this species from the sea.

The creek front in Creekside Park is a popular spot.
On a Friday, you can hire an abra for the morning at
the Bur Dubai or Deira landing steps and ask your
driver to take you to the mouth of the creek. You could
also consider a deep-sea fishing trip with one of the
charter companies listed under Tours.

For more competitive anglers, the UAQ Marine Club
(uaqmarineclub.com) sponsors a fishing competition
twice a year, in April and October. Call 06 766 6644
for more details. A good selection of fishing rods,
tackle and equipment is available at Barracuda Dubai
(barracudadubai.com). You can even post your catch
of the day on their website.

Licence To Krill
To throw a fishing line into the water you'll first need a
fishing licence from Dubai government. Either that or
go with a registered fishing charter. There are different
permits for leisure boats and offshore fishing. Both are
free and can be applied for through the government
portal, dm.gov.ae.

Club Joumana
JA Jebel Ali Golf Resort Mena Jabal Ali **04 8836000**
jaresortshotels.com
Metro **Jebel Ali**
Budding fishermen will soon be reeling them in by
chartering one of these fully-equipped fishing boats
complete with experienced crew and refreshments.
Serious contenders can fish under IGFA rules.

Dubai Creek Golf & Yacht Club
Nr Deira City Centre Port Saeed **04 295 6000**
dubaigolf.com
Map **2 M7** Metro **Deira City Centre**
Charter the club's yacht, Sneak Away, and head out
into the Arabian Gulf for big game sport fishing. The
32 foot Hatteras carries up to six passengers and
the Dhs.3,500 hire fee includes four hours at sea (or
Dhs.4,500 for eight hours) plus tackle, bait, ice, fuel
and a friendly crew.

Ocean Active
Al Qouz Ind. 3 **050 559 1375**
oceanactive.com
Map **1 S6** Metro **First Gulf Bank**
This experienced boat charter company offers live-
aboard and day fishing trips to locations in the UAE
and Oman. Fishing charters across the Middle East are
also available.

Deep Blue Fishing
Fisherman Village, Umm Suqeim 2 **052 889 8973**
deepbluefishing.ae
Map **1 T4** Metro **Noor Bank**
Guaranteeing you will catch a lot of fish on your trip
on the water, this company owns a fleet of vessels and
offers four hour (half day) and seven hour (full day)
trips. It costs Dhs.400 per hour.

Xclusive Yachts Sport Fishing & Yacht Charter
Marina Yacht Club Marsa Dubai **04 432 7233**
xclusiveyachts.com
Map **1 K5** Metro **Jumeirah Lakes Towers**
Two-hour cruises and four-hour fishing trips are
available. An impressive 37 foot sport fishing boat
operates from the Dubai Marina Yacht Club.

Football
Football (or soccer) is much loved here in the UAE.
Teams train and compete on a regular basis and
you'll see plenty of impromptu kickabouts in parks.
Insportz (insportzclub.com) in Al Qouz has five indoor
five-a-side pitches, and some universities and schools
rent out their outdoor and five-a-side pitches. If you'd
rather watch than play, the UAE league has regular
fixtures in Dubai. Gaelic Football fans should contact
Dubai Celts GAA.

Dubai Amateur Football League

dubaifootball.leaguerepublic.com
The 'Expat League' hosts two divisions of 12 teams. It runs an 11-a-side league and cup games between September and April at various locations, and seven-a-side games during the summer.

Dubai Schools Football League

04 296 6804
dsfl.leaguerepublic.com
This is the umbrella organisation that oversees league football for girls and boys in Dubai. Children wishing to participate in school league football should do so through their schools, but questions about league set-up, results and fixtures can usually be answered here.

Dubai Women's Football Association

Hessyan 1 **050 659 8767**
dubaiwfa.com
Features 15 women's teams that compete across two divisions. Players train once a week, and play weekly matches. Matches take place at the Jebel Ali Centre of Excellence, in the Jebel Ali Shooting Club.

Duplays

Indigo Icon Tower JLT, Al Thanyah 5 **04 447 2394**
duplays.com
Map **1 K5** Metro **Jumeirah Lakes Towers**
Duplays runs competitive and recreational five-a-side indoor and seven-a-side outdoor leagues, and has recently added a women's five-a-side league as well as the Mighty Eagles, an outdoor flag football league.

E-Sports Football Academy

04 443 4188
esportsfootballacademy.com
This company provides comprehensive training for youngsters at various locations. Players are encouraged to join one of the teams competing in the Dubai Junior Football League. A 15 week course costs Dhs.1,400 for one session a week or Dhs.2,500 for two sessions a week.

Football Planet Academy

Mirdif City Centre Mirdif **800 586**
theplaymania.com
Map **2 P12** Metro **Rashidiya**
Playnation at Mirdif City Centre is where you'll find this fun football activity centre, which is a big hit with families and groups of youths. It's also a fantastic place for boys' birthday parties. Participants undergo a series of challenges to improve skills. If the Training Academy and Powerplay simulated stadium experience whet the appetite, there's a huge indoor multisports pitch that can be hired for matches.

International Football Academy

04 454 1683
ifasport.com
Offers training for four- to 16-year-olds from internationally qualified coaches. Provides tailored coaching to schools, as well as existing teams. Teams play in several leagues. Pitch hire is also available and the academy can organise birthday parties packed full of events.

Dubai has many football camps for kids

It's Just Football
JA Centre of Excellence Mena Jabal Ali **055 296 2963**
itsjustfootball.com
Metro **Jebel Ali**
Welcomes beginners through to elite players, with
sessions running throughout the week. The dedicated
UEFA, A & B licensed coaches have all played and
coached at the highest levels and bring years' of
experience to their training. The club also offers the
chance to take coaching qualifications, and hosts
tournaments, social events, and regular fitness
training.

McGettigan Irish Football Club
mcgettigans.com
Dubai Irish consists of players of all nationalities and
participates in the Dubai Amateur Football League.
Despite competing in the more competitive division
one, the team welcomes players of all skill levels.

Socatots
Sports City, Al Hebiah 4 **04 448 1555**
footballacademydubai.com
Map **1 M12**
This is a fun, musical, soccer play programme for
toddlers from walking age to five years. It covers
aspects of physical, mental and social development
and involves parent participation. Sessions, held from
Thursdays to Saturdays, also take place at Emirates
International School.

Soccer Kids Dubai
055 207 3168
soccerkidsdubai.com
Soccer Kids Dubai offers soccer training in locations
across Dubai for ages three to 16 years. Soccer camps
during the school holidays are also available. The
school also offers children's parties.

Gaelic Games

Dubai Celts GAA
055 660 8357
dubaicelts.com
Dubai Celts GAA holds games and organises training
in men's and ladies' Gaelic football, hurling and
camogie. Monthly matches are played within the UAE,
and international tournaments are held in Bahrain
(November) and Dubai (March) each year. Training
sessions are held every Monday and Wednesday at
7pm. To join, call the above number.

Gymnastics
Whether you're looking for professional coaching,
something to keep the kids active or to just try out a
new activity, there are gymnastics classes for every
skill level.

Dubai Olympic Gymnastics Club
Al Raya Girl's School, 12A St Al Wasl
050 765 1515
dubai-gymnastics.com
Map **2 F5** Metro **Burj Khalifa/Dubai Mall**
UK gymnastics champion Dean Johnstone runs this
club which offers courses for gymnasts of all levels.
Classes correspond with school terms as they are
geared towards children.

DuGym Gymnastics Club
050 553 6283
dugym.com
Gymnastics and trampoline coaching for children of
all abilities is offered during classes from Sunday to
Thursday. DuGym runs gym tots lessons as well as
club competitions throughout the year at locations
including the GEMS World Academy, the Jumeirah
English Speaking School and Emirates International
School. Contact Suzanne for more info.

GymnastEx
Prism Tower Business Bay **04 445 8244**
Map **2 E6** Metro **Business Bay**
GymnastEx combo classes blend three disciplines
– rhythmic, acrobatics and sports aerobics – in one
session. Martial arts instruction for boys and yoga
for parents is also available, as well as classes for
babies. The classes are suitable for pre-school children
between two and five years old.

Hashing
Billed as 'drinking clubs with a running problem', Hash
House Harriers is a global network of clubs with an
emphasis on taking part and socialising afterwards,
rather than serious running. A fun way to get fit and
meet people.

Creek Hash House Harriers
Nadd Al Shiba 4 **050 451 5847**
creekhash.net
Map **2 B8** Metro **Noor Bank**
This men-only group meets every Tuesday, and runs
take pace in the desert around sunset for around
45 minutes. They then gather around a camp fire to
socialise. They also hold regular curry nights and spit-
roast dinners.

Desert Hash House Harriers
050 614 6621
deserthash.org
This group runs every Sunday, an hour before sunset.
Prior to the run, one or more members, the Hares, set
a trail using straws, paint, chalk or flour. This trail is
then followed by the remainder of the group. The fee
is Dhs.50 including refreshments. There's no need to
worry if you're not an athlete – everyone is welcome.

Hockey

Dubai Hockey Club
Nr Cricket Stadium Sports City, Al Hebiah 4
055 917 0622
dubaihockeyclub.com
Map **1 L11**
The club plays in local tournaments on grass and takes part in friendly games. Club training sessions are every Sunday and Wednesday evening. All abilities are welcome. Men and women can join. International tours to locations such as Singapore, Hong Kong and the UK are organised fairly regularly.

Horse Riding

There are a number of excellent stables and equestrian clubs in Dubai. While keeping your own horse can be very expensive, you may find that riding lessons cost less here than in your home country. Though there may be a waiting lists for lessons. There are a few places, such as The Desert Palm Riding School, where you can take your kids for a 10 minute horse ride around the track. If you are a dressage rider and would like to get involved in shows in the UAE contact stables such as Godolphin (godolphin.com), the Abu Dhabi Equestrian Club (emiratesracing.com), or Al Zobair Stud Farm in Sharjah (alzobairstud.com). Horse racing in Dubai is extremely popular. Most races, including the Dubai World Cup – the richest horse race in the world – take place at the Meydan racetrack.

Al Ahli Horse Riding Club
Nr LuLu Hypermarket Al Nahda 1 **04 298 8408**
alahliriding.com
Map **2 R7** Metro **Stadium**
A well-established club offering a wide range of activities including bare back lessons, dressage and jumping. There's also pony clubs and horsemanship clubs for riders aged four and up.

Al Jiyad Stables
Nr Dubai International Endurance City Al Yalayis 2
050 599 5866
aljiyad.com
Offers lessons for riders of all levels of experience. It also runs individual or group desert hacks. The excellent stables are home to more than 60 horses.

Al Sahra Desert Resort Equestrian Centre
Al Sahra Desert Resort Al Yufrah 2
04 427 4055
alsahra.com
Horse riding for individuals and groups is available at this eco-tourism resort in the Dubai desert. Private livery is also offered for a limited number of horses, and corporate team-building exercises are available.

The Desert Equestrian Club
Wadi Al Amardi Mushrif **050 309 9770**
If you have your own horse, the Desert Equestrian Club offers livery services for Dhs.1,500 a month. Accomplished riders can pay Dhs.100 to use one of the stable's horses. Private lessons are Dhs.80 for adults and Dhs.50 for children under 16.

The Desert Palm Riding School
Desert Palm Warsan 2 **04 323 8010**
desertpalm.ae
This state-of-the-art riding school offers group or semi-private classes for all ages, and one-to-one sessions. Prices are Dhs.95 per 30 minutes for child beginners and Dhs.175 per hour for adults, including all equipment. Relax after riding in the club's Lime Spa, or enjoy dinner at the Arabian-influenced restaurant.

Dubai Polo & Equestrian Club
Al Qudra St Arabian Ranches, Al Hebiah 2
04 361 8111
poloclubdubai.com
Map **1 N13**
This top-notch centre features a sandplast arena (one of the best surfaces to ride on), a riding school and a polo club. Horseriding lessons are available for all abilities. Beginners' courses start at Dhs.1,400 for 10 lessons. Enjoy a picnic pitchside during chukkas, held every weekend during the winter. Bring your own sandwiches or order bespoke picnics through the website. The club also houses several top-quality restaurants and a branch of Angsana Spa, and the venue is available for weddings and conferences.

Emirates Equestrian Centre
Nr Bab Al Shams Desert Resort & Spa Mugatrah
050 553 7986
emiratesequestriancentre.com
This centre is home to more than 80 horses. Facilities include an international size floodlit arena, a riding school, and dressage and lunging rings. It can cater to very small children and hosts regular competitions, gymkhanas and shows. The centre also has regular clinics and stable management courses.

Hoofbeatz
Umm Al Daman **050 181 0401**
hoofbeatz.com
Map **1 N13**
The Hoofbeatz Horsemanship Club runs every Friday and Saturday, from 4pm until 6pm, for beginner and novice horse lovers aged eight to 18 years. The centre also runs an all-round horsemanship course covering stable management and caring for horses. If you're unfamiliar with horses, then try the two-hour 'Meet the Horse' experience. Also on offer are birthday parties, educational visits for schools, and holiday camps.

JA Jebel Ali Golf Resort
Nr Palm Jebel Ali Mena Jabal Ali **04 814 5555**
jaresortshotels.com
Metro **Jebel Ali**
The riding centre has nine horses and air-conditioned stables. Instructors give private lessons from Tuesday to Sunday, while experienced riders can tackle one-hour desert rides. Half-hour lessons cost Dhs.200 (private) and Dhs.150 (semi-private).

Jebel Ali Equestrian Club
Nr Jebel Ali Hospital Jabal Ali 1 **04 884 5101**
Map **1 N7** Metro **Ibn Battuta**
Qualified instructors teach all levels of dressage, jumping, gymkhana games and hacking. Newcomers can try one lesson, after which a 10 lesson package costs Dhs.800 for children and Dhs.1,000 for adults, plus a Dhs.120 annual registration fee.

Riding for the Disabled Association of Dubai
Desert Palm Warsan 2 rdad.ae
A charity that uses horseriding and hippotherapy (physical and speech therapy using the movement of a horse) to achieve therapeutic goals for those suffering from autism, cerebral palsy, Down's Syndrome, spina bifida and learning disabilities. The aim is to improve poise, posture, strength and flexibility while boosting confidence. Classes last around 45 minutes.

Ice Hockey
Ice hockey has been a fixture on the local sports scene ever since Al Nasr Leisureland opened in 1979. With the opening of Dubai Ice Rink, teams now have two Dubai venues. The Skate Shop next to the ice rink at The Dubai Mall stocks hockey kit including skates, sticks, body armour, jerseys and helmets for children and adults. Call Dubai Ice Rink for stock details (04 448 5111).

Dubai Mighty Camels Ice Hockey Club
Al Nasr Leisureland Oud Metha
dubaimightycamels.com
Map **2 L6** Metro **Oud Metha**
This amateur ice hockey league has more than 120 members and competes in the Emirates Hockey League (EHL). The club also hosts an annual tournament in April, which attracts up to 20 teams from the Gulf, Europe and the Far East.

Dubai Sandstorms Ice Hockey Club
Oud Metha **050 775 8713**
eteamz.com/dubaisandstorm
Map **2 L6** Metro **Oud Metha**
Practice sessions are held twice a week for youngsters aged four to 18. The emphasis is on teamwork and sportsmanship. Matches are played against teams from Dubai, Abu Dhabi, Al Ain Oman and Qatar. The Sandstorms website has a noticeboard for buying and selling ice hockey equipment.

Kayaking
See Activities, Things To See & Do.

Kitesurfing
See Activities, Things To See & Do.

Martial Arts
Aspiring Bruce Lees are well catered for with many centres offering courses in judo, aikido, karate, kickboxing and other martial arts. In addition, many fitness clubs and gyms offer Thai boxing, kung fu, self-defence alongside their group exercise programmes. For kids, the Active Sports Academy has an excellent range of disciplines for all ages and runs after-school classes as well as holiday camps.

Colosseum Muay Thai Health & Fitness Club
Zaabeel St Al Karama **04 337 2755**
colosseumuae.com
Map **2 L6** Metro **BurJuman**
Classes are daily from 8.30pm to 10pm, except Fridays (Dhs.50). Personal training is available for those over eight years old.

Dubai Karate Centre
Nr Safa Park Al Safa 1 **04 344 7797**
dubaikarate.com
Map **2 C5** Metro **Noor Bank**
This club is a member of the Japanese Karate Association (JKA) and has a team of black belt, JKA qualified instructors who teach a range of martial arts that include shotokan karate, taekwondo, aikido, Muay Thai, judo, kudo, iado, laido and wingtzun. This centre also runs regular self-defence courses. Registration Dhs.100. Monthly memberships from Dhs.380.

Dubai Kendo Club
050 900 2661
The focus here is on a martial art based on the ancient Japanese swordsmanship traditions. The club meets Wednesdays at 7.45pm and Saturdays at 4pm at Emirates International School Jumeirah. The two-hour classes cost Dhs.50 for adults, Dhs.30 for children.

EBMAS School Of Self Defense
DUCTAC Al Barsha 1 **055 605 8128**
ebmas-selfdefense.com
Map **1 R6** Metro **Mall of the Emirates**
Emin Boztepe Martial Arts System (EBMAS) is a popular form of self-defence that is now taught in more than 40 countries. This school teaches armed and unarmed forms of EBMAS. Classes are held on Sundays and Wednesdays.

Golden Falcon Karate Centre
Nr Choithrams Al Karama **04 336 0243**
goldenfalconkarate.com
Map **2 L5** Metro **ADCB**
Established in 1990, the centre is affiliated with the
International Karate Budokan and the UAE Judo,
Taekwondo & Karate Federation. The centre is open
throughout the week. Training costs Dhs.150 for two
classes per week. Classes are also taught at Jabal Ali,
Meadows, Oud Metha and JLT.

Golden Fist Karate Club
Al Riffa Plaza Al Raffa **04 452 5599**
goldenfistkarate.net
Map **2 L4** Metro **Al Raffa**
This club is popular for the flexible times it provides for
training in martial arts including karate and kung fu.
A nine-month black belt crash course is available too.
Two and six classes a week, from Dhs.150 to Dhs.320
per month (plus a Dhs.50 admission fee). For those
of a more gentle disposition, yoga, swimming and
aerobics classes are also offered.

Team Nogueira Dubai
Sheikh Zayed Road 04 338 8967
Map **2 B6** Metro Noor Islamic Bank
This martial arts and fitness academy is located in a
huge warehouse on Sheikh Zayed Road, complete
with a mixed martial arts cage, boxing ring, Jiu-Jitsu
mats, Muay Thai area, and cafe. Blending martial arts
and fitness, the classes and training sessions cater to
men, women and children, with the overall aim to
boost fitness levels.

Zanshinkan Aikido Club Dubai
Al Razi Boys School Al Safa 1 **050 795 2716**
aikido.ae
Map **2 C5** Metro **Business Bay**
Classes for children and adults are held throughout
the week at the Dubai Karate Centre. Once-only
registration Dhs.100. Kids' classes are Dhs.350 for eight
classes a month and adult training costs Dhs.500 for
12 sessions a month.

Motorsports

Automobile & Touring Club of The UAE
Al Wuheida St Al Mamzar **04 296 1122**
atcuae.ae
Map **2 R6** Metro **Al Qiyadah**
The club is the UAE's FIM (Fédération Internationale
de Motocyclisme) representative. Regular motocross
and off-road enduros are held between September
and April, and activity centres at the DMX Club and
in Umm Al Quwain host quad and drag races. It
organises the Abu Dhabi Desert Challenge, and the
opening round of the FIA Cross Country Rally.

Dubai Autodrome
Shk Mohammed Bin Zayed Rd MotorCity,
Al Hebiah 1 **04 367 8700**
dubaiautodrome.com
Map **1 N12**
Dubai's motorsport home in MotorCity has six track
configurations, including a 5.39km FIA-sanctioned GP
circuit, state-of-the-art pit facilities and a 7,000 seat
grandstand. Events hosted include rounds of the FIA GT
Championship.

Dubai Motocross Club (DMX)
Nr Jebel Ali Go Kart Track Hessyan 1 **055 388 6279**
Metro **Jebel Ali**
Dubai Motocross (DMX) runs classes for cadets,
juniors, 65cc, 85cc, 125cc and adults. The facility
features two tracks, one for juniors and one for seniors,
and organises eight championship events per year.
The entry fee is Dhs.150 for members and starts at
Dhs.250 for non-members. Practice fees for members
are Dhs.50 during the week and Dhs.75 at weekends.
Non-members pay Dhs.100 or Dhs.150.

Emirates Motor Sports Federation
Villa 1, 21A St Al Garhoud **04 282 7111**
emsf.ae
Map **2 M8** Metro **GGICO**
Emirates Motor Sports Federation organises events
throughout the year, such as the 4WD 1000 Dunes
Rally, the Champions Rally for saloon cars, road safety
campaigns and classic car exhibitions. Membership
including competition licence is Dhs.500 per year;
non-members can race for a fee.

The Chase street-racing festival at Dubai Autodrome

Harley Owners Group Dubai Chapter
04 339 1909
hogdubai.com
The group meets at various locations for rides across the region, including the Middle East HOG Rally in Fujairah. See its website for a full events calendar and map links to meet locations.

Royal Enfield Dubai
Nr Times Square Al Qouz Ind. 1 **04 340 1855**
royalenfielduae.com
Map **1 U6** Metro **Noor Bank**
The social club organises city rides, long-distance trips and informal gatherings, as well as an annual gala. Although the club is named Royal Enfield Dubai, riders of any bikes are welcome.

Netball
Netball is not just for school girls – here in Dubai it's alive and kicking for all age groups, and is a well-established sport. Even if you've no prior experience, you'll be welcomed by Dubai's teams if you want to give it a try.

Dubai Netball League
The Sevens Al Marmoom **055 884 2474**
dubainetballleague.com
Four divisions compete between September and May. Training is on Sundays or Mondays. League nights are on Wednesdays. Players also have the chance to be selected for the annual inter-Gulf championship. New players of all levels are welcome.

Duplays
Indigo Icon Tower JLT, Al Thanyah 5 **04 447 2394**
duplays.com
Map **1 K5** Metro **Jumeirah Lakes Towers**
Duplays' competitive women's league plays Sunday evenings, and games in the recreational league take place on Monday evenings. Players can sign up as individuals and be allocated to a team for Dhs.450. Enter a full team for Dhs.3,900 per season.

Polo

Dubai Polo & Equestrian Club
Al Qudra St Arabian Ranches, Al Hebiah 2
04 361 8111
poloclubdubai.com
Map **1 N13**
The very best players in the world are attracted to this venue's regular local and international polo competitions held on its two full-sized pitches. Coaching is offered for all levels, from 40 minute lessons to six-day courses. An introductory 1.5 hour lesson is Dhs.800.

Polo
For a fun twist on the game, head to the Dubai Polo and Equestrian Club for a spot of camel polo. It's not as fast-paced as the real thing but you'll come away with plenty of good stories. Any group of eight or more is welcome to book a session. Call 04 404 5880 for reservations or for more details email camelpolo@gulfventures.com.

Rugby

Dubai Exiles Rugby Football Club
dubaiexiles.com
The Exiles is Dubai's most serious rugby club and has a 1st and 2nd XV that competes in the AGRFU leagues. It also has a veterans, U19s, ladies', girls' U17s and a minis and youth section. The Exiles club also hosts a tournament alongside the annual Dubai IRB Sevens Tournament.

Dubai Hurricanes Rugby Football Club
The Sevens Al Marmoom **050 794 0823**
dubaihurricanes.com
Having started as a social outfit, the Hurricanes now compete in the Dubai Sevens. The club also has a ladies' team and players aged from four to over 50 and all abilities are welcome. Training is on Mondays and Wednesdays at 6.30pm. Touring is a key activity of the club and is used to develop the Midi and Youth sections – tours to date include Australia, Japan, Spain and more.

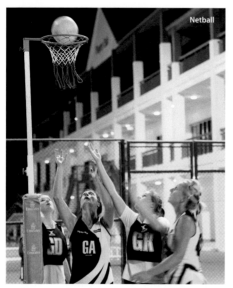
Netball

Running

For more than half the year, Dubai's weather is perfect for running. There are lots of groups to try and a number of events to train for, such as the excellent Creek Striders Half Marathon (dubaicreekstriders@gmail.com), the Dubai Marathon (dubaimarathon.org), and the Wadi Bih Race (wadibih.com). For suggestions of places to run, see askexplorer.com.

Dubai Creek Striders

dubaicreekstriders.org

The Striders meet Friday mornings (on the road opposite the Novotel next to the Trade Centre) for a long-distance run. This club started in 1995 and training is designed for members to take part in the 42.2km Dubai Marathon in January. For more info email them on dubai.creek.striders@gmail.com.

Dubai Road Runners

Jumeira Beach Park Jumeira 2 **050 624 3213**
dubai-road-runners.com
Map **2 D4** Metro **Business Bay**
Meet up with the Road Runners on Saturdays at 6.30pm by gate 4 of Safa Park to run between 3.4km and 7km (the park charges Dhs.5 entrance fee). For fun, runners predict their times, with a prize for the winner.

Nike+ Run Club

facebook.com/nikerunning
Beginners or intermediates are best suited to these sessions at Festival City (Tuesday evenings) and Downtown (Friday mornings) and are expertly coached, not to mention free.

Reebok Running Club

055 886 9158
urbanenergyfitness.com
Map **1 K5** Metro **Jumeirah Lakes Towers**
Ignite your passion for running with this club for all abilities and fitness levels. Members meet twice a week at Dubai Marina Mall to run in a fun, motivating atmosphere and share advice on training, nutrition and health tips. Organised in partnership with fitness experts Urban Energy.

Stride For Life

050 657 7057
strideforlife.com
Stride for Life offers aerobic walking and running for people of all ages and abilities. Anyone interested in joining should first undergo a fitness assessment. Following this, a thrice-weekly programme is recommended. Stride for Life also does Nordic and mall walking, and 'training journeys' for novices preparing for long distance events. Fees are Dhs.1,600 for a one-year membership.

Ski Dubai

Sailing

See Activities, Things To See & Do.

Skating & Rollerblading

See Activities, Things To See & Do.

Skiing

Dubai Ski Club

Al Barsha 1
dubaiskiclub.com
Map **1 R6** Metro **Mall of the Emirates**
The club has over 1,400 members and meets at 6pm on the last Saturday of every month, next to Ski Dubai's ticket counter, for social skiing or snowboarding, race training and races, followed by apres ski. Membership benefits include a reduced fee for the slope pass and use of the 'advance booking' lane when purchasing tickets, plus special offers on equipment, clothing, accessories and holidays. Membership is Dhs.300. Club ski and snowboard trips to Europe are also arranged.

Softball

Duplays

Indigo Icon Tower JLT, Al Thanyah 5 **04 447 2394**
duplays.com
Map **1 K5** Metro **Jumeirah Lakes Towers**
Located in Jumeirah Lakes Towers, Duplays runs a mixed recreational softball league on Wednesdays. Matches are held at the sports field near Business Bay on Sheikh Zayed Road.

Squash

Dubai Squash
The Greens, Al Thanyah 3
dubaisquash.com
Map **1 N6** Metro **Nakheel**
The league has been active in Dubai and Sharjah since the 1970s and is run by the UAE Squash Association. Around 250 competitors in 25 teams play three 10 week seasons. Teams meet on Mondays at 7.30pm.

Emirates Golf Club
Emirates Hills **04 380 1919**
dubaigolf.com
Map **1 M6** Metro **Nakheel**
The Fit Lab Squash Facility at Emirates Golf Club hosts regular member and inter-club competitions. Annual membership is Dhs.3,000, which includes unlimited squash and access to the monthly league.

Surfing
See Activities, Things To See & Do.

Swimming
Dubai has some great swimming spots at various public beaches, private pools, at beach clubs or one of the beach parks. The water temperature rarely dips below 20°C in winter, although during the summer it can feel like stepping into a bath. Be aware that rip tides and undertows in the sea can catch out even the strongest swimmer, so never ignore flags or signs ordering you not to swim.

You might also run into quite a lot of jellyfish towards the end of the summer. Around the UAE there are occasional outbreaks of red tide, a naturally occurring algal bloom which turns the water red and gives it an unpleasant smell. These generally affect the east coast and are relatively uncommon in Dubai.

Many hotels, beach clubs and health clubs have swimming pools open to the public for a day entrance fee. Swimming lessons are available from health and beach clubs too. For children's lessons, check with your school. Keen swimmers can sign up for the Wild Wadi Swim Around the Burj annual challenge, held each February in aid of Medecins Sans Frontieres (swim.msf-me.org). There are two distances to choose from – an 800m swim and a 1,600m swim – and swimmers are given plenty of encouragement from spectators watching from the beach.

Active Sports Academy
Al Rebat St Al Kheeran **050 559 7055**
activeuae.com
Map **2 M9** Metro **Emirates**
Classes, held in various locations, include water babies, parent and toddlers, and lessons for beginners to advanced swimmers.

Aqua Sports Academy
King's Dubai Umm Suqeim 3 **050 574 7942**
aquaswim.ae
Map **1 S5** Metro **First Gulf Bank**
Aqua Sports runs mainly from the 25m pool at Kings' School in Umm Suqeim. Sessions include everything from parent-and-baby sessions, kids' swim lessons and one-to-one clinics, competitive squads and holiday camps. It also runs the city's most popular masters' swim programme for swimmers aged 16 and up. Casual, keep-fit swimmers and competitive age-group swimmers and triathletes all welcome. See the website for session times and special events.

Australian International Swim Schools
Al Shafar Tower 1 Al Thanyah 1 **04 368 9226**
aiss.ae
Map **1 N6** Metro **Dubai Internet City**
AUSTSWIM-certified instructors provide swimming lessons at pools throughout Dubai. This company also runs many of the schools' swimming programmes. Swimming training is provided at all levels, from classes for parents and babies, to adult triathlon swimming squads. Lessons are available in Al Qouz, Jumeira, The Lakes, Emirate Hills, Springs, Victory Heights, Sharjah, Mirdif and Al Twar.

Dawn Venturas
050 509 5673
dawnventuras.com
Swimming coach Dawn Venturas comes from a competitive swimming and waterpolo background. She specialises in baby and toddler classes, from as early as eight weeks old. Group lessons are held at various location across Dubai. Private lessons can also be arranged.

Excel Sports
050 223 9235
excelsportsuae.com
Excel Sports offers coaching in swimming, cricket, soccer and gymnastics. The emphasis is firmly on having fun and being confident in the water. The company also runs holiday camps that include swimming in the programme, as well as other activities such as tennis, soccer and softball.

Hamdan bin Mohammed Sports Complex
Nr Emirates Rd Umm Nahad 2 **04 306 2666**
hamdansc.com
The HSC is the largest sports Aquatic Sports Centre in the world. It houses three swimming pools and specialises in swimming, diving, water polo and synchronised swimming. It also offers track and field sports and hosts events. A monthly swimming pass is Dhs.200 – see the website for further prices.

Hamilton Aquatics
04 450 8832
hamiltonaquaticsdubai.com
Hamilton Aquatics is currently one of the largest swimming academies in the Middle East. Hamilton's Learn to Swim Academy develops children and adults from non-swimmers to advanced swimmers with over 210 classes and 1,200 spaces a week for every level of swimmer. Operating across numerous locations in Dubai, it runs a swim development programme to enhance swimming skills and a dedicated Squad Academy for elite swim training.

Speedo Swim Squads
04 354 9525
speedodubai.net
Map **1 Q13**
This private club offers tuition for all ages and abilities, from 'duckling' to squad training. It also offers ASA teacher training and water polo classes. Lessons take place at a number of locations including Horizon School, Uptown High School, Dubai International Academy and Emirates International School.

Synquatics
Raffles International School
Umm Suqeim 3 **055 448 5381**
synquatics.com
Map **1 S5** Metro **First Gulf Bank**
Opened in 2012 by former Olympian sisters, Sarah and Hebel Abdel Gawad, this club teaches synchronised swimming; a hybrid of swimming, dance and

gymnastics. Locations include Safa School, Raffles and Fitness First (Meadows). Swimmers can choose to train either once, twice or three times a week in 60 minute sessions, though during term time only block bookings are accepted.

Table Tennis
Table tennis can be played for Dhs.40 per hour, including equipment, at Insportz just behind Dubai Garden Centre on Sheikh Zayed Road. Booking is required. Several of the older leisure clubs provide table tennis, although the equipment is usually a bit rusty. The UAE Table Tennis Association is in Dubai (04 254 7111), and can provide information on how to get into leagues and high level competitions, but unfortunately most of the local clubs only accept UAE Nationals.

Tennis
Dubai is firmly established on the international tennis circuit, with the annual Dubai Duty Free Tennis Championships attracting the best players in the world. There are plenty of venues to enjoy a game. Outdoor courts are available at most health and beach clubs, many of which are floodlit. There are indoor courts for hire at InSportz (04 347 5833).

Ace Sports Academy
055 452 2066
acesportsacademy.com
Map **2 G6** Metro **Burj Khalifa/Dubai Mall**
This tennis school offers everything from tots' tennis and junior development to ladies' mornings,

Emirates Golf Club

adult lessons and tournaments. The Cardio Lessons, designed to keep the heart rate up for optimal fitness, are very popular. Private, semi-private and family lessons are available, and ball machines can be hired. Membership and lesson costs vary. Check the website for details. Also at Mirdif Tennis Courts, near Mirdif City Centre.

The Atlantis Tennis Academy
Atlantis Nakhlat Jumeira **04 426 1433**
Map **1 N1** Metro **Nakheel**
Provides world-class coaching for players of all ages and levels. The state-of-the-art facilities include the latest court surfaces plus video technology for technique analysis. The academy also organises social events and tournament afternoons for members.

Clark Francis Tennis Academy
04 282 4540
clarkfrancistennis.com
This tennis school offers group and individual tennis coaching for children and adults. A ladies' morning is held at the Grand Hyatt on Mondays from 8.15am. Cardio Tennis classes (a cross between tennis and circuit training) are every Tuesday from 6.45pm at the Aviation Club. It also organises competitive leagues in a variety of categories including juniors. Ball kid training (for the Dubai Tennis Championships) is available, and the service centre can have your racket restrung and returned to you within 12 hours.

Dubai Tennis Academy
American University Al Sufouh 2 **04 399 1125**
dubaitennisacademy.com
Map **1 M5** Metro **Nakheel**
Become a better tennis player at this expertly run academy. Provides training for all levels, with internationally qualified coaches, at American University Dubai, and the five-star Grand Hyatt hotel Dubai (which has four courts). Programmes include private lessons, group clinics, competitions, ladies' tennis mornings and school holiday camps. Check the website for prices for members and non-members. The academy sometimes offers discounts and promotions on its website.

Emirates Golf Club
Shk Zayed Rd Al Sufouh 2 **04 417 9999**
dubaigolf.com
Map **1 M6** Metro **Nakheel**
The Elite Tennis Academy at Emirates Golf Club is open to non-members of all levels for coaching by qualified USPTR professionals. The centre has four courts. Two teams play in the ladies' Spinneys League and one in the men's Prince League. Private and semi private lesson packages, group lessons, ladies mornings, social mixers, tournaments and camps are all available.

Tennis 360
Meydan Racecourse, Al Meydan Road **04 381 3500**
tennisthreesixty.com
Map **2 E10**
Opened in January 2012, Tennis 360 aims to teach key tennis skills, mental conditioning, and good nutrition, to create a love for the game in both adults and children. The facility boasts a championship court, five regular courts, two mini courts, and one enclosed padel court for doubles.

Wilson Tennis Academy
Le Royal Meridien Beach Resort & Spa, Jumeira Beach **055 675 3885**
wilsondubaitennis.com
Map **1 L5** Metro **DAMAC**
Located at Le Royal Meridien Beach Resort & Spa, the academy offers private and group instructions, instructional clinics, and social events.

Triathlon

SuperTRI
050 873 1989
supertriuae.com
If you fancy getting really fit this year then train with certified triathlon coach, Trace Rogers, who can help you gain the skills and techniques you need to perform in a triathlon and reach your best ever time. Training focuses on all areas of swimming, running and biking and programmes are offered to suit your lifestyle and budget.

TriDubai
tridubai.org
Support for everyone from complete beginners to world-class athletes; for those training for sprint distance to Ironman races (or just training for the love of it); for those starting out, starting again or wanting to break records. The club welcomes new members and training sessions are free of charge.

Ultimate Frisbee

Duplays
Indigo Icon Tower JLT, Al Thanyah 5 **04 447 2394**
duplays.com
Map **1 K5** Metro **Jumeirah Lakes Towers**
Duplays (duplays.com) organises a friendly league which you can enter as a team or individual and be placed in a team. Games are on Monday nights on the field near Business Bay. Pickup games are held in Safa Park on Saturday afternoons.

Watersports
For information on diving, kayaking, kitesurfing and other watersports, see Activities, Things To See & Do.

Hobbies

Arts & Crafts

There's a thriving arts and crafts scene in Dubai with classes available for beginners and children. During the hot summer months, an arty activity could be just what you need to keep occupied. And, if you need to buy supplies, see our Shopping section for listings.

Art Labs

04 374 6208
artlabs.me
Courses are held at Dubai Ladies Club and The Pavillion Downtown on everything from *sospeso trasparente* and sugar wires to jewellery making and decorating techniques. There's also an online store to buy supplies. The group creates beautiful, glitzy accessories for weddings and corporate events, as well as invites – some of which are decorated with Swarovski crystals.

Cafe Ceramique

Town Centre, Jumeira Beach Road
04 344 7331
cafe-ceramique.com
Map **2 F4** Metro **Emirates Towers**
Paint your own teapot or a whole dinner set. Choose your piece of blank pottery, which the cafe will glaze and fire for you after you decorate it. Events include Art4fun Workshops and the Kidz4art Summer Camp. The cafe also serves a great selection of healthy breakfasts, lunches and snacks to keep you energised while you get creative.

Cafe Ceramique

Craft Land

Town Centre Jumeirah Jumeira 1 **04 342 2237**
mycraftland.com
Map **2 F4** Metro **Burj Khalifa/Dubai Mall**
Everything you'd like to learn about machine sewing, quilting, hand embroidery, knitting and crocheting is taught here. There are needlecraft workshops, courses, clubs and clinics. Classes are for beginners and the more experienced. Most sessions last around 90 minutes. Some are charged per class (roughly Dhs.40) while for others you pay for a full course (prices vary). Club meetings are Tuesday mornings and Saturday afternoons and membership is Dhs.50.

Creative Hands

Mayfair Bldg Dubai Investment Park 1 **04 884 9343**
creativehandsdubai.com
Map **1 G10** Metro **Ibn Battuta**
Creative Hands has a store in The Green Community and another online. The company also offers workshops and sessions in crafts such as scrapbooking and card making.

Dubai Community Theatre & Arts Centre

Mall of the Emirates Al Barsha 1 **04 341 4777**
ductac.org
Map **1 R6** Metro **Mall of the Emirates**
Decorative arts, drawing, painting, photography, sculpture, paper craft and the performing arts are just some of classes DUCTAC runs for adults and children. Details are listed online and updated regularly. DUCTAC also has a theatre, art galleries and studios for exhibitions and performances. There's a cafe, art supplies shop and The Old Library, an English language lending library run by volunteers. DUCTAC is open daily 9am to 10pm and 2pm to 10pm on Fridays.

Dubai International Art Centre

Villa 27, Street 75B Jumeira 1 **04 344 4398**
artdubai.com
Map **2 F4** Metro **Financial Centre**
Villa-based art centre offering six- to eight-week courses in more than 70 subjects, including painting, drawing, dressmaking, etching, pottery and photography. Annual membership starts from Dhs.350 for adults, Dhs.450 for families and Dhs.120 for under 18s.

the jamjar

Nr Dubai Garden Centre Al Qouz Ind. 3 **04 341 7303**
thejamjardubai.com
Map **1 S6** Metro **First Gulf Bank**
A canvas, paints and the obligatory jam jar are yours starting at Dhs.195 for four hours of self-inspired creativity. All you need to bring is your inspiration. The 'Jam-To-Go' service brings the experience to you – a novel idea for a party or corporate event. Open

weekdays from 10am to 8pm; Fridays 2pm to 8pm; closed on Sundays.

Objects & Elements
Street 8 Al Qouz Ind. 1 **04 323 6182**
objectsandelementsgroup.com
Map **1 U6** Metro **Noor Bank**
A sewing group where you can get your 'sewing machine driving licence' and learn how to make everything from ironing board covers to retro soft toy owls. They also teach embroidery.

Paper at Artisans of the Emirates
Time Square Center Al Qouz Ind. 1 arte.ae
Map **1 T6** Metro **Noor Bank**
Paper@ARTE is part of ARTE Souk, held at the Times Square Center or Festival Centre most Fridays. All scrapbookers can join the workshops.

Paper Lane
Town Centre Jumeirah Jumeira 1 **04 344 3633**
mypaperlane.com
Map **2 F4** Metro Burj Khalifa/Dubai Mall
One of the city's biggest scrapbooking shops, Paper Lane carries all the materials you'll need to create a memorable album. It also runs classes for all ages and levels. Families welcome.

reMADE DXB
Objects & Elements, Al Qouz 1 **055 615 5711**
remadedxb.com
Map **1 U6** Metro **Mall of the Emirates**
This Al Qouz crafting company runs regular workshops, with subjects including machine sewing, book binding, decoupage, bunting making, and much more. There are also classes arranged for children.

Birdwatching

Emirates Bird Records Committee
uaebirding.com
Local and visiting birders are invited to submit details of sightings to this committee which collates information on birds in the UAE and on request. A weekly roundup of bird sightings and a monthly report are available via email from Tommy Pedersen at 777sandman@gmail.com.

Bridge

Dubai Ladies Bridge Club
Jumeira 1 **050 659 1300**
Map **2 F4** Metro **Business Bay**
The sociable females of Dubai meet for ladies-only bridge mornings at 9am on Sundays and Wednesdays. Contact Marzie Polad on the number above or Jan Irvine on 050 645 4395.

Chess

Dubai Chess & Culture Club
Nr Century Mall Al Mamzar **04 296 6664**
dubaichess.ae
Map **2 R6** Metro **Al Qiyadah**
The home of the UAE's national chess team. Members can play at the club seven nights a week, and competitions are organised on a regular basis. The club also promotes international competitions, including the Dubai International Open, Emirates Open and Dubai Junior Open. Membership costs Dhs.100 a year.

Cooking Classes

Many hotels run cookery classes by special request if you particularly like one of their dishes, or as an organised series of classes. There are also wine tasting classes and courses for budding oenophiles or those just wanting to up their dinner party game.

Armani Hotel Dubai
Downtown Dubai, Burj Khalifa **04 888 3888**
dubai.armanihotels.com
Map **2 F6** Metro **Burj Khalifa/Dubai Mall**
The teams of chefs at several of the Armani Hotel's most popular restaurants teach students how to make some of their specialities at home. Between Saturdays and Wednesdays, 4.30pm to 6pm, you can learn to prepare a classic three-course Italian meal, master Indian cuisine or perfect the intricacies of Japanese fare. Classes range from Dhs.1,100 to Dhs.1,300.

Asado
The Palace Downtown Dubai **04 428 7888**
theaddress.com
Map **2 F6** Metro **Burj Khalifa/Dubai Mall**
Master the art of Argentinean cooking with Chef Gabriel Stivala at Asado. Available daily with registration in advance, the classes give an insight into the skills required to prepare dishes from every region of Argentina, from the south to the north. Costs Dhs.345, including food.

The Balance Cafe Cookery School
Oasis Centre Al Qouz 1 **04 515 4051**
balance-wellness-centre.com
Map **2 C6** Metro **Noor Bank**
Award-winning chefs from restaurants across Dubai, including Carluccio's, Ushna and Mango Tree offer hands-on training in a variety of cuisines such as Thai, Italian, sushi and Indian, all with a focus on healthy eating. The Balance Cafe cookery courses are designed for everyone, from amateurs to professionals, with prices starting at Dhs.250 per class and Dhs.800 for any four classes.

Blue Elephant

Al Bustan Rotana Al Garhoud **04 282 0000**
blueelephant.com
Map **2 N7** Metro **Airport Terminal 1**
Al Bustan Rotana offers cookery classes at its classic Thai restaurant on the first Saturday of every month. The cost per person is Dhs.199. Participants take away a new set of recipe ideas for the kitchen, a souvenir goody bag, and a certificate of attendance.

Blue Flame

Jumeirah Creekside Al Garhoud **04 230 8459**
jumeirah.com
Map **2 M7** Metro **GGICO**
Learn the secrets of preparing gourmet dishes such as brick baby chicken and seafood papillote at the Blue Flame cookery school. Classes are held every day at 7pm in a state-of-the-art cooking pod. Prices start at Dhs.300, which includes a signed copy of the menu and Blue Flame apron.

Cooking At Home

056 244 5082
Learn how to prepare traditional Italian family recipes, with two-hour weekly classes for Dhs.150 or weekend courses for Dhs.180. Private classes are also available.

Children's Classes

Kids can learn to cook at Le Meridien Dubai's Little Pastry Chef sessions at L'atelier des Chefs (atelierdeschefsdubai.com, Dhs.150). They also teach adults if you're inspired by your little one's new skills!

De Dietrich Cuisine Academy

Dubai Ladies Club Jumeira 1 **050 550 1612**
de-dietrich-academy.ae
Map **2 D4** Metro **Business Bay**
Brush up on your culinary skills with courses in French, Italian, Asian, sushi and special pastries. Learn how to make the perfect seasonal menu, prepare mocktails, cook fresh and healthy cuisine, or make special meals for kids. Classes cost from Dhs.130 to Dhs.350, and special packages for birthdays, baby showers and bridal parties are also available.

Jamie's Italian

Jumeirah Beach Hotel **04 380 8890**
jamieoliver.com/italian/dubai
Map **1 R4** Metro **First Gulf Bank**
Jamie's Italian hosts cookery classes within its Jumeirah Beach Hotel branch. The price of Dhs.299 per person includes a meal, goody bag of ingredients, and certificate. Classes are run several times per month and are popular, so make sure you register in advance.

Jones The Grocer

Shk Zayed Rd Al Manara **04 346 6886**
jonesthegrocer.com
Map **1 T6** Metro **First Gulf Bank**
Australia's gourmet deli and cafe hosts weekly cooking classes where you can master the art of pastries and breads, learn how to make pasta, or create your own soups. Classes start at 6pm and cost Dhs.375, and prior booking is necessary.

L'atelier des Chefs

Le Meridien Al Garhoud **056 690 0480**
atelierdeschefsdubai.com
Map **2 N7** Metro **Airport Terminal 1**
This French cooking school offers a wide range of classes including Arabic, Indian and French cuisine, plus sushi, seafood and pastry making. Classes cost from Dhs.120 for half an hour to Dhs.350 for two hours, depending on the type of class.

Nobu

Atlantis Nakhlat Jumeira **04 426 2626**
atlantisthepalm.com
Map **1 N1** Metro **Nakheel**
If you've always wanted to learn the art of sushi making, Nobu will show you how it's done. Chef de Cuisine Herve Courtot, and his team of expert Japanese chefs teach students at the restaurant's three-hour class on the first Saturday of every month. Costs Dhs.1,250 per person with lunch.

Prego's

Media Rotana, Al Thanyah 1 **04 435 0201**
rotana.com
Map **1 P6** Metro **Dubai Internet City**
Cooking has been in Chef Mauro's family for generations, and he makes for a charismatic and easy guide through some of his kitchen's most famous Italian dishes.

Thiptara

The Palace Downtown Downtown Dubai, Burj Khalifa **04 888 3444**
Map **2 F6** Metro **Burj Khalifa/Dubai Mall**
Culinary classes with Chef Mac cost Dhs.295, including the two-hour demonstration, some hands-on practice, lunch and a diploma in Thai cuisine.

Zuma

Gate Village Bldg 6 DIFC, Zaa'beel 2 **04 425 5660**
zumarestaurant.com
Map **2 G6** Metro **Financial Centre**
As the man behind arguably the city's best sushi counter, Zuma's Masaharu Kondo is the perfect host for these two-hour sushi masterclasses which cost Dhs.500 and allow for plenty of delicious sampling.

Dance

Whether you prefer to tap your feet to classical or contemporary rhythms, all dancing tastes are catered for in Dubai. Dancing schools, health clubs, restaurants and even bars hold weekly sessions in flamenco, salsa, samba, jazz dance, ballroom and so much more.

Belly Dancing

The ancient art of belly dancing is a great way to keep fit. The Ballet Centre (04 344 9776) holds lessons for Dhs.40 on Tuesdays and Saturdays. Milla Tenorio teaches at the Rotana Towers on Sundays and Tuesdays at 6pm; classes cost from Dhs.50 (050 395 5983). Nora Dance Group also offers belly-dancing classes and Exhale Fitness offers belly-dance fitness classes (exhaledubai.com).

The Address Dubai Marina
Nr Dubai Marina Mall Marsa Dubai **04 436 7777**
theaddress.com
Map **1 K5** Metro **Jumeirah Lakes Towers**
Every Wednesday is Havana Night at Blends with instructor Aloy Junco, Cuban-Latino sounds and complimentary Cuban salsa classes and beverages for the ladies, from 7pm till midnight.

Arthur Murray Dance Centre
201 Reef Tower JLT, Al Thanyah 5 **04 448 6458**
arthurmurraydubai.com
Map **1 K5** Metro **Jumeirah Lakes Towers**
Teaches rhythm and Latin, smooth and standard, country western and speciality dances in line with the Arthur Murray method. There's a second branch at Souk Al Bahar (04 450 8648).

The Ballet Centre
Nr Jumeira Plaza Jumeira 1 **04 344 9776**
balletcentre.com
Map **2 H4** Metro **World Trade Centre**
Study ballet, tap, modern, salsa, Irish, jazz and belly dancing. Classes are for adults, and children three years and over. Training for the Imperial Society for Teachers of Dancing (ISTD) and the Royal Academy of Dance examinations is encouraged.

BNF Dance School
Al Sufouh 2 **04 364 4881**
facebook.com/bnfdubai
Map **1 N5** Metro **Dubai Internet City**
The BNF is a celebrated Columbian dance school. The Dubai branch offers private and group instruction in tango, salsa and belly dancing, among other styles. The school also provides shows and entertainment for private events.

Cello Music & Ballet Centre
Oasis Centre Al Qouz 1 **04 380 8282**
cellodubai.com
Map **2 C6** Metro **Noor Bank**
Established in 2007, Cello Music & Ballet Centre offers dance and music classes to children and adults of all ages, at eight locations across Dubai: Springs, Lakes, Arabian Ranches, JBR, Umm Suqeim, Marsa Dubai, Palm Jumeirah, Al Qouz and Sheikh Zayed Road. There are also classes in belly dance, jazz, modern, tap dance, Irish dance, hip-hop and martial arts.

Ceroc Arabia
Trade Center 1 **050 659 5406**
Map **2 G5** Metro **Financial Centre**
Specialising in the modern jive, this Trade Center dance group offers classes, socials, and private tuition. The dance style is easy to learn and similar to salsa, but without the fancy footwork. It can be danced to all kinds of different music, including club and chart hits, classics, swing, Latin and rock 'n' roll.

Dance Horizons
Al Wasl **04 360 7691**
dancehorizons.ae
Map **2 D5** Metro **Business Bay**
A specialist ballet school that offers the Royal Academy of Dance Examination syllabus for beginners and advanced dancers, and a specialised music and movement programme for age three and older. Classes are at Horizon School near Safa Park and Safa School on Meydan Road in fully equipped ballet studios with sprung floors, barres and mirrors, and are led by highly qualified, RAD-registered teaching staff.

Dance Studios in Dubai
Jumeirah Lake Towers **04 457 9228**
Map **1 K5** Metro **Jumeirah Lake Towers**
Offering group and private lessons in ballroom dancing to both adults and children, this Jumeirah Lakes Towers based dance group currently has over 1,000 registered students learning to dance. There is a social dance every Wednesday at 9pm, where you can practice the steps you learnt in class with different partners in a relaxed, easy atmosphere. This is complimentary to students.

Dubai Liners
Al Satwa **055 700 6114**
Map **2 G5** Metro **Financial Centre**
It's not all country and western at this Al Satwa based line dancing group, which has been around since 1997. Attendees can line dance to disco, rock 'n' roll, salsa, jazz, R&B and waltzes. Beginners' classes are held on Saturdays from 9.30am to 11.30am, and intermediates dance from 11am to 1pm, with another class on Wednesdays from 7pm to 8.30pm.

Familia De La Salsa
050 277 7475
familiadelasalsa.com
Formed in Dubai in 2003, Familia De La Salsa is a one-stop dance academy for learning salsa and other Latin dancing styles from around the world in a relaxed environment at locations across Dubai. Regular social dances and events are organised by the company for fans of Latin dance. There are also children's dancing classes at the Dubai Ballet Centre every Saturday. Classes start from Dhs.40.

First International Dance Studio
One Lake Plaza Al Thanyah 5 04 252 5080
firstids.com
Map 1 L5 Metro Jumeirah Lakes Towers
Hip-hop and breakdance are the main disciplines offered at this school, but other modern and classical styles are also available. Dhs.800 per month for three group classes a week; get a taster with a free introductory lesson. Classes are for kids, teenagers and adults.

James & Alex Dance Studios
Media City, Al Sufouh 2 04 447 0773
jamesandalex.com
Map 1 M5 Metro Nakheel
With three studios in Media City, salsa-dancing partners James and Alex offer a variety of classes for adults and children from ballet and jazz to belly dance and salsa. There's also pole fitness classes for beginners and intermediates, as well as private classes for one-on-one tuition, such as first dance choreography for weddings. Studios are spacious and airy.

Malecon
Dubai Marine Beach Resort Jumeira 1 04 346 1111
dxbmarine.com
Map 2 H4 Metro Emirates Towers
Head to this Dubai Marine Beach Resort restaurant to enjoy salsa dancing every Saturday night from 10pm onwards for Dhs.40. Dancing is free if you order food, with Latin DJs providing the soundtrack.

Nora Dance Group
050 875 0111
noradancegroup.com
Nora Dance Group has been teaching dance in Dubai since 2006. Pick from classes in hip-hop, ballet, jazz, tango and modern freestyle, as well as belly dancing and Bollywood. Classes are held at Knowledge Village, DUCTAC and Dubai Marina Mall. There are classes for all age groups and skill levels, and also provides corporate and custom events and choreography for large scale events including, flash mobs and big productions.

Prima Performing Arts
Dubai Investments Park 1 055 771 4526
primauae.com
Map 1 F9
Prima Performing Arts offers a fun way for children to dance. There are classes for all ages, with Dinky Dances for babies aged 18 months, fun movement classes for mums and toddlers, and ballet classes for three to 18 year-olds. The dance academy also holds annual exams and performances in hip-hop, contemporary, dance/gymnastics, musical theatre, jazz and tap.

Ritmo De Havana
DUCTAC Al Barsha 1 050 696 3520
ritmo-de-havana.com
Map 1 R6 Metro Mall of the Emirates
Del Piero is a certified instructor. His courses start from Dhs.600 per person and run in batches so check the website for the most up-to-date timings.

Salsa Dubai
Umm Hurair 2 050 565 6420
Map 2 L7 Metro Dubai Healthcare City
Instructor Phil has 13 years' experience in Cuban, New York and Spanish dance styles. Classes are tailored to the individual, and members can learn the famous La Rueda Cuban dance. Find schedules on 'The Original Salsa Dubai' Facebook page.

Savage Garden
Capitol Madinat Dubai Al Melaheyah 04 346 0111
Map 2 J4 Metro Al Jafiliya
On Monday, Tuesday, Thursday and Friday nights, this Latin American restaurant and nightclub serves up Latino food with a side order of salsa and merengue classes. Beginners' lessons are from 8pm to 9pm and intermediate and advanced dancers take to the floor from 9pm to 10pm. Classes cost Dhs.40 a pop. Contact George or Tatiana on 050 597 5058 for more details.

Solid Rock
Pinnacle Bldg Al Barsha 1 04 395 7808
solidrockdubai.com
Map 1 Q6 Metro Sharaf DG
A complete performing arts studio offers music and dance, with hip-hop, salsa and jazz on the menu. The first group lesson is free, so you can try before you buy. Classes are available from beginners through to advanced dancers.

Tango Dubai
DUCTAC Al Barsha 1 050 451 6281
tangodubai.com
Map 1 R6 Metro Mall of the Emirates
Tuesday classes are held for beginners and advanced dancers at Evory Bar, Kempinski Hotel and at DUCTAC,

Mall of the Emirates. Call Eleanor on the number listed, or Maya on 050 622 3679. Lessons cost Dhs.200 for four beginners' classes and Dhs.240 for advanced. Tango Dubai also runs dance nights at Sezzam and Pachanga restaurants.

Turning Pointe Music
Russia Cluster Warsan 1 **04 422 1592**
turningpointe.ae
Metro **Rashidiya**
Turning Pointe has over 35 studios throughout the UAE, offering everything from ballet for children aged three and over (with Royal Academy of Dance Syllabus and Examinations). There's also hip-hop, street jazz and Jazz2Pop, plus the popular TP Glee Club! All teachers fully qualified and recruited from the UK.

Salsa
If you fancy a bit of salsa there are a number of places you can learn seriously, or just have a bit of fun. Check out dubaisalsa.com for more information.

Drama

Drama Dubai
The Courtyard Al Qouz Ind. 1 **050 986 1761**
dramaworkshopsdubai.com
Map **1 R6** Metro **Mall of the Emirates**
This very active drama school runs classes for children and adults on the elements and techniques of acting. School workshops include circus fighting, comedy and Shakespeare. Private tuition and corporate training can be arranged.

DUCTAC

Dubai Drama Group
DUCTAC Al Barsha 1
dubaidramagroup.com
Map **1 R6** Metro **Mall of the Emirates**
Members of this group include actors, directors, singers, dancers and backstage crew. Dubai Drama Group stages four productions a year, and there are workshops, socials and an internet forum. Annual membership is Dhs.100.

Manhattan Film Academy
Al Sufouh 2
mfacademy.com
Map **1 N5** Metro **Dubai Internet City**
The Dubai branch of this world-famous New York film school offers workshops in screenwriting, directing and acting.

Flying

Al Jazirah Aviation Club
Jazirah Airport Ras Al Khaimah **07 244 6416**
jac-uae.net
Dedicated solely to microlight/ultralight flying. The club also offers training and pleasure flights. A Microlight Pilot's Licence course, with around 25 hours flying time, costs Dhs.500 per hour.

Emirates Aviation Services
Dubai International Airport **04 299 5155**
emiratesaviationservices.com
Map **2 N8** Metro **Airport Terminal 1**
The only approved flight training institution in Dubai offers private and commercial licences, and will convert international licences to the UAE equivalent. A Private Pilot's Licence course costs upwards of Dhs.48,720.

Environment
In recent years, the determined clamour of environmentally conscious campaigners and groups has begun to make an impact in a country where concepts like carbon-offsetting, recycling and re-using are still nascent. In 1998, HH Sheikh Mohammed bin Rashid Al Maktoum, then Crown Prince of Dubai, established an environmental award which recognises an individual or organisation for work carried out on behalf of the environment. At an everyday level, there are increasing numbers of glass, plastic and paper recycling points around the city, mainly around shopping centres. However, overall, little seems to be done to persuade the average citizen to be more environmentally active, for instance by encouraging the reduction of littering. If you want to take action, there are a couple of groups, including Emirates Environmental Group, who always need volunteers and funds.

Dubai Natural History Group
Umm Suqeim 3
dnhg.org
Map **1 S5** Metro **First Gulf Bank**
Learn more about the UAE's fascinating natural history at monthly meetings where experts lecture about flora, fauna, geology, and archaeology. Members go on regular field trips and can borrow from a library of natural history publications. Annual membership is Dhs.100 for a family and Dhs.50 for individuals. Contact chairman Gary Feulner (04 306 5570; grfeulner@gmail.com).

Emirates Environmental Group
Villa 68-117A Jumeira 1 **04 344 8622**
eeg-uae.org
Map **2 G4** Metro **Emirates Towers**
A voluntary organisation devoted to helping protect the environment through education, action programmes and community involvement. Activities include evening lectures and special events such as recycling collections and clean-up campaigns. Annual membership costs Dhs.300 for adults and Dhs.100 for college students.

Music
There are a number of specialist music schools in Dubai where you and your kids can have lessons. In addition, you may find that some schools offer extra-curricular music programmes (for a fee) for students.

Brooklyn Melodies Music Centre
Mirdif 04 288 8951
brooklynmelodies.com
Map **2 R13** Metro **Rashidiya Metro Station**
This centre was founded in 2007 in Mirdif, but has since grown to nine locations across Dubai. Learn to play the piano, guitar (classical, electric and bass), violin, flute, drums, and percussion instruments.

Centre For Musical Arts
Al Qouz Ind. 3 **04 341 8872**
cmadubai.com
Map **1 S6** Metro **Mall of the Emirates**
Budding musicians can get instruction in string, woodwind and brass instruments, as well as piano. Group lessons start at Dhs.975 and individual lessons from Dhs.1,625 per term. Visit the website for details of their popular Saturday Sessions.

Dubai Music School
Stalco Bldg, Zabeel St Al Karama **04 396 4834**
dubaimusicschool.com
Map **2 L6** Metro **ADCB**
This school offers one-hour lessons in guitar, piano, organ, violin, brass, drums, singing and composing, leading to Trinity College of Music examinations.

Juli Music Center
Nr Mazaya Shopping Centre Al Wasl **04 321 2588**
imi-jmc.net
Map **2 F6** Metro **Burj Khalifa/Dubai Mall**
Juli Music Center offers lessons in various instruments from Dhs.180 per hour. They also sell a variety of musical instruments including new and used pianos, brass, woodwind, strings, and percussion.

Jumeirah Music Centre
Jumeirah Plaza Jumeira 1 **04 349 2662**
jumeirah-music.com
Map **2 H4** Metro **Emirates Towers**
Lessons in piano, guitar, flute, violin, drums and voice for all ages at Dhs.90 per half hour. All children are welcome to audition for the choir, which puts on a concert every year.

The Music Chamber
Time Square Center Al Qouz Ind. 1 **04 346 8056**
musicchamber.net
Map **1 T6** Metro **Noor Bank**
The Music Chamber gives lessons in all instruments, from electric and classical guitar to cello, piano and percussion. The school is recognised by the Associated Board of Royal Schools of Music in London. It boasts a large variety of instruments, accessories and books. It also offers vocal training and theory lessons.

The Music Institute
Murjan 1 Plaza Marsa Dubai **04 424 3818**
tmi.ae
Map **1 K4** Metro **Jumeirah Lakes Towers**
Piano, violin, guitar and drum lessons with musical theory for all ages, plus group guitar and violin lessons. Practice rooms available to hire. Recitals are also held.

Popular Music Institute
Umm Hurair 2 **04 324 2626**
Map **2 L7** Metro **Dubai Healthcare City**
Thomsun Pure Music is in Wafi and runs the Popular Music Institute and the Sing & Swing Training Centre. Students can learn to play instruments, musicianship, theory and performance, and prepare for music exams.

Solid Rock
Pinnacle Bldg Al Barsha 1 **04 395 7808**
solidrockdubai.com
Map **1 Q6** Metro **Sharaf DG**
Teaches modern music and dance at its Al Barsha studios. There is a particular focus on piano, guitar and drums – the staples of rock music. Private and group classes are available, and the school offers the first group session for free, so you can check it out before you sign up.

Orchestras & Bands

Centre For Musical Arts
Al Qouz Ind. 3 **04 341 8872**
cmadubai.com
Map **1 S6** Metro **First Gulf Bank**
The centre is home to a number of adult and children's musical groups, including ensembles for string, flute, saxophone and guitar players. It also offers instrumental and choral tuition and has an instrument hire and repair service.

Dubai Chamber Orchestra
Safa School, Meydan Street, Al Safa
The chamber orchestra practises every Wednesday evening and gives three public performances a year. It was founded by an international group of musicians now residing in the UAE. There are currently more than 40 members hailing from more than 15 countries and more are always welcome. Its varied programme includes chamber and modern orchestral pieces.

Dubai Classical Guitar Orchestra
DUCTAC Al Barsha 1 **04 341 4666**
dcgo.ae
Map **1 R6** Metro **Mall of the Emirates**
This classical guitar ensemble rehearses at DUCTAC every Tuesday from 6pm to 8pm. People of all ages and levels of skill are welcome to join or learn. Regular performances are also staged.

Dubai Drums > p.xiv
Building 8 Media City, Al Sufouh 2 **04 347 4790**
dubaidrums.com
Map **1 M5** Metro **Nakheel**
Dubai Drums runs African Djembe drumming circles every Monday. A leader guides the group from simple rhythms right through to more complex performances. Classes cost Dhs.50 with drums provided. On Saturdays, Kidz Drum Club is held at DUCTAC, from 10.15am to 11.15am. Cost Dhs.50. Dubai Drums organises other events throughout the year, such as Full Moon and Desert Drumming.

Gardening

Dubai Gardening Group
Villa 97, 16D St Jumeira 1 **04 344 5999**
Map **2 G4** Metro **Emirates Towers**
This group shares its communal gardening know-how in a friendly and informal atmosphere, with seminars and practical demonstrations from experts, trips to garden nurseries and members' gardens also arranged. If you want advice on how to improve your gardening skills, or just want to mingle with other green-fingered Dubaians and chat plants, then this group is for you.

Photography & Film
Photography and film are increasingly popular in the region. Although three film festivals, DIFF, ADFF and Gulf Film Festival shine an encouraging spotlight on the region's filmmaking, there is still a dearth of serious funding. For amateur film fans, there are groups that bring the filmmaking community together for screenings, workshops and presentations.

Photography
For photographers, Emirates Photography Club (meetup.com/emiratesphotoclub) is a web-based community where local photography enthusiasts can exchange tips and ideas. The group meets twice a month on alternating Tuesdays.

Gulf Photo Plus
Alserkal Avenue Al Qouz Ind. 1 **04 380 8545**
gulfphotoplus.com
Map **1 U6** Metro **Noor Bank**
Digital photography classes for beginner to intermediate photographers, and workshops and events with master photographers. Introductory classes to Photoshop are also available. Check out their store selling lenses, lights and literature.

the jamjar
Nr Dubai Garden Centre Al Qouz Ind. 3 **04 341 7303**
thejamjardubai.com
Map **1 S6** Metro **First Gulf Bank**
The award-winning filmmaker, Mahmood Kabour, holds a film series called Mahmovies! at the jamjar (an art studio space). He screens art house offerings for the general public in an informal atmosphere; totally free of charge and encourages discussion amongst viewers. Mahmood is the director of the documentary Champ of the Camp – a film about life in the UAE's labour camps. Further details are available on the Mahmovies! group Facebook page (facebook.com/mahmovies).

Lightform
facebook.com/lightformmediamarketing
An International Filipino Photographer's Guild photographic society, it organises regular workshops, field trips and events for members. Members must complete a basic class to join.

The Picturehouse
Dubai Mall Downtown Dubai, Burj Khalifa
reelcinemas.ae
Map **2 F6** Metro **Burj Khalifa/Dubai Mall**
The Picturehouse at Reel Cinemas in Dubai Mall screens arthouse films and documentaries that don't make it onto the main screens.

SAE Institute Dubai
Knowledge Village, Al Sufouh 2 **04 361 6173**
dubai.sae.edu
Map **1 N5** Metro **Dubai Internet City**
The world's largest private college for film and audio production, animation and multimedia offers a degree in filmmaking, as well as photography bootcamps.

The Scene Club
Knowledge Village, Al Sufouh 2 **04 391 0051**
thesceneclub.com
Map **1 M5** Metro **Nakheel**
Dubai's first film club for true movie buffs offers workshops as well as screenings of films and documentaries that may not make box office history but are felt to be culturally significant. Screenings generally take place once a month.

Shelter Dubai
Alserkal Ave Al Qouz Ind. 4 **04 380 9040**
shelter.ae
Map **1 U6** Metro First Gulf Bank
Shelter (shelter.ae) has a small screening room and holds regular film nights which are open to non-members. Visit their website for schedules.

Scrabble

Dubai Scrabble League
050 653 7992
Meets once a month for friendly games between players of all levels. Regular competitions are held, and players also attend competitions overseas. The UAE Open is the qualifier for the Gulf Open in Bahrain. For more information, contact Selwyn Lobo.

Singing

Dubai Chamber Choir
facebook.com/groups/dubaichamberchoir
Established in 2003, the choir provides choral education and training, and performs concerts throughout the year. The seasonal Christmas series is a highlight. Contact the choir if you're interested in joining up. There are a limited number of members, so auditions are held for all new members, and re-auditions for the full choir on a biennial basis.

Dubai City Sound
Al Safa 1 **056 690 7052**
dubai-harmony.com
Map **2 C5** Metro **Noor Bank**
A barbershop quartet-style group with an all-female ensemble. New members are always welcome and previous musical training is not required – just the desire to sing with enthusiasm.

Dubai Singers
Kindermusik, **15B Street** Umm Suqeim 3 **04 344 8883**
dubaisingers.info
Map **1 S5** Metro **First Gulf Bank**
This is a group of amateur singers who meet regularly to create music in a variety of styles. Repertoire includes requiems, choral works, Christmas carols, musicals and variety shows. Membership is open to everyone; sheet music is provided.

Snooker

Dubai Snooker Club
Nr Karama Post Office Al Karama **04 337 5338**
dubaisnooker.com
Map **2 L6** Metro **Oud Metha**
The club's facilities include 12 tournament-class snooker tables, 13 pool tables, two private snooker rooms and a private pool room. Table charges are Dhs.30 per hour, and food is available. You don't have to be a member to play.

Take A Shot
Knight Shot (04 343 5678) sells all manner of pool and billiards equipment. As one of the main sponsors of the games in the region, it's worth chatting to staff and find out about local tournaments.

Yoga
A low-impact (but deceptively challenging) form of holistic exercise, yoga involves holding sequences of poses or 'asanas' that, combined with breathing exercises, gently but powerfully help your body become stronger and more flexible. Many health and fitness clubs offer yoga as part of their weekly schedule, as do some alternative therapy centres.

Bharat Thakur's Artistic Yoga
800 9642
artisticyoga.com
The latest twist in this flexible form of inner and outer exercise combines ancient yogic techniques with modern cardio training. Morning and evening classes, from Dhs.65, are held at Angsana Spa, Body & Soul Spa Al Ghusais and Al Hana Centre.

Club Stretch
Nr Mercure Hotel, Al Mina St Al Hudaiba **04 345 2131**
clubstretch.ae
Map **2 J4** Metro **Al Jafiliya**
A popular studio offering Bikram yoga, which is practised in a hot room to aid muscle warming and stretching. Pilates is also offered. An unlimited 10 day introduction pass costs Dhs.120.

Advanced yoga

Exhale

Marsa Dubai **04 424 3777**
exhaledubai.com
Map **1 K4** Metro **DAMAC**
This ladies-only fitness offering vinyasa, ashtanga and power yoga, as well as yoga for pregnant women. The cost per session is Dhs.75, with packages of 10 costing Dhs.650 and valid for two months.

Fitness First

DIFC, Zaa'beel 2 **04 363 7444**
fitnessfirstme.com
Map **2 G6** Metro **Financial Centre**
Great for yoga newbies, hatha classes are held most days of the week, with power yoga also available. Prices start at Dhs.100 for non members. Other studios at The Meadows and Lakes.

Gems of Yoga

White Crown Bldg, Shk Zayed Rd Trade Center 1
04 331 5161
gemsofyogadubai.com
Map **2 H5** Metro **Emirates Towers**
Hatha, ashtanga and power yoga as well as classes for ladies, children and the elderly. Dhs.650 for 10 classes.

Rawr Yoga

Concord Tower Media City, Al Sufouh 2 **04 423 2808**
rawryoga.com
Map **1 N5** Metro **Nakheel**
A stylish, state-of-the-art Bikram yoga studio in the heart of Media City. Offers 90 minute Bikram yoga classes, as well as hour-long express classes and a few

other types of yoga. Open to all ages and levels of fitness, with a range of membership packages from its Dhs.125 introductory offer to Dhs.700 for unlimited monthly membership.

Yoga Room

Swiss Tower JLT, Al Thanyah 5 **050 518 9966**
yogaroom.ae
Map **1 L6** Metro **DAMAC**
Ashtanga and vinyasa yoga for all levels and workshops hosted by visiting yoga experts. Packages start from Dhs.80 for a single class.

Yogalates Bliss

Fraser Suites Al Sufouh 2 **050 328 9642**
yogalatesblissindubai.com
Map **1 P5** Metro **Dubai Internet City**
Yogalates is a fusion of yoga and pilates to relieve muscular tension, improve core and pelvic floor strength and inspire balance. Classes are on an outdoor terrace. There's also Funky Fireflies kids yoga, as well as yoga teacher training workshops.

Zen Yoga

BBC Bldg Dubai Media City, Al Sufouh 2 **04 367 0435**
yoga.ae
Map **1 P5** Metro **Dubai Internet City**
Zen Yoga is a yoga and pilates specialist. Its three modern centres have mirrored walls to help you check your posture. A one-month unlimited yoga trial costs Dhs.750 and regular classes are Dhs.80. The studios are in Emirates Hills (04 422 4643), Dubai Media City (04 367 0435), and Town Centre Jumeirah (04 349 2933).

WORKING IN DUBAI

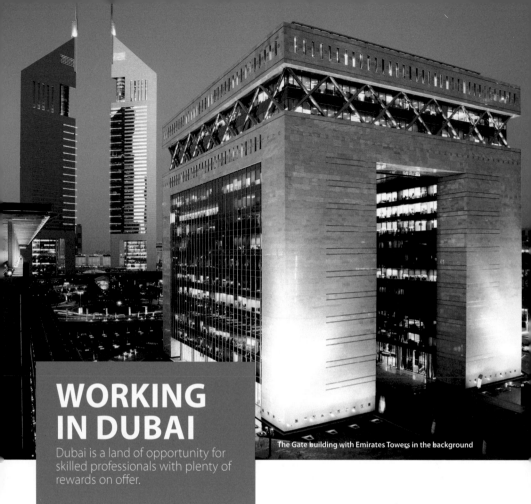

WORKING IN DUBAI

Dubai is a land of opportunity for skilled professionals with plenty of rewards on offer.

The Gate building with Emirates Towers in the background

Expat workers come to Dubai for a number of reasons: to advance their career, enjoy a higher standard of living, or to take advantage of new opportunities. Whatever the reason, there are various advantages to making the move.

While the biggest bonus of working in Dubai may seem to be tax-free salaries, the cost of living (or your newly acquired lifestyle) can somewhat balance out this benefit. All-inclusive packages with accommodation and education allowances are not as common as they once were, although basic benefits still apply (such as annual flights home, health insurance and around 22 calendar days of annual leave). That said, Dubai is still very much a land of opportunities for skilled professionals. It is comparatively easier to change industries, as skill sets are less 'pigeon-holed' than in other countries, and

jobs in certain industries (such as construction and property) are more readily available.

Expats can work in either the public (government) or private sectors; many companies in the private sector operate within Free Trade Zones (FTZs), where foreigners can work, trade or establish their business under more relaxed laws.

To work anywhere in Dubai you need to be aged 18 to 65 years, be sponsored by an employer, and have a residence visa. The visa permits you to live and work anywhere in the UAE; it is valid for two years (or three years for those working in some free zones or in government jobs). All companies are governed by UAE Labour Law, although there is a noticeable difference in salaries, benefits, holidays, annual leave, and end of service payments between the public (government) and private sectors.

EMPLOYMENT

Getting Started

If you're looking to live and work in Dubai you have three options. You can search for jobs while in your home country; you'll often be interviewed by phone or Skype, rather than here in the UAE. Once you have a job offer, your employer will start to process your residence visa. Depending on your contract, your employer may pay for your flight to Dubai (and often tickets for any family members), one month's temporary accommodation, shipping costs, vehicle hire, and the services of a relocation company to help you find a new home. Alternatively, you can arrive in Dubai on a visit visa, which means that you have 30 days (or up to 60 days if you renew it) to legally look for work and live in the country. Or, you may already be living and working in the UAE and looking to transfer jobs. In this instance, you will need to cancel your existing residence visa; your new employer will then sponsor you on a new residence visa.

Job Hunting

Start by registering with a recruitment agency in Dubai. The agency will then set up an interview where you are usually required to fill out a form summarising your CV; you will also need a few passport photos. The agency takes its fee from the registered company once the position has been filled. It is illegal for a recruitment company to levy fees on candidates for this service, although be warned that some might try.

Boutique Recruitment Services

If your field is office support, but you are looking for an executive position, then Miller Hay (millerhay. com) could be the best recruitment company for you to contact. They specialise in finding high-calibre secretarial and office support staff.

Employers also use local newspapers and headhunters (also known as executive search companies) to advertise job opportunities, as well as their own websites. It is easier to look for a job once you are in Dubai. Get your hands on the Gulf News appointments supplement (gncareers.com), published every day except Fridays and Saturdays, or the Khaleej Times Appointments (khaleejtimes.com) every day except Friday. The National has a careers section that is available to those who subscribe online.

Also, check listings on online versions of international newspapers as companies within the UAE often post jobs on these sites. Websites for The Guardian (guardian.co.uk) and The Times (timesonline. co.uk) newspapers in the UK and The Washington Post (washingtonpost.com) in the US are often a good resource. You can also upload your CV to sites like monstergulf.com, naukrigulf.com, bayt.com and gulftalent.com. Job advertisements are posted on dubizzle.com and expatwoman.com. Also try contacting companies directly and start networking, using sites such as linkedin.com.

What To Expect

According to the Bayt.com Job Index Survey (August 2013), the time is ripe for many jobseekers. There is a demand for qualified professionals in the UAE, as engineering (27%), business management (24%) and commerce (23%) top the list of most desirable qualifications among UAE employers. The most attractive industries in the UAE for jobs are perceived to be banking and finance (34%), construction (33%) and oil, gas and petrochemicals (33%). Recruitment agency Charterhouse lists the following average monthly salaries for key sectors:

HR Manager: Dhs.25,000
Head Of Corporate Bank: Dhs.60,000
Senior Civil/Structural Engineer: Dhs.35,000
Financial Accountant: Dhs.20,000
Finance Director: Dhs.50,000
Senior Project Engineer: Dhs.55,000
Senior Architect: Dhs.30,000
Legal Secretary: Dhs.20,000
General Manager (Construction): Dhs.75,000
Designer: Dhs.18,000
Key Account Manager: Dhs.20,000
Head of IT: Dhs.20,000-30,000
Communications Manager: Dhs.22,000-35,000
Marketing Manager: Dhs.25,000
Partner (Law Firm): Dhs.60,000-70,000 plus

Recruitment Agencies

BAC Middle East Liberty House, Zaa'beel 2, 04 439 8500, *bacme.com*
Bayt.com Grosvenor Business Tower, Al Thanyah 1, 04 449 3100, *bayt.com*
Charterhouse Middle East > *p.202, 213* Maze Tower, Shk Zayed Rd, Trade Center 1, 04 372 3500, *charterhouseme.ae*
Hays Middle East Dubai Knowledge Village, Al Sufouh 2, 04 361 2882, *hays.ae*
Manpower Middle East Dubai Internet City Bldg 1, Al Sufouh 2, 04 391 0460, *manpower-me.com*
Parsons Brinckerhoff The H Dubai Office Tower, Trade Center 1, 04 376 7222, *pbworld.com*

Permit To Work

Once you receive a job offer, your employer, and sponsor, will start to process your residence visa with the General Directorate of Residency and Foreigners Affairs (GDRFA). All the paperwork should be taken care of by your PRO (see Getting Started); you will need to take a medical test and hand over your passport and attested education certificates. Your labour card or free zone ID – your permit to work – will be processed at the same time. Your PRO should also help with your application for your Resident ID.

Labour Card

Employees working outside a free zone will receive a labour card, processed by the Ministry of Labour. If you work in a free zone, however, you will receive a free zone ID, which is processed by the free zone authority and can be ready in as little as 24 hours. Both cards feature your photo and details of your employer. The labour card costs Dhs.1,000 (paid for by your company) and is valid for as long as your residence visa is. A free zone ID is valid for either one, two or three years.

You will need to sign your labour contract before the labour card/free zone ID is issued. This contract is printed in both Arabic and English. The plan is for labour cards to be phased out in favour of the Resident ID, but, for now, the labour card is still required. There is now an electronic e-labour card, which is designed to replace the tangible cards. However, it is only available to companies on the mainland and not those residing in free zones.

Family Sponsored

If you are sponsored by your husband or wife on a family visa, you can still legally work. Your employer will simply need to apply for your labour card; you will need an NOC from your sponsor as well as your passport with residence visa, your sponsor's passport and your attested education certificates.

Temporary Work Permits

Non-GCC nationals who are above 18 years of age can now enter the UAE on a short-term work permit which is valid for 60 days; these can be extended/renewed up to six times (subject to a fee and bank guarantee).

Employment Contracts

Once you have accepted a job offer you will be asked to sign an employment contract; this should list the starting date, type of employment, location, terms and conditions, duration and the salary. This is a legally binding agreement that should be written in both Arabic and English. You can check or print your labour contract and card online at mol.gov.ae. There is often confusion over the offer letter and the contract. An offer letter should give details of the terms of the job you are being offered, such as salary, leave, hours and other benefits; if you accept the terms of this offer, it becomes a legally binding contract.

An employment contract can be terminated if both parties agree, provided that the employee's written consent is given; the employer will then need to cancel your residence visa. See Changing Jobs.

Probation

Probation periods can be set for a maximum of six months. Some companies delay the residency process until the probation period is up, which can make settling in difficult – no residency means you can't sponsor family members, buy a car or get a bank loan.

By law, employees are not entitled to paid sick leave during probation and most firms do not grant paid annual leave to be taken during this time – you will continue to accrue annual leave though that you can take over the course of the year.

Leave

While on sick leave, the first 15 days are with full pay, the next 30 days are with half pay, and any subsequent days are unpaid. Annual holiday starts at one calendar month per year, roughly 22 working days.

Working Hours

Working hours differ dramatically between companies; straight shifts vary from 7am to 2.30pm for government organisations to the common 9am to 6pm for private companies. Most retail outlets tend to be open from 10am to 10pm but often operate shifts. Teachers start early at around 7.30am and classes finish around 2.30pm, although their hours aren't as predetermined as other roles. Although less common nowadays, some offices and shops operate split shifts, which allow for a longer break in the afternoon (hours are usually 8am to 1pm and 4pm to 7pm).

The maximum number of hours permitted per week according to UAE Labour Law is 48, although some industries, such as hospitality and retail, have longer stipulated hours. Annual holiday allowance starts at one calendar month per year, or roughly 22 working days. Some employees, especially those in management, have more than this and long service usually adds to holiday allowance.

Friday is the Islamic holy day and therefore a universal day off for offices and schools. Consumer demand means that the hospitality and retail industries are open seven days a week. Saturday is the second day of the weekend; some companies work five and a half days a week and some operate a six-day week, taking only Friday as a rest day. Public holidays are set by the government, while the timing of religious holidays depends on the sighting of the moon. This can mean that it is difficult to plan holidays, as confirmation of public holidays can come just days before the event. All employees (even non-Muslims) are entitled to a shorter working day during Ramadan, although lawyers would advise you not to insist on this if you are not fasting.

Health Insurance

A new health insurance law (Insurance System for Advancing Healthcare in Dubai – ISAHD) is currently being rolled out in Dubai, which makes it compulsory for employers to provide all workers, and their spouses and dependants, with basic health insurance; this covers all businesses in the emirate including those in free zones. Under the law, employers must pay for private health cover with any insurance company holding a health insurance permit from the DHA. This mandatory health cover also applies to domestic workers such as maids and nannies. The first stage was implemented in October 2014, requiring 200 or so companies in Dubai's mainland and freezone with more than 1,000 employees to provide health cover for workers.

Gratuity Payments

An employee on a fixed-term contract, who has completed one or more years of continuous service, will be entitled to 21 days pay for each of the first five years of service, and 30 days pay for each additional year as an end-of-service gratuity payment; this compensates for the lack of a pension system. This is based on your basic salary (not including basic housing, transport and utilities). The total end-of-service gratuity should not exceed the salary of two years. Leaving before the end of your fixed-term contract or being fired for breaking UAE Labour Law could result in the loss of your gratuity payment.

Maternity Leave

Under UAE Labour Law, women are entitled to 45 days maternity leave, on full pay, once they've completed one year of continuous service. Fathers are not entitled to paternity leave. If you've been with your employer for less than a year you can claim 45 days on half pay.

UAE Labour Law

The UAE Labour Law outlines information on employee entitlements, employment contracts and disciplinary rules. The law is employer friendly, but it also clearly outlines employee rights. You can download a copy of the document from the Ministry of Labour website (mol.gov.ae); the document has not been fully updated for some time but amendments and additions are often posted on the site.

If you find yourself in the situation where you have not been paid (including women on maternity leave), you can file a case with the UAE Labour Department which will take the necessary action. You could also get a lawyer to deal with the claim on your behalf. Although lawyers are expensive in Dubai, the employer will have to bear the cost if the case is settled in your favour.

Changing Jobs

If you decide to leave a company before the end of your contract you will require permission from your existing employer in the form of an NOC. Your employer will also need to cancel your residence visa. You will then be able to switch to a new job and your new employer will process a new residence visa and labour card.

Officially, anyone working in the private sector who breaks their contract could face a six month ban from working for any other company in the UAE (if you are working in a free zone, this ban may be restricted to jobs within that free zone only). However, banning rules are increasingly relaxed and job transfers have become much more flexible. Stay on good terms with your employer, and you shouldn't face a problem. If you complete your contract period, either two or three years, you can legally move jobs without an NOC.

Always check if there is a non-compete clause in your contract, particularly if your new role is with a direct competitor to your current employer.

There are some exceptions where you can transfer your sponsorship without the approval of your current sponsor; such as death of your sponsor, change of company ownership, company closure and cancellation of your company's trade licence.

Transferring A Visa

If you are planning to transfer your visa, your new employer will first need to gain permission from your previous employer, after getting approval from the Ministry of Labour. Free zone visas can usually be transferred from one employer to the next. However, the previous employer needs to agree to the transfer and may need to provide a no objection certificate (NOC). Keep in mind that this NOC may also need to be translated into Arabic, on headed notepaper, and signed by the local sponsor.

Non-free zone visas need to be cancelled before you can apply for a new one. You should also sign a document instructive of a six-month work ban. This ban can be lifted with an NOC from a previous employer. When a non-free zone visa is cancelled, the new employer may have to pay a fine for the duration of the remainder of the visa, if the employee has not completed a specified period of work.

Absconding

Anyone leaving the country or their job permanently without informing their employer and cancelling the residence visa with their sponsor will be classed as 'absconding' and may receive a ban; employers or sponsors have to report absconders who have left the country within 10 days, not within three months as was previously the case.

Absconders are reported to the Ministry of Labour, who then pass information on to the GDRFA and the Dubai police. If a ban is on your computer file, any applications from a new employer for a residence visa and labour card will be refused. Also, if you leave the country or are unaccountable for seven days in a row or 20 days in total, your company can terminate your employment contract without awarding you gratuity pay or any outstanding benefits.

Company Closure

If the company you work for closes, you are still entitled to outstanding holiday pay and gratuity. The Ministry of Labour would need to be involved though. You are allowed to transfer sponsorship to a new employer; but if you can't find a new job your visa will be cancelled and you will have to leave the country (though some nationalities are allowed to re-enter on a tourist visa straight away). To transfer the visa you'll need an attested certificate of closure, issued by the court and submitted to the Ministry of Labour. If your company were to close without cancelling their trade licence, you could receive a short-term ban from taking a new role with a new employer. Consult the appropriate government offices to get your paperwork right, or consider investing in the services of a specialist labour lawyer.

Redundancy

If you are made redundant, the first thing to discuss with your employer is whether they are prepared to be flexible with your visa status. If you have a good relationship with your company, you should have room to negotiate the terms under which you are leaving, and it's a good idea to request a few months leeway so that you have the opportunity to find a new employer and sponsor. If this is not possible and your company wishes to cancel your visa immediately, you have a standard 30 day grace period within which to leave the country before incurring any fines for overstaying your visa. Similarly, if you are in company accommodation, try to negotiate the date on which you need to move out. If your company has paid for your villa or apartment up front, they may let you stay for a fixed period.

It is always a good idea to plan for every eventuality by putting money aside to act as a buffer should you lose your job; rather than incur large debts, this money can help pay for key bills like rent and car loans.

FREE ZONES

Dubai is home to more than 20 free zones, which service a wide range of industries, including healthcare, education, commodities and technology

Dubai Media City

companies. Unique laws regarding taxation, recruitment of labour, and income apply to these areas. Various benefits make free zones an ideal option for companies wishing to establish a distribution, manufacturing and service base for trade outside of the UAE.

Free zones in the UAE work on a 'one-stop shop' principle – so, as an employer or company owner, you'll only have one authority to deal with. This should simplify the process of running your business considerably. If you want to work as a consultant or you wish to set up a small business, free zones are your best bet. The process and fees for getting a visa varies between each free zone. Note that the cost of commercial property can be quite high in popular free zones, such as Dubai Media City and the Jebel Ali Free Zone.

Employees of companies in free zones have different sponsorship options to choose from, depending on which free zone they inhabit. For example, in the Jebel Ali Free Zone you can either be sponsored by an individual company or by the free zone authority itself.

Whether you are in the Jebel Ali Free Zone, Dubai Internet City, Dubai Media City, Knowledge Village, Healthcare City or any other free zone, the respective authority will process your residence visa directly through the General Directorate of Residency and Foreigners Affairs (GDRFA), without having to get employment approval from the Ministry of Labour. This speeds up the process significantly, and residence visas can sometimes be granted in a matter of hours.

Once the GDRFA has stamped your residence visa in your passport, the free zone will issue your free zone ID – this also acts as your security pass for entry to the free zone. A big advantage of working in a free zone is the lack of red tape encountered if you move jobs to another free zone company. This is because the free zone itself is actually your sponsor, so when you switch jobs to another employer you won't be switching sponsors.

The validity of a free zone residence visa permit will depend on how long the labour card is valid for (either one, two or three years, depending on the zone).

Designed to encourage investment from overseas, free zones allow 100% foreign ownership and exemption from taxes and customs duties. There are plenty to choose from in Dubai: the most well-known being Dubai Media City and Jebel Ali Free Zone.

Choosing A Free Zone

If the idea of working for yourself in a free zone appeals to you, then begin by checking out the Dubai free zones' individual websites or see uaefreezones.com, which provides a fact sheet on each zone. This will give you a good idea of which zone is best suited to your business plan, as well as the conditions to fulfil to obtain a licence. Licences

for businesses vary from Dhs.5,500 in the Jebel Ali Free Zone to Dhs.20,000 in JLT.

Freelance Work

Freelancers can apply for a work permit and residence visa from a select number of free zones in Dubai, including International Media Production Zone, Dubai Technology and Media Free Zone, Dubai Media City and Knowledge Village. Your profession needs to be related to these free zones' activities, which are predominantly media-related: artists, editors, directors, writers, engineers, producers, photographers, camera operators and technicians in the fields of film, TV, music, radio and print media.

Freelancers are granted a freelance permit, which identifies you as a sole practitioner and enables you to conduct your business in your birth name as opposed to a brand name. You will also be given a UAE residence visa, and have access to a 'hot desk' and business facilities (including a PO Box address) within the free zone that sponsored you. Both the permit and visa are valid for one year. This costs between Dhs.20,000-30,000. The process varies between free zones, and check individual websites for specific requirements and to download forms.

An alternative option, depending on your line of work, may be to set up or register your own Dubai-based company. This has become a little easier to do than it used to be (check out Explorer's *Dubai How-To* guide for step-by-step information on setting up a company). Or, contact the Department of Economic Development (dubaided.gov.ae) to get started. See also Part-time work in this chapter for other options.

Virtuzone

Virtuzone is officially part of Fujairah Creative City free zone, and was set up with the express aim of helping those who want to either set up a small company or relocate it to the UAE while keeping costs as low as possible. Start-up costs begin at around Dhs.10,000 and Virtuzone looks after the whole process; significantly, there's no need for a UAE sponsor, companies can be 100% foreign owned and there are no corporate or income taxes. Also, there's no requirement to take commercial premises – something that really drives up the price of setting up in other free zones.

If you're looking to move your small business from your home country or are thinking about taking a skill and going solo, it's probably the easiest and cheapest way to set up. Visit vz.ae or the physical office on The Walk at JBR.

Dubai Media City

Media professionals in the following categories are eligible to apply for a freelance permit and visa in

Dubai Media City: artists, editors, directors, writers, engineers, producers, photographers, camera operators and technicians in the fields of film, TV, music, radio or print media. They will be subject to the conditions listed below:
- The freelance permit includes a residence visa, access to 10 shared work stations, and a shared PO Box address and fax line
- A minimum of three hours per week and no more than three hours per day must be spent at the hot desk
- A business plan, CV, bank reference letter and portfolio must be submitted along with your application

Costs at DMC include:
- Dhs.5,000 security deposit (refundable)
- Dhs.5,000 joining fee (one-off payment)
- Dhs.8,000 annual freelance permit fee
- Dhs.4,000 annual membership fee

Working On The Move

MAKE Business Hub (makebusinesshub.com) near JBR at The Walk offers freelancers a workspace and a cafe rolled into one; there are work stations, work pods for private meetings and a tasty menu serving breakfast through to dinner.

Part-time Work

In the past, it has been extremely difficult to organise part-time work. What little there is has been offered 'off the books' to those already in Dubai under their partner's sponsorship. But new legislation now allows residents to take on work part-time in Dubai.

Since January 2011, teenagers from 15 to 18 years of age can find jobs in the UAE upon obtaining a teenage work permit from the Ministry of Labour. Part-time work permits can be also be issued for any of the following: workers below the age of 65 with valid residence visas who are registered with the Ministry of Labour; government workers; or women living with their parents, husbands, sons or daughters with valid residence visas.

However, part-time work is still a relatively new concept in Dubai and it may be a while until there's the wide variety of casual work available that you'll find in most other countries, but there are an increasing number of opportunities. For more information, contact the General Directorate of Residency and Foreigners (dnrd.ae).

It is up to the employer to pay for the part-time work permit (which costs Dhs.500) rather than the employee. It's also essential that both sign a contract which explicitly states the wage before the permit can be issued. To request a part-time work permit, visit the

Ministry of Labour website (mol.gov.ae). You will need to provide a number of documents including copies of the company's trade licence, a photo of the employee as well as a copy of his passport and his education certificates attested by the Ministry of Foreign Affairs.

BUSINESS

Business Culture

Like anywhere in the world, doing business in the UAE has its own unique idiosyncrasies. Even if you work for a western company, the chances are that some of your business transactions will be with Emiratis, whether on a customer or client basis.

One of the key aspects to realise is that family ties, friendship, honour and trust are crucial. So much so that those who have built good relationships can often see rules bent; the system of favours being given and not forgotten is an integral, if unspoken, part of things. Age, money and social connections are also significant in establishing your status, and older people are treated with respect. Often elders in a room are greeted first and served first at meals.

All of this can mean that things can take longer to get done than expats are used to; which can, in turn, lead to frustrations and difficulties meeting expected deadlines if you work for a western company.

Networking is important

Entrepreneurs' Guide

Dubai is one of the most exciting cities in the world for entrepreneurs and start-up companies. The fast-changing nature of the region means that opportunities abound for small business ventures here. It is advisable to do your market research before you arrive and then come along with endless endurance to tackle the bureaucratic procedures that will need to be followed.

Getting started

All companies setting up outside a free zone in Dubai must have a trade licence, which determines which business activities you are permitted to practise. One of your first points of call should be the Department of Economic Development (DED) which issues trade licences and is the integral authority for business in the UAE.

You will need sponsorship from a UAE national (who will have a 51% stake in your business) if setting up a Limited Liability Company (LLC) or public/private shareholding company. Alternatively, you will need sponsorship from a local service agent if setting up a branch company, sole proprietorship or civil business.

Applying for a trade licence

This is a multi-step process that requires you to register your trade name, apply for an Initial Approval Certificate, rent/buy commercial premises, and obtain special licensing approvals (if required). These procedures are dealt with by the DED and Ministry of Economy, Only then will you receive a full trade licence. This is usually valid for one year.

Getting a PO Box

You will need to organise a company PO Box as part of the set-up procedure. All mail is then sent to a PO Box address, registered at your company premises. See emiratespost.ae for details.

DCCI

All commercial and industrial businesses in Dubai must be registered with the Dubai Chamber of Commerce & Industry (DCCI), responsible for registering and attesting members, and recording information on companies.

Setting up in a free zone

Free zones offer business licences to companies 100% owned by foreign nationals. This negates the need for a UAE national sponsor or local service agent; you simply apply to the relevant Free Zone Authority (FZA) – there are more than 20 to choose from in Dubai, each designed around one or more industries. While the initial minimum capital requirement to set up in a free zone can be substantial, there are plenty of benefits.

Get, set, go!

The following companies can assist you in setting up a business, dealing with licensing, start-up and free zone applications, as well as offering ongoing services such as audits and accounting, HR and recruitment:

Commitbiz *commitbiz.com*
Healy Consultants *healyconsultants.com*
HLB Hamt Chartered Accountants *hlbhamt.com*
Middle East and Africa Monitor *meamonitor.com*

For the full procedure of how to set up your business, see Explorer's *Dubai How-To* guide.

Warm greetings are commonplace, with long handshakes, effusive compliments and enquiries about the health of families. Avoid enquiring after female family members though, as this is kept extremely private. Similarly, when meeting someone of the opposite sex, it's likely that a handshake will not be given and is best to refrain unless they extend their hand to you. Always use your right hand to meet, eat or hand over items as Muslims reserve the left hand for bodily hygiene and consider it unclean. Avoid showing the bottom of your shoes in meetings too, as this is considered an insult.

If you're attending a business meeting at an Arab-owned company, it's likely that you'll be served traditional Arabic coffee, or *kahwa*. Sharing coffee is an important social ritual in the Middle East so you should drink some when offered. Cups should be taken in the right hand and if there is a waiter standing by, replenishing your cup, there are two ways to signal that you have had enough: either leave a small amount of coffee in the bottom of your cup or gently tip the cup from side to side.

Networking & Events

With Dubai still being a relatively small city, made up of communities that are smaller still, networking is critical, even across industries. Everyone seems to know everyone else and getting in with the corporate 'in-crowd' definitely has its plus points.

Business acumen here can, at times, be more important than specific industry knowledge so it pays to attend business events and trade shows. Make friends in government departments and this will often land you in the front line for opportunities.

Likewise, bad news is rarely made public here, so staying in tune with the grapevine can help prevent wrong decisions. Social networking sites such as LinkedIn (linkedin.com) are a great resource when looking for new jobs or contacts, whilst Eleqt.com is an exclusive social networking site for high-level executives and entrepreneurs willing to pay the Dhs.18,000 joining fee.

Business Councils

American Business Council of Dubai & The Northern Emirates 04 379 1414, *abcdubai.com*
Arab Business Club 04 358 3000, *arabbusinessclub.org*
Australian Business Council Dubai 04 390 0467, *abcduae.com*
British Business Group 04 397 0303, *britbiz-uae.com*
Canadian Business Council 04 359 2625, *cbc-dubai.com*
Danish Business Council Dubai 050 625 0092, *danishbusinessdubai.com*

French Business Council Dubai & The Northern Emirates 04 312 6700, *fbcdubai.com*
German Emirati Joint Council For Industry & Commerce 04 447 0100, *vae.ahk.de*
Indian Business & Professional Council 04 332 4300, *ibpdubai.com*
Iranian Business Council 04 335 9220, *ibc.ae*
Italian Business Council 04 321 3082, *italianbusinesscouncil.com*
Malaysia Business Council 04 335 5528, *mbc-uae.com*
Netherlands Business Council 050 559 2272, *nbcdubai.com*
Pakistan Business Council Dubai 056 109 3017, *pbcdubai.com*
Singapore Business Council *sbcuae.com*
South African Business Council 050 259 4280, *sabco-uae.org*
Spanish Business Council 04 330 0110, *spanishbusinesscouncil.ae*
Swedish Business Council 056 114 5395, *sbcuae.se*
Swiss Business Council 04 368 7702, *swissbcuae.com*

STARTING A BUSINESS

Starting a business requires meticulous market research, a strict and realistic business plan and responsive action to take advantage of fleeting openings in the market. Bankruptcy laws are not as defined as in other countries and mismanagement of funds could result in harsh repercussions, including deportation or even jail time.

These days there is legislation which aids the start-up process – for example, there is no minimum capital requirement to start a business, unless you opt for a Limited Liability Company, in which case the capital requirement is Dhs.300,000.

One of the main hesitations that entrepreneurs have about starting a business here is the traditional requirement of having a local sponsor control a majority stake of the company. An eagerly awaited revamp of the commercial companies' law is in the drafting, although clauses removing the requirement for a local sponsor or a local service agent have already been rejected by the Federal National Council.

The exception to the above are free zones, where full private foreign ownership is already permitted. The licensing process for opening a business in a free zone is also more streamlined and helped by the free zone organisation. Government and privately sponsored initiatives are also helping

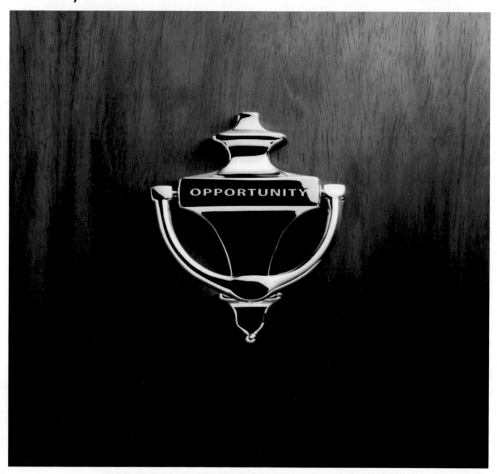

to spur growth and educate potential business owners. The Mohammed Bin Rashid Establishment for SME Development (sme.ae) was set up to help entrepreneurs understand the procedures and potential costs of setting up in Dubai. The organisation provides guidance and information to Emiratis and expats hoping to start their own business. If you want someone to handle all of the red tape for you, companies like Sentinel Business Centres (sentinelbusinesscentres.com) and Creative Zone (creativezone.ae) can help you set up in a free zone or even help find a local sponsor for your business.

There are various business groups in Dubai that help facilitate investments and provide opportunities for networking. Some provide information on trade with their respective countries, as well as business opportunities in Dubai and internationally. Most arrange social and networking events. Before you set up, contact the Dubai Chamber of Commerce & Industry (dubaichamber.com) and the Ministry of Economy (economy.gov.ae). Both can offer excellent advice. Embassies or consulates can also be a good business resource and may be able to offer contact lists for the UAE and the country of representation. For further information, refer to Explorer's *UAE Business Guide*, the Dubai Commercial Directory or the Hawk Business Pages.

Business Domain Name

You can register your domain name through Etisalat (etisalat.ae) which handles domain name registration through UAEnic (United Arab Emirates Network Information Center), or through du (du.ae) which is an accredited registrar of the .ae Domain Administration (.aeDA). It can also register other top-level domains such as those ending with .com and .net.

Consultants & Chartered Accountants

It pays in the long run to get professional advice if you want to set up your own business or become a freelancer. Listed below are just some of the consultants who can help and advise. For more, see askexplorer.com.

Commitbiz Dubai World Trade Centre, Trade Center 2, 04 386 7444, *commitbiz.com*
Future Way Business Services LLP, Golden Motor Building, Frej Al Murrar Deira, *www.futurewbs.com*
Healy Consultants Dubai World Trade Center, Trade Center 2, *healyconsultants.com*
HLB Hamt Chartered Accountants City Tower 2, Trade Center 1, 04 327 7775, *hlbhamt.com*
LLC Licence Set Up, 401 Al Zarouni Business Centre Sheikh Zayed Road, *cigdubai.ae*
Middle East & Africa Monitor *meamonitor.com*

VOLUNTARY & CHARITY WORK

There are a number of opportunities to do voluntary or charity work in Dubai and the organisations listed below are always looking for committed volunteers. The Dubai Volunteering Centre, run by the Community Development Authority (CDA), regulates, promotes and encourages people to get involved in voluntary work. To register as a volunteer, call the CDA on 800 2121 or visit the website at cda.gov.ae.

If you're not entirely sure which charity you'd like to help, or want to volunteer for more than one charity, check out volunteerindubai.com – the website matches volunteers with the needs of specific drives or events.

All As One
Fairmont Dubai Trade Center 1 **04 311 6707**
allasone.org
Map **2 H5** Metro **World Trade Centre**
A non-profit organisation that cares for abandoned, disabled, abused and destitute children of Sierra Leone at the All As One Children's Centre. Operating costs are funded through donations, child sponsorship and charity events.

Breast Cancer Arabia
055 147 6435
breastcancerarabia.com
A charity that raises money to pay for breast cancer treatment for women who cannot afford it. Monies are raised at events such as golf days organised by the Breast Cancer Arabia Foundation, as well as through donations. Email foundation@breastcancerarabia.com for further information.

Feline Friends Dubai
050 451 0058
felinefriendsdubai.com
This non-profit organisation, with volunteers who rescue and re-home stray cats and kittens, promotes the control of street cats by sterilisation and provides care and relief to sick and injured cats. Rescue volunteers and foster homes are always needed.

Gulf for Good
Century Village Al Garhoud **04 368 0222**
gulf4good.org
Metro **Jebel Ali**
This organisation raises funds for selected worthy causes around the world by organising sponsored expeditions and treks to locations across the globe.

Challenges include hikes in the Himalayan foothills and a trek through Palestine's remote highlands, wadis and deserts.

K9 Friends > *p.155*
04 887 8739
k9friends.com

A group of volunteers who rescue, care for and re-home unwanted dogs from all over the UAE. Running costs are met entirely through public donations and corporate sponsors. Assistance is always welcome.

Medecins Sans Frontieres (MSF)
Al Shafar Bldg, Shk Zayed Rd Al Thanyah 1
04 457 9255
msf-me.org
Map **1 N6** Metro **Dubai Internet City**

An international, non-profit emergency medical relief organisation. Volunteers can become involved locally with fundraising and awareness campaigns. Annual events include the Dubai Vertical Marathon, where participants climb the Emirates Towers' 1,334 steps, and Wild Wadi's Swim Burj Al Arab.

Riding for the Disabled Association of Dubai
Desert Palm Retreat Warsan 2
rdad.ae

Launched by HH Sheikha Hassa bint Mohammed bin Rashid Al Maktoum, the association provides therapeutic benefits for children with special needs through gentle horse riding. Reliable volunteers are always needed to lead the horses and assist riders.

Women for Women International
050 342 4949
womenforwomen.org

Informal charity events organised by a group of ladies to help Women for Women International, a charity giving aid to war survivors. Contact Julie Wilkinson for details on 050 342 4949 or at jwilkinson@valleyforge.com.

Environmental Groups

The UAE government and local municipalities have started making efforts towards reducing waste and consumption and raising environmental awareness. Masdar City in Abu Dhabi is being hailed as a groundbreaking green project and will be one of the world's most sustainable places to live, powered by renewable energy sources (masdarcity.ae).

In Dubai, The Change Initiative is a flagship store in Al Barsha for environmentally friendly services and products. The first company of its type in the region, it specialises in eco-friendly goods including sustainable cleaning products, solar panels, household appliances and building solutions.

Dubai's Emirates Environment Group (eeg-uae.org) is devoted to environmental protection through education, action and community involvement. It also has a recycling centre. Call 04 344 8622.

Dubai Desert Conservation Reserve (ddcr.org) allows visits and sometimes accepts volunteer workers to help with the monitoring of endangered species.

In neighbouring Abu Dhabi the government effort is being accelerated by various environmental organisations who aim to protect the environment, as well as to educate the population about environmental issues. The Environment Agency Abu Dhabi (ead.ae) assists the Abu Dhabi government in the conservation and management of the emirate's natural environment, resources, wildlife and biological diversity.

Sir Bani Yas Island, which is part of the Abu Dhabi emirate, is home to an internationally acclaimed breeding programme for endangered wildlife. Created as a private wildlife sanctuary by the late Sheikh Zayed, it is now an exclusive eco-resort (call 02 801 5400 or visit anantara.com).

Emirates Wildlife Society is a national environmental NGO that operates in association with the WWF (panda.org). In addition, The Breeding Centre for Endangered Arabian Wildlife (06 531 1212) at Sharjah Desert Park has a successful breeding programme for wildlife under threat, particularly the Arabian leopard. The breeding centre is off-limits to visitors but the Arabian Wildlife Centre (06 531 1999), also at the Desert Park, is open to the public.

Several environmental groups help native wildlife

Shows & Exhibitions

The MICE industry in Dubai is growing rapidly, as both local and international companies choose to host events in the emirate.

With its vast transport hub, Dubai is an increasingly popular location for international trade fairs and conferences. The emirate's central location and abundance of five-star accommodation options means worldwide organisations are likely to choose Dubai as their meeting point.

There are a growing number of industry and trade events in Dubai that are lucrative for companies – or a fantastic day of entertainment for local families.

The Dubai World Trade Centre hosts more than 500 events every year, receiving more than 1.4 million visitors and about 6,000 exhibitors.

Each year the Abu Dhabi National Exhibition Centre (ADNEC) also stages more than 100 events, which bring millions of dollars to the UAE capital.

The Big Three

Gitex Shopper
Residents wait for Gitex Shopper so they can purchase electronics or IT goods. This is where manufacturers release their latest products and retailers offer them at discounted prices. In 2014, there were two events, one in April and another at the end of September. Gitex Shopper retailers reported sales in excess of Dhs.101 million at the April event alone; an increase of 10% on sales in 2013.

Arabian Travel Market (ATM)
The leading international travel and tourism event in the Middle East for inbound and outbound tourism professionals from across the globe. Residents also flock to see what travel promotions are running in tandem with the exhibition. With Dubai winning the right to host the World Expo 2020, this event is even more important as a way for the city to market itself to visiting tourism authorities.

Big Boys Toys
If it's fast, powerful or expensive, you'll find it at Big Boys Toys – the showcase of sleek and luxurious products. Check out the latest Lamborghini or the biggest from Bang and Olufsen. Other interesting products previously showcased include the smallest folding electric bike in the world.

2015 Highlights

March
Dubai International Boat Show 3-7 March *boatshowdubai.com*
Cabsat Mena 10-12 March *cabsat.com*
Dubai International Horse Championship 19-21 March *dihf.ae*
ARABLAB 23-26 March *arablab.com*
The Bride Show Dubai 25-28 March *thebrideshow.com*
International Property Show 30 March-1 April *internationalpropertyshow.ae*

April
GITEX Shopper 1-4 April *gitexshopperdubai.com*
Gulf Education & Training Exhibition 15-17 April *mygetex.com*
Cityscape Abu Dhabi 21-23 April *cityscapeabudhabi.com*

May
Arabian Travel Market (ATM) 4-7 May *arabiantravelmarket.com*
INDEX International Design Exhibition 18-21 May *indexexhibition.com*
Beauty World Middle East 26-28 May *gulfbeautyexpo.com*

June
Dubai Summer Surprises June and July *mydsf.ae*
Middle East Event Show 2-3 June *me-eventshow.com*

October
GITEX Technology Week 18-22 October *gitex.com*
Big Boys Toys (Exact date TBC) *bigboystoysuae.com*

November
Dubai Airshow 8-12 November *dubaiairshow.aero*

MICE Venues

Aside from the Dubai World Trade Centre, Dubai has many hotels that offer conference and event facilities, which are suitable for events ranging from 20 people in a boardroom meeting, to 500-plus at a company conference.

The Fairmont (fairmont.com) in Dubai offers 'sustainable meetings' packages for socially and environmentally conscious delegates, or you could arrange a seminar in JA Jebel Ali Golf Resort's (jaresortshotels.com) bio garden.

Sheikh Zayed Rd skyline

táaleem
inspiring young minds

Inspiring the learners of today to become the leaders of tomorrow.

All Taaleem schools aim to inspire young minds to become active and compassionate lifelong learners who help to create a better, more peaceful world through intercultural understanding and respect.

As one of the UAE's largest education providers, we are passionate about offering our students the very best learning environments in which to flourish. The IB, NEASC and CIS accredit our schools and our students are accepted into Oxbridge and Ivy League universities.

We invite you to join the Taaleem family where together we create the environment to be 'Be Extraordinary'.

For more information, visit www.taaleem.ae

Inspiring young minds for
10 YEARS

The Taaleem family of schools:

International Baccalaureate World Schools
Dubai
Greenfield Community School
www.gcschool.ae

Uptown School
www.uptownschool.ae

Jumeira Baccalaureate School
www.jbschool.ae

Abu Dhabi
Raha International School
www.ris.ae

National Curriculum for England
Dubai British Foundation
www.dubaibritishfs.ae

Dubai British School Jumeirah Park
www.dubaibritishschooljp.ae

Dubai British School
www.dubaibritishschool.ae

American Curriculum
Al-Mizhar American Academy
www.americanacademy.ae

International Curriculum for Languages and Creative Arts (ICLCA)

The Children's Garden
www.childrensgarden.ae
www.tcgbarsha.ae
www.tcgjumeira.ae

Scan for our
extraordinary video

EDUCATION

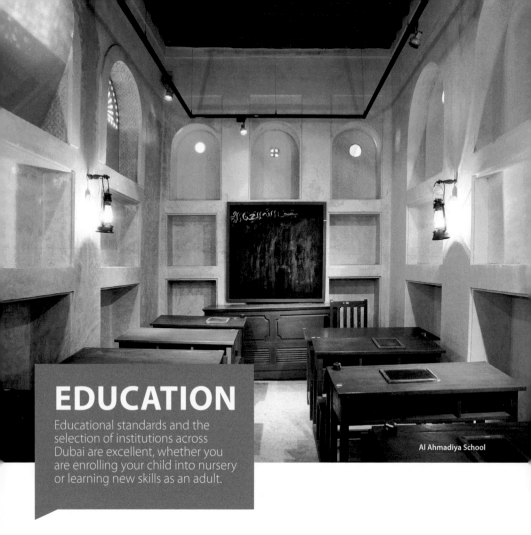

Al Ahmadiya School

EDUCATION

Educational standards and the
selection of institutions across
Dubai are excellent, whether you
are enrolling your child into nursery
or learning new skills as an adult.

Dubai is home to various international and
government nurseries, schools and universities
offering top quality education. There has been a
high level of investment and rapid expansion within
a relatively short time frame in the emirate – and
the educational landscape continues to change and
improve. School inspections are now compulsory,
and teachers will soon have to be 'licensed' (as in
western countries).

Local schools are restricted primarily to Arabic
speaking Emiratis, so you will need to enrol your
child in a private school. Although prices can be
high, your child will learn Arabic and other languages
from a young age, the facilities are world-class, and
schools are a melting pot of nationalities. There are
currently 225,000 students enrolled in private schools
across the emirate – and plans to build more new

schools by 2020. There is also a growing number of
internationally accredited colleges and universities
offering courses in the arts, sciences, business and
engineering sectors. Although the majority of
university places in Dubai are filled by locals, there are
both expat and mature students studying here too.

The first thing anyone will tell you about education
in the UAE is to get your child's name on several
schools' waiting lists as soon as possible. The
demand for spaces at the more popular schools is
high, and you can never apply too early. Secondly,
try to negotiate school fees in your employment
package with your employer. Also, check to see if your
company has a corporate debenture with a particular
place, as that will move you up the waiting list.

Whether you are a parent or a mature student, this
chapter will guide you on the path to education...

NURSERIES & PRE-SCHOOLS

Some nurseries, or kindergartens, accept babies from as young as three months, although most prefer to take on children who have started walking (around 12 months). Fees and timings vary dramatically, so it's best to call around and visit a few nurseries to get an idea of what's available. As a general rule of thumb, most nurseries are open for four or five hours in the morning and charge anything from Dhs.3,000 to Dhs.12,000 per term. You can pay extra in many nurseries if you need to drop your child off earlier (for a 7am breakfast club) or collect them later, often until 6pm. In general, classes of between 10 and 20 children are staffed by a nursery teacher and as many as three teaching assistants.

The more popular nurseries have unbelievably long waiting lists, so, if you're after a particular establishment, it may be necessary to enrol your child before he or she is even born just to make sure you get a spot. Some of the bigger primary schools also have nursery sections or an affiliated nursery – if you've got a primary school in mind for your child, it is worth checking to see if they have a nursery, as this may help you secure a place in the school itself a few years down the line.

Selecting A Nursery

The Ministry of Social Affairs is currently developing a nursery rating system to help you choose a school but, for the time being, parents will have to make this decision based on their own research. This chapter should serve as a useful guide.

Some nurseries in Dubai only operate morning hours, which may rule them out if you are working full time. However, many will also run late classes until 6pm for an extra fee and a number of them have early-bird drop-offs. They may also organise summer camps and other sessions during the holiday periods.

Don't be surprised if your child starts learning Arabic or even French from as young as one. Another factor worth thinking about when selecting your child's nursery is whether or not they provide meals – having to make a packed lunch every morning when you're trying to get ready for work may not be suitable for you.

The location of your nursery will also be a key factor in your decision making progress. You may prefer a nursery that is within walking distance of your home or en route to the office. Bear in mind that traffic can often get very congested at pick-up and drop-off time during term time.

International

Most nurseries will follow one particular curriculum – mainly International, English (Early Years Foundation Stage) or Montessori – so bear that in mind. Quite often there will be an amalgamation of approaches with more of a focus on children's social and personal development than on any one particular country's curriculum. Kidville Nursery (kidville.com) in Marsa Dubai, for example, runs its Kidville University programme with a focus on preparing toddlers for the transition to school through creativity and play.

Early Years Foundation Stage

In line with the National Curriculum for England, children between the ages of three and five follow the EYFS (Early Years Foundation Stage) curriculum, which is specifically designed to prepare them for entry to Key Stage 1 (Years 1 & 2) at school. EYFS focuses on: communication and language, and physical, personal, social and emotional development. Regular assessments help teachers understand the child and tailor a curriculum to suit their development. In line with a new KHDA rule, children can attend Foundation Stage 1 (FS1) from the age of three (at nursery or primary school) and Foundation Stage 2 (FS2) from the age of three years and eight months on 31 August (four years old on 31 December).

Alphabet Street Nursery
Villa 11, Al Manara St Al Manara **04 348 5991**
alphabetstreetnursery.com
Map **1 U5** Metro **Noor Bank**
Alphabet Street employs the UK's Early Years Foundation Stage Programme to develop each child's communication, control and coordination. Facilities include a library, computer room and paddling pool. The school offers the possibility of a 7.30am start, and also provides holiday care outside of term time. A late class is available until 5.30pm. **Age:** 6 months to 3 years. **Fees:** Available on request.

Blossom Children's Nursery
Villa 37, 10A St Umm Al Sheif
04 348 6275
theblossomnursery.com
Map **2 B5** Metro **First Gulf Bank**
Structured play programmes include dance, drama, music, water play, and foreign languages. A smartbook keeps parents informed of their child's development and there's a big focus on sensory learning. There are also branches in Downtown and Umm Suqeim; its Early Learning Centre at Academic City teaches up to FS2 level. **Age:** 6 months to 4 years. **Fees:** Available on request.

British Orchard Nursery

Nr Al Karama Metro Station Al Mankhool
04 398 3536
britishorchardnursery.com
Map **2 K5** Metro **ADCB**
Timings are from 8am to 12.30pm and there are two out-of-school daycare clubs, Little Apples and Breakfast Club, which run from 7.30am to 5pm. Parents can log on to a secure website to see their children through the in-class CCTV. There are also branches in Jumeira, Silicon Oasis and Media City. **Age:** 6 months to 4 years. **Fees:** Available on request.

Building Blocks Nursery & Child Enrichment Centre

Apex Atrium MotorCity, Al Hebiah 1 **04 453 4363**
building-blocks.ae
Map **1 N11**
Building Blocks follows the UK's Early Years Foundation Stage curriculum framework, which concentrates on helping babies and toddlers to learn and grow through play. The nursery has an 'enrichment centre' where children can learn the basics of dance, music, sport, language and cooking. **Age:** 4 months to 5 years. **Fees:** Dhs.7,000-13,700/term.

Burj Daycare Nursery

Downtown Dubai, Burj Khalifa **04 431 8320**
burjdaycarenursery.com
Map **2 F6** Metro **Burj Khalifa/Dubai Mall**
Open 8am until 2pm, this one-classroom nursery follows the UK's Early Years Foundation Stage programme, including classes in music and movement, Kidzart and French. There's a dedicated outdoor space with plenty of shade, which includes a wave pool and 'splash maze', as well as an area for bikes and push-along toys. The nursery offers flexible hours, and packages for those that would prefer not to commit to regular hours. **Age:** 18 months to 4 years. **Fees:** Dhs.10,000-42,000/year.

The Children's Garden

Green Community Dubai Investment Park 1
04 885 3484
childrensgarden.ae
Map **1 F10**
The Children's Garden was Dubai's first multilingual preschool and has three branches: Green Community, Barsha (tcgbarsha.ae, 04 399 0160), and Jumeira (tcgjumeira.ae, 04 349 2985). The syllabus officially offers children exposure to multiple languages: English, Arabic, French and German. In total, the staff speak 19 languages. The school implemented the preschool ICLA in 2005 – the International Curriculum for Languages and Creative Arts – under the auspices of Taaleem, a UAE school management organisation. **Age:** 2 to 5 years. **Fees:** Available on request.

Children's Oasis Nursery > p.x, 225

22nd St Umm Suqeim 2 **04 348 8981**
childrensoasisnursery.com
Map **1 T5** Metro **Noor Bank**
The founders of this nursery have 20 years' experience in early childhood education. The nursery offers a flexible timetable, and caters for four age groups: babies; toddlers; nursery age; and Foundation Year 1. **Age:** 3 months to 4 years. **Fees:** Available on request.

Curious Minds Nursery

Villa 31A, St 13 Al Safa 1 **04 321 6630**
thecuriousmindsnursery.com
Map **2 C5** Metro **Noor Bank**
Offers the Bidayaat Early Learning Experience and has large bright classrooms as well as specially designed 'experiential areas'. The curriculum is developed from a child's point of view and presents lots of opportunities for children to explore. There are full and half-day options, plus a nutritious meal and a transport service. **Age:** 4 months to 4 years. **Fees:** Dhs.29,250-44,600/year.

Emirates British Nursery

Umm Suqeim St Umm Al Sheif **04 348 9996**
emiratesbritishnursery.com
Map **1 R6** Metro **Mall of the Emirates**
This nursery regards playtime as an important factor in a child's early development. Its three locations (including Mirdif and MotorCity) offer multilingual staff, an in-house nurse, a pool and a soft 'sensory' room. A summer school is available during July and August **Age:** 3 months (Mirdif & Motor City) to 4 years. **Fees:** Available on request.

Golden Beach Nursery

17A St Umm Suqeim 3 **04 380 9336**
goldenbeachnursery.com
Map **1 S5** Metro **First Gulf Bank**
Follows the British Early Years Foundation Stage curriculum, with a focus on qualified staff and healthy meals. Facilities include two indoor play areas and a large outdoor shaded play area, and the curriculum includes water play, music, French and art classes. Open 50 weeks a year (7am to 6pm). **Age:** 14 months to 5 years. **Fees:** Dhs. 8,166-11,666/term.

Home Grown Children's Eco Nursery

Villa 33, 9C St Umm Suqeim 2 **04 330 7008**
homegrownnursery.ae
Map **1 U5** Metro **Noor Bank**
Billed as Dubai's first 'eco-nursery', Home Grown follows the British Early Years Foundation Stage curriculum, uses eco-friendly resources and equipment, and many of the activities are focused on nature and the outdoors. **Age:** 12 months to 4 years. **Fees:** Dhs.470-17,000/term.

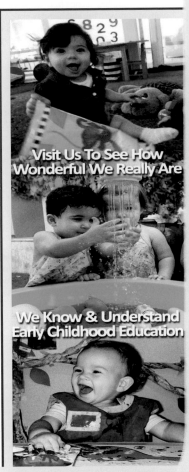

Jumeirah International Nursery School

Villa 8, 13 St Al Wasl **04 349 9065**
jinspire.com
Map **2 F5** Metro **Burj Khalifa/Dubai Mall**
One of the oldest in Dubai, this nursery follows the UK's Ofsted standards; individual attention is given in a safe and balanced environment. Classes run from 8am to 12.30pm. There are also branches near Safa Park (04 394 5567) and in Downtown (04 456 4955).
Age: 6 weeks to 4 years. **Fees:** Available on request.

Kensington Nursery

Umm Al Sheif St Umm Suqeim 1 **04 394 4473**
thekensingtonnursery.com
Map **2 B5** Metro **Noor Bank**
With locations in Umm Suqeim and Dubai Silicon Oasis, this nursery follows the Bidayaat curriculum, EYFS from the UK and High Scope from the USA. It is open 7.30am to 6pm with full and half-day options, operates a transport service, and runs holiday camps. **Age:** 4 months to 4 years. **Fees:** Dhs.28,080-42,440/year.

Kids Island Nursery

Jumeira St Jumeira 3 **04 394 2578**
kidsislandnursery.com
Map **2 B5** Metro **Noor Bank**
This nursery school follows a British curriculum and is open all year, with late classes running until 1pm. There are large, shaded outdoor play areas, an activity room and a playroom. It is partnered with Cocoon Nursery in Jumeirah 3 (04 394 9394). **Age:** 12 months to 4 years. **Fees:** Available on request.

Kids Zone Nursery

The Villa Community Wadi Al Safa 5
04 452 6474
kidszonenursery.com
Map **2 A13**
Kids Zone Nursery uses the British Early Years Foundation Stage curriculum and also adopts the Reggio approach to teaching. The school runs holiday programmes outside of term time. Timings are from 8am to 1pm with early drop off times from 7.30am and extended pick-up options until 6pm. **Age:** 6 months to 4 years. **Fees:** Available on request.

Little Discoverers Nursery

Villa 38, 35th St Al Safa 1 **04 394 6066**
littlediscoverers.com
Map **2 B6** Metro **Noor Bank**
Open between 7am and 6pm, this nursery follows the British curriculum and kids can enjoy a wide range of facilities including themed classrooms, a jungle gym, herb garden, small world and role play area, and bike tracks. There's also an indoor play area, themed classrooms and a cosy library. **Age:** 4 months to 4 years. **Fees:** Available on request.

Little House Nursery

10A St Umm Al Sheif **04 388 7130**
littlehousenursery.ae
Map **1 S6** Metro **First Gulf Bank**
This nursery follows the Early Years Foundation Stage Curriculum, with an emphasis on learning through play. Children are encouraged to experiment and explore the world around them. The nursery also offers music, art and dance classes. You can book a tour through their website. **Age:** 4 months to 4 years. **Fees:** Available on request.

My Nursery

Al Wasl St Jumeira 1 **04 344 1120**
mynursery.ae
Map **2 H4** Metro **Emirates Towers**
This nursery delivers a bilingual English-Arabic curriculum aimed at educating children to the same level of proficiency in both languages. After-school care and school transport are available. **Age:** 2 to 4 years. **Fees:** Available on request.

Raffles International School

Nr Burj Al Arab, Street 20 Umm Suqeim 3
04 427 1228
rafflesis.com
Map **1 S5** Metro **First Gulf Bank**
Raffles operates nine nurseries at various locations throughout Dubai, including Arabian Ranches, Marsa Dubai, Springs, Lakes, and Umm Suqeim. Nursery timings are 8am to 2pm, and there is a choice of two curriculums: the British Early Years Foundation Stage and Montessori. **Age:** 18 months to 4 years. **Fees:** Dhs.36,000/year approx.

Safa Kindergarten Nursery

Nr Shangri-La Al Satwa **04 344 3878**
safanurseriesdubai.ae
Map **2 G5** Metro **Burj Khalifa/Dubai Mall**
This British curriculum nursery uses the popular Montessori learning principles. Activities include educational play, water play and singing. Arabic or French as a second language is introduced to children when they turn three. **Age:** 12 months to 4.5 years. **Fees:** Available on request.

Seashells Nursery

Nr Mall of the Emirates Al Barsha 2 **04 341 3404**
seashellsnursery.com
Map **1 R7** Metro **Mall of the Emirates**
Seashells Nursery follows the British curriculum. It has indoor playrooms, an indoor gym, a project room for cooking and experiments, and shaded outdoor play areas. There are organised field trips too. After-school activities include football, gym and languages, and a school holiday programme is also available. **Age:** 18 months to 4 years. **Fees:** Available on request.

children's oasis
nursery

The First ISO Certified Nursery in the Middle East

ISO 9001
BUREAU VERITAS
Certification

Excluding Design

Two locations in Umm Suqeim, Dubai
Children's Oasis Nurseries
Umm Suqeim Branch: +971 4 348 8981
Burj Branch: +971 4 379 0790

* Excellent qualified staff to student ratio
* Age appropriate furniture and equipment in each classroom
* Spanish program available
* Arabic, Music, Football & Movement activities offered at no additional cost

* Outdoor wonderland
* Stimulating environment
* Activities to suit your child's needs
* Variation of timings available
* Sunday - Thursday
* 7:30am - 5:00pm
* 2 months - 4 years

Email: caitriona@childrensoasisnursery.com Website: www.childrensoasisnursery.com

Small World Nursery
Nr Archaeological Site Jumeira 2 **04 349 0770**
smallworldnurserydubai.com
Map **2 D4** Metro **Business Bay**
Small World combines academic learning with physical education. Facilities include a discovery garden, swimming pool and outside play area. There is a late class until 1.30pm. Another branch in Umm Suqeim (04 348 0788) offers the UK curriculum with the Waldorf-Steiner philosophy, a swimming pool, and a late class until 3pm. **Age:** 1 to 4 years. **Fees:** Dhs.8,100-9,775/term approx.

Willow Children's Nursery
Villa 75, Al Wasl St Umm Suqeim 2
04 346 5078
willownurserydubai.com
Map **1 U5** Metro **Noor Bank**
This bright and pleasant nursery, with large gardens and play areas, is run by British staff teaching the Early Years Foundation Stage curriculum. Flexible hours are offered and a home-cooked lunch can be provided. There is a dedicated baby area, Little Willows. **Age:** 45 days to 3 years. **Fees:** Available on request.

Yellow Brick Road Nursery > *p.223*
Nr Irish Village Al Garhoud **04 282 8290**
yellowbrickroad.ws
Map **2 N8** Metro **Airport Terminal 1**
This huge and popular British curriculum nursery (with a long waiting list) accommodates 180 children in nine classes and a dedicated baby room. A cooked breakfast and lunch are provided. Late classes run until 6pm. It was the first of the 'Beautiful Minds' nurseries, others include: Emerald City Nursery (04 349 0848) in Jumeira 2, as well as Cyrstal Valley Nursery, in Mizhar, and Indigo Valley Nursery near Terminal 2. **Age:** 2 months to 4 years. **Fees:** Dhs.28,500/year.

Montessori

Montessori is a popular teaching method that encourages a more flexible approach to learning than a strict academic curriculum. Children are encouraged to discover new things through imaginative play, social interaction and physical activity. The method is also used to help children to develop their own instinct to learn and is a good foundation for the International Baccalaureate curriculum.

Baby Land Nursery
Al Wasl St Al Manara **04 348 6874**
babylandnursery.com
Map **1 T5** Metro **Noor Bank**
Children participate in a series of practical activities specially designed to improve their independence,

concentration, hand-eye coordination, fine motor skills, patience and judgement. Baby Land offers late classes until 4pm and a summer school during the holidays. There's also a large, supervised outdoor play area. **Age:** 12 months to 4.5 years. **Fees:** Available on request.

Canadian Montessori Center
Villa 40, Al Waheeda St Al Waheeda 04 239 9102
canadianmontessoricenter.com
Map **2 R5** Metro **Al Qiyadah**
This Al Waheeda-based nursery is the second Canadian Montessori Center in the UAE, with the first located in Sharjah. Catering to children aged 2-6, the nursery has both Western and Middle Eastern staff to develop children's communication and language skills. **Age:** 2 to 6 years. **Fees:** Available on request.

First Steps Nursery Dubai
Villa 10, Nr Burj al Arab Umm Suqeim 3 **04 348 6301**
Map **1 S5** Metro **Mall of the Emirates**
This Montessori nursery opens from 7.30am to 6pm. It encourages child development through arts and crafts, reading, educational videos and indoor and outdoor play areas. The nursery is open on Saturdays too, when it also accepts children up to the age of 10. In addition, it runs summer camps during the holidays. **Age:** 18 months to 3+ years. **Fees:** Available on request.

GEMS Modern Nursery > *p.237*
Nadd Al Shiba 3 **04 326 3339**
Map **2 H13**
Dubai Modern High School in Nadd Al Shiba offers a one year pre-kindergarten programme to help prepare children for kindergarten by having them spend some time away from home. It follows the self-directed learning principles of both the Reggio and Montessori methods. The nursery runs regular field trips, with the aim being that children will become confident individuals and independent learners from an early age. **Age:** 3 to 4 years old. **Fees:** Available on request.

Gulf Montessori Nursery
Nr Choithrams Al Garhoud **04 282 7046**
gulfmontessori.com
Map **2 N8** Metro **Airport Terminal 1**
This Gulf Montessori Nursery has fully equipped classrooms and its facilities include a dedicated art room, swimming pool, nurse room, play areas, and a large shaded outdoor play and activity area. The nursery follows the Indian curriculum and takes a child-centred approach to academic and social development, and children attending the nursery are required to wear a uniform every day. **Age:** 2 to 5 years. **Fees:** Available on request.

Hope Montessori Nursery
Nr Children's Library Al Mankhool **04 398 2494**
hopemontessorinursery.ae
Map **2 K5** Metro **ADCB**
This private multicultural, multilingual nursery located in a quiet area of Bur Dubai follows an English-speaking, Montessori curriculum. There are a wide variety of activities on offer, including water play, arts and crafts, aerobics and even yoga. The school organises a number of extracurricular activities for after nursery hours. In addition, there is a fully equipped clinic with a nurse on the premises and a full-time senior paediatrician. **Age:** 2 to 4 years. **Fees:** Available on request.

Kidz Venture > p.239
Ibn Battuta Jabal Ali 1 **04 368 4130**
kidzventure.ae
Map **1 G5** Metro **Ibn Battuta**
Children are free to experiment through multiple activities like gardening, music, drama, cooking and games at this nursery for infants through to pre-schoolers. It offers a Montessori programme as well as the British Early Years Foundation Stage curriculum. Open 8am to 5pm Sunday to Thursday. The nursery also operates an Activity Centre, which doesn't require booking and is available 1pm to 9pm Monday to Wednesday and 10am to 10pm during weekends and holidays. **Age:** 6 months to 4 years. **Fees:** Available on request.

Ladybird Nursery
Villa 8, 25A St Al Wasl **04 344 1011**
ladybirdnursery.ae
Map **2 E5** Metro **Business Bay**
Ladybird strikes an interesting balance between a traditional nursery and a Montessori school by providing a bright and cheerful environment, toys, dressing-up clothes and soft play. The nursery school has branches in Jumeirah 1, Umm Suqeim 3 and a purpose-built nursery school presently under construction in Jumeirah Village Circle. Late classes are available until 1.30pm. **Age:** 1 to 4 years. **Fees:** Available on request.

Little Land Nursery & Montessori Centre
Nr Saga World Umm Suqeim 1 **04 394 4471**
littlelandnursery.com
Map **1 U4** Metro **Noor Bank**
At Little Land Nursery there are six classrooms, three of which are traditional nurseries for toddlers aged from 14 months old, and three Montessori classrooms for kids aged from 2.5 years old. There is also a spacious play area outside, divided into four large shaded areas. All of the teachers have pre-school teaching qualifications. **Age:** 14 months to 4 years. **Fees:** Available on request.

SELECTING A SCHOOL

Things to consider when selecting a school:
Curriculum Pick the best curriculum for your child based on your nationality and future plans; there are as many as 15 curriculae on offer.
KHDA rankings The government inspected all schools in 2014 and rated them accordingly.
School fees These can vary considerably between schools, and primary and secondary.
School transport Dubai's rush-hour traffic can turn a short journey into a tedious trek every day – check for the availability of school transport.

Curriculum

There is a wide choice of international curriculums at Dubai's primary and secondary schools, but you will find that many schools follow either the English (UK) National Curriculum, American Curriculum or International Baccalaureate Programme (IB). International schools are typically open to all nationalities, and so the choice is yours. To help you get started, this chapter features an overview of schools teaching the English, American and IB curriculums; see also askexplorer.com for a more comprehensive list covering other curriculums.

Other curriculums include the Indian CBSE/ICSE, which is taught at Apple International School (apple.sch.ae) amongst others; the German International School Dubai (germanschool.ae) is based on the curriculum of the German federal state of Thuringia, and the Lycee Francais International de Dubai (aflec-fr.org/lfidubai) teaches the French syllabus. There is also the Japanese School Dubai (japanese.sch.ae), the Russian International School Dubai (dubairuschool.com) and the Swedish School in Dubai (svenskaskolandubai.com). For full details on these and other schools, visit askexplorer.com.

Indian Curriculum
The CBSE/ICSE is an ideal option for Indian nationals who want to continue their children's education internationally, but expect to settle back in India. It educates students to CBSE and ICSE level to the end of Year 12. There are many choices for Indian schools in the emirate, including The Indian High School – Dubai, Our Own Indian High School – Dubai, and Global Indian International School – Dubai.

KHDA Rankings

The Knowledge and Human Development Authority (KHDA) is Dubai's regulatory body for private education at all levels, from early childhood to adult learning. Since inspections began in 2008, KHDA reports have ranked every school in Dubai from Outstanding and Good to Acceptable and Unacceptable; schools that perform well can increase their fees at a steeper percentage than poorer schools. School inspections are carried out annually by the Dubai Schools Inspection Bureau (DSIB). Assessments are based on a wide range of criteria, from academic achievements in core subjects to the attitude of students; higher rankings often come hand in hand with the quality of teaching of Islamic and Arabic subjects. See khda.gov.ae for more information and for a breakdown of each school's result.

British schools can now apply for inspection and British School Overseas certification by the British government; the KHDA plans to make this compulsory and also to introduce a similar quality assurance scheme for US curriculum schools. According to the KHDA rankings for 2013/14, nine out of the 12 Outstanding schools in Dubai follow a UK curriculum.

Top Scores

In the latest 2013/14 report, the 12 schools awarded an Outstanding rating are the same 12 awarded Outstanding in 2012/13. These schools include Dubai English Speaking College, Kings School Dubai, Horizon English School and The Indian High School. The number of pupils at Good and Outstanding schools in Dubai is increasing steadily, with the figure rising by 19% since 2008. According to the KHDA, 49% of all private school students are now studying at either Good or Outstanding schools in the city.

School Fees

School fees are a contentious issue for many. For a good school, you can expect to pay Dhs.25,000 plus per year during the primary years, Dhs.30,000 and up for the middle primary years, and as much as Dhs.60,000 per year for secondary school. Ouch! If you're lucky, your company may include an education allowance for school fees as part of your employment package, so it's worth trying to negotiate for this when accepting a job offer. However, you should note that this is no longer very common. Additionally, you will usually pay around Dhs.500 to put your child's name on a waiting list, and a registration fee (around Dhs.2,000), which is deducted from your annual costs. Crucially, you must sign your child up for your chosen school as soon as you can (sign-up is usually in February) as competition for places is extremely fierce.

Financial Headache

They say what goes up must come down, but not when it comes to UAE school fees, it seems. A recent survey found that fees are causing parents a great deal of financial worry. WhichSchoolAdvisor.com surveyed 1,072 UAE parents. Results revealed that 90% said school fees were a source of financial stress, one in three said they paid fees late, and two out of 10 have taken personal loans to pay them. A total of 77% said they never sent their kids on a school trip and 19% never sent them to extracurricular activities, due to the cost. UAE schools don't usually offer grants, bursaries and scholarships.

Parents struggling with fees are advised to notify the school, which may agree to a payment plan. Banks can advise on a savings scheme or loans; Barclays, for example, offers an Education Loan.

OUTSTANDING SCHOOLS

The Knowledge and Human Development Authority (KHDA) ranks every school as Outstanding, Good, Acceptable or Unacceptable. The schools below were ranked Outstanding, and are shown with highlights from the report. See whichschooladvisor.com for the latest rankings.

Dubai College	Large proportion of leavers enrol in high ranking 'red brick' UK universities
GEMS Jumeirah Primary School	A unique parental engagement programme to boost achievement
GEMS Wellington Int'l School	State-of-the-art facilities and a reputation for academic excellence
Jumeirah College	Consistently high grades with a strong emphasis on personal development
JESS Jumeirah	Ranked Outstanding three years in a row. Hugely popular with parents
Kings' Dubai	Renowned for engaging curriculum and positive attitudes of students
Dubai English Speaking College	Exceptional achievement in core subjects, teaching standards and parent support
Horizon School	High quality student-staff relationships promote personal development
JESS Arabian Ranches	Over 99% of students achieved 5 grades A* to C at GCSE in 2013
GEMS Dubai American Academy	Renowned for high IB diploma pass rate and modern facilities
GEMS Modern Academy	Praised for outstanding leadership of staff and high attainment
The Indian High School	Exceptional attainment in core subjects and notable students' work ethic

School Transport

If you are not able to do the school run every day, you can make use of the bus services offered by most schools. The advantages are that you avoid having to deal with heavy traffic, and strict regulations mean that bus safety standards are high.

The disadvantages are that it can be very expensive – you pay the same fees regardless of how close you live to the school – and if your child is one of the first to be picked up, it will mean an early start and a long journey while the bus collects the other kids.

The very identifiable bright yellow school buses are heavily regulated: bus drivers must have valid school bus driver permits, a supervisor must accompany pupils below the age of 11, and drivers are not permitted to exceed a speed of 80km/h.

Drive Safe

School Transport Services LLC (STS) is used by over 40 schools in the UAE. You can visit schooltransportservices. com to register your child and make online payments; you can also see the existing routes and pick-up times.

PRIMARY & SECONDARY SCHOOLS

Having selected a school, you will need to register your child on the waiting list (there's usually a Dhs.500 non-refundable fee). If places are available, your child will be assessed and then either offered a place or placed on a waiting list. Assessments are usually held at the child's nursery or at the school, and tend to just 'observe' the child at play. It's a stressful time for parents, especially as schools' registration procedures happen at different times of the year; apply to three or four schools and you are more likely to get a place. Your chances increase with siblings, who get priority, or if your child is in an affiliated nursery.

School Regulator

Education standards in private schools are high. The Knowledge and Human Development Authority (KHDA) has been set up to ensure that education in Dubai is delivered consistently and to an acceptable standard. All schools have to apply to the KHDA if they want to increase their fees; these can be upped annually based on each school's ranking. Outstanding schools are allowed an increase of up to 6%, schools

assessed as good get up to 4.5%, and those in the acceptable and unsatisfactory category can ask for a 3% increase.

School Uniforms

Most private schools here in Dubai will insist on students wearing the official school uniform. Each school will use a particular uniform supply shop, and this will be the only place where you can buy official school items. Before heading out and spending a fortune on uniforms, check with the school and with other parents which items are compulsory and which are not: a sturdy pair of black school shoes and a pair of non-marking trainers are usually essential items, whereas a branded school bag is often not.

Uniforms bought from the official suppliers are usually priced very highly, and can often be of poor quality, so if your school offers any flexibility on the uniform issue (such as your child wearing a plain white collared shirt as opposed to a white shirt with the school badge on the pocket), you may want to take it. A final word on uniforms: if you leave your uniform shopping until the last few days before the beginning of term, chances are you'll get to the uniform shop to find several items have sold out. This is definitely one task where it pays to shop in advance. Find out from your school who its uniform supplier is, and stock up as early as possible.

School Lunches

Many private schools in Dubai do not offer school meals, so children have to bring a packed lunch. This is worth bearing in mind if you know you won't have time to prepare packed lunches every morning when you're busy getting your children ready for school and yourself ready for work.

Holiday Calendar

Be prepared to accept that there are a lot of school holidays here in Dubai. The summer holidays stretch for 10 long weeks over the hottest months of July and August, when many kids return to their home countries for extended holidays, or attend summer camps. There are also holidays in April and December.

Schools close for at least a week twice a year for Eid Al Fitr and Eid Al Adha, and will most likely also open for reduced hours during the month of Ramadan. If one of you is a stay-at-home parent, then this poses few problems in terms of childcare; however, if both of you work, you will need to make sure that you have alternative arrangements for childcare during school holidays and random days off.

Schools which follow an Indian or Pakistani curriculum follow a different academic calendar, with the term starting in April and ending in March the following year. As a result, they follow different schedules for school exams and holidays too.

School Transfers

If you are transferring within Dubai, you will need a transfer certificate. If you are leaving Dubai, you may need a 'student leaving certificate' to prove the years of study in school in Dubai. In both cases, the school supply these and verify them through the KHDA.

Other Options

Boarding Schools

Repton School Dubai was the first boarding school to open in Dubai, and has boarding facilities for up to 100 boys and 20 girls. Abu Dhabi also has its own boarding schools, with the Junior School at Saadiyat Island, Cranleigh Abu Dhabi, as well as the Senior School having recently opened their doors. The school will cater for over 1,600 boys and girls aged three to 18, on the UAE's largest school campus. Most will be day students. Boarding fees for Cranleigh Abu Dhabi are between Dhs.65,000-Dhs.80,000 for FS1 to year nine. Repton Dubai charges up to Dhs.161,000 per year.

Some parents opt to send their children abroad – usually back to their home country – for a boarding school education. There are various boarding school agents in the UAE who provide impartial advice and guidance on selecting a school, such as Sue Anderson Consultants (andersoneducation.co.uk). For the past nine years the UK Boarding School Exhibition Dubai has also been held in the city, with over 30 UK schools represented at the last event.

Raffles International School

Home Schooling

One of the main reasons for home schooling in the UAE is to avoid the hefty private school fees. There are very few private schools in Dubai that offer home schooling curriculums. K12 in Knowledge Village offers some online courses (visit k12.com/int/arabian_gulf//index.html). The Ministry of Education offers home schooling for all nationalities but the curriculum is only available in Arabic.

Schools in your home country will be able to provide you with the curriculum, materials and online testing, for a fee. Many expats with multiple children find that whilst nurseries tend to be more affordable than in their home countries, when it comes to schooling it makes more financial sense to return home, where free public education is often available.

American Curriculum

A popular curriculum, the American curriculum is an option that is well-suited to parents who are thinking of moving Stateside before their children graduate.

Students aged four start in KG1 and progress through to Grade 12 when, aged 17, they take their High School Diploma exams. There is some variation in US curriculums and students might be tested in a range of methods from IQ assessments to exams based on understanding and recollection. Usually private schools in Dubai will choose the curriculum of one of the larger accreditation bodies in the US, such as the New England Association of Schools and Colleges or the Middle States Association of Colleges and Schools. For younger children, there is a greater emphasis on learning through play, with a gradual move to more formal education as they get older.

As well as developing students' core and essential skills, the American system has a well-regarded holistic approach to learning, cultivating a capacity for critical thinking and creativity as well as promoting students' characters, their skills as young leaders, and their sense of civic responsibility.

Al Mizhar American Academy > p.149, 218
Algeria St Al Mizhar 1 04 288 7250
americanacademy.ae
Map 2 R12
Located in Mizhar and offering an American curriculum, Al Mizhar American Academy has a co-educational early years programme for dual language learners leading to an all-girls school. It is well equipped for sporting activities including swimming and basketball. There are also computer labs, interactive whiteboards, art and music studios, science labs, and a mini auditorium. Age: 3 to 18 years (Pre-KG to Grade 12). Fees: Dhs.35,530- 55,385. Transport: Bus. KHDA ranking: Good.

American International School

Nr Lulu Hypermarket Al Qusais 1 **04 298 8666**
aisch.net
Map **2 R7** Metro **Stadium**
Established almost a decade ago, AISCH follows a
curriculum that leads to both US and UAE High School
Diplomas, making this school popular with Americans,
Canadians and Emiratis. **Age:** 4 to 18 (KG1 to Grade
12). **Fees:** Available on request. **Transport:** Bus. **KHDA
ranking:** Acceptable.

American School of Dubai

Nr Saudi German Hospital Al Barsha 1 **04 395 0005**
asdubai.org
Map **1 P6** Metro **Dubai Internet City**
The school's 23-acre site includes two multipurpose
gyms, a 700-seat performing arts theatre, an indoor
climbing wall and two 25m swimming pools. After
Grade 6 there is a 1:1 laptop programme. **Age:** 4 to
18 years (KG1 to Grade 12). **Fees:** Dhs.34,172-65,073.
Transport: Bus **KHDA ranking:** Good.

Bradenton Preparatory Academy

Sports City, Al Hebiah 4 **04 818 3600**
bradentonprepdubai.com
Map **1 M12**
The curriculum is based on the American Common
Core standards, with venues for art, music, drama,
laboratory sciences, as well as a library and full-sized
gym. The academy has small class sizes. On graduating
students receive the American High School Diploma.
Age: 4 to 18 (KG to Grade 12). **Fees:** Dhs.30,000-
70,790. **Transport:** NA. **KHDA ranking:** Acceptable.

Dovecote Green Primary School > *p.235*

Green Community, DIP 1 056 464 8707
dovecotegreen.org
Map **1 F10** Metro **Energy**
This British school is managed by Evolvence
Knowledge Investments who own Repton School and
Foremarke School. It has a gym, two pools, a library, a
music room, and is also adding multipurpose outdoor
sports courts. **Age:** FS1 to Year 1 **Fees:** 42,000-44,000
Transport: Bus.
KHDA ranking: Not available.

Dubai American Academy

First Al Khail St Al Barsha 1 **04 347 9222**
gemsaa-dubai.com
Map **1 R7** Metro **Mall of the Emirates**
DAA offers the International Baccalaureate Diploma
and an enriched American curriculum; there is also an
extensive after-school programme. Facilities include
computer and science labs, a gymnasium, library,
pool, athletics track and an auditorium. **Age:** 4 to 18
years (KG1 to Grade 12). **Fees:** Dhs.18,688-69,186.
Transport: Bus. **KHDA ranking:** Outstanding.

DWC High School > *p.233*

Al Nahda 2 **04 208 9700**
dwchighschool.hct.ac.ae
Map **2 S7** Metro **Al Nahda**
Located on the campus of the HCT Dubai Women's
College, one of the major education institutions for
young UAE women. The school shares facilities with
the college, which includes a well-stocked library,
cutting-edge technology, state-of-the-art fitness
centre, swimming pool and a cafeteria – all in a
landscaped setting. Uniquely, the school offers a dual
curriculum, which allows its students to follow the
UAE Ministry of Education syllabus in parallel with a
US syllabus through a hybrid learning model. **Age:** 14
to 17 years (Grade 9 to 12). **Fees:** Dhs.50,000 approx.
Transport: Bus. **KHDA ranking:** Not available.

International School of Arts & Sciences

Al Warqa'a 1 **04 280 0185**
isas.sch.ae
Map **2 M13** Metro **Rashidiya**
ISAS follows an American, English-speaking curriculum
with additional subjects such as Arabic and Islamic
Studies set according to UAE Ministry of Education
guidelines. It boasts outstanding facilities including
four modern science laboratories, two computer labs, a
visual arts centre, a library and a medical clinic staffed
by a full-time doctor and nurse. There's also an indoor
swimming pool and three indoor playgrounds. **Age:**
KG1 to Grade 12. **Fees:** Dhs.28,200-51,465.
Transport: Bus. **KHDA ranking:** Acceptable.

Universal American School Dubai

Nr Al Badia Residence Al Badia, Al Kheeran
04 232 5222
uasdubai.ae
Map **2 M10** Metro **Emirates**
UASD follows an American curriculum culminating
with the American High School Diploma. The campus
has a gymnasium, Olympic-size track and football
field, as well as computer and science labs, libraries
and a swimming pool. **Age:** 4 to 18 years old (Pre-KG
to Grade 12). **Fees:** Dhs.31,000-69,320. **Transport:** Bus.
KHDA ranking: Good.

English National Curriculum

Taught by many private schools in Dubai and in
British schools around the world, the English National
Curriculum or British Curriculum is popular with
many nationalities. It encourages children to reach
educational milestones each year and standardised
tests assess students, who are assigned targets suited
to their academic performance.

The Early Years Foundation Stage (EYFS, Foundation
Stages 1 and 2) for children aged three to five, is

focused on developing the social and academic skills of young children through the use of milestones and communication with parents, with an emphasis on play as well. Students then move on to the Key Stages 1 to 4, until they complete their GCSEs, aged 16 and A-Levels, aged 18.

Cambridge International School Dubai
Al Rebat St Al Garhoud
04 282 4646
gemscis-dubai.com
Map 2 M8 Metro GGICO
This school follows the English National Curriculum and aims to encourage creativity and critical thinking alongside academic rigour. Set in a spacious campus, the school is divided into two sections: Primary and Secondary. There's a variety of activities and good facilities. **Age:** 3 to 18 (FS1 to Year 13). **Fees:** Dhs.16,000-25,000 approx. **Transport:** Bus. **KHDA ranking:** Good.

City School International
Nadd Al Hamar 04 289 9722
tcs-uae.com
Map 2 L12 Metro Rashidiya
A Pakistan-based organisation with sister schools in Pakistan, Saudi Arabia, Malaysia, Bangladesh and the Philippines, the school follows a UK-based curriculum leading to IGCSE exams in Grade 11. A fairly limited range of subjects is offered – in addition to the compulsory, which include English, Maths and ICT, students also have to choose one of three pairs: chemistry/accounting, physics/economics and biology/business. **Age:** 4 to 17 years. **Fees:** Dhs.12,349-21,892. **Transport:** Bus. **KHDA ranking:** Acceptable.

Dubai British School > p.149, 218
Springs 3 Al Thanyah 4 04 361 9361
dubaibritishschool.ae
Map 1 K8 Metro Jumeirah Lakes Towers
Offering high quality facilities and set in a convenient location for residents in the Emirates Living area, DBS follows the English National Curriculum. Modern facilities include a swimming pool, gymnasium and library. **Age:** 3 to 18 years old (FS1 to Year 13). **Fees:** Dhs.38,843-58,265. **Transport:** Bus. **KHDA ranking:** Good.

Dubai British Foundation (DBF) > p.149, 218
Jumeirah Islands 04 399 5170
dubaibritishfs.ae
Map 1 K8 Metro Jumeirah Lakes Towers
DBF, a Taaleem school, opened in 2014, offering the Early Years Foundation Stages One and Two of the National Curriculum for England. Facilities include: large, multi-purpose indoor hall; spacious classrooms; shaded outdoor learning spaces; specialist music room;

specialist language room; swimming pool; indoor learning spaces; and a creative outdoor play area on split levels including a bicycle track. Dubai British Foundation **Age:** 3-5 years old, **Fees:** Dhs.55,000. **KHDA ranking:** Not yet available as school is new.

Dubai British School Jumeirah Park (DBSJP) > p.149, 218
Behind Jumeirah Park Pavilion, 04 552 0247
www.dubaibritishschooljp.ae
Map 1 J8 Metro Jumeirah Lakes Towers
A Taaleem school, DBSJP will open in September and offers the National Curriculum for England. There's a performing arts theatre, swimming pool and a food technology room with professional-standard kitchen. **Age:** 5 to 17. **Fees:** Dhs.65,000-75,000. **Transport:** Bus. **KHDA ranking:** NA.

Dubai English Speaking College
Dubai International Academic City
Al Rowaiyah 2 04 360 4866
descdubai.com
This English curriculum secondary school opened in 2005. It has been praised for the quality of teaching, student behaviour and partnerships with parents. There's a dedication to sport with top notch facilities (a 25m pool, several pitches and double sports hall). The school also offers rugby, football, netball, basketball, badminton and volleyball. **Age:** 11 to 18 (Year 7 to 13). **Fees:** Dhs.66,061-71,003. **Transport:** Bus. **KHDA ranking:** Outstanding.

Dubai English Speaking School
Oud Metha St Umm Hurair 2
04 337 1457
dessdubai.com
Map 2 L7 Metro Oud Metha
DESS is a highly respected school offering the English National Curriculum. It's renowned for the positive attitudes of students and consistently high attainment in core subjects. Facilities and activities include IT labs, music, swimming, dance and a library, and the school is successful at sport. **Age:** FS1 to Year 6. **Fees:** Dhs.31,500-37,325. **Transport:** Bus. **KHDA ranking:** Good.

Dubai Gem Private School > p.237
Nr Iranian Club Oud Metha 04 337 6661
dubaigem.org
Map 2 L7 Metro Oud Metha
This established school has a reputation for strong attainment in English, maths and science. It follows the British curriculum, leading to IGCSE exams in Grade 11, AS Levels in Grade 12 and A-Levels in Grade 13. There's a range of facilities, including computer rooms, art rooms, and a sports centre. **Age:** 3 to 18 years. **Fees:** Dhs.10,000-20,366. **Transport:** Bus. **KHDA ranking:** Good.

Dovecote Green
PRIMARY SCHOOL

Looking for a British School that provides an excellent education and a nurturing environment?

Dovecote Green Primary School is now in your community.

Book your School Tour today by contacting us on
**04-883-7474 or
admissions@dovecotegreen.org**

Located adjacent to Green Community West, DIP.

Foremarke
Dubiotech Al Barsha South 2 **04 818 8600**
foremarkedubai.org
Map **1 R10**
Foremarke is a co-educational junior school, which opened in September 2013. It is partnered with Foremarke Hall in the UK and follows the English National Curriculum. Years 3 to 5 start September 2014. **Age:** FS1 to Year 6. **Fees:** Dhs.65,000-85,000. **Transport:** NA. **KHDA ranking:** NA.

GEMS Jumeirah Primary School > p.237
Nr Park N Shop Al Safa 1 **04 394 3500**
jumeirahprimaryschool.com
Map **2 C5** Metro **Noor Bank**
GEMS Jumeirah Primary School teaches the National Curriculum for England. The school has excellent facilities, including a library and Discovery Centre and 25m swimming pool. The whole campus is bright, spacious and comfortable. **Age:** 3 to 11 (FS1 to Year 6). **Fees:** Dhs.32,775-41,315. **Transport:** Bus. **KHDA ranking:** Outstanding.

GEMS New Millennium School Al Khail > p.237
Hadaeq Sheikh Mohammed Bin Rashid 04 339 6533
gemsnewmillenniumschool-alkhail.com
Map **1 U9** Metro **Noor Bank**
This school takes on students from kindergarten to Year 7, and there are plans to expand to Year 12 in the future. The English National Curriculum is followed, and there are state-of-the-art facilities including music rooms, sports fields, libraries and a pool. **Age:** FS1-Year 7. **Fees:** 20,000-27,000. **Transport:** Bus. **KHDA ranking:** NA.

GEMS Royal Dubai School > p.237
Nr Arabian Centre Al Mizhar 1 **04 288 6499**
royaldubaischool.com
Map **2 S13**
GEMS Royal Dubai School offers high quality education in line with the English National Curriculum. The school employs British-trained, experienced teachers and the spacious building provides cutting-edge facilities. **Age:** 3 to 11 (FS1 to Year 6). **Fees:** Dhs.31,438-39,639. **Transport:** Bus. **KHDA ranking:** Good.

GEMS Wellington Academy > p.237
Silicon Oasis Nadd Hessa **04 515 9000**
gemswellingtonacademy-dso.com
Metro **Rashidiya**
GEMS Wellington Academy – Silicon Oasis offers the English National Curriculum, and educates children from Foundation Stage to Sixth Form. Students benefit from excellent, purpose-built facilities, including a swimming pool and visual arts suite. **Age:** 3 to 18 (FS1 to Year 12). **Fees:** Dhs.31,000-70,000. **Transport:** Bus. **KHDA ranking:** Good.

GEMS Wellington International School > p.237
Shk Zayed Rd Al Sufouh 1 **04 348 4999**
wellingtoninternationalschool.com
Map **1 Q5** Metro **Sharaf DG**
Following the English National Curriculum, and the International Baccalaureate programme in Years 12 and 13, students have access to digital editing suites, and a television studio and radio station. Other facilities include an indoor swimming pool, state-of-the-art gym and three science laboratories. **Age:** 3 to 18 (FS1 to Year 13). **Fees:** Dhs.35,244-76,675. **Transport:** Bus. **KHDA ranking:** Outstanding.

GEMS Wellington Primary School > p.237
Nr Shangri-la Al Satwa **04 343 3266**
gemswps.com
Map **2 G5** Metro **Financial Centre**
The curriculum at GEMS WPS complies with the National Curriculum in England. It has well-equipped music, art and IT departments, as well as a library, gymnasium, shaded play areas and two swimming pools. **Age:** 3 to 11 (FS1 to Year 6). **Fees:** Dhs.36,063-45,458. **Transport:** Bus. **KHDA ranking:** Good.

GEMS Winchester School Dubai > p.237
Nr American Hospital Oud Metha **04 337 4112**
gemswinchesterschool-dubai.com
Map **2 L7** Metro **Oud Metha**
One of the most recent additions to the GEMS network of international schools. The school follows the Early Years Foundation Stage set by the English National Curriculum. Years 10-13 are set to open in 2014. **Age:** 3 to 14 (FS1 to Year 9). **Fees:** Dhs.9,377-15,104. **Transport:** Bus. **KHDA ranking:** Acceptable.

Horizon International School Umm Sheif
10A St Umm Al Sheif **04 348 3314**
horizonintlschool.com
Map **1 S6** Metro **First Gulf Bank**
Formally Star International School Umm Sheif, Horizon International teaches the Early Years Foundation Stage and the National Curriculum of England. Facilities include splash pools, a large indoor play area, an ICT suite with programmable robots, and sports hall. **Age:** 3 to 15 years (F1 to Year 9). **Fees:** Dhs.30,000-50,000. **Transport:** Bus. **KHDA ranking:** Good.

Horizon School
Nr Safa Park Al Wasl **04 342 2891**
horizonschooldubai.com
Map **2 D5** Metro **Business Bay**
Horizon is based in a large complex, and offers the British curriculum to primary students. Facilities include a fantastic music room, library and outdoor pool. **Age:** 3 to 11 (FS1 to Year 6). **Fees:** Available on request. **Transport:** Bus. **KHDA ranking:** Outstanding.

Let's talk about the most creative people on earth.

A child's creativity is the most inspiring thing, full of joy and wonder. Nothing is impossible! Imagine if that survived the rigours of growing up. Imagine if they held on to that sense of curiosity and self-belief. Imagine how happy they'd be... and what a difference they could make!

We think about this a lot at GEMS schools. Because although we believe our people, our track record and our choice of curricula are beyond compare, what's really mattered, for 55 years, is how your children feel when they're in our care.

We unlock the potential of 140,000 students across 19 countries each and every day. Our students have been accepted into 860 Universities across 47 countries including:

- 12 of the top 15 in the world
- 37 of the top 50 in the US
- attended 6 of the top 8 Ivy League
- top 50 universities in the UK

Over **20,000** GEMS Alumni are changing the world - for the better.

For more information go to:
gemseducation.com/enquiry

Call **600 567 771** for enrolment enquiries

Jebel Ali Primary School
Jabal Ali Village, Jabal Ali 1 **04 884 6485**
jebelalischool.org
Map **1 F6** Metro **Ibn Battuta**
JAPS teaches the English National Curriculum as well as offering an excellent range of after-school activities, including football, netball, golf, gymnastics, swimming, squash, drama, dance, cooking, and music. **Age:** 4 to 11 (Reception to Year 6). **Fees:** Dhs.36,297. **Transport:** Bus. **KHDA ranking:** Good.

Jumeirah College
Nr Park N Shop Al Safa 1 **04 395 5524**
gemsjc.com
Map **2 C5** Metro **Noor Bank**
Jumeirah College uses the English National Curriculum. The student body is multicultural with members from more than 59 countries represented, and the school has a reputation for high academic standards. **Age:** 11 to 18 (Year 7 to 13). **Fees:** Dhs.58,542-73,177. **Transport:** Bus. **KHDA ranking:** Outstanding.

Jumeirah English Speaking School
16th St Al Safa 1 **04 394 5515**
jess.sch.ae
Map **2 C5** Metro **Noor Bank**
JESS is one of the most in-demand British schools in Dubai, with a long waiting list. The campus has a gymnasium, music rooms, playing areas, a football pitch and a swimming pool. **Age:** 3 to 11 (FS1 to Year 6). **Fees:** Dhs.32,043-40,164. **KHDA ranking:** Outstanding.

Jumeirah English Speaking School
Arabian Ranches Wadi Al Safa 6 **04 361 9019**
jess.sch.ae
Map **1 Q13**
This second JESS school offers the English National Curriculum, with facilities including a swimming pool, tennis and netball courts. The majority of the pupils live within the Arabian Ranches complex, making it a close-knit community. **Age:** 3 to 11 (FS1 to Year 13). **Fees:** Dhs.32,043-78,741. **Transport:** Bus. **KHDA ranking:** Outstanding.

Kings' School Dubai
Umm Suqeim 3 04 348 3939
kingsdubai.com
Map **1 S5** Metro **First Gulf Bank**
Also known simply as Kings' Dubai, this popular school teaches the English National Curriculum through an innovative, creative approach. It is the only school to achieve the Outstanding ranking five years in a row. Facilities include a swimming pool and sports fields. **Age:** 3 to 11 years (FS1 to Year 6). **Fees:** Dhs.33,441-50,892. **Transport:** NA. **KHDA ranking:** Outstanding.

Kings' School Nad Al Sheba
Nr Repton School Nadd Al Shiba 3 **04 327 1841**
kingsdubai.com
Map **2 H13**
This new project from the renowned Kings' School opened in September 2014, along with Kings' School Al Barsha. Both offer classes from Foundation stage to Year 9. Parents are advised to apply early, as waiting lists for the original Kings' School are long. **KHDA ranking:** New school. Assessment due.

Nord Anglia International School Dubai
Hessa St Al Barsha South 3 **04 361 4330**
nainternationalschool.ae
Map **1 P10** Metro **Dubai Internet City**
Founded in 1972, Nord Anglia Education is a family of 27 international schools providing a premium education to more than 16,000 students around the world. This new Dubai school opened in September 2014, offering both British and IB curriculum. **Age:** 3 to 13 years (up to Year 8). **Fees:** Dhs.60,000-80,000. **Transport:** Bus. **KHDA ranking:** NA.

Finding it hard to study?
MacKenzie Art can provide dreamy abstract artwork paintings and motivational mural designs to help you focus on your work and studies. Or to brighten up recreational areas. Innovative solutions and consultations available. Call 04 341 9803 mackenzieart.com

Oasis School
8B St Al Safa 1 **04 388 1388**
oasisschool.ae
Map **2 C5** Metro **Noor Bank**
The Oasis School offers the English National Curriculum with a full inclusion approach for special needs students. Students can obtain either their AS and A-Levels or vocational qualifications such as Edexcel and BTEC. **Age:** FS2 to Year 13. **Fees:** Dhs.35,244 – 65,874. **Transport:** Not in 2014. **KHDA ranking:** NA.

Pristine Private School
6ASt Al Nahda 2 **04 267 4299**
pristineschool.com
Map **2 S7** Metro **Stadium**
One of the most affordable Dubai schools with the 'Good' KHDA ranking. It follows the National Curriculum for England and Wales, as well as the Ministry of Education Framework for Islamic Education and Arabic. Support for students with special educational needs is good, and facilities include art studios, computer labs, a swimming pool and a grand auditorium. **Age:** FS1 to Year 13. **Fees:** Dhs.8,500-16,000. **Transport:** Bus. **KHDA ranking:** Good.

Early Learning Center

Open For FS1 & FS2 Registrations

Kids Club Opening Soon April 2015 @ Double Tree by The Hilton The Walk, JBR

- Highly experienced & qualified teacher
- Exciting & diverse enrichement activities
- Flexible timings
- Extended hours of operation
- French & Arabic Lessons
- After school programs
- P.E. Lessons at foundation stage

- Book club
- Montessori certified educational toys
- Teaching aids for children with special needs
- Full time registered nurse
- CCTV controlled facilities
- Bus service available
- Junior holiday camps

Offering Montessori & EYFS Curriculum

Open: 8am - 6pm | Ibn Battuta Mall, Egypt Court | 04 3684130 | www.kidzventure.ae

Raffles International School
21st St Umm Suqeim 3 04 427 1200
rafflesis.com
Map 1 S5 Metro First Gulf Bank
The South Campus follows the Cambridge Curriculum at primary and secondary level, and offers the Montessori programme at preschool. There is a theatre, art rooms, dance studio, swimming pools, tennis courts and sports hall. **Age:** 4 to 12 years (KG1 to Grade 10). **Fees:** Dhs.26,807-63,050. **Transport:** Bus. **KHDA ranking:** Good.

Regent International School
The Greens Al Thanyah 3 04 360 8830
risdubai.com
Map 1 N6 Metro Dubai Internet City
Regent International School offers the English National Curriculum for students between FS1 and Year 12 and 13. Facilities include state-of-the-art technology, multimedia zones, library, computer, science and language labs, as well as a football pitch, playing fields, gymnasium and a swimming pool. **Age:** 3 to 18 years (FS1 to Year 13). **Fees:** Dhs.34,172-78,375. **Transport:** Bus. **KHDA ranking:** Good.

Repton School
Nr ENOC Petrol Station Nadd Al Shiba 3 04 426 9393
reptondubai.org
Map 2 H13
This prestigious school offers the English National Curriculum and has premium educational and sporting facilities on its vast campus, including sports fields, performing arts centre, music room and library.

Dubai International Academic City

Repton offers places to children between the ages of 3 and 18 years old – and it is also the first school in Dubai to offer boarding for students from 11. Each boarding house is also home to a Housemaster or Housemistress, with a matron available 24 hours a day. **Age:** 3 to 18 years (FS1 to Year 13). **Fees:** Dhs.47,599-95,199. **Transport:** Bus. **KHDA ranking:** Good.

Safa Community School
Arjan, Al Barsha South 3 04 388 4300
safaschooldubai.com
Map 2 D7 Metro Business Bay
This British school has a football pitch, pool, sports courts, sprinting track and a dance studio, an ICT suite and many other facilities, which are available for hire by parents. The school works in collaboration with families and the local community. They also hold themed days: Community Day, Health Day, World Book Day, Science Day, Maths Day, Mini-Enterprise Week and a Culture & Creative Arts Week. **Age:** FS1 to Year 8. **Fees:** Dhs.38,500-65,000 per year. **Transport:** Bus **KHDA ranking:** Not available.

Safa School
Meydan St Al Qouz 1 04 388 4300
safaschooldubai.com
Map 2 D7 Metro Business Bay
Also known as Al Safa Private School, this Al Qouz establishment follows a British curriculum and its largest demographic comes from the UK. It has been recognised for the quality of its teaching and student support, as well as consistent attainment in core subjects. **Age:** FS1 to Year 8. **Fees:** Dhs.24,787-47,547. **Transport:** Bus **KHDA ranking:** Good.

Sheffield Private School
Doha St Al Nahda 2 04 267 8444
sheffield-school.com
Map 2 T8 Metro Dubai Airport Freezone
Sheffield Private School follows the English National Curriculum. Its campus facilities include music and art studios, an ICT lab, covered play areas and swimming pools. **Age:** 3 to 18 years (FS1 to Year 12). **Fees:** Dhs.19,117-36,050. **Transport:** Bus. **KHDA ranking:** Acceptable.

St Mary's Catholic High School
Oud Metha St Umm Hurair 2 04 337 0252
stmarysdubai.com
Map 2 L6 Metro Oud Metha
St. Mary's retains the discipline of a convent education but welcomes all students of all religions. The school teaches the English National Curriculum and offers sports activities alongside drama, music, debating class, cookery and chess. **Age:** 5 to 19 (1st – 12th Grade). **Fees:** Dhs.7,485-12,850. **Transport:** Bus. **KHDA ranking:** Good.

SWISS
INTERNATIONAL
SCIENTIFIC SCHOOL
— DUBAI —

BILINGUAL
EXCELLENCE
SUSTAINABILITY
TOGETHER

Bilingual
Understanding the Global World

At Swiss International Scientific School in Dubai, we offer the full continuum International Baccalaureate (IB) curriculum section:

- French - English
- German - English
- English

As global citizens, we celebrate diversity, treating all languages and cultures with equal respect.

Our school values – Bilingual, Excellence, Sustainability, Together - are at the heart of everything we do. This B.E.S.T. approach to education recognizes the importance of developing lasting human values alongside academic success.

Contact the Admissions Team to learn more!

www.sisd.ae   +971 (0)4-375 0600   admissions@sisd.ae

Admission Centre Al Habtoor Business Tower, Floor 25, Dubai Marina
School Address Dubai Healthcare City, Phase 2 – Al Jaddaf
School opening and operations are subject to the completion of the building and final approval from KHDA.

Victory Heights Primary School
Dubai Sports City, Al Hebiah 4 **04 423 1100**
vhprimary.com
Map **1 M11**
At this relatively new primary school, the curriculum is based on the English National Curriculum, but expands upon it to recognise Dubai's diverse population. There's a strong emphasis on personal and social, as well as academic, development. Modern facilities including a library, art studio, music room and science lab. **Age:** FS1 to Year 6. **Fees:** 33,000-45,000. **Transport:** Bus. **KHDA ranking:** NA.

Westminster School
10th St Al Qusais 1 **04 298 8333**
gemsws-ghusais.com
Map **2 R7** Metro **Al Nahda**
The spacious premises provide separate facilities for boys and girls from Year 5 onwards and, with students from over 72 nationalities, the school has a rich, multicultural environment. **Age:** 3 to 18 (FS1 to Year 13). **Fees:** Dhs.5,557-10,484. **Transport:** Bus. **KHDA ranking:** Acceptable.

Winchester School
The Gardens, Jabal Ali 1 **04 882 0444**
thewinchesterschool.com
Map **1 G6** Metro **Ibn Battuta**
Winchester School provides a high quality, relatively affordable education to students of all nationalities, following the English National Curriculum. It has a multipurpose auditorium for indoor games, when students aren't developing their musical and theatrical talents, as well as science laboratories, arts and crafts rooms and multiple sports fields. **Age:** 3 to 18 years (FS1 to Year 13). **Fees:** Dhs.11,789 to 26,298. **Transport:** Bus. **KHDA ranking:** Good.

International Baccalaureate Programme

A third option is the International Baccalaureate, also known as the IB curriculum, which is the best choice for parents who don't know where they will be in the next few years. It is compatible internationally, so your child should be able to fit into any school around the world. The programmes, aimed at students aged three to 19, aim to develop the intellectual, personal, emotional and social skills of children. They focus on a range of subjects including literature, arts, humanities, sciences and mathematics, with the choice to take certain subjects as specialist options. The IB Primary Years Programme is designed for students aged three to 12, and the IB Middle Years Programme, aimed at students aged 11 to 16, then prepares these final year students for the IB Diploma.

Dar Al Marefa Private School
58C St Mirdif **04 288 5782**
daralmarefa.ae
Map **2 R13** Metro **Rashidiya**
Dar Al Marefa Private School offers a bilingual education in Arabic and English, with a strong emphasis on respecting local culture and values. The curriculum includes all major areas of study such as languages, maths, science, technology and the arts. There's a range of facilities including sports fields, outdoor playgrounds, a library and clinic. **Age:** KG1 to Grade 10. **Fees:** 25,750.00-50,000.00. **Transport:** Bus. **KHDA ranking:** Good.

Deira International School
Vista Boulevard, Al Badia, Al Kheeran
04 232 5552
disdubai.ae
Map **2 M11** Metro **Rashidiya**
DIS offers GCSE/IGCSE, A-Levels and the International Baccalaureate programme. Facilities within the school include a gymnasium, a full-sized track and football field, music rooms, computer and science labs, libraries, a large auditorium and a swimming pool. **Age:** 3 to 18 (FS1 to Year 13/IB2). **Fees:** Dhs.34,765-70,050. **Transport:** Bus. **KHDA ranking:** Good.

IGCSE
The International General Certificate of Secondary Education (IGCSE) is recognised as being equivalent to the English system of GCSEs. It prepares students for further academic study, including progression to AS Level and A Level, and the IB Diploma Programme, and is taught at several schools in Dubai.

Delhi Private School Academy
Dubai Intl Academic City Al Rowaiyah 2 **04 326 5556**
dpsacademy.ae
This school follows the Indian Curriculum laid down by the Central Board of Secondary Education (CBSE), with the aim being to create a lifelong love of learning. Plenty of modern facilities include a well-equipped sports field, vibrant learning rooms, computer labs and science labs. **Age:** KG1-Grade 7. **Fees:** Dhs.21,000-30,000. **Transport:** Bus. **KHDA ranking:** Good

Dubai International Academy
Nr Jebel Ali Racecourse Al Thanyah 4
04 368 4111
diadubai.com
Map **1 M7** Metro **DAMAC**
DIA delivers the full IB curriculum, from primary to secondary. The school has more than 80 classrooms, as well as music, art, and drama rooms, science and computer labs, libraries, swimming pools, playing

fields, basketball and tennis courts. **Age:** 3 to 18 years (KG1 to Year 13). **Fees:** Dhs.33,618-59,565. **Transport:** Bus. **KHDA ranking:** Good.

Emirates International School – Jumeirah

Al Thanya St Umm Al Sheif **04 348 9804**
eischools.ae
Map **1 T6** Metro **First Gulf Bank**
EIS-Jumeirah was the first school in Dubai to be authorised to offer the International Baccalaureate Diploma Programme. It accepts children at primary, middle school and senior school levels and runs an alumni programme for graduates. **Age:** 4 to 18 years (KG1 to Grade 13). **Fees:** Dhs.30,140-63,870. **Transport:** Bus. **KHDA ranking:** Good.

Emirates International School – Meadows

1st St Emirates Living, Al Thanyah 4
04 362 9009
eischools.ae
Map **1 K6** Metro **Jumeirah Lakes Towers**
The Meadows campus of EIS offers the International Baccalaureate curriculum. The school facilities include large classrooms, computer and science labs, a library and a theatre, alongside a free after-school activity programme offering sporting, artistic, cultural and social activities. **Age:** 3 to 18 years (KG1 to Grade 13). **Fees:** Dhs.23,647-70,129. **Transport:** Bus. **KHDA ranking:** Good.

GEMS International School Al Khail

Al Khail Rd Mohammed Bin Rashid Garden, Hadaeq Sheikh Mohammed Bin Rashid **04 339 6200**
gemsinternationalschool-alkhail.com
Map **1 U9** Metro **Noor Bank**
This establishment's curriculum is currently under development with the intention to follow the International Baccalaureate programmes, making it a good choice for expats who are not sure which country they may move to next. The core subjects are language arts (English and Arabic), maths, science and social studies. **Age:** KG1-Grade 8. **Fees:** Dhs.46,000-6000. **Transport:** Bus. **KHDA ranking:** NA.

GEMS Modern Academy

Nr ENOC Petrol Station Nadd Al Shiba 3
04 326 3339
gemsmhs.com
Map **2 H13**
GEMS Modern Academy, previously Dubai Modern High, teaches the Indian School Certificate Examinations and the IB syllabus. The school teaches academics in the morning, then Activities for Curriculum Enrichment (ACE), which includes a supervised study session with clubs and games. **Age:** 2 to 18 years (Pre-KG to Grade 12). **Fees:** Dhs.26,780-43,513. **Transport:** Bus. **KHDA ranking:** Outstanding.

GEMS World Academy Dubai

Al Khail Rd Al Barsha South 1 **04 373 6373**
gemsworldacademy-dubai.com
Map **1 Q9** Metro **Sharaf DG**
The GWA Discovery World is at the heart of this IB school, with computer rooms, a robotics lab, and design and technology studios. There's also a planetarium, rooftop peace garden and music centre. **Age:** 3 to 18 years (Pre-KG to Grade 12). **Fees:** Dhs.56,831-98,649. **Transport:** Bus. **KHDA ranking:** Good.

Greenfield Community School > p.149, 218

Green Community Dubai Investment Park 1
04 885 6600
gcschool.ae
Map **1 F12**
Located in Dubai Investments Park just beyond the Green Community, Greenfield Community School teaches the IB curriculum. GCS has excellent facilities and a progressive special needs policy. **Age:** 4 to 18 years (KG1 to Grade 12). **Fees:** Dhs.37,878-69,754. **Transport:** Bus. **KHDA ranking:** Good.

The Indian Academy

Nr Madina Mall Muhaisanah 4 **04 264 6746**
indianacademydubai.com
Map **2 T9** Metro **Al Qusais 1**
Offers the Indian Certificate of Secondary Education. Its focus is on holistic learning, with an emphasis on social, emotional and physical development as well as academic. Facilities include a music room, library and an after school kinder club for foundation stage children. **Age:** KG1-Grade 7. **Fees:** Dhs.10,000-16,000 **Transport:** Bus. **KHDA ranking:** Acceptable.

JSS International School

Al Barsha South 1 **04 325 6886**
jssisdubai.com
Map **1 P9** Metro **Sharaf DG**
This private school in Barsha follows the Indian Central Board of Secondary Education Curriculum. English is the primary language – secondary languages include Arabic, Hindi, French and (from Grade 6) Sanskrit. There's a good selection of extra-curricular activities. **Age:** KG1 – Grade 12. **Fees:** Dhs. 13,476-32,500. **Transport:** Bus. **KHDA ranking:** Acceptable.

Jumeira Baccalaureate School

53B St Jumeira 1 **04 344 6931**
jbschool.ae
Map **2 G4** Metro **Financial Centre**
This co-educational school offers the English Early Learning Goals at kindergarten level, the International Primary Curriculum, and the International Baccalaureate Middle Years and Diploma Programmes. **Age:** Pre-KG to Grade 12. **Fees:** Dhs.50,000-75,000. **Transport:** Bus. **KHDA ranking:** Good.

Raffles World Academy

7th St Umm Suqeim 3 **04 427 1300**
rafflesis.com
Map **1 U5** Metro **Noor Bank**
This is an authorised World School for the International Baccalaureate Diploma Programme (IBDP), offering the Primary Years Programme (PYP), the Cambridge Secondary 1(CS1) and the International General Certificate of Secondary Education (IGCSE). **Age:** 4 to 18 (KG1/IB PYP to Grade 12/IB2). **Fees:** Dhs.26,807-75,059. **Transport:** Bus. **KHDA ranking:** Good.

Swiss International Scientific
School Dubai > p.241

Dubai Healthcare City, Zone 2 Al Jadaf **04 375 0600**
sisd.ae
Map **2 K8** Metro **Creek**
Due to open in September 2015 for pre-kindergarten to age six, the Swiss International Scientific School follows the International Baccalaureate programme. Students can study their subjects in English, French and German and have the option to graduate with a bilingual Matura. The school boasts vast sports fields. **Age:** 3 to 18 **Fees:** Dhs.55,000-85,000 **Transport:** Bus. **KHDA ranking:** Not yet available.

Special needs education is available

Special Needs Education

The UAE boasts an excellent private school system for expats; however, it is sometimes more difficult to find quality education for children with special needs. There is increasing awareness, and so the situation does seem to be slowly improving.

If your child has physical or learning difficulties, there are several organisations that can help; the Dubai Dyslexia Support Group, for example, holds regular meetings for families affected by dyslexia. There are also schools that seem to be leading the way in terms of opening doors to children with special needs, while certain other private schools in Dubai will offer places to children with mild dyslexia or Down's syndrome.

Unfortunately, the picture is not so bright for children with more severe learning difficulties or special needs. While in an ideal world it may be desirable for these children to attend 'normal' schools, the truth is that the majority of private schools in the UAE do not have sufficient facilities or support to cope with severe disabilities or to meet the special needs of some children. While this may result in, for example, a child with a physical disability not being able to attend a mainstream school despite not having any cognitive impairment, some parents feel that there is little point pushing the issue.

Organisations such as the British Institute for Learning Development aim to bridge a gap between private schools that may lack adequate facilities and more extreme solutions in the form of centres for children with severe disabilities. Although it focuses more on learning support and sensory therapy than on helping children with physical disabilities, the institute seeks to address children's learning and behavioural problems through occupational therapy and neuro-developmental therapy (Sensory Integration). Students are supported through work with speech therapists, psychologists and specially qualified teachers.

Al Noor Training Center for Children with Special Needs

23rd St Al Barsha 1 **04 340 4844**
alnoorspneeds.ae
Map **1 R6** Metro **Mall of the Emirates**
This centre provides therapeutic support, and educational and vocational training to special needs children from three to 18 years of age. The centre is also active in the community with fundraisers, various events such as swimming galas, programmes to help parents learn how best to support their children, and a summer camp.

All 4 Down Syndrome Dubai

050 880 9228
all4downsyndrome.com
This support group is open to families whose lives have been affected by Down's syndrome. The group is part of an awareness-raising campaign, and offers advice on health, education and care for people with Down's. Social mornings are held every Sunday.

Dubai Autism Center

6B St Hudaiba **04 398 6862**
dubaiautismcenter.ae
Map **2 J4** Metro **ADCB**
This non-profit organisation provides a variety of
services for children with autism including diagnosis,
family support, training and school services.

Dubai Centre for Special Needs

Nr Gulf News Al Wasl **04 344 0966**
dcsneeds.ae
Map **2 D5** Metro **Business Bay**
A learning institution offering individualised
therapeutic and educational programmes to its 130
students. A pre-vocational programme is offered for
older students, including arranging work placements.

Rashid Paediatric Therapy Centre

Umm Suqeim St Al Barsha 1 **04 340 0005**
rashidc.ae
Map **1 R6** Metro **Mall of the Emirates**
An educational centre that runs classes for students
with learning difficulties aged between three and 15,
and a senior school offering functional academic and
practical life skills education for 13 to 17 year olds.
Classes are taught in both Arabic and English.

Riding for the Disabled Association of Dubai

Desert Palm Warsan 2
rdad.ae
Metro **Rashidiya**
A unique and therapeutic riding programme designed
to help children with disabilities and special needs,
such as autism, cerebral palsy and spina bifida to
develop their abilities through interaction with horses.
Sessions usually take place at Desert Palm Dubai.
For more information, please contact the instructors at
lessons@rdad.ae.

Special Needs Future Development Centre

Karama Centre Al Karama **04 334 9818**
snfgroup.com
Map **2 L5** Metro **ADCB**
An educational and vocational training centre for
children and young adults with special needs. The
centre also aims to help the families and communities
of children with special needs.

After-School Activities

Most schools pride themselves on offering a broad
spectrum of after-school extracurricular activities and
often see these as important parts of a child's overall
development. Activities include anything from sports
teams, drama and computer clubs to dance lessons,
singing or even gardening classes. According to the
recent whichschooladvisor.com Fees and Financing
Survey, 70% of UAE parents pay less than Dhs.1,000 per
month for extra-curricular activities, with others paying
far more. One in 10 respondents claims to be spending
more than Dhs.30,000 annually. If your school doesn't
offer anything suitable, there are plenty of independent
options, such as sports academies like the Clark Francis
Tennis Academy. Budding Beckhams can hone their
skills with the International Football Academy or the
UAE English Soccer School of Excellence, and Turning
Pointe run ballet classes in several Dubai schools.

Many schools have also embraced the UK's Duke
of Edinburgh Award youth achievement programme.
Established in 1956 by Queen Elizabeth's husband, the
scheme encourages youngsters to learn skills, build
confidence and engage in voluntary work.

Scouts & Guides

The majority of Scout and Guide groups in Dubai are
held at schools, so check with your kids' school to find
our if they run a programme. Alternatively, you can
contact the British Guides in Foreign Countries (bgifc.
org.uk) and the Scouts Association (scouts.org.uk).

Summer Camps

Due to the sweltering hot weather, children can
find themselves cooped-up indoors for much of
the long summer holidays – but fortunately many
of Dubai's nurseries and schools offer camps and
activities during this and all other holidays to keep
them entertained. See Family & Parenting for more
information on independent summer camps.

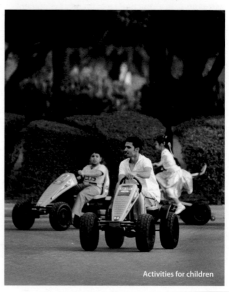
Activities for children

UNIVERSITIES & COLLEGES

In the past, the vast majority of expat teenagers returned to their home countries when moving from secondary to tertiary education. Now, a growing number of institutions within Dubai and the other emirates entice more people into studying in the UAE, with degrees and diplomas offered in the arts, sciences, business, and engineering and technology. There are also a number of opportunities for post-graduate study here in the UAE. Many institutions are based at Knowledge Village near Media and Internet Cities, and Dubai International Academic City, on the outskirts of Dubai.

Public institutions are free for UAE citizens, but the amount of international universities is increasing in Dubai as the interest in higher education grows. In particular, many UK institutions are looking to tap into the growing number of business schools in Dubai; the London Business School (london.edu) is based in DIFC, as is Cass (cass.city.ac.uk, formerly City University Business School). The latter specialises in energy and Islamic finance. Warwick Business School (wbs.ac.uk) has been offering MBAs in Dubai since 2003. In addition, there are also plenty of college options available.

Some of the universities, including several of the ones above, offer students the opportunity to study part-time, or in a structured e-learning environment through the use of a range of learning strategies. International correspondence courses and distance learning schemes, are other available options for learning skills and gaining new qualifications.

The UK-based Open University (open.ac.uk) is a popular choice, as is the South African-based UNISA (University of South Africa). UNISA recently opened an office in Dubai (unisa.ac.za). *Gulf News'* classifieds section carries adverts for the numerous other study options for short courses.

Education UK Exhibition

Organised annually by the British Council, Education UK Exhibition (EDUKEX) is part of an initiative to enhance educational relations between the UK and the Middle East. Students from across the region can attend the event to gather information on UK universities, whether they have campuses in the UAE or in the UK. The event usually takes place in January at the Dubai International Convention and Exhibition Centre. See britishcouncil.org.

Getting A Place

Typically, in Years 11 and 12 students take an interests test and psychometric evaluation to help them select their A-Levels or equivalent. In Year 13, many schools invite universities to come for an open day, after which students can draw up a shortlist of the five that they will apply for; the universities will tell the student what grades they are expected to achieve. The majority of students opt for the UK, as well as universities in the US, Australia, Canada, New Zealand and Hong Kong – but some do stay here in the UAE.

Fashion: An Opportunity

If you're interested in studying fashion, keep an eye out for the latest short courses offered by the London School Of Fashion in Dubai. Programmes last between one and five days, and cover a whole range of subjects including: fashion journalism, fashion communication and PR, luxury brand management, fashion marketing, design and styling, and starting your own fashion label. The courses are all led by tutors who have extensive experience in the fashion world, including designers, journalists and image consultants. The programmes are held throughout the year, so check the website (fashion.arts.ac.uk) for up to date news and how to register.

Academic City

Dubai International Academic City (diacedu.ae) hosts international universities including: American University in the Emirates, Cambridge College International Dubai, Dubai English Speaking College, EHSAL, French fashion university Esmod Dubai, Hamdan Bin Mohamed e-University (HBMeU), Heriot-Watt University, Hult International Business School, the Institute of Management Technology, Islamic Azad University, JSS Education Foundation, Mahatma Gandhi University, MAHE, Manipal-Dubai Campus, Manchester Business School Worldwide, Michigan State University Dubai, Middlesex University, Murdoch University International Study Centre Dubai, PIM International Center, S P Jain Center of Management, SAE Institute, Saint-Petersburg State University of Engineering and Economics, Shaheed Zulfikar Ali Bhutto Institute of Science and Technology (SZABIST), Syrian Virtual University, the British University in Dubai, the University of Exeter, the University of Wollongong in Dubai (UOWD), Universitas 21 Global Pte Ltd, University of Bradford and University of Phoenix.

Knowledge Village

Knowledge Village prides itself on creating an environment conducive to education, the business of education and networking. The operating rules and regulations are relatively straightforward

CANADIAN
UNIVERSITY DUBAI
Your portal to Canadian education

Say Hello to a successful future
with a degree from Canadian University Dubai

We bring the best of Canadian higher education to you here in the UAE, with programs in the Schools of:

- Business Administration
- Environment and Health Sciences
- Liberal Arts and Sciences

- Architecture and Interior Design
- Engineering and Applied Science and Technology
- Graduate Studies

Whether you are starting your higher education or continuing it, come and explore our range of Bachelors and Masters degree programs.

Your University, Your Future
Canadian University Dubai

Connect with us to find out more:

Call +971 4 321 9090, write to apply@cud.ac.ae
Visit CUD, 1st Interchange, Sheikh Zayed Road, Dubai

www.cud.ac.ae

Accredited by the UAE Ministry of Higher Education and Scientific Research
مرخصة من وزارة التعليم العالي والبحث العلمي

INSPIRING MINDS
TRANSFORMING LIVES

and they simplify the application process for a one-year student's resident visa, too. Some of the tertiary institutions to be found here are: European University College Brussels, Institute of Management Technology, Islamic Azad University, Mahatma Gandhi University, UAE University, Royal College of Surgeons and the University of New Brunswick in Dubai. Find out more at kv.ae.

Transform Your Life

If you want to enhance personal and professional skills, increase your capabilities, fulfil your highest potential and promote creativity, innovation and transformational change, then sign up for a course at the Transformations Institute (04 344 0115). As well as counselling and therapy, they offer career and life make-overs and professional development courses. See transforminst.com for more information.

International Universities

A number of leading international universities have an established presence in the emirate, and are open to students of all nationalities.

American University in Dubai

Shk Zayed Rd Al Sufouh 2 **04 399 9000**
aud.edu
Map **1 M5** Metro **Nakheel**
With its impressive main building that has become something of a landmark along Sheikh Zayed Road, the American University in Dubai is a well-established institution with over 2,000 students of various nationalities. The campus boasts excellent sporting facilities and the university offers a number of courses including business, engineering, information technology, visual communication, interior design and liberal arts. **Best for:** Engineering

Overseas Study

For students looking to travel further afield within the Middle East, there are several higher education institutions in Qatar. Virginia Commonwealth University (qatar.vcu.edu) specialises in research and education in art and design; UCL Qatar (ucl.ac.uk), the first British university to open a campus in Qatar, offers postgraduate degree programmes in archaeology, conservation, cultural heritage and museum studies; and Carnegie Mellon University (qatar.cmu.edu) offers full-time, coeducational, English-language undergraduate degree programmes in business administration and computer science in Doha.

American University of Ras Al Khaimah

Shk Saqr Bin Khalid Rd, Seih Al Hudaibah
Ras Al Khaimah **07 2210 900**
aurak.ac.ae
Set up in 2009, the American University of Ras Al Khaimah offers a wide variety of degree courses including BScs in Biotechnology, Business Administration, Computer Engineering, and Electronics and Communications Engineering. There are also BAs in English Language and Communication. **Best for:** Sciences.

American University of Sharjah

Sharjah **06 515 5555**
aus.edu
This university offers a wide range of undergraduate programmes in areas such as language, literature, communications, business, finance and engineering. Postgraduate courses are also offered from the schools of Arts and Sciences, Architecture and Design, Business and Management, and Engineering. **Best for:** Commerce, Art and Culture.

Amity University

Block 10 Academic City, Al Rowaiyah 2 **04 455 4900**
amityuniversity.ae
With campuses in Dubai and India, Amity University offers a wide range of MBA, BBA and B Tech courses in subjects as wide-ranging as hospitality, tourism, real estate, civil engineering and aerospace. Open evenings are held every Thursday. **Best for:** Technology.

The British University in Dubai

Block 11 Academic City, Al Rowaiyah 2 **04 391 3626**
buid.ac.ae
Map **1 N5** Metro **Dubai Internet City**
The British University In Dubai, established in 2004, is the region's first postgraduate research-based university. BUID offers postgraduate degrees including an MSc in Environmental Design of Buildings, MSc in Information Technology and various PhD programmes, and welcomes international students from outside the UAE. **Best for:** Postgrad research.

Canadian University of Dubai > p.247

Nr Shangri-La Hotel Al Satwa **04 321 9090**
cud.ac.ae
Map **2 G5** Metro **Burj Khalifa/Dubai Mall**
CUD is one of the few Canadian universities within the UAE and strives to create an international academic experience for its students, with credit transfer if you wish to continue your studies in Canada. It offers various accredited degrees including business and marketing, human resource management, interior design and architecture, telecommunication engineering and health management. As well as

academic achievement, the importance of extra-curricular activities such as sport, music and drama is also emphasised. **Best for:** Business and marketing.

Cass Business School City University London
DIFC Zaa'beel 2 **04 401 9316**
cass.city.ac.uk
Map **2 G6** Metro **Financial Centre**
Part of City University London, the Cass Executive MBA is targeted towards Middle East business executives, with a focus on Islamic Finance or Energy. It's a two-year course and the lectures are delivered over the weekends to avoid disruption to the working week. Students have direct access to City of London contacts, and students can take electives at the London campus. Degrees include accounting, business studies, and actuarial science.
Best for: Middle East-focused business.

Libraries
There are a number of libraries in Dubai. Several come under the jurisdiction of Dubai Culture & Arts Authority and can be found at dubaipubliclibrary.ae. For French books go to the Alliance Francaise Dubai (afdubai.org), and find English books at The Old Library (theoldlibrary.ae) in Mall of the Emirates. For a full list of libraries in Dubai see askexplorer.com.

Esmod Dubai
Academic City, Al Rowaiyah 2 **04 429 1228**
esmod-dubai.com
The French Fashion University is the only university in the Middle East that is dedicated to fashion. Accredited by the French Ministry of Education, it offers three-year BA courses, fashion workshops, trend forecasting master classes, merchandising training sessions, and an MBA in Fashion Management. Three and six-month courses are also available, plus classes on everything from make-up to marketing. One-month summer workshops can provide a foundation for the three-year course. **Best for:** Fashion.

European University College
Ibn Sina Bldg Umm Hurair 2 **04 362 4787**
euc.ac.ae
Map **2 L7** Metro **Dubai Healthcare City**
Formerly Nicholas & Asp University College, this is the first postgraduate dental institution to offer international training programmes in the UAE, including masters degrees, speciality training, certificates, diplomas, and CPD courses. Other areas covered include oral implantology, paediatric dentistry, and orthodontics. There is also an associate degree in dental assisting. **Best for:** Dentistry.

Heriot Watt University Dubai Campus
Academic City, Al Rowaiyah 2 **04 435 8700**
hw.ac.uk
One of the UK's oldest universities, Heriot-Watt offers undergraduate and postgraduate courses in business, management, finance, accounting, and IT at its purpose-built campus in the heart of Dubai International Academic City. Comprehensive English language programmes are also available. **Best for:** Business.

Hult International Business School
Dubai Internet City Al Sufouh 2
04 427 5800
hult.edu
Map **1 N5** Metro **Dubai Internet City**
This highly-ranked global business school offers US accredited further education. Courses offered at the Dubai campus include a one-year, full time MBA programme, a part-time Executive MBA programme, and a Master's degree in International Marketing and International Business. Students can choose to take electives at the school's campuses in London, Boston, San Francisco and Shanghai. **Best for:** Business.

Manchester Business School
Knowledge Village, Al Sufouh 2 **04 446 8664**
mbs.ac.uk
Map **1 N5** Metro **Dubai Internet City**
Affiliated to the UK's University of Manchester, this business school was established in Knowledge Village in 2006, and offers a range of MBAs in subjects including engineering, construction, sports and finance, plus doctoral programmes and executive education courses. **Best for:** Business.

Manipal University Dubai Campus
Academic City, Al Rowaiyah 2 **04 429 0777**
manipaldubai.com
A branch of India's Manipal University, this campus offers certificate programmes and bachelor's and master's degree programmes in a range of subjects including information systems, engineering, bio-technology, media and communications, as well as fashion and interior design. **Best for:** Technology

Michigan State University Dubai
Knowledge Village, Al Sufouh 2 **04 446 5147**
dubai.msu.edu
Map **1 N5** Metro **Dubai Internet City**
This non-profit institution offers UAE and international students bachelor's and master's degree programmes in line with those at MSU in the US. Programmes covered include business administration, computer engineering, construction management, media management, human resources and family community services. The university encourages a

combination of teaching methods including lectures and seminars, online classes, and internship/study abroad options.
Best for: Engineering and construction.
(Masters program for Public Health & Law only)

Middlesex University Dubai

Knowledge Village, Al Sufouh 2 **04 367 8100**
mdx.ac
Map **1 N5** Metro **Dubai Internet City**
The UK's Middlesex University recently opened a campus at Knowledge Village. Students have the option of studying for single or joint honours degrees in various subjects including accountancy, business studies, tourism, human resource management, journalism, advertising, public relations and media, marketing and computing science. Student accommodation is available at The Halls, on the outskirts of the city.
Best for: Public relations and media.

Murdoch University International Study Centre Dubai

Block 10 Academic City, Al Rowaiyah 2 **04 435 5700**
murdoch.edu.au
Murdoch University offers undergraduate degrees in business, environmental management, information technology and media, and postgraduate degrees in business and media. Their impressive campus houses a fully professional HD TV studio, an advanced editing suite and three radio studios. Students can transfer all credits to Murdoch in Australia if they wish to continue their studies there. **Best for:** Business and media.

New York University Abu Dhabi

Markaziya West Abu Dhabi
02 628 4000
nyuad.nyu.edu
This research university's arts and science undergraduate programmes are affiliated with the US campus. The university aims to give students the full, traditional college experience and its approach is firmly set on creating a campus where students will learn and develop in residences, clubs and campus events, as well as in lectures. Although it does not currently offer a graduate programme, most of NYU's selective graduate and professional schools will offer special consideration to applications from NYU Abu Dhabi graduates.
Best for: Arts and sciences.

Paris Sorbonne University Abu Dhabi

Abu Dhabi 02 656 9555
sorbonne.ae
The legendary Sorbonne arrived in Abu Dhabi in 2006. This French-speaking university focuses on a wide range of majors in humanities and law, with undergraduate and master's degrees in subjects such as archaeology and history of arts, economics and management, French and comparative literature, international business and languages. Classes are either in French (with translation) or in English.
Best for: Arts and social sciences.

University of Wollongong in Dubai > *p.251*

Knowledge Village, Al Sufouh 2 **04 278 1800**
uowdubai.ac.ae
Map **1 N5** Metro **Dubai Internet City**
The University of Wollongong offers undergraduate and postgraduate programmes in business and IT, in addition to certificates and awards in accounting, banking and management. This Australian university was on Jumeira Road, but moved its campus in 2005, making it one of the more established universities in the city. **Best for:** Business and IT.

Public Universities

The Higher Colleges of Technology (HCT) and Zayed University are the two most prominent local universities in Dubai. The HCT is the largest, with around 16,000 students (all UAE nationals) studying at 16 campuses; it offers higher diplomas, bachelor's and master's degrees across over 80 different programmes. Prior to 2009, Zayed University only offered its degree programmes to UAE nationals; however, it now invites all UAE residents and international students to apply.

Dubai Women's College – HCT

Baghdad St Al Nahda 2 **04 267 2929**
dwc.hct.ac.ae
Map **2 S7** Metro **Al Nahda**
With more than 20,000 students studying at 16 campuses across the UAE, HCT is the largest higher education institution in the UAE. English-taught programmes include Applied Communication, Business, Computer & Information Science, Engineering Technology, Health Sciences and Education at various levels. **Best for:** Technology.

Zayed University

Knowledge Village Al Sufouh 2
04 402 1111
zu.ac.ae
Map **1 P5** Metro **Dubai Internet City**
This university was established in 1998 and has a solid reputation. Zayed University's campuses in Academic City and Abu Dhabi Khalifa City now accept female and male students of all nationalities, whether international or UAE residents. It offers bachelor's and master's programmes in the arts, sciences, business, media, sustainabilty, education and IT. **Best for:** Media and communications.

WELCOME TO THE FAMILY
WE'RE 7,500 STRONG AND STILL GROWING

As Dubai's oldest private university, we've seen over 7,500 students
pass through our doors.

Graduate from UOWD and become part of a global network of leaders.

Connect with us to find out more about our undergraduate and postgraduate programs in
Business, Finance, IT, Engineering, International Studies, Media and Communications.

Call 04-2781800, email info@uowdubai.ac.ae or visit Block 15, Dubai Knowledge Village
www.uowdubai.ac.ae

UOWD - Your Australian University in Dubai

UNIVERSITY OF
WOLLONGONG
IN DUBAI

Institutes & Colleges

Recently, more and more expat students have been considering staying in Dubai to continue their education once they have left school. Traditionally many ventured further afield, or travelled back to their home countries, but as the choice of further education institutes in Dubai grows, so does the appeal of staying.

American College of Dubai
Al Rebat St Al Garhoud **04 282 9992**
acd.ac.ae
Map **2 M8** Metro **Airport Terminal 1**
The American College of Dubai offers courses that will provide students with university-level credits, allowing them to transfer to institutions in the US, UK, UAE, Canada, Europe, India, or elsewhere in the world. Additionally, associate degrees in the liberal arts, business and information technology are also available.

Moving With Kids?
Moving with children doesn't have to be stressful. At Allied Pickfords, they've come up with some easy ways to incorporate your kids into the moving process. Asking for their help, fun projects and small packing tasks can all help your kids to feel part of the move. They recommend involving your children in all aspects of your relocation, if possible, including house-hunting, planning the move, and tasks that are age-appropriate. Contact them to receive all their tips. (04 818 0400, alliedpickfords.ae).

Dubai School of Dental Medicine
Building 34 Healthcare City, Umm Hurair 2
04 424 8777
dsdm.ac.ae
Map **2 L7** Metro **Dubai Healthcare City**
This home-grown dental institution was launched in 2013. The postgraduate school offers students a three-year MSc degree in a range of specialisations such as oral surgery, orthodontics, paediatric dentistry, and fixed and removable prosthodontics. Students will have the opportunity to sit a membership examination in their dental speciality from The Royal College of Surgeons of Edinburgh.

EMDI Institute of Media & Communication
Knowledge Village, Al Sufouh 2 **04 433 2833**
emdiworld.com
Map **1 N5** Metro **Dubai Internet City**
EMDI specialises in providing education and qualifications in media and communications. Full-time and part-time courses are available in everything from journalism, advertising and PR, through to graphic design, DJing, events and wedding planning. There's also a range of journalism courses to arm students with the fundamental skills of print, broadcasting and new media.

European University College
Ibn Sina Bldg Umm Hurair 2 **04 362 4787**
euc.ac.ae
Map **2 L7** Metro **Dubai Healthcare City**
This pioneering college offers master's degrees, speciality training, certificates, diplomas, and CPD courses, and is a reputable college to attend in order to train for a career in dentistry. Students also study oral implantology, paediatric dentistry, endodontics, and orthodontics or dental assisting. For additional information refer to the listing under International Universities previously in this chapter.
Best for: Dentistry.

Lotus Educational Institute
Knowledge Village, Al Sufouh 2 **04 391 1718**
lotus.ae
Map **1 N5** Metro **Dubai Internet City**
Located in Knowledge Village, Lotus Educational Institute provides professional training in arts and design subjects, development programmes in business studies and holistic self development, as well as preparatory classes in English and IT. There's a strong focus on painting, with courses in classical, abstract and cubist art as well as workshops to introduce students to various techniques.
Best for: Art and design.

University of Wollongong in Dubai

Mohammad Bin Rashid School of Government

Convention Tower Trade Center 2 **04 329 3290**
mbrsg.ae
Map **2 J6** Metro **World Trade Centre**
Mohammad Bin Rashid School Of Government
(formerly known as the Dubai School Of Government)
is a research and teaching institution that focuses on
Arab world politics, public policy and administration,
and economics. It offers two graduate programmes,
the Master of Public Administration, in cooperation
with Harvard Kennedy School, and the Executive
Diploma in Public Administration. Its executive
education programmes provide courses in public
policy, leadership and management for government
and non-government leaders.

Rochester Institute of Technology

Techno Point Bldg Silicon Oasis, Nadd Hessa
04 371 2000
dubai.rit.edu
Currently RIT Dubai mirrors the degree programmes
of RIT in the United States, offering master's degrees in
Business Administration (MBA), engineering (electrical
and mechanical), fine arts, architecture, science,
service leadership and innovation and networking
and systems administrations. An undergraduate
programme is also offered in subjects as diverse
as accounting, ceramics, 3D digital graphics,
woodworking, and furniture design.

SAE Institute Dubai

Knowledge Village, Al Sufouh 2 **04 361 6173**
dubai.sae.edu
Map **1 N5** Metro **Dubai Internet City**
This large and respected Australian film institute,
which has branches on every continent, has an
impressive multimedia training facility in Dubai's
Knowledge Village. The perfect choice for budding
movie makers, SAE offers degree courses in audio
engineering, digital animation, film making and web
development, with short courses available too. Online
courses in music, film, 3D animation, games and
business are also on offer.

Language Courses

As you would expect from a city with such a diverse
range of nationalities, there are plenty of options if
you would like to learn a different language. While
English is widely spoken by many in the workplace,
some people may need to hone their English-speaking
skills at a language centre. Living in Dubai can also
be a great reason to give Arabic lessons a go, or to
learn the mother tongue spoken in your next port of
call. Most institutes cater for adults as well as children

with a range of classroom times, making morning,
afternoon or evening lessons possible.

Generally speaking, a course will cover between 28-
36 hours with varying levels of intensity. Some will last
just seven weeks while others will run over 12 weeks.
Expect to pay between Dhs.1,800 and Dhs.2,000 for
your chosen course.

You can also opt for private one-to-one lessons, but
these will cost more.

International House Dubai

Addiyar Bldg Al Wasl **04 321 3121**
ihdubai.com
Map **2 D6** Metro **Business Bay**
With a team of teachers speaking 16 different
languages, including Arabic, English, Spanish, Hindi,
Farsi and Japanese, IH Dubai specialises in teaching
languages, teacher training and industry-specific
professional qualifications. It also delivers the
National Development Programme, with tailormade
induction courses to help Emirati nationals to enter
the workforce.

Teaching English

If you're interested in a career move or would like to
expand your skill set, consider a TEFL (Teaching English
as a Foreign Language) or TESOL (Teaching English to
Speakers of Other Languages) course offered at plenty
of institutions within Dubai's Knowledge Village (kv.
ae). The four-week courses cost around Dhs.9,000. If
you can't find anything to suit in Dubai, Abu Dhabi
Men's College (hct.ac.ae) offers courses, as do the British
Council (britishcouncil.org) and Abu Dhabi Higher
Colleges of Technology (hct.ac.ae).

Alliance Francaise Dubai 18th St, Oud Metha,
04 335 8712, *afdubai.org*
Arabic Language Centre Shk Rashid Tower, Trade
Center 2, 04 331 5600, *arabiclanguagecentre.com*
Berlitz Language Center Nr Dubai Zoo, Jumeira 1,
04 344 0034, *berlitz-uae.com*
British Council Nr Rashid Hospital, Umm Hurair 2,
600 529 995, *britishcouncil.org/uae*
Confucius Institute University of Dubai, Riggat Al,
Buteen, 04 207 2678
Dar El Ilm School Of Languages Shk Rashid Tower,
Trade Center 2, 04 331 0221, *dar-el-ilm.com*
Eton Institute Knowledge Village, Al Sufouh 2,
04 438 6800, *etoninstitute.com*
Goethe-Institut German Language Center Dubai
Al Raffa, 04 325 9865, *goethe.de*
Inlingua Sultan Business Centre, Oud Metha,
04 334 0004, *inlingua.com*
Lotus Educational Institute Knowledge Village,
Al Sufouh 2, 04 391 1718, *lotus.ae*

THE RIGHT TIME IS RIGHT NOW.
GET FIT WITH MODELL'S TODAY.

THINGS TO
SEE & DO

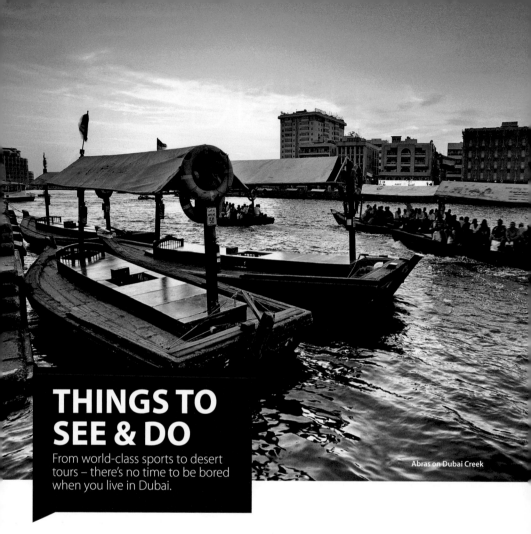

THINGS TO SEE & DO

From world-class sports to desert tours – there's no time to be bored when you live in Dubai.

Abras on Dubai Creek

Dubai has put itself well and truly on the global map over the past decade as one of the top places to visit. Its desire to build the biggest and best of everything has, as planned, caught much of the world's attention. The city's ever-growing skyline, audacious man-made islands, mega malls, seven-star service and permanently sunny weather have combined with its position as a major airline hub to transform Dubai into an international holiday destination, a regional shopping magnet, and the Middle East's most ostentatious, glamorous party capital.

Expats can also enjoy the emirate's culture and traditions as well as a host of leisure activities. The city's art scene is growing too, with more modern galleries popping up in the industrial area of Al Qouz, and there's a full calendar of international events to keep sports fans happy. During the cooler months,

there are some excellent outdoor options for get-togethers with family and friends; Dubai's green parks are superbly maintained, while the beaches draw crowds of sunbathers and swimmers at the weekends. There's family fun to be had at the various water parks, aquariums and amusement centres. The larger attractions (and many hotels) often offer discounted residents' rates. You're not likely to tire of enjoying the urban attractions anytime soon, but even if you do, there's a huge adventure playground just beyond the city limits that's waiting to be explored. Head off-road to make the most of the awe-inspiring desert sands and wadi beds, hike in the mountain peaks, go camping or take to the sea for some excellent diving, snorkelling and sailing. And that's just Dubai – there are six other emirates to get to know too – see the Out Of The City section to find out more.

PLACES OF INTEREST

To get a sense of the city, simply exploring is a good place to start. There's a definite divide between the old and the new parts of town. Head to the creek and its surrounding areas of Deira and Bur Dubai for a flavour of what Dubai used to be like. Souks, narrow side streets, heritage sites, local restaurants and a bustling waterway make this a great part of town to investigate. In contrast, the mind-boggling modern developments that make up new Dubai – Downtown Dubai, Palm Jumeirah and Marsa Dubai accommodate spectacular buildings, first-class hotels, shopping delights, and more besides.

Deira & The Creek

Once the central residential hub of Dubai, Deira remains an incredibly atmospheric area. Narrow convoluted streets bustle with activity while gold, spices, perfumes and general goods are touted in its numerous souks. Likewise, Dubai Creek, beside which Deira sits, was the original centre of Dubai commerce, and it still buzzes today with boats plying their transport and cargo trades. Both sides of the creek are lined by corniches that come alive in the evenings as residents head out for a stroll and traders take stock. Take the time to meander along the Deira side, where men in traditional south Asian garb unload wooden dhows docked by the water's edge, tightly packed with everything from fruit and vegetables to televisions and maybe even a car or two, often traded with Iran, the UAE's neighbour across the Gulf.

Creek Tours

A cruise on Dubai Creek is a wonderful way to enjoy views of new and old parts of the city side by side. Many of the tours are in traditional wooden dhows, but even these often have air conditioning inside to avoid the summer heat and humidity. Prices per adult range from about Dhs.45 for a daytime trip to Dhs.325 for a top-class evening cruise with fine food. For more information see Boat Tours.

Across the creek in Bur Dubai you'll find a multitude of nationalities squeezed together alongside busy shopping streets, seedy bars in older hotels, and some of the best historical and cultural attractions in Dubai. A walk along the Corniche between Al Fahidi and Shindagha will take you through crowds of people buying and selling fabrics from the Textile Souk, jostling to board an abra, or heading for prayers at one of the mosques or the atmospheric Hindu temple.

Dubai's Oldest History

For a full creek experience, start at Al Fahidi Historical Neighbourhood (formerly Bastakiya), where you'll step out of the modern world and into a pocket of the city that harks back to a bygone era. Situated in Bur Dubai by the creek, it is one of the oldest heritage sites in Dubai and certainly the most atmospheric. The area dates from the early 1900s when traders from the Bastak region of southern Iran were encouraged to settle there by tax concessions granted by Sheikh Maktoum bin Hashar, the ruler of Dubai at the time.

The area is characterised by traditional windtower houses, built around courtyards and clustered together along a winding maze of alleyways. The distinctive four-sided windtowers (*barjeel*), seen on top of the traditional flat-roofed buildings, were an early form of air conditioning. There are some excellent cultural establishments in and around the area, including Dubai Museum and XVA Gallery.

Water Taxis

A fleet of James Bond-style water taxis serve waterfront destinations from Al Mamzar and the creek all the way to Jabal Ali. The smart-looking taxis are available for private hire with fares starting from Dhs.50 and rising to Dhs.570 for the longest distance. They can also be hired on an hourly basis, starting at Dhs.400 per hour. Passengers can call the RTA on 800 9090 to be picked up from one of 23 taxi stops.

Souk Up The Atmosphere

From Al Fahidi, wander through the Textile Souk and then on to Shindagha, another interesting old area where you'll find Sheikh Saeed Al Maktoum's House and the Heritage & Diving Villages. Then take an abra towards Deira; a must for Dubai residents, you can make a single crossing on a communal abra for Dhs.1, or take a private tour between Maktoum Bridge and Shindagha (the official RTA rate is Dhs.100 for an hour).

Once on the Deira side, cross the corniche and head towards the souk district. First stop is the Spice Souk, where the aroma of saffron and cumin fills the air. Nearby, the streets in and around the Gold Souk are crammed with shops shimmering with jewellery.

Take a wander around the area behind the souks to discover alleyways with shops that deal in almost any kind of goods imaginable. Tiny cafeterias, old barbershops and odd knick-knack stores appear around almost every corner, and life in general seems to move at its own energetic pace.

Deira Tower on Al Nasr Square is worth a visit if you're after rugs. Around 40 shops offer a colourful profusion of carpets from Iran, Pakistan, Turkey and Afghanistan. For dinner with a view, head to the top of the Hyatt Regency where Al Dawaar hosts an incredible buffet within its rotating dining room. Afterwards, you can burn off the buffet belly by strolling along the Gulf-side Deira corniche, where you'll find the atmospheric Fish Market and Al Mamzar Beach Park, a great spot for a day out by the sea.

Good As Gold

The Gold Souk is an Aladdin's cave of gold shopping. Bargaining is expected, and discounts depend on the season and the international gold rate. Dubai Shopping Festival and Dubai Summer Surprises are the main periods for low prices, when huge discounts attract gold lovers from around the world. Individual pieces can be made, or copies made to your own specifications, within a few days. Even if you aren't buying, an evening stroll through the Gold Souk, when it's glistening, is worth the experience.

Architectural Delights

Further up the creek, on the other side of the souks, are some fascinating buildings that seemed years ahead of their time when they were built. The large golf ball that sits atop the Etisalat building is testimony to the unique imagination of Dubai's modern architecture. The sparkling glass building housing the National Bank of Dubai (known fondly as the 'pregnant lady') is a sculptural vision, standing tall like a magnificent convex mirror that reflects the bustling activity of the creek.

It is also in this area that you can find three of Dubai's original five-star hotels: Hilton Dubai Creek, Sheraton Dubai Creek, and the Radisson Blu, Dubai Deira Creek. Nearby is the dhow wharfage area where more of the large wooden trading boats dock.

Inland is Deira City Centre, one of Dubai's first mega malls, while bordering the creek for about 1.5km between Maktoum and Garhoud bridges is an enticing stretch of carefully manicured greenery, home to the Dubai Creek Golf & Yacht Club. The impressive golf clubhouse is based on the shape of a dhow sail (the image of this famous building is found on the Dhs.20 note), while the yacht club is aptly in the shape of a yacht. This is also the site of one of the city's top five-star hotels, the Park Hyatt Dubai, which features Mediterranean-style low buildings offering creek views and some great restaurants.

To the south-west of Bur Dubai is Port Rashid, where you'll find the Dubai Ports Authority building, a large glass and chrome construction imaginatively designed like a paddle steamer.

Downtown Dubai

This spectacular mix of shops, restaurants, entertainment and architecture is a showstopper destination that attracts hordes of tourists and residents every day.

At the heart of Downtown is the world's tallest tower, the shimmering Burj Khalifa, which points like a needle more than 800m skywards and contains exclusive apartments, the At The Top Burj Khalifa SKY observatory, and the Armani Hotel Dubai. By its base are The Dubai Mall and Old Town, while the centrepiece is the spectacular Dubai Fountain, which draws crowds to witness the regular evening shows where jets of water shoot 150m into the air along the length of Burj Lake to modern and Arabic music. Take a seat at any of the restaurant terraces that line the lake for a perfect view; Mango Tree at Souk Al Bahar is particularly well placed.

Inside The Burj Khalifa

After growing like a beanstalk before the eyes of residents over the years, the Burj Khalifa reached its zenith in 2010, and at over 828m in height, is officially the world's tallest building. Visitors can ride high-speed lifts all the way to observation decks At The Top (124th floor) and Burj Khalifa SKY (148th floor) to take in the staggering 360° views (burjkhalifa.ae). Fine dining restaurant At.mosphere, found on the 122nd floor, is officially the world's highest restaurant from ground level, too.

The Dubai Mall, one of the largest malls in the world, is full of top-end retail brands, an array of excellent eateries and some fantastic entertainment options such as Dubai Aquarium & Underwater Zoo, Dubai Ice Rink, Reel Cinemas and SEGA Republic.

The Dubai Fountain

The world's largest dancing fountain is located in Burj Lake. The very best views are from either the restaurants on the waterfront promenade of The Dubai Mall, or those that line Souk Al Bahar. You can get an entirely different view if you head for drinks at Neos, The Cigar Lounge or At.mosphere, or time your ascent of the Burj Khalifa. Set to modern, Arabic and classical music, the fountain sends spray up to 150m, with 22,000 gallons of water airborne at some points, all lit up by 1.5 million lumens of projected light. Performances are daily at 1pm and 1:30pm, and then every 30 minutes from 6pm.

There are two Address hotels in the area, and the views from the 63rd floor Neos bar at The Address

Downtown are well worth taking in. Old Town, which is home to the atmospheric Souk Al Bahar, takes strong influences from traditional Arabia, with windtowers, mosaics, courtyards, passageways and fortress-like finishes, all of which are beautifully lit at night. Other hotels in the area include The Palace and Al Manzil, which are home to Asado steakhouse and upmarket sports bar Nezesaussi Grill respectively. Circling the Downtown complex is Sheikh Mohammed bin Rashid Boulevard, which has a growing number of alfresco eateries and hangouts, including the ever-popular Reem Al Bawadi. It's a wide and pleasant place to stroll, and popular with joggers.

Just behind Downtown, the buzzing strip over on Sheikh Zayed Rd is known for the striking architecture of its high-rise residential buildings, office towers and top-class hotels including Jumeirah Emirates Towers and the Shangri-La. From Dubai World Trade Centre to Interchange One (known as Defence Roundabout), the wide, skyscraping 3.5km stretch is the subject of many a photo, as well as after-hours hook ups in the various happening hotspots.

With so many residents, tourists and business people around, this area really comes to life at night, as the crowds flit from restaurants to bars to clubs.

Marsa Dubai

Known by most as Dubai Marina, this area has been renamed under the new addressing system as 'Marsa Dubai'. The epitome of new Dubai's rise to modern

prominence, apartment buildings line every inch of the man-made waterway, while between the marina and the shore is the massive Jumeirah Beach Residence (JBR) development, which dwarfs nearby beach resorts, such as the Hilton and the Ritz-Carlton.

The pedestrianised walkways that run around the marina and parallel to the coast have evolved into lively strips of cafes and restaurants, which throng with people in the evenings when the lit-up skyscrapers are at their most impressive.

Marina Walk boulevard provides continuous pedestrian access around the 11km perimeter of the water and is a popular circuit for morning joggers, skaters and cyclists. It is a great place for a stroll any time, but it really comes to life in the evenings and cooler months when you can sit and gaze out across the rows of gleaming yachts and flashing lights of high-rise hotels and apartments. Dubai Marina Mall sits along the walkway with a number of alfresco cafes connecting the mall with the boulevard bustle. Nearby, The Walk at JBR is an outdoor parade of shops, restaurants and hotels parallel to the beach that has become a huge leisure-time draw for Dubai visitors and residents. Shopping and dining complex The Beach at JBR opened in 2014, providing a plethora of new food and shopping options. Located right on the beach, the new development also boasts a jogging track, public changing facilities and toilets, outdoor cinema, and water play area for children.

The beach itself is massively popular during the cooler months. The spaces in front of the hotels are reserved for guests, but there are areas in between

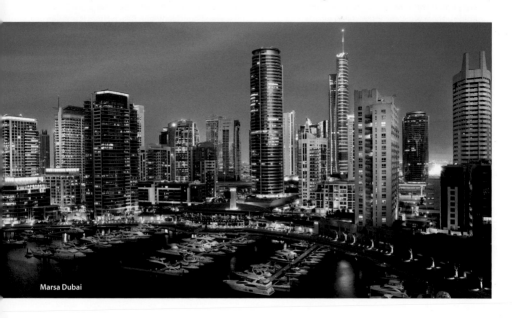

Marsa Dubai

that fill with crowds of families and groups of friends at weekends. The waters are fairly calm here and the shallow areas are scattered with bathers, while the hotels offer a variety of watersports such as parasailing and boat rides that anyone can sign up for.

Construction continues on the Dubai Eye project, which will see the building of Bluewaters Island off the southern canal entrance to hold the world's tallest observation wheel, along with leisure amenities and residential developments.

Jumeira

Jumeira might not have the exotic atmosphere or history of Deira, but its beaches, shopping centres and pleasant, wide streets make up for it. The area is traditionally one of the most desirable addresses for well-off expats, and the origin of the infamous 'Jumeira Jane' caricature – well-to-do expat women who fill their days shopping, spa-ing or lunching with fellow Janes in the establishments along Jumeira Beach Road. The area is home to a range of stylish boutiques and shopping centres, Mercato Shopping Mall, and excellent cafes such as The Lime Tree Cafe & Kitchen and THE One restaurant.

It's a great part of town for hitting the beach too. The popular Jumeirah Open Beach has showers and lifeguards, but it unfortunately attracts a few voyeurs, so you may prefer to try the more private Jumeirah Beach Park opposite Chili's, where you can hire sun loungers and parasols.

That's not to say Jumeira is all sun, sea and shopping – there are some interesting cultural spots here too. Jumeirah Mosque is one of the most recognisable places of worship in the city and welcomes visitors with tours and educational programmes, while a couple of galleries will keep art enthusiasts happy.

Jumeirah Corniche

Opened in late 2014, the new corniche runs from Dubai Marine Beach Resort down to the Burj Al Arab hotel. The walkway, with jogging and cycle tracks, is now the longest beachfront in Dubai.

Just outside Jumeira, on the border with Satwa, lies 2nd December Street. It offers a completely different vibe to the sedate Jumeira suburbs; it's a hectic thoroughfare lined with shops and restaurants, and is the main destination for anyone needing to feed their post-club hunger, show off their expensive customised car, or watch the city pass by as they enjoy some street-side Lebanese fare. If you're out past midnight, don't miss having a bite at either Al Mallah

Burj Khalifa from the beach

or the Dubai institution that is Ravi's.

At the other end of Jumeira is Umm Suqeim, where the ultimate attraction has to be the iconic Burj Al Arab – be sure to visit its restaurants or spa at least once while you live here.

Souk Madinat Jumeirah is a picture perfect leisure destination in itself, brimming with popular bars and restaurants amongst its waterways and Arabesque architecture, and packed with shops and stalls.

The wave-shaped Jumeirah Beach Hotel is another popular spot for dining and nightlife and is home to 360 Bar & Lounge, which sits at the end of its own pier and has fabulous views of the city's shoreline.

Sun and water lovers are well catered for in this area too, with a great public beach that has views of the Burj Al Arab, and the excellent water park, Wild Wadi.

Streetlife: Karama and Satwa

They may not offer too much in the way of spectacular modern developments or five-star luxury, but for a dose of interesting street life, plus a real flavour of the Indian subcontinent and the Philippines, Karama and Satwa are well worth a visit.

Karama mainly consists of low-rise apartment buildings, but is also home to a range of shops selling all kinds of cheap clothing and goods – not always the genuine article. Karama's merchants are a far cry from their mall counterparts, and you can expect to have to haggle to get your bargain. The other big draw for Karama is the range of excellent, low-budget south Asian restaurants, serving fiery Indian, Sri Lankan and Pakistani fare. Highlights include Saravana Bhavan and Karachi Darbar.

Satwa's character shines through on its busy main thoroughfares, 2nd December Street, Plant Street and Satwa Road. 2nd December Street is the heartbeat of the area, where people go to eat, socialise and be seen. Satwa Road branches off this road, and Plant Street runs parallel; here you'll find pots and plants, pet shops, fabric shops and hardware outlets, and a small area full of car repair shops. It's also a great spot to find a bargain tailor. Head here on a Saturday evening to soak up the atmosphere, but women are advised to cover up to avoid being stared at.

Dubai Canal

Dubai Creek is being extended from Business Bay to Jumeira beach. The 3km stretch of water will cut through Sheikh Zayed Road, Safa Park, Al Wasl Road and Jumeira Road and will be peppered with pedestrian bridges and waterside walkways leading to new hotels, malls and restaurants. The whole project is due for completion by 2017 and will be known as Dubai Canal.

Palm Jumeirah

Stretching several kilometres out to sea between Marsa Dubai and Al Sufouh is the Palm Jumeirah, Dubai's original, mind-boggling man-made island built in the shape of a palm tree. Stretching out along the exclusive 'fronds' are countless luxury villas, while the 'trunk' is lined with desirable apartments along the

Golden Mile (accessed by the left fork onto the Palm) and the Shoreline.

Standing boldly at the seaward-most point of the island is the Disney-esque Atlantis hotel, which has become an icon in itself. Dotted along the east and west 'crescents', are a raft of deluxe hotels including One&Only The Palm, Jumeirah Zabeel Saray, the Kempinski, and gorgeous new offerings from Sofitel and Anantara.

Aquaventure is Atlantis' thrilling water park, and you can get up close to the marine life at Dolphin Bay and The Lost Chambers aquarium.

The Palm is also home to several top restaurants, including Nobu at Atlantis and West 14th at Oceana, as well as more relaxed hangouts such as Aussie surf shack-inspired BidiBondi and Riva Beach Club along the same strip as the Shoreline Apartments.

You can drive the length of the Palm and around its perimeter for great views back to the shore, and the sea wall here has a pleasant sidewalk for a stroll. Plans are afoot to widen this into a boardwalk that will be dotted with kiosks, and for two piers to be built into the water.

If you want to avoid having to drive, you can take a ride on the monorail for a more interesting trip up the Palm, and for an elevated view of the luxury-villa-lined fronds. The picturesque Al Ittihad Park, which stretches beneath the monorail, may not have the open lawns and acres of space found elsewhere, but it bustles with dog walkers, joggers making use of the springy, 2.9km running track and exercise equipment, and kids enjoying the shady play areas dotted the length of the park.

Atlantis The Palm

Al Qouz – The Unlikely Art District

Some of Dubai's most significant culture is hidden away among the sand-covered warehouses and factories of Al Qouz.

Tucked away in massive warehouses – often out of sight – are a collection of galleries and impressive interior design shops that are some of Dubai's best bets for truly joining the global arts landscape. Add to that an endless selection of cheap south Asian cafeterias, several trendy cafes, the Gold & Diamond Park, Times Square Center, the treasure trove of goods at Dubai Antique Museum and community arts hub The Courtyard, Al Qouz quickly becomes a destination worth exploring.

Although less-publicised than massive state-sponsored cultural projects in Abu Dhabi or Doha, the Al Qouz art scene, and Alserkal Avenue in particular, are the heart of the Arab art world. It is here that lesser-known artists can find exhibition space, and the galleries are working to promote Arab art on an international scale.

At one end of the spectrum sit smaller galleries such as **4 Walls Art Gallery** (4walls-dubai.com) and, at the other end, are the well-known, more established galleries that have experienced art collectors as their main clients. One of the best recognised is **The Third Line**. The gallery itself is impressive and contains some of the most innovative art in the city, representing contemporary Middle Eastern artists locally, regionally and internationally. In addition to monthly exhibitions, the gallery hosts programmes including film screenings, debates and international multimedia forums, all promoting interaction between regional artists and the public.

Al Qouz is aiming to be the new Soho. It's not quite there yet, but along with the promotion and exhibition of regional art, the industrial zone has managed to become a centre for the creative process, be it art, acting or music.

the jamjar offers an extensive schedule of workshops and open studio sessions geared towards amateur artists looking for a welcoming outlet. Workshops range from advanced painting skills to the basics of lomography. the jamjar also hosts several exhibitions each year in its gallery space.

Shelter (shelter.ae) promotes regional creatives with a host of entrepreneurial services including office space, business setup assistance and an environment to nurture contacts. . Elsewhere in Al Qouz, you'll find great galleries like **Artsawa**.

Alserkal Avenue

This arts district is home to around 20 creative spaces, and it's a great place to spot new talent from the UAE and abroad. The easiest way to explore it is with the aid of ArtMap (visit artinthecity.com).

There's **Salsali Private Museum**, a non-profit museum, and hip gallery **Mojo**, both of which are known for championing local artists.

Gulf Photo Plus is a photography studio and gallery that runs courses as well as exhibitions, and **The Fridge** has become something of a hidden gem for performance art and music events.

Ayyam Gallery runs the Shabab Ayyam Project, a programme that encourages the development of new talent in the region, while **Carbon 12 Dubai** states its mission as bringing together a colourful variety of international movements with one common point: contemporary at its best.

Gallery Isabelle Van Den Eynde has become a significant player, credited with discovering and nurturing the talent of some of the most promising figures in the Middle East's contemporary art scene – including Rokni and Ramin Haerizadeh, Reza Aramesh and Lara Baladiwell.

Green Art Gallery represents a multi-generational mix of artists from the Middle East, North Africa, South Asia, Turkey and beyond, and **Lawrie Shabibi** focuses on modern art, supporting established and emerging contemporary artistic talent within its 3000 square foot warehouse space.

The Courtyard

A stone's throw from Alserkal is The Courtyard, home to the Total Arts Gallery, which has long showcased Middle Eastern art with an emphasis on Iranian artists, and the venue frequently exhibits traditional handicrafts and antique furniture. There's also an innovative performing arts theatre here, The Courtyard Playhouse, which specialises in Improvisation but also hosts poetry workshops.

Trendy tastes

Popular cafes in the area include a few cafes along the road from the Gold & Diamond Park, hip newcomer Tom & Serg (behind ACE Hardware) and Lime Tree Cafe. All are worth the trip into dusty Al Qouz.

Highlights of Al Qouz

1. Alserkal Avenue
2. Artsawa
3. The Third Line
4. 4 Walls Art Gallery
5. the jamjar
6. The Courtyard
7. Dubai Garden Centre
8. ACE Hardware
9. Tom & Serg
10. THE One Deli
11. J+A Gallery
12. Meem Gallery
13. Lime Tree Cafe

AL WASL ST
D92
Choithrams
AL WASL ST
J3 Mall
Medi Clinic
Synergy Integrated Medical Centre
8B
8A
25
15
33
Princess Haya Bint Al Hussein Cultural & Islamic Centre
AL THANYA ST
AL MANARA
Al Sha'arawi School
AL MANARA ST
33
14C
10A
Emirates Intl School
14A
21B
7
UMM AL SHEIF
39
SHK ZAYED RD
43
Al Manara
4
FGB
31
Times Square
8
9
10
13
15A
11
Bur Dubai Traffic Dept
Gold & Diamond Park
7
42
3
7
6A
6
4
5
17A
Cemex Readymix
NBM Santa Margarita
FIRST AL KHAIL ST
1
FIRST AL KHAIL ST
Home Centre
ARABTEC Construction
AL QOUZ IND 3
Jotun Powder Coatings
AL MARABEA ST
2
6
AL QOUZ IND 1
DUTILE
Al Nahda International Chemicals
18
United Precast Concrete
27
22
Explorer
JK Metal Industries
11B
12
UMM SUQEIM ST
Al Qouz Mall
17B
D65
28A
AL ASAYEL ST
D72
AL ASAYEL ST
17A
Grand City Mall
Al Ahli Driving Centre
AL QOUZ IND 2
14C
18B
33B
Emirates Printing Press
26

0   1km

© Explorer Group Ltd. 2015

AL KHAIL RD

ART & CULTURE

Along with well-curated heritage sites and some fascinating museums, there's a thriving art scene in the city that's well worth exploring.

Art Galleries

While there's nothing like the Tate or the Louvre in Dubai yet, there are a number of galleries that have interesting exhibitions of art and traditional Arabic artefacts, and more are springing up, particularly in the Al Qouz area. Most operate as a shop and a gallery, but some also provide studios for artists and are involved in the promotion of art within the emirates. The Majlis Gallery, The Courtyard and the XVA Gallery are all worth visiting for their architecture alone; they provide striking locations in which you can enjoy a wide range of art, both local and international, while at Opera Gallery you'll find the odd Renoir and Picasso. Many art shops also have galleries as well.

Modern Art

Dubai is following in Abu Dhabi's footsteps with plans for a new cultural district in the emirate. The Opera House District, which is under construction in Downtown Dubai, will include a 2,000 seat opera house (due to open in 2015), a modern art museum, two 'art hotels' and several new galleries.

Alserkal Avenue

First Al Khail St Al Qouz Ind. 1 **04 416 1900**
alserkalavenue.ae
Map **1 U6** Metro **Noor Bank**
This cool complex off Manara Road is home to several galleries and event spaces. See the feature on the previous page for more information about this thriving arts centre.

Art Couture

Al Badia Golf Club Al Kheeran **04 601 0101**
artcoutureuae.com
Map **2 M10** Metro **Emirates**
With a number of regional and international solo and group exhibitions each year, this gallery also hosts the interesting Art & Coffee mornings that offer art fans a chance to chat to artists, watch live demonstrations and participate in discussions around a set theme.

Artsawa

Al Marabea St Al Qouz Ind. 1 **04 340 8660**
artsawa.com
Map **1 T7** Metro **Noor Bank**
Artsawa focuses on the promotion of contemporary Arab art in a variety of mediums including collage, etching, installation, painting, photography, sculpture and video. It also hosts performing arts performances, music recitals and educational workshops aimed at engaging the local and international communities.

Abu Dhabi Art

Establishing itself as a major artistic centre is high on the agenda for Abu Dhabi. Exciting attractions to come are branches of the Louvre and the Guggenheim at Saadiyat Cultural District on Saadiyat Island, which are due in 2015 and 2017 respectively. Emirates Palace already regularly plays host to some excellent international exhibitions in association with some of the world's leading institutions, while Manarat Al Saadiyat is already making waves (saadiyatculturaldistrict.ae). There's also an increasingly important annual event on the calendar, Abu Dhabi Art (abudhabiartfair.ae), which is held in November.

DIFC Gate Village

DIFC Zaa'beel 2
difc.ae
Map **2 G6** Metro **Emirates Towers**
An arts hub to service the trendy DIFC area, Gate Village is home to several impressive spaces and hosts regular events. Artspace is one of Dubai's most sophisticated galleries, specialising in showcasing contemporary art from Middle Eastern artists. Cuadro Fine Art Gallery has a space every bit as beautiful as the art it displays. Exhibitions concentrate on contemporary pieces focusing on painting, paper, photography and sculpture. These are enhanced by the Cuadro Education Program, which organises lectures, workshops and panel discussions.

The Empty Quarter deals exclusively in fine art photography, staging exhibitions from both emerging and established artists from across the globe and works from abstract art to photo journalism. The Farjam Foundation features rotating exhibitions from the private collection of a local arts patron, including Quranic scripts, regional art and international masterpieces. The gallery hosts guided tours and an art camp for kids in the summer.

Opera Gallery is part of an international chain, and has a permanent collection of art on display and for sale, mainly European and Chinese, with visiting exhibitions changing throughout the year. The permanent collection also includes several masterpieces, so look out for the odd Dali or Picasso.

Rira Gallery hosts solo and group exhibitions featuring a strong selection of emerging and well-known artists from the Arab world. Its monthly exhibitions and programme of alternative events are making it a notable player in the Dubai art scene.

Dubai International Art Centre

Nr Mercato Shopping Mall Jumeira 1 **04 344 4398**
artdubai.com
Map **2 F4** Metro **Burj Khalifa/Dubai Mall**
This large gallery and shop has eight showrooms with a wide range of original art, framed maps, and Arabian antiques and gifts. The gallery specialises in the restoration of antiques and furniture, and also offers picture framing.

The Flying House

House 18, 25 Street Al Qouz 1 **050 651 9935**
flyinghouse.net
Map **2 C6** Metro **Business Bay**
A non-profit organisation dedicated to contemporary Emirati artists, with a collection of important Emirati works that have been assembled over a period of 30 years. This includes early works by some of the pioneers of contemporary art in the UAE, and recent works by both established and young artists.

◄ The ArtBus

The ArtBus runs regular art gallery tours and offers transport to the major exhibitions during the annual art fairs including Art Dubai and Abu Dhabi Art Fair. For more information, visit artinthecity.com.

Hunar Gallery

Villa 6, Nadd Al Hamar St Al Rashidiya **04 286 2224**
hunargallery.com
Map **2 P10** Metro **Rashidiya**
Open since 1998, this gallery features international portraits, landscapes, calligraphy and abstract art, as well as promoting up and coming local artists and works by women. There have been exhibitions from artists from many continents. Open Saturday to Thursday from 9am to 8pm, and Friday by appointment.

J+A Gallery

Warehouse 15, St 4A Al Qouz Ind. 1
055 395 0495
ja-gallery.com
Map **2 A6** Metro **Noor Bank**
With a focus on rare industrial antiques and vintage items from the early 20th century, this gallery highlights the transition from traditional craft to industrial mass production after the First World War. There's also an impressive collection of contemporary German art.

the jamjar

Nr Dubai Garden Centre Al Qouz Ind. 3 **04 341 7303**
thejamjardubai.com
Map **1 S6** Metro **First Gulf Bank**
A studio and workshop space for creatives, the jamjar also hosts several exhibitions each year in its gallery, as well as hosting other arts events such as film screenings. Team-building days can be organised, and it's also a great place to introduce kids to the joys of art, with painting sessions and parties available.

The Majlis Gallery

Al Fahidi Neighbourhood Al Souk Al Kabeer
04 353 6233
themajlisgallery.com
Map **2 M4** Metro **Al Fahidi**
A converted traditional house with windtowers, the building also has small whitewashed rooms leading off the central courtyard where exhibitions by contemporary artists are held. You can also see hand-made glass, pottery, fabrics and unusual furniture.

Meem Gallery

Umm Suqeim St Al Qouz Ind. 3 **04 347 7883**
meemartgallery.com
Map **1 S7** Metro **First Gulf Bank**
Features work from modern and contemporary Middle Eastern artists. It's also home to The Noor Library of Islamic Art, which houses a comprehensive collection of books, journals and catalogues on regional and Islamic art. Open Saturday to Thursday.

Miraj Islamic Art Centre

12A St Umm Suqeim 1 **04 394 1084**
mirajislamicartcentre.com
Map **2 B4** Metro **Noor Bank**
A fantastic collection of Islamic art objects from silver, metalware and marble, to intricate astrolabes (ancient astronomical 'computers'), painstakingly crafted carpets and textiles, and displays of calligraphy and engraving.

New Masters Art Gallery

Majestic Al Mankhool **04 359 8888**
Map **2 L5** Metro **Al Fahidi**
An offering of collectible European, Asian and American art within a reasonable price range. The gallery also provides art advice and education.

The Pavilion Downtown Dubai

Emaar Boulevard Burj Khalifa **04 447 7025**
pavilion.ae
Map **2 F6** Metro **Burj Khalifa/Dubai Mall**
A non-profit contemporary art space that not only showcases new regional artists but provides a space for artists and aficionados to meet, with a restaurant, cinema, library, espresso cafe and lounge.

Pro Art

Palm Strip Mall Jumeira 1 **04 345 0900**
proartuae.com
Map **2 H4** Metro **World Trade Centre**
This fine art gallery in the well-to-do Jumeira area
is a lovely space where you can browse and buy
artworks from more than 50 international artists from
15 countries, including several masters and street
artists. It also has a framing service, and organises
lectures and conferences.

Read All About It

The Archive (thearchive.ae) is a library dedicated to
Middle Eastern and North African art literature. Located
near Gate 5 in Safa Park, it hosts various activities and
events including public art initiatives as well as live
music jams, magazine fairs and food markets. There is
also a modern cafe and espresso bar.

Tashkeel

Nr Nad Al Sheba Health Center Nadd Al Shiba 1
04 336 3313
tashkeel.org
Map **2 F11**
A creative hub for artistic activity, members have
access to fantastic studio facilities and resources,
including a dark room. Public creative workshops are
also hosted by practising artists, and there are regular
exhibitions. There's a great skatepark onsite that's free
to use all day, every day, and the peaceful location
complements the relaxed, creative atmosphere.

The Third Line

The Third Line

Warehouse 8 St 6 Al Qouz 3 **04 341 1367**
thethirdline.com
Map **1 U6** Metro **Noor Bank**
One of the leading lights of the Dubai art scene,
this gallery in Al Qouz hosts exhibitions by artists
originating from or working in the Middle East. There
are indoor and outdoor spaces for shows. Open
Saturday to Thursday 10am to 7pm.

Total Arts

The Courtyard Al Qouz Ind. 1 **04 347 5050**
Map **1 U6** Metro **Noor Bank**
Occupying two floors of The Courtyard in Al Qouz. This
large gallery exhibits works from a variety of cultures
and continents, although there is a leaning towards
regional talent (particularly Iranian). There are over
300 paintings on permanent display, and regular
shows of traditional handicrafts and antique furniture.
One of the main attractions is the beautiful cobbled
courtyard itself, surrounded by different facades
showcasing building styles from around the world.

Art Dubai

This annual get-together of industry people from across
the Middle East and Asian art world is held in March at
Madinat Jumeirah. Several exhibitions and events also
run alongside the forum, drawing thousands of visitors.

XVA Gallery

Al Fahidi Neighbourhood Al Souk Al Kabeer
04 353 5383
xvagallery.com
Map **2 M4** Metro **Al Fahidi**
Located in the centre of Al Fahidi Historical
Neighbourhood (formerly Bastakiya), this is one
of Dubai's most interesting galleries. A restored
windtower house, it is worth a visit for its architecture
and displays of local and international art. The gallery
hosts many exhibitions throughout the year, as well as
free film screenings. It is also home to Dubai's hippest
hotel and a great cafe. Another branch is open at DIFC.

Heritage Sites

Old Dubai features many fascinating places to visit,
offering glimpses into a time when the city was
nothing more than a small fishing and trading port.
Many of the pre-oil heritage sites have been carefully
restored, paying close attention to traditional design
and using original building materials. You'll marvel at
how people coped in Dubai before air conditioning.
Most of these attractions are closed on Friday
mornings, and they charge a nominal entrance fee.

Al Ahmadiya School & Heritage House

Nr Dubai Public Libraries Al Ras **04 226 0286**
dubaiculture.ae
Map **2 M4** Metro **Al Ras**

This was the earliest regular school in the city, established in 1912 for Dubai's elite. Situated in what is becoming a small centre for heritage in Deira (Al Souk Al Kabeer), it sits just behind the Heritage House, an interesting example of a traditional Emirati family house and the former home of the school's founder, Mr Ahmadiya, dating back to 1890. Both buildings have been renovated and are great places for a glimpse of how life used to be. Admission to both is free. Open Saturday to Thursday 8.30am to 8.30pm and 2pm to 8.30pm on Friday.

Al Fahidi Historical Neighbourhood

Nr Ruler's Court, Al Souk Al Kabeer **04 353 9090**
dubaiculture.ae
Map **2 M4** Metro **Al Fahidi**

Escape the skyscraper valleys of the city centre and travel back in time with a trip to Al Fahidi, previously known as Bastakiya. This atmospheric area in Bur Dubai is one of the oldest heritage sites in the city, with a neighbourhood that dates back to the early 1900s. A wander around offers a beguiling glimpse into the Dubai of a bygone era, with its traditional windtowers, bustling courtyards and maze of winding and beautiful alleyways.

There are some great cultural attractions to visit in the area, including the Dubai Museum. Located in Al Fahidi Fort, this family friendly attraction showcases all aspects of traditional Emirati life, from souks and oases to archaeological finds and local wildlife. After a wander around the museum, head for the art galleries. The Majlis Gallery and XVA Gallery are in restored traditional houses and both host a variety of contemporary art. There are also several shops selling good quality handicrafts and souvenirs.

Heritage & Diving Villages

Nr Shindagha Tunnel, Al Khaleej St Al Shindagha **04 393 7139**
dubaiculture.ae
Map **2 M4** Metro **Al Ghubaiba**

For a fascinating glimpse into Dubai's history, the Heritage & Diving Villages are an excellent spot to spend the day. Located near the mouth of Dubai Creek, this cultural attraction focuses on Dubai's maritime past, pearl diving trade, arts, customs and architecture. Here you can observe potters and weavers practising their craft the way it has been done for centuries, get close to local wildlife or sample genuine Emirati cuisine served by local women in traditional dress.

The best and liveliest time to visit is during the Dubai Shopping Festival or Eid celebrations, when it comes alive with a variety of performances including traditional sword dancing. Open daily 8am to 10pm (Fridays 3.30pm to 10pm).

Jumeirah Mosque

Nr Palm Strip, Jumeira St Jumeira 1 **04 353 6666**
cultures.ae
Map **2 H4** Metro **World Trade Centre**

The much-photographed Jumeirah Mosque is one of Dubai's most famous landmarks and features on the Dhs.500 note. The Sheikh Mohammed Centre for Cultural Understanding organises tours for non-Muslims everyday at 10am, except for Fridays, during which you'll be guided around the impressive building and given a talk on Islam and prayer rituals.

Pre-booking is recommended and there is a registration fee of Dhs.10. It is essential that you dress conservatively and remove your shoes before entering. Do not wear shorts or sleeveless tops, and women must cover their heads with a scarf or shawl.

Majlis Ghorfat Um Al Sheif

Al Mehemal St Jumeira 3 **04 852 1374**
dubaiculture.ae
Map **2 C4** Metro **Business Bay**

Constructed in 1955 from coral stone and gypsum, this simple building was used by the late Sheikh Rashid bin Saeed Al Maktoum as a summer residence. The ground floor is an open veranda (known as a *leewan* or *rewaaq*), while upstairs the Majlis is decorated with carpets, cushions, lanterns and rifles. The roof terrace was used for drying dates and even sleeping on and the site has a garden with a pond and traditional *falaj* irrigation system.

The Majlis is located just inland from Jumeira Road on Street 17, beside Reem Al Bawardi Restaurant – look for the brown municipality signs. Entry is Dhs.1 for adults and free for children under six years old.

Sheikh Mohammed Centre For Cultural Understanding > *p.xxviii*

Al Fahidi Neighbourhood Al Souk Al Kabeer **04 353 6666**
cultures.ae
Map **2 M4** Metro **Al Fahidi**

Located close to Dubai Museum, the SMCCU was established to help visitors and residents understand the Emirati culture, as well as the customs and religion of the UAE, by involving expats in various activities. These include cultural meals, fascinating and informative tours of Dubai's historic district, and a Jumeirah Mosque visit programme. The building that houses the centre is also worth a look for the *majlis*-style rooms located around the courtyard and great views through the palm trees and windtowers. Open Sunday to Thursday 9am to 5pm and Saturday 9am to 1pm.

Don't Leave Dubai Without…

There are some attractions that you simply must see during your time in Dubai to get the whole experience.

Burj Khalifa
You'll spend a lot of time gazing at the tallest tower in the world, if only to get your bearings from practically any point in the city. But you can't leave Dubai without visiting the observation decks on either the 124th floor (At The Top) or 148th floor (Burj Khalifa SKY).

Desert safari
Dubai's biggest playground is waiting to be explored, whether you go bashing through the dunes in a 4WD or rampaging through the sands on a dune buggy. End the day with shisha and Arabic entertainment as the sun sets and the rolling dunes take on a lustrous orange hue.

Ski Dubai > p.175, 293
To try an experience that is beyond comprehension, skiing in the desert tops the lot. Leave the bikini at home, don some thermal gear, and take to the snowy slopes of Ski Dubai, where the temperature hovers around a chilly -3 degrees.

Dubai Museum/Al Fahidi/Creek
Get to the heart of Dubai with a wander around the creek area. This ancient trading hub oozes character, from the old traditional windtowers of Al Fahidi Historical Neighbourhood to the abras that continue to transport people across the water.

Downtown Dubai
After a day spent navigating Dubai Mall, marvelling at the enormous window of Dubai Aquarium and having fun at SEGA Republic, watching the Dubai Fountain is a must. Join the crowds lining Burj Lake, waiting for the nightly spectacular to begin, or settle on the candlelit terrace at Souk Al Bahar's Mango Tree or Rivington Grill for a romantic evening.

Skydive Dubai
For the ultimate in adrenaline experiences, it doesn't get more exciting – or maybe just plain scary – than a UAE skydive and nothing says you've 'done Dubai' like plummeting towards it from 12,000 feet. Take in the stupendous views of the desert, the city and the sea, while the perfectly formed Palm Jumeirah is laid out beneath you.

High tea at the Burj Al Arab
This Dubai icon is as extravagant inside as its spectacular architecture suggests. Head to Sahn Eddar for a champagne afternoon tea, followed by a cocktail at the Skyview Bar to enjoy the stunning vistas. It's the pinnacle of the Dubai high life.

Aquaventure
This sprawling water park at the famous Atlantis, The Palm is worth visiting for its multitude of adrenaline-fuelled rides. Take the monorail for a great view of the Palm Jumeirah's exclusive fronds and then head to the top of the Tower of Neptune for panoramic views of the Dubai skyline – before whizzing down the Leap of Faith through tunnels surrounded by shark-infested waters.

Souks
You may have shopped till you drop in one of the city's gigantic malls, but you haven't had the true Middle East experience until you've haggled in one of the souks – head to the Gold and Spice souks in Deira, or the Textile Souk across the creek.

Dhow cruise
Step aboard an atmospheric wooden dhow and cruise the calm waters of the creek amid the twinkling evening lights. Dhow dinner tours also take place along Dubai Creek and from Marsa Dubai at the other end of town. Traditionally trading crafts that ship cargo between the Gulf and Iran, these dhows have been converted to become floating restaurants; the two to three hour tours typically see diners sit on the top deck, beneath the stars, while an Arabian buffet is served up.

Friday polo
The Dubai Polo & Equestrian Club stages Friday and Saturday chukka events during the polo season (the cooler winter months) and rather spiffing events they are too. Don't worry if you don't know the first thing about polo – you'll be in good company, plus polo events are all about the social aspect anyway. For Dhs.50, you can drive pitchside and set up your picnic chairs and blanket, bringing along a cool box full of the finest fare you could find.

Burj Khalifa and Downtown

Sheikh Saeed Al Maktoum House

Nr Heritage & Diving Villages Al Shindagha
04 393 7139
dubaiculture.ae
Map **2 M4** Metro **Al Ghubaiba**
This 19th century restored house-turned-museum
was constructed in a way typical of the time and
era, using coral covered in lime and sand-coloured
plaster. Located in Shindagha, one of the oldest
neighbourhoods in Dubai, the house was once home
to the visionary leader Sheikh Saeed Al Maktoum
and centuries ago it provided the ruling family with
unparalleled views of the shipbuilding district and
Arabian Gulf.

Today, it is home to an impressive collection of
Emirati artefacts including historic documents and
maps, and wonderful rare photographs that capture
the Dubai of a bygone era. Entry is Dhs.2 for adults.

Ramadan Timings

During Ramadan, timings for many companies change
significantly. Museums and heritage sites usually open
slightly later in the morning than usual, and close earlier
in the afternoon.

Museums

Dubai Moving Image Museum

MCN Hive Bldg TECOM, Al Thanyah 1 **04 421 6679**
dubaimovingimagemuseum.com
Map **1 P6** Metro **Dubai Internet City**
This rich museum in TECOM charts the history of the
moving image prior to the advent of cinema. There's
an incredible array of lovingly preserved antiques,
some from as early as 1730, and the museum explores
how light and shadow have been played around
with to create moving images for millennia. There are
some cool reproductions to play with, optical illusions
and videos to watch. Entry costs Dhs.50 (Dhs.25 for
students and children under 18) and it's worth paying
the extra Dhs.10 for the guided tour.

Dubai Museum

Al Fahidi St Al Souk Al Kabeer **04 353 1862**
definitelydubai.com
Map **2 M4** Metro **Al Fahidi**
Housed in Al Fahidi Fort, a traditional Arabic fort
that dates back to 1787, this family friendly museum
was once the home of the ruler of Dubai and also
functioned as a sea defence. Today, the impressive
building presents all manner of interesting artefacts
and relics from Dubai's past. Galleries and dioramas
have been used to depict life from a bygone era; you'll
find souks from the 1950s, stroll through an oasis, step

into a traditional house and even get up close to local
wildlife. Tickets cost just Dhs.3 for adults and Dhs.1 for
children under six.

Falcon & Heritage Sports Centre

Nr Nad Al Sheba Market Nadd Al Shiba 1
800 900
Map **2 D9**
A hub for breeders and owners, this heritage landmark
of Dubai offers a truly Arabian falconry experience.
The centre has a souk for falcon traders and falcon
breeders, as well as a small mosque, (a replica of the
old Masjid Bin Suroor in Shindagha), a cafe and gift
shop. Be dazzled by falconry displays in the outdoor
courtyard and learn all about these fascinating birds at
the museum, which showcases the history of falcons
in three halls and a 3D light and sound show. The souk
is open from 9am to 10pm every day, except Friday,
with some shops closing between 12pm and 2pm.

Naif Museum

Naif Fort Naif **04 227 6484**
dubaiculture.ae
Map **2 N4** Metro **Baniyas Square**
Situated in the heart of Deira, Naif Fort gives a
fascinating insight into the history and development
of Dubai's police force, as well as the city's justice
system. Built in 1939, almost entirely of clay, the fort
is home to life-size models, interactive exhibits and
museum displays. The fort, which has been extensively
restored, was the former police headquarters and has
also served as a prison. Open Saturday to Thursday
8am to 7.30pm, and Friday 2.30pm to 7.30pm.

Dubai Museum

15 rides, hundreds of games & tons of fun for everyone!

Are you ready to be thrilled?

Enjoy a fun-filled day out with the whole family at the largest indoor theme park in Dubai.

- 15 fun-filled rides
- Hundreds of exciting games
- Soft play area for little ones
- From virtual reality to adventure rides
- Giant Slider – the tallest indoor-slide in the UAE

There is something for the whole family.
Come visit us at Level 2, The Dubai Mall.

Follow "SEGA Republic Dubai" on 🅕 🅣 🅑 📺
www.segarepublic.com

INDOOR THEME PARK

ATTRACTIONS

There's no shortage of fun to be had in Dubai, whatever your age and interests. The whole family will find more than enough thrills and spills at the water parks such as Wild Wadi, and theme parks like SEGA Republic.

Several family attractions get you pretty close to some wildlife too, from swimming with dolphins at Dubai Dolphinarium to feeding rays at The Lost Chambers aquarium.

Amusement Centres

There are plenty of children's play zones around the city, from parks to soft play areas, and you can find more information on these in Family and Parenting, as well as outdoor activities and summer camps. The following amusement centres offer fun for the whole family.

Aquaplay
Mirdif City Centre Mirdif **04 231 6307**
theplaymania.com
Map **2 P12** Metro **Rashidiya**
An indoor play centre that's dedicated to water fun; kids will love it here. Perfect for two to eight year olds, Aquaplay features a variety of interactive and educational games and water rides. There are arcade-style amusement games with an aqua twist, as well as an experimentation 'lab' with water guns, a swinging pirate ship, a seahorse carousel, and a more boisterous bumper boat ride that's fun for mums and dads too. Rides cost between Dhs.10 and Dhs.35.

Children's City
Gate 1, Creek Park Umm Hurair 2 **04 334 0808**
childrencity.ae
Map **2 L7** Metro **Dubai Healthcare City**
This themed activity centre in Creek Park is the first of its kind and offers kids their own learning zone and amusement facilities. It's designed to complement what they've been learning at school, with interactive, hands-on displays to keep things interesting. A planetarium focuses on the solar system and space exploration, a nature centre provides information on the world around them, and the Discovery Space explores the miracles and mysteries of the human body. There's something to suit everyone; while the exhibition space is aimed at visitors aged five to 15, toddlers and older teens are also well catered for.

Extreme Fun
Nr Spinneys MotorCity, Al Hebiah 1 **04 452 5543**
extremefunuae.com
Map **1 N12**
Big, bright and noisy, Extreme Fun is every child's dream. There are play areas, a birthday party room and kiddie rides, as well as arcade games and a Kidz Kutz salon. There's also plenty for youngsters to do with soft play and toddler areas, while parents can enjoy a relaxing coffee or snack in the cosy cafe.

Fun City
Mercato Shopping Mall Jumeira 1 **04 349 9976**
funcity.ae
Map **2 F4** Metro **Al Jafiliya**
A combination of rides, games, sports and an indoor playground, Fun City caters to all younger family members and is especially popular for kids' parties, with a range of packages available from Dhs.55 per child. The daily (Sunday to Thursday) Mother's Club coffee mornings are also popular. There are branches at malls across the city, including Ibn Battuta Mall, Arabian Center, Reef Mall, Lamcy Plaza and BurJuman.

KidZania > p.273
Dubai Mall Downtown Dubai, Burj Khalifa **04 448 5222**
kidzania.ae
Map **2 F7** Metro **Burj Khalifa/Dubai Mall**
A truly unique attraction that will keep the kids entertained for hours, this fantastic edutainment zone gives kids the chance to become adults for the day. Billed as a 'real-life city' for children, youngsters can dress up and act out more than 80 different roles, including everything from a policeman or fireman in an emergency response team – compete with a fire truck and fake fire – to being a pilot, doctor or a designer.

Little Explorers
Mirdif City Centre Mirdif **800 386**
theplaymania.com
Map **2 P12** Metro **Rashidiya**
Little Explorers offers an exciting mix of education and entertainment for children from two to seven, this bright and spacious attraction is divided into five zones, and each one is packed with fun learning experiences, such as the building site with foam bricks, chutes and miniature wheelbarrows. There are more than 80 different activities in all, and you can leave the kids under supervised care.

Magic Planet
Deira City Centre Port Saeed **04 295 4333**
magicplanet.ae
Map **2 M7** Metro **Deira City Centre**
There are branches of this entertainment hub in various malls throughout the UAE, including Mirdif City Centre, Deira City Centre and Mall of the Emirates.

What would you like to be today? Over 80 professions to choose from!

Get Ready for a Better World!

In KidZania, children can understand the world of grown-ups better through activities based on role-playing. A child can become a chef, surgeon, radio host, firefighter and a whole lot more, all in the course of a day.

Bring your children to KidZania. Let them be adults for a day!

KidZania
Dubai

LEVEL 2 | THE DUBAI MALL

It's a blaring, boisterous play area that's hugely popular with kids accompanying their mums and dads on long shopping trips.

There are various rides, bowling lanes and the latest video games. Entry is free, and you can use the facilities on a 'pay as you play' basis, or buy a Dhs.85 special pass for unlimited fun and entertainment.

Playnation
Mirdif City Centre Mirdif **800 5347873**
theplaymania.com
Map **2 P12** Metro **Rashidiya**
A dedicated leisure and entertainment destination at Mirdif City Centre, Playnation offers a range of exciting activities (and not just for younger family members). There are five 'experiences': indoor skydiving at iFLY Dubai (see Sports & Leisure), Soccer Circus Dubai, Little Explorers edutainment centre, Yalla! Bowling and Magic Planet, which includes the nerve-wracking Sky Trail attraction. Parents can even drop their children off at Playnation while they enjoy a movie at VOX Cinemas – see the website for more information.

Theme Parks
SEGA Republic
Dubai Mall Downtown Dubai, Burj Khalifa
04 448 8484
segarepublic.com
Map **2 F7** Metro **Burj Khalifa/Dubai Mall**
Don't be fooled by the somewhat dated, amusement arcade feel to this indoor theme park located in The Dubai Mall – SEGA Republic is really, really fun and, unlike many other shopping mall amusement centres, is for all ages.

Big kids as well as little ones will find enough thrills to satisfy, with some familiar characters for company. There are some genuinely unique rides at SEGA Republic, including the dizzying Halfpipe Canyon, which sees you working your 'snowboard' to spin higher and faster in order to beat your opponent. SpinGear goes beyond the usual arcade racing game, flipping you 360 degrees as you race your opponents on a virtual bobsled run. There's also a soft play area and more than 170 amusement games that allow you to win tickets to exchange for prizes.

Water Parks
Aquaventure
Atlantis Nakhlat Jumeira **04 426 0000**
atlantisthepalm.com
Map **1 N1** Metro **Nakheel**
The ultimate destination for thrill-seekers. To get the adrenaline pumping, there's the Leap Of Faith, a near-

vertical drop that shoots you through a series of tunnels surrounded by shark-infested waters, or try the largest waterslide in the world. There's rapids and a lazy river for those who want something calmer.

Out of the water, there's the longest zip line in the Middle East, or you can make use of a sun lounger on the park's private beach. Splashers is a giant water playground with slides specifically for little ones.

Splash Land
WonderLand Umm Hurair 2 **04 324 3222**
wonderlanduae.com
Map **2 L8** Metro **Dubai Healthcare City**
It may feel at times like a bit of a ghost town, but the water park within WonderLand offers fun for kids and adults with nine rides, including slides and twisters, a lazy river, an adults' pool and a children's activity pool with slides, bridges and water cannons. Alternatively, you can just relax by the pool and sunbathe. Lockers and changing rooms are available.

Water, Water Everywhere
Taken the Leap Of Faith so often you're on first-name terms with the sharks? It's time for a new water challenge. Umm Al Quwain is home to Dreamland Aqua Park, with over 30 rides and attractions, plus camping facilities. Also, Ice Land Water Park in Ras Al Khaimah is just 80km from Dubai and features more than 30 slides, plus water football and a rain dance pool. Or, you can pop to Yas Waterworld Abu Dhabi and brave the Liwa Loop – a full 360 degree looping waterslide.

Aquaventure

TAKE A DAY TRIP TO ANOTHER WORLD

Encounter. Experience. Explore.

Make a new friend at **Dolphin Bay** and **Sea Lion Point.** Experience a close encounter that you'll treasure for a lifetime.

Release the thrill-seeker in you with **NEW** record breaking rides at **Aquaventure Waterpark,** the No.1 waterpark in the Middle East.

Rediscover the explorer in you at **The Lost Chambers Aquarium,** home to a mythical lost city and 65,000 amazing marine animals.

Book today on atlantisthepalm.com for best Available Rates

ATLANTIS
THE PALM, DUBAI

Wild Wadi > *p.277*
Nr Burj Al Arab Umm Suqeim 3 **04 348 4444**
wildwadi.com
Map **1 S4** Metro **First Gulf Bank**
There's fun for all ages at this perennially popular
water park beside Jumeirah Beach Hotel. The highlight
is the Jumeirah Sceirah, the tallest and fastest freefall
slide outside of the United States. A trapdoor floor
opens to shoot you down a 120m long slide at speeds
of up to 80kph. For something more sedate, float
round the lazy river or simply bob about in the wave
pool. There's also a great water play area for younger
kids, and life jackets are available.

Wildlife & Sealife

While Dubai Zoo may not be the best facility in the
world, there are several places beyond the city limits
that are worth a visit for animal lovers. Al Ain Zoo
contains excellent facilities for an impressive range of
animals from around the globe, including rare breeds
like the white lion, or there's Emirates Park Zoo in Abu
Dhabi, which lets you get pretty close to a lot of the
animals. Sharjah has its own aquarium; plus Arabia's
Wildlife Centre and Children's Farm; and Al Tamimi
Stables, with pony rides, nature trails, a petting farm,
equestrian and falconry shows. See Out of the City for
more information on these.

Closer to Dubai is Ras Al Khor Wildlife Sanctuary, a
stopping off point for thousands of migrating birds
each year, including about 1,500 flamingos. There are
a number of hides from where to view the action: one

Dubai Aquarium

beside Ras Al Khor Road, and two off Oud Metha Road
(wildlife.ae, 04 606 6822/26).

Al Hurr Falconry Services
Falcon & Heritage Sports Centre Nadd Al Shiba 1
04 323 4829
alhurrfalconry.com
Map **2 D9**
Located in Nadd Al Shiba, Al Hurr is where you can
discover all you've ever wanted to know about falcons
and falconry – one of the traditional symbols of
Arabia. The trained handlers educate visitors about the
majestic falcons and it's well worth visiting to see the
amazing shows these graceful creations put on.

Desert Ranch
Al Sahra Heritage Vision, Al Yufrah 2 **04 427 4055**
alsahra.com
This eco-tourism concept is part of Jebel Ali
International Hotels. The 2.4 sq km Desert Ranch runs
a wide variety of fun, desert-themed nature activities
ranging from campfire Fridays, family picnics and
educational field trips, to horse riding, children's clubs,
ranch tours, Bedouin farm tours and camel cuddling.

Dolphin Bay
Atlantis Nakhlat Jumeira **04 426 1030**
atlantisthepalm.com
Map **1 N1** Metro **Nakheel**
Playing with a bottlenose dolphin at Dolphin Bay is an
unforgettable experience. Touching, hugging, holding
'hands', playing ball and feeding are all encouraged,
under the supervision of the marine specialists. A 90
minute session will set you back Dhs.790 per person
(with discounts for hotel guests) and is open to all
ages. Your family and friends can watch and take
photos from the beach for Dhs.300, but this also
grants them access to Aquaventure and the private
beach. There's a deep water experience too, where
visitors can swim and snorkel alongside the mammals
with the aid of an underwater scooter.

Dubai Aquarium & Underwater Zoo
Dubai Mall Downtown Dubai, Burj Khalifa
04 448 5200
thedubaiaquarium.com
Map **2 F6** Meto **Burj Khalifa/Dubai Mall**
Located, somewhat bizarrely, in the middle of The
Dubai Mall, this aquarium displays over 33,000 tropical
fish to passing shoppers free of charge. For a closer
view of the main tank's inhabitants, which include
fearsome looking sand tiger sharks, you can pay to
walk through the 270° viewing tunnel and see them
swimming overhead. Also well worth a look is the
Underwater Zoo, which is home to residents such as
penguins, turtles and alligators. You can also scuba
dive in the tank (call ahead to book), and even take a

HUGE FUN ON YOUR DOORSTEP

Easy to get to, easy to get around, easy to enjoy. Wild Wadi is all family fun and excitement. Watch the kids shriek and scream their way through the best day of their lives. Book your tickets at: **wildwadi.com** or call 04 348 4444

Wild Wadi
WATERPARK
Life. Refreshed.

15 YEARS AND STILL DUBAI'S FAVORITE

2014 TRAVELERS' CHOICE
tripadvisor

PADI diving course. For those who don't fancy being eyed up as a shark's potential dinner, you can cage snorkel or take a ride in a glass-bottomed boat.

Dubai Dolphinarium > p.279
Gate 1, Creek Park Umm Hurair 2 **04 336 9773**
dubaidolphinarium.ae
Map **2 L7** Metro **Dubai Healthcare City**
Swimming with Flipper will get any child excited and Dubai Dolphinarium is absolutely guaranteed to delight the kids. The main attraction is the seal and dolphin show, when you meet the resident Black Sea bottlenose dolphins and northern fur seals. It takes place three times daily. Afterwards, you can have your picture taken with them, or even jump in for playtime, and grab a fin to be whizzed across the pool.

The Dolphinarium has some additional fun attractions, including a Mirror Maze, 5D and 7D cinemas (where you might even feel the rain and wind blowing over you), a soft play area and an onsite restaurant and gift shop too. The Dolphinarium also runs an exotic bird show in Creek Park, where you can watch a cockatoo paint. They also host birthday parties.

Dubai Zoo
Jumeira St Jumeira 1 **04 349 6444**
dm.gov.ae
Map **2 G4** Metro **Financial Centre**
This is an old-fashioned zoo, with lions, tigers, giraffes, monkeys, deer, snakes, bears, flamingos, giant tortoises and other animals housed in small cages. The curator and his staff do their best to look after the animals with woefully inadequate space and resources, but it's not a place that animal lovers will enjoy. The ageing zoo will be replaced by a safari-style park in Al Warqa in 2015. Entry costs Dhs.2 per person, under twos go free. Closed on Tuesdays. Female visitors must cover shoulders and knees.

The Lost Chambers Aquarium
Atlantis Nakhlat Jumeira **04 426 1040**
atlantisthepalm.com
Map **1 N1** Metro **Nakheel**
The ruins of the mysterious lost city provide the theme for this enormous aquarium at Atlantis, The Palm. Guests can see quite a lot from the hotel windows, but it's worth splashing out for the views inside. A maze of underwater halls and tunnels provide ample opportunity to get up close to the aquarium's 65,000 inhabitants, ranging from sharks and eels to rays and piranhas, as well as multitudes of exotic fish. For an insight into the aquarium's residents, join one of the hourly guided tours, and there's also a twice-daily show at the Seven Sage Chamber. Other activities are available at extra cost, including a behind-the-scenes tour with the animal experts.

PARKS & BEACHES

Blessed with warm weather, calm ocean waters and long stretches of sand, Dubai offers its residents the choice of several beautiful beaches. There are three types of beach to choose from: public beaches (limited facilities but no entry fee), beach parks (good facilities and a nominal entrance fee), and private beaches (normally part of a hotel or resort).

Free wifi is being made available at 17 beaches, parks and municipal centres, and there's also a new app called Dubai Parks and Beaches that allows you to search for certain activities available at parks and beaches, as well as see weather updates.

Beaches

Several beaches in Dubai have been awarded the Blue Flag award for cleanliness and safety: JA Jebel Ali Golf Resort, Jumeirah Open Beach, Al Mamzar Beach Park, Le Meridien Mina Seyahi, Jumeirah Beach Hotel, Le Royal Meridien and the Sheraton Jumeirah Beach Resort; Sofitel Dubai The Palm Resort & Spa; and Atlantis The Palm Dubai Hotel & Resort.

Regulations for public beaches are quite strict. Dogs are banned and so is driving on the sand. Officially, other off-limit activities include barbecues, camping without a permit and holding large parties. Contact the Public Parks & Recreation Section (04 221 5555) for clarification. It is fine to wear swimming costumes and bikinis on the beach, as long as you keep both parts on.

Swim Safely
Although the waters off the coast generally look calm and unchallenging, very strong rip tides can carry the most confident swimmer away from the shore very quickly and drownings have occurred in the past. Take extra care when swimming off the public beaches where there are no lifeguards.

Black Palace Beach
Al Sufouh St Al Sufouh 1
Map **1 P4** Metro **Dubai Internet City**
This section of public beach, known unofficially as Black Palace Beach or 'secret beach', is on Al Sufouh Road, in a gap amid the grand palaces between Madinat and the Palm. There are no facilities whatsoever, but the beach gets nice waves and has a great view of the Palm and the Burj Al Arab.

JBR Beach
Nr The Walk at JBR Marsa Dubai
Map **1 K4** Metro **DAMAC**
The waters are fairly calm here and the shallow
areas are scattered with bathers, while the hotels
offer a variety of watersports such as parasailing,
wakeboarding and banana boating that anyone can
sign up for, as well as camel rides. It is by far one of
the most fun, family friendly beaches in Dubai, and
the skyscrapers of Marsa Dubai provide a spectacular
backdrop to your activities. With the opening of JBR
The Beach in 2014, the beach has only got better,
with wide walkways to stroll, shower and toilet
facilities, play areas for children, and a large choice of
restaurants, cafes, and boutiques to dine or browse in.
Behind it, original development The Walk at JBR offers
even more restaurants and coffee shop options.

Jumeirah Beach Park
Jumeira Rd Jumeira 2 **04 349 2555**
dm.gov.ae
Map **2 D4** Metro **Business Bay**
One of Dubai's most popular outdoor spaces for the
past 25 years, Jumeirah Beach Park is currently closed
to make way for the city's ambitious canal project.
When it reopens, which is estimated to be in 2016,
residents will once again be able to enjoy the winning
combination of grassy areas and vast expanses of
pristine, palm-lined beach with clear blue waters that
are perfectly safe for swimming.

Kite Beach
Nr Dubai Offshore Sailing Club Umm Suqeim 1
thekitebeach.com
Map **2 A4** Metro **Noor Bank**
Dubai's sportiest beach – also known as Woollongong
Beach – is by far its coolest, and a favourite with
local kitesurfers. The long sweeping stretch of
uninterrupted sand makes it the perfect playground,
or if you prefer to stay on dry land it's also a great
spot for flying a kite. Family events are held here
throughout the year. There are kayaks for hire, a small
kids' play area, volleyball and a Dutch waffle kiosk, as
well as showers and toilets. Be careful not to get in the
way of the kitesurfers, though!

Mamzar Beach Park
Al Khaleej Rd Al Mamzar **04 296 6201**
dm.gov.ae
Map **2 T4** Metro **Al Qiyadah**
With four clean beaches, green spaces, chalets for hire
and play areas, this is a park and a half, and can be
pleasantly empty during the week. The well-maintained
beaches have sheltered, safe areas for swimming and
there are also two swimming pools with changing
rooms with showers, plus parasols and lifeguards. There
are barbecue areas, a restaurant and several snack bars.

Umm Suqeim Beach
Nr Jumeirah Beach Hotel Umm Suqeim 3
Map **1 T4** Metro **First Gulf Bank**
This popular stretch of sand, also known as Sunset
Beach or Surfers' Beach, is one of the busiest public
beaches at weekends. Extending from Jumeirah Beach
Hotel to Dubai Offshore Sailing Club, its spot next
to the Burj Al Arab allows for some stunning photos.
There aren't any cafes or toilet facilities, but there are
plenty of options on Jumeirah Beach Road for picking
up a picnic. You will also find surfers out whenever
there's a swell, though the surf club is currently closed
until they can get new permissions to re-open. The
beach is also popular with stand up paddleboarders.

Blue Flag Status
Al Mamzar Beach Park and Jumeirah Open Beach, as
well as several Dubai hotel beaches – Jumeirah Beach
Hotel, Le Royal Meridien, the Sheraton Jumeirah Beach
Resort, Sofitel Dubai The Palm Resort & Spa, Atlantis
The Palm Hotel & Resort – have the internationally
recognised Blue Flag for cleanliness, safety and
environmental management.

Beach Clubs
Many beachfront hotels in Dubai offer annual
membership and day passes. From Dhs.13,000 (single)
for Dubai Marine Beach Resort to Dhs.22,000 for the
Ritz-Carlton Beach Club, you can use the hotels and
the facilities. Day passes start at around Dhs.100, but
average at around Dhs.300.

Barasti
Le Meridien Mina Seyahi Marsa Dubai **04 399 3333**
barastibeach.com
Map **1 M5** Metro **Nakheel**
The best value beach 'club' by far as it's free. This
small beach by the hugely popular bar is scattered
with sun loungers and square sunbeds large enough
for two. It gets really busy from 2pm onwards on
weekends when the beach starts to fill, the music
starts playing, and there's a lively atmosphere. People
come here to relax rather than swim, and under 21s
are not allowed entry.

Dubai Marine Beach Resort & Spa
Jumeira St Jumeira 1 **04 346 1111**
dxbmarine.com
Map **2 H4** Metro **World Trade Centre**
Pay for a day pass here (from Dhs.100 on weekdays)
and you get the run of three great swimming pools,
a private beach, a pool bar, and loads of restaurants
and bars. Highly recommended is Flooka for

some delicious, fresh Arabic cuisine. There's also a supervised play room where you can leave kids in air-conditioned comfort.

Meydan Beach
The Walk at JBR Marsa Dubai **04 433 3777**
meydanbeach.com
Map **1 K4** Metro **DAMAC**
Arriving at this beach club feels as if you've been superimposed onto an art deco painting. The please-dive-in infinity pool, complete with floating sun loungers and delightfully manicured green lawns, creates a picture postcard setting for the ultimate beach club experience. It's Monaco in the heart of JBR, and this celeb-style living will set you back Dhs.495 for a day pass, but this includes Dhs.250 credit on food and drink.

Nasimi Beach
Atlantis Nakhlat Jumeira **04 426 2626**
atlantisthepalm.com
Map **1 N1** Metro **Nakheel**
The beach of the 'it' crowd – complete with white four-poster beds to lounge on. A DJ spins chilled tracks all day, cocktails are sipped by elegant clientele in floaty dresses and the Mediterranean kitchen turns out fancy food for diners on the beach terrace. The calm waters of the Palm are easy to swim in, and mainland Dubai's city skyline makes a great backdrop for your photos. Access is free with an obligatory minimum spend of Dhs.150 during the week and Dhs.200 on Fridays and Saturdays.

Riva Beach Club
Shoreline Apartments Nakhlat Jumeira **04 430 9466**
riva-beach.com
Map **1 N3** Metro **Nakheel**
This standalone beach club on the Palm Jumeirah has a laid back feel, and manages to accommodate both families and the fashionable crowd. For Dhs.150 (Dhs.100 on weekdays) you can make use of the chilled swimming pool, sun lounger bar service and private beach. Go for a yummy Pina Colada served in a pineapple. Also in the building are a couple of spas, a gym, a restaurant and a great cafe called Sophie's.

Rixos The Palm Dubai
The Crescent East Nakhlat Jumeira **04 457 5555**
rixos.com
Map **1 P3** Metro **Nakheel**
With a great location at the end of Palm Jumeirah, this beach club is well worth the drive. Members get access to the gym, the longest private beach on the Palm, a lap pool, the spa, tennis courts, beach volleyball and beach football areas. You also get 20% discount on dining at Rixos' restaurants and bars. Annual membership starts from Dhs.20,000, or day passes are available from Dhs.175.

Parks

Dubai has a number of excellent parks, with lush green lawns and a variety of trees and shrubs creating the perfect escape from the concrete jungle of the

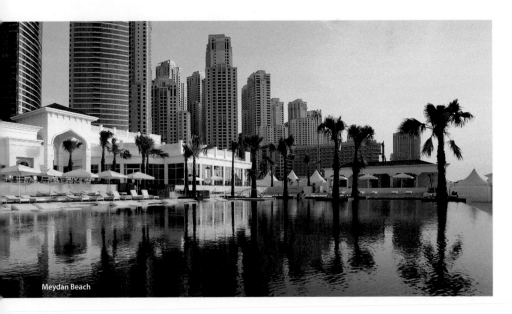

Meydan Beach

city. Children's play areas and even fitness equipment are often provided. In the winter months, the popular parks are very busy, especially at weekends. Most have a kiosk or cafe selling snacks and drinks, and some have barbecue pits (take your own wood or charcoal, and remember that it is forbidden to cook pork at public barbecue areas).

Regulations at the parks vary, with some banning bikes and rollerblades, or limiting ball games to specific areas. Pets are not permitted and you should not take plant cuttings. Some parks have a ladies' day when entry is restricted to women, girls and young boys, and certain smaller ones actually ban anyone other than ladies through the week, while allowing families only at the weekends. Entrance to the smaller parks is generally free, while the larger ones charge up to Dhs.5 per person. Opening hours of most parks change during Ramadan.

Al Barsha Pond Park
23rd Street Al Barsha 2
Map **1 Q7** Metro **Sharaf DG**
A welcome focal point for the Al Barsha community, this compact, but incredibly well-equipped park has tennis and basketball courts and football pitches (book at the onsite office) as well as a cushioned 1.5km running track and additional cycling path. Scattered around a large central lake are lots of green spaces to enjoy picnics on (as hundreds of families do at the weekend), kiosks and play areas to keep children amused.

Al Ittihad Park
Nr Shoreline Apartments Nakhlat Jumeira
nakheel.com
Map **1 N4** Metro **Nakheel**
This serene park on the Palm Jumeirah boasts more than 60 species of indigenous trees and plants. Located between the Golden Mile and Shoreline residential developments, and running under the track for the Palm Jumeirah Monorail, the park covers around 10 hectares and has a cushioned 3.2km jogging track. It's free, open 24 hours a day and features various play areas for children, and fitness equipment is scattered throughout.

Al Qouz Pond Park
Al Khail Rd Al Qouz 2 **050 852 8513**
Map **2 C7** Metro **Business Bay**
In an unlikely semi-industrial location in Al Qouz 2, at the intersection of Al Khail Road and Al Meydan Street, is this peaceful and little-known park. It's free to enter and there's a large fenced-off pond, which is encircled by a cushioned running track. You'll also find green lawns, flowers and a scattering of trees, as well as a toilet and drinking water fountain. A handy lunchtime escape if you're working in Al Qouz.

Creek Park
Nr Al Garhoud Bridge Umm Hurair 2 **04 336 7633**
dm.gov.ae
Map **2 L7** Metro **Dubai Healthcare City**
Situated in the heart of the city, but blessed with acres of gardens, fishing piers, jogging tracks, barbecue sites, children's play areas, mini golf, restaurants and kiosks. Get a bird's eye view of the park, the creek and Old Dubai in a scenic half-hour cable car ride, and check out some more traditional attractions: a mini falaj system of canals, a desert garden and camel and pony rides near Gate 1. Four-wheel cycles can be hired, and the park is also home to Dubai Dolphinarium and Children's City.

Jumeirah Lakes Towers Park
Al Thanyah 5
Map **1 K5** Metro **Jumeirah Lakes Towers**
Where 'Lake C' once commanded attention at the centre of the JLT development, a new JLT park now stands in its place and, in the process, has become the longest public park in the vicinity and is a popular place for dog-walkers.

Miracle Garden
Arjan Al Barsha South 3 **04 422 8902**
dubaimiraclegarden.com
Map **1 P11**
This explosion of colour has been developed with the vision of becoming the world's biggest flower garden – no mean feat in the arid climate of Dubai. The sheer volume of blooms is astonishing, and you can walk under beautifully designed flower-covered arches and blooms fashioned into the shapes of hearts and stars.

Mushrif Park
Al Khawaneej St Mushrif **04 288 3624**
dm.gov.ae
Spread over 526 hectares, this desert park near Mirdif is full of surprises, including play areas, a 5km walking, cycling and jogging track, two 25-metre swimming pools (Dhs.10 for adults and Dhs.5 for children), Mushrif Equestrian and Polo Club, and even a miniature village. The park is so vast you can drive through it, and there's a petting zoo and aviary.

Safa Park
Al Wasl St Al Wasl **04 349 2111**
dm.gov.ae
Map **2 D5** Metro **Business Bay**
This huge artistically landscaped park is a great place to escape the commotion of nearby Sheikh Zayed Road. Its sports fields, barbecue areas and play areas make it one of the best parks in the city. There's lots to entertain the kids, including a boating lake in the centre and a small maze. The Archive arts library and

cafe (thearchive.ae) makes for a welcome pit stop, especially for breakfast (try the eggs Benedict), and regular markets run throughout the winter months. Bikes are available for hire, and there's a great running track around the park's perimeter. However, sections of the park are currently closed for construction of the Dubai Canal project. Entrance is Dhs.3.

Umm Suqeim Park

Nr Jumeirah Beach Hotel Umm Suqeim 2
04 348 4554
dm.gov.ae
Map **1 T4** Metro **First Gulf Bank**
This ladies' park is closed to men except for at weekends. It is fairly large and has three big, well-equipped sandy playgrounds. There are also plenty of shady, grassy areas so that mums can sit and rest while the kids let off steam. Entrance is free.

Zabeel Park

Shk Rashid Rd Al Kifaf **04 398 6888**
dm.gov.ae
Map **2 K6** Metro **Al Jafiliya**
This green oasis straddles Sheikh Zayed Road in the shadow of Trade Centre roundabout. The northern half of the park is home to a well-shaded children's play area, with all kinds of obstacles and some funky slides. There's also a large amphitheatre and a football pitch. Cross the pedestrian bridge over the highway (or catch the mini train) and explore the southern half, which has a serene lake with motorised boats available for hire and a great view of the SZR skyline.

Al Barsha Pond Park

SPORTS & LEISURE

There is one dedicated sports hub in the emirate, Dubai Sports City, which will feature four stadia: a 60,000 seat multi-purpose outdoor stadium for rugby, soccer and track and field events, a swimming pool, a 25,000 seat capacity dedicated cricket stadium, a 10,000 seat multi-purpose indoor arena for hard court games, ice hockey, concerts and other events, and a rugby stadium. So far the Dubai International Cricket Stadium, the 18 hole championship golf course, The Els Club and Fit Republik (fitrepublik.com) are all open.

Elsewhere in the emirate there is the Etisalat Academy Sports & Leisure Club (eacademy.ae), The Aviation Club (aviationclub.ae) and the Dubai Ladies Club (dubailadiesclub.com). There's also a multitude of sports and leisure facilities within Dubai's malls, hotels and park areas. With everything from bowling and paintballing to skiing and skydiving, there's no time to get bored.

Archery

Dubai Archers

Nr Sharjah National Park Sharjah **050 454 3099**
dubaiarchers.com
Dubai Archers meet at Sharjah Wanderers Golf Club, just inside the E611 on the Sharjah-Al Dhaid Road, every Friday. Timings change according to the season, but are usually around 9am to noon and cost Dhs.70 for two hours including equipment and instruction for those who require it.

Sharjah Golf & Shooting Club

Shk Mohammed Bin Zayed Rd Sharjah **06 548 7777**
golfandshootingshj.com
The shooting club's indoor range offers target practice at Dhs.60 for 20 arrows for members and Dhs.70 for non-members. You can try your hand at pistol and rifle shooting, and there's also several superb arenas for paintballing.

Bowling

There are a number of places that you can go bowling. At independent centres, the lanes are cheap and you can have an alcoholic drink while you play. If you want to join a bowling league, contact Dubai International Bowling Centre and they will put you in touch with Dubai's leagues.

Al Nasr Leisureland
Nr American Hospital Oud Metha **04 337 1234**
alnasrll.com
Map **2 L6** Metro **Oud Metha**
This large leisure complex has eight lanes and the
bonus of a licensed bar. Booking is recommended,
and the first game costs Dhs.15, including shoe rental.
The complex also houses an outdoor swimming pool
with a wave machine, slides and a baby pool, plus
an Olympic-size ice skating rink, squash and tennis
courts, arcade games and restaurants.

Bowling City
Dubai Festival City Mall Al Kheeran **04 232 8600**
bowling-city.com
Map **2 L9** Metro **Emirates**
Located on the balcony level, this centre has 12 hi-
tech bowling lanes with various special effects to jazz
up the experience, including synchronised coloured
lighting and fog and mist effects. Bumpers and ramps
are available for beginners and little ones, and there
are billiard tables, PlayStation booths, a 24 station PC
gaming network and karaoke cabins.

Dubai Bowling Centre
Meydan St Al Qouz 1 **04 339 1010**
bowlingdubai.com
Map **2 D6** Metro **Business Bay**
With 24 professional-series lanes you can either bowl
for fun or compete in a league. The centre caters for
professional tournaments, corporate events and kids'
parties – there's also a gaming area. Prices are from
Dhs.15 per game or Dhs.130 per hour for a lane.

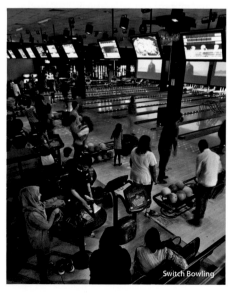

Switch Bowling

Dubai International Bowling Centre
Nr Century Mall Al Mamzar **04 296 9222**
Map **2 R6** Metro **Al Qiyadah**
Dubai's biggest bowling centre boasts 36 state-of-the-
art computerised lanes as well as amusement games,
snooker, billiards and food outlets. Several of Dubai's
clubs and leagues are based here and the centre hosts
regular competitions.

Funky Lanes Bowling Centre
Arabian Center Al Mizhar 1 **04 239 3636**
Map **2 R13** Metro **Rashidiya**
This 10 lane bowling centre also has a billiards lounge,
arcade games zone and a private party room. It runs
a daily Ladies' Happy Hour offering free bowling for
women between 10am and 2pm.

Magic Planet
Mall of the Emirates Al Barsha 1 **04 341 4444**
magicplanet.ae
Map **1 R6** Metro **Mall of the Emirates**
Magic Planet has bowling lanes in its games arcade.
Prices per player per game start at Dhs.20 on
weekdays and Dhs.25 on weekends.

Switch Bowling Dubai
Ibn Battuta Mall Jabal Ali 1 **04 440 5961**
switchbowlingdubai.com
Map **1 G5** Metro **Ibn Battuta**
Set within the Indian Court, Switch Bowling has
state-of-the-art lighting and sound effects, and 12
glow-in-the-dark lanes that are served by waiters who
bring food and refreshments. The decor is pretty funky
too, and there are professional billiard tables, network
gaming facilities, private karaoke and PlayStation
rooms, and a cafe and lounge area. From Dhs.25 per
game.

Yalla! Bowling Lanes & Lounge
Mirdif City Centre Mirdif **04 231 6316**
theplaymania.com
Map **2 P12** Metro **Rashidiya**
Yalla! is within Mirdif City Centre's Playnation. It
features 12 illuminated lanes of dayglo bowling, along
with video simulators, video games and pool tables.
Open daily 10am to midnight.

Golf

Design collaborations with stars such as Colin
Montgomerie, Ernie Els and Ian Baker-Finch have
helped cement Dubai as a world-class golf destination.
Several of the game's biggest events are hosted here,
including the annual Dubai Desert Classic at Emirates
Golf Club, and the DP World Tour Championship
at Jumeirah Golf Estates. For amateur enthusiasts

there are local monthly tournaments and annual competitions open to all such as the Emirates Mixed Amateur Open, the Emirates Ladies' Amateur Open (handicap of 21 or less), and the Emirates Men's Amateur Open (handicap of five or less).

To get your official handicap in the UAE, register with Emirates Golf Federation and submit three score cards. You will then be issued with a member card and handicap card enabling you to enter competitions.

If you don't want to join a golf club – and the fees are pretty steep – you can join an amateur golf society such as the Kegs or Dubai Divots, or start one yourself as large groups can often get concessionary rates.

The Address Montgomerie Dubai

Emirates Hills Al Thanyah 4
04 390 5600
theaddress.com
Map **1 L7** Metro **DAMAC**
Set on 265 acres of land, the 18-hole, par 72 course has some unique characteristics, including the mammoth 656 yard 18th hole. Facilities include putting greens and a swing analysis studio. The clubhouse is managed by The Address and boasts an Angsana spa and a number of places to dine, including Nineteen.

Al Badia Golf Club By InterContinental Dubai Festival City

Al Badia Blvd, Al Kheeran 1 **04 601 0101**
albadiagolfclub.ae
Map **2 M10** Metro **Emirates**
This Robert Trent Jones-designed course features a plush clubhouse, 11 lakes and eco-friendly salt-tolerant grass, meaning the 7,303 yard, par 72 championship course can be irrigated with sea water.

Arabian Ranches Golf Club

Arabian Ranches 1 Wadi Al Safa 6 **04 366 3000**
arabianranchesgolfdubai.com
Map **1 Q13**
Designed by Ian Baker-Finch and Nicklaus Design, this par 72 grass course incorporates natural desert terrain and indigenous plants. Facilities include an academy, an extensive short-game practice area, GPS-enabled golf carts and a pleasant clubhouse.

Dubai Creek Golf & Yacht Club

Nr Baniyas St Port Saeed **04 295 6000**
dubaigolf.com
Map **2 M7** Metro **Deira City Centre**
Offers one of the most scenic 18-hole championship courses in Dubai, and it's in the heart of the city. Peak winter rates are Dhs.795 for an 18-hole round, but nine-hole rounds and off-peak rates are also available. There's also a par 3 (Adults: Dhs.80; members and juniors: Dhs.60). For bookings, call 04 380 1234 or email golfbooking@dubaigolf.com.

The Els Club

Dubai Sports City Al Hebiah 4 **04 425 1000**
elsclubdubai.com
Map **1 L11**
This 7,538 yard, par 72 signature course in Sports City was designed by Ernie Els and includes a Butch Harmon School of Golf for players of all ages and skills. It also includes a Mediterranean-style clubhouse managed by Troon Golf.

Emirates Golf Club

Nr American University of Dubai, Al Sufouh 2
04 417 9999 dubaigolf.com
Map **1 M6** Metro **Nakheel**
Home of the European Tour Omega Dubai Desert Classic, this club has two of the city's best courses. Peak winter rates including green fees, cart hire and range balls are Dhs.995 for a round on the Majlis course and Dhs.695 on the Faldo course. Look out for off-peak or night golf reductions. For bookings, call 04 380 1234 or email golfbooking@dubaigolf.com.

Emirates Golf Federation

Creek Golf & Yacht Club Port Saeed **04 295 2277**
egfgolf.com
Map **2 M7** Metro **Deira City Centre**
Affiliated to R&A (golf's rulemaking body) and the International Golf Federation, this non-profit organisation is the governing body for amateur golf in the UAE. It supports junior players, develops the national team and issues official handicap cards. It also has a hole-in-one club for golfers to record their glorious moments. The affiliate membership rate is Dhs.200 for a quarter.

JA Jebel Ali Golf Resort

Nr Palm Jebel Ali Mena Jabal Ali **04 814 5555**
jaresortshotels.com
Metro **Jebel Ali**
Peacocks and Gulf views may be a little distracting at this nine-hole, par 36 course which hosts the Jebel Ali Golf Resort & Spa Challenge, and the Omega Dubai Desert Classic Challenge Match, the curtain raiser to the main event. For family members who take their golf a little less seriously, there's a mini golf course too.

Jumeirah Golf Estates

Nr Dubai Sports City Me'aisem 1 **04 375 9999**
jumeirahgolfestates.com
Map **1 H9**
The home of the DP World Tour Championship offers themed courses designed by Greg Norman. The Fire course features desert terrain and greens, with red sand bunkers; Earth is reminiscent of European parklands. The Wind and Water courses are under construction. Annual membership packages include access to both courses.

Spectator Sports

From local competitions to world-class headliners, Dubai's sports calendar draws crowds from across the globe.

The UAE's sunny winter climate, central location, excellent sporting facilities and ability to stump up monstrous sums as prize money mean the country is growing ever more attractive as a venue for international sporting events. From headliners like the Dubai Desert Classic to tennis tournaments and international cricket, and even local horse and camel racing meets, there's an awful lot going on.

Camel racing

This local sport is serious business, with racing camels changing hands for as much as Dhs.10 million each, while up to Dhs.25 million in prizes is won each year. Races take place during the winter months, usually early on Thursday and Friday mornings, and admission is free. Dubai's camel racetrack is on the Al Ain Road, just past the Sevens (take the Al Lisali exit).

Cricket

Dubai Sports City is home to the world-class, 25,000 seat Dubai International Cricket Stadium (dubaisportscity.ae), and well as the headquarters of the International Cricket Council, which runs a cricket academy at the stadium, creating a global hub for the sport. The stadium hosts its fair share of major international matches; the likes of India, Pakistan, England, Australia, South Africa and Sri Lanka have played here.

Football

Football is as popular in the UAE as it is the world over. There's a strong domestic competition – the Arabian Gulf League – and attending one of these games makes for a really colourful experience.

Golf

Each February, the Dubai Desert Classic is staged at Emirates Golf Club (dubaidesertclassic.com). Part of the European PGA Tour, previous winners include Tiger Woods and Rory McIlroy. The DP World Tour Championship, staged annually at the Jumeirah Golf Estates, is the culmination of the European Tour's Race To Dubai. Golf fans also have another major international tournament to look forward to: the Abu Dhabi HSBC Golf Championship, staged at Abu Dhabi Golf Club each January.

Horse racing

The richest horse race in the world, the glitzy Dubai World Cup, is held at the Meydan Racecourse in March, and there are also race nights throughout the season. Futuristic trackside The Meydan Hotel offers special racing packages; gambling is not allowed in the UAE, but there are raffles and cash prizes.

For horse excitement of a different kind, Dubai Polo & Equestrian Club stages Friday chukka events during the polo season. For Dhs.50 you can drive pitchside and set up your picnic chairs and blanket.

Motorsports

Dubai's own Autodrome hosts events such as the Dunlop 24H endurance series, for which admission is free, but the real action is down on Abu Dhabi's Yas Island, where the Formula 1 Grand Prix takes place at Yas Marina Circuit each November.

Rugby

The Sevens stadium on the Al Ain Road is host to the Emirates Airline Dubai Rugby Sevens (dubairugby7s. com) – three days of rugby and revelry. This 'light' version of the sport is fast paced and competitive, with young, up-and-coming international stars taking centre stage. As much about the atmosphere as the sport, it's a great day out for groups of friends.

Tennis

Dubai Duty Free Tennis Championships, which is held at The Aviation Club every February, is a great opportunity to catch some of the top players in the game at close quarters, and features both men's and ladies' tournaments. Tickets for the later stages sell out in advance so keep an eye out for sale details, although entrance to some of the earlier rounds can be bought on the day. See dubaidutyfreetennischampionships.com.

Watersports

An important part of Dubai's heritage, many sailing and dhow racing events take place off Dubai's shoreline, including the 10 day Maktoum Sailing Trophy, which takes place every February (dimc.ae).

The emirate's waters are also a venue for the Class 1 World Powerboat Championship (class-1.com).

UIM Class 1 World Powerboat Championship

The Track Meydan Golf
Meydan St Nadd Al Shiba 1 **04 381 3733**
meydangolf.com
Map **2 E10**
This 'pay-and-play' golf course designed by Peter
Harradine can be played as nine or 18 holes. Located
at the famous Dubai racecourse, it challenges golfers
of all skill levels as it works its way between a series
of natural lakes. There's no membership fee, so casual
golfers can simply book a tee time to play. Tuition
packages and one-off lessons are also available.

Ice Skating

Al Nasr Leisureland
Nr American Hospital Oud Metha **04 337 1234**
alnasrll.com
Map **2 L6** Metro **Oud Metha**
This Olympic-size rink is part of a large leisure complex
that includes a bowling alley. Entry is Dhs.10 for adults
and Dhs.5 for children under 10, with skate hire at
Dhs.20 for two hours. There is a skating school and
regular ice shows. Call ahead as the rink is sometimes
closed for practice sessions.

Dubai Ice Rink > p.289
Dubai Mall Downtown Dubai, Burj Khalifa **04 448 5111**
dubaiicerink.com
Map **2 F7** Metro **Burj Khalifa/Dubai Mall**
An Olympic-sized arena on the ground floor of The
Dubai Mall. Skating aids are available to help little
ones feel safe on the ice and there are also Mom and
Tots sessions. Regular public sessions are held at
various times during the day, and on certain days the
rink is transformed into an ice disco with a DJ. Lessons
are available for skaters of all different abilities.

The Galleria Ice Rink
Hyatt Regency Al Corniche **04 209 6550**
Map **2 N4** Metro **Palm Deira**
Public skating costs Dhs.35 per person (including
skate hire). Membership rates start at Dhs.400
per month, or Dhs.2,075 per year, with unlimited
skating. Lessons are available and start at Dhs.200 for
members and Dhs.300 for non-members for five 15
minute classes. Other packages include figure skating
coaching, birthday celebrations, and disco nights.

Queen Of Ice World
Nr Al Nasr Leisureland Oud Metha **04 358 4778**
Map **2 K6** Metro **Oud Metha**
Everyone from toddlers to experienced skaters
looking to jump, spiral and dance are catered for in
classes run by the Queen of Ice World school at Al Nasr
Leisureland. The school is also the biggest supplier of
skating equipment and clothing in the Middle East.

Karting

Emirates Kart Zone
Al Wasl Sports Club Oud Metha St, Al Jadaf
050 426 3424
emirateskartzone.net
Map **2 J7** Metro **Dubai Healthcare City**
Operating under the Emirates Motor Sports
Federation, this is a huge, state-of-the-art floodlit
outdoor track, where visitors of all ages can take
on a Formula 1-style circuit, complete with hairpin
turns and chicanes. Professional and junior karts
are available – and at the end of each session,
participants can gather around big screens to check
out computerised race results that reveal the fastest
lap times.

Blokarting
Get involved with the latest extreme sports craze in
Dubai. Blokarting, or landsailing, takes the principles of
windsurfing and applies them on land – or to a buggy
on land, to be specific. A Blokarting experience for
two costs Dhs.550 through Dreamdays (dreamdays.
ae) and once you've got the bug, join Duplays' blokart
racing league at Jumeirah Beach Park. Find out more at
duplays.com

Kartdrome
Dubai MotorCity Al Hebiah 1 **04 367 8744**
Map **1 N12**
The Autodrome in MotorCity has a 500 metre
indoor circuit as well as a 1.2km outdoor track with
a challenging 17 corners. After a safety briefing,
you take to your 390cc kart (there are 120cc karts
for kids over seven years) and hit the tarmac to
test your skill and speed. There are timed races for
the International Leisure Ranking, plus the Dubai
Autodrome Championship for more serious racers.
Races are Dhs.100 (indoor track) or Dhs.110 (outdoor
track), including kart and clothing, and they last 15
minutes. Those with their own karts can use the track
at certain times.

Mini Golf
Hyatt Regency Dubai Golf Park
Hyatt Regency Al Corniche **04 209 6817**
Map **2 N4** Metro **Palm Deira**
Bring your own clubs and golf balls for the nine-hole
pitch-and-putt grass course (Dhs.30 for one round)
or rent it all at the 18-hole crazy golf course (Dhs.15
per person). The lush surroundings also make an
ideal venue for corporate team-building events. No
membership required.

GET BACK ON THE ICE

COME ALIVE ON THE ICE AT THE ALL NEW DUBAI ICE RINK

With improved facilities and newly remodeled skating spaces, enjoy a fun time with our DJ nights, special events and parties on the ice. You can also enroll for skating and ice-hockey training courses at our new Dubai Ice Rink Skating Academy.

For details call us on +971 4 448 5111 or visit **www.dubaiicerink.com**
Follow 'Dubai Ice Rink' on f t 🅜 📷 YouTube

DUBAI ICE RINK

Co-sponsor

Official Timekeeper

JA Jebel Ali Golf Resort
Nr Palm Jebel Ali Mena Jabal Ali **04 814 5555**
jaresortshotels.com
Metro **Jebel Ali**
Right on the beach in the serene gardens of the resort, this course features a range of obstacles, from awkward bends and jumps, to tricky loops and putts. Prices start at Dhs.20, although you will have to pay for a day pass at Jebel Ali Golf Resort on top, with rates starting at Dhs.180 (weekdays) for non-members (Dhs.90 for children).

Play A Round @ Some Place Nice
Jewels Tower 2 Marsa Dubai **04 457 0455**
playaround.ae
Map **1 J5** Metro **Jumeirah Lakes Towers**
Intended as a space for parents and kids to play together, Play A Round is an indoor, neon nine-hole mini golf course with an underwater theme. There are also arts and crafts activities, a soft play area and a cafe.

Tee & Putt Mini Golf
Wafi Umm Hurair 2 **04 357 3290**
teeandputt.com
Map **2 N7** Metro **Airport Terminal 1**
A glow-in-the-dark world of UV lights and surreal outer space designs, all set to a lively pop soundtrack. There are 18 holes, all with different obstacles that follow the space theme. There's also the opportunity for kids to paint their own designs onto glow-in-the-dark t-shirts or get their faces painted, and the venue has a space for hosting parties.

Motorsports

Dubai Autodrome
MotorCity Al Hebiah 1 **04 367 8700**
dubaiautodrome.com
Map **1 N12**
Dubai's motorsport home has six track configurations, including a 5.39km FIA-sanctioned GP circuit, state-of-the-art pit facilities and a 7,000 seat grandstand. The venue hosts events including rounds of the FIA GT Championship. A number of experiences are available, from getting behind the wheel of an Audi R8 V10 to trying out an F1-style single seater.

Multi-sports

The Aviation Club
Al Rebat St Al Garhoud **04 230 8560**
jumeirah.com
Map **2 M8** Metro **GGICO**
This leisure facility offers more activities than your average gym – beach volleyball, bocce, badminton,

croquet, along with tennis and some great swimming pools – even a glass-bottomed rooftop one.

Dubai Ladies Club
Jumeira St Jumeira 1 **04 349 9922**
dubailadiesclub.com
Map **2 D4** Metro **Business Bay**
There's lots going on at this club exclusive to the fairer sex, including facilities for squash, tennis and volleyball, with tournaments organised regularly for members. There's also a 1km running track, swimming pool and wellness centre with a group fitness studio.

Etisalat Academy Recreation & Sports Complex
Off Shk Mohd Bin Zayed Rd Muhaisanah 2
04 204 3491
eacademy.ae
Map **2 S10** Metro **Etisalat**
This large sports and recreation facility close to the Dubai International Airport is open to visitors, with football, volleyball, basketball and squash courts, as well as a running track and swimming pool.

Shooting, Paintballing & Laser Games

JA Shooting Club
Nr Jebel Ali Golf Resort Hessyan 1 **04 883 6555**
jaresortshotels.com
Metro **Jebel Ali**
If you are ready to feel like a champ, the JA Shooting Club is one of the most popular destinations in Dubai. There are five floodlit clay shooting ranges, consisting of skeet, trap and sporting clays. Instructors give detailed lessons. Both members and non-members are welcome.

Laserdrome Dubai
Indoor Kartdrome Al Hebiah 1 **04 436 1422**
Map **1 N12**
Players wear special vests that detect their enemies' lasers. At the end of each round, contestants can see how many times they got shot and who shot them. The charges are Dhs.80 per person for 15 minutes.

Pursuit Games
Jabal Ali Shooting Club Hessyan 1 **04 324 4755**
paintballdubai.com
Map **2 L8** Metro **Jebel Ali**
The Pursuit Games version of paintball is a combination of speedball and paintball and this arena capitalises on the desert terrain. Sessions start at Dhs.90 for two hours, including 100 paintballs and all the necessary gear. Different game scenarios such as 'prison break' and 'total elimination' add variety.

Dubai Ice Rink at The Dubai Mall

Mini Golf

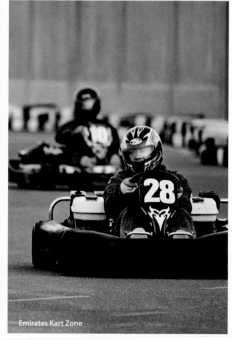

Emirates Kart Zone

Thrill Zone
Oasis Centre Al Qouz 1 **04 388 3551**
thrillzoneuae.com
Map **2 C6** Metro **Noor Bank**
A dinosaur-themed laser tag centre that's suitable for
the whole family – and great for competitive groups
of friends looking for a fun afternoon. There's also a
6D cinema, a party area and a cafe. Prices for laser tag
start at Dhs.55 per person.

Sharjah Golf & Shooting Club > p.vi, vii
Shk Mohammed Bin Zayed Rd Sharjah **06 548 7777**
golfandshootingshj.com
Trigger-happy activities are well served with superb
shooting facilities and three fantastic paintball parks.
The shooting range boasts indoor pistols, rifles and
revolvers, and 25m and 50m ranges. Thirty minute
beginner lessons with .22 calibre weapons cost
Dhs.170 for non-members and Dhs.130 for members.
Twenty-five shots with standard weapons are charged
at Dhs.90 for non-members and Dhs.70 for members.
For paintball, there are two innovative outdoor parks
to choose from: a World War I battlefield and a giant
outdoor jungle. Indoors, there's a London-themed
battlefield complete with black taxis, red telephone
booths and even a Harrods to hide in.

Skateparks

Dubai's many parks provide some excellent locations
for skating. The likes of Creek Park and Safa Park
have plenty of wide pathways, relatively few people
and enough slopes and turns to make it interesting.
Alternatively, check out both sides of Dubai Creek,
the seafront near the Hyatt Regency Hotel or the
promenades at the Jumeira Beach corniche and in
Deira along towards Al Mamzar Beach Park, where the
views are an added bonus. Sheikh Mohammed bin
Rashid Boulevard, running through the Downtown
area, The Walk at Jumeirah Beach Residence, and the
promenade running around Marsa Dubai also have
wide promenades that are great for skating. Dubai
also has a women's roller derby team. Not sure what
that is? Check out dubairollerderby.com for more.

Rage Bowl
Dubai Mall Downtown Dubai, Burj Khalifa **04 434 1549**
rage-shop.com
Map **2 F7** Metro **Burj Khalifa/Dubai Mall**
This indoor skateboarding bowl is open Sunday to
Wednesday, 10am to 10pm, and until midnight at
weekends. Two-hour sessions cost Dhs.25; helmets
can also be hired for Dhs.10. Lessons are available
at Dhs.85 per hour on weekdays and Dhs.125 on
weekends, and no previous experience is required.
Check the website for happy hour timings.

Tashkeel
Nr Nadd Al Sheba Health Centre Nadd Al Shiba 1
04 336 3313
tashkeel.org
Map **2 F11**
Art meets skateboarding at this gallery in peaceful
Nadd Al Shiba. The creative hub has a fantastic, free-
to-use skate ramp and bowl that's open every day.
Skate lessons are available, and so is equipment.

Skiing

Ski Dubai > p.175, 293
Mall of the Emirates Al Barsha 1 **04 409 4090**
skidxb.com
Map **1 R6** Metro **Mall of the Emirates**
Leave the sun and sand outside and head to this
winter wonderland, complete with 22,500 sq m of
real snow, where the temperature hovers around -2°C.
Competent skiers and boarders can choose between
five runs of different difficulty (there's even a black
run) and a freestyle area, but lessons are available for
beginners. There's also a huge Snow Park, where you
can take little ones tobogganing and get up close with
penguins. If you don't ski, you can even roll down the
slope inside a giant inflatable ball or zip line on the
brand new Snow Bullet. Slope pass and lesson prices
include the hire of jackets, trousers, boots, socks,
helmets and equipment, but it's worth bringing your
own gloves, as you'll be charged extra for the hire of
these.

Skydiving

iFLY Dubai
Mirdif City Centre Mirdif **04 231 6292**
theplaymania.com
Map **2 P12** Metro **Rashidiya**
Like the idea of a skydive but don't have the budget
or the head for heights? Visit iFLY at Playnation.
Giant vertical wind tunnels simulate the sensation
of jumping from a plane – you hover over powerful
fans while being blasted up to 10 metres in the air by
winds of up to 200kph. It's a remarkable sensation
and it may sound scary, but instructors are on hand to
help. You can even take kids as young as three.

SkyDive Dubai
Nr Grand Beach Resort Marsa Dubai **04 377 8888**
skydivedubai.ae
Map **1 L4** Metro **DAMAC**
Stunning skydives over The Palm Jumeirah and Marsa
Dubai. A first-time tandem jump costs Dhs.1,999 (with
photos and DVD). You can also sign up for skydive
school, and licensed jumpers can rent gear.

SPOIL YOURSELF.
BECOME A MEMBER.

SKI DUBAI سكي دبي
DO SOMETHING DIFFERENT

ACTIVITIES

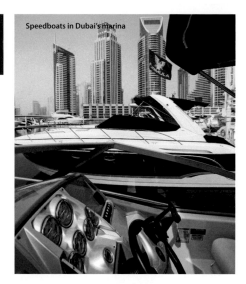
Speedboats in Dubai's marina

The UAE's diverse topography lends itself perfectly to a wide range of outdoor pursuits, including mountain biking, dune bashing, wadi driving and camping. Thanks to the endless kilometres of coastline, watersports are particularly popular as well, with scuba diving, sailing, wakeboarding and kayaking all firmly within the realms of possibility. With so many different cultures converging in Dubai, it's little surprise that there is such a diverse range of activities available to fill your free time with.

Biking

Away from the cities, the UAE has a lot to offer outdoor enthusiasts, especially mountain bikers. On a mountain bike it's possible to see untouched places that are not even accessible in 4WDs.

Beginner bikers: head to the Hatta Fort Hotel, a secluded mountain retreat which has an off-road bike track on its grounds.

Advanced bikers: from super-technical rocky trails in areas like Fili and Siji, to mountain routes like Wadi Bih, which climb to over 1,000m and can be descended in minutes, there really are plenty of fantastic routes for experienced riders to try where riding is mainly rocky and quite challenging. Even if you are experienced, always be sensible and go prepared – the sun is strong, you will need far more water than you think, and it's easy to get lost. Wide, knobbly tyres work much better on the loose, sharp rocks. For further information on mountain biking in Dubai, including details of possible routes, refer to the *UAE Off-Road Explorer*. See also the Clubs & Groups section in this book for more details of other biking groups.

Boating

With calm waters and year-round sunshine, the UAE offers ideal conditions for those wishing to sample life on the ocean waves. An evening aboard a dhow, either on Dubai Creek or sailing along the coast, is a wonderfully memorable experience. A number of companies in Dubai provide boat charters, offering everything from sundowner cruises of a couple of hours and overnight trips with snorkelling stopovers, to scuba diving excursions to remote destinations such as Musandam. Large sailing yachts, catamarans, speedboats and other motorboats can be hired for

private charter and corporate events; other companies offer outings on dhows and also cater to weddings and birthday parties. Fishing trips and watersports packages are also available. If you're on the east coast and fancy a traditional boating experience, large independent groups can charter a dhow from the fishermen at Dibba. If you're a boating enthusiast, make sure you pick up Explorer's *UAE Boating & Yachting* book.

Membership at one of Dubai's sailing clubs allows you to participate in club activities and to rent sailing and watersports equipment. You can also use leisure facilities and the club's beach, and moor your boat at an additional cost. If you've not found your sea legs but would like to, there are a few places that will teach you.

Exclusion zones

There are many exclusion zones set around the offshore sites, such as the Palms, The World and other in-water development sites around Dubai's coast. These exclusion zones not only detract sightseers, but are also in place for the safety of the boat owner, so it is advisable to stay well clear. Approaching any oil installations areas is strictly prohibited.

Dubai International Marine Club
Al Sufouh St Marsa Dubai **04 399 5777**
dimc.ae
Map **1 M5** Metro **Nakheel**
Offers sailing lessons for children. A 12 hour course sets members back Dhs.1,500. See the website for more details on lessons and membership.

Dubai Offshore Sailing Club

Jumeira St Umm Suqeim 1 **04 394 1669**
dosc.ae
Map **2 B4** Metro **Noor Bank**

This Royal Yachting Association Training Centre offers dinghy and keelboat courses throughout the year. Members enjoy weekly regattas and a busy social calendar. The restaurant is very reasonably priced and has a large terrace with views over the quaint marina. There's also a small private beach and private function area. To gain membership, you have to prove that you're an active sailor and gain points in your sailing logbook in order to be considered.

Sailing Events

Sailing is an important part of Dubai's heritage and this is reflected in the number of sailing events that take place each year. The traditional dhow races are an exciting spectacle, while the long distance races such as the annual Dubai to Muscat race attracts many sailors. The emirate's waters are a major venue for the popular Class 1 World Power Boating Championship (class-1.com). These stylish heavyweights of the powerboating world race around a grand prix circuit through Mina Seyahi lagoon at speeds of up to 257kph, just metres from the beach. Held at the end of November, the twin Dubai competitions represent the finale of the European circuit, which has seen Dubai's Victory Team win the series eight times.

In Sharjah, the UIM F1 H2O World Championship takes place every December as part of Sharjah Water Festival. For a quieter but still vigorous display of boating prowess, look out for the various dragon boat events held throughout the year (dubaidragonboat. com), and keep an eye open for the many sailing and dhow racing events that take place off Dubai's shoreline, including the 10-day Maktoum Sailing Trophy, which takes place every February (dimc.ae).

Ports Of Call

If you've already established that sailing is your pastime, and you either have a boat or are currently looking to buy one, you're going to need to store it somewhere. There are still waiting lists at a few of the UAE's most established marinas but, by and large, there is availability. Rates start from Dhs.245 per month.

Buying A Boat

Whether you're purchasing your first vessel, or you're a serious skipper, there are a few rules and regulations you need to be aware of. You will need the following:

- Marine craft registration and licence
- Marine craft inspection report
- Coastguard approved transponder
- Boat insurance
- Permit to sail
- Marine driver's licence

Both private vessels – also known as 'pleasure', leisure or marine craft – and commercial vessels, must be registered annually with the Dubai Maritime City Authority (DMCA) before they can be used. As part of this process, you will need to insure your vessel (Dubai Insurance and AXA Gulf both offer boat insurance), take it to the DMCA at the dry docks for a marine inspection report, and get a transponder fitted.

Before you reach the water, you will need to obtain a permit to sail, which is authorised by the Dubai Coastguard; its patrol boats are often on the look out to make sure boat owners have complied with all these regulations. You will also need to apply to the DMCA for a marine driver's licence, a relatively new rule to ensure that all boat owners have the theoretical and practical knowledge and expertise to drive light marine vessels and leisure crafts.

Explorer's *Dubai How-To* guide gives full information on all procedures required in buying and registering a boat and a jet ski.

Camping

To really appreciate the surroundings that Dubai has to offer, you need to venture out and experience the natural wonders of the Arabian countryside for at least a night or two. There are an awe-inspiring array of safe and secluded locations to make camping a much-loved activity in Dubai and the UAE. While the weather is rarely bad – there's hardly ever any rain – the ideal time for a camping trip is between October and April. Such warm temperatures mean you can camp with much less equipment and preparation than in other countries, and many first-timers or families with children find that camping becomes their favourite weekend break.

Choose between the peace and tranquillity of the desert, or camp among the wadis and mountains next to trickling streams in picturesque oases. Generally speaking, there are no restrictions on where you can camp, with the exception of some beaches, but obviously people's privacy and property need to be respected at all times.

About 140km west of Abu Dhabi, Mirfa is a small, quiet town located on the coast. While there are not a lot of attractions, the long stretch of beach is a kitesurfer's paradise and many choose to pitch tents here, especially during the popular Al Gharbia Watersports Festival which takes place in March each year. Or head to Ras Khumais. Turning off the main road 15km after Sila (6km before the Saudi Arabia boarder), this small road takes you up to the headland of Ras Khumais. Before you hit the military post, there are a few areas where you can drive onto the beach and camp right beside the sea while watching pink flamingos as they bob around in the turquoise sea.

Luckily, in the UAE there's a great selection of stores that offer a huge variety of camping equipment whatever your budget. Head to the Shopping section for listings.

Child's Play
The long stretch of beach in Fujairah is ideal for those travelling with kids. Hotels line some of these beaches and, so, if your attempt at a beach BBQ goes awry, you can always head to a restaurant to fill empty bellies. Toilets in the hotels can also be a sight for sore eyes for those with kids too. Other good locations include Jabal Ali and Hatta, as they all have hotels nearby.

Glamping
Love camping but hate pitching? In these parts, you can always take to the great outdoors with a few extra luxuries. There are several tour companies that organise desert camping trips, which make for a completely hassle-free experience all round. These firms usually offer a full desert safari, complete with dune bashing, camel riding, belly dancers and a BBQ dinner, as well as an overnight stay, but usually tourists choose to skip the staying over part. Check the list of tour companies for more. For those who want to try the very best in glamping experiences try Banyan Tree Al Wadi, where tented luxury awaits. Expect four-poster beds, tent-service and unrivalled extravagance.

Places To Pitch Up
You can camp just about anywhere, but there are some stand-out spots that are super places to pitch up. Many good camping spots are easily accessible from tarmac roads too, so a 4WD is not always required. Jebel Yibir is the UAE's highest peak and, as such, camping out on the mountain (there's a road up to the summit) is a good option for the warmer months as the temperatures up there are much cooler than down below. The Wadi Sidr off-road route leads to a plateau that offers some good places to camp, with great views, while both Fossil Rock and the drive from Madam to Madah provide terrific, accessible dune driving and camping spots.

The ultimate camping experience, however, is to be had in the sea of dunes at Liwa, where you can go to sleep beneath a starry sky and wake up completely surrounded by one of the world's most mesmerising dunescapes (see Out Of The City). For more information on off-road adventuring and camping, refer to the *UAE Off-Road Explorer*.

Don't forget that while the UAE has comparably low rainfall, care should always be taken in and near wadis as flash floods, although rare, can occur; remember, it may be raining in the mountains miles from where you are.

Caving
The cave network in the Hajar Mountains is extensive and much of it has yet to be explored. Some of the best caves are near Al Ain, the Jebel Hafeet area and just past Buraimi near the Oman border. Many of the underground passages and caves have spectacular displays of curtains, stalagmites and stalactites, as well as gypsum flowers.

In Oman, the range includes what is still believed to be the second-largest cave system in the world, as well as the Majlis Al Jinn Cave – the second-largest chamber in the world.

Within the region, caving ranges from fairly safe to extremely dangerous and, as no mountain rescue services exist, anyone venturing out into the mountains should always be well-equipped and accompanied by an experienced leader.

Mountain High Middle East
050 659 5536
mountainhighme.com
A company providing exciting adventure experiences and motivational and teambuilding activities. Mountain-climbing and trekking are just some of the trips they can organise.

UAE & Oman Rock Climbing & Outdoor Adventures
Abu Dhabi **055 770 8629**
Providing rock climbing adventures around the UAE, Oman and further afield, UAE & Oman Rock Climbing & Outdoor Adventures welcomes everyone from beginners to experienced climbers. The type of climbing includes traditional, bouldering, DWSing, sport climbing, spelunking, and aid climbing, and the company aims to build a large community of keen climbers in the region.

Climbing
Excellent climbing can be found in various locations around the UAE, including Ras Al Khaimah, Hatta and the Al Ain/Buraimi region. More than 600 routes have been recorded since the 1970s. These vary from short outcrop routes to difficult mountain routes of alpine proportions. Most range from very severe up to extreme. There are several easier routes for beginner climbers, especially around Wadi Bih and Wadi Khab Al Shamis.

To meet like-minded people, head to Wadi Bih where you'll find climbers nearly every weekend, or go to one of the climbing walls listed below. For more information, contact John Gregory on 050 647 7120. Other excellent resources are uaeclimbing.com and the book UAE Rock Climbing by Toby Foord-Kelcey.

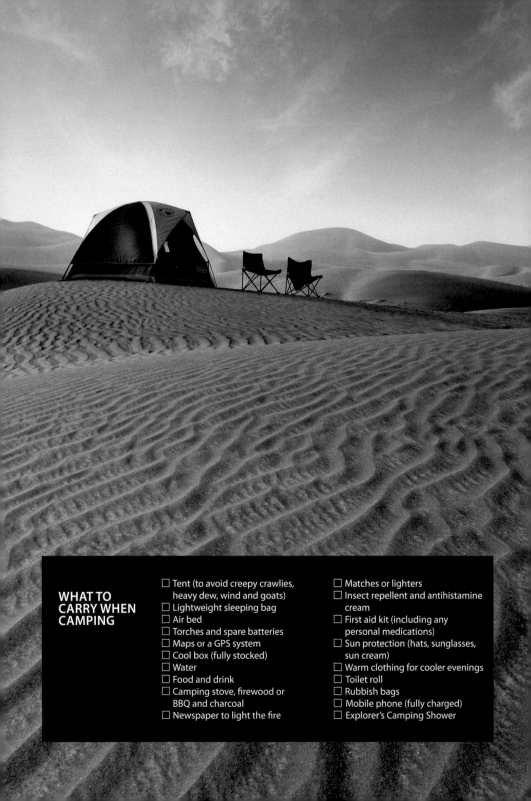

WHAT TO CARRY WHEN CAMPING

- ☐ Tent (to avoid creepy crawlies, heavy dew, wind and goats)
- ☐ Lightweight sleeping bag
- ☐ Air bed
- ☐ Torches and spare batteries
- ☐ Maps or a GPS system
- ☐ Cool box (fully stocked)
- ☐ Water
- ☐ Food and drink
- ☐ Camping stove, firewood or BBQ and charcoal
- ☐ Newspaper to light the fire

- ☐ Matches or lighters
- ☐ Insect repellent and antihistamine cream
- ☐ First aid kit (including any personal medications)
- ☐ Sun protection (hats, sunglasses, sun cream)
- ☐ Warm clothing for cooler evenings
- ☐ Toilet roll
- ☐ Rubbish bags
- ☐ Mobile phone (fully charged)
- ☐ Explorer's Camping Shower

Climbing wall at Playnation

Adventure HQ
Times Square Centre Al Qouz Ind. 1 **04 346 6824**
adventurehq.ae
Map **1 T6** Metro **Noor Bank**
As well as being arguably the best place in the UAE to
pick up climbing gear, Adventure HQ has a state-of-the-
art climbing wall and cable obstacle course. Climbing
rates starting from Dhs.50 per person. Test your
climbing gear for cold conditions in the Chill Chamber.

Cleopatra's Spa & Wellness
Wafi Umm Hurair 2 **04 324 7700**
cleopatrasspaandwellness.com
Map **2 K7** Metro **Dubai Healthcare City**
The indoor climbing wall at Cleopatra's Spa and
Wellness in Wafi offers courses for all abilities,
including beginners' classes as well as sessions for
experienced climbers. The wall has routes of varying
difficulty and crash mats are provided for bouldering.
Lessons cost Dhs.62 per hour and are limited to six
people per instructor.

Climbing Dubai
The Apartments Trade Center 2 **04 306 5061**
dorellsports.com
Map **2 H6** Metro **World Trade Centre**
The Middle East's tallest outdoor climbing wall can be
found at Dubai World Trade Centre Hotel Apartments.
Learn to scale the impressive 16 metre wall with an
introductory lesson for Dhs.85. Courses for adults are
Dhs.350 for five classes and for kids are Dhs.250 for
five classes. A day pass costs Dhs.60. Climbing Dubai

also has an eight-metre climbing tower at Horizon
School Dubai, next to Safa Park Gate 4 (050 659 8500).

Playmania
Mirdif City Centre 800 386
theplaymania.com
Map **2 P12** Metro **Rashidiya**
The 8-metre climbing wall at this popular kid's activity
centre leads to Sky Trail; a thrilling obstacle course
that is suspended 13 metres above the ground. Little
adventurers can test their head for heights by scaling
the wall to reach it, before negotiating their way around
the aerial frames and walkways. Single sessions start
at Dhs.25 - and birthday parties can also be arranged,
starting at Dhs.90 per child.

Desert Activities

When it comes to the UAE, there's one place that
demands our attention more than any other: the
desert. It makes up more than 90% of the country
and it's the biggest outdoor adventure playground
you could imagine. In all directions the desert offers
a varied and fascinating landscape that has great
potential for exploring and leisure-time activities. In
Dubai, there are a number of organisations who offer
professional desert driving and off-road courses (see
opposite for details). A number of tour companies
provide desert safari trips, or lease out dune buggies
and quad bikes; these companies are listed under
Desert & Mountain Tours.

Al Futtaim Training Centre
Nr Dubai Duty Free Umm Ramoul **04 292 0555**
traininguae.com
Map **2 N9** Metro **Emirates**
Classroom and practical tuition for off-road driving
enthusiasts to learn how to venture safely out and into
the desert.

Desert Rangers
Churchill Business Tower Business Bay **04 357 2200**
desertrangers.com
Map **2 K6** Metro **Business Bay**
Experience a four-hour desert driving safari with the
chance to spend an hour behind the wheel. The costs
are Dhs.1,000 with own vehicle, or Dhs.1,800 without.

Emirates Driving Institute > *p.101*
Nr Galadari Engineering Al Qouz Ind. 3 **04 340 0449**
edi-uae.com
Map **1 T7** Metro **First Gulf Bank**
Offers an eight-hour desert driving course from
Dhs.500 or Dhs.550 on Fridays.

OffRoad-Zone
8th Street Al Qouz Ind. 1 **04 339 2449**
offroad-zone.com
Map **2 A6** Metro **Noor Bank**
Drivers are taught how to handle a 4WD on a training
course in Jabal Ali, which covers all terrains from deep
water crossings to sandy descents. Bring your own
4WD or rent one from OffRoad-Zone. Dhs.850 per
person for three hours.

◤
Drive WIth Care
To protect the environment from damage, you should
try to stick to existing tracks rather than create new
tracks across virgin countryside. While it may be hard
to deviate from the track, dunes are ever changing so
obvious paths are less common. Although the sandy
dunes may look devoid of life, there is a surprising
variety of flora and fauna that exists. Check out
Explorer's *UAE Off-Road* series for more information.

Desert Driving
Dune bashing, desert driving or off-roading is one of
the toughest challenges for both car and driver, but
once mastered, it's great fun if you do it safely. Taking
special off-road driving lessons enables you to make
the most of your 4WD and learn how to tackle driving
in the desert without getting stuck in the sand. Learn
what to do if you do get bogged in, or learn more
about driving your own vehicle safely in the sand – a
good idea if you plan to go camping. See Off-roading
for some of the best and most peaceful places in the
region to visit away from the city.

Dune Buggying
Unless you've got Dhs.60,000 to spare for a neat
motorised vehicle used solely for the pleasure of
revving up and down dunes, chances are you've not
got a dune buggy, but ask almost every adventure
junkie in the UAE and they'll tell you that getting out
to the dunes to shred some sand is top on their list
on fun. Dune buggying is a full-on adrenaline bender
spent rocketing across the desert plains in custom-
made two-seater buggies that resemble something
you might see on a lunar landing. See Desert &
Mountain Tours.

Quad Biking
More adrenaline-fuelled than a desert hack and
closer to the action than a 4WD tour, on a quad you're
down at sand level feeling every dune contour. It is
especially exciting as the routes get more challenging.
Just remember to listen to the instructions of the
professionals accompanying you.

Sandboarding
Sandboarding is a sport of its own and requires
balance, strength and no small amount of tenacity.
Once you climb your way to the top of the dune, it's
best to wax the bottom of the board to reduce friction
between the board and the sand. Strap your feet onto
the board, bending your back knee slightly and slide
on down, using your heels and toes to turn. All major
tour operators in Dubai (see Desert & Mountain Tours)
offer sandboarding experiences with instruction.

Mountain Biking
Away from the city, Dubai also has a lot to offer
mountain bikers. On a mountain bike, it's possible
to see the most remote and untouched places that
are not even accessible in 4WDs. For hardcore,
experienced bikers there is some good terrain from
super-technical rocky trails to mountain routes above
the desert. See Biking for further details.

Diving
The UAE's coastal waters are home to a variety of
marine species, coral life and shipwrecks. You'll see
some exotic fish, like clownfish and seahorses, and
possibly even spotted eagle rays, moray eels, small
sharks, turtles, dolphins, barracuda, jellyfish, sea
snakes and stingrays.
   Most of the wrecks are on the west coast, while the
beautiful flora and fauna of coral reefs can be seen
on the east coast. Cement Barge, Mariam Express and
the MV Dara wreck are some of the more popular
dive sites. Off the east coast, one well-known dive
site is Martini Rock, a small, underwater mountain
covered with colourful soft coral, with a depth range

of three to 19 metres. North of Khor Fakkan is the Car Cemetery, a reef that has thrived around a number of cars placed 16 metres below water. Visibility off both coasts ranges from five to 20 metres.

Another option for diving enthusiasts is to take a trip to Musandam. This area, which is part of the Sultanate of Oman, is often described as the 'Norway of the Middle East' due to the fjord-like inlets and the way the sheer cliffs plunge directly into the sea. It offers some spectacular dive sites. Straight-down wall dives with strong currents and clear waters are more suitable for advanced divers, while the huge bays, with their calm waters and shallow reefs, are ideal for the less experienced. Visibility here is between 10 and 35 metres. The further north you go, the more likely you are to see large pelagics.

If you plan to travel to Khasab, the capital of the Musandam region, you may not be able to take your own air tanks across the border and will have to rent from one the dive centres there. You may also require an Omani visa. Alternatively, from Dibba on the east coast, you can hire a fast dive boat to take you anywhere from five to 75km up the coast. The cost ranges from Dhs.150 to Dhs.500, for what is usually a two-dive trip.

There are plenty of dive companies in the UAE that can help you should you want to try diving for the first time, or improve on your existing diving skills (see below). PADI training is available from beginner level through to instructor qualifications. Most companies offer both tuition and straightforward dive outings, with equipment. Online PADI e-learning courses are also available via Al Boom Diving (alboomdiving.com).

Diving

7 Seas Divers
Nr Al Safeer Centre, Khor Fakkan **09 238 2971**
7seasdivers.com
This PADI dive centre offers day and night diving trips to sites around Khor Fakkan, Musandam and Lima Rock. Training is provided from beginner to instructor level, in a variety of languages.

UAE Diving book
Check out the *UAE Diving* book for further information on the best diving and snorkelling sites in the area as well as detailed info on diving companies and clubs. Go to askexplorer.com to purchase a copy.

Al Boom Diving
Nr Iranian Hospital Jumeira 1 **04 342 2993**
alboomdiving.com
Map **2 H4** Metro **World Trade Centre**
Al Boom's Aqua Centre on Al Wasl Road (there are centres in Fujairah, Dibba and Jabal Ali too) is a school and diving shop. PADI certification starts from Dhs.1,750 for Scuba Diver; novices can try a discovery dive experience for Dhs.150. Al Boom also runs the Diving With Sharks experience in Dubai Aquarium at The Dubai Mall, where you can experience a 40 minute dive in a tank filled with these sharp toothed creatures.

Al Mahara Diving Centre
Al Nahyan Abu Dhabi **02 643 7377**
divemahara.com
An excellent dive centre run by very experienced staff that offers diving in Dubai's waters as well as boat trips to some lesser-known coral-filled spots amongst Abu Dhabi's islands.

Arabian Divers & Sportfishing Charters
Marina Al Bateen Abu Dhabi **050 614 6931**
fishabudhabi.ae
This dive centre has a complete range of diving courses and adventure packages, all based in the waters surrounding the Musandam Peninsula. Guests can enjoy a fusion of Caribbean and Arabian seafood onboard, as well as activities such as environmental education classes.

Atlantis Dive Centre
Atlantis Nakhlat Jumeira **04 426 3000**
atlantisthepalm.com
Map **1 N1** Metro **Nakheel**
This top level, accredited PADI facility is one of the best equipped in the country, with indoor saltwater pools, classrooms, good quality equipment and boat rental. All major courses are available from discovery to advanced, as well as a variety of trips and tours. Its Family Fun Days provide a free introduction to diving.

BSAC 406 Sharjah Dive Club
Shj Wanderers Sharjah **06 566 2105**
bsac406.com
This club is a member of the British Sub Aqua Club and follows its training, certification and diving practices. Clubhouse facilities include a training room, social area, equipment room, compressors, dive gear and two dive boats. The club dives mainly shipwrecks in the Arabian Gulf, and launches boats from both Sharjah and Dubai, depending on which dive site they are visiting.

Desert Sports Diving Club
St 40A Al Qouz 1 desertsportsdivingclub.net
Map **2 C7** Metro **Noor Bank**
Dubai's only independent diving group meets on Mondays and Wednesdays at the clubhouse near Sheikh Zayed Road to plan dives. The group has two boats in Dubai and one on the east coast. A Dhs.1,000 fee entitles members to unlimited free dives on club boats. Guests pay Dhs.200 per dive.

The Dive Centre
Dubai International Marine Club
thedivecentre.ae
Map **1 L4** Metro **Nakheel**
A professional centre with experienced instructors who are especially knowledgeable about the wreck dives along the west coast of Dubai.

Divers Down UAE
Iberotel Miramar Al Aqah Fujairah **09 237 0299**
diversdownuae.com
Offers PADI courses for all abilities, and organises a variety of diving adventures including wreck dives, wall dives, deep dives and night dives, as well as dives in the Gulf of Oman. It runs two boats, operates three dives per day, and is open seven days a week; transport can be provided. In 2013, a centre also opened at RIVA Beach Club on the Palm Jumeirah.

Emirates Diving Association
Al Shindagha **04 393 9390**
emiratesdiving.com
Map **2 M4** Metro **Al Ghubaiba**
A non-profit organisation that seeks to protect the UAE's marine resources. It runs a coral monitoring project and annual Clean-Up Arabia campaigns. Divers are encouraged to join for Dhs.100 per year.

Freediving UAE
Abu Dhabi **050613 0486**
freedivinguae.com
This Abu Dhabi-based company teaches you how to dive deep without the aid of scuba equipment. Allowing divers to enjoy a whole new sense of freedom, freediving is rapidly gaining in popularity. Freediving UAE offers all levels of training courses.

Freestyle Divers
Royal Beach Fujairah **09 244 5756**
freestyledivers.com
A quality dive centre with learning premises on Al Wasl Road, as well as a dive centre at the Royal Beach Hotel in Dibba. Offers courses and certification from beginner to advanced divers and organises regular trips. The full PADI Open Water Diver course costs Dhs.2,100.

Nomad Ocean Adventures
Nr The Harbour, Al Biah Dibba **+968 26 836 069**
discovernomad.com
This very friendly dive centre offers dive, dhow and overnight camping trips which can be tailored for individual parties. A two-dive trip with equipment starts at Dhs.450, a beginner's trial dive costs Dhs.500. You can also spend the weekend at its wonderfully charismatic eco-lodge and complete your open water course (including nine dives and certification). Rates for this start at Dhs.1,800. Call Christophe on the number above or +968 98 155 906.

The Pavilion Dive Centre
Jumeirah Beach Hotel Umm Suqeim 3 **04 406 8828**
jumeirah.com
Map **1 S4** Metro **First Gulf Bank**
This PADI Gold Palm IDC Centre is run by PADI course directors. Daily dive charters for certified divers are available in Dubai; charters to Musandam can be organised upon request from Dhs.650 with equipment. Open Water certification is Dhs.1,850.

Prodive Middle East
Pinnacle Bldg Al Barsha 1
prodiveme.com
Map **1 Q6** Metro **Sharaf DG**
Prodive is run by an instructor with more than 25 years' experience. Trips can be tailored for individuals, groups and corporate clients, and chocolate brownies are offered to all their divers!

Sandy Beach Diving Centre
Sandy Beach Fujairah **09 244 5555**
sandybm.com
Located in a chalet beach resort, the centre, which sells dive equipment, is open year-round. Nearby Snoopy Island, alive with hard coral and interesting marine life, is an excellent spot for snorkelling and diving.

Scuba 2000
Al Bidiya Beach, Al Bidiyah Fujairah **09 238 8477**
scuba-2000.com
This east coast dive centre provides daily trips to Dibba and Khor Fakkan, as well as a range of courses starting at Dhs.400 for Discover Scuba and rising to Dhs.2,200 for Open Water certification.

Scubatec Diving Center
Sana Fashion Bldg Al Karama **04 334 8988**
scubatecdiving.com
Map **2 K5** Metro **Al Jafiliya**
A five-star IDC operator, licensed by PADI and TDI, offering courses from beginner to instructor level. Dives are available in Dubai and on the east coast.

Sheesa Beach Dive Centre
Karsha Dibba **968 26836551**
sheesabeach.com
The perfect dive centre for those wanting to explore the amazing dive sites of Musandam – said to be amongst the world's very best. As well as its resort in Dibba, Sheesa offers all manner of diving, from kids' courses and speciality diving to PADI certification. It also offers more private trips on speedboats, as well as social dhow trips, from a few hours' duration to a full weekend or several days.

Decompression Sickness
While diving is generally a safe sport, there is always a risk of decompression sickness if a diver stays too deep for too long or ascends too rapidly. One of the first symptoms is aches and pains in the joints, and following that there may be a skin rash or dizziness and other neurological symptoms.

If you notice any of these symptoms after diving, consult a doctor as soon as possible – it is likely that you will need oxygen and possibly hyperbaric re-compression. Before you can receive treatment in a re-compression chamber, a qualified diving doctor must sign a consent form – there's no point just turning up at the chamber.

In Dubai you can contact Dr Barbara Karin Vela for diving-related questions at Dubai London Clinic and Speciality Hospital on Jumeirah Beach Road in Umm Suqeim (800-DLC/800-352). In an emergency, call 050 885 8172. The UAE only has two hyperbaric re-compression chambers – one at Zayed Military Hospital in Abu Dhabi (02 444 8100) and another at Aqua Marine Diving Services in Al Qouz industrial area (04 323 3100 or 04 323 3200, aqua-diving-services.com).

Snorkelling
If you'd like a glimpse of underwater life without making the investment to become a certified diver, snorkelling is the way to go. It's a great hobby regardless of your age or fitness level and you can pretty much snorkel anywhere off a boat – all you need is a mask and fins. The dive sites listed before are perfect for snorkellers and divers alike. Snorkelling offers a different experience to diving, with many interesting creatures such as turtles, rays and even sharks seen near the surface. It's also a great way for the family to enjoy an activity together, and all you need is some basic equipment.

The east coast is a great area for snorkelling and has the most diverse marine life compared to Dubai's coast. Most dive centres take snorkellers out on their boats (along with divers) and the trip last for about two hours. Some centres can make arrangements to take you to Shark Island (also called Khor Fakkan Island) where you can spend the day.

You can also go to Sandy Beach Hotel in Fujairah and spend the day on the beach and swim out to Snoopy Island, just a short distance from shore. In winter time, the water recedes a long way and the distance you have to swim is even less – but the water temperature will be considerably cooler too. Musandam offers good snorkelling too, but the waters can have strong currents so it's a good idea to go with a tour company and have a guide to point out the best sites. The best fish life is to be found between the surface and 10 metres below, so try to snorkel along the side of rocks and islands. There are a number of tour companies that offer dhow trips for dolphin watching and snorkelling, and the boats usually moor in areas that are safe for snorkelling in.

Hiking
It's easy in Dubai to get out of the habit of walking, and so even the most gentle of hikes can be good for the heart. Unsure where to go? Join an organised hike.

Safety First
As with any trip into the UAE 'outback', take sensible precautions. Tell someone where you are going and when you should be back, and don't forget to take a map, compass, GPS equipment and robust hiking boots. Don't underestimate the strength of the sun – take sunscreen and, most importantly, lots of water. Be particularly careful in wadis (dry riverbeds) during the wet season (November to January) as flash floods can immerse a wadi in seconds. Also note that there are no mountain rescue services in the UAE.

Despite Dubai's flat terrain, spectacular hiking locations can be found just a few hours outside the city limits. In the very north of the UAE, the Ru'us Al Jibal Mountains contain the highest peaks in the area, standing proud at over 2,000m, while the impressive Hajar Mountains stretch from Musandam in the north all the way down to the Empty Quarter desert in the south. Inland, Al Ain provides some excellent hiking routes, with plenty of mountains, including the imposing Jebel Hafeet, teamed with seven lush oases. Routes range from short, easy walks leading to spectacular viewpoints, to all-day treks over difficult terrain, and can include major mountaineering.

Some hikes follow centuries-old Bedouin and Shihuh mountain paths, a few of which are still being used.

One of the easiest places to reach is the foothills of the Hajar Mountains on the Hatta Road, near the Oman border. After passing through the desert, the flat, stark, rugged outcrops transform the landscape. Explore any turning you like, or take the road to Mahdah, along which you'll find several hiking options. Other great areas for hiking and exploring include the mountains in and around Musandam, and the mountains near the east coast. You can find details of local hikes in the *UAE Off-Road Explorer*; and for somewhere a bit further afield see *Oman Trekking*, a guide book from Explorer with pull-out maps covering major signed routes in Oman.

Absolute Adventure

SIT Tower Silicon Oasis, Nadd Hessa **04 392 6463**
adventure.ae
Map **2 J5** Metro **Business Bay**
This adventure tour operator offers a range of treks, varying in difficulty, including extreme trekking at Jebel Qihwi and an eight-hour coastal village trek. The activity centre, right on the beach at Dibba, can accommodate 14 people for group stays – and beach barbecues. The group also organises treks for serious hikers to destinations further afield, such as Nepal. Check the website for details of upcoming trips.

Arabia Outdoors

Various locations 055 955 6209
arabiaoutdoors.com
Organises individual, group and corporate hikes along routes such as Jebel Qihwi, Jebel Hafeet and Stairway To Heaven. Other activities include camping, climbing and kayaking, and team-building camps and events.

Desert Rangers

Churchill Business Tower Business Bay **04 456 9944**
desertrangers.com
Map **2 K6** Metro **Business Bay**
Offers hikes for individuals and groups of up to 100 people by dividing them into smaller teams to tackle different trails to the summit. A variety of routes are offered according to age and fitness. Locations include Fujairah, Dibba, Masafi, Ras Al Khaimah and Al Ain, with prices starting at Dhs.275 per person.

Off-roading

Getting out into the deserts and wadis by 4WD is a must-do while you're a Dubai resident and, once you're out there, there are some super hiking and camping spots to take advantage of too. If you're desert driving for the first time, go with an experienced person – driving on sand requires very different skills to other surfaces. Tour companies offer a range of desert and mountain safaris (see Tour Operators). 4WDs can be hired from most car hire companies (see Car Hire Companies).

OffRoad-Zone

If you're really keen to learn to off-road in a controlled environment, then OffRoad-Zone (offroad-zone.com) runs a driving centre at the Jebel Ali Shooting Club where you can practise tackling all manner of obstacles that you might find while off-roading, including deep water, loose rocks and steep descents. Tutors are on hand to show you the proper technique too.

Northern Emirates: For a weekend away, with some of the best driving in the UAE, combine the mountains around Wadi Bih, near Ras Al Khaimah, with one of the interesting wadi routes on the east coast.
East Coast: From Dubai, the east coast can be reached in about two hours. The mountains and beaches are fantastic spots for camping, barbecues and weekend breaks, as well as various other activities. There are some great wadi and mountain routes here, and the area is also renowned for its diving and snorkelling opportunities, particularly around Snoopy Island.
Hatta: The Hatta region is home to the popular Big Red sand dune, a huge draw and a must-do challenge for off-roaders and quad bikers, as well as the Hatta Pools, a great swimming spot in the Hajar Mountains.
Al Ain: The oasis town is worthy of a visit in its own right, but nearby the imposing Jebel Hafeet and Hanging Gardens have great trekking spots.
Liwa: A trip to Liwa is one you'll never forget – it's one of the few remaining chances to experience unspoiled dunes. The drive from Dubai is long, more suitable for a two or three day camping trip, but the journey is worth it. Prepare for the most adventurous off-road driving the UAE has to offer. For further information and tips on driving off-road, check out both the *UAE Off-Road Explorer* and the *Oman Off-Road Explorer*. These books feature a multitude of detailed routes and give advice on how to stay safe, where to camp and things to do along the way. If you want a wilderness adventure but don't know where to start, contact any of the major tour companies. All offer a range of desert and mountain safaris.

Top Day Trips

If you want more ideas for the best day trips in Dubai and the region, get a copy of Explorer's *UAE Day Tripper*. The book features detailed reviews of some of the region's top attractions and sightseeing highlights. See askexplorer.com.

Water Activities

Temperatures throughout the year make Dubai the perfect place for sailing, swimming and watersports generally. The emirate's stunning stretch of beaches offer plenty of opportunities for water-based fun, from the latest craze of flyboarding to the more relaxed thrills of stand up paddleboarding, and the different ocean breaks allow for a wide range of activities to take place within close proximity.

Before grabbing your kayak or board and making a dash for the ocean, make sure that you are allowed to kitesurf or surf there. Some beaches have restrictions in place to protect swimmers, so check the signs before hitting the waves. Also remember that some beaches in the UAE may not be open to the public, or if they are, are not patrolled as diligently as some European beaches (if at all).

Swimming

Dubai has some great swimming spots, whether it's at the public beaches, in the private pools, in a beach club, or at a beach park. The water temperature rarely dips below 20°C in winter, although during the summer it can feel like stepping into a bath. As with sea swimming elsewhere, rip tides and undertows can catch out even the strongest swimmer, so never ignore flags or signs ordering you not to swim. You might also run into quite a lot of jellyfish towards the end of the summer.

For details on where to swim or where to go to for swimming lessons in Dubai, see Clubs and Groups.

Swim Around The Burj Challenge

Keen swimmers can sign up for the annual Wild Wadi Swim Around The Burj challenge, usually held in February each year in aid of Medecins Sans Frontieres (swim.msf-me.org). Over 500 participants tackle the 1km distance and all swimmers are given plenty of encouragement from beach spectators.

Fishing

A boat isn't necessarily required to enjoy a great afternoon or evening of fishing. There are plenty of places along Dubai's coast where fishermen tend to congregate, but be aware that you must first obtain a recreational licence. You can apply and pay online (it costs Dhs.250) for a fishing licence via Dubai Municipality at dm.gov.ae/en. September to April is the peak fishing season here, although it's still possible to catch queenfish and sailfish in the summer months.

For a chance of hooking bigger bites, or to let someone else handle the licence admin, it's best to get out on the water and hire a fishing guide or charter a boat. For more information see Clubs & Groups.

Canoeing and Kayaking

Canoeing and kayaking are great ways to get close to the varied marine and birdlife of the UAE. Khor Kalba on the east coast is a popular canoeing spot, as are the mangrove-covered islands in Umm Al Quwain. Sea canoes can be used in Musandam to visit secluded bays and spectacular rocky coastlines where many species of turtles can often be found soaking up the sun. There are a number of specialist tour companies who offer canoeing and kayaking trips to all of these areas, including Desert Rangers and Noukhada. Alternatively, you can test your skills at the artificial whitewater rafting venue at Wadi Adventure (wadiadventure.ae).

For leisurely paddles along the coastline, many of the beach hotels provide hourly kayak hire (from around Dhs.100 per hour). Kite Beach, for instance charge Dhs.25 per hour and an adult must show ID or a driver's licence before heading out. A particularly pleasant kayaking route starts at the Hilton hotel along JBR and follows around clockwise past the Skydive Dubai centre, into the marina and out the other side back onto JBR. It's a peaceful route that should take a beginner kayaker an hour to complete. Just beware of the water taxis and other large vessels sailing swiftly in the marina.

Kitesurfing

Kitesurfing is an extreme sport that fuses elements of windsurfing, wakeboarding and kite flying. You may see kitesurfers showing off along several of Dubai's beaches, but the Kite Beach in Umm Suqeim (behind Sunset Mall, between the Dubai Offshore Sailing Club and Jumeirah Beach Park) is the only place where kiting is officially permitted. The Dubai Kite Forum (dubaikiteforum.com) is a good place to find out the latest on regulations. Kite People (kitepeople.ae) and Kitesurfing in Dubai (dubaikiters.com) are good online resources for buying equipment and locating IKO instructors.

Stand Up Paddleboarding

For a great workout and a good way to get out on the water when conditions are less than ideal for surfing or kitesurfing, the new craze of stand up paddleboarding or SUP, as it has become known, is a welcome addition to the watersport scene. Since the length and width of the board is a generous size, balancing on top of one is far easier than a surfboard. Get in contact with Surfing Dubai (surfingdubai.com) and Dukite (dukite.com/standup-paddle) for lessons, demos, sales and rentals. If you fancy getting your pulse racing a little harder, head to the Black Palace beach in between the Palm and Madinat Jumeirah with Oceanman UAE (oceanmanuae.com) where the team combine paddleboarding with an on-beach fitness regime comprising burpees, sprints and push

Watercooled

to consider whether you have any personal liability insurance in case you injure a third party. There are several places that offer jet ski rental, with prices varying significantly.

Flyboarding
Flyboarding is the new craze in watersports, where you'll be strapped onto a miniature wakeboard that's connected to a giant hose, that in turn is connected to a jet ski. As soon as your jet-skier flips the throttle, water is sent through the hose at a very high pressure into the board on your feet giving you powerful propulsion. Your job? Harness that power, balance on a cushion of water pressure – and fly. Check out flyboards-uae.com for information. Sessions start at Dhs.300 per 30 minute experience.

Surfing
Dubai isn't well-known as a surfing destination, but if you're looking to catch some waves, you'll find an enthusiastic community of surfers who are out whenever there's a swell. Dubai Municipality has also periodically cracked down on surfing at public beaches in the past – check with Surfing Dubai for the latest before paddling out. Sunset Beach (Umm Suqeim open beach) has smallish but decent waves, as does the Sheraton Beach between the Hilton and Sheraton in Marsa Dubai.

ups. Oceanman UAE also organises the popular monthly full moon paddleboarding sessions which take paddlers out to the Burj Al Arab towards Pierchic under the stars and moonlight. Don't forget to bring your glow sticks and a head torch.

Wakeboarding
Wakeboarding is the cool, young upstart that has become the newest, hippest watersport around. If you don't have a boat, you'll find that many of the big hotels' beach clubs offer the sport with a going rate of about Dhs.140 for 15 minutes. Better still, there are now are few excellent wakeboarding-specific companies that offer hourly sessions with equipment hire included. See Watersports Centres and Companies at the end of this section for details.

Cable-Boarding
A popular sport in the US and Europe, cable-boarding allows you to wakeboard while being pulled along by a zip line. The Al Forsan International Sports Resort in Abu Dhabi has two excellent – and world-renowned – cable-boarding lakes.

Jet-skiing
Due to complaints of noise pollution and safety issues concerning swimmers, the Dubai Maritime City Authority has introduced licences and regulations for jet-skiing. You must now obtain a licence through DMCA (dmca.ae) and are only allowed to jet-ski within restricted areas between sunrise and sunset. If you do go jet-skiing, it may be worth checking that your medical insurance covers you. You may also want

Watersports Centres and Companies

Al Forsan International Sports Resort
Khalifa City, Abu Dhabi **02 556 8555**
alforsan.com
If you've tried wakeboarding behind a boat, then you'll already have the general gist of what is required to cable board. The main difference, of course, is that there is no need for a boat and, instead, the strong cable links that are wired around the lakes pull you along.

Bristol Middle East Yacht Solution
Marina Heights Tower Marsa Dubai **04 368 2480**
bristol-middleeast.com
Map **1 L5** Metro **DAMAC**
Has a watersports division that covers water skiing, wakeboarding, surf skiing, kneeboarding, banana boating, donut rides and speed boat trips.

Club Joumana
JA Jebel Ali Golf Resort Mena Jabal Ali **04 883 6000**
jaresortshotels.com
Metro **Jebel Ali**
Windsurfing, waterskiing, kayaking, catamaran, Laser sailing and banana boat rides are available at this club at JA Jebel Ali Golf Resort. Non-residents are charged an additional fee for day access to the beach and pools.

Dubai International Marine Club
Al Sufouh St Marsa Dubai **04 399 5777**
dimc.ae
Map **1 M5** Metro **Nakheel**
DIMC is the home of Mina Seyahi Watersports Club.
Kayaks, surfskis, Lasers, catamarans, wakeboards, jet
skis and kneeboards are available to hire.

Dubai Offshore Sailing Club
Jumeira St Umm Suqeim 1 **04 394 1669**
dosc.ae
Map **2 B4** Metro **Noor Bank**
DOSC opened its doors in 1974 with no more than
a barasti shade on the beach and a few small sailing
boats. The Royal Yachting Association Training Centre
now offers dinghy and keelboat courses throughout
the year. See Boating in this chapter for more
information.

Dubai Surfski & Kayak Club
Nr Saga World Umm Suqeim 1 **055 498 6280**
dskc.net
Map **1 U4** Metro **Noor Bank**
This club has a paddling school offering training for
surfski or kayak beginners, and coaching for advanced
paddlers. Activities include the 10km DSKC Squall on
the last Friday of every month at Mina Seyahi.

Duco Maritime
Jumeira 3 **050 870 3427**
ducomaritime.com
Map **2 B4** Metro **Business Bay**
Classes are available every day by request on beaches
in Dubai, RAK and Abu Dhabi. Two-hour lessons by IKO
qualified instructors are available for beginners,
charged at Dhs.300 per hour including equipment.
Stand up paddleboarding lessons also available.

Explorer Tours
Nr Nadd Shamma Park Umm Ramoul **04 286 1991**
explorertours.ae
Map **2 N10** Metro **Emirates**
Take a canoe or kayak trip in Umm Al Quwain from
Dhs.300 per person with transport, or Dhs.200 per
person without. Explore the tranquil mangroves of the
east coast, famous for its variety of birds and marine life.

Sea Riders
Dubai Marina Mall Dubai Marina **055 510 3739**
searidersuae.com
Sea Riders has been in operation since summer 2013
but its fully-loaded boat complete with enormous
speakers and laid back staff will no doubt make it a
Dubai favourite. Sessions cost Dhs.500 for one hour
(weekdays) and Dhs.550 per hour (weekends). Sea
Riders also offer excellent private fishing and boating
charters for competitive prices.

Sky & Sea Adventures
Hilton Dubai Jumeirah Marsa Dubai **04 399 9005**
watersportsdubai.com
Map **1 K4** Metro **Jumeirah Lakes Towers**
Offers bodyboarding, kayaking, waterskiing,
snorkelling, parasailing, windsurfing and wakeboarding.

Surf House Dubai
Jumeira St Umm Suqeim 2 **050 504 3020**
surfingdubai.com
Map **1 T4** Metro **First Gulf Bank**
Due to a change in the law in 2013, surf lessons in
Dubai are currently on hold, so Surf House Dubai
(previously Surf Dubai) has moved with the times
and launched a facility for the surfing community to
once again come together. You can buy, rent or store
boards and stand up paddles (SUP's) at the Umm
Suqeim-based facility. The company also organise
corporate surf and SUP packages for groups, offer
courses of yoga classes on the beach, and serve a
good cup of coffee. The founders of the company have
been surfing in Dubai since 1992, with the company
launching in 2005, so you can expect experienced
advice when you step inside the facility.

Ignite Surf School UAE
Riva Beach Club Nakhlat Jumeira **055 601 0997**
surfschooluae.com
Map **1 N3** Metro **Nakheel**
Owned and managed by keen and experienced
surfers, and certified by the International Surf
Association. Surf lessons are currently on hold due to
a municipality ruling, but stand up paddleboarding
lessons are available at Riva Beach Club on Palm
Jumeirah. Keep an eye out for the latest on surfing
and SUP in Dubai to see if the situation changes.

Wadi Adventure
Jebel Hafeet Al Ain **03 781 8422**
wadiadventure.ae
The waves aren't always reliable in Dubai, unless you
head for the hills that is. Located near Jebel Hafeet,
entry to Wadi Adventure costs Dhs.50 to Dhs.100, with
an hour in the surf pool (where waves reach three
metres) costing Dhs.100 further, including equipment.

Watercooled
JA Jebel Ali Golf Resort Mena Jabal Ali **04 887 6771**
watercooleddubai.com
Metro **Jebel Ali**
Offers a good range of watersports – from dinghy
and catamaran sailing to wakeboarding – as well as a
variety of RYA courses. Call in advance to reserve the
kit you want. There's also a small bar with delicious
mocktails, and guests can use the facilities at the
adjacent JA Jebel Ali Golf Resort hotel for a limited
time if hiring equipment at Watercooled.

Your WOW moment is in your hands...

Experience the beautiful deserts of Dubai, up close & personal, in a thrilling Adventure with our 1500cc, manual transmission, purpose built dune buggies! Try out the loops and drops on these mystical dunes, in a convoy with these brilliant machines. All our dune buggies are equipped with roll cages, safety harnesses, helmets and an experienced crew to provide you a safe & unforgettable trip.

Contact us for the various options to choose from & select your perfect WOW moment.

RECOMMENDED ON

DELTA
ADVENTURES
(a division of Delta Travel & Holidays L.L.C.)

www.deltaadventures.ae   info@deltaadventures.ae   +971.55.6988330   +971.4.3980909

TOURS

As befits a leading international tourist destination, Dubai is well geared up for taking people on tours of its attractions and highlights. It's generally a rite of passage for Dubai residents to go on a desert safari, and there are plenty of other popular options for seeing the country via land, sea or air.

Tour Tips

If you are booking a tour, make sure you ring around to get the best price. Dubai is dedicated to discounts and you can often get a better rate as a resident. Just remember it is all about putting on the charm – not being a cheeky customer.

Some tours are offered by most operators, particularly desert experiences and dhow cruises; both of these are great options for when you have guests in town. Other companies run memorable, specialised tours, such as diving trips, aerial sightseeing and trekking, while almost all the firms listed here will tailor programmes to suit individual needs.

Bus

If you've got visitors here on a short visit or on a whirlwind stopover in Dubai before they jet off elsewhere, a bus tour of the city is a great way to take in all the highlights in one go. It's also a good way to get acquainted with what's where when you first move to Dubai.

Shopping Tours

Dubai's reputation as the shopping capital of the Middle East is well deserved. From designer clothes, shoes and jewellery in the malls, to electronics, spices and gold in the souks, everything is available. A half-day shopping tour takes you round some of the best shopping spots.

ArtBus
04 341 7303
artinthecity.com
This service runs from the jamjar to galleries across town and Madinat Jumeirah during major art festivals and exhibitions.

Big Bus Tours
04 340 7709
bigbustours.com
A fleet of double-decker buses that provide a hop-on hop-off service, with audio commentary, to major attractions across town. Tickets are valid for either 24 or 48 hours. Take the Day Tour to visit all the places that interest you, or join the Night Tour with a live-guided commentary that showcases illuminated Dubai.

Easy Tour Dubai
04 388 3410
easytour.ae
Easy Tour Dubai offer day and night guided bus tours around Dubai at 10am, 2.30pm, 4pm and 8pm. The four and two-hour round trips include free entrance to Dubai Museum and a walking tour in The Dubai Mall. Commentary is in English, with ticket prices very reasonable. Free refreshments are provided throughout the trip. Expect to see the best of old and new Dubai, with stops including Jumeirah Mosque, Burj al Arab, Emirates Towers, and the historical area of Al Bastakiya.

Wonder Bus Tours
Al Mankhool **04 359 5656**
wonderbustours.net
Map **2 L5** Metro **Al Fahidi**
You can't miss the bright yellow amphibious Wonder Bus Tour Buses, which travel along, and on Dubai Creek. The two-hour mini tour covers Creek Park and Dubai Creek Golf & Yacht Club, and then heads under Maktoum Bridge towards Garhoud Bridge, before returning to BurJuman. The buses are equipped with air conditioning, restrooms, and DVD players.

Desert & Mountain

Desert safaris are by far the most popular variety of tours available, perhaps because a good safari offers many activities in one day. Expert drivers blast 4WD vehicles up, down and around massive dunes (dune bashing) while passing old Bedouin villages and pointing out beautiful natural attractions. Mountain safaris lead passengers through the narrow wadis and steep passes of the Hajar Mountains.

Some tours include sand skiing or boarding and end the day at a replica Bedouin camp where you can watch a belly dancer, eat Arabic delicacies, hold a falcon, ride camels and smoke shisha. Many operators even run overnight safaris that combine desert and mountain safaris. Most driving safaris include pick-up from your place of residence and lunch. The approximate cost for a desert safari is Dhs.150 to Dhs.350 (overnight up to Dhs.500). Most

Think you know Dubai?
Wait till you experience
it with us.

We've been thrilling visitors to the United Arab Emirates and Oman for over two decades. Off-road desert action; polo and golf to camel-trekking and sandboarding; incredible rides by balloon and sea-plane; wedding celebrations and days that end in the romance of our Bedouin desert camp. All of this tailored to groups, families, couples or solo travellers. And wrapped in luxurious hospitality.

Call us today and discover why Gulf Ventures is your natural partner.

Use the booking code **EG2015** to get an exclusive **10% discount** on any desert experience

T: +971 4 404 5880
E: tours@gulfventures.com

gulfventures.com

Leisure Services / Event Services / Tours & Excursions

GULF VENTURES

Destination Management Specialists

tour operators offer variations on the main types of excursions: city tours, desert safaris and mountain safaris. Some offer more unique activities, such as fishing or diving trips, expeditions to the Empty Quarter, helicopter tours and desert driving courses.

Alpha Tours
Al Owais Bldg, Ittihad St Port Saeed **04 294 9888**
alphatoursdubai.com
Map **2 K7** Metro **Deira City Centre**
Alpha Tours provides a full range of tours, including shopping trips, desert safaris, flights and cruises.

Arabian Adventures > p.IBC
Emirates Holiday Bldg Business Bay **04 343 9966**
arabian-adventures.com
Map **2 E6** Metro **Business Bay**
This company offers a range of tours and itineraries, including desert safaris, city tours, sand skiing, dhow cruises, camel riding, and wadi and dune bashing.

Dadabhai Travel
Sama Bldg, Ittihad St Al Nahda 1 **04 220 9393**
dadabhaitravel.ae
Map **2 R7** Metro **Stadium**
An operator with one of the most extensive range of tours in Dubai, covering everything from shopping and culture, to overnight desert camps. The company has a great Bedouin camp, based out near Al Aweer.

Delta Adventures > p.307
New Ruler Bldg Al Hudaiba 1 **04 398 0909**
delta.ae
Map **2 K5** Metro **Al Jafiliya**
Enjoy a thrilling ride in a dune buggy, followed by sand boarding. Also offers other sporting activities, cultural tours and trips to neighbouring emirates.

Desert Adventures
Al Barsha Boutique Bldg Al Barsha 1 **04 450 4450**
desertadventures.com
Map **1 Q6** Metro **Sharaf DG**
Desert Adventures offers a full range of city and desert tours throughout the emirate, with interesting and creative city tours. The company can also arrange trips to Oman and Jordan if you want to travel further afield.

Desert Rangers
Nr American Hospital Oud Metha **04 357 2200**
desertrangers.com
Map **2 K6** Metro **Oud Metha**
Desert Rangers runs a wide variety of standard and specialist desert and mountain tours, including desert safaris with dinner, dune buggy safari, overnight desert safari, wadi and mountain safaris, Dubai dhow dinner cruise, rock climbing, helicopter tours and kayaking.

Desert Safari Abu Dhabi & Dubai
Lake View 316 Bldg Al Thanyah 5 **04 361 7530**
desertsafariabudhabi.ae
Map **1 M5** Metro **Jumeirah Lakes Towers**
Specialising in desert safaris, dune bashing and dune buggying, this company also offers city tours and water-based excursions.

Dream Explorer
Al Musalla Tower Al Hamriya **04 354 4481**
dreamexplorerdubai.com
Map **2 H5** Metro **Al Fahidi**
Try dune buggying or white-knuckle jet boat rides. A luxury option combines dune driving with a visit to the Bab Al Shams Desert Resort.

Dubai Tourism & Travel Services > p.313
Al Abbar Bldg Al Karama **04 336 7727**
dubai-travel.ae
Map **2 K6** Metro **ADCB**
City shopping tours, tours of key city attractions, creek dinner cruises, cultural tours to Sharjah and Ajman, plus desert, mountain and east coast excursions.

Gulf Ventures > p.309
Business Bay **04 404 5880**
gulfventures.com
Map **2 D6** Metro **Business Bay**
Gulf Ventures offer a wide range of activities including Bedouin camps, creek cruises and east coast tours on land and sea, plus fishing, polo and ballooning. More unusually, camel polo is a fun-packed day out.

Lama Tours
Al Sayegh Bldg Oud Metha **04 334 4330**
lamadubai.com
Map **2 L6** Metro **Oud Metha**
Tours include an excellent desert safari experience, dhow cruises, city excursions and fishing tours.

Net Tours > p.311, 315, 481
Emarat Atrium Al Wasl **04 376 2333**
nettoursuae.ae
Map **1 Q6** Metro **Sharaf DG**
Offers mountain tours and treks, theme park excursions, helicopter and balloon flights, dhow dinner cruises and desert safaris, plus of course the usual Bedouin desert campsite experience.

Oasis Palm Tourism
Royal Plaza Bldg, Al Rigga St Al Rigga **04 262 8889**
opdubai.com
Map **2 N5** Metro **Al Rigga**
One of the biggest and best known tour operators, Oasis Palm offers desert safaris, dhow dinner cruises and wadi trips, plus east coast tours, diving and deep sea fishing trips.

Life is **a safari,**
let's conquer it **together**

nettours
L e a d i n g   t h e   w a y . . .

Head Office – Dubai
Al Barsha Boutique Bldg., Office# 105
P.O.Box: 50777
T: +971 04 425 4450
F: +971 04 427 0411

Abu Dhabi Branch:
Khalifa Street, Opp. Sheraton Hotel
P.O.Box: 37907
T: +971 02 679 4656
F: +971 02 671 1232

Orient Tours

Liberty Bldg Al Garhoud **04 282 8238**
orient-tours-uae.com
Map **2 N7** Metro **GGICO**
Orient Tours offers city tours, including trips to the horse and camel races, desert safaris, sea safaris around Musandam, off-road trips to Hatta and day tours of the Empty Quarter in Liwa.

Planet Travel & Tourism

Abulhoul Bldg, Airport St Al Garhoud **04 282 2199**
planetgrouponline.com
Map **2 N7** Metro **GGICO**
A large travel company with plenty of resources to call on, Planet Travel offers coach, heritage and shopping tours within Dubai, as well as a range of safari and desert tours.

Dune Dinners

Enjoy some thrilling off-road desert driving before settling down to watch the sun set behind the majestic Arabian dunes. Starting around 4pm, tours typically pass camel farms and fascinating scenery that provide great photo opportunities. At a traditional Arabian campsite, enjoy a delicious dinner and the calm of a starlit desert night, before returning around 10pm. Make sure you remember your camera to capture the desert bathed in a stunning orange light as the sun sets.

Full-Day Safari

This day-long tour usually passes through traditional Bedouin villages and camel farms in the desert, with a drive through sand dunes of varying colours and heights. Tours often visit either Fossil Rock or the Hajar Mountains. A cold buffet lunch may be provided in the mountains before the drive home.

Hatta Pools Safari

Hatta is a quiet, old-fashioned town nestled in the foothills of the Hajar Mountains, famed for its fresh water rock pools that you can swim in. The full-day trip usually includes a stop at the Hatta Fort Hotel, where you can enjoy the pool, landscaped gardens, archery, and nine-hole golf course. Lunch is served either in the hotel, or alfresco in the mountains. The trip costs Dhs.260-Dhs.350.

Mountain Safari

Normally a full-day tour takes you across to the east coast, heading inland at Dibba and entering the spectacular Hajar Mountain range. You will travel through rugged canyons onto steep winding tracks, past terraced mountainsides and old stone houses. It returns via Dibba, where the journey home to Dubai stops off at the quaint Masafi Market on the way, where you can buy everything from rugs to beach inflatables.

Overnight Safari

This 24 hour tour starts at about 3pm, with a drive through the dunes to a Bedouin-style campsite. Dine under the stars, sleep in the fresh air and wake to the smell of freshly brewed coffee, before heading for the mountains. The drive takes you through spectacular rugged scenery, past dunes and along wadis, before stopping for a buffet lunch and returning to Dubai.

Boat

An evening aboard a dhow, either on Dubai Creek or sailing along the coast, is a wonderfully atmospheric experience. Some companies run regular, scheduled trips, while others will charter out boats to private parties. Many boats also offer dinner cruises from the Bur Dubai side of the creek. Charters of luxury yachts, catamarans and fishing boats are available from several operators, and many firms will consider letting out their tour boats for the right price. If you want to go further afield, a dhow cruise in Musandam is a must and some dhow cruise companies offer transfers from Dubai. Alternatively, a number of dive companies, such as Al Boom Diving, offer sightseeing cruises – either as part of a dive trip or as a separate offering.

4Yacht Arabia

JAFZA View 18 Jabal Ali Ind. 2 **04 886 5755**
4yachtarabia.ae
Map **1 B7** Metro **Jebel Ali**
A luxury yacht charter and sales company with five Dubai-based yachts for charter, plus water taxis, and three vessels moored in Greece, if you fancy a cruising holiday.

Al Boom Tourist Village

Shk Rashid Rd Umm Hurair 2 **04 324 3000**
alboom.ae
Map **2 L8** Metro **Dubai Healthcare City**
Operates several dhows on the creek, with capacities ranging from 20 to 350 passengers. Various packages are available.

Al Marsa Tours & Cargo

University City Rd Sharjah **06 544 1232**
almarsamusandam.com
Runs dhow voyages off Musandam for divers, snorkellers and sightseers, lasting from half a day to a whole week.

Al Wasl Cruising & Fishing

Al Owais Bldg Port Saeed **04 239 4760**
cruiseindubai.com
Map **2 P6** Metro **Deira City Centre**
Specialises in a variety of deep sea fishing trips and yacht charters with a fleet of modern vessels.

ART Marine
Shk Zayed Rd Al Qouz Ind. 1 **04 338 8955**
artmarine.net
Map **2 A6** Metro **Noor Bank**
Offers chartered yacht experiences from locations around the region, including Jumeirah Beach Hotel in Dubai, Emirates Palace and Yas Marina in Abu Dhabi, and the stunning Zighy Marina in Oman.

Athena Charter Yacht
Marina Yacht Club Marsa Dubai **04 362 7900**
Map **1 K5** Metro **Jumeirah Lakes Towers**
A 50 foot yacht available for cruises around Marsa Dubai, the Palm Jumeirah and along the Jumeira coastline, for up to 12 people at a time. On-board dining is also available.

Bateaux Dubai
Nr British Embassy Al Hamriya **04 814 5553**
bateauxdubai.com
Map **2 M5** Metro **BurJuman**
This sleek sightseeing vessel offers daily tours, but it's the dinner cruises that offer the best and most unique experience. The boat can also be privately chartered to cater for parties of up to 300 people.

Bristol Middle East Yacht Solution
Marina Walk Marsa Dubai **04 366 3538**
bristol-middleeast.com
Map **1 L5** Metro **DAMAC**
This Marina-based company offers charters and packages on boats of all shapes and sizes, from luxury yachts to its old wooden dhow, Captain Jack, which regularly takes one-hour pleasure cruises along the coast from Marsa Dubai. The firm puts together land and air tours too.

Cruise With Nakheel
Nakheel Sales Centre Al Sufouh 2
nakheel.com
Map **1 N5** Metro **Nakheel**
Experience striking views of the Palm Jumeirah from the deck of a double-decker houseboat or smaller vessel. The 'Cruise with Nakheel' service runs trips for groups of up to 12, 15 and 30 people around the landmark island, with prices starting from around Dhs.1,000 per boat.

Divaz
Jebel Ali Golf Resort Mena Jabal Ali **04 814 5555**
Metro **Jebel Ali**
More of a floating party than traditional boat trip, Divaz offers chilled dining experiences including a seafood buffet with a selection of fresh fish for only Dhs.250 per person. It also caters for raucous brunches or elegant night-time gatherings., all out on the open waves.

El Mundo
DIMC Marsa Dubai **050 551 7406**
elmundodubai.com
Map **1 M5** Metro **Nakheel**
El Mundo is a 60 foot catamaran that offers four-hour cruises on Thursdays and Fridays, and can be privately chartered for all manner of occasions.

JA Jebel Ali Golf Resort
Nr Palm Jebel Ali Mena Jabal Ali **04 814 5555**
jaresortshotels.com
Metro **Jebel Ali**
One or two-hour long leisure boat trips for up to seven people on board Club Joumana's 36ft fishing boat.

Khasab Travel & Tours
Al Muraqqabat **04 266 9950**
khasabtours.com
Map **2 P6** Metro **Al Rigga**
Runs a dhow cruise from Khasab in Musandam that includes lunch, refreshments, snorkelling gear and a spot of fishing. Khasab Travel & Tours can also organise pick-ups from Dubai.

OCEAN Independence
Wafi Residences Umm Hurair 2 **04 324 3327**
oceanindependence.com
Map **2 L7** Metro **Dubai Healthcare City**
Provides a range of luxury yacht charters from short trips to overnight stays and holidays on the water. Also sells vessels and runs charters internationally.

Sheesa Beach Dive Center
Musandam Dibba **050 333 6046**
sheesabeach.com
Exceptionally fun day, overnight and week-long dhow cruises in Musandam, with transfers from Dubai available. Diving trips, PADI training and camping are also offered.

Tour Dubai
Oud Metha **04 336 8407**
tour-dubai.com
Map **2 L6** Metro **Oud Metha**
Offers a variety of creek dhow tours and charter packages that range from romantic dinners for two to corporate hospitality for up to 200 guests.

Ultimate Charter
Fairmont Trade Center 1 **04 346 4194**
dubaiultimatecharter.com
Map **2 H5** Metro **World Trade Centre**
As well as two-hour dhow dinner cruises along Marsa Dubai and the Palm Jumeirah, there are catamaran party cruises, luxury motor yachts, super yachts and mega yachts available for charter, and fishing boats offering a guaranteed catch.

Life is **a safari,**
let's conquer it **together**

nettours
Leading the way...

Waterworld Yacht Rental
Marina Yacht Club Marsa Dubai **04 422 8729**
waterworldyachtrental.com
Map **1 K5** Metro **Jumeirah Lakes Towers**
As well as yacht rentals from Dhs.699 per hour, this
company offers deep sea fishing trips, BBQ cruises and
dhow dinner cruises.

Xclusive Yachts Sport Fishing & Yacht Charter
Marina Yacht Club Marsa Dubai **04 432 7233**
xclusiveyachts.com
Map **1 K5** Metro **Jumeirah Lakes Towers**
Offering everything from 22ft to 90ft boats, Xclusive
can organise sightseeing or fishing trips for groups
of family or friends, or you can simply charter a boat
and follow your own itinerary. Watersports including
banana boating and parasailing can be included.

Dhow And Out
An option for large independent groups is to charter
a dhow from the fishermen at Dibba on the east coast
to travel up the coast to Musandam. If you're prepared
to haggle you can usually knock the price down
substantially, especially if you know a bit of Arabic.
Expect to pay around Dhs.2,500 per day for a dhow
large enough to take 20-25 people, or Dhs.100 per
hour for a smaller one. You'll need to take your own
food and water, as nothing is supplied onboard except
ice lockers suitable for storing supplies. Conditions are
basic, but you'll have the freedom to plan your own
route and see the beautiful fjord-like scenery of
Musandam from a traditional wooden dhow.

The waters in the area are beautifully clear and
turtles and dolphins can often be seen from the boat,
although sometimes unfavourable weather conditions
can seriously reduce visibility for divers. If you leave
from Dibba (or Daba), Omani visas are not required,
even though you enter Omani waters.

It is also possible to arrange stops along the coast
and it's worth taking camping equipment for the
night, although you can sleep on board. This kind
of trip is ideal for diving, but you should hire any
equipment you may need before you get to Dibba. If
diving is not your thing, you can just spend the day
swimming, snorkelling and soaking up the sun.

Aerial Tours
With its soaring skyscrapers, rolling sand dunes and
spectacular man-made islands, Dubai from the air
is an impressive and truly unique sight. Swoop over
the cityscape in a helicopter, fly along the coast in a
seaplane, or take in the serenity of the desert from
a graceful hot air balloon flight – any one of these
experiences will live long in the memory.

Aerogulf Services
Dubai International Airport **04 877 6120**
aerogulfservices.com
Map **2 N7** Metro **GGICO**
Based at Dubai International Airport, this company
provides helicopter tours over the city and its main
landmarks. A half-hour tour for four people costs
Dhs.3,200 or you can opt to charter a chopper by the
hour and choose your route.

Amigos Balloons
04 289 9295
amigos-balloons.com
Take a dawn hot air balloon flight over the desert out
near Fossil Rock and watch the changing colour of the
sands as the sun rises. Flights operate from September
to June and cost Dhs.950 per person.

Balloon Adventures Emirates
12th St Al Rashidiya **04 285 4949**
ballooning.ae
Map **2 P11** Metro **Rashidiya**
There's nothing better than taking in the serenity
of the desert from a graceful hot air balloon flight.
Balloon Adventures Emirates organises tours, with
flights departing before sunrise. Flights depart before
sunrise between October and May, and are followed
by dune driving.

Fujairah Aviation Academy
Fujairah **09 222 4747**
fujaa.ae
This company offers an enthralling bird's-eye view of
Fujairah's coastline, rugged mountains, villages and
date plantations. Flights can accommodate one to
three people.

Gulf Ventures > p.309
Business Bay **04 404 5880**
gulfventures.com
Map **2 D6** Metro **Business Bay**
In addition to offering desert and mountain tours,
Gulf Ventures also offers several ways for you to view
the emirate from great heights. Fly over Fossil Rock in
a hot air balloon, take a private helicopter along the
coastline and over the Palm and Burj Al Arab, or soar
through the sky in a sea plane.

Seawings
JA Jebel Ali Golf Resort Mena Jabal Ali **04 807 0708**
seawings.ae
Metro **Jebel Ali**
A Seawings flight is often top on most residents'
bucket list. Take off from the water in a seaplane from
Jabal Ali or Dubai Creek for spectacular flights over the
Gulf and city. Various package options are available for
a memory that will last a lifetime.

HOTELS

Hotels in Dubai, range from one of the most superlative and opulent in the world, the Burj Al Arab, with a rack rate in the region of Dhs.11,000 for a night in a standard suite, right down to the cheapest digs in areas such as Deira costing under Dhs.200 a night. There are an increasing number of internationally branded budget hotels, plus a handful of B&Bs. While the hotels at the higher end of the market offer superb surroundings and facilities, those at the cheaper end vary – you get what you pay for. There are dozens of the world's leading hotel brands to be found here, many of them housed in some of the city's most iconic buildings.

The Dubai Department of Tourism & Commerce Marketing (DTCM) oversees a hotel classification system that gives an internationally recognised star rating to hotels and hotel apartments. This is being updated to include a budget hotel category, and Gold and Platinum Accolades for outstanding hotels and resorts.

Record breakers

Dubai's penchant for showing off has resulted in some stupendously extravagant places to stay. From one of the most expensive hotels in the world, the Burj Al Arab, to the tallest hotel in the world, the JW Marriott Marquis. Then there's The Meydan Hotel, which hosts the richest horse race in the world, the Dubai World Cup, and the Armani Hotel, nestled at the base of the tallest man-made structure in the world, practically every inch of which has been personally designed by Armani himself. And that's before you head out to Atlantis on the Palm Jumeirah – once the world's largest man-made island.

Staycations

Forgo the hassle of travel and take a staycation. Many hotels also offer seasonal discounts to GCC residents, particularly in the hot summer months when prices can be 50% lower than at peak times for a bargain weekend 'away'. These hotels are the best Dubai has to offer for a luxurious beach break.

Anantara Dubai The Palm
The Crescent East Nakhlat Jumeira **04 567 8888**
anantara.com
Map **1 Q3** Metro **Nakheel**
This stunning hotel on the eastern crescent of Palm Jumeirah combines the hospitality of Thailand,

the luxury of Arabia and the iconic over-water accommodation of the Maldives. Splash out on a villa on stilts hovering above the ocean, or opt for a lagoon villa, where you can step straight into the pool from the balcony of your stylish room. Impeccable service, a stunning infinity pool and beach side dining round off the incredible experience.

Atlantis The Palm > p.275
Crescent St Nakhlat Jumeira **04 426 0000**
atlantisthepalm.com
Map **1 N1** Metro **Nakheel**
With a staggering 1,539 rooms and suites, all with views of the sea or the Palm Jumeirah, Atlantis is certainly one of Dubai's grandest hotels. It has no less than four fancy restaurants featuring the cuisine of Michelin-starred chefs, including a branch of the world-famous chain Nobu. It is also home to Aquaventure and the Lost Chambers aquarium. The dance and rock music event, Sandance is held on the hotel's Nasimi Beach.

Burj Al Arab
Jumeira St Umm Suqeim 3 **04 301 7777**
jumeirah.com
Map **1 S4** Metro **First Gulf Bank**
Standing on its own man-made island, this dramatic Dubai icon's unique architecture is recognised around the world. Suites have two floors and are serviced by a team of butlers. To get into the hotel as a non-guest, you will need a restaurant reservation.

Dubai Marine Beach Resort
Jumeira St Jumeira 1 **04 346 1111**
dxbmarine.com
Map **2 H4** Metro **World Trade Centre**
This beachside hotel has 195 villa-style rooms nestled among lush, green landscaped gardens, waterfalls and streams. The grounds offer three swimming pools, a spa, a health club and a small private beach. The restaurants and bars are perennially popular, especially the Ibiza-esque Sho Cho and beautiful hangout, Boudoir.

Fairmont The Palm
The Trunk Nakhlat Jumeira **04 457 3388**
fairmont.com
Map **1 N3** Metro **Nakheel**
Located on the trunk of the Palm Jumeirah, this hotel enjoys impressive views of Marsa Dubai, with the skyscrapers of JBR as a backdrop. Relax and unwind at the Willow Stream Spa; enjoy the great outdoors at the hotel's private beach club with four swimming pools and outdoor leisure facilities; and take your pick from seven restaurants and lounges, serving Brazilian, pan-Chinese, Middle Eastern, Indian, Mediterranean and Asian cuisine. Service is attentive, and the sea views (especially from upper floors) are stunning.

Jumeirah Beach Hotel
Jumeira St Umm Suqeim 3 **04 348 0000**
jumeirah.com
Map **1 S4** Metro **First Gulf Bank**
Shaped like an ocean wave, with a fun and colourful
interior, the hotel has 598 rooms and suites and 19
private villas, all with a sea view. It is also home to
some excellent food and beverage outlets, including
Jamie's Italian restaurant, Uptown for happy hour
cocktails and a great view of the Burj Al Arab. The
popular 360° nightclub is perched at the end of a
walkway out into the sea. You haven't done Dubai
until you've danced on its open-air terrace.

Jumeirah Zabeel Saray
The Crescent West Nakhlat Jumeira **04 453 0000**
jumeirahzabeelsaray.com
Map **1 L3**
So opulent, it was used for the lavish party scenes in
Mission Impossible: Ghost Protocol, Zabeel Saray is an
architectural wonder, drawing on Arabic and Turkish
influences. It's a huge hotel with a gorgeous outdoor
pool overlooking the sea. There are several excellent
outlets including the super cool Voda bar, although
the real draw is the spa which is one of the world's
biggest and best.

Madinat Jumeirah
Jumeira St Al Sufouh 1 **04 366 8888**
jumeirah.com
Map **1 R5** Metro **Mall of the Emirates**
This extravagant resort has two hotels, Al Qasr and
Mina A'Salam, with no fewer than 940 luxurious rooms
and suites, and the exclusive Dar Al Masyaf summer
houses, all linked by man-made waterways navigated
by wooden abra boats, which whisk guests around
the resort. Nestled between the two hotels is the
Souk Madinat, with a plethora of popular shops, bars
and restaurants all located inside a faux Arabian-style
market. There's also a theatre that hosts international
musicals, comedy shows and dance events. A third
hotel is due to open in 2015.

One&Only Royal Mirage > p.173
Al Sufouh St Al Sufouh 2 **04 399 9999**
oneandonlyresorts.com
Map **1 M5** Metro **Nakheel**
This stunningly beautiful resort is home to three
different properties: The Palace, Arabian Court, and
the Residence & Spa. The service and dining (opt for
the Beach, Bar & Grill for a romantic evening out; try
delectable Moroccan cuisine in the opulent Tagine;
or enjoy cocktails with a view in The Rooftop and
Sports Lounge) are renowned, and a luxury spa
treatment here is the ultimate indulgence. Its equally
extravagant sister property sits across the water on
the outer reaches of the Palm Jumeirah.

Rixos The Palm
The Crescent East Nakhlat Jumeira **04 457 5555**
rixos.com
Map **1 P3** Metro **Nakheel**
Located on the eastern crescent of the Palm
Jumeirah, Rixos The Palm boasts incredible views in
all directions – the Arabian Gulf, the Palm and the
Dubai coastline – with many of the city's landmarks
in sight, not least the Burj Al Arab, Burj Khalifa and
Marsa Dubai. It is a relaxing resort on a peaceful slice
of beach, with a few dining options, great lounging
areas and luxurious spa.

Sofitel The Palm
The Crescent East Nakhlat Jumeira **04 455 6677**
sofitel.com
Map **1 P1** Metro **Nakheel**
The sunny Polynesian island theme to this hotel, with
its fresh flowers on the walls and Maui beach bar,
makes this a great escape from the city – especially
due to its location right on the top of the Palm, which
gives the feeling of being on an island out at sea with
Dubai viewed in the distance.
   Lounge in private cabanas discretely dotted around
the large main pool, find yourself one of the secret
Jacuzzi pools, or take a pedalo from the beach jetty.
By night, you can enjoy sundowners on the rooftop
bar before dining at one of Dubai's most fantastic
restaurants (you will be wowed), Studio du Chef. Hong
Loong is the hotel's Chinese restaurant and is also
exceptionally good. The kids' pool with waterslides is
more than enough to keep the little ones happy, too.

Visitors In Town?

You may soon find a continual stream of friends
and family arriving and needing a place to stay. We
recommend a range of hotels that offer something to
visitors, be it great spa facilities or popular restaurants,
at a variety of budgets.

The Address Downtown Dubai
Shk Mohd Bin Rashid Blvd Downtown Dubai, Burj
Khalifa **04 436 8888**
theaddress.com
Map **2 F7** Metro **Burj Khalifa/Dubai Mall**
With three main properties in prime glitzy locations,
this group of hotels is sure to please. The Address
Downtown has breathtaking views of the Burj Khalifa,
beautiful interiors and eight dining outlets (including
Neos, the panoramic bar on the 63rd floor), while
The Address Dubai Mall and The Address Dubai
Marina are handily attached to major shopping and
leisure hotspots making them a perfect choice for
shopaholics. The marina location has a terrific infinity
pool overlooking the stunning Marsa Dubai skyline.

The Address Downtown Dubai and Dubai Fountain

One&Only Royal Mirage Dubai

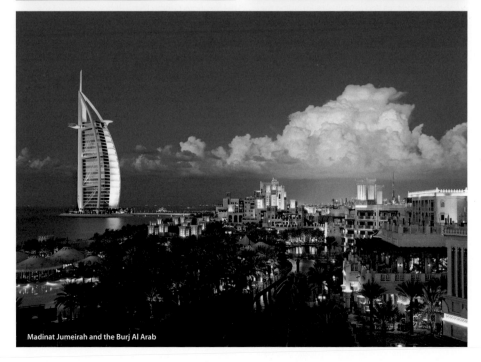

Madinat Jumeirah and the Burj Al Arab

Al Bustan Rotana
Casablanca St Al Garhoud **04 282 0000**
rotana.com
Map **2 N8** Metro **Airport Terminal 1**
A central location near the airport, Deira City Centre and the Dubai Creek makes this hotel accessible for tourists and business visitors. Renowned for its good restaurants, with Benihana (Japanese), Blue Elephant (Thai) and Rodeo Grill (steakhouse) standing out.

Al Manzil Downtown Dubai
Downtown Dubai, Burj Khalifa
04 428 5888
almanzilhotel.ae
Map **2 F7** Metro **Burj Khalifa/Dubai Mall**
In the heart of Old Town, this beautiful four-star hotel is conveniently located for business and leisure trips. It also houses Nezesaussi Grill, the popular Antipodean sports bar, and The Courtyard, a beautiful and atmospheric mezze and shisha cafe.

Al Murooj Rotana
Al Sa'ada St Trade Center 2 **04 321 1111**
rotana.com
Map **2 G6** Metro **Burj Khalifa/Dubai Mall**
A luxurious resort hotel that is popular with both leisure tourists and business travellers, being ideally located right between Downtown and DIFC. It has a number of good bars and restaurants, including the popular and often raucous Double Decker bar.

Amwaj Rotana Jumeirah Beach Residence
Al Mamsha St, JBR Marsa Dubai **04 428 2000**
rotana.com
Map **1 K5** Metro **Jumeirah Lakes Towers**
Located on the bustling strip along new Dubai's seafront, this smart 200 room hotel features an outdoor pool, a fitness centre and great dining venues including Italian terrace bar Rosso and teppanyaki restaurant Benihana.

Armani Hotel Dubai
Downtown Dubai, Burj Khalifa **04 888 3888**
dubai.armanihotels.com
Map **2 F6** Metro **Burj Khalifa/Dubai Mall**
This luxurious hotel in the world's tallest tower, is remarkably without pretension, but its designer credentials are noticeable down to the nuts and bolts. As well as elegant suites kitted out with Armani/Casa goods, it is home to an Armani spa and excellent dining.

Asiana Hotel
Salah Al Din Al Muraqqabat **04 238 7777**
asianahoteldubai.com
Map **2 N5** Metro **Salah Al Din**
With a choice of four restaurants specialising in Chinese, Filipino, Japanese and Korean, this Deira-

based five-star hotel is worth the trip. And if the quality, value and variety of food doesn't lure you in, then the trendy decor with Asian flair will do its very best to.

Bonnington Jumeirah Lakes Towers
Cluster J JLT, Al Thanyah 5 **04 356 0000**
bonningtontower.com
Map **1 K5** Metro **Jumeirah Lakes Towers**
Containing both hotel suites and serviced apartments, as well as six restaurants and bars and a leisure deck with infinity pool, it has great connections to Marsa Dubai via the nearby metro.

City Seasons Hotel
Al Maktoum St Port Saeed 1 **04 294 2777**
cityseasonshotels.com
Map **2 N6** Metro **Deira City Centre**
A decent and clean hotel with great customer service in the bustling area of Deira, not far from the airport. A good value for money option. City Seasons also has partner hotels in Al Ain, Abu Dhabi and Muscat.

Conrad Dubai
Shk Zayed Rd Trade Center 1 **04 444 7444**
hilton.com
Map **2 H5** Metro **Emirates Towers**
For stunning views over the sea and skyline, head to the luxurious Conrad Dubai. It boasts some of the best nightlife spots in the city, including the Parisian-inspired bar Cave and the Marco Pierre White Grill. There's a luxury spa, yoga and fitness instruction, and a hidden oasis on the sixth floor.

Al Manzil Downtown Dubai

Crowne Plaza Dubai

Shk Zayed Rd Trade Center 1 **04 331 1111**
ihg.com
Map **2 H5** Metro **Emirates Towers**
One of Dubai's older five-star hotels, with an excellent
collection of food and beverage outlets including
Trader Vic's, Wagamama and Oscar's Vine Society. It's
centrally located on Sheikh Zayed Road, so it's only a
short drive to the beaches, malls and nightspots.

Crowne Plaza Dubai Festival City

Nr Dubai Festival City Mall, Al Kheeran **04 701 2222**
ihg.com
Map **2 L9** Metro **Emirates**
On the banks of the Creek, this Crowne Plaza is
excellently positioned within the Festival City
complex. One of its highlights is the Belgian Beer Cafe,
an atmospheric bar that serves a great selection of
European beers and is extremely popular with Dubai
residents and visitors alike.

Dubai Marriott Harbour

Al Sufouh St Marsa Dubai **04 319 4000**
dubaimarriottharbourhotel.com
Map **1 L5** Metro **DAMAC**
With 261 spacious suites, each with its own fitted
kitchen, staying in The Harbour is like having your very
own luxury apartment. The hotel is home to a range
of dining options including The Observatory (offering
great views from the 52nd floor) and 24 hour deli
Counter Culture.

Dusit Thani Dubai

Shk Zayed Rd Trade Center 2 **04 343 3333**
dusit.com
Map **2 G6** Metro **Burj Khalifa/Dubai Mall**
This member of the upmarket Thai hotel chain is
situated in the 'clasped hands' (or 'pair of trousers')
building on the main stretch of Sheikh Zayed Road.
It features 321 rooms, and several food and beverage
outlets including Benjarong, the 'royal Thai' restaurant
and the Champagne Lounge. The hotel is walking
distance from the metro and the Burj Khalifa.

Emirates Grand Hotel

Shk Zayed Rd Trade Center 2 **04 323 0000**
emiratesgrandhotel.com
Map **2 G6** Metro **Financial Centre**
Next to the Burj Khalifa and the Dubai Mall, this
non-alcoholic hotel boasts serious style. The rooftop
terrace is a must-see for its panoramic city and sea
views, and you can also relax there with a traditional
Arabic shisha. Chill out further at the wellness centre
with its sauna, hot tub and steam room, or pump
some iron at the gym. The hotel is completed with four
restaurants, which serve a variety of food including
Lebanese and Turkish.

Fairmont Dubai

Shk Zayed Rd Trade Center 1 **04 332 5555**
fairmont.com
Map **2 H5** Metro **World Trade Centre**
Home to the legendary Spectrum On One restaurant,
a beautiful rooftop pool and the renowned The Spa at
Fairmont Dubai, this hotel is as notable for its modern
interior as it is for its striking architecture, which is
based on traditional Arabian windtowers.

Gloria Hotel

Shk Zayed Rd Al Sufouh 2 **04 399 6666**
gloriahoteldubai.com
Map **1 P5** Metro **Dubai Internet City**
With a spa, gym, pool and excellent location next to
the metro, this is a good hotel for those wanting easy
links to Dubai's top attractions.

Grand Excelsior

Nr Mall of the Emirates Al Barsha 1 **04 444 9999**
grandexcelsior.ae
Map **1 R7** Metro **Mall of the Emirates**
This 230 plus room hotel offers luxury amenities
including a pretty rooftop swimming pool and a
well-equipped gym. F&B outlets include an all-day
dining restaurant, the Oak 'n' Barrel pub, and a
Mediterranean venue.

Grand Hyatt

Shk Rashid Rd Umm Hurair 2 **04 317 1234**
dubai.grand.hyatt.com
Map **2 L8** Metro **Dubai Healthcare City**
The hotel is a strange shape when viewed from
ground level, but from the air the shape of this
building spells out the word 'Dubai' in Arabic. It
has excellent leisure facilities, a great selection of
restaurants, and one of the most impressive lobbies
in Dubai.

Grosvenor House

Al Sufouh St Marsa Dubai **04 399 8888**
grosvenorhouse-dubai.com
Map **1 L5** Metro **DAMAC**
This neon-blue skyscraper at the mouth of Marsa Dubai
is run by Le Meridien group, and features guest rooms,
serviced apartments and some iconic nightlife venues:
Buddha Bar, Gary Rhodes' Mezzanine and the crow's
nest Bar 44 are all well worth a visit, with a second
tower adding the likes of Toro Toro and Embassy. There's
also a branch of luxury male-only spa 1847 here.

H Hotel

Shk Zayed Rd Trade Center 1 **04 501 8888**
h-hotel.com
Map **2 J5** Metro **World Trade Centre**
Previously The Monarch, this stylish hotel may have
changed names, but its popular restaurants including

Okku and Ruth's Chris, thankfully, stay the same. With 236 rooms and suites, including 53 serviced residential apartments, this hotel has one of the most desirable addresses in Dubai: One Sheikh Zayed Road.

Habtoor Grand Beach
Al Sufouh St Marsa Dubai **04 399 5000**
habtoorhotels.com
Map **1 L4** Metro **DAMAC**
The twin-towered Habtoor Grand, on the beach at the northern end of Marsa Dubai, offers 442 spacious rooms and suites with garden or sea views. Pools, restaurants and bars are set amid the hotel's tropical gardens bordering the Arabian Gulf, while The Underground bar draws in the expat football fan crowd for its multiple screens.

Hilton Dubai Creek
Baniyas St Riggat Al Buteen **04 227 1111**
hilton.com
Map **2 M6** Metro **Al Rigga**
With very flash yet understated elegance, this ultra-minimalist hotel features interiors of wood, glass and chrome. Centrally located and overlooking the Dubai Creek, with splendid views of the Arabian dhow trading posts, the hotel has two renowned restaurants: Glasshouse Brasserie and the Dubai gastronomic darling, Table 9.

Hilton Dubai Jumeirah Resort
Al Mamsha St, JBR Marsa Dubai **04 399 1111**
hilton.com
Map **1 K4** Metro **Jumeirah Lakes Towers**
Situated between The Walk and the JBR beach, the Hilton Dubai Jumeirah features excellent restaurants, including the Italian BiCE and the Latin American meat feast venue Pachanga, as well as a sports bar, Studio One. There's a beach bar too – Wavebreaker – which is a great spot for sundowners. New mall development The Beach at JBR is on its doorstep.

Hyatt Regency
Al Khaleej St Al Corniche **04 209 1234**
dubai.regency.hyatt.com
Map **2 N4** Metro **Palm Deira**
The restaurants alone in this hotel are well worth fighting the Deira traffic for – particularly Al Dawaar, Dubai's only revolving restaurant which boasts amazing views of the creek and coast. All 400 rooms have creek views too.

InterContinental Dubai Festival City
Nr Dubai Festival City Mall, Al Kheeran **04 701 1111**
ichotelsgroup.com
Map **2 L9** Metro **Emirates**
Worth a visit if only to taste fine fare served up in Michelin-starred chef Pierre Gagnaire's excellent

restaurant, or to enjoy the panoramic views from the Eclipse bar. The hotel also features an excellent spa, and access to the Festival Waterfront Centre.

JA Ocean View
Al Mamsha St, JBR Marsa Dubai **04 814 5599**
jaresortshotels.com
Map **1 K5** Metro **Jumeirah Lakes Towers**
A great location right on the edge of The Walk and The Beach at JBR, this hotel boasts to be 'Dubai's only four-star hotel on the beach'. All rooms have sea views, and aqua-lovers can enjoy the swimming pool, the local beach or jump on a complimentary shuttle to the private beach at JA Jebel Ali Golf Resort. Dining highlights include Fogo Vivo, a Brazilian steakhouse with an open kitchen, and The Whistler, a cheese and wine bar. Popular with families, the hotel has a shaded children's pool and kids' club for three to 11 year olds.

Jumeirah Creekside
Al Rebat St Al Garhoud **04 230 8555**
jumeirah.com
Map **2 M8** Metro **GGICO**
A sleek yet eclectically designed hotel with an abundance of venues. Start your day at the lively Italian cafe, go light and healthy on lunch at Plumeria, choose either steak or seafood at Blue Flame or south Asian flavours at Nomad for dinner, and then finish off the evening with mint and rum infused mojitos at the rooftop lounge Cu-ba. From the statement art, to the personalised service, to the new concept menus, this hotel breathes boutique and is sure to 'wow'.

Jumeirah Emirates Towers
Shk Zayed Rd Trade Center 2 **04 330 0000**
jumeirah.com
Map **2 H6** Metro **Financial Centre**
Sophisticated and elegant, this hotel forms one part of Dubai's iconic twin skyscrapers. It has 400 rooms, some excellent restaurants and bars (including Harry Ghatto's for hilarious karaoke nights), as well as an exclusive shopping mall. Other leisure facilities include the Talise spa and health club, offering massage treatments and a sauna.

JW Marriott Marquis
Shk Zayed Rd Business Bay **04 414 0000**
marriott.com
Map **2 D6** Metro **Business Bay**
This long awaited five-star hotel which opened in 2012, rises above Business Bay at a staggering 355m, making it the world's tallest freestanding hotel. Spread across two iconic towers, there are some top-notch restaurants, including the hyped restaurant Rang Mahal by Atul Kochhar, the fine-dining steakhouse Prime 68 and the impressive and elegant Italian restaurant, Positano.

JW Marriott Marquis

Kempinski Mall of the Emirates
Shk Zayed Rd Al Barsha 1 **04 341 0000**
kempinski.com
Map **1 R6** Metro **Mall of the Emirates**
The hotel has more than 400 deluxe rooms, a spa, infinity pool, fitness centre, tennis court and the attached Ski Dubai. Check into one of the 15 unique ski chalets, remove your snow boots, put your feet up by the (fake) fire and tuck into an après-ski afternoon tea while enjoying the view of the piste from your room.

Le Meridien Dubai
Airport St Al Garhoud **04 217 0000**
lemeridien-dubai.com
Map **2 N8** Metro **Airport Terminal 1**
Just a stone's throw from Dubai Airport and the Aviation Club, guests and visitors can enjoy many excellent restaurants inside the hotel, many of which share a large alfresco terrace in the cooler months. With 383 rooms, the hotel is also home to trendy nightspot Warehouse and Antipodean restaurant Yalumba, which offers a famous Friday brunch.

Le Meridien Mina Seyahi
Al Sufouh St Marsa Dubai **04 399 3333**
lemeridien-minaseyahi.com
Map **1 M5** Metro **Nakheel**
Home to legendary beach bar and ever-popular expat hangout, Barasti, this hotel has a great stretch of beach overlooking the Palm, with watersports on offer. There's also a rooftop pool and some rooms come with a personalised butler service.

Le Royal Meridien Beach Resort
Al Sufouh St Marsa Dubai **04 399 5555**
leroyalmeridien-dubai.com
Map **1 L5** Metro **DAMAC**
Large-scale beach resort at Marsa Dubai. Good leisure facilities and a big selection of bars and restaurants including Mexican Maya and seafood outlet Me Vida. A shuttle bus transfers guests through the Marina to allow access to the facilities of the Grosvenor House.

Media One
Dubai Media City Al Sufouh 2 **04 427 1000**
mediaonehotel.com
Map **1 M5** Metro **Nakheel**
This fun, funky and functional hotel is great if you need to be in reach of Media City. The rooms are geared towards the business traveller's needs, with workspaces, wi-fi and flat screen TVs, but they certainly don't lack style. Z:ONE and the Dek on 8 are popular post-work haunts, while The Med hosts a fun Friday brunch.

Media Rotana
Hessa St TECOM, Al Thanyah 1 **04 435 0000**
rotana.com
Map **1 P6** Metro **Dubai Internet City**
Ideally located close to Dubai Media City and Dubai Internet City, this city hotel boasts an outdoor pool and massage rooms. On the dining front, Prego's restaurant offers a cosy ambience with an open kitchen; Channels features live cooking; or you can try designer beers at Nelson's pub. Hugely popular is the alfresco brunch on The Terrace, held every Friday.

Melia Dubai
Kuwait St Al Raffa **04 386 8111**
melia-dubai.com
Map **2 K4** Metro **Al Fahidi**
Contemporary and elegant, the Melia stands out in Bur Dubai for all the right reasons. Featuring two high-profile restaurants – Titanic and Signature – and a luxurious spa, this is a hidden gem worth discovering. The rooms are tastefully decorated, and the TVs disguised as mirrors add a stylish touch.

The Meydan
Meydan St Nadd Al Shiba 1 **04 381 3333**
meydanhotels.com
Map **2 D10**
There's no better place to watch the racing action at The Meydan horserace track than from the rooftop infinity pool of this decadent, five-star, landmark hotel, but the striking modern design, spa and excellent outlets including Prime and Shiba make this hotel a deluxe destination in itself. Guests can also enjoy The Track; the hotel's stunning pay-to-play golf course for all abilities. Guests can make use of free shuttle buses to destinations around Dubai.

Movenpick Hotel Ibn Battuta Gate
Nr Ibn Battuta Mall Jabal Ali 1 **04 444 0000**
moevenpick-hotels.com
Map **1 G5** Metro **Ibn Battuta**
This five-star hotel is themed on the territories to which the 14th century explorer Ibn Battuta travelled. The pool terrace offers stunning views over 'new Dubai' and its food outlets represent the cuisines of the world. Guests can also take the free shuttle to the Palm and use the facilities at Oceana Beach Club.

Movenpick Hotel Jumeirah Beach
Al Mamsha St JBR, Marsa Dubai **04 449 8888**
moevenpick-hotels.com
Map **1 K5** Metro **Jumeirah Lakes Towers**
Situated on The Walk at JBR this five-star, 300 room hotel has much to recommend it, not least its beachfront location and stunning sea-view pool bar, but also a couple of decent restaurants.

The Oberoi
The Oberoi Centre Business Bay **04 444 1444**
oberoihotels.com
Map **2 E6** Metro **Business Bay**
The latest hotel to open up in the Business Bay district is The Oberoi Dubai – the first high-end Indian hotelier to hit the UAE's shores. Everything from the beautifully modern decor to the perfectly mannered staff ensures that a stay here is a peaceful and magical one. In addition to the pampering services of an on call butler – yes, each of the hotel's 252 rooms are sated with this gem – there's also in-room check-in, famous

nightclubs and a fantastic tapas-style brunch at Nine7One. Dubai Mall is only a 10 minute drive away.

One&Only The Palm
The Crescent West Nakhlat Jumeira **04 440 1010**
oneandonlyresorts.com
Map **1 L3** Metro **Nakheel**
A stunning boutique resort at the end of the west crescent on the Palm intended to create an intimate and indulgent setting. Designed in an Andalusian style, the 64 rooms, 26 suites and four beachfront villas feature free-standing bath tubs and rain showers, plus private terraces or balconies that take in the lights of Marsa Dubai. Among the highlights is restaurant STAY by Yannick Alléno and the romantic alfresco 101 Dining Lounge and Bar.

The Palace Downtown Dubai
Nr Dubai Mall Downtown Dubai, Burj Khalifa **04 428 7888**
theaddress.com
Map **2 F6** Metro **Burj Khalifa/Dubai Mall**
Palatial indeed, The Palace, and many of its luxurious and beautifully designed suites look out onto the mighty Burj Khalifa and the Dubai Fountain, and boasts a beautiful spa – guests can even have a treatment at a poolside cabana while the Dubai Fountain is in full swing. There are some excellent restaurants, including the renowned Argentinian restaurant Asado and Thiptara.

Park Hyatt Dubai
Nr Dubai Creek Golf & Yacht Club Port Saeed **04 602 1234**
dubai.park.hyatt.com
Map **2 M7** Metro **GGICO**
Enjoying a prime waterfront location within the grounds of Dubai Creek Golf & Yacht Club, the Park Hyatt is Mediterranean in style with low-rise buildings, natural colours and stylish decor. The hotel has 225 rooms and suites, all with beautiful views, as well as some great dining outlets and a luxurious spa. Excellent restaurants include The Thai Kitchen and Traiteur.

Pullman Deira City Centre
Ittihad St Port Saeed **04 294 1222**
pullmanhotels.com
Map **2 N7** Metro **Deira City Centre**
The Pullman is in a great spot overlooking Dubai Creek and the Golf & Yacht Club. Its vibrant, modern and spacious rooms have fantastic creek views and the 24 hour chic lobby lounge always has a welcoming coffee on hand. The hotel's Medley restaurant offers the added entertainment of live cooking stations and after dinner, guests can enjoy the stunning rooftop bar Azure – a great place to watch the dusk roll in. Relaxation is available at Soma Spa.

Radisson Royal

Shk Zayed Rd Trade Center 1 **04 308 0000**
radissonblu.com
Map **2 H5** Metro **Emirates Towers**
Within walking distance of the World Trade Centre
Metro Station, this city centre hotel is a popular choice
with business travellers. But its appeal is far-reaching,
thanks to its spa, Japanese restaurant Icho and, above
all, trendy London nightclub Mo*Vida.

Ramada Plaza JBR > p.397

Bahar 7, Jumeirah Beach Residence Marsa Dubai
04 439 8888
ramadaplazajbr.com
Map **1 K5** Metro **Jumeirah Lakes Towers**
Dubai's marina and pedestrianised leisure areas The
Beach and The Walk are on the doorstep. There are
five international restaurants, a heated outdoor pool,
health club, sauna, and children's playground.

Ritz-Carlton Dubai

Al Mamsha St, Jumeirah Beach Residence
Marsa Dubai **04 399 4000**
ritzcarlton.com
Map **1 L4** Metro **DAMAC**
Even though it is the only low-rise building amid the
sea of marina towers behind it, all 138 rooms have
beautiful views of the Gulf – The Ritz-Carlton was,
after all, here years before the rest of Marsa Dubai was
built. Afternoon tea in the Lobby Lounge is a must,
and there are several other excellent restaurants and a
very good spa onsite. The Ritz-Carlton has also added
another property to its offerings, with a 341 room
hotel in the DIFC area.

Shangri-La

Shk Zayed Rd Trade Center 1 **04 343 8888**
shangri-la.com
Map **2 G6** Metro **Burj Khalifa/Dubai Mall**
Featuring great views of the coast and the city from
Sheikh Zayed Road, this hotel has 301 guest rooms
and suites, 126 serviced apartments, a health club and
spa, two swimming pools and a variety of restaurants
and bars including majestic Moroccan Marrakech and
seafood specialist Amwaj.

Sheraton Jumeirah Beach

Al Mamsha St Marsa Dubai **04 399 5533**
sheratonjumeirahbeach.com
Map **1 K4** Metro **Jumeirah Lakes Towers**
An older waterfront resort right at the southern end
of JBR beach, this hotel has a secluded stretch of
the golden sands to itself, plus green gardens and
a couple of decent restaurants, including Peacock
Chinese Restaurant and The Grill Room. It hosts a chill-
out evening on Fridays, Ocean Club, which is popular
with local residents.

Sofitel Jumeirah Beach

JBR Marsa Dubai **04 448 4848**
sofitel-dubai-jumeirahbeach.com
Map **1 K5** Metro **Jumeirah Lakes Towers**
This chic, five-star, seafront property stands tall on
Jumeirah Beach Residence's The Walk, and the hotel
offers direct access to the beach as well as a host of
boutiques and cafes along the promenade. It features
a beauty salon, a pool bar, and popular Irish sports
bar The Hub.

Waldorf Astoria Palm Jumeirah

The Crescent East Nakhlat Jumeira **04 818 2222**
waldorfastoria3.hilton.com
Map **1 P1** Metro **Nakheel**
This iconic brand's first foray in Dubai is an opulent
affair that oozes class and benefits from a stunning,
peaceful location on the Palm Jumeirah. The hotel
boasts the luxurious Waldof Astoria Spa, a stretch of
private beach, and 3-starred Michelin cuisine at Social
by Heinz Beck. The Waldorf Astoria New York-inspired
brunch is the latest to join the ever popular Friday
brunch scene in the city.

Westin Dubai Mina Seyahi

Al Sufouh St Marsa Dubai **04 399 4141**
westinminaseyahi.com
Map **1 M5** Metro **Nakheel**
Set on 1,200 metres of private beach, The Westin has
294 spacious rooms and suites with all the luxury
amenities you would expect of a five-star hotel,
including the aptly named Heavenly Spa. Ample
dining venues include perennially popular Italian
Bussola and wine and cheese bar Oeno.

Other Options

Bur Dubai and Deira have plenty of notable (and
affordable) hotels for guests staying in this buzzing
end of town. The Crowne Plaza Dubai Deira is home to
legendary buffet restaurant Spice Island, and the JW
Marriott Hotel Dubai is known for its theme nights and
brunches. The Grand Excelsior Hotel Bur Dubai and the
Park Regis Kris Kin Hotel also offer great facilities with
rooms available at competitive prices.

Radisson Blu (radissonblu.com), Novotel, Rotana
(rotana.com), Sheraton and Holiday Inn all have
various branches around the main areas of the city,
each with its own popular brunch options and bars.

Guesthouses are not hugely common in Dubai but
are becoming more popular. Smaller in size, B&Bs offer
a homely feel and are ideal for guests who want to see
more of the 'real Dubai'. Located in residential areas,
they won't have access to private beaches, but there
is no shortage of good public beaches to enjoy. Some
will have their own pool, while owners will be only too
happy to give personal recommendations on what to
see, and things to do.

HOME OF ELEGANT RETAILERS AND UPSCALE DINING

Shop in the contemporary beauty of Sunset Mall.

Visit our boutiques and you're sure to find a style of shopping that suits your taste:

Provedore, Taste of Fame, Arabesque, Ahmed Seddiqi & sons, and more

Jumeirah Beach Road, Jumeirah 3

www.sunsetmall.ae

SHOPPING

Souk Madinat Jumeirah

SHOPPING

Spending money is something of a national sport in the UAE; whatever your budget, you'll find no shortage of opportunity when it comes to opening those purse strings.

Dubai is well and truly positioning itself as the retail capital of the world – where else would you get a festival dedicated specifically (and reverently) to shopping? The largest shopping mall in the world is here, as well as plenty more leisure and retail havens. Dubai's development is inextricably linked to shopping, and with each new development comes a new mall.

Practicality plays a large part in the mall culture; during the hotter months, malls are oases of cool in the sweltering city – somewhere to walk, shop, eat and be entertained.

But it doesn't end there – the city's shopping highlights include traditional souks and quirky markets, boutiques, a few thrift shops, a plethora of designer names and a growing number of original independent stores. There are new unique shopping hubs cropping up all the time, and several residential areas now have something akin to a high street.

The thing that makes shopping here so appealing is the fantastic range of products; there is very little that is not available and for most items there is enough choice to fit any budget, from the streets of Karama with its fake designer goods, to the shops in the malls that sell the real thing.

With the population being largely transitory, there is no shortage of second-hand goods, and it's worth venturing out of the city for bigger items; Sharjah and Ajman are known for their cheaper prices.

One thing's for sure, there are not many places that can beat Dubai's range of goods and services. You'll be spoilt for choice, and the frequency of sales means that if you look in the right places at the right time, you'll be sure to bag a bargain.

NEED TO KNOW

Most shops are open until 10pm every night and even later at the weekends. You can often do your grocery shopping till midnight, and a few of the major supermarkets are open 24 hours a day. The malls are particularly busy at the weekend, especially on Friday evenings. Things change slightly during Ramadan, when some shops close from noon until around 7pm.

You may find that imported items and brands, particularly from the international high-street stores, carry an extra few dirhams to compensate for the cost of importing the goods.

Bizarrely, the fashions here follow the European seasons, so just as the weather cools down from the extreme heat of the summer and you're ready to get kitted out for the beach, you'll find the stores are full of winter boots and heavy coats. You may want to stock up at the beginning of summer.

How To Pay

You'll have few problems parting with your money. Credit cards (American Express, Diners Club, MasterCard and Visa) and debit cards (Visa Electron) are accepted in shopping malls, supermarkets and many independent shops. Cards mainly use the chip-and-pin system. Aramex also offers a Web Surfer card, a pre-paid MasterCard for use online.

It's better to pay with cash for fuel at petrol stations, although some are now offering card payment. You are never too far from an ATM in the city and it is preferable to pay with cash in souks and smaller shops – try to have a variety of denominations, because it is better to hand over close to the exact amount. US dollars and other foreign currencies are accepted in some larger shops (and in airport duty free).

Loyalty Cards

Many stores and malls in the UAE participate in nationwide loyalty card schemes. These allow you to earn points while shopping, which can then be redeemed against purchases, and so can be well worth collecting. Shukran, from the Landmark Group, has lots of participating shops from fashion to electronics, including Iconic, New Look, Centrepoint and Emax, as well as restaurants. Alshaya is another popular card with H&M, Debenhams, Boots and many more participating stores. Several brands have their own loyalty schemes, including Virgin Megastore, and Carrefour with its MyClub loyalty card.

Bargaining

Bargaining is common practice in the souks and shopping areas of the UAE; you'll need to give it a go to get the best prices. Before you take the plunge, try to get an idea of prices from a few shops, as there can often be a significant difference. Once you've decided how much to spend, offer an initial bid that is roughly around half that price. Stay laidback and vaguely uninterested. When your initial offer is rejected (and it will be), keep going until you reach an agreement or until you have reached your limit. If the price isn't right, say so and walk out – the vendor will often follow and suggest a compromise price. The more you buy, the better the discount. When the price is agreed, it is considered bad form to back out of the sale.

Bargaining isn't commonly accepted in malls and independent shops. However, some shops such as jewellery stores and smaller electronics stores do operate a set discount system so you never know: ask whether there is a discount on the marked price and you may bag a bargain.

Canny Coupons

It's no secret that there are bargains to be had across the city. As well as the Entertainer books and app, check out groupon.ae and cobone.com for discounts on everything from shopping to dentistry to holidays.

Shopping Events

At certain times of the year, Dubai sees sweeping discounts and promotions. It can be worth holding out for these events to buy certain items, including cars and electronics. While prices are slashed in the shops, many malls hold raffles for big prizes when you spend money – these include cars and large cash prizes. The malls are pretty busy during these periods.

Art Dubai

Madinat Jumeirah Al Sufouh 1 **04 384 2000**
artdubai.ae
Map **1 R5** Metro **Mall of the Emirates**
A commercial art fair that draws together artwork from many of Dubai's galleries. The event will run from 18 to 21 March 2015, and is a great opportunity to check out the variety of art on offer in the city.

Dubai Shopping Festival

600 555 559
dubaievents.ae
A month dedicated to consumerism that takes place annually between January and February. There are sweeping discounts, entertainment and promotions across the entire city.

Dubai Summer Surprises
600 555 559
dubaievents.ae
Another city-wide event that takes place in the summer months, aimed at attracting visitors despite the sweltering heat. There are vast sales and promotions, as well as all sorts of family entertainment to draw shoppers into the malls.

Online Shopping

Without the local presence of online stores like Amazon and ASOS, knowing where to go online for what is perhaps a little trickier than at home. But there's still plenty of choice locally, and delivery is available to your home or office. More online stores are cropping up all the time, and the range is always improving. Geant is the first hypermarket to offer online grocery shopping, with delivery across Dubai (geantonline.ae).

International websites are a popular option (such as Amazon UK or US), and while not all companies ship to the UAE (or they charge high prices), there are several options for getting round this. Aramex provides a 'Shop & Ship' service which sets up a mailbox in both the UK and US, great for dealing with sites which do not offer international shipping. Borderlinx (borderlinx.com) provides a similar service for stores that will only ship to the USA.

There are sites based in the UAE that will arrange for gifts to be delivered both here and internationally, such as quickdubai.com and papagiftexpress.com, which delivers to India, Sri Lanka, Qatar, Oman and the UAE. International sites such as moonpig.com and Interflora are great for sending cards and gifts within the delivery country, often with same or next day delivery.

Deliveries & Shipping

The high number of international and local shipping and courier agencies means it is possible to transport just about anything. Both air freight and sea freight are available; air freight is faster and you can track the items, but it's more expensive and not really suitable for large or heavy objects. Sea freight takes several weeks to arrive but it is cheaper and you can rent containers for larger items. It is worth getting a few quotes and finding out what will happen when the goods arrive; some offer no services at the destination while others, usually the bigger ones, will clear customs and deliver right to the door. See the Getting Started section for more information. The companies listed above (right) are best to use for sending small packages.

Aramex
HP Bldg Dubai Media City, Al Sufouh 2 **600 544 000**
aramex.com
Offers a great service called 'Shop & Ship'. For a one-off payment of $45, Aramex will set up a mailbox for you in both the UK and US. Deliveries can be arranged up to three times a week; packages can be tracked. There are branches in Media and Internet Cities, and also in Garhoud.

Empost
Deira Main Post Office Bldg Hor Al Anz **600 565 555**
empostuae.com
Offers both local and international courier and air freight services – its prices are competitive and packages can be tracked.

Refunds, Exchanges & Consumer Rights

Policies on refunds and exchanges vary from shop to shop. It is common to be offered an exchange or credit note rather than a refund. Even with tags attached, many stores will not even consider an exchange unless you have the receipt. For some items, such as those in sealed packages, shops insist that the packaging should be intact so that the item can be resold – a fairly illogical stance if the item proves to be faulty.

If you're having no success with customer services, ask to speak to the manager, as the person on the shop floor is often not authorised to deviate from standard policy whereas managers may be more flexible.

The Consumer Protection Department of the UAE Ministry of Economy has been established to safeguard the interests of shoppers. The department tracks and regulates retail prices and has rejected planned price increases for staple goods. It has also mandated that all retail outlets display a notice of their consumer rights policy in the store. Consumers wishing to complain about a retailer can complete a form on the website economy.gov.ae, send an email to consumer@economy.ae, or call the free phone hotline on 600 522 225. In Dubai, the Consumer Rights Unit at the Economic Development Department (600 545 555, dubaided.gov.ae) primarily deals with unfit food, but can be contacted to report faulty goods or to complain if a guarantee is not honoured.

Buyer Beware

Traps for the unwary shopper do exist. Some of the international stores sell items that are far more expensive than in their country of origin (you can often even still see the original price tags). Prices can be as much as 30% higher, so beware.

Getting Started: 10 Shops to Set You Up

Whether you're waiting for your freight to arrive from overseas, or are staring at a big empty apartment, you'll need to turn your house into a home. Pretty much anything you'll ever need can be found in these convenient and affordable stores, and at the lowest prices in the city save some serious haggling at the souks. Delivery on larger items is usually free, too.

IKEA
Budget-friendly, well-designed furniture you can take straight home. Also stock up on bits for the house – from towels to tealights, cutlery to curtains.

Carrefour
Stock up on home appliances: toaster, kettle and fridge, and fill your kitchen cupboards with good international branded products as well.

Sharaf DG
Appliances, electronics and related accessories at very welcoming prices.

ACE Hardware > p.367
Everything you need for DIY around the house, plus garden furniture and plants, as well as outdoor equipment to get you ready for some exploring in the desert.

Home Centre
Put the finishing touches on your new home with items from this classy but affordable range of essential homeware.

Centrepoint
This is a one-stop shop for several handy and affordable brands – clothe your kids, stock up on baby essentials and decorate the home.

LuLu Hypermarket
Great for all the household essentials – cleaning products and cheap necessities – as well as stocking up on tins and basics. The fruit and veg section is also brilliant.

Emax
A wide range of electronic brands to get your home entertainment sorted, from TVs and games consoles to wireless routers, plus a range of cameras to document your UAE adventures with.

Modell's Sports
Prepare yourself for Dubai's outdoors and active lifestyle by stocking up on trainers, sportswear and all kinds of sports equipment.

dubizzle.com
Absolutely anything you can think of – from cars to furniture, someone will be selling theirs at a pre-owned price on this online expat institution.

Shop Online
Check out these local online stores and you won't even need to leave the house.

carrefouruae.com
tejuri.com
souq.com
alshop.com
ikea.com
dbbabies.com
geantonline.ae

Groceries
Chances are high that your local convenience store will deliver to your door, night and day. Pop inside and ask for a phone number, and you'll never need to nip out for milk again.

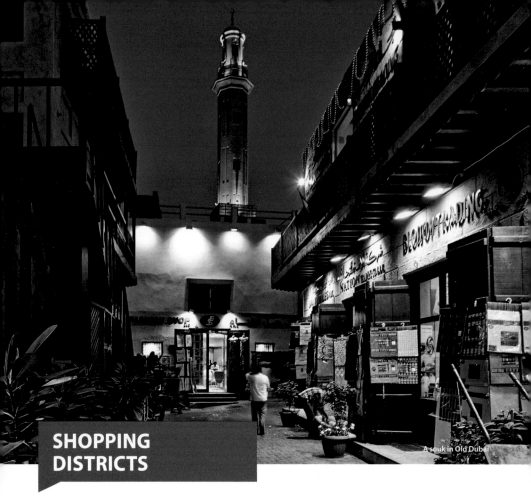

A souk in Old Dubai

SHOPPING DISTRICTS

If you're moving to a new area in Dubai or just planning a shopping trip, it helps to know what your options are across the city. While there is generally a mall or shopping centre within striking distance of anywhere you end up, different areas can also conjure up some different shopping treats.

If venturing into the gargantuan Dubai Mall exhausts you at the very thought, try Dubai Marina Mall, handy for the Marsa Dubai end of town, or Mercato Shopping Mall towards the northern end of Jumeira Road. Both are a more manageable size and usually pretty calm, but have a good range of shops.

For a breath of fresh air – literally – head to Wasl Square or Citywalk, both in Jumeira. These outdoor complexes have a more interesting range of shops, as well as lovely alfresco cafes and several amenities.

For the true Middle Eastern shopping experience, head for Dubai Creek, where the buzzing souks of Deira and Bur Dubai are and haggle to your heart's content.

Al Barsha

The main draw in this area is the city's second biggest shopping hub, Mall of the Emirates, but the neighbourhood has an urban residential feel with lots of cafes and independent shops. The huge LuLu Hypermarket just off Umm Suqeim Road is worth the journey, and there's a cluster of handy shops accessed from this main artery, including furniture emporium, Pan Emirates.

Al Barsha Mall
23rd St Al Barsha 2 **04 455 7151**
Map **1 Q7** Metro **Mall of the Emirates**
A large Union Co-operative Society supermarket is the main draw for this handy community mall, plus there's a range of services available, a few fashion brands, electronics store Sharaf DG, Japanese value store Daiso and some rides to entertain the kids.

Al Qouz

Head into this industrial wilderness and you'll find some real gems, which make use of the space and versatility of the warehouses. Al Qouz 1 is home to The Courtyard, which has some interesting shops and galleries, and hosts a farmers' market on Saturdays. Nearby Dubai Antique Museum is an enormous wonderland of furniture, souvenirs and much more, and then there's Alserkal Avenue, with a host of edgy art galleries.

Lining Sheikh Zayed Road are a number of retail outlets and car dealerships; dig a little deeper and you'll find stores such as Safita, which sells well-priced wooden Indian furniture. Kidz Inc sells furniture and toys for children, while Just Kidding has all the latest baby equipment. The nearby branch of Lime Tree Cafe has some lovely edible and kitchen goodies that make great gifts. Dubai Garden Centre has everything for the garden, and the Sun & Sand Sports outlet behind the Gold & Diamond Park has lots of bargains.

Gold & Diamond Park > p.371
Nr First Gulf Bank Metro Station
Al Qouz Ind. 3 **04 362 7777**
goldanddiamondpark.com
Map **1 S6** Metro **First Gulf Bank**
Gold & Diamond Park (at junction four on Sheikh Zayed Road) has branches of many of the same shops as the Gold Souk but in a calmer, air-conditioned atmosphere. You can still barter, and there is the added bonus of cafes nearby on the road parallel to Sheikh Zayed Road. There are a few other shops, such as Just Kidding.

Oasis Centre
Al Waha St Al Qouz Ind. 1 **04 515 4000**
oasiscentremall.com
Map **2 C6** Metro **Noor Bank**
A good selection of outlets including Home Centre, New Look, Carrefour Express and Centrepoint. A small food court offers the usual fast food outlets, or head to Balance Cafe for a guilt-free, healthy lunch.

Times Square Center
Shk Zayed Rd Al Qouz Ind. 1 **04 341 8020**
timessquarecenter.ae
Map **1 T6** Metro **Noor Bank**
Outdoor and adventure sports megastore Adventure HQ, which has a climbing wall and aerial obstacle course, is the biggest draw for this small but modern mall. You'll find large branches of Sharaf DG, Intersport, Toys R Us and Yellow Hat (for car accessories), and a good branch of Al Manama Hypermarket. Head to the Chillout ice lounge (unlicensed) for a sub-zero mocktail. The ARTE craft market takes over the ground floor once a month.

Bur Dubai

Al Fahidi Street is perfect for a bit of local colour and some great shopping. It is part of the commercial area that runs from Al Fahidi Historical Neighbourhood (formerly Bastakiya) all the way to Shindagha and takes in Dubai Museum, the Electronics Souk and the Textile Souk. There is a good range of inexpensive places to eat, including some fantastic vegetarian restaurants. This area is always busy, but it really comes to life at night – if you're not sure you're in the right place, just head for the neon lights.

Karama is one of the older residential districts in Dubai, and is one of the best places to find a bargain. The best spot is the Karama Complex, a long street running through the middle of the district that is lined by shops on both sides. The area is best known for bargain clothing, sports goods, gifts and souvenirs (from toy camels to mosque alarm clocks and stuffed scorpions to pashminas) and it is notorious for being the hotbed of counterfeit items in Dubai. As you wander round you will be offered 'copy watches, copy bags' with every step, and if you show any interest you will be whisked into a back room to view the goods. If you're not interested, a simple 'no thank you' will suffice, or even just ignore the vendor completely – it may seem rude, but sometimes it's the only way to cope with the incessant hassle. The most popular shops are Blue Marine, Green Eye and Asda. With loads of small, inexpensive restaurants, you won't go hungry while pounding the streets of Karama. Try Chef Lanka, Aryaas or Saravana Bhavan, or head for the large fish, fruit and vegetable market.

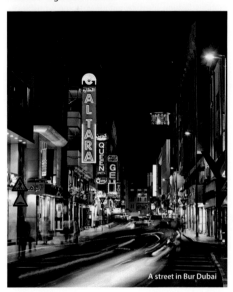
A street in Bur Dubai

Lamcy Plaza
Shk Rashid Rd Oud Metha **04 335 9999**
lamcyplaza.com
Map **2 K6** Metro **Oud Metha**
Large and consistently popular, there's a great variety
of shops and entertainment. Services include a play
area, pharmacy, a money exchange, a florist and a post
office counter. There's fashion stores aplenty, including
Dorothy Perkins, Aldo and Levi's; baby stores include
Mothercare and Pumpkin Patch. Peacocks and Matalan
sell reasonably priced fashion, while sharp menswear
can be found at Pierre Cardin and Ted Lapidus.

Deira

This chaotic urban jungle is crammed with
independent shops that cater to all tastes and
budgets, and the area hides some great shopping
centres, both large and small. While Deira City Centre
has all the modern amenities and attractions, a major
draw is the atmospheric district that incorporates the
winding Gold Souk, where you can barter for some
bargain bling, and the fragrant Spice Souk on the
banks of the Creek.

Century Mall
Nr Al Shabab Club, Al Wuheida Rd Al Mamzar
04 296 6337
mysafeer.com
Map **2 R6** Metro **Al Qiyadah**
Shopping meets entertainment here, with 75
speciality stores selling the latest in electronics,
mobiles, fashion, lifestyle, gift ideas, home furnishings,
jewellery, and health and beauty products. There's
a Carrefour, a foodcourt and an indoor themed
amusement centre.

Madina Mall
Beirut St Muhaisnah 4 **04 238 1111**
madina-mall.com
Map **2 T9** Metro **Al Qusais**
This strikingly designed shopping mall is packed with
outlets selling everything from homewares to fashion,
and is home to the Middle East's first Poundstretcher,
a popular UK bargain basement brand. There's also a
Carrefour and a family entertainment area.

Reef Mall
Salah Al Din St Al Muraqqabat **04 224 2240**
reefmall.com
Map **2 N5** Metro **Salah Al Din**
This surprisingly large mall has branches of Daiso,
Babyshop, Home Centre and a range of fashion
brands. There's a huge Fun City for kids to burn off
a bit of energy, plus a small foodcourt, several cafes
and a supermarket.

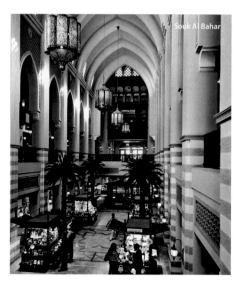
Souk Al Bahar

Downtown Dubai

This area has grown into a key place to meet, eat
and shop. The Dubai Mall won't disappoint with
its extensive store listing. For a more laidback
atmosphere, Souk Al Bahar's passageways,
resembling a traditional souk, cater well to tourists.
Some great restaurants are here, with prime position
over the nightly Dubai Fountain show. The Boulevard
is also lined with cafes, shops and hotels. Further
afield, Jumeirah Emirates Towers has a promenade of
high-end shops.

Dubailand

This enormous development that stretches down
the desert side of the city has a long way to go to
completion, but there are some great pockets of
leisure and retail. With a slightly out of town location,
they are surprisingly easy to get to and for the most
part traffic free. Check out Global Village during the
winter months, a major attraction with plenty of
shopping, plus fairground rides and entertainment.

Dubai Investments Park
Dubai Investments Park 1 **04 885 1188**
dipark.com
Map **1 F10**
Park n Shop fans should head here for the brand's
large and blissfully quiet Cash and Carry branch (04
805 1000). There's a Carrefour Market here too, and a
pleasant local shopping centre at Green Community.

Uptown MotorCity
Al Hebiah 1 **04 885 1555**
Map **1 N12**
This neighbourhood has become desirable thanks to its pleasant high street. With a huge Spinneys at one end, the promenade is lined with cafes, shops and useful services.

Marsa Dubai & JBR

This trendy residential district is a hub of retail and leisure. Dubai Marina Mall is a manageable size, and outside there's plenty more along the waterways.

Marina Walk
Marsa Dubai
Map **1 L5** Metro **DAMAC**
By night the promenade that hugs the waters of Marsa Dubai is buzzing with strolling families and friends enjoying the alfresco lifestyle at the many cafes and restaurants that line the Walk. In the cooler months it's a popular spot for jogging or rollerblading.

The Beach
Jumeirah Beach Residence Marsa Dubai
04 431 0190
thebeach.ae
Map **1 K4** Metro **DAMAC**
A new open-air mall, with retail stores, restaurants, a Reel Cinemas and direct access to JBR beach and its watersports. There's a market lining the waterfront, and more outdoor terraces than you can count.

The Walk at Jumeirah Beach Residence
Jumeirah Beach Residence Marsa Dubai
04 390 0091
dubaipropertiesgroup.ae
Map **1 K4** Metro **Jumeirah Lakes Towers**
This cobbled strip embraces alfresco cafe culture, with street-side shops, cute stalls and plenty of outdoor restaurant seating. Outlets are either on the ground level or on the plaza level of six clusters of towers called Murjan, Sadaf, Bahar, Rimal, Amwaj and Shams.

Jumeira & Umm Suqeim

This area has a community feel, though the whole strip is a bit long to walk (Jumeirah Road and Al Wasl Road stretch from Souk Madinat Jumeirah up to 2nd December Street). There are clusters of stores, restaurants and cafes, as well as several small malls, including the luxury Saga World mall (sagaworldonline.com) near Kite Beach. Many businesses in the area are located in villas; these are mostly spas, dentists, hairdressers, and cosmetic surgery clinics.

On Al Wasl Road there are art galleries, garden stores, hair salons, dentists and vets. Expat favourites are the popular Spinneys Centre and Al Safa Centre, a shopping centre that's home to Park n Shop and Pizza Express. At the Satwa end of Al Wasl Road is the Al Ghazal Complex, well known by partygoers for Mr Ben's Costume Closet. Supermarkets in the area include Choithrams, Waitrose and the Union Co-operative Society.

Beach Centre
Nr Dubai Zoo, Jumeira St Jumeira 1 **04 344 7077**
Map **2 G4** Metro **Emirates Towers**
This mall sells everything from books to furniture and jewellery. Two branches of White Star Bookshop stock craft materials and teachers' supplies respectively. It also houses the Music Room, which has the largest supply of sheet music in Dubai, plus Kuts 4 Kids, a children's hairdressers, an opticians and a pharmacy.

Citywalk
Al Safa St Al Wasl
citywalk.ae
Map **2 F5** Metro **Burj Khalifa/Dubai Mall**
This low-rise retail space on Al Wasl Road is characterised by pleasant open spaces, water features, play areas, alfresco cafes and boutiques.

J3 Mall
Al Wasl St Al Manara **04 388 4433**
j3mall.com
Map **1 U5** Metro **Noor Bank**
This compact shopping centre has a good Choithrams, funky women's sportswear at Lorna Jane, SPERA fashion boutique and an indoor play centre for kids.

The Walk at JBR

Jumeira Plaza

Jumeira St Jumeira 1 **04 349 7111**
Map **2 H4** Metro **Emirates Towers**

The 'pink mall' has an interesting range of independent shops selling everything from furniture to greeting cards. Prose is a popular second-hand bookshop; Melange has an interesting selection of clothing, jewellery and soft furnishings from India. There's a play area for kids, a Dome Cafe and a small branch of the Dubai Police – great for paying fines without having to queue.

Jumeirah Centre

Jumeira St Jumeira 1 **04 349 0766**
gmg.ae
Map **2 H4** Metro **Emirates Towers**

Packs a lot into a small space. Chains like Benetton and Nike join a number of independents, including Elves & Fairies for crafts and hobbies, Panache for accessories made only from natural materials, and the Wedding Shop. Kazim has a good range of stationery and art supplies, and there are some interesting clothes shops, plus a gallery.

Palm Strip

Jumeira St Jumeira 1 **04 346 1462**
dipllc.ae
Map **2 H4** Metro **World Trade Centre**

Across the road from Jumeirah Mosque, this shopping arcade is dominated by upmarket boutiques, plus there are beauty salons and a pharmacy. Often quiet during the day, it gets a little livelier in the evenings with the popular Japengo Cafe. Other outlets include: Beyond the Beach, Elite Fashion, Oceano and Zara Home.

Shops are open late in Dubai

Spinneys Centre

Al Wasl St Al Safa 2 **04 394 1657**
spinneys-dubai.com
Map **2 B5** Metro **Noor Bank**

Just off Al Wasl Road, there's a number of shops centred around a large Spinneys supermarket, including Early Learning Centre and Mothercare, Tavola (for kitchenalia), and Disco 2000, one of Dubai's better music and DVD shops. There are branches of both MMI and A&E, a large play area, and services include dry cleaning and a pharmacy.

Sunset Mall > p.326

Jumeira St Jumeira 3 **04 330 7333**
sunsetmall.ae
Map **2 C4** Metro **Business Bay**

Stretching along Jumeirah Road, this boutique mall has a sleek glass and steel exterior, and is home to premium fashion and lifestyle brands as well as unique dining experiences in town. Provedore, a delicatessen with a difference, Taste of Fame, a unique celebrity themed restaurant, and other niche venues such as I Love F Cafe, Gizia, Valleydez, West L.A. and more, are featuring at this elegant and stylish shopping destination.

Town Centre Jumeirah

Jumeira St Jumeira 1 **04 344 0111**
towncentrejumeirah.com
Map **2 F4** Metro **Burj Khalifa/Dubai Mall**

This community mall has an interesting blend of outlets and several cafes, including Cafe Ceramique where you can customise a piece of pottery while you dine. There are beauty salons, as well as clothing shops including Heat Waves (for beachwear), Anne Klein (fashion accessories), TKD Lingerie for the more well-endowed lady, a large branch of Paris Gallery plus an Empost counter and an Etisalat machine.

Village Mall

Jumeira St Jumeira 1 **04 344 9514**
Map **2 H4** Metro **Emirates Towers**

With its Mediterranean theme, this has more of a community feel than many of the malls in Dubai. The niche boutiques are great for something different, whether it's clothing or something for the home, with outlets like S*uce, Ayesha Depala and Shakespeare & Co. There's a bright and fun children's play area for younger children and a number of places to eat.

Wasl Square

Nr Al Safa Park, Al Wasl St Al Safa 1 **800 9275**
waslproperties.com
Map **2 D5** Metro **Business Bay**

This lovely open-air development next to Safa Park has a number of interesting stores, restaurants and services, including S*uce Gifts, a gourmet butcher, a Japanese bakery and salons for men and women. There are several cafes, including popular gourmet venue The Pantry and Bookmunch, where you can peruse and purchase books while you eat.

Mirdif

The family suburb of Mirdif is mostly collections of small cornershops and supermarkets, usually centred around a mosque, but Uptown Mirdiff is a pleasant open-air complex, and the huge Mirdif City Centre mall is a destination worth heading to, especially for the variety of attractions at Playnation.

Arabian Center
Al Khawaneej St Al Mizhar 1 **04 284 5555**
arabiancenter.ae
Map **2 R13** Metro **Rashidiya**
This small mall still manages to tick all the boxes. You can pick up home appliances or creature comforts (Homes R Us, Sharaf DG and Eros Digital) as well as high-street fashion including New Look and Mango. A good selection of sports stores includes Adidas. There's also a cinema, hypermarket, a play area for kids and a salon.

Bin Sougat Centre
Airport St Al Rashidiya **04 286 3000**
binsougatcenter.com
Map **2 P10** Metro **Rashidiya**
Anchored by a large Spinneys, there is an interesting mix of stores including Emirates Trading which sells professional art supplies and equipment, Dubai Library Distributors, which is excellent for stationery, and Orient Curios Furniture. There is also a Secrets Boutique which sells a limited range of lingerie in larger sizes.

Etihad Mall
Al Khawaneej St Muhaisnah 1 **04 284 3663**
etihadmall.ae
Map **2 R12** Metro **Rashidiya**
A community mall with numerous fashion brands – including several aimed squarely at the Arab market – as well as services like opticians, banks and pharmacies. There's an indoor amusement centre for kids, and a good sized foodcourt.

Uptown Mirdiff
Nr Uptown Primary School Mirdif **04 288 9333**
uptownmirdiff.ae
Map **2 Q13** Metro **Rashidiya**
This open-air complex has a sense of community about it that attracts plenty of families living in the area. It has all the essentials: a Spinneys, an A&E liquor store, banks, pharmacy, gym, cafes and restaurants.

Satwa

One of Dubai's original retail areas, Satwa has something of a village feel about it. It is best known for its fabric shops and tailors, but holds a real mix of stores. The area tends to cater to the lower end of the market and is great fun to look around. Popular reasons to visit Satwa include buying traditional *majlis* seating and getting your car windows tinted. The pick of the fabric shops is Deepak's, with an amazing range, reasonable prices and helpful staff.

There are a number of shops on 'Plant Street' with good indoor and outdoor plants; this is also the street for upholstery and paint. Animal lovers should probably avoid the pet shops – conditions are awful, despite regulations, and the animals are often in a sorry state. Shop around, because whatever you are looking for there's bound to be more than one outlet selling it and prices vary.

Satwa is renowned for its fast food outlets and reasonably priced restaurants. Ravi's is an institution in Dubai, serving good Pakistani food at incredible prices; Mini Chinese has been going for years and Rydges Plaza Hotel has a number of popular, licensed bars and restaurants. Satwa is also home to some great salons, where you can get various treatments at low prices. They might not be as smooth as the upper-end salons, but they are great for a quick fix.

2nd December Street (still often called by its former name, Al Diyafah Road) is a great place for a lively evening stroll. There's an eclectic mix of shops and fast food outlets; Al Mallah, a popular Lebanese restaurant, is highly recommended (arguably the best falafel and shawarma in Dubai).

Out Of Town

Venture slightly out of the city and you can find some serious bargains. Dubai Outlet Mall is 15 minutes along the Al Ain Road and great for cut-price labels, or head to Sharjah or Ajman for cheap furniture, carpets and electronics.

Dragon Mart
Ras Al Khor Rd Warsan 1 **04 433 6200**
dragonmart.ae
This huge concentration of Chinese traders (shaped like a dragon and over a kilometre long) is vaguely divided into zones by commodity; from building materials to toys, household items to quad bikes, everything is available – and cheaper than elsewhere in the city. There's an incredible amount of tat, but if you're looking for something cheap and for the short haul, you can't go wrong. Items worth looking out for include garden furniture and fancy dress costumes. See the website for opening hours.

The waterfall at The Dubai Mall

PLACES TO SHOP

Depending on what you need to buy, or how you want to spend your day, Dubai has a place to shop that will match your mood. While the magnificent malls are fantastic places to be entertained, eat and buy from many top international stores, there are also smaller shopping centres, hypermarkets and souks to help you spend your dirhams.

The souks and markets offer a surprisingly authentic Middle Eastern shopping experience – bargaining can be fun and rewarding, and you never know what you might come home with, from fresh fish to Iranian plant pots. The hypermarkets, on the other hand, stock all manner of international brands and you can shop knowing what to expect.

Overall, don't panic that you can't head to your favourite organic grocery store or department store – you're bound to have a new favourite in no time, and many of the chains you are used to are right here.

Department Stores

Department stores are at the heart of some of Dubai's biggest malls and in addition to British stalwarts like Marks & Spencer and Debenhams, South Africa's trusted Woolworths and regional powerhouse Jashanmal provide essentials for the whole family.

Bloomingdale's
The Dubai Mall Burj Khalifa 04 350 5333
bloomingdales.com
Map 2 F7 Metro Burj Khalifa/Dubai Mall
The first Bloomingdale's to open outside the USA brings with it the exclusivity that attracts well-heeled New Yorkers. Three storeys of high-end lines of fashion include jewellery, accessories and homewares. Classic touches include the store's famous 'big brown bags' and a taste of Manhattan at Magnolia's Bakery.

Centrepoint

Oasis Centre Al Qouz 1 **04 809 4000**
Map **2 C6** Metro **Noor Bank**
Shopaholics will love this store, a one-stop shopping destination that houses Babyshop, Splash, Lifestyle, Shoe Mart and Beautybay all under one roof. You can dress your family head to toe in one easy shopping trip – and without breaking the bank. Also at Mall of the Emirates and Mirdif City Centre.

Debenhams

The Dubai Mall Burj Khalifa **04 339 9285**
debenhams.com
Map **2 F7** Metro **Burj Khalifa/Dubai Mall**
A mainstay of the British high street, it's a go-to for perfumes, cosmetics, homewares and clothing for men, women and children. Brands include Evans, for plus-size clothing, Warehouse and Miss Selfridge, as well as John Rocha and Jasper Conran. Also located at Deira City Centre, Ibn Battuta Mall, Mirdif City Centre and Mall of the Emirates.

Galeries Lafayette

The Dubai Mall Burj Khalifa **04 339 9933**
galerieslafayette-dubai.com
Map **2 F7** Metro **Burj Khalifa/Dubai Mall**
This French department store adds more designer brands to The Dubai Mall's extensive store list; from glamorous frocks and stylish shoes to cosmetics, children's wear, lingerie and a homeware section. The Lafayette Gourmet food store stocks a range of original and innovative edible treats, and there's the option to dine in too.

Harvey Nichols

Mall of the Emirates Al Barsha 1 **04 409 8888**
harveynichols.com
Map **1 R6** Metro **Mall of the Emirates**
The epitome of chic shopping, 'Harvey Nics' offers a large selection of high-rolling fashion (for men, women and kids), beauty and homeware brands. You'll find Jimmy Choo and Diane Von Furstenberg rubbing shoulders with other swish brands. There is a small range of gourmet products in the Foodmarket and restaurant Almaz by Momo.

Jashanmal

Dubai Festival City Mall Al Kheeran **04 232 9023**
jashanmalgroup.com
Map **2 M9** Metro **Emirates**
The go-to shopping destination for dinnerware, cookware, bed and bath accessories, home appliances as well as luggage. It also sells a small range of clothing and underwear, perfume and books, and its luggage section is particularly good. Also located at Mall of the Emirates, The Dubai Mall, Mirdif City Centre and Al Ghurair Centre.

Marks & Spencer

The Dubai Mall Burj Khalifa **04 339 8890**
marksandspencerme.com
Map **2 F7** Metro **Burj Khalifa/Dubai Mall**
A renowned UK brand, 'M&S' sells clothes and shoes for men, women and children, including a revered underwear range, along with a small selection of food and sweets. It's a good bet for seasonal items such as Christmas cards and Easter eggs. Also at Wafi, Mall of the Emirates, Festival City, Mirdif and Deira City Centre.

Mudo City

The Dubai Mall Burj Khalifa **04 325 3246**
mudo.com.tr
Map **2 F7** Metro **Burj Khalifa/Dubai Mall**
One of the most famous brands in Turkey, Mudo City is a lifestyle store with a collection of furniture, home furnishings, kitchen, bathroom and personal accessories, and home textiles. It's an eclectic mix of fashion and home decor, all with a modern-classic style; you can pick up an affordable T-shirt for Dhs.70 or a quirky designer table for Dhs.10,000.

Redtag

Ibn Battuta Mall Jabal Ali 1 **04 445 6966**
redtag.ae
Map **1 G5** Metro **Ibn Battuta**
A big name in fashion in Saudi Arabia, with more than 40 stores across the Kingdom, this store offers value ranges of men's, women's and children's clothing. It's a popular regional choice, with several locations including Ibn Battuta Mall, Arabian Centre and Lamcy Plaza.

Saks Fifth Avenue

BurJuman Al Mankhool **04 501 2700**
saksfifthavenue.com
Map **2 L5** Metro **BurJuman**
Even in Dubai's cultured retail sector, this store has an air of sophistication. Along with cosmetics, perfumes, designer sunglasses and the Saks Nail Studio, there are boutiques from Jean Paul Gaultier, Prada and D&G, plus children's designer clothes, a men's store, and a chocolate bar and cafe. There's also an exclusive bridal salon that stocks Vera Wang gowns.

Salam Studio & Stores

Wafi Umm Hurair 2 **04 704 8349**
salams.com
Map **2 K7** Metro **Dubai Healthcare City**
This local department store has a swanky decor and a good mix of brands, including LA brand Gypsy 05 and designer names such as Betsey Johnson, Roberto Cavalli and Missoni. Its spacious store in Wafi stocks a good range of homeware and jewellery, as well as a particularly good selection of photography accessories from well-known brands.

Hypermarkets

For a one-stop shop for almost anything you can think of, hypermarkets are the place to go. With a range that goes far beyond food, most sell a variety of electronics and home appliances at competitive prices, as well as toys, homewares, luggage, clothes, shoes, music and DVDs and much, much more.

Carrefour

Mall of the Emirates Al Barsha 1 **800 73232**
carrefouruae.com
Map **1 R6** Metro **Mall of the Emirates**
Renowned for its competitive pricing and special offers, branches of this French chain can be found throughout the city. As well as a good range of French food products there's a comprehensive range of electronics and household goods. Camping gear, car accessories, garden furniture and hardware are also on sale. Non-food items can be ordered online. Also located in Mirdif and Deira, and new to BurJuman.

Geant

Ibn Battuta Mall Jabal Ali 1 **04 368 5880**
geant-uae.com
Map **1 G5** Metro **Ibn Battuta**
Stocks a massive selection of products. It is well worth a visit for the cheap fruit and vegetables and the huge selection of nuts (great almonds). You'll also find very reasonably priced towels and bedding, a good selection of electronics, a car accessories section and it's also a good destination for DVD box sets. Comprehensive online grocery shopping is also available – a first for the UAE.

HyperPanda

Dubai Festival City Mall Al Kheeran **04 232 5997**
panda.com.sa/dubai
Map **2 M9** Metro **Emirates**
Enormous but quieter than similar stores, so it's a good choice when you need hypermarket shopping without the hyperactive crowds. The selection of produce isn't as extensive as in some of the other hypermarkets, but it does have a healthcare department, electronics and more than the basic range of goods.

LuLu

Nr Mall of the Emirates Al Barsha 1 **04 341 8888**
luluhypermarket.com
Map **1 R6** Metro **Mall of the Emirates**
Great for those on a budget; LuLu's hot food counters, salad bars and fishmonger are particularly good value, as is the wide-ranging fruit and vegetable section. While you may not find all of your favourite Western brands, it stocks a good range of ethnic food. Most stores have a range of home appliances. Also located in Mirdif, Karama and Al Qusais.

Fruit and veg is imported

Convenience Stores

Dubai has a huge number of convenience stores selling basic food and drink. If you live close to a convenience store it's quite usual that you can phone them up and have them deliver. There are also branches of Spinneys Market, Carrefour Market and Carrefour Express around the city.

Al Maya

Reef Mall Al Muraqqabat **04 2229898**
almaya.ae Map **2 N5** Metro **Al Rigga**
This city-wide chain can be relied on for a good range of items, a bakery and fresh meat and fish. It also has a pork section selling a wide range of goods. Many of its branches are open 24 hours and offer free home delivery for a minimum order of Dhs.50.

Blue Mart

Al Barsha 1 **04 442 5303**
bluemartgroup.com Map **1 Q7** Metro **Mall of the Emirates**
One of the fastest growing supermarket chains in Dubai with branches also in Motor City, Al Marsa and Tecom, Blue Mart offers a decently priced shopping and delivery service experience, and stock a host of high quality products, from fruit and veg to toiletries.

All Day Mini Mart > p.345

Branches city-wide
alldayuae.com
There are around 29 branches of this convenience store across Dubai. Stocks basic groceries, chilled products and toiletries.

Spinneys
The fresher experience

NO
ADDED
HORMONES

spinneys FOOD

GREAT TASTE, NATURAL AND HEALTHY

All our meat is responsibly farmed and free from Hormonal
Growth Promonants (HGPs). Freshness, quality and taste at
no additional cost.

Supermarkets

Unlike hypermarkets, supermarkets concentrate solely on food and domestic necessities such as cleaning products and toiletries. They all tend to have their own kitchens that cook up freshly baked goods, with some larger stores offering quite an impressive range of pies, samosas and pasties. Some even have fish and meat counters for you to peruse. Carrefour Market (with various locations) is a more condensed and less frantic version of the hypermarket.

You may find that the prices between different brands of supermarket can vary quite dramatically, while the quality of some items like fruit and vegetables can be equally varied; this means it can pay to visit a couple of different supermarkets to get the best balance of quality and price when completing the grocery run.

Choithrams

Nr Al Safa Park, Al Wasl St Jumeira 3 **04 394 3852**
choithram.com
Map **2 D5** Metro **Business Bay**
With branches across the city, Choithrams stores are renowned for stocking British, American and Asian products that can't be found elsewhere (such as the Quorn range), but they are also known for being fairly expensive. Stores have pork sections and a great range of baby products – particularly food and formula. The large branch opposite Safa Park is open until 1am.

Park n Shop > p.343

Dubai Investments Park **04 805 1000**
Map **1 G9** Metro **Energy**
The Park n Shop Cash n Carry at Dubai Investments Park (04 805 1000) is huge, blissfully quiet, and has a loyalty scheme. Also find branches at JLT, TECOM, and a superb supermarket in Jumeira (04 394 5671), which has great prices and is worth a trip simply because it has the best bakery (famous for birthday cakes, fresh goodies and seasonal treats) and butchery in the city. The butchery has a Christmas ordering service for your turkey and ham. All branches have a great selection of treats from home that you might not find elsewhere.

Spinneys > p.341

Nr Centrepoint Al Mankhool **04 351 1777**
spinneys-dubai.com
Map **2 L5** Metro **ADCB**
With branches across Dubai, this high-end supermarket (with prices to match) has a great range of South African and Australian, as well as British and American items and a selection of Waitrose products. The freezer section and vegetarian options are both good, along with the deli counter. If you stay in town for Christmas you can order your seasonal goodies from here. Most branches have a pork section.

Union Co-operative Society

Rashidiya Shopping Centre Al Rashidiya **800 8889**
ucs.ae
Map **1 P11** Metro **Rashidiya**
It may lack the shine of other hypermarkets, but it's great for shaving a few dirhams off your grocery bill. The huge fruit and veg section is packed with farm-fresh produce at great prices, and it has a superb selection of Arabic cheeses, olives, and family size bargain packs. The Al Wasl Road branch is open 24 hours a day, and a new branch is due to open in Umm Suqeim.

Waitrose

The Dubai Mall Burj Khalifa **04 434 0700**
waitrose.com
Map **2 F7** Metro **Burj Khalifa/Dubai Mall**
This upmarket UK chain is well known for its premium range of British produce and gourmet goods, and this, along with the ease of shopping experience, is reflected in the price. It has a well-stocked deli filled with hot and cold selections of pre-made dishes and a great selection of baked goods, meat and cheese. There's a large, quiet branch in Umm Suqeim and several more around the city.

Delicatessens, Gourmet & Health Foods

If you have tastebuds that can only be satisfied by the best or healthiest ingredients, you'll find several stores dedicated to organic products and gourmet options. The main supermarkets also stock increasing varieties of speciality foods, including organic products and breads made from spelt or rye, and they all now carry products for diabetics.

The range of health food is improving; prices are generally high, but it is worth shopping around as costs vary. Nutrition Zone and Holland & Barrett have a good selection of vitamins, health supplements and detoxifying products and carry a range of health food, grains, gluten and wheat-free products, as well as some ecological household products.

Jones The Grocer

Indigo Central 8, Nr Times Square, Shk Zayed Rd Al Manara **04 346 6886**
jonesthegrocer.com
Map **1 T6** Metro **First Gulf Bank**
The Australian gourmet foodstore brings its artisan products to Dubai, with an extensive selection of deli items and fresh produce. It has an on-site bakery and cafe, and also offers a catering service. This is the perfect food emporium for connoisseurs looking to shop for a picnic basket or alfresco dining at home. Also holds food-related events.

The Biggest Specialty Food Mart in Dubai

DISCOVER IN-HOME EXPERIENCES OUT-OF-HOME

More British and American brands than any other supermarket in Dubai

Park .n. Shop
THE SPECIALITY FOOD MART

Al Safa Centre	Dubai Investment Park	Jumaira Lakes Tower	Tecom
+971 4 394 5671	+971 4 805 1000	+971 4 447 1424	+971 4 450 8560

Market & Platters
Pinnacle Tower Marsa Dubai **04 450 4466**
marketandplatters.com
Map **1 M5** Metro **DAMAC**
This store sells platters of sushi freshly prepared on-site, choice seafood and cheese, as well as beautifully presented fruit and vegetables, quality teas and other gourmet products. Their fish and cheese selection is quite extensive, and they make fresh bread daily. Grab a tasty salad or sandwich to go during your lunch break, or make this place a pit stop on your way to a picnic or beach day out.

Maybury Fresh Food Store
Ariyana Tower Marsa Dubai **04 423 8073**
facebook.com/MayburyStore
Map **1 L5** Metro **DAMAC**
This is a high-end store in a funky, urban space in the marina that stocks organic products, fresh halal meats, seafood, locally grown produce, cheeses, salads, freshly baked bread and fresh flowers. The Maybury Deli Cafe features regular new menus from head chef Varinder Patiel, and there is even a cooking studio on the premises catering to those wanting to learn more about creating their own plates.

Milk & Honey
Shoreline Bldg 10 Nakhlat Jumeira **04 432 8686**
milkandhoney.ae
Map **1 N3** Metro **Nakheel**
Open 24 hours a day and with a delivery service, this boutique supermarket has a range of organic products and everyday household essentials, with a focus on high-end brands and gourmet living.

Organic Foods & Cafe
Shk Zayed Rd Al Quoz 3 **04 338 2911**
organicfoodsandcafe.com
Map **2 G4** Metro **Emirates Towers**
Great for stocking up on fresh organic fruit, veggies, meat, fish and bread. Weekly specials and 20% off events every third Saturday of the month make guilt-free grocery shopping far more affordable. The adjoining cafe serves food prepared with organic ingredients too. Also at The Village-Jumeirah 1 and the Greens.

Cakes & Breads
There's a fantastic choice of bakeries, including the Yamanote Japanese Bakery in Wasl Square, Belgian outlet Maison Mathis at Arabian Ranches, the Lebanese bakery Al Reef on Al Wasl Road, and Le Succes French Bakery & Pastry at MotorCity. And you're never more than a few metres away from a good cupcake with branches of Hummingbird Bakery, Magnolia and Kitsch Cupcakes across the emirate.

Farm Shops
As demand for organic and locally grown produce increases in Dubai, so does the number of shops offering these healthier options. Prices may be higher, but it's a real treat to be able to buy fresh and organic fruit and veg in the middle of the desert.

downtoearthorganic.ae
These guys arrange for choice organic products and fresh produce to be delivered right to your door via its online store.

Greenheart Organic Farms
The Light Building, Arjan Al Barsha 2 **056 640 7060**
greenheartuae.com
Map **1 P11**
For everything fresh, nutritious and delicious. This farm shop in Arjan, Al Barsha 2, sells produce within hours of being harvested, and holds regular tasting events and demonstrations, as well as offers some fab promotions. You can put together your own mixed box or bag of produce on-site, as well as online. Opening times are Monday, Wednesday and Saturday from 11.30am to 5pm. Online delivery is available.

Ripe
Al Wasl St Al Manara **04 380 7602**
ripeme.com
Map **1 U6** Metro **Noor Bank**
Having served the Dubai community with fresh produce at its regular markets, Ripe's shop serves as a permanent base for fans.

Organic products are available

refresh... on the go...allday.

Markets

Western-style markets are becoming more and more popular in Dubai and are usually based around crafts or gourmet food and are often seasonal. These are less daunting than the souks and a good place to find unique items and fresh produce.

The Fish Market and the Fruit & Vegetable Market, however, are pretty old school, and bustling with traders and restauranteurs picking up fresh produce.

Artisans of the Emirates (ARTE)

Times Square Center Al Qouz Ind. 1
arte.ae
Map **1 T6** Metro **Noor Bank**
Taking place fortnightly (alternating between Dubai Festival City Mall and Times Square Center) this is where you'll find all manner of individual and quirky products unlike anything you'll find in any of the bigger markets; from hand-printed cards or personalised artwork to bags, cushions and jewellery created by talented local designers.

Cultural Night Market

Safa Park Al Wasl **055 5019408**
greateventsdubai.com
Map **2 D5** Metro **Business Bay**
Providing an urban public space for local and international artists to develop and showcase their art, the Cultural Night Market offers music, paintings, sculptures, dance and theatre, as well as a world food market. There's a kids' corner, artistic market, books area and live performances in the park amphitheatre. Held every last Friday and Saturday of the month, 3pm to 11pm, September through to April. Admission costs Dhs.15 per person; free for children under 10.

Dubai Designer Market

The Beach Centre Jumeira 1 **050 251 2480**
dubaidesignermarket.com
Map **2 G4** Metro **Emirates Towers**
Thrifty fashionistas should head here for chic and boutique designer goods at affordable prices. Think rails of high-end brands like Gucci, Prada, and Chanel, as well as vintage items and collections by young, up and coming designers. The Market has a strict original brands and high-end goods only policy, so no fakes allowed! Every second Saturday of the month at the Beach Centre, Jumeira.

Dubai Flea Market

Safa Park Al Wasl **04 452 6030**
dubai-fleamarket.com
Map **2 D5** Metro **Business Bay**
One man's junk is another man's treasure, and this is certainly true here. Winter sessions are at Safa Park on the first Saturday of the month. During the summer, the market takes place at Dubai World Trade Centre, on the first Friday of the month. From furniture and trinkets to clothes, toys and even household appliances, anything goes and you don't know what you might find.

The Farmers' Market

Emirates Towers Trade Center 2 **04 427 9856**
bakerandspiceme.com
Map **2 G6** Metro **Emirates Towers**
Taking place every Friday from 9am to 1pm during winter at Emirates Towers, The Farmers' Market On The Terrace sells local produce grown on UAE farms, as well as fresh bread and cakes baked by Baker & Spice and Sweet Connections Gluten Free Baking, plus more stalls packed with goodies. Produce is harvested just hours before the market and the farmers are on hand to answer any questions.

Fish Market

Nr Al Shindagha Tunnel Al Corniche **800 900**
dm.gov.ae
Map **2 N4** Metro **Palm Deira**
To get the freshest fish for your evening meal, and to experience the vibrancy of this working market, head down early in the morning or late at night as the catch is coming in. There is an incredible range of seafood on display and the fish can be cleaned and gutted for you.

Fruit & Vegetable Market

Ras Al Khor Rd Ras Al Khor Industrial 3
Map **2 K13** Metro **Rashidiya**
Located off Sheikh Mohammed bin Zayed Rd in Al Aweer, there is a huge variety of produce on offer that is usually fresher than in the supermarkets. Be sure to haggle; you can often tell if you have paid more than the trader thinks the goods are worth if they give you freebies. It is well signposted as you drive along the Dubai-Hatta Road and mornings are the best time to visit.

Ripe

Al Wasl St Al Qouz Ind. 1 **04 380 7602**
ripeme.com
Map **1 U6** Metro **Noor Bank**
Ripe hosts a farmers' market every Saturday at The Courtyard, Al Qouz, and every Friday in Zabeel Park during the winter months, selling cardboard boxes packed with fresh local fruit and vegetables. Produce varies according to the season and can include anything from leafy, fragrant basil and irregular-sized courgettes to potatoes with the dirt still clinging to them. There are also stalls selling tasty treats such as locally made cheeses, olives and chutneys, as well as designer gifts and kitsch crafts. Zabeel Park also houses a boating lake. Park entry is Dhs.5.

Fish Market

Traditional items

Ripe Vegetable Market

Souks

The souks are the traditional trading areas, the closest you'll get to an authentic, old world Arabian experience. In keeping with tradition, bargaining is expected and cash gives the best leverage.

The Gold, Spice and Textile Souks line either side of the creek, but parking is limited, so if possible it is better to go to these areas by taxi or, if you are visiting all three, park on one side of the creek and take an abra to the other side.

The modern souks tend to be more like malls with high-end shops and a nod to traditional architecture.

Al Fahidi Souk

Al Souk Al Kabeer **800 900**
dm.gov.ae
Map **2 L4** Metro **Al Fahidi**
This heritage-themed souk in Al Fahidi is opening slowly, and at the time of going to print is only open on Saturdays from 10am until sunset. Built to resemble Naif Souk, it uses many traditional architectural cues.

Gold Souk

Nr Baniyas Square, Al Sabkha
goldsouks.com
Map **2 M4** Metro **Baniyas Square**
This is Dubai's best-known souk and a must-do for every visitor. It's a good place to buy customised jewellery for unique souvenirs and gifts at a reasonable price. On the Deira side of the creek, the meandering lanes are lined with shops selling gold, silver, pearls and precious stones. These can be bought as they are or in a variety of settings so this is definitely a place to try your bargaining skills – but don't expect a massive discount. Gold is sold by weight according to the daily international price and so will be much the same as in the shops in malls – the price of the workmanship is where you will gain more bargaining power. Most of the outlets are closed between 1pm and 4pm. The Gold Souk is always busy, and it is shaded.

Khan Murjan

Wafi Umm Hurair 2 **04 3279795**
Map **2 K7** Metro **Dubai Healthcare City**
For something a little different, head to Wafi's underground souk. Khan Murjan's magnificent stained glass ceiling (which stretches 64 metres) and long curved arches help make this an atmospheric place to shop. Over 150 stalls sell jewellery, antiques, Arabic perfume and souvenirs. It is particularly good if you wish to spice up your home with traditional arts and crafts; there are workshops where artisans can create various bits of arts and crafts on site. The open air marble courtyard in the centre houses the highly recommended Khan Murjan Arabic restaurant.

Naif Souk

Nr Naif Police Station Naif
Map **2 M4** Metro **Baniyas Square**
This souk in the heart of Deira re-opened in 2010, two years after the original burned down in a fire that destroyed most of the buildings. Before the inferno, this souk was a big draw for visitors and locals alike, and the new facilities – more modern, less rustic than the Naif of old – still bring crowds of shoppers and tourists back to look for bargains from the range of goods on sale.

Souk Al Bahar > p.349

Shk Mohd Bin Rashid Blvd Burj Khalifa **04 362 7011**
soukalbahar.ae
Map **2 F6** Metro **Burj Khalifa/Dubai Mall**
Not exactly a souk in conventional terms, Souk Al Bahar in Downtown Dubai is an Arabian-style mall with many shops catering to tourists as well as a few international brands and the odd funky boutique. There are a number of useful outlets catering for residents including a Spinneys. Most folk head here for the views of the Burj Khalifa, Dubai Fountain and the fantastic range of eateries, cafes and bars.

Souk Madinat Jumeirah

Jumeira St Al Sufouh 1 **04 366 8888**
madinatjumeirah.com
Map **1 R5** Metro **Mall of the Emirates**
A recreation of a traditional souk complete with narrow alleyways, authentic architecture and motorised abras. The blend of outlets is unlike anywhere else in Dubai, with boutique shops, art galleries, souvenir stalls, and popular cafes, restaurants and bars. During the cooler months the doors and glass walls are opened to add an alfresco element and there is shisha on offer in the courtyard.

There are more than 20 waterfront cafes, bars and restaurants to choose from, including some of Dubai's hottest night spots, and you'll find Left Bank, Trader Vic's and Barzar to name a few. There's also the impressive Madinat Theatre which sees international and regional artists and theatre companies perform everything from ballet to comedy.

Spice Souk

Nr Gold Souk Al Ras
Map **2 M4** Metro **Al Ras**
The narrow streets and exotic aromas are a great way to get a feel for the way the city used to be. Vendors are usually happy to give advice on the types of spices and their uses, and the experience of buying from the Souk is more memorable than picking a packet off a shelf. You may even be able to pick up some saffron at a bargain price. The shops operate split shifts but, whether you visit in the morning or the evening, this is a bustling area of the city.

Al fresco dining
with the best views
of Burj Khalifa &
The Dubai Fountains

SOUK AL BAHAR

Abd El Wahab | Bice Mare | Café Habana | Claw
Caribou Coffee | Eugenie | Fuego | Icons | Coffee Couture
Kanpai | Karma Kafé | La Postreria | Left Bank | Mango Tree
Patiala Restaurant | The Meat Co. | Rivington Grill | Starbucks Coffee
Al Malouf Restaurant | Tolosa | Urbano | Baker & Spice | Sammach
Bon Patisserie & Café | Entourage | Loca | Muze | Shakespeare and Co.
Serafina | Shake Shack | Zahr El Laymoun

For more information   04 362 7011 / 12   www.soukalbahar.ae
SoukAlBahar   @soukalbahardubai   #SoukAlBahar

THE OLD TOWN
AT DOWNTOWN DUBAI

EMAAR
MALLS

Textile Souk

Ali Bin Abi Talib St Al Souk Al Kabeer
Map **2 M4** Metro **Al Ghubaiba**
This souk in Bur Dubai is stocked with every fabric
and colour imaginable. The textiles are imported
from all over the world, with many of the more
elaborate designs coming from the subcontinent and
the Far East. There are silks and satins in an amazing
array of colours and patterns, velvets and intricately
embroidered fabrics. Prices here are somewhat
negotiable, but it is worth having a look in a few
shops before parting with your cash as they may have
different stock and at better prices. The mornings tend
to be a more relaxed time to browse.

Shopping Malls

Malls are not just places to shop; a huge mall culture
exists here, and they are places to meet, eat and
mingle. Many malls provide entertainment for people
of all ages. With so much choice out there, malls make
sure they can offer something unique to shoppers to
draw the crowds. From one-of-a-kind attractions such
as indoor skiing, and theme parks to unique shops,
restaurants and bars, each mall has its own feel and its
own pulling power. Most malls will have branches of
the major banks, pharmacies and other services such
as dry cleaning.

Special events are held during Dubai Shopping
Festival, Dubai Summer Surprises and Ramadan, with
entertainment for children, special offers and longer
opening hours. These are peak shopping times and an
evening in the larger malls at this time is not for the
faint-hearted. Most of the malls have plenty of parking
– often stretched to the limits at the weekends; all
have taxi ranks (be warned that queues can be very
long at chucking-out time on the weekends) and
many are handy for bus and metro routes.

Al Ghurair Centre

Al Rigga St Al Muraqqabat **800 24227**
alghuraircentre.com
Map **2 N5** Metro **Union**
Housing an eight-screen Novo Cinemas, a Spinneys,
and a good range of shops, this two-storey mall
has the maze-like quality of a souk. There are a
number of international brands, including Bhs and
Mothercare, along with smaller boutiques. A major
recent expansion has brought several new brands
to the mall, including popular British supermarket
fashion brand George, a branch of Marks & Spencer,
Mango and Iconic, and the mall plans to have an
ongoing programme of street theatre and other
unique entertainment. There's also a Sparky's family
entertainment centre with an ice rink, as well as rides
that include an outdoor rollercoaster.

BurJuman

Shk Khalifa Bin Zayed St Al Mankhool **04 352 0222**
burjuman.com
Map **2 L5** Metro **BurJuman**
Renowned for its blend of designer and high-street
brands, BurJuman attracts many a well-heeled
shopper. There are famous brands such as Versace
and Ralph Lauren, as well as some interesting smaller
shops and New York department store Saks Fifth
Avenue. Gap and Zara lead the way in everyday
fashion. There are some independent music shops
plus a branch of Virgin Megastore, while home
stores include THE One. There is a Fitness First gym,
and services include a pharmacy. Restaurants cater
to all tastes, from Noodle House to Masala House,
and the mall has direct access to the Dubai Metro.
Major renovation and expansion works continue
and a section of the mall remains closed, although a
Carrefour recently opened in the new wing.

Deira City Centre

Ittihad St Port Saeed **04 295 1010**
deiracitycentre.com
Map **2 N7** Metro **Deira City Centre**
This popular mall attracts the most cosmopolitan
crowd. Three floors offer a diverse range of shops
where you can find anything from a postcard
to a Persian carpet. There's a cinema, children's
entertainment centre Magic Planet, with an eight-lane
cosmic bowling arena, a jewellery court, a textiles
court and an area dedicated to local furniture, gifts
and souvenirs. It is all anchored by a huge Carrefour
hypermarket, a Debenhams department store and
Paris Gallery. Most of the high-street brands are
represented, including New Look and River Island,
plus a number of designer boutiques. The mall has
two foodcourts, one serving mainly fast food, and one
featuring several good sit-down restaurants such as
Noodle House and Japengo. Deira City Centre Metro
station offers easy access.

Dubai Festival City Mall

Crescent Drive Al Kheeran **800 332**
festivalcentre.com
Map **2 M9** Metro **Emirates**
The biggest shopping draw here is Dubai's only
IKEA store, but this waterfront destination features a
number of useful retail outlets and plenty of alfresco
restaurants, including Jamie's Italian and the hugely
popular Hard Rock Cafe. There's a broad range of
fashion, electronics and homeware outlets, and it is
home to an enormous HyperPanda hypermarket, a
large Plug-Ins, and the largest ACE store outside of
North America, making it a great stop for setting up
home. There is also a large modern gold souk where
you can peruse gold from all over the world, and the
monthly community ARTE craft market is worth a look.

BurJuman Mall

Festival City Mall

Al Ghurair Centre

The mall also features Brit favourite Marks & Spencer and designer stores like Marc By Marc Jacobs. You'll find a branch of the Dubai London Clinic here too, a pharmacy, banks and dry cleaners.

There is a Grand Cinemas and a 10 lane bowling alley, and plenty more for kids too, from Toys R Us to the Cool Times soft play area, which has an art zone.

The Dubai Mall

Financial Centre St Burj Khalifa **04 362 7500** thedubaimall.com
Map **2 F7** Metro **Burj Khalifa/Dubai Mall**
This colossal shopping centre is one of the largest in the world, and buzzes at weekends with the entire cross-section of Dubai society. The complex also houses an Olympic-size ice rink, an enormous aquarium and underwater zoo, a 22 screen cinema, indoor theme park SEGA Republic and unique children's 'edutainment' centre, KidZania.

Unique to The Dubai Mall are the regional flagship stores for New York department store Bloomingdale's, French department store Galeries Lafayette, and the world-renowned toy shop Hamleys. You'll find all of the haute couture designer brands along Fashion Avenue, as well as high-street favourites like Topshop and Forever 21, and a sprawling gold souk. There are branches of the major banks on the ground floor, a large Waitrose supermarket and a huge variety of fast food outlets, cafes and restaurants.

The fountain show beside the Burj Khalifa is a must-see, and starts at 6pm and runs every half hour.

For a complete contrast, cross the wooden bridge over the Burj Lake to Souk Al Bahar, offering a more relaxing stop after the onslaught of the mall.

Dubai Marina Mall > p.353

Al Marsa St Marsa Dubai **04 436 1020**
dubaimarinamall.com
Map **1 K5** Metro **Jumeirah Lakes Towers**
Located in Marsa Dubai's thriving community, and within walking distance of The Walk, Jumeirah Beach Residence, this manageably compact mall's outlets offer a mix of plush designer goods and high-street regulars. It offers Marina residents some good local, reasonably priced fashion outlets without having to venture far, but is worth a visit from further afield if you're this end of town.

Options include shops like New Look and Reiss, while kids' clothes and toys can be found at Mamas & Papas and Mothercare. There are banks, an exchange centre, opticians, a travel agency, a tailor and dry cleaner on site – all handy local amenities for local residents. The Waitrose supermarket is a huge draw for expats. Dining options range from the usual fast food suspects at the foodcourt to Carluccio's and Gourmet Burger Kitchen, while the connecting Address hotel has some upmarket venues. The latest destination for foodies is Pier 7.

A play area provides plenty of entertainment for kids, and you can drop them off while you shop, or alternatively there's a small offshoot of SEGA Republic by the cinema.

Dubai Outlet Mall

Dubai – Al Ain Rd Umm Nahad 1 **04 423 4666**
dubaioutletmall.com
In a city where the emphasis in on excess, it is refreshing (not only for the wallet) to find a mall dedicated to saving money. Dubai's first 'outlet' concept mall may be a way out of town (15 minutes down the Al Ain road) but it's worth the drive. Big discounts on major retailers and labels are available; think T-shirts for under Dhs.30 and Karama-esque prices for Marc Jacobs handbags.

High-street shops including Massimo Dutti, Giordano and Dune sit alongside designer names such as Tommy Hilfiger and DKNY, with city style and sports casual equally catered for. Pick up trainers from Asics, Adidas, Nike and Puma, reduced eyewear from Al Jaber or Magrabi, homewares from THE One and a range of electronics. There are some bargains to be had on trendy surf brands as well, including Billabong, Roxy and Quiksilver.

To keep the little ones happy there's US institution Chuck E Cheese serving up food and entertainment.

Ibn Battuta Mall

Off Shk Zayed Rd Jabal Ali 1 **04 362 1900**
ibnbattutamall.com
Map **1 G5** Metro **Ibn Battuta**
A theatre-like mall with whacky themed zones. There is a good range of mostly international stores and several anchor stores such as Debenhams and a huge Geant hypermarket. Shops are loosely grouped: China Court is dedicated to entertainment, with several restaurants (including the excellent Finz), a Fitness First gym and a large cinema; the IMAX screens regular blockbusters. The fashion conscious should head to Persia and India Courts for high street favourites such as H&M and Oasis. Persia Court is styled as the lifestyle area – when you get to Starbucks, look up to see the ceiling detail. Egypt Court is for sporty types; Andalusia Court covers life's necessities such as banking, dry cleaning, key cutting, and DVD and video rental.

The six zones of the mall are each based on a region that explorer Ibn Battuta visited in the 14th century. Guided tours that illuminate the mall's unusual features, such as the full-size replica of a Chinese Junk and Al Jazari's Elephant Clock, are available.

Food courts are located at either end of the mall, and there's a Fun City in Tunisia Court. It is an enjoyable mall to wander around, but its long, linear design means it can be a long way back if there's something you've missed.

DUBAI MARINA MALL

Your mall
in the heart of the marina

Mall of the Emirates

Shk Zayed Rd Al Barsha 1 **04 409 9000**
malloftheemirates.com
Map **1 R6** Metro **Mall of the Emirates**

This lifestyle destination houses an indoor ski slope (Ski Dubai), a huge VOX Cinemas and the Dubai Community Theatre & Arts Centre. There are hundreds of outlets selling everything from forks to high fashion, and further expansion is under way. Label devotees should head to Via Rodeo and the Fashion Dome for designer labels like Burberry, Versace and Louis Vuitton. High-street fashion is covered with two H&M stores, Zara, the largest Dune store in the world, and much more.

The mall is anchored by Carrefour hypermarket, Dubai's largest branch of Debenhams, upmarket Harvey Nichols, and Centrepoint. Entertainment centre Magic Planet includes a bowling alley and a myriad of games and rides. Electronics stores are grouped handily into a corner, as are the homewares shops. A wide range of dining options encompass everything from the Swiss chalet feel of Apres to popular American eatery The Cheesecake Factory, as well as three separate foodcourts.

Mall Parking

Some malls, including Mall of the Emirates and Deira City Centre, charge for parking, but even at these it's free on weekends and public holidays, and for the first four hours on weekdays.

Mercato Shopping Mall

Jumeira St Jumeira 1 **04 344 4161**
mercatoshoppingmall.com
Map **2 F4** Metro **Financial Centre**

The Renaissance-style architecture really makes this mall stand out and, once inside, the huge glass roof provides a lot of natural light, enhancing its Mediterranean feel.

The mall is anchored by Spinneys which has a dry cleaners, photo lab and music shop; a large Virgin Megastore (that has a decent book department); Laura Ashley Home, and Gap. There are also a few good options for kids such as Early Learning Centre, Toy Store Express and Armani Junior. It's a good stop for high-street brands, from Pull & Bear and Mango to Jack Wills.

There is a foodcourt and a number of cafes and restaurants, including Paul Patisserie, and American burger favourite Shake Shack. VOX Cinemas and a large Fun City play area should keep most of the family occupied. There is also a nail salon, hair salon and mother and baby room on the upper floor, in addition to ATMs, a money exchange and a key cutting and shoe repair shop.

Mirdif City Centre

Shk Mohd Bin Zayed Rd Mirdif **04 602 3000**
mirdifcitycentre.com
Map **2 P12** Metro **Rashidiya**

This large and spacious mall is Mirdif's very own slice of upmarket retail action. Key anchor outlets include a large Carrefour, Debenhams, Emax and Centrepoint; there are some great home stores here too, including Home Centre, Pottery Barn and Crate & Barrel. High street fashion is comprehensive, with dozens of fashion outlets including Miss Selfridge and Forever 21. There's a huge foodcourt plus more upscale eateries such as MORE Cafe, Mango Tree Bistro and Butcher Shop & Grill.

Kids won't mind being dragged shopping here too; the VOX Cinemas houses 10 screens, and the Playnation centre has a number of fantastic attractions including a fun water play area called Aquaplay, footy-based Soccer Circus, a bowling alley, Little Explorers children's activity centre and even an indoor sky diving facility, iFLY Dubai.

Wafi

Shk Rashid Rd Umm Hurair 2 **04 324 4555**
wafi.com
Map **2 L7** Metro **Dubai Healthcare City**

Wafi's Egyptian theme, designer stores and layout make this one of the more interesting malls to wander around, and it rarely feels busy. The distinctive building has three pyramids forming part of the roof and a large stained glass window. Two of the pyramids are decorated with stained glass, depicting Egyptian scenes – best viewed during daylight.

From jewellery to couture, the likes of Versace and Roberto Cavalli mix with well-known high-street shops like Oasis and a large branch of UK stalwart Marks & Spencer. THE One, a popular Dubai furniture store, has a branch here, as does Villeroy & Boch and Tanagra. For something different head to Khan Murjan, the mall's impressive underground souk.

There are a number of cafes and restaurants, including Biella and the highly recommended Khan Murjan Arabic restaurant, where you can enjoy your meal in an alfresco dining area. Children's play area Kids Connection keeps little ones very happy, and events include the Return of the Pharaohs light show and Movies Under the Stars screenings on the rooftop.

Wafi is also home to the exclusive Raffles Dubai hotel, with its Raffles Spa and Fire and Ice restaurant.

Appy Shopper

Some malls have their own apps, with information on shops and discounts. Visit mall websites to find out more. Or try ShopperInput and get paid for being a mystery shopper!

Mercato Mall

Mall of the Emirates

Mirdif City Centre

Traditional carpets

BUYERS' GUIDE

From antiques to technology, and from tools to toys, the aim of this section is to let you know what's out there and the best places to buy. It's by no means an exhaustive list, but is designed to help you find those items that, while in your home country you just know how to find, in a new city can be harder to figure out.

Hypermarkets such as Carrefour and LuLu are a good place to start, and ACE Hardware and IKEA are also great for the things you didn't even know you needed. We've referred to the main stores in each category, but many have branches all over the city. See askexplorer.com for a complete list of store locations.

Quick Reference

Alcohol

If you're over the age of 21 you can buy alcohol in Dubai's restaurants and licensed bars, and some sports clubs, for consumption on the premises. If you wish to drink at home you will need a liquor licence; how much you are permitted to buy is dependent on your monthly salary and Muslims are not allowed to apply.

Two companies operate liquor stores in Dubai: African + Eastern (A+E) and Maritime & Mercantile International (MMI). Both have branches in several locations around the city, the most handy being the ones near supermarkets. The selection is decent, and prices are not so bad: wine costs from around Dhs.35 and upwards; vodka from Dhs.60; whisky from Dhs.80; and beer from Dhs.4 to Dhs.8 per can or Dhs.100 to Dhs.135 per case. Alcohol is, however, subject to 30% tax on the marked price.

There is a good selection of alcohol available at the airport Duty Free. The alcohol available at the airport is similar in price to the shops in town, but you don't pay the tax.

There are also a number of 'hole in the wall' stores close to Dubai (in the northern emirates of Ajman, Ras Al Khaimah and Umm Al Quwain) that sell duty-free alcohol to members of the public, even if you don't have a licence. Prices are reasonable and there is no tax. You won't need to worry about being busted buying booze illegally, but you should be careful when driving home; it is the transporting of alcohol that could get you into trouble, especially if you are stopped within the borders of Sharjah, which is a 'dry' emirate. There have been reports of random police checks on vehicles driving from Ajman into Sharjah. Also, if you have an accident and you're found to have a boot full of liquor, your day could take a sudden turn for the worse.

African + Eastern > p.xii, 45, 359
Spinneys Centre Al Safa 2 04 394 2676
africaneastern.com
Map 2 B5 Metro Noor Bank
With convenient locations across Dubai, a wide variety of products and regular promotions, A+E outlets remain a good place to purchase wine, spirits and beer. Its stores sell the typical brands and a few imports of Japanese and German beer.

Al Hamra Cellar
Al Hamra Village Ras Al Khaimah 07 244 7403
mmidubai.com
Around an hour's drive from Dubai along Sheikh Mohammed bin Zayed Rd, this licence-free store stocks an amazing selection of beers, spirits and award-winning wines at fantastic tax-free prices – including wine specially selected by guru Oz Clarke.

Barracuda Beach Resort
Nr Dreamland Aqua Park, Khor Al Baida
Umm Al Quwain 06 768 1555
barracuda.ae
A tax-free, licence-free booze emporium that is popular with Dubai's residents. There is a superb selection, including the regular brands of beer, wine and spirits.

Centaurus International
Ras Al Selaab Ras Al Khaimah 07 228 3117
centaurusint.info
Another licence-free 'hole in the wall' outlet that offers a good range of products. You can view its range of wine, beer and spirits on its online shop, and it also offers a delivery service.

Le Clos
Nr Gate 214 Dubai International Airport 04 220 3633
leclos.net
Map 2 P8 Metro Airport Terminal 3
This exclusive store in Emirates Terminal 3 offers a premium selection of alcohol that can only be pre-ordered on departure and collected on arrival at the terminal. See the website for more details.

MMI
Trade Centre Rd Al Mankhool 04 352 3091
mmidubai.com
Map 2 L5 Metro ADCB
Similar to A+E, with a broad selection of international drink brands and some lesser known names. To get the best value for money, look for its special 'bin' with discounts on wine where you can select new or not as known brands that are on promotion. Don't forget your liquor licence. See website for other stores.

Arts & Crafts

A number of shops sell a good range of art and craft supplies, with everything from paints and crayons for children to top-quality oils available. Particularly good places to find materials are Bin Sougat Mall in Rashidiya and the Holiday Centre on Sheikh Zayed Road. For DIY picture framing, Rafi Frame Store, aka Al Warda Gallery, in Karama is the place to find the necessary equipment, including mountboards.

Craft Land
Town Centre Jumeirah Jumeira 1 04 342 2237
mycraftland.com
Map 2 F4 Metro Burj Khalifa/Dubai Mall
Supplies materials, machines, tools and gadgets for a host of needle crafts, including knitting, sewing, embroidery, quilting and crochet, and also offers classes, clinics and clubs for keen crafters.

Creative Minds

Beach Centre Jumeira 1 **04 344 6628**
creativemindsdubai.com
Map **2 G4** Metro **Emirates Towers**
With stores in Al Barsha 1 (on Umm Suqeim Road) and at Beach Centre in Jumeira, Creative Minds is convenient for several areas of the city. Both stores stock a wide range of products, as well as school supplies and even fancy dress.

Emirates Trading Establishment

Villa 27, Nr Mercato Shopping Mall, St 75B
Jumeira 1 **04 344 1052**
emirates-trading.com
Map **2 F4** Metro **Burj Khalifa/Dubai Mall**
Stocks everything from children's crayons to industrial spray booths and it is a supplier of Windsor & Newton and Daler-Rowney products.

White Star Bookshop (Wasco)

Beach Centre Jumeira 1 **04 342 2179**
Map **2 G4** Metro **Emirates Towers**
Stocks craft supplies that are suitable for children's projects and difficult to find elsewhere. Prices can be expensive for some speciality items, such as mosaic tiles, but art materials are reasonably priced.

ARTE Souk

Artisans of the Emirates (ARTE) occasionally sets up markets selling arts and crafts in Times Square Center and Dubai Festival City Mall. These stalls sell a range of items including photographs, jewellery and a variety of art and everything is locally handmade. For more information on the stalls and market dates and locations, visit arte.ae.

Books, Music & DVDs

You'll find both international bookstores and good local stores in Dubai. All malls feature at least one bookstore, and if you cannot find a publication, the larger stores let you place an order or enquire whether it is available in another branch. Dubai's transitory residents furnish the second-hand bookshops – you'll find a wide range of books, particularly fiction, many of which have only been read once. There are regular charity book sales, the most notable being the ones organised by Medecins Sans Frontieres (msf-me. org). They are held several times throughout the year, usually in the Dune Centre in Satwa. A small selection of books, DVDs and games sell in the supermarkets and hypermarkets.

Unless you have particularly obscure taste, you should find a satisfying collection of music in the city's supermarkets and record stores. Music and DVDs are generally more expensive than they are in other countries, but the advantage of Dubai's multicultural society is that you can open yourself up to new genres – Arabic dance music for example, is very popular. Everything has to go through the censor, so any music or DVDs deemed offensive will not be sold here, unless it can be edited to make it more acceptable. Retailers will order titles that are on the approved list for the UAE. Bollywood films are extremely popular and available in most shops.

Online shopping is an alternative if you can't find an item and you'll find more variety on sites like Amazon (amazon.com and amazon.co.uk), which delivers to the UAE. Delivery rates are cheaper from the UK site than the US site. Your package may be inspected by UAE customs. The UAE iTunes store sells a limited selection of music, TV shows, movies and iBooks, but you can log in to the UK or US sites for the extensive library – you'll need a UK or US registered credit card for these.

You can also buy guide books and photography books by Explorer in most of the bookstores listed below, or order online at askexplorer.com.

Movie Rentals

There are a few places where you can rent DVDs in the city; Spinneys stores often have rental sections where you can sign up. Some supermarkets have a self service DVD dispenser from Moviebank or Davina Box, where you pay to join and you are charged by the day – you simply return the DVD to the dispenser when you are finished. If DVDs are too old school for you, the On Demand services from OSN and du allow subscribers to rent movies and series through their cable or satellite receiver. See TV in Living in Dubai for more info.

Book Munch

Wasl Square Al Safa 1 **04 388 4006**
bookmunchcafe.com
Map **2 D5** Metro **Business Bay**
Dubai's first literary cafe is situated in a lovely spot not far from Safa Park. It houses a big collection of hand-picked titles that cater to all ages in addition to offering mouthwatering dishes for breakfast, lunch and dinner. You can peruse the titles while you eat, but be mindful of leaving the books in a saleable condition. Also hosts regular events for book lovers.

Book World

Nr Satwa Flower Shop Al Bada' **04 349 1914**
Map **2 H5** Metro **World Trade Centre**
A literary paradise for all bookworms; browse an assortment of pre-loved titles and new books, as well as a fascinating collection of comics.

AFRICAN + EASTERN STORES ARE ALL OVER TOWN!

And where there's African + Eastern, there's always an extensive portfolio of labels across ales, grape, malt and more from all over the world. Visit your nearest neighbourhood store for all the brands you love.

For more information call us on **800 CHEERS** (243377) or ask our staff in-store.

Al Wasl Road* · Arabian Ranches* · Bur Dubai* · Burj Views* · Deira* · Dubai Marina Mall*
Dubai Marina Walk* · Green Community** · Jumeirah* · Karama · Le Méridien Dubai** · Mirdif · TECOM*

*Stores also open on Fridays from 2:00pm - 9:00pm
**Stores open Saturday to Thursday from 2:00pm - 9:00pm

african eastern
INSPIRING GREAT BLENDS

Books Kinokuniya > *p.386*
The Dubai Mall Burj Khalifa **04 434 0111**
kinokuniya.com
Map **2 F7** Metro **Burj Khalifa/Dubai Mall**
The biggest bookshop in Dubai, this Japanese chain stocks a variety of international titles and a great selection of comics, as well as stationery, magazines and journals, and a fantastic range of childrens' books.

Booksplus
Dubai Festival City Mall Al Kheeran **04 232 5563**
appareluae.com
Map **2 M9** Metro **Emirates**
A fairly comprehensive range of titles and international magazines are stocked at this small bookstore. This is a perfect place to pick up light reads and popular titles.

Bookworm
Park n Shop Al Safa 1 **04 323 5305**
Map **2 C5** Metro **Noor Bank**
A great store for inspiring kids to read with an extensive range of titles for very young kids up to young adults, plus educational books and a fun selection of toys and gifts.

Borders > *p.444*
Mall of the Emirates Al Barsha 1 **04 341 5758**
almaya.ae
Map **1 R6** Metro **Mall of the Emirates**
This US chain sells a vast variety of books and a fantastic selection of the latest international magazines. The store stocks a good range of Paperchase stationery items and a small gift range.

Culture & Co
Umm Hurair St Oud Metha **04 357 3603**
culturecodubai.net
Map **2 L6** Metro **Oud Metha**
A great option for French speakers and readers, or students of the language, this bookshop in Oud Metha sells a good selection of French novels, guidebooks, magazines and papers.

Duflix Movies
Spinneys Centre Al Safa 2 **04 394 0139**
duflix.com
Map **2 B5** Metro **Noor Bank**
Stocks a good range of items, particularly BBC and children's titles, and also has a rental section.

House Of Prose
Dubai Garden Centre Al Qouz Industrial 3
04 340 0006
Map **1 S6** Metro **First Gulf Bank**
A huge collection of second-hand books; there's a great choice of English fiction for children and adults.

Most of the stock is in excellent condition, and you may even find a new release.

Jashanmal Bookstores > *p.385*
Mall of the Emirates Al Barsha 1 **04 340 6789**
jashanmalbooks.com
Map **1 R6** Metro **Mall of the Emirates**
A wide-ranging selection, with international books and magazines. Head here during the sales and you can grab some really good bargains.

Magrudy's
Nr Jumeira Centre, Jumeira Rd Jumeira 1
04 344 4193
magrudy.com
Map **2 H4** Metro **Emirates Towers**
A local chain offering new releases, travel, fiction, children's books and more. Outlets include a dedicated educational resource centre. There's an annual warehouse sale for discounted books, toys and gifts.

Ohm Records
Nr BurJuman Al Karama **04 397 3728**
ohm-records.com
Map **2 L5** Metro **BurJuman**
Vinyl and electronic mixing fans should head to this speciality shop; you can buy processors and turntables, as well as record bags and accessories. Also stocks mainstream DVDs and a few independent films.

The Archive
Safa Park Al Wasl
04 349 0433
thearchive.ae
Map **2 D5** Metro **Business Bay**
The Archive serves as a cafe and library, with a good selection of art history and cultural books.

The Old Library
DUCTAC, Mall of the Emirates Al Barsha 1
04 341 4777
theoldlibrary.ae
Map **1 R6** Metro **Mall of the Emirates**
Nestled within DUCTAC at Mall of the Emirates, this library has a collection of over 19,000 fiction and general reference books. There's also a selection of second-hand books for sale.

Virgin Megastore
Mall of the Emirates Al Barsha 1 **04 341 4353**
virginmegastore.me
Map **1 R6** Metro **Mall of the Emirates**
The widest selection of mainstream music is stocked at this store, as well as an excellent range of DVD box sets and an interesting selection of books related to music and popular culture. There's also a selection of quirky gifts and branded T-shirts.

LOCATION. LOCATION. LOCATION.

With 15 great locations we've got Dubai covered.

AL THANYA — Tel No: 04 380 7655
Sat – Thu 10am - 9pm, Fri 2pm - 9pm

AL WASL — Tel No: 04 394 0351
Sat - Thu 10am - 9pm, Fri 2pm - 9pm

BUSINESS BAY - NEW SHOP — Tel No: 04 321 4805
Sat – Thu 10am - 9pm, Fri 2pm - 9pm

BUR DUBAI — Tel No: 04 393 4361
Sat - Thu 11am - 9pm

DEIRA — Tel No: 04 294 0390
Sat - Thu 11am - 9pm

DUBAI FESTIVAL CITY — Tel No: 04 232 5522
Sat - Thu 11am - 9pm

DSO COMMUNITY CENTRE — Tel No: 04 326 4583
Sat - Thu 11am - 9pm, Fri 2pm - 9pm

DSO CEDRE — Tel No: 04 326 1103
Sat - Thu 10am - 9pm, Fri 2pm - 9pm

GREEN COMMUNITY — Tel No: 04 885 4550
Sat - Thu 2pm - 9pm

IBN BATTUTA MALL — Tel No: 04 368 5626
Sat - Thu 11am - 9pm, Fri 2pm - 9pm

KARAMA — Tel No: 04 335 1722
Sat - Thu 11am - 9pm

MALL OF THE EMIRATES — Tel No: 04 341 0371
Sat - Thu 10am - 9pm, Fri 2pm - 9pm

MOTOR CITY — Tel No: 04 447 4900
Sat - Thu 11am - 9pm, Fri 2pm - 9pm

SHEIKH ZAYED ROAD — Tel No: 04 321 1223
Sat - Thu 11am - 9pm

TRADE CENTRE ROAD — Tel No: 04 352 3091
Sat - Thu 11am - 9pm, Fri 2pm - 9pm

For directions please call the shop or visit Find our shops on our website.

 mmidubai.com /mmidubai @mmi_dubai MMIDubai

Camera Equipment

From single-use cameras to darkroom equipment, photographers can usually find most things in Dubai. Prices vary between the larger outlets, where they are fixed, and the electronics shops of Bur Dubai. However, while you might be able to bag a bargain from the independent retailers using your superior powers of negotiation, you will ultimately get more protection buying from the larger outlets. The most important consideration, if you are buying the camera to take abroad, is to ensure your warranty is international; and don't just take the retailer's word for it, ask to read the warranty to make sure.

For second-hand equipment, gulfphotoplus.com (an essential site for all photography enthusiasts) has an equipment noticeboard, as well as being a great source of information.

Grand Stores

The Dubai Mall Burj Khalifa **04 339 8614**
grandstores.com
Map **2 F7** Metro **Burj Khalifa/Dubai Mall**
The main retailer for Nikon, Grand Stores also stocks Fuji, Canon and Mamiya. You can have your camera cleaned and repaired in its outlets, which can be found in several locations across Dubai.

MK Trading

Nr Twin Towers, Baniyas Rd Al Rigga **04 222 5745**
mktradingco.com
Map **2 N5** Metro **Union**
This store is the place to purchase Sigma cameras and lenses, as well as other leading brands; it also stocks a particularly good selection of filters. The store offers a repair facility.

National Store

Khansaheb Bldg, Al Fahidi St Al Souk Al Kabeer
04 353 4168
jksons.ae
Map **2 L4** Metro **Al Ghubaiba**
This store is a distributor of Canon products and you'll find a good selection of cameras, printers and camera accessories from the well-known brand. There are several branches of this store in Dubai.

Salam Studio & Stores

Wafi Umm Hurair 2 **04 704 8349**
salams.com
Map **2 K7** Metro **Dubai Healthcare City**
Stocking a complete range of professional-grade camera and studio equipment, this department store is considered the most comprehensive photography store in the city. It carries Bronica, Leica, Minolta and Pentax, and there's a good selection of filters, tripods and studio equipment.

Car Accessories

Cars and their accessories are big business in Dubai, so you won't struggle to find the accessories you need. ACE Hardware and Carrefour have large departments selling everything from steering wheel covers to fridges that run off the car battery, and there is a wide selection of tools in larger stores and in the smaller shops in Satwa. Further out in Sharjah industrial area you'll find slightly cheaper outlets than in Dubai.

GPS systems are available from Picnico or mainstream shops like Plug-Ins and Sharaf DG. Car stereos are widely available, and are sold by most electronics shops, with some of the car dealerships stocking alternative models for their cars. To have them fitted, head either to the workshops of Rashidiya or Satwa, or AAA and the dealers – it should cost around Dhs.500 if you are providing all the parts.

Many car owners try to beat the heat by having their car windows tinted. The legal limit is 30% tint; if you get your windows tinted any darker you could be fined, and your car won't pass its annual inspection. Be aware though that company-owned cars are not allowed tinted windows. The options range from the Dhs.75 plastic film from the workshops in Satwa, to Dhs.1,300 to Dhs.1,500 at After Dark (covered by a 10-year warranty), and up to Dhs.5,000 at V-KOOL which is also covered by warranty, and its clear film is more heat resistant than the tinted one.

If you are just looking for some memorabilia, or if you simply love fast cars, Ferrari has stores selling memorabilia and accessories. Head to Al Qouz and Rashidiya to customise your car by increasing its performance – West Coast Customs (as featured on the MTV series Pimp My Ride) now has a showroom and workshop in Al Qouz.

AAA Service Center > *p.103*

Nr Honda Trading Enterprises Umm Ramoul
04 285 8989
aaadubai.com
Map **2 N9** Metro **Rashidiya**
Sells specialist sand tracks and heavy duty jacks and winches – if your car is fitted with a GPS system the company can rescue you from the most remote dune or wadi.

Yellow Hat

Times Square Center Al Qouz Industrial 1
04 341 8592
yellowhat.ae
Map **1 T6** Metro **Noor Bank**
A one-stop shop for car accessories, supplying everything from tyres and sound systems to engine tuning. Head here to pick up breakdown kits, steering wheels, air filters or alloy wheels. The store also offers car cleaning and servicing.

Clothing & Shoes

You'll find no shortage of options when it comes to fashion in Dubai. For high-end brands and designer names, BurJuman is popular, as is Fashion Avenue and Level Shoe District at The Dubai Mall, and the Fashion Dome at Mall of the Emirates. Department stores like Saks Fifth Avenue, Harvey Nichols and Bloomingdale's stock a wide range of cutting-edge couture, and there are several boutiques dotted around Jumeira, such as Ayesha Depala Boutique and Boutique 1. TKD Lingerie at Town Centre Jumeirah stocks larger cup sizes that can be otherwise hard to find. Maktoum Road is lined with stores selling men's designer clothing, and there are also plenty of options inside the Twin Towers Mall in Deira.

For fashion that's less mainstream, head to stores like Kitsch, S*uce and Five Green for their eclectic mix of funky fashion. You can get beautiful hand-crafted fabrics and traditional Indian clothing at Fabindia on Al Mankhool Road, or Melangé in Jumeirah Plaza.

For high-street fashion head to any of the major malls, and many of the smaller ones, where you'll find pretty much all of the most popular international chains, such as Topshop, H&M, Forever 21, New Look, Pull & Bear and Mango.

For cut-price designer labels, Dubai Outlet Mall has all sorts of bargains, from designer to high street. Also check out My Ex Wardrobe (myexwardrobe.com) for pre-loved labels. The streets of Karama are crammed with designer fakes, ranging from cheap knock-offs to good quality copies.

All of the main hypermarkets stock affordable clothing and shoes, and Lamcy Plaza is a real bargain-hunter's mall – Mexx for Less, Peacocks and Factory Fashions are all excellent.

Shopping events such as Dubai Shopping Festival at the beginning of the year and Dubai Summer Surprises bring city-wide sweeping sales across all retail sectors; a great time to bag a discount.

Electrical Goods & Appliances

Whether you are setting up home or moving house, you'll have to spend some time looking for white goods. In Dubai, unfurnished really means unfurnished and you'll have to fork out for even the most standard items, like curtain rails for your windows. Unsurprisingly, there are plenty of places where you can buy goods and most international brands are sold here. Competition is high, so prices are reasonable and most dealers will offer warranties – some will offer a warranty extension for an extra year or two. You'll find a similar range of products in all of the electronics stores.

There are several stores dedicated to electronics and appliances in each of the larger malls and you'll find large sections in the hypermarkets, including Carrefour, Geant and HyperPanda, which stock a superb selection of goods from well-known brands (and some lesser known ones that also do the job) and usually offer a delivery and installation service. Everything from top-of-the-range high-definition televisions to games consoles, fridges and ovens to irons, water coolers and so on. It's worth waiting for the sales as there can be a noticeable drop in prices.

Bang & Olufsen and Bose offer a pricey, but undeniably stylish, range of goods for the home. You'll also find some high-end brands like Gaggenau on Jumeira Road and Miele at Trade Centre roundabout. For stylish kitchen appliances, head to Tavola, Bloomingdale's and Galeries Lafayette.

Many stores offer delivery and installation services, which take the hassle out of mounting a plasma screen or setting up your surround sound system.

Check that the warranty is valid internationally if you wish to take items back to your home country. Also check that the item will work in all areas of the world and whether you will have to pay any import duty if you return back home. Find out who will service the items if there are problems. For second-hand items, check the adverts placed on supermarket noticeboards and online classifieds, like dubizzle.com.

Al Ain Mall in Bur Dubai is dedicated to computer equipment, and several places do repairs and upgrades.

A Greener Future

The Change Initiative (thechangeinitiative.com) is a one-stop eco-store, offering environmentally-friendly and sustainable products. There's a range of household goods, appliances and building solutions that combine technology and good design, from ideas to improve insulation and lessen energy use, to eco-friendly furniture, paints and fashion accessories. Shop online or visit the store in Al Barsha 1, near the Ibis on Sheikh Zayed Rd.

ALSHOP

Burj Khalifa **800 257 467**
alshop.com Map **2 E7** Metro **Business Bay**
This online store is great for Apple products and the latest gadgets at competitive prices. Deliveries are prompt – usually within a few days, if not same day.

Better Life

Mall of the Emirates Al Barsha 1 **04 341 0716**
betterlifeuae.com
Map **1 R6** Metro **Mall of the Emirates**
This reliable store stocks the most popular brands, and its worth bartering for a discount if you're buying lots of items at once – good if you're setting up home.

Dubai Audio

Nr Safestway, Shk Zayed Rd Al Wasl 04 343 1441
dubaiaudio.com
Map **2 E6** Metro **Business Bay**
A super stylish range of designer electronics from
premium brands including Lexicon, Conrad Johnson
and Linn. The range includes luxury home cinema and
audio equipment and multi-room audio systems.

Jacky's Electronics

The Dubai Mall Burj Khalifa 04 434 0222
jackys.com
Map **2 F7** Metro **Burj Khalifa/Dubai Mall**
A wide range of electronics from well-known brands
– particularly Sony products. The store offers home
delivery and installation for some of its products, as
well as warranties and protection plans.

Jumbo Electronics

Al Mankhool 04 352 1323
jumbocorp.com
Map **2 L5** Metro **Al Fahidi**
A vast selection of popular entertainment brands, with
good deals and helpful staff. A good place to head to
if you are looking for Sony LCD televisions and home
theatre systems.

Plug-Ins

Dubai Festival City Mall Al Kheeran 04 206 6777
pluginselectronix.com
Map **2 M9** Metro **Emirates**
A comprehensive range of electronics, including the
latest products from Panasonic, Bose, Sony and LG.

Sharaf DG

Times Square Center Al Qouz Ind. 1
04 341 8060
sharafdg.com
Map **1 T6** Metro **Noor Bank**
A great first port of call because of its range of
appliances and gadgets, from plasma TVs and laptop
computers to mobile phones, washing machines,
cookers and irons. Staff are helpful and prices are
competitive, so you're sure to find what you're looking
for. Also very good for camera equipment.

Furniture & Homewares

This is one of Dubai's most buoyant retail sectors;
most tastes are catered for, from everyone's favourite
Swedish flatpack store to unique ethnic pieces, to
the latest designer concepts and specialist children's
furniture stores.

The industrial area between interchanges three
and four of Sheikh Zayed Road is home to a number
of furniture warehouses, many of which sell pieces
crafted from Indonesian teak. Their hot, dusty
warehouses are not the most chic of all options,
but prices are excellent and after a good polish
the furniture looks fabulous. Genuine antiques are
available but very rare (and therefore very expensive);
including pieces from Oman and Yemen.

Most shopping areas will have at least one furniture
store, and you'll be spoilt for choice in the larger malls.
Dubai Festival City Mall has the city's only IKEA, as well
as several other furniture and home accessories stores.

Jacky's Electronics

Real investment pieces that you'll want to keep and take back home can be bought at Natuzzi (04 338 0777) in Al Qouz. For exotic designs, try Safita Trading Est (04 339 3230, Al Qouz) which stocks a range of exotic items from India and the Far East. For unusual designer items, head to THE One Fusion in Al Qouz. Another warehouse worth visiting is Dubai Antique Museum – an enormous treasure trove of furniture and quirky pieces, as well as souvenirs and lots more.

Panache Interiors (050 351 7100) offers design services and ready-made home accessories. BAFCO is the place to hit if you're looking for office furniture with added style.

The transient nature of some of Dubai's population results in an active second-hand furniture market. Items are advertised in the classified sections of the local newspapers and on websites like dubizzle.com, but supermarket noticeboards are the best source; this is also the place to find garage sales – you can get some real bargains.

BAFCO

Al Karama **04 335 0045**
bafco.com
Map **2 L6** Metro **BurJuman**
Originally known as 'the office furniture people', BAFCO are experts at creating stylish and practical workspaces for their customers.

Crate & Barrel

Mall of the Emirates Al Barsha 1 **04 399 0125**
crateandbarrel.com
Map **1 R6** Metro **Mall of the Emirates**
Contemporary, stylish and functional sums up the modern designs of this American home store. From classic to hip and trendy styles, furniture, home decor, gifts, or housewares – there is something for all tastes. Another outlet is located at Mirdif City Centre.

Home Centre

Mall of the Emirates Al Barsha 1 **04 341 4441**
homecentrestores.com
Map **1 R6** Metro **Mall of the Emirates**
These large and inspiring stores are filled with a huge assortment of items and ideas. There are large ranges of bath towels, accessories and kitchenware in both traditional and modern styles. There's also plenty of furniture for the whole house.

Homes R Us

Mazaya Centre Al Wasl **04 321 3444**
ww.homesrusgroup.com
Map **2 F6** Metro **Burj Khalifa/Dubai Mall**
A complete, one-stop lifestyle destination showcasing a wide range of home furniture, furnishings and accessories at reasonable prices. There are also stores at Ibn Battuta Mall and Arabian Centre, Mirdif.

IKEA

Dubai Festival City Mall Al Kheeran **04 203 7555**
ikea.com
Map **2 M9** Metro **Emirates**
This enormous showroom sells a great range of good value furniture and home accessories, suitable for most budgets; it stocks everything from Dhs.1 tealight holders to Dhs.20,000 kitchens. It's also good for reasonably priced kids' furniture.

THE One

Mall of the Emirates Al Barsha 1 **04 341 3777**
theoneplanet.com
Map **1 R6** Metro **Mall of the Emirates**
A favourite among the expat crowd because of its funky, modern style and good selection of home accessories. Partner store THE One Fusion in Al Qouz Industrial 1 stocks an imaginative range of quirky collectables and cool one-offs.

Pan Emirates

Umm Suqeim St Al Barsha 1 **04 383 0800**
panemirates.com
Map **1 R6** Metro **Mall of the Emirates**
A wide range of furniture and accessories, from stylish and modern to the more traditional, to some grander, more gaudy affairs. Also sells a small range of garden furniture. Also located at Ibn Battuta Mall.

Pottery Barn

Mirdif City Centre Mirdif **800 802**
potterybarn.me
Map **2 P12** Metro **Rashidiya**
An American giant that sells a good range of quality household furniture and accessories, and also has an in-store design studio where customers can get advice on their home furnishing needs and ideas. There's also a big branch at The Dubai Mall.

United Furniture

Nr Oasis Centre Al Qouz 3 **04 338 9690**
unitedfurnitureco.com
Map **2 B6** Metro **Noor Bank**
A wide-ranging collection of home and office furniture and accessories. There's styles to suit international tastes, from the contemporary to the classic, and at affordable prices. Also features a variety of kids bedroom interiors.

Bloomingdale's The Dubai Mall, Burj Khalifa, 04 350 5333, *bloomingdales.com*
Debenhams Deira City Centre, Port Saeed, 04 294 0011, *debenhams.com*
Harvest Home Trading Jumeirah Centre, Jumeira 1, 04 342 0225
Tavola Spinneys Centre, Al Safa 2, 04 394 8150, *tavola.ae*

Designer Furniture

BoConcept
Shk Zayed Rd Al Safa 2 **04 388 4522**
boconcept.ae
Map **2 A6** Metro **Noor Bank**
A varied selection of urban and contemporary, Danish designed and manufactured sofas, tables, chairs, beds and accessories all created for the design conscious, but without a price tag to match. The store also offers an interior decoration service.

IDdesign
Mall of the Emirates Al Barsha 1 **04 341 3434**
iddesignuae.com
Map **1 R6** Metro **Mall of the Emirates**
A selection of modern furniture for the home or office, and a decent range of outdoor furniture. The store also offers an interior design service, furniture re-upholstery, and custom-made curtains, pillows and other accessories. Other outlets are located at Mirdif City Centre and Al Khabaisi.

Aati Nr Karama Fish Market, Za'abeel Rd, Al Karama, 04 337 7825, *altayer.com*
Armani/Casa The Dubai Mall, Burj Khalifa, 04 339 8121, *armanicasa.com*
B&B Italia Mall of the Emirates, Al Barsha 1, 04 341 2445, *baituti.com*
B5 The Art Of Living Sidra Tower, Shk Zayed Rd, Al Sufouh 1, 04 447 3973, *b5living.com*
Ethan Allen The Dubai Mall, Burj Khalifa, 04 330 8871, *ethanallen.com*
Filini Nr Times Square Center, Al Qouz Ind. 1, 04 323 3636, *filini.com*
Hastens Dubai Sunset Mall, Jumeira 3, 04 380 9565, *hastensdubai.com*
Irony Home The Dubai Mall, Burj Khalifa, 04 434 0166, *ironyhomelifestyle.com*
Kart Furniture Villa 746, Jumeira St, Umm Suqeim 2, 04 348 8169, *kartdesign.net*
Muri Lunghi Italian Furniture Al Reem Residency Bldg, Shk Rashid St, Al Karama, 04 358 2341, *murilunghi.com*
Natuzzi Nr Bosh Service Centre, Al Qouz 3, 04 338 0777, *int.natuzzi.com*
Objekts Of Design Al Kuthban Bldg, Shk Zayed Rd, Al Qouz Ind. 1, 04 328 4300, *od.ae*
Roche Bobois Nr Sharaf DG Metro Station, Al Barsha 1, 04 399 0393, *roche-bobois.com*
Singways Mall of the Emirates, Al Barsha 1, 04 340 9116, *singways.com*
Traffic 179 Umm Suqeim Rd, Al Qouz Ind. 4, 04 347 0209, *viatraffic.org*
Zen Interiors Essa Lutfi Bldg, Nr Sharaf DG Metro Station, Shk Zayed Rd, Al Barsha 1, 04 340 5050, *zeninteriors.net*

Wooden Furniture

Falaknaz – The Warehouse
Shk Zayed Rd Al Qouz Ind. 1 **04 328 5859**
falaknazthewarehouse.com
Map **2 A6** Metro **Noor Bank**
A big depot in Al Qouz, full to the brim with colonial-style teak home furniture and a good range of outdoor garden items. You can also have furniture custom-made by its factory in Indonesia.

Lucky's Furnitures & Handicrafts
Nr China Mall, Ind. Area 11 Sharjah **06 534 1937**
luckyfurnitureuae.com
This store in Sharjah is popular with expats seeking well-priced furniture. The range is vast, but the staff will happily explain the origin and design of the pieces, and can paint, varnish or make alterations.

Marina Exotic Home Interiors
Mall of the Emirates Al Barsha 1 **04 341 0314**
marinahomeinteriors.com
Map **1 R6** Metro **Mall of the Emirates**
Items here will add an exotic touch to your home and are generally more individual than you'll find at the usual furniture stores. You can pick up large wardrobes, tables, ornate chests and garden furniture. Other locations include Souk Al Bahar and The Walk at JBR.

Pinky Furniture
Nr Dubai American Academy Al Barsha 1 **04 422 1720**
pinkyfurnitureuae.com
Map **1 R7** Metro **Mall of the Emirates**
Much like Lucky's, Pinky has long been an expat favourite for traditional, hand-made Indian furniture. The new Barsha showroom saves customers the trip into Sharjah.

Kids

Kidz Inc > *p.x, 225*
Nr ACE Hardware, Al Qouz Ind. 1 **04 328 5775**
kidzincdubai.com
Map **1 U6** Metro **Noor Bank**
This shop is the sole agent for Haba – its German, hand-made, wooden furniture doesn't come cheap but all pieces meet European and American safety standards and come with a warranty. Especially good is the range of themed beds (think pirate ships and flowery glades), with matching furniture and unique and inspirational accessories.

Bellini The Dubai Mall, Burj Khalifa, 04 325 3222
Indigo Living Oasis Centre, Al Qouz 1, 04 339 7705, *indigo-living.com*

Thinking hardware? Think again.

There's certainly more to ACE than just a hardware store. From automotive accessories to kitchen appliances, camping gear to barbeques, outdoor furniture to paints and plants, gardening items to pet accessories. There's so much to choose from all under one roof. **ACE. The helpful place.**

Just Kidding Gold & Diamond Park,
Al Qouz Ind. 3, 04 341 3922, *justkidding-uae.com*
Laura Ashley The Dubai Mall, Burj Khalifa,
04 325 3245, *lauraashley.ae*
THE One Junior THE One Fusion, Al Qouz Ind. 1,
04 346 8977, *theone.com*
Pottery Barn Kids The Dubai Mall, Burj Khalifa,
04 325 3720, *potterybarnkids.me*

Art

Several galleries in Dubai sell traditional and
contemporary art by Arabic and international artists,
and there's an annual art fair called Art Dubai. You
can also find information on art auctions, art fairs and
gallery openings at artinthecity.com.

Souk Madinat Jumeirah has a large concentration
of boutiques selling art, glass and photographs, both
originals and reproductions. The style and subjects
are diverse, from traditional to modern, Arabic to
international. And Dubai's up-and-coming art district
in Al Qouz is home to a variety of galleries.

Many galleries and showrooms have a framing
service. There are some excellent framing shops on
Plant Street in Satwa and in Karama – they can frame
anything from prints to sports jerseys. You can also
create your own art by transferring your photos onto
canvas. There are a few stores that offer the service
including Riot Studio (04 445 8488, riotstudio.com), as
well as Portfolio (portfolio-uae.com) in Festival Centre
and Mercato Shopping Mall.

MacKenzie Art

For a specially commissioned artistic touch why not
contact MacKenzie Art? You can order individually
designed paintings with either classical or contemporary
designs. Artworks can be painted directly on canvas or
walls, or on ceilings as murals, in a colourful or subdued
style. Check out previous projects at mackenzieart.com
or call 04 341 9803 for further information.

Dubai Art

London +**44 20 8740 8708**
dubaiart.org
Specialises in commissions and bespoke art, from
personal portraits to commercial paintings.

E-Walls Studio

API Business Suites, 403 Al Barsha 1 **04 399 4748**
ewalls-s.com
Map **1 P6** Metro **Dubai Internet City**
This local company designs wall stickers for the home
and office. Designs are for the living room, bedroom,
kitchen, bathroom and kids' room, or you can have your
own customised. There are even designs for parties and
celebrations. Delivery is available throughout the UAE.

Gallery One

Souk Madinat Jumeirah Al Sufouh 2 **04 368 6055**
g-1.com
Map **1 R5** Metro **Mall of the Emirates**
A selection of stylish photographs and canvas prints.
Particularly good if you want images of the region.

The Majlis Gallery

Al Fahidi Historical Neighbourhood
Al Souk Al Kabeer **04 353 6233**
themajlisgallery.com
Map **2 M4** Metro **Al Fahidi**
A great venue for fine art, hand-made glass, pottery
and other unusual pieces.

Boutique 1 Gallery The Walk at JBR, Marsa Dubai,
04 425 7888, *boutique1.com*
XVA Gallery Al Fahidi Historical Neighbourhood,
Al Souk Al Kabeer, 04 353 5383, *xvagallery.com*

Outdoor

ACE Hardware > *p.367* Nr Times Square Center,
Shk Zayed Rd, Al Qouz Ind. 1, 04 341 1906, *aceuae.com*
Ambar Garden Furniture Umm Suqeim Rd,
Al Qouz Ind. 3, 04 323 2405, *ambargardenfurniture.com*
B&B Italia Mall of the Emirates, Al Barsha 1,
04 341 2445, *baituti.com*
Desert River Nr Times Square Center, Al Qouz Ind.1,
04 323 3636, *desertriver.com*
Finasi Al Ittihad Rd, Al Khabaisi, 04 297 1777, *finasi.ae*
Haif Hospitality Furnishings Al Nasr Plaza,
Oud Metha, 04 357 3221, *hhfuae.ae*
Nakkash Gallery Nr Indian Palace Restaurant, Shk
Rashid Rd, Al Garhoud, 04 282 6767, *nakkashgallery.com*
Parasol Garden Furniture Umm Suqeim Rd,
Al Qouz Ind. 4, 04 347 9003, *parasoldubai.com*
Rainbow Play Systems Dubai Investment Park 1,
050 450 7610, *rainbowplayuae.com*
Royal Gardenscape Nr ENOC Petrol Station,
Al Qouz Ind.4, 04 340 0648, *royalgardenscape.com*
Soubra Tents & Awnings Nr Leader Sports,
Al Khabaisi, 04 266 5347, *soubra-uae.ae*
Sultan Garden Center Nr Dubai Zoo, Jumeira 1,
04 344 5544, *sultangardencenter.com*

Gardens & Pools

Hardware retailers such as ACE Hardware stock a good
range of outdoor furniture and gardening accessories,
as do the major hypermarkets such as LuLu and
Carrefour. IKEA has a good plants section and sells
candles, watering cans and other useful items, and
there are plenty of companies to call on for swimming
pool installation and maintenance. Head to Plant
Street in Satwa for all kinds of foliage and plant pots.

Dubai Garden Centre
Nr Commercial Bank of Dubai Al Qouz Ind.3
04 340 0006
desertgroup.ae
Map **1 S6** Metro **First Gulf Bank**
A good bet for all your gardening needs, and also sells garden furniture.

Sultan Garden Center Nr Dubai Zoo, Jumeira 1, 04 344 5544, *sultangardencenter.com*

Hardware & DIY

With a number of companies offering handyman services, it may be easier and cheaper to find a 'man who can' rather than invest in the tools and materials you need for DIY jobs. If you'd rather do it yourself, there's a range of places to go, and the larger hypermarkets, such as Carrefour, often have a DIY section. There are numerous independent shops selling a broad range of items in Satwa, and Dragon Mart has a section for builder's merchants where you can find tiles, power tools and other hardware items.

ACE Hardware > p.367
Dubai Festival City Mall Al Kheeran **800 27 5223**
aceuae.com
Map **2 M9** Metro **Emirates**
DIY enthusiasts will find all the tools they need to get the job done. There's another large branch off Sheikh Zayed Rd, close to Times Square Center. Customised paints, glazes, electronic tools and hardware materials can also be found here, as well as some garden furniture and other household items.

Speedex
Nr Oasis Centre Al Qouz 1 **04 339 1929**
speedextools.com
Map **2 C6** Metro **Noor Bank**
Stocks comprehensive ranges of tools for everything from gardening to carpentry, along with all the nails, nuts, bolts and screws you may need.

Jewellery

Dubai is the world's leading re-exporter of gold and you'll find at least one jewellery shop in even the smallest malls, and large dedicated areas in the bigger malls. Gold is sold according to the international daily gold rate, so wherever you buy it there will be very little difference in the price of the actual metal. Where the price varies is in the workmanship that has gone into a particular piece.

While gold jewellery may be the most prevalent, silver, platinum, precious stones, gems and pearls are all sold, either separately or crafted into jewellery. Most outlets can make up a piece for you, working from a diagram or photograph. Just ensure that you are not obliged to buy it if it doesn't turn out quite how you had imagined. A pendant with your name spelled out in Arabic, or some jewellery crafted with black pearls, are traditional gifts. The Gold Souk in Deira is the best place to start in terms of choice, but some of the air-conditioned alternatives may be preferable in the summer, including the Gold & Diamond Park.

Many of the world's finest jewellers are represented in Saks Fifth Avenue's jewellery department, such as Cartier, Tiffany & Co, Graff and De Beers. For watches, whether it's a Rolex, Tag Heuer, Swatch or Timex, you'll find most models here. Costume jewellery and watches can be found in most department stores; there's a beautiful Swarovski range at Tanagra (04 324 2340), in Wafi. Several fashion stores also stock a small range of jewellery, and branches of Accessorize and Claire's Accessories can be found in many of the malls.

Al Fardan Jewels & Precious Stones Deira City Centre, Port Saeed, 04 295 3780, *alfardangroup.com*
Al Futtaim Jewellery Deira City Centre, Port Saeed, 04 295 2906, *watches.ae*
Damas The Dubai Mall, Burj Khalifa, 04 339 8846, *damasjewellery.com*
Golden Ring Jewellery Deira City Centre, Port Saeed, 04 295 0373
Liali Jewellery Mercato Shopping Mall , Jumeira 1, 04 344 5055, *lialijewellery.com*
Mansoor Jewellers Mall of the Emirates, Al Barsha 1, 04 341 1661

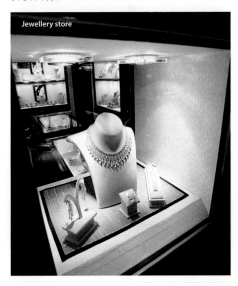
Jewellery store

Paris Gallery Deira City Centre, Port Saeed, 04 295 5550, *parisgallery.com*
Prima Gold BurJuman, Al Mankhool, 04 355 1988, *primagold.co.th*
Pure Gold Mercato Shopping Mall, Jumeira 1, 04 349 2400, *pugold.com*
Raymond Weil Deira City Centre, Port Saeed, 04 295 2906, *raymond-weil.com*
Saks Fifth Avenue BurJuman, Al Mankhool, 04 501 2700, *saksincorporated.com*
Tanagra Wafi, Umm Hurair 2, 04 324 2340, *chalhoub-group.com*
Vhernier Jumeirah Emirates Towers, Trade Center 2, 04 354 4017, *vhernier.com*

All That Glitters

The Gold & Diamond Park (at junction four on Sheikh Zayed Road) has branches of many of the same shops as the Gold Souk in Deira, but in a calmer, air-conditioned atmosphere. You can still barter, and there is the added bonus of cafes to wait in while the jeweller makes any alterations. This is also a good spot to head for if you are looking for engagement or wedding rings and, like at the outlets in the souk, you are able to commission pieces. (goldanddiamondpark.com)

Kids

When it comes to clothing, there is plenty of choice, from high-end designer fashion to factory seconds from Sana. Many of the department stores have children's departments and, for real indulgence, The Dubai Mall has a section dedicated to premium brands such as Armani Junior.

School Supplies

Most schools will suggest a preferred supplier for its school uniforms, and Dar Al Tasmim Uniforms, Magrudy's and Zaks produce uniforms for many in Dubai. You can also buy generic uniforms from Marks & Spencer. Most hypermarkets stock a plethora of branded school bags and stationery items, especially in the 'back to school' promotions of summer, while Creative Minds stocks harder to find stationery and art materials that can come in useful for homework.

Creative Minds The Beach Centre, Jumeira 1, 04 344 6628, *creativemindsdubai.com*
Dar Al Tasmim Uniforms 04 285 9624, *ouruniform.com*
Magrudy's Nr Jumeira Centre, Jumeira 1, 04 344 4193, *magrudy.com*
Marks & Spencer The Dubai Mall, Burj Khalifa, 04 339 8890, *marksandspencerme.com*
Zaks Jumeira 1, 04 342 9828, *zaksstore.com*

Toys

As well as the major toy stores and kids' clothes shops, you'll find a wide range in the larger hypermarkets and supermarkets, including Park n Shop, as well as bookshops and places like Virgin Megastore.

IKEA and Kidz Inc in Al Qouz carry good quality toys that are built to last, whereas the little shops around Karama and Satwa are excellent for cheap toys that probably won't. Remember that not all toys conform to international safety standards and therefore should only be used under supervision.

Early Learning Centre

Wafi Umm Hurair 2 **04 324 2730**
elc.com
Map **2 K7** Metro **Dubai Healthcare City**
Stocks a good range of educational products and toys that stimulate play and imagination, and has a good reputation for the quality of its products, especially wooden toys. You'll also find inflatable pools, swimming jackets and arm bands. Plenty of locations include a large branch at Deira City Centre.

Hamleys

The Dubai Mall Burj Khalifa **04 339 8889**
hamleys.com
Map **2 F7** Metro **Burj Khalifa/Dubai Mall**
Hold on to your kids, this British store is well known for offering the best, and the biggest, variety of toys. There's a plethora of toys and games for pre-schoolers through to early teens.

The Toy Store

Mall of the Emirates Al Barsha 1 **04 341 2473**
mytoystore.com
Map **1 R6** Metro **Mall of the Emirates**
Recognisable by the large toy animals peering out of its store front, it's a great place to amaze kids. The Mall of the Emirates branch is large and filled with a broad variety of toys.

Toys R Us

Dubai Festival City Mall Al Kheeran **04 206 6568**
toysrusuae.com
Map **2 M9** Metro **Emirates**
This well-known emporium is guaranteed to get your little ones excited. The range is comprehensive so whatever you are looking for, from small toys and games to bikes, you're likely to find it.

Can't Find What You Need?

If you've scoured the city for a particular item and still not found it, log on to askexplorer.com and ask advice from your fellow expats. If we've missed your favourite store, log on and let us know why you love it.

A dazzling display
of craftsmanship

ZaZeeZou
Jumeirah Centre Jumeira 1 **04 344 0204**
harvesthomegroup.com/zaazeezou/
Map **2 H4** Metro **Emirates Towers**
A treasure trove of unique toys, nursery products and children's clothes from a range of independent brands, including Emma Bridgewater's children's crockery and wooden toys by French brand Moulin Roty.

Mother & Baby

Big business in Dubai, there are a multitude of shops selling baby paraphernalia, and many brands you'll know from your home country. You shouldn't have trouble finding nursery essentials like bottles, buggies, changing bags, clothes, cots, prams, rocking chairs and travel cots, and there are plenty of shops selling maternity ranges.

Supermarkets stock formula, nappies and wipes and many sell a good range of bottles and feeding equipment. Choithrams has the best selection of formulas, stocking popular UK brands SMA and Cow & Gate. Pharmacies sell baby essentials and some have breast pumps.

Safety 1st and Maxi Cosi car seats are widely available and should fit most cars; you can also rent car seats, buggies, strollers and other equipment from Rentacrib (rentacrib.ae) – if you hire a car seat its staff will fit it for you free of charge.

For clothing, The Dubai Mall has a very good selection of well-known stores that are grouped in one area on the top floor, and a range of high-end brands like Cacharel Paris and Burberry. Pablosky, Okaidi and Pumpkin Patch sell colourful and practical clothes.

Second-hand Stuff
Second-hand baby items are widely available in Dubai – you just need to know where to look. There are classifieds listings on dubizzle.com and expatwoman.com, and then of course there's always the supermarket noticeboards.

IKEA has a small range of nursery furniture such as cots, changing tables and bathtubs, plus a selection of cot sheets and blankets and some baby-safe toys.

Many retailers have jumped on the maternity fashion bandwagon and now offer fashionable outfits for mums-to-be, including many high street stores, the main department stores and the popular baby shops. And you can shop online at blushandbloom.com and luxelittle.com for fashionable maternity lingerie, nightwear, dresses and 'mama and baby' twinsets. TKD Lingerie offers a pretty maternity range.

Storage bags for breast milk are widely available in Dubai (Playtex, Medela and Avent brands). Boppy breastfeeding pillows are available in Toys R Us, and Arabian Home Health Care (arabianhomecare.com), opposite Rashid Hospital, also stocks pillows for breastfeeding – ask for them when you go in.

Other essential accessories for pregnancy include a 'Bump Belt', a device that redirects your car seatbelt under your bump for protection, and which can be found in Mothercare and some Spinneys stores.

Babies R Us
Toys R Us Port Saeed **04 236 4166**
toysrusuae.com
Map **2 N7** Metro **Deira City Centre**
Usually found inside Toys R Us, stocks a wide range of products, from pushchairs to baby bottles, cots to travel accessories. The quality of the items is good and most conform to international safety standards.

Babyshop
Mall of the Emirates Al Barsha 1 **04 341 0604**
babyshopstores.com
Map **1 R6** Metro **Mall of the Emirates**
Sells low-cost baby clothing and essentials such as feeding items, clothing, toys and baby monitors. Its affordable newborn items come in value packs, and it's worth waiting for Babyshop's sales, held several times a year.

Blossom Mother & Child
The Dubai Mall Burj Khalifa **04 434 0103**
blossommotherandchild.com
Map **2 F7** Metro **Burj Khalifa/Dubai Mall**
A premium range of maternity items is sold at this store, all from well-known designers. The store also has a denim bar which features popular brands like J Brand Jeans and 7 For All Mankind, customised with the Blossom Band.

DbBabies
Town Centre Jumeirah Jumeira 1 **050 600 3199**
dubaibabies.com
Map **2 F4** Metro **Burj Khalifa/Dubai Mall**
This online boutique stocks a fabulous range of products including feeding essentials, slings and skincare products. There's also a good selection of gifts for baby showers and new parents. Offers free delivery within Dubai.

Goodbaby
Nr Abu Hail Centre Hor Al Lanz
04 397 5653
goodbabydubai.com
Map **2 Q6** Metro **Abu Hail**
A great store for key items like car seats and changing mats, and with a large selection of buggies from Maclaren, Quinny and Phil & Teds. The store also stocks stairguards, cots and engaging toys.

Jenny Rose
Mall of the Emirates Al Barsha 1 **04 341 0577**
jennyrose.net
Map **1 R6** Metro **Mall of the Emirates**
Fashionable mums should head to this store for
classy clothes for the day or night. Its collection is
particularly suitable for Dubai's warm climate and
you'll find a good assortment of dresses, sleeveless
tops and comfortable trousers. It is a good place to
find speciality items such as swimwear, lingerie and
evening wear.

Just Kidding
Gold & Diamond Park Al Qouz Industrial 3
04 341 3922
justkidding-uae.com
Map **1 S6** Metro **First Gulf Bank**
Not for the budget conscious, with baby items, furniture
and clothes from Europe, including Bugaboo buggies
and Stokke high chairs. Also stocks interesting toys and
a catalogue of maternity wear, gift sets and slings.

Mamas & Papas
Mercato Shopping Mall Jumeira 1 **04 344 0981**
mamasandpapas.com
Map **2 F4** Metro **Financial Centre**
A household name for well-designed, stylish products
for babies and mums-to-be. The store stocks all you
need from toys, car seats, pushchairs, cribs, nursery
items and decorations to maternity clothes and
feeding items.

Mothercare
The Dubai Mall Burj Khalifa **04 339 9812**
mothercare.com
Map **2 F7** Metro **Burj Khalifa/Dubai Mall**
A reliable place to shop for baby essentials, with a
particularly good selection of clothes. Many of its
larger stores stock breast pumps, cots, prams and car
seats, and you can order items you've seen online or in
a UK catalogue.

Mumzworld
04 449 3150
mumzworld.com
Has a huge range of products and is great for all those
baby essentials, from walkers and playpens to clothing
and skincare.

Organic Foods & Cafe
The Village Jumeira 1 **04 338 2911**
organicfoodsandcafe.com
Map **2 G4** Metro **Emirates Towers**
Sells a wide selection of natural and eco-friendly
baby items, including biodegradable and terry
cloth nappies, wooden toys, organic baby food and
children's mattresses made from organic fibres.

Pregmamma
J3 Mall Al Manara **04 388 3993**
pregmamma.com
Map **1 U5** Metro **Noor Bank**
A complete maternity range for mums-to-be, all with
a comfortable and fashionable touch. Shop in-store or
order online.

Musical Instruments

There are some great specialist shops selling
good quality musical instruments, as well as sheet
music – and some offer lessons. Prices for pianos
are considerably lower than elsewhere in the
world. Sharaf DG, Carrefour, Geant and other large
supermarkets stock basic keyboards and guitars,
which are fine for beginners, as do some toy shops
such as Toys R Us. Virgin Megastore also stocks a
range of instruments.

Juli Music Center
Nr Mazaya Centre Trade Center 1 **04 321 2588**
Map **2 F6** Metro **Burj Khalifa/Dubai Mall**
This store on Sheikh Zayed Rd stocks a good range of
instruments and can also arrange lessons for various
instruments. Particularly useful is its 'hire before you
buy' policy.

The Music Chamber
Times Square Center Al Qouz Ind. 1
04 346 8056
musicchamber.net
Map **1 T6** Metro **Noor Bank**
Sells instruments such as guitars, pianos and ouds, as
well as sheet music, strings, tuners and many other
accessories. Brands stocked include Godin, Seagull,
Ritmuller, D'Addario, Jinbao and Oud Sekar.

The Music Institute
The Walk at JBR Marsa Dubai **04 424 3818**
tmi.ae
Map **1 K4** Metro **DAMAC**
A small range of items are stocked here such as digital
pianos, guitars, violins and guitar accessories, but the
range is primarily to support its students.

The Music Room
Majestic Hotel Tower Dubai Al Mankhool
04 501 2529
Map **2 L5** Metro **Al Fahidi**
Run by an experienced music teacher, this shop has
the widest range of sheet music in Dubai. It stocks a
range of instruments including clarinets, flutes, violins,
trumpets and guitars, and their associated accessories.
It is an agent for Steinway & Sons pianos, and also
stocks Kawai grand, upright and digital pianos.

Sadek Music
Souk Madinat Jumeirah Al Sufouh 1 **04 368 6570**
sadek-music.com
Map **1 R5** Metro **Mall of the Emirates**
Stocks an assortment of eastern and western
instruments, including a good selection of guitars. The
store offers a repair service and music lessons, and you
can also rent a selection of its instruments.

Thomsun Pure Music
Dubai Festival City Mall Al Kheeran **04 232 9900**
thomsunmusiconline.com
Map **2 M9** Metro **Emirates**
A wide range of mainly Yamaha instruments, from
pianos to drum kits and guitars, and also sells mixing
decks and equipment for digital music-making.

Thomsun Pure Music
Ibn Battuta Mall Jabal Ali 1 **04 366 9385**
thomsun.com
Map **1 G5** Metro **Ibn Battuta**
One of the largest distributors in the Middle East for
Yamaha musical instruments, Thomsun offers a huge
selection of grand pianos, keyboards, guitars, violins,
percussion and wind instruments, plus accessories
and home audio systems.

Turning Pointe Music
Bldg V23, Russia Cluster Warsan 1 **04 422 1592**
turningpointe.ae
Metro **Rashidiya**
Sells everything ranging from guitars and string
instruments, through to keyboards and brass
instruments, in addition to stands, cases, strings, picks
and oils. Also leases instruments to students.

Zak Electronic & Musical Instruments
BurJuman Al Mankhool **04 336 8857**
zakelectronics.com
Map **2 L5** Metro **BurJuman**
This store carries grand pianos, keyboards, amplifiers
and guitar accessories. You'll also find a good range of
brands including Roland, Kawai and Fender.

Parties

Accessories
Party accessories are available in most supermarkets
and toy shops but there are several specialist stores
that stock everything for children's or adults' parties.
Carrefour, Park n Shop and Toys R Us all sell themed
party essentials, such as paper cups, gift bags,
balloons and plates, and for certain occasions like
Halloween and Easter, really get into the spirit of
things, selling a range of costumes and accessories.

Fabric is inexpensive and it doesn't cost much to
hire the services of a tailor, so you can easily have a
costume made. See Textiles, Tailoring and Repairs for
more information on where to go for this.

Balloon Lady
Jumeira Plaza Jumeira 1 **04 344 1062**
balloonladyme.com
Map **2 H4** Metro **Emirates Towers**
This store is the place to buy balloons and seasonal
items; you can also hire bouncy castles and purchase
costumes for special events. The store offers a balloon
decoration service and can also customise balloons.

Mr Ben's Costume Closet
Al Ghazal Complex & Shopping Mall Al Bada'
04 346 3494
mrbenscostumecloset.com
Map **2 J4** Metro **World Trade Centre**
The ultimate store for fancy dress outfits and
accessories – available for adults and children to buy
or rent. From character outfits to historical garbs,
wigs to masks, there is an overwhelming choice of
costumes to suit each and every occasion.

Party Centre > *p.375*
Nr Welcare Hospital Al Garhoud **04 283 1353**
mypartycentre.com
Map **2 N7** Metro **GGICO**
This enormous store stocks everything you will need,
no matter what the occasion. This is a one-stop shop for
decorations and party accessories, as well as children's
fancy dress outfits. There's a second store at TECOM (04
453 3373) and two in Garhoud (04 297 9125).

Party Zone
The Dubai Mall Burj Khalifa **04 325 3443**
partyzone.ae
Map **2 F6** Metro **Burj Khalifa/Dubai Mall**
A good place for getting party supplies such as fancy
dress outfits and themed table decorations.

Tickles & Giggles
The Walk at JBR Marsa Dubai **04 432 8681**
ticklesandgiggles.com
Map **1 K4** Metro **Jumeirah Lakes Towers**
A party zone for kids that also has a well-stocked party
accessories store.

Celebration Cakes
Baskin Robbins Deira City Centre, Port Saeed,
04 295 1326, *baskinrobbinsmea.com*
Boulevard Gourmet Radisson Blu Hotel Dubai Deira
Creek, Al Rigga, 04 222 7171,
radissonblu.com/hotel-dubaideiracreek
Caesars Al Mankhool, Bur Dubai, 04 3259400,
caesars-uae.com

Coco's Restaurant Deira City Centre, Port Saeed, 04 295 3777
French Bakery Interchange 1, Al Safa St, Al Satwa, 04 343 6444, *frenchbakery.ae*
Hey Sugar The Village, Jumeira 1, 04 344 8204
The House Of Cakes Block D-04, China Cluster Warsan 1, 04 420 6973, *houseofcakesdubai.com*
Park n Shop > *p.343* Al Safa Centre, Al Safa 1, 04 394 5671, *facebook.com/parknshopdxb*

Perfumes & Cosmetics

This is big business here, from local scents like frankincense and oud, to the latest designer offerings. Local scents tend to be strong and spicy – you can often locate the stores by the smell of the incense they burn in their doorways.

Department stores such as Harvey Nichols, Saks Fifth Avenue, Bloomingdale's and Debenhams, as well as local chains such as Areej and Paris Gallery stock the most comprehensive ranges of international brand perfumes and cosmetics. Larger supermarkets and pharmacies stock skincare products and some makeup. Anti-allergenic ranges are available at some of the larger pharmacies. Most needs are covered but if yours aren't, specialist retailers often have online shopping facilities or you may find products available at your local beauty clinic. Glambox.me has an online cosmetics store, and also runs a service where, for a certain amount each month, they deliver a box of samples for you to try. Prices for perfumes and cosmetics are similar to those in some other countries. There are no sales taxes, so there is rarely a difference between duty free and shopping mall prices.

Amouage
Deira City Centre Port Saeed **04 295 5550**
amouage.com
Map **2 N7** Metro **Deira City Centre**
'The world's most valuable perfume,' Amouage is made in Oman. The luxurious brand has a standalone store at The Dubai Mall and is sold in Paris Gallery stores, as well as Dubai and Abu Dhabi Duty Free.

Bath & Body Works > *p.377*
Mirdif City Centre Mirdif **04 231 6751**
facebook.com/BathAndBodyWorksMiddleEast
Map **2 P12** Metro **Rashidiya**
A one-stop shop for all things scented, this US-based store is present in Mall of the Emirates, Deira City Centre, Ibn Battuta Mall and The Dubai Mall. All kinds of lovely bath and beauty products are available here, including a men's range, and there's the option to 'spray before you pay'. Their candles smell wonderful! Follow them on twitter.com/bbwmena and http://instagram.com/bbwmena to see what's new in store.

Paris Gallery
Ibn Battuta Mall Jabal Ali 1 **04 368 5500**
parisgallery.com
Map **1 G5** Metro **Ibn Battuta**
Although it stocks a wide selection of perfumes and cosmetics (and a good range of shoes, eyewear and jewellery), its stores never feel too busy, which allows plenty of freedom to browse. Outlets are located all over the city.

Wojooh
Mall of the Emirates Al Barsha **04 347 1225**
wojooh.com
Map **1 R6** Metro **Mall of the Emirates**
Formerly known as Faces, all manner of lotions and potions are sold in this store. Get all of your monthly makeup, perfume and skincare buys here, from brands like Clarins, Lancome, Givenchy and Clinique. There is another branch within The Dubai Mall.

Boots Mall of the Emirates, Al Barsha 1, 04 340 6880, *me.boots.com*
L'Occitane The Dubai Mall, Burj Khalifa, 04 339 8148, *loccitane-me.com*
Lush Mercato, Jumeira 1, 04 344 9334, *lush.com*
M.A.C Mall of the Emirates, Al Barsha 1, 04 409 8931, *maccosmetics.com*
Sephora Dubai Festival City Mall, Al Kheeran, 04 232 6023, *sephora.com*

Pets

Most supermarkets carry basic ranges of cat, dog, bird and fish food, although the choice is limited. If your pet has specific dietary requirements, many of the veterinary clinics carry specialist foods. There are pet shops dotted around the city which can supply most items you need for your pet, with Pet Land being well known for aquariums and Tetra products for fish keeping. While there are good pet shops, some can be a little depressing with animals kept in conditions that may make you feel uncomfortable. The pet shops along Plant Street in Satwa are notoriously the worst offenders and animals purchased there are often malnourished and diseased. On principal, it might be better to spend your money elsewhere. Below is a list of the better pet shops.

Pampered Pets
Dreams Tower 2, Nr Emaar Yacht Club Marsa Dubai **04 447 5330**
pamperedpets.ae
Map **1 K5** Metro **Jumeirah Lakes Towers**
A range of couture pet beds and exclusive accessories and fashion for a pooch with a taste for the finer things in life.

Animal World Nr Jumeirah Centre, Jumeira 1, 04 344 4422

Glam Paws UAE 050 344 1984, *glam-paws.wix.com*

Paws & Claws Uptown Mirdiff, Mirdif, 04 288 4885, *pawsnclawspets.com*

Pet's Delight Arabian Ranches Community Centre, Wadi Al Safa 6, 04 361 8184, *pets-delight.com*

Petland Nr Health Mart, Shk Zayed Rd, Al Qouz 3, 04 380 4343, *petlanduae.com*

Petzone Nr Mazaya Center, Shk Zayed Rd, Downtown Dubai, 04 321 1424, *petzoneonline.com*

World of Pets Nr Dr Nicholas Clinic, Jumeira Rd, Jumeira 3, 04 395 5701, *worldofpetsme.com*

Second-hand

There is an extremely active second-hand market in Dubai, as people are always leaving, redecorating or downsizing, and need to get rid of their stuff. Noticeboards in supermarkets and apartment complexes are a great place to start, as many people post 'for sale' notices with pictures. Garage sales are also popular on Fridays and you'll notice signs going up in your neighbourhood from time to time.

For the Dhs.5 entry fee into Zabeel Park you can peruse the monthly flea market (see dubai-fleamarket.com for additional locations), and a car boot sale is held every Friday in the cooler winter months at the Autodrome which is free for shoppers. There are also a number of websites with classifieds sections; dubizzle.com is the main one, and expatwoman.com is another good one. Here you'll find absolutely anything, from appliances to furniture, cars and toys.

There are a number of second-hand shops, often linked to churches and special needs schools, but the opening hours can be somewhat eccentric. Second-hand bookshops such as Book World, House of Prose and Book & Bean buy books in good condition for 50% of the purchase price.

Al Noor Charity Thrift Shop
Al Barsha 1 **04 340 4844**
alnoorspneeds.ae
Map **1 R6** Metro **Mall of the Emirates**
Raises funds for the Al Noor School for Special Needs, and always welcomes donations of second-hand clothing in good condition.

Dubai Charity Centre
Nr Al Karama Fish Market, Al Karama **04 337 8246**
Map **2 K6** Metro **ADCB**
The biggest of the charity shops, this store supports the students who attend The Dubai Centre for Special Needs, and finances a number of places for those who are unable afford them. It stocks a good range of clothes, books and toys.

Holy Trinity Thrift Centre
Nr Dubai English Speaking School Oud Metha **04 337 8192**
holytrinitychurchdubai.org
Map **2 L7** Metro **Oud Metha**
Good for high-quality items and books in particular, and proceeds go towards a number of orphanages supported by the church. The shop gives you back 50% of what your items sell for.

Rashid Paediatric Therapy Centre
Nr Mall Of The Emirates Al Barsha 1 **04 340 0005**
rashidc.ae
Map **1 R6** Metro **Mall of the Emirates**
Has a decent range of items and raises money for projects at the centre.

Soft Furnishings

Carpets, Rugs & Curtains

Carpets are one of the region's signature items. The ones on sale here tend to be imported from Iran, Turkey, Pakistan and Central Asia. A carpet will vary in price depending on a number of factors such as its origin, the material used, the number of knots, and whether or not it is hand-made. The most expensive carpets are usually those hand-made with silk, in Iran.

Inspect carpets by turning them over – if the pattern is clearly depicted on the back and the knots are neat, the carpet is of higher quality than those that are indistinct. Try to do some research so that you have a basic idea of what you're looking for before you go, just in case you happen to meet an unscrupulous carpet dealer who could take advantage of your naivety.

Fortunately, carpet conmen are rare, and most will happily explain the differences between the rugs and share their extensive knowledge with you. If you ask the dealer, you can often garner some interesting information about the carpets and where they were made – for example, some carpets have family names sewn into the designs.

National Iranian Carpets has a section on its website (niccarpets.com) about the history and development of carpets from the various regions.

Ask to see a variety of carpets so that you can get a feel for the differences between hand-made or machine-made, silk, wool or blend carpets. Of course, asking may not be necessary, since carpet vendors will undoubtedly start unrolling carpets before you at a furious pace.

Carpets range in price from a few hundred dirhams to tens of thousands. It is always worth bargaining; make sure the seller knows you are not a tourist, and remain polite at all times to maximise the success of your haggling.

Deira Tower on Al Nasr Square has a huge number of carpet outlets under one roof, and the Blue Souk in Sharjah also has a great range. If you happen to venture further out, the road to Hatta is lined with stalls selling carpets and the Friday Market in Fujairah is also a good place to pick them up.

Mall of the Emirates and The Dubai Mall have a selection of shops selling traditional carpets, as does Souk Al Bahar, but just bear in mind that prices will be steeper here.

Occasionally, you might get a travelling carpet seller ringing your doorbell – they usually drive around an area in a truck that is packed to the roof with carpets. The quality isn't great, and if you show the slightest bit of interest they'll keep coming back.

You may want to invest in blackout curtains as the early morning light is very bright and will wake even the deepest sleeper.

Carpetland Pyramid Centre, Oud Metha, 04 337 7677, *aaf-me.com*
Mostafawi Al Karama, 04 334 9888
National Iranian Carpets Souk Madinat Jumeirah, Al Sufouh 1, 04 368 6003, *niccarpets.com*
The Orientalist Woven Art Jumeirah 1, 04 394 6989, *theorientalist.com*
Pride Of Kashmir Mall of the Emirates, Al Barsha 1, 04 341 4477, *prideofkashmir.com*
Qum Persian Carpets & Novelties Sheraton Dubai Creek Hotel & Towers, Al Rigga, 04 228 1848, *qumcarpets.com*
Dubai Blinds Silver Tower, Al Thanyah 5, 04 368 8759, *dubaiblinds.com*

Cute souvenirs

Souvenirs

From typical holiday trinkets to tasteful keepsakes, there is a huge range of souvenirs in Dubai. Many of the items are regional rather than local, and several are mass produced in India, Pakistan and Oman. You will find a good selection of traditional gifts like antique wooden wedding chests or pashminas, as well as the typical buys like fridge magnets, T-shirts and soft toys. Tourist hotspots like Souk Madinat Jumeirah and the major malls all have a variety of shops and stalls that sell a good selection, or head to the traditional souks around the Creek for a more authentic experience.

Camels feature heavily in souvenir shops; wooden carvings, camel pot stands and even carvings made from camel bones, and are great as novelty presents. Perhaps the tackiest souvenirs are plastic alarm clocks in the shape of a mosque – they only cost Dhs.10 and they wake you up with a loud call to prayer.

Coffee pots are symbols of Arabic hospitality and another popular souvenir item. Prices vary enormously from Dhs.100 for a brand new, shiny one, to several thousand dirhams for a genuine antique. Traditional silver items, such as the Arabic dagger (khanjar) and silver wedding jewellery, are excellent souvenirs, and are available both framed and unframed.

Wooden items are popular and representative of the region; trinket boxes (often with elaborate carvings or brass inlays) start from around Dhs.10. Elaborate Arabic doors and wedding chests, costing thousands, are also popular. The doors can be hung as art, or converted into tables or headboards.

While carpets are a good buy, it is worth doing some research before investing (see Soft Furnishings for more information). For a smaller, cheaper option, many shops sell woven coasters and camel bags, or you can buy a Persian carpet mouse pad.

You can hardly walk through a mall or shopping area without being offered a pashmina – they are available in an abundant range of colours and styles. Most are a cotton or silk mix and the ratio dictates the price. It is a good idea to check out a few shops before buying as prices vary and, as with most items, the more you buy the cheaper they are. For a decent quality pashmina, prices start from around Dhs.50. Shisha pipes make fun souvenirs and can be bought with various flavours of tobacco, such as apple or strawberry. Both functional and ornamental examples are on sale, prices start from around Dhs.75 in Carrefour.

Local scents, like oud and frankincense, make good gifts and are widely available in outlets such as Arabian Oud and Paris Gallery, while Amouage produces some of the world's most valuable perfumes, made with rare ingredients.

Explorer publishes a number of great, multi-language coffee table books, calendars and postcards with stunning photos depicting the diversity of this vibrant city. Visit askexplorer.com to order copies.

Al Jaber Gallery
The Dubai Mall Burj Khalifa **04 339 8566**
aljabergallery.ae
Map **2 F7** Metro **Burj Khalifa/Dubai Mall**
This eclectic store is good for a browse if you're short on inspiration. From tacky (plastic replicas of the Burj and 'I love Dubai' fridge magnets) to tasteful (colourfully painted mezze bowls and embroidered pashminas), it's a good spot to take out of town visitors.

Antique Museum
Nr Kanoo Bldg, Al Qouz Ind. 1 **04 347 9935**
fakihcollections.com
Map **1 U7** Metro **Noor Bank**
Upon entering this store's gilded doors, you'll be met by an eclectic maze of products. It has a large section devoted to teak Indian furniture and silver chests, plus a fantastic selection of token holiday tat, but you can also pick up pashminas, Omani silver boxes, Arabian lanterns and other traditional souvenirs.

The Sultani Lifestyle Gallerie
Souk Al Bahar Burj Khalifa **04 420 3676**
Map **2 F6** Metro **Burj Khalifa/Dubai Mall**
Head here for good quality traditional souvenirs, carpets and exotic items from the region. The store also carries a good selection of postcards and elaborate home furnishings.

Sports & Outdoor Equipment

Dubai is a great place for a variety of sports, from common activities such as tennis, sailing, golf or football to exploring the great outdoors hiking or mountain biking – a popular pastime in the UAE, especially when the weather cools.

General sports shops are found all over the city and stock a good variety of items including rackets, swimming essentials or sports clothing. You can also find specialist sports shops that offer diving, sailing and desert sport equipment. Many of the major brand names have multiple outlets in Dubai, including Adidas, Nike and Timberland. You can also pick up a few basic items at Carrefour, especially camping gear and various accessories.

A growing range of camping and off-roading accessories is available at askexplorer.com, as well as several essential guides and apps to help you get the best of the great outdoors.

Clubs that organise specialist sports, such as Dubai Surfski Kayak Club (dskc.hu), can often be approached for equipment. Golf is extremely popular and clubs,

balls and bags are available in most sports shops. Golf House (04 434 0655) and the pro shops are the best places for decent kit.

ACE Hardware > p.367
Nr Times Square Center, Shk Zayed Rd
Al Qouz Ind. 1 **04 341 1906**
aceuae.com
Map **1 T6** Metro **Noor Bank**
You can buy all the basic equipment you need for a jaunt in the desert at this store, including tents, sleeping bags and cool boxes. The store also stocks a good range of hardware and accessories.

Adventure HQ
Times Square Center Al Qouz Ind. 1 **04 346 6824**
adventurehq.ae
Map **1 T6** Metro **Noor Bank**
An outdoor sport and camping specialist, you'll find everything here from tents, sleeping bags and hiking boots to full climbing gear, kayaks and paddleboards. There's a good range of Merida and BMC bikes, covering everything from mountain bikes to hybrids and high-end road racers, and it offers servicing and bike rental.

Decathlon Dubai
Mirdif City Centre Mirdif **04 283 9392**
Map **2 P12** Metro **Rashidiya**
The French sporting giant has a cavernous Mirdif City Centre store. Covering everything from tracksuits and trainers to camping, climbing and equestrian gear, Decathlon has several of its own value brands as well as big name brands.

Models Sporting Goods > p.254
Ibn Battuta Mall Jabal Ali 1 **04 368 5344**
Map **1 G5** Metro **Ibn Battuta**
The most comprehensive collection of sports goods, selling equipment for popular sports like running, basketball and tennis, and it also stocks cycling, camping and golfing gear. Has a large bike section and a workshop in its Mall of the Emirates store.

Intersport
Times Square Center Al Qouz Ind. 1 **04 341 8214**
intersport.ae
Map **1 T6** Metro **Noor Bank**
Intersport is the world's largest sports retailer, and so these superstores cover practically everything - football, rugby, basketball, running, racket sports, cycling, camping, watersports and more. You'll find all the major international labels, as well as services including footscan technology, racket stringing, jersey printing and bike maintenance/fitting.
The concept store in Festival City has an outdoor activity and demo area.

Knight Shot

Nr Mazaya Centre, Shk Zayed Rd Al Wasl
04 343 5678
knightshot.com
Map **2 F6** Metro **Burj Khalifa/Dubai Mall**
For fans of table sports, this is the must-know store in the UAE, selling everything from snooker, pool and table tennis tables (plus dartboards, table football and air hockey tables) to cues, bridges, chalk and apparel. Its experts can also re-tip your cues or service, clean and re-felt tables.

Lorna Jane

J3 Mall Al Manara **04 388 3006**
lornajane.com.au
Map **1 U5** Metro **Noor Bank**
Ladies will be pleased with the arrival of this Australian sportswear brand known for its bright, funky colours and flattering styles designed for various different sports, from running to yoga.

Picnico General Trading

Al Faraidooni Bldg, Shk Zayed Rd Al Barsha 1
04 395 1113
picnico.ae
Map **1 P6** Metro **Dubai Internet City**
An outdoor specialist stocking a good range of Coleman and Campingaz equipment like cooler bags, tents and accessories. The store also stocks GPS systems, rock climbing gear and footwear. It has one of the largest ranges of hydration packs and it carries Dakine kitesurfing kit, sea kayaks, diving gear and angling equipment.

Stadium

Deira City Centre Port Saeed **04 295 0261**
Map **2 M7** Metro **Deira City Centre**
Along with sister store Studio R (located at BurJuman, Dubai Outlet Mall and Ibn Battuta Mall), Stadium sells brands that cater to those with an active lifestyle, with a range of well-known clothing labels and sports brands (Quiksilver, Adidas, New Balance and Speedo). It also stocks Teva, which make a range of practical sandals. Sales throughout the year see heavy discounts. Further outlets are located at The Dubai Mall and Dubai Marina Mall.

Sun & Sand Sports

Ibn Battuta Mall Jabal Ali 1 **04 366 9777**
sunandsandsports.com
Map **1 G5** Metro **Ibn Battuta**
One of the larger sports stores in the city with a good range of sportswear and home gym equipment, as well as a limited range of pool and snooker tables. Further branches are located at The Dubai Mall and Mirdif City Centre, and there's an outlet store in Al Qouz 3, behind the Gold & Diamond Park.

Adventure HQ

Timberland

The Dubai Mall Burj Khalifa **04 434 1291**
timberland.com
Map **2 F7** Metro **Burj Khalifa/Dubai Mall**
Get dressed for the great outdoors with this timeless collection of hiking boots, outdoor clothing and sporting products for men, women and children. Branches include Mall of the Emirates, Ibn Battuta Mall, Arabian Centre and Dubai Outlet Mall.

yApparel

Jumeirah Centre Jumeira 1 **04 344 4130**
yapparel.com
Map **2 H4** Metro **Emirates Towers**
Tucked away inside the Jumeirah Centre is this new, multi-brand yoga and fitness boutique apparel store – the first in the UAE that is solely dedicated to providing a range of high-quality athletic wear and accessories to the growing yoga and pilates community. Brands include Liquido and Wellicious.

Yas Sports

Nr Al Karama Bus Stand Al Karama **04 396 8009**
yassports.ae
Map **2 K6** Metro **ADCB**
Although this store specialises in cricket equipment, it also stocks equipment for many other sports, including kit that can be harder to find. The store can also supply sports teams with personalised kits, and manage bulk orders.

Rage The Dubai Mall, Burj Khalifa, 04 434 1549, *rage-shop.com*
Golf House The Dubai Mall, Burj Khalifa, 04 434 0655

Biking

For serious bikers, there are several shops selling specialist equipment and accessories, including BMXs, that are listed below. Many also do repairs. Joining a cycling club (see Clubs & Groups) can also help you find the bikes or accessories you need.

For the casual cyclist, various sports shops sell more basic models at reasonable prices. Children's bicycles are widely available in bike and sports shops, while the likes of Babyshop and Toys R Us have a range for tiny Bradley Wiggins wannabes, as do some hypermarkets, such as Carrefour. Both adults' and children's helmets are available at the main retailers. Supermarket noticeboards and online classifieds, such as dubizzle. com, are good places to look for second-hand bikes.

Probike

Shk Juma Bin Ahmed Al Maktoum Bldg Al Barsha 1
04 325 5705
probike.ae
Map **1 R6** Metro **Mall of the Emirates**
Run by biking enthusiasts, Probike stocks mountain, road and triathlon bikes for all levels, as well as shoes, helmets, apparel and components. Probike is the UAE dealer for Planet X bikes, which are renowned for their value for money. Both bike servicing and a professional fitting service are available and good road bikes can be rented by the day.

Ride Bike Shop

Mirdif City Centre Mirdif **04 284 0038**
ridebikeshop.com
Map **2 P12** Metro **Rashidiya**
A good range of stock for both serious cyclists and those who just need something for recreational use, and staff will advise on the most suitable bike for your needs. The in-store workshops at both Mirdif City Centre and Sheikh Zayed Road branches offer a high standard of maintenance to ensure that you are constantly kept on your saddle. Brands include Topeak, Crank Brothers, WeThePeople Bike Company and CycleOps.

Wolfi's Bike Shop

Nr Oasis Centre, Shk Zayed Rd Al Qouz 3
04 339 4453
wbs.ae
Map **2 B6** Metro **Noor Bank**
For the cycling community, Wolfi's is more of an institution than simply a shop, although it is also the UAE's biggest dedicated cycle store, where you'll find everything from kids' and leisure bikes to hardcore carbon time trial machines, and plenty in between. The store specialises in top-end brands like Scott, Felt, Storck, Profile Design and Zipp, and staff are all passionate cyclists who are happy to assist. Bike fitting, servicing and bike hire are also available in-store.

The Cycle Hub MotorCity, Al Hebiah 1,
04 425 6555, *thecyclehub.com*
Kona Bikes Nr Rashid Hospital, Oud Metha,
04 335 0399, *bikes.konaworld.com*
Revolution Cycles Apex Atrium, MotorCity,
Al Hebiah 1, 04 369 7441
Trek Bike Shop Oud Metha, 04 335 0399, *trekbikes.ae*

Boating

There's a cluster of marine equipment stores in Al Jaddaf, so it's a good place to head for all manner of boat related requirements, from fenders and ropes to upholstery services and anti-fouling services. There's also a few around Marsa Dubai, Deira and Al Qouz Industrial. Adventure HQ also sells a broad range of fishing equipment.

ACT Marine Marsa Dubai, 04 424 3191
Al Boom Marine Nr Coca Cola, Al Kheeran,
04 289 4858, *alboommarine.com*
Al Hamur Marine & Sports Equipment Jumeira 1,
04 344 4468
Dubai Creek Marina Dubai Creek Golf & Yacht Club,
Port Saeed, 04 295 6000, *dubaigolf.com*

Diving

Al Boom Diving

Nr Iranian Hospital Jumeira 1 **04 342 2993**
alboomdiving.com
Map **2 H4** Metro **World Trade Centre**
The main outlet of the region's major diving company sells a good range of sub-aqua and watersports gear. All the main brands of technical scuba equipment can be found, including Technisub and GoPro, as well as kitesurfing equipment and beachwear.

The Dive Shop

Dubai Investment Park 1 **04 813 5474**
thediveshopdubai.com
Map **1 F9**
A small and friendly scuba dive shop selling snorkels, masks, regulators, fins and all other accessories.

Watersports

While sports shops such as Adventure HQ, Sun & Sand Sports and Intersport stock some gear, there are several stores dedicated to watersports equipment. Check dubizzle.com for second-hand equipment too.

Leisure Marine

The Walk at JBR Marsa Dubai **04 424 3133**
leisuremarine-me.com
Map **1 K4** Metro **DAMAC**
As well as larger boats, dinghies and kayaks, this store stocks a range of accessories from popular boating and watersports brands.

Surf Shop Arabia

Nr Time Square Center, Al Manara St Al Qouz Ind. 1
04 379 1998
surfshopdubai.com
Map **1 U6** Metro **Noor Bank**
Surf Shop Arabia stocks a wide range of new and
used surfboards, as well as surfing products, stand up
paddleboard (SUP) boards, kitesurfing gear and surf
ski accessories. Boards can even be custom made.
They intend to relocate soon, with no location yet
confirmed, so best to phone ahead before
dropping in.

Textiles, Tailoring & Repairs

If you are looking for fabric, you have several options,
including the Textile Souk near Al Fahidi Street, Satwa,
or the shopping malls, most of which have at least
one fabric outlet. Prices start from a few dirhams for a
metre of basic cotton. The Textile Souk can get busy,
but the sheer range of fabrics makes it worthwhile.
There are several haberdashery shops in the same
area should you wish to buy matching buttons, bows
or cotton.

Satwa Road has a good collection of general fabric
stores and a few good haberdashers; Plant Street is
the place to go for upholstery. IKEA and Fabindia also
stock a range of vibrant fabrics that can be used for
cushions, curtains or bedding.

Tailors can be found in most areas, but there is a
concentration of stores in the Textile Souk, and on
the main street in Satwa. For simple alterations and
repairs, such as hemming, head to one of these areas

Colourful garments

and take your pick – for simple work, the general
standard is fine. For anything more complex, the best
way to select a tailor is by recommendation. A good
tailor can make a garment from scratch, either from a
photo or by copying an existing garment. It may take
a few fitting sessions and alterations to get it just right,
but it's worth the effort, and with tailoring services so
cheap compared to other international cities, it's well
worth getting some custom-made clothes while living
in Dubai. Shirts usually start from Dhs.30 and suits
from Dhs.500.

Deepak's Textiles

Nr Emarat Petrol Station Al Bada' **04 344 3536**
deepakstextiles.com
Map **2 H5** Metro **Jafiliya**
Well-stocked with a fantastic range of fabrics – from
casual denim to more glamorous silks, chiffons and
pure linen. Also offers a tailoring service.

Dream Girl Tailors

Meena Bazaar Al Souq Al Kabeer
04 388 0048 dreamgirltailors.com
Map **2 L4** Metro **Al Fahidi**
Popular store that will take on all tailoring jobs from
taking up trousers to making ball gowns.

Lobo Tailors

Meena Bazaar Al Souk Al Kabeer **04 352 3760**
Map **2 L4** Metro **Al Fahidi**
This is good for suits, which range from Dhs.1,500-
2,500 including fabric and stitching.

Regal Textiles

Nr Habib Bank, Al Fahidi St Al Souq Al Kabeer
04 353 4894 regaldubai.ae
Map **2 L4** Metro **Al Fahidi**
Stocks a good selection of fabrics including French
chiffon, printed silks, Swiss cotton and French lace.

Rivoli Textiles

Nr Mashreq Bank, Zabeel St Al Karama **04 335 0075**
rivoligroup.com
Map **2 L6** Metro **ADCB**
This classy store has a broad range of fabrics and a
personalised tailoring service. Its Satwa store caters to
women. For a suit, head to the Marsa Dubai branch.

Al Masroor Textiles Murshid Bazaar, 04 225 5343,
almasroorgroup.com
Deepas Textile & Tailoring Nr Emirates Post Office,
Al Bada', 04 349 9733, *deepastailoring.com*
Savile Row The Walk at JBR, Marsa Dubai,
04 423 3813, *savilerow.ae*
Stitches The Village, Jumeira 1, 04 342 1476
Whistle & Flute Nr Iranian Hospital, Al Satwa,
04 342 9229

Cobblers

Locksmiths in the city often offer a shoe repair service and you'll find stores in Satwa and Karama.

Minutes

Mall of the Emirates Al Barsha 1 **04 340 8281**
Map **1 R6** Metro **Mall of the Emirates**
Offers shoe repairs in addition to its key cutting service and it has outlets located in many of the main malls.

NDust Shoe Repairs

Nr LuLu Hypermarket Al Barsha 1 **04 325 5016**
ndustshoes.com
Map **1 R6** Metro **Mall of the Emirates**
Offers a handy collection and delivery service.

60 Second Lock & Shoe Repair Opp Ramada Hotel, Al Mankhool 04 355 2600
Al Fareed Shoes Musalla Road, Al Souq Al Kabeer, 04 353 2302

Weddings

For dresses, shoes and accessories, a good bet is Jumeira Road where you'll find several bridal stores, or for designer gowns head to Saks Fifth Avenue's bridal department, which stocks or can order the latest off-the-peg designer wedding gowns by Vera Wang and Reem Acra. The bride will need to attend a number of fittings, but alterations are done in-house and they are up to couture standards.

Some of the city's tailors are able to work from pictures to create your ideal dress; a traditional wedding dress will cost upwards of Dhs.2,000 (including tailoring and fabric), reaching in excess of Dhs.10,000 for a complex design and expensive fabric. It's a good idea for the bridesmaids' dresses, too.

For the groom, there are several shops where formal wear can be hired, including The Wedding Shop, Elegance and Formal Wear on 2nd December Street. Debenhams and Monsoon both sell girls' bridesmaids' dresses, and cater well to mothers of the bride and groom.

Magrudy's and Susan Walpole stock invitations, guest books and photo albums, while The Paper Room in The Dubai Mall has a particularly good range of stationery. Debenhams and THE One both offer wedding registry services.

As well as offering wedding venue and planning services, several of the city's hotels can be commissioned to make the wedding cake. Most of the city's florists can turn their hands to wedding bouquets and arrangements, with certain florists like Mamosa Flowers (mamoso.com) specialising in weddings. Discuss your requirements with them to find out what will be available.

Dresses

The Bridal Showroom

Jumeirah Business Center 2 Al Thanyah 5 **04 457 9400**
dubaibridalshowroom.com
Map **1 L5** Metro **DAMAC**
Their expert consultants will help you find the perfect dress for your big day. Book an appointment to try on a range of beautiful gowns from designers including James Clifford, Sophia Tolli, David Tutera, Ellis Bridals and more. There's also a stunning collection of bridal accessories, flower girl outfits and evening gowns.

Frost

Wasl Square Al Safa 1 **04 345 5690**
frostdubai.com
Map **2 H4** Metro **Emirates Towers**
Head here if you want contemporary wedding dresses from some of the top US and European designers. The store has a great set-up for trying dresses on with exceptionally friendly staff on hand. There's also a decent selection of evening gowns and bridesmaid dresses.

Arushi Couture

Al Urouba St Jumeira 1 **04 344 4103**
Map **2 G4** Metro **Financial Centre**
Arushi Couture is renowned as one of the best of several specialist bridal designers with workshops in Dubai. You can select the fabric yourself or it can be selected during the first meeting with the designer. Gowns take around one month to make, but as Arushi is so popular, there is often a waiting list.

Services

Studio Sol

055 314 9444
studiosol.me
These guys will consult with you on your wedding theme and design all of your stationery from scratch.

Cadorim

The Village Jumeira 1 **04 349 3333**
Map **2 H4** Metro **Emirates Towers**
Creates tailor-made favours and ring boxes. They also sell trendy wrapping paper, tasteful greeting cards and other delicate trinkets.

The Wedding Shop

Jumeirah Centre Jumeira 1 **04 344 1618**
theweddingshop.ae
Map **2 H4** Metro **Emirates Towers**
A great place to get confetti, guest books and photo albums, not to mention a healthy dollop of inspiration.

Reading a good book is like taking a journey

Your fondest memories are probably the ones where you've curled up with a good book and lost yourself in its world. For children, a book is more than just a tool, it is a gateway to a magical place where learning and wonderment go hand in hand. Give your child the perfect start in life with our excellent selection of children's books.

Mall of the Emirates 04 3406789 • Selected Spinneys Supermarkets

A massive 68,000 ft² wide paragon book gallery with stocks of more than half a million books in English, Arabic, Japanese, French, German and Chinese.

Shop more. Read more.

GOING OUT

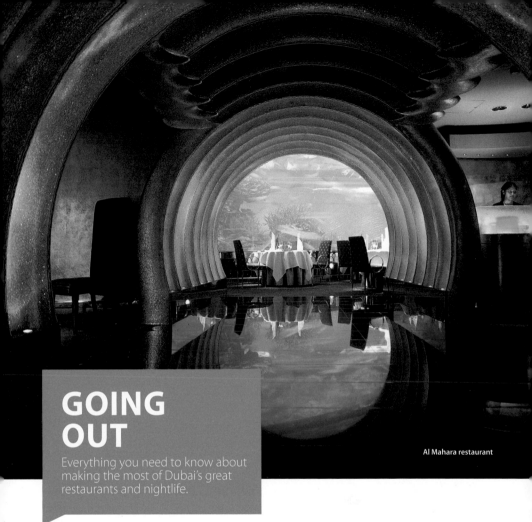

GOING OUT

Everything you need to know about
making the most of Dubai's great
restaurants and nightlife.

Al Mahara restaurant

Exploring the many entertainment options in Dubai is
one of the best parts of living here. Whether you want
to eat, party or stay overnight, this chapter will help
guide you on your going out missions.

Dining & Dancing

The launch of numerous new hotels in Dubai over
the last few years has seen the number of culinary
treats on offer skyrocket. At one end of the spectrum,
celebrity chefs, picturesque cocktail lounges and
well-appointed clubs compete for your hard-earned
dirhams. At the other end, bargain eateries, drink-deal
bars and bang-for-your-buck brunches are there to
help at the end of the month.

The licensing laws in Dubai mean that if you like
a glass of grape with your meal, you will inevitably
have to seek out a restaurant located within a hotel

or leisure club. However, don't make the mistake of
missing out on some of the culinary delights which
can be found in non-licensed independent restaurants
and cafes – you will find the bill is generally much
more wallet-friendly, as a decent bottle of wine can
often cost more than your whole meal.

When eating out in hotels, bear in mind that not
only will your bottle of local water cost up to 10
times more than in the supermarket, you will also be
stung with a 10% tourism fee, as well as a 10% service
charge. Taxis are cheap and plentiful, so leave the car
at home to avoid spending a night in the cells – the
UAE has a zero-tolerance policy on drink driving. The
legal drinking age is 21, and it's best to avoid getting
staggeringly drunk; raucous behaviour is not tolerated
and will land you in hot water. Clubs and bars close at
about 1am, although some go on until 3am.

RESTAURANTS

While Dubai is well known for its high-end dining options, don't let first impressions deter you from giving some of the budget establishments around town a go. Food and drink outlets are subject to regular checks, so basic hygiene requirements are usually met; a good barometer is to choose an establishment which has a large number of hungry eaters wolfing down their dinner, so you know that the turnover of ingredients is high.

If you suffer from food allergies, don't assume that serving staff have understood your requirements, or that the menu will be suitably labelled.

Vegetarians are generally well catered for, as Dubai is home to a large population from the subcontinent who are vegetarian by religion. It's a good idea to confirm ingredients with staff, just in case meals which at first appear vegetarian may in fact have been cooked using animal fats. Arabic cuisine, although heavy on meat-based mains, offers a great range of mezze that are mostly vegetarian.

You will find that restaurants tend to fill up later in the evening, with the hip Lebanese crowd often not eating before 10pm at the weekends.

Wherever you're heading to dine, it's generally best to leave the flip-flops and shorts on the beach and trade up to smart trousers and shiny shoes – you may get some funny looks if you turn up looking like you've just rolled off your sun lounger.

New smoking laws have been introduced and since mid-2014 smoking is not allowed in any restaurant smaller than 1,000 square feet; those restaurants that do have smoking areas will have to limit the area to a maximum of 50% of the dining area. Currently, you can still smoke in pubs and bars. Also, hotels with up to three stars have been banned from serving shisha.

Read the following pages, which give you an all-round taster of restaurants in Dubai, whether you want alfresco dining, somewhere to take the kids, a romantic rendezvous, or a cheap and cheerful bite to eat before the cinema or night out on the town.

The Yellow Star

The yellow star highlights the Dubai gems that merit extra praise. It might be the atmosphere, the food, the cocktails, the music or the crowd, but any review that you see with the star attached is sure to be for somewhere that's a bit special.

Ramadan Timings

During Ramadan, opening and closing times of restaurants change considerably. Because eating and drinking in public is forbidden during daylight hours, many places only open after sunset, then keep going well into the early hours. Restaurants in some hotels remain open, but will be screened off from public view. Live entertainment is not allowed, so while some nightclubs remain open, all dancefloors are closed.

Taxes & Service Charges

Look out for the small print on the bill and you may spot the words 'prices are subject to 10% service charge and 10% tourism fee'. This service charge is rather misleading as it isn't passed onto the staff, and there's no option to opt out if you're not happy with the service. If you do want to tip the waiting staff though, 10% is the norm – and try to give them cash if you can. Tourism tax is only levied in hotels.

Feast of Festivals

Dubai gastrophiles should look forward to the month of March as that's when the Taste of Dubai Festival hits the city. This three-day culinary tour de force sees Michelin-starred and celebrity chefs from restaurants across Dubai showcase their skills at Dubai Media City. Taste some signature dishes, enjoy a cookery class, participate in beverage tastings and see world-famous chefs share their secrets live on stage. See tasteofdubaifestival.com for more information.

In the UAE capital, Gourmet Abu Dhabi (gourmetabudhabi.ae) is a 10 day festival in February that showcases world-renowned chefs and their culinary skills.

Cultural Meals

While it is possible to find pretty much any national cuisine you can imagine in the city, there are certain areas that cater best for those in search of some local flavour. Al Fahidi Historical Neighbourhood, formerly known as Bastakiya, is a great place to grab a bite to eat and soak up some culture.

This traditional part of the city is best experienced by strolling through the streets, visiting the museums and historical buildings, and dining at one of the many cafes – a culinary and cultural experience rolled into one. Alternatively, you can simply visit the Sheikh Mohammed Centre for Cultural Understanding. As well as organising tours of Jumeirah Mosque, the centre also hosts regular cultural meals to introduce visitors to the national cuisine, where you can chat to your local Emirati host about the culture and traditions.

The Department of Tourism & Commerce Marketing also works closely with the Emirates Culinary Guild (emirates-culinaryguild.com) and a few chefs to promote Emirati cuisine in Dubai.

CUISINE FINDER

Celebrities restaurant

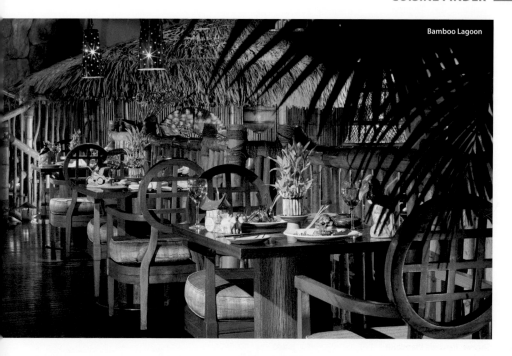

Bamboo Lagoon

Pakistani
Ravi Restaurant, Nr Satwa — p.419

Russian
Troyka, Ascot — p.413

Seafood
Al Bandar Restaurant, Al Shindagha — p.409
Al Mahara, Burj Al Arab — p.416
Aprons & Hammers, DIMC — p.394
Aquara, Marina Yacht Club — p.394
Asmak, Al Garhoud — p.394
Beach Bar & Grill, The Palace At
One&Only Royal Mirage — p.399
Fish Market, Radisson Blu Deira Creek — p.408
Moana, Sofitel — p.415
Ossiano, Atlantis — p.417
Pierchic, Al Qasr — p.417
Wheeler's, Gate Village — p.403

South American
Asado, The Palace Downtown — p.408
Beach House Cabana, Clubhouse Azraq,
Shoreline Apartments — p.399

Spanish
Al Hambra, Al Qasr — p.412
El Sur, The Westin — p.401

Sri Lankan
Chef Lanka, Nr LuLu Supermarket Al Karama — p.404

Steakhouse
Center Cut, Ritz-Carlton DIFC — p.408
Porterhouse, Sofitel The Palm — p.416
Prime 68, JW Marriott Marquis — p.409
Rare Restaurant, Desert Palm — p.416
Seafire, Atlantis — p.401
The Butcher Shop & Grill,
Mall of the Emirates — p.410
The Meat Co, Downtown Dubai — p.398

Tex-Mex
Shooters, Hessyan 1 — p.412

Thai
Blue Elephant, Al Bustan Rotana — p.408
Lemongrass, Nr Lamcy Plaza Oud Metha — p.405
Pai Thai, Al Qasr — p.416
Smiling BKK, Al Wasl Rd — p.405
The Thai Kitchen, Park Hyatt — p.402

Turkish
A La Turca Restaurant, Rixos The Palm — p.394

Vietnamese
Voi, Jumeirah Zabeel Saray — p.398

Yalumba

Alfresco

If the weather is cool enough, head outside onto a terrace or balcony for breakfast, lunch or dinner and you'll feel the vacation vibe flow over you.

A La Turca Restaurant   Turkish

Rixos The Palm Nakhlat Jumeira **04 4575 555**
rixos.com
Map **1 P3** Metro **Nakheel**
Indulge in mouthwatering mezze and succulent kebabs at Rixos The Palm's all-day dining restaurant. It's predominantly a buffet concept that serves up the usual mix of Middle Eastern dishes, but also worth a try is the homemade Turkish thin crust pizza. You'll need your appetite because it comes on a one metre-long platter! Outside there's a laidback, alfresco dining experience where gorgeous views of the cityscape create a lovely backdrop to your meal.

Al Muna   Buffet

Madinat Jumeirah, Al Sufouh 1 **04 366 6730**
jumeirah.com
Map **1 R4** Metro **Mall of the Emirates**
Al Muna offers an indulgent buffet of international cuisine, as well as a 24 hour a la carte menu catering to those who want a more personalised experience. Like every other venue in Madinat Jumeirah, it comes in a nice posh package with elegant decor and an inviting terrace to match. Book a table outside for the ever-popular Friday brunch and you can observe the abras and dhows drift by along the water while you tuck in.

AOC

AOC   French

Sofitel Jumeirah JBR, Marsa Dubai **04 448 4848**
sofitel-dubai-jumeirahbeach.com
Map **1 K4** Metro **Jumeirah Lakes Towers**
The staff are friendly and the venue, especially the terrace, is excellent but you should know that the a la carte menu serves up largely European main courses rather than anything authentically French. The wine list and desserts do their best to return a touch of 'ooh la la' to proceedings.

Aprons & Hammers   Seafood

DIMC Marsa Dubai **04 454 7097**
apronsandhammers.com
Map **1 L4** Metro **DAMAC**
Soak up some incredible views on board this traditional dhow – from the dazzling skyscrapers of Marsa Dubai, to the Palm Jumeirah stretching out to sea. A visit here is a true must-do for seafood fans – armed with a wooden hammer and a giant bib, diners are served huge buckets of delicious crab and other fresh catch, and invited to get cracking.

Aquara   Seafood

Marina Yacht Club Marsa Dubai **04 362 7900**
dubaimarinayachtclub.com
Map **1 K5** Metro **Jumeirah Lakes Towers**
Aquara is chic but understated, allowing the views of the marina's skyscrapers and million-dirham yachts to speak for themselves. It specialises in seafood, most of which is served with an Asian twist. Friday brunch is excellent – the centrepiece is the seafood bar with lobster, oysters, prawns, crab, clams, sushi and sashimi. A great terrace too.

Asmak   Seafood

Al Garhoud **04 282 5377**
centuryvillage.ae
Map **2 N8** Metro **GGICO**
Asmak's simple, calm blue and white decor hides a quaint little place serving succulent seafood as well as a variety of hot and cold mezzes. The spicy garlic potatoes are a must-try but best avoided on any sort of romantic outing! Choose between indoor seating or alfresco dining on a beautiful wooden deck.

AZ.U.R   International

Marriott Harbour Marsa Dubai **04 319 4794**
azur.dubaimarriottharbourhotel.com
Map **1 L5** Metro **DAMAC**
Boasting a fantastic wooden floored terrace with great views of the marina, AZ.U.R is a popular spot for outdoor dining during the cooler months. The restaurant offers a selection of Spanish, Moroccan, Mexican and Italian inspired chicken, vegetarian, meat and seafood dishes. It's a child-friendly venue too, offering high chairs as well as a kids' menu.

Take A Stroll

Got the munchies? Head to The Walk, or The Beach; Dubai's latest places to be that are packed with a multitude of restaurants and cafes.

One of the most popular areas in Dubai for going out is the recently built The Beach (thebeach.ae); a pedestrianised zone of shops and restaurants on the beachside opposite JBR's The Walk. Restaurants include The Cheescake Factory, Aprons & Hammers and Le Paradis du Fruit; there's an Adventure HQ packed with beach games and bikinis; and a 10 screen Reel Cinemas; and an outdoor cinema screen as well as yoga events, markets and access to the real beach and its watersports.

It stretches from the Hilton down to the Shams court at JBR. It's all open-air, rather than being housed in a mall, and so is very popular. There is underground parking, but be prepared for queues to get to it along the JBR strip at weekends.

Still as popular as ever is the 1.7km pedestrian-friendly boulevard that lies between the JBR residential development and The Beach. Crowds come for the atmosphere, the relaxed alfresco eating and drinking, and a stroll along the strip.

Starting at the Dubai end of the strip, the first JBR court is Murjan. This is where the designer boutiques and home accessory stores congregate. There's also a cluster of international dining options to choose from here: Da Shi Dai (Chinese); Umi Sushi (Japanese); Suvoroff (Russian); Scoozi (Italian-Japanese fusion); The Fish & Chip Room (British); and On The Border (Mexican). There's also a cigar lounge here, La Casa Del Habano.

The next court, Sadaf, has its outlets tucked away up on the plaza level, including branches of the excellent Lebanese chain Automatic and the burger-and-shake joint Fuddruckers. Wedged among the JBR courts is Oasis Beach Tower, which contains some popular (and, unlike the JBR outlets, licensed) restaurants, including Frankie's, Wagamama and Trader Vic's Mai-Tai Lounge. Next there's New Zealand's 'healthy' burger chain, Burger Fuel, and the popular Canadian coffee and donuts chain Tim Hortons.

JBR continues with Bahar and Rimal courts, which feature a great stretch of alfresco eating. Packed tables spread out onto the wide pavement, and it is perhaps The Walk's busiest section in the evenings and for leisurely weekend breakfasts. Highlights include Il Caffe Di Roma, Paul, Le Pain Quotidien, The Butcher Shop and Grill, Sukh Sagar and El Chico.

Things descend into more of a fast food frenzy by the time you reach Amwaj and Shams courts, with a selection of the usual suspects – Hardee's, Cinnabon, KFC, Pizza Hut, Figaro's Pizza – plus decent breakfast spot Coco's. If the endless options along The Walk are not enough to satisfy your appetite, there are plenty more cafes and restaurants by the water at Marina Walk, while the beachfront hotels – Amwaj Rotana, Sofitel, Habtoor Grand, Le Royal Meridien, Ritz-Carlton, Hilton and Sheraton – house a more upmarket selection of restaurants and bars.

Fogueira

Ba
Chinese

Fairmont The Palm Nakhlat Jumeira 04 457 3338
dineatba.com
Map **1 N3** Metro **Nakheel**

Upstairs is a sumptuous lounge serving cocktails topped with gold leaf, while downstairs the vast oriental restaurant sprawls out onto a wonderfully situated terrace with sea views as far as Marsa Dubai. Chefs from all provinces of China showcase their unique skills in a range of Chinese cuisine.

Caramel Restaurant & Lounge
American

DIFC Zaa'beel 2 04 425 6677
caramelgroup.com
Map **2 G6** Metro **Financial Centre**

This is where those who work hard, come to play even harder. Stylish wooden furniture spills out from the bar onto the terrace, where trendy cabanas and warm lighting set the mood for stylish lounging. From the mac and cheese to the lobster tacos, expect high-quality dishes with American flair. Dress to impress.

Da Gama
International

Al Garhoud 04 282 3636
Map **2 N8** Metro **GGICO**

The Da Gama menu mixes traditional Portuguese dishes with Mexican favourites and Asian fusion options. Outside is for family dining, but inside is a nightclub-style bar complete with dancefloor. The tantalising selection of sweet and spicy delights includes edamame, Asian duck salad, miniature burgers, succulent steaks, mixed quesadillas and fajitas. The *espatada* skewers are Portuguese perfection.

The Deck
International

JA Ocean View JBR, Marsa Dubai 04 814 5590
jaresortshotels.com
Map **1 J4** Metro **Jumeirah Lakes Towers**

Enjoy the panoramic views of The Deck, where the stylish yet relaxed seating area overlooks the Palm Jumeirah and a stunning infinity pool. A tempting selection of bar snacks are available throughout the day – and breakfast is served here too. But the real draw is the a la carte menu of Ocean-meets-Arabic gourmet fare, including authentic Arabic salad, Burrata Caprese, and mains of everything from baked gnocchi to fresh, juicy grilled salmon.

Eauzone
Asian

Al Sufouh 2 **04 399 9999**
oneandonlyresorts.com
Map **1 N5** Metro **Nakheel**

Dine beneath softly lit canopies overlooking a network of waterways for a truly romantic meal. This beachside restaurant has a casual ambience by day and a more stylish feel after sunset. The Thai and Japanese fusion dishes are best accompanied by an unusual sorbet such as chilli and raspberry, or some sake. Groups should try dining at the teppanyaki station, from Dhs.250 per head.

Elia
Greek

Majestic Al Mankhool **04 501 2529**
dubaimajestic.com
Map **2 L4** Metro **Al Fahidi**

Sit inside in the slightly over-air-conditioned dining area or, better still, out on the terrace, which manages to be serene despite its view looking out over Bur Dubai. The selection of Greek dishes is served with zesty olive oils, fluffy breads and includes succulent meatballs and moreish dolma.

Fogueira Restaurant & Lounge
Brazilian

Ramada Plaza Marsa Dubai **04 439 8888**
ramadaplazajbr.com
Map **1 K4** Metro **Jumeirah Lakes Towers**

Located on the 35th level with stunning views of Dubai Marina and Palm Jumeirah, this Brazilian Churrascaria offers authentic all-you-can-eat Brazilian barbeque along with traditional appetisers and a salad bar. There's a live band from Monday to Saturday and a Samba dance show every Thursday and Friday.

Luciano's
Italian

Habtoor Grand Marsa Dubai **04 399 5000**
habtoorhotels.com
Map **1 L4** Metro **DAMAC**

Traditional and good-quality dishes from across Italy are served at this reasonably priced poolside restaurant, including seafood, meat and pasta. The portions are generous and the starters deserve a

5 Flavors.. 1 Destination

Whether you are looking for a leisurely dining experience with stunning views of Dubai Marina & The Palm Jumeirah or a great time out with your family; the choice is yours at **Ramada Plaza JBR**.

Call 04 439 8888

special mention. The real stars of the show are the thin-crust pizzas. When the temperature permits, ask for a table outside underneath the fairy light bedecked palm trees.

The Meat Co   Steakhouse
Downtown Dubai, Burj Khalifa **04 420 0737**
themeatco.com
Map **2 F6** Metro **Burj Khalifa/Dubai Mall**
While you're choosing the country you'd like your steak to come from, the cut, and how you want it prepared, enjoy the beautiful view of the Burj Khalifa from the terrace. You can't go wrong with anything on the Connoisseur's Choice menu. While it isn't cheap, many consider this one of the best steak joints in the city. There's also a branch at Souk Madinat Jumeirah (04 368 6040).

Meridien Village Terrace   Buffet
Le Meridien Al Garhoud **04 702 2455**
meridienvillageterrace-dubai.com
Map **2 N8** Metro **Airport Terminal 1**
Set in the middle of Le Meridien's outdoor dining area, the huge buffet switches nightly between culinary themes including BBQ, Asian and Latino. Only open in winter, this is one of the best buffets in town. The Flames Band serenades diners throughout the evening, and keeps dancers on their feet after dinner.

Olives > p.175   Italian
The Palace At One&Only Royal Mirage Al Sufouh 2 **04 399 9999**
royalmirage.oneandonlyresorts.com
Map **1 M4** Metro **Nakheel**
There's an air of a riviera coastal cafe at Olives, with its dramatic archways, indoor foliage and white ceramic tiles, as well as a lovely outdoor terrace overlooking the gardens and pool. Pizzas and pastas are the highlight of the Mediterranean menu, but you shouldn't miss the braised lamb shank with roasted garlic salad and an orange rosemary jus – the chef's signature dish. Open for breakfast, lunch and dinner.

Voi   Vietnamese
Jumeirah Zabeel Saray Nakhlat Jumeira **04 453 0444**
jumeirah.com
Map **1 L3** Metro **Nakheel**
The focus here is on upscale Vietnamese with French influences, using high-quality fresh ingredients. Seafood dishes are particularly impressive and, if you are feeling adventurous, go for the chef's tasting menu. The atmosphere is as opulent as the food, with ornately designed ceilings and walls centred around a crystal chandelier, and the dramatic all-white dining room is straight out of a palatial French film set. Voi is especially suited to a romantic night out, as several candle-lit outdoor tables overlook the resort's grounds.

Watatsumi   Japanese
Marsa Dubai **04 399 3373**
watatsumi.ae
Map **1 M4** Metro **Nakheel**
At Watatsumi, you'll find traditional Japanese dishes with a contemporary twist that take you on a culinary journey far beyond the usual sashimi and sushi.

The interior is opulent and the adjoining terrace has a funky vibe, lit by orange lanterns and kept buzzing by the sound of music from nearby Barasti bar. Ample greenery and a balmy sea breeze bring a tropical feel to the evening's festivities. Pair your dishes with Japanese-inspired cocktails or a choice of tasty (and potent) sakes.

Waterfront

Dubai has plenty of coastline which has spawned a clutch of very special beachfront restaurants. There's also a choice of eateries with marina and creek views.

25°55° Cafe Bistro   European
Marina Yacht Club Marsa Dubai **04 362 7955**
dubaimarinayachtclub.com
Map **1 K5** Metro **Jumeirah Lakes Towers**
Whether you come to enjoy a pie and pint while watching the big match or for a must-have full-English breakfast after a big night out, this bistro/pub/yacht club restaurant will satisfy your hunger. It's not about the location – although the terrace affords a stunning view overlooking the marina – but rather about the hearty dishes and warm atmosphere.

Al Muntaha

Al Mansour Dhow
Middle Eastern

Radisson Blu Deira Creek Al Rigga 04 205 7033
radissonblu.com
Map **2 M5** Metro **Union**

This two-hour creek trip features dinner aboard a traditional dhow operated by Radisson Blu. Great views, atmospheric oud music, a buffet of Middle Eastern and Indian food, and shisha make this a memorable evening. The ship sails at 8.30pm.

Al Muntaha
Mediterranean

Burj Al Arab Umm Suqeim 3 04 301 7600
jumeirah.com
Map **1 S4** Metro **Mall of the Emirates**

The breathtaking coastline view from the top of Burj Al Arab goes some way to excusing the grand yet eccentric decor. The Mediterranean menu, with its Atlantic lobster and sweetbread ravioli or 'wild sea bass three-ways', offers a fresh twist on simple flavours and ingredients.

Beach Bar & Grill
Seafood

The Palace At One&Only Royal Mirage Al Sufouh 2 04 399 9999
royalmirage.oneandonlyresorts.com
Map **1 M4** Metro **Nakheel**

Seafood lovers must take a trip to this opulent, romantic beach bar. There are seafood platters to share, and surf and turf options for people who can't pick just one dish. The chef's recommendation is the cataplana of shellfish – clams, mussels, prawns, scallops and crabs with cooked beef chorizo, tomatoes, vegetables and fresh herbs.

Beach House Cabana
South American

Clubhouse Azraq, Shoreline Apartments Nakhlat Jumeira 04 361 8856
emiratesleisureretail.com
Map **1 N4** Metro **Nakheel**

Perfect for a laidback evening with friends. Hot and cold tapas, hearty mains, reasonable prices and a good cocktail selection add to the convivial feel at this South American eatery. Devour peri-peri chicken stuffed with sun-blushed tomatoes, served with Mexican rice, or a Caribbean pumpkin and feta cheese salad. Once the sun goes down, salsa music entices diners onto the dancefloor.

Beachcombers
Asian

Jumeirah Beach Hotel Umm Suqeim 3 04 406 8999
jumeirah.com
Map **1 S4** Metro **First Gulf Bank**

This breezy shack has an idyllic location right on the beach with fantastic views of the Burj Al Arab from its deck terrace. Expect excellent far eastern buffets with live cooking stations for stir-fries and noodles. The Peking duck, curry hotpots and satay are highly recommended. Kids will love the ice cream machine, while you relax with a sundowner cocktail.

Boardwalk
Mediterranean

Creek Golf Club Port Saeed 04 295 6000
dubaigolf.com
Map **2 M7** Metro **Deira City Centre**

Boardwalk's water views are unmatched as it stands on wooden stilts overlooking the creek. The menu features an array of generous and well-presented starters and mains including seafood and vegetarian options. The restaurant doesn't take reservations but you can grab a drink at QD's while you wait.

Bussola
Italian

The Westin Marsa Dubai 04 511 7136
bussoladubai.com
Map **1 M4** Metro **Nakheel**

Adventurous, delicious Sicilian-influenced pizzas served alfresco on a terrace by the sea – Arabia doesn't get much more Mediterranean than this. Upstairs the open-air deck offers a relaxed atmosphere, with more formality and a fuller menu downstairs. The desserts are excellent whatever floor you're on and the food is certified by the Italian Cuisine Academy.

Honyaki
Japanese

Souk Madinat Al Sufouh 1 04 366 6730
jumeirah.com
Map **1 R4** Metro **Mall of the Emirates**

It would be easy for Honyaki to rely purely on its breathtaking views from the terrace overlooking the Madinat amphitheatre and Burj Al Arab, but this authentic Japanese restaurant goes further, preparing its miso, sashimi and maki with delightful twists. The mochi icecream is a must.

Nomad
International

Jumeirah Creekside Al Garhoud 04 230 8571
jumeirah.com
Map **2 M8** Metro **GGICO**

Set by Dubai Creek, Nomad has romantic waterside dining, cosy fireside lounging and an upbeat DJ. Starters include sushi and seafood tempura, and favourites such as nasi goreng and Singapore noodles complement a number of a la carte meat and fish dishes. The venue also hosts an Asian tapas wine bar, New York-style deli, an Asian pool grill, and a dim sum trolley.

The Observatory
International

Marriott Harbour Marsa Dubai 04 319 4795
observatory.dubaimarriottharbourhotel.com
Map **1 L5** Metro **DAMAC**

It's all about the views at this atmospheric 52nd floor gastro-lounge. Spectacular 360° vistas over the marina and Palm Jumeirah accompany the menu. Come just before sunset then stay for evening cocktails.

Villa Beach
Mediterranean

Jumeirah Beach Hotel Umm Suqeim 3 **04 406 8999**
jumeirah.com
Map **1 S4** Metro **First Gulf Bank**
With a prime location on the sand just a stone's throw from the Burj Al Arab, you can dine alfresco and appreciate the architectural wonder much more than if you were inside it. Villa Beach's simple wooden beach-hut decor has an almost Polynesian vibe although the menu is purely Mediterranean. This is a good choice for romantic reverie or to drop the jaws of out-of-towners. The service is swift and the dishes are presented with a finesse befitting the surroundings. The scenery doesn't come cheap, but the food is almost worth the price.

Brunch

A Friday ritual, all-you-can-eat (and drink) brunches are infamous in Dubai – you may struggle to find room for everything on offer.

Al Badia Golf Club By InterContinental Dubai Festival City
International

Al Badia, Al Kheeran **04 601 0101**
albadiagolfclub.ae
Map **2 M10** Metro **Emirates**
Blades at Al Badia puts a Dubai spin on the traditional picnic and serves up a smorgasbord of delights in a casual, family-friendly brunch. Find a shady spot on the grassy lawns overlooking the golf course and lake, relax on the blanket around a low level table, and work your way through a heavily laden traditional wicker hamper; from the picnic staples of scotch eggs and pork pate to the more contemporary offerings of lentil crackers and fresh crab meat – it's a feast. Kids also get their own miniature hamper. Leave room for the BBQ.

Blurring The Boundaries

In the same vein as its counterparts in Istanbul, Amsterdam, Los Angeles, San Francisco and London, the ultra-cool Supperclub (04 451 1100, supperclub. com) offers more than just fine dining. This is a cultural experience, founded by artists, that also functions as a cocktail bar, club, gallery and performance art venue. You literally kick off your shoes and eat while lounging on a large white bed. The food and cocktails shout 'innovation', the vibe is relaxed, and you never know what kind of entertainment will appear next. Find it at Zabeel Saray, West Crescent, Palm Jumeirah. And of course, being the Palm, the sea is never far away.

Al Qasr
International

Madinat Jumeirah Al Sufouh 1 **04 366 8888**
jumeirah.com
Map **1 R5** Metro **Mall of the Emirates**
The brunch at Al Qasr attracts the glitzier end of the brunching spectrum and has won numerous 'best brunch in Dubai' awards. Three ground floor restaurants offer an impressive array of delicately

The Observatory

constructed dishes, which you can wash down with a deliciously dangerous mix of caipirinhas and mojitos. Face painting will keep children occupied.

The China Club
Chinese

Radisson Blu Deira Creek Al Rigga **04 205 7033**
radissonblu.com
Map **2 M5** Metro **Union**

A chic space with subtle touches of authenticity, the China Club serves tasty favourites as well as new creations. The excellent Peking duck is theatrically carved tableside. It's also one of the best value Friday brunches – if you're not interested in sampling the house beverages or bubbly – with an all-you-can-eat deal for Dhs.140 per head excluding alcohol.

El Sur
Spanish

The Westin Marsa Dubai **04 399 7700**
elsurdubai.com
Map **1 M5** Metro **Nakheel**

The Westin's newest dining spot serves up contemporary Spanish fare at a Saturday brunch that's perfect for ladies who lunch. Offering a more relaxed meal on a Mediterranean-style terrace, plates of tapas from traditional meats, breads and olives to calamari, paella and prawns, are all brought to the table. Order your main courses, choosing from a selection of Spanish-style fish, meat and vegetarian delights, and then squeeze in a taster of the delicious desserts. The all-inclusive menu also includes a rather upmarket choice of drinks and cocktails, including the restaurant's popular free-flowing sangria.

Farriers
International

Meydan Nadd Al Shiba 1 **04 381 3111**
meydanhotels.com
Map **2 E10** Metro **Business Bay**

Does Dubai really need another posh brunch? Yes, it does, if it's from the Meydan's stylish restaurant Farriers, with its free-flowing bubbly, live jazz and a kids' club. On other days, dine in the bright, airy interior or on the track-side terrace. Sample delicious signature dishes courtesy of vast interactive buffet stations. Once you're done, head for the hotel's Shiba bar, where brunchers can enjoy discount on drinks.

Flow Kitchen
International

Fairmont The Palm Nakhlat Jumeira **04 457 3457**
fairmont.com
Map **1 N3** Metro **Nakheel**

An innovative brunch concept where waiters bring tasters to your table, such as the unique vegetable salad, crafted to look like a miniature garden complete with chocolate soil. You can also order classics such as eggs Benedict from the menu, and finish off your leisurely brunch with dessert. Kids will love the interactive juice bar.

Imperium
French

Jumeirah Zabeel Saray Nakhlat Jumeira **04 453 0444**
jumeirah.com
Map **1 L3** Metro **Nakheel**

Located in the opulent and ever-impressive Jumeirah Zabeel Saray, the brunch at Imperium is an altogether refined affair. While the free-flowing bubbly and mixed drinks are undoubtedly delicious, the emphasis here is firmly on the food, with a host of French-inspired dishes and a delicious selection of seafood. There's also a hot food and carving grill, as well as a tempting desserts station. One for those in search of a less rowdy, crowded weekend.

Mazina
International

The Address Dubai Marina Marsa Dubai **04 888 3444**
theaddress.com
Map **1 K5** Metro **DAMAC**

The Saturday brunch at Mazina is perfect for families. Enjoy a long, hearty lunch while the young ones jump on the bouncy castle or get competitive on the Wii. Choose from never-ending salad options, dim sum, a variety of roasts, and a delicious array of desserts.

The MED
Mediterranean

Media One Al Sufouh 2 **04 4271000**
Map **1 M5** Metro **Nakheel**

On the eighth floor of Media City's latest hotspot, The MED serves up a fun, energetic and good-value menu of Mediterranean classics, served with enough Gallic flare to reveal the chef's nationality. Head here on Fridays for a lively brunch.

MORE Cafe
International

Mall of the Emirates
04 395 0967
morecafe.co
Map **1 R6** Metro **Mall of the Emirates**

A homely and popular cafe with an extensive breakfast, lunch and dinner menu. The huge portions of home-made, wholesome food could set you up for a full day of swimming, cycling and other activities – all of which you will probably not get around to doing because you'll want to stay for dessert. They offer a loyalty card which gives you freebies once you have 10 stamps. The menu is vast, so it's easy to keep going back for your stamps.

Seafire > p.275
Steakhouse

Atlantis Nakhlat Jumeira **04 426 2626**
Map **1 N1** Metro **Nakheel**

Dinner at this friendly New York-style eatery starts with extravagant, delicious appetisers – just try to resist the succulent fillet or seafood grill. The Atlantis strip sirloin is one of the finest steaks you'll ever taste, and the sides are delicious. Seafire is mainly for beef lovers, but it does offer other meats as well as vegetarian options.

Do You Drunch?

If you think brunch is simply a portmanteau of 'breakfast' and 'lunch', you clearly haven't been in Dubai that long. Here, 'brunch' has evolved one step further into 'drunch', an amalgamation of 'drinking' and 'brunch'. The act of 'drunching' is a hobby, a social skill, a weekend institution – the calorific glue that holds the weekend together. All for a set price. So raise your fork, pop your cork, and get stuck in.

The Thai Kitchen   Thai
Park Hyatt Port Saeed **04 317 2221**
restaurants.dubai.hyatt.com
Map **2 M7** Metro **Deira City Centre**
A decent range of Thai delicacies with rich, authentic flavours. The decor is stylish and modern, portions are perfect for sharing and the Friday brunch, from 12.30pm to 4pm, is a delight – more refined than most.

Yalumba   International
Le Meridien Al Garhoud **04 702 2328**
yalumba-dubai.com
Map **2 N8** Metro **Airport Terminal 1**
This Friday feast consists of a grand selection of seafood, international buffet options and desserts, complemented by four types of world-class champagne. At Dhs.499 per person, it certainly isn't the cheapest option; and there's no alcohol-free price. Diners can get quite rowdy after a drink or five.

Zuma   Japanese
Gate Village DIFC, Zaa'beel 2 **04 425 5660**
zumarestaurant.com
Map **2 G6** Metro **Financial Centre**
Despite being a perfect way to sample this sushi restaurant's legendary menu, the Zuma brunch is certainly not the place for you if you are looking for a smash and grab all-you-can-eat (and drink) affair. Dining is a combination of a la carte and buffet, and you are unlikely to end the afternoon having to trade up a clothing size. Delicate, stylish and sophisticated are the overwhelming themes in this trendy eatery.

Celebrity Chef

Big name celebrity chefs rub shoulders with Michelin-starred culinary giants in Dubai, including the likes of Marco Pierre White and Sanjeev Kapoor.

Frankie's   Italian
JBR, Marsa Dubai **04 399 4311**
Map **1 K5** Metro **Jumeirah Lakes Towers**
Grab a vodka Martini and pizza in the bar at this stylish joint, co-owned by Frankie Dettori and Marco

Pierre White, then head into the main restaurant for classic Italian dishes and new favourites such as duck ravioli. With its sultry interior, pianist and good quality Friday brunch, this is a classy establishment with a welcoming vibe.

Jamie's Italian   Italian
Dubai Festival City Mall Al Kheeran **04 232 9969**
jamieoliver.com
Map **2 M9** Metro **Emirates**
Unlike many celeb chefs before him, Jamie Oliver has opted not to chase after the big bucks, but has instead gone for the mid-range and family markets with Jamie's Italian. The restaurant is both chic and homely. The menu features some outstanding antipasti and a great selection of tasty traditional and innovative pastas.

Khazana Indian
Oud Metha **04 336 0061**
khazanadubai.com
Map **2 L6** Metro **Oud Metha**
Indian celebrity chef Sanjeev Kapoor's eatery specialises in cuisine from north India. Try grilled tandoori seafood and gravy-based dishes, as well as the kebabs and Anglo-Indian novelties such as 'British raj railroad curry'.

Maya Modern Mexican Kitchen & Lounge   Mexican
Le Royal Meridien Marsa Dubai **04 316 5550**
richardsandoval.com/mayadubai
Map **1 L4** Metro **DAMAC**
Maya – from US chef Richard Sandoval – is a standout in Dubai. The food is a contemporary take on the dishes of rural Mexico. Forget fajitas. Dive into lobster with chilli chipotle or langoustine tacos. The *crepas con cajeta* is super sumptuous and the lovely terrace is perfect for margaritas.

Nobu > p.275   Japanese
Atlantis Nakhlat Jumeira **04 426 2626**
atlantisthepalm.com
Map **1 N1** Metro **Nakheel**
Nobuyuki Matsuhisa, the godfather of sushi, has upped the ante for Japanese food aficionados with his Dubai offering. You'll love the exceptional quality, attention to detail and huge menu of sushi, sashimi and tempura. Despite its reputation for exclusivity, Nobu is not restricted to celebrities – as long as you can get a reservation.

Reflets Par Pierre Gagnaire French
InterContinental Festival City Al Badia, Al Kheeran **04 701 1127**
diningdfc.com
Map **2 L9** Metro **Emirates**
From the Michelin-starred grandfather of molecular gastronomy, Pierre Gagnaire, comes a magical,

imaginative and highly conceptual dining experience incorporating French cuisine. Bold purple carpet and pink chandeliers along with floor-to-ceiling mirrors and white tablecloths are the backdrop to a menu that strives to be a work of art. The romantic waterfront setting is the perfect place to sample the superb wines.

Ronda Locatelli — Italian
Atlantis Nakhlat Jumeira **04 426 2626**
atlantisthepalm.com
Map **1 N1** Metro **Nakheel**
Giorgio Locatelli's cavernous restaurant can seat hundreds of diners in its raised alcoves or at tables surrounding a huge stone-built wood-fired oven. There's a charmingly rustic vibe and the casual menu offers a good range of authentic starters, pasta and mains, as well as a selection of small dishes that are perfect for sharing. A great comfort food venue with top-quality dishes.

Signature By Sanjeev Kapoor — Indian
Melia Al Raffa **04 386 8111**
sanjeevkapoor.com
Map **2 K4** Metro **ADCB**
The aptly named Signature, Sanjeev Kapoor's latest Dubai restaurant, bears all the hallmarks of its progressive and eclectic chef, with traditional Indian dishes given an innovative makeover. Samosas and bhajis take a back seat to such modern delights as tandoori wasabi lobster, basil pepper hammour tikka, honey mustard chicken chat puffs or paneer tikka with asparagus fritters and avocado mousse. Main courses continue the trend. It's traditional but with a twist – so

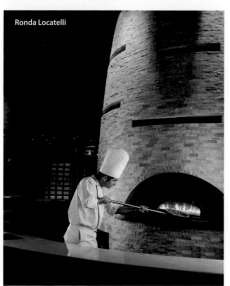

Ronda Locatelli

expect to find paneer cooked in a butternut pumpkin and tomato sauce, goat shanks simmered in kashmiri and chilli onion gravy, and mutton cubes fried in pepper. Every inch the fine-dining restaurant.

STAY By Yannick Alleno — French
One&Only The Palm Nakhlat Jumeira **04 440 1030**
Map **1 L3** Metro **Nakheel**
Yannick Alleno, with three Michelin stars to his name, has brought his contemporary French restaurant STAY to Dubai's dining scene. Located in the opulent One&Only The Palm, the emphasis is on impeccably selected ingredients cooked to perfection. Seasons dictate the menu but signature dishes are constant; the Black Angus beef fillet 'cafe de Paris' is recommended. Leave enough room for something sweet – the open Pastry Library allows you to participate in the dessert making process.

Drinking Water

Bottled water seems to rocket in price in the five-star venues, and if you ask for water you'll often be given an imported brand, costing up to Dhs.40 a bottle. You should specify 'local' water when ordering, but even then you can expect to pay Dhs.10 or Dhs.20 for a bottle of still water that costs less than Dhs.2 in the supermarket.

Wheeler's — Seafood
Gate Village Trade Center 2 **04 386 0899**
wheelersdubai.com
Map **2 G6** Metro **Financial Centre**
This trendy Marco Pierre White eatery serves perfect seafood and posh British nosh to happy post-work revellers in DIFC. With a buzzing, post-work drinks atmosphere, this is a good place to head with friends for a rowdy supper. There are some British classics, such as beer battered fish and triple cooked chips, as well as enough vegetarian and carnivorous options to keep most diners happy.

Cheap & Cheerful

There's a huge mix of chain and independent restaurants in the city where two people eat well for less than Dhs.100 – perfect for a casual bite.

Al Safadi Restaurant — Middle Eastern
Al Kawakeb Bldg, Shk Zayed Rd Trade Center 2
04 343 5333
alsafadi.ae
Map **2 G5** Metro **Financial Centre**
Function rules over form at big and busy Al Safadi, but it's the high-quality Arabic food that people come

here for. Street-side tables are perfect for more relaxed dining, shisha and people watching. Another branch is on Al Rigga Road in Deira (04 227 9922).

Aryaas   Indian
Al Nakheel Bldg, Zabeel Rd Al Karama **04 335 5776**
Map **2 L6** Metro **ADCB**
This Indian chain has served excellent fare since 1959, and, despite its austere decor, the food is excellent. The house speciality is thali, small pots of different flavours into which you dip naan bread or rice. Around Dhs.15 will buy enough to fill you up for the day.

Automatic   Middle Eastern
Beach Centre Jumeira 1 **04 349 4888**
Map **2 G4** Metro **Emirates Towers**
This popular chain continues to serve high-quality Arabic food in various locations in Dubai. The vast range of mezze is accompanied by mountainous portions of salad, and grilled meat, fish and kebabs. The atmosphere is minimalist but clean and bright, with family-friendly amenities and good service.

Benihana   Japanese
Amwaj Rotana JBR, Marsa Dubai **04 428 2000**
rotana.com
Map **1 K4** Metro **Jumeirah Lakes Towers**
Dining at Benihana is a pleasure and an experience. The restaurant is part of an internationally renowned chain, and the quality is excellent. It's also great value for money. The terrace is lovely, or sit at the teppanyaki grills where the chefs cook your food in front of you, with liberal amounts of cheeky banter and utensil trickery. There are live sushi, sashimi and Robatayaki stations at brunch every Friday from 12pm-4pm. If you're too full to move, then book their chauffeur service to take you home. There's another branch at Al Bustan Rotana (04 282 0000).

Street Food
Shawarma is a popular local snack consisting of rolled pita bread filled with lamb or chicken carved from a rotating spit, vegetables and tahina sauce. You'll see countless roadside stands offering shawarma for as little as Dhs.5 each, and they make a great alternative to the usual fast food staples. In residential areas, the small cluster of shops beside a mosque is often a good bet to find your local shawarma outlet. These cafes and stands usually sell other dishes, such as falafel (or *ta'amiya*), which are small savoury balls of deep-fried chickpeas, also sold separately or in a pita bread sandwich. Many offer freshly squeezed fruit juices for around Dhs.10. For a really unique version, check out Al Shera'a Fisheries Centre on Al Muraqqabat Road (04 227 1803) – the only place in town that offers fish shawarmas.

Bistro Domino   French
Ibis Deira City Centre Port Saeed **04 292 5000**
ibishotel.com
Map **2 N7** Metro **Deira City Centre**
A hearty selection of dishes is served here that will leave you warm, satisfied and wishing you were tucking into your meal in a rustic chateau. The tempting menu is an authentic mix of typical French dishes (including deliciously buttery escargot) and fabulously rich desserts.

The Bombay   Indian
Marco Polo Al Muteena **04 272 0000**
marcopolohotel.net
Map **2 P5** Metro **Salah Al Din**
The Bombay is an unassuming restaurant that packs quite a punch and is a favourite destination for Indian food lovers in the know. The dishes are well priced, generous and authentic, and the laid-back atmosphere lends itself to a convivial night out with friends.

Caravan   International
Ritz Carlton Dubai Hotel Marsa Dubai **04 318 6150**
ritzcarlton.com
Map **1 K4** Metro **Jumeirah Lake Towers**
Located in an opulent seafront setting, Caravan's menu is as lavish as its expansive gardens. As the name suggests, Caravan is a journey through the continents of cooking. For buffet or a la carte, sample Big Rami's chicken shawarma, slow-cooked Moroccan couscous or a home-cooked chicken tikka. The crispy Porchetta is not to be missed neither is the Sicilian pistachio tart. Feeling adventurous? Try the Canoodle camel milk dessert. Their rotisserie Friday brunch is a real draw.

Channels   International
TECOM, Al Thanyah 1 **04 435 0201**
rotana.com
Map **1 P6** Metro **Dubai Internet City**
This all-day diner makes up for rather drab surroundings and a flat atmosphere with its great value buffets four nights a week. The spread is staggering, the desserts in particular, and the price (from Dhs.175 including house drinks) makes it a great option for big groups.

Chef Lanka   Sri Lankan
Nr LuLu Supermarket Al Karama **04 335 3050**
Map **2 L6** Metro **ADCB**
This is a smart, clean, Sri Lankan restaurant with inexpensive, tasty food. The lunch buffet is just Dhs.16 and dinner costs Dhs.30. Alternatively, you can order a la carte for your desired spiciness. The excellent king fish curry and koththu roti (chopped roti bread stir-fried with chicken, leeks, tomatoes and carrots), come highly recommended.

Chili's American

Nr Welcare Hospital Al Garhoud **04 705 9656**
chilisuae.com
Map **2 N7** Metro **GGICO**

Known all around the world and all over Dubai, Chili's delivers its winning formula for inexpensive, all-American tucker in generous portions and in family friendly surroundings. Takeaway and home delivery (600 561 112) are also available. See the website for locations throughout Dubai.

Lemongrass Thai

Nr Lamcy Plaza Oud Metha **04 334 2325**
lemongrassrestaurants.com
Map **2 K6** Metro **Oud Metha**

One of the better – and cheapest – Thai restaurants in Dubai, the menu at Lemongrass offers a typical range of decently executed Siamese dishes served in a casual dining atmosphere. There's no alcohol, but the fruity mocktails compensate. The setting is bright, inviting and comfortable, and the service unobtrusive. Also at Ibn Battuta Mall (04 368 5616).

Mannaland Korean Restaurant Korean

Al Mina Rd Madinat Dubai Al Melaheyah **04 345 1300**
Map **2 J4** Metro **Al Jafiliya**

A real find, for a truly unique Dubai dining experience, this Korean restaurant in Satwa offers traditional floor seating and excellent, authentic food cooked at your table. This is the place to try *kimchi* – a dish made of fermented vegetables, said to be a superfood. Wash it all down with a teapot of 'special brew'. Great value too.

Nando's International

Nr Four Points Sheraton Trade Center 1 **04 321 2000**
nandos.ae
Map **2 G6** Metro **Financial Centre**

Famous for its tasty flame-grilled chicken, Nando's has branches across the city, including The Dubai Mall, Greens and Novotel Suites Al Barsha. Delivering the same delicious Afro-Portuguese peri-peri chicken that is a trademark of Nando's across the world, it's a firm family favourite. The good news is they even deliver too, so if you want your chicken to come to you, call for delivery on 600 542 525.

Pax Italian

Dusit Thani Trade Center 2 **04 343 3333**
dusit.com
Map **2 G6** Metro **Burj Khalifa/Dubai Mall**

Pax does traditional Italian dishes in less than traditional sizes to give punters a pick 'n' mix of tastes. The style is called bocconcini (little delicacies), and with appetisers starting at Dhs.70, and most mains costing less than Dhs.200, a hearty feed is not prohibitively expensive. There's also an extensive wine list.

Smiling BKK Thai

Al Wasl Rd Al Wasl **04 349 6677**
smilingbkk.com
Map **2 E5** Metro **Burj Khalifa/Dubai Mall**

This outstanding Thai pad near Safa Park is a rare thing: great food topped with good humour and superb service. The cheekily named dishes are reasonable at around Dhs.30, but with gossip mag pages for place mats and theme nights such as 'sing for your supper', it's the spirit that sets Smiling BKK apart. Check out its Facebook page for details of the hilarious menu.

Tagpuan Filipino

Karama Complex Al Karama **04 337 3959**
Map **2 K6** Metro **ADCB**

Tagpuan serves home-style Filipino cooking at great prices. The tiny tables inside this miniscule eatery fill up quickly, but the outside area on the terrace offers more space. Come here to try simple but tasty versions of Filipino home favourites including *adobong pusit* (squid), fried *tilapia* (fish) or *pinakbet* (mixed vegetables).

Family Friendly

Family is a huge part of Dubai life and many restaurants offer kids' menus, high chairs, changing facilities and child-friendly entertainment.

A La Grand International

Grand Excelsior Al Barsha 1 **04 444 9999**
grandexcelsior.ae
Map **1 R7** Metro **Mall of the Emirates**

A La Grand offers a refined atmosphere; while it's not Michelin-starred stuff, the menu offers wholesome European food made using excellent ingredients and delivered to the table in a professional but friendly manner. The heartier meat-based mains are tasty and generous, so you won't leave hungry. The restaurant is open all day, has a good children's menu and also offers a good brunch.

Applebee's American

Shk Issa Tower Trade Center 1 **04 343 7755**
applebees.com
Map **2 H6** Metro **Financial Centre**

This restaurant has everything you'd expect of the crowd-pleasing chain – friendly staff, a lively atmosphere and a familiar menu of kid-friendly favourites. It's easy to keep the whole clan with Applebee's huge portions of Tex-Mex fare, burgers, and other crowd pleasers. Wash it all down with an Oreo milkshake. The big screen TVs, and great kids' and dessert menus make this a winning choice for lunch or dinner.

Blades — International
Al Badia Golf Club Al Badia, Al Kheeran **04 601 0101**
albadiagolfclub.ae
Map **2 M10** Metro **Emirates**
Delicious Asian noodles, steaks and tasting platters feature prominently in this fine-dining eatery that also makes children feel welcome with a healthy kids' menu and colouring books. Diners can look out over the golf course and its picturesque waterfalls, and during the cooler months adults can enjoy a shisha on the terrace. Excellent service for all ages and not a chicken nugget or plastic toy in sight.

Carnevale — Italian
Jumeirah Beach Hotel Umm Suqeim 3 **04 406 8999**
jumeirah.com
Map **1 S4** Metro **First Gulf Bank**
This family-friendly, award-winning Italian offers upmarket Italian food, swift service and views of the Burj Al Arab from the adjoining indoor terrace. Dishes include home-made fettuccine, served with garlic prawns, asparagus, tomato and fresh basil and other traditional favourites. Despite its exclusive, Venetian-themed interior, families and children are welcome.

The Farm — International
Nr Falcon City Al Barari, Wadi Al Safa 3 **04 392 5660**
thefarmdubai.com
Map **2 A13**
Located within the new uber-luxurious Al Barari residential area, and hidden in an oasis of running water, frangipani trees and sprawling greenery, The Farm serves wholesome, tasty treats. From sensational seafood creations such as saffron shrimp curry and to marvellous meat feasts like rib eye steak and honey glazed duck, pretty much every palate is catered for.

Johnny Rockets — American
J3 Mall Jumeira 1 **04 388 1696**
johnnyrockets.com
Map **2 H4** Metro **Emirates Towers**
This 1950s inspired American diner, with its classic decor, red vinyl booths and jukeboxes, transforms a casual family meal into a novelty experience. Fresh burgers, great milkshakes, reasonable prices, and impromptu outpourings of dance to Staying Alive by friendly, bow-tied staff will brighten up anybody's evening. See the website for other locations.

La Veranda — Italian
Jumeirah Beach Hotel Umm Suqeim 3 **04 406 8999**
jumeirah.com
Map **1 S4** Metro **First Gulf Bank**
This cosy restaurant right on the beach serves large portions of inexpensive pizza, pasta and seafood with marina views. Children are well catered for with typical treats like burgers and fish fingers on the menu.

Living Rooms Video Games Cafe — Cafe
Al Badia, Al Kheeran **04 232 9291**
livingroomscafe.com
Map **2 M9** Metro **Emirates**
Gamers will love this: state-of-the-art video game systems and the latest games to play on Sony Playstation®, Nintendo Wii or Microsoft XBOX. Simply book one of the gaming rooms, plug in and battle it out with your friends as if you were in your own living room. For old school, pre-Playstation® fun, you can also play chess, Monopoly, Scrabble, Risk or dominos instead. Fizzy drinks and snacks are on the menu.

Max's Restaurant — Filipino
Khalid Bin Al Waleed Rd Al Karama **04 325 7797**
maxschicken.com
Map **2 L5** Metro **BurJuman**
This family-friendly diner is a firm favourite with the Filipino community and the food is plentiful and tasty. Max's serves up favourites such as fried chicken served with rice or kamote fries (yummy sweet potato fries). The menu also boasts traditional dishes such as kare-kare (oxtail and tripe stew) and lumpiang ubod (crab meat sauteed with fresh coconut).

Mosaico — Italian
Emirates Towers Trade Center 2 **04 319 8088**
jumeirah.com
Map **2 H6** Metro **Financial Centre**
Open from 6am to 5pm, Mosaico blends Italian flavours with Spanish flamboyance. The Mediterranean buffet incorporates freshly prepared tapas, pastas and pizzas made to order, and honey-drizzled profiteroles. There's a special combo menu for kids too.

Orchid Restaurant — International
Ramada Downtown Downtown Dubai, Burj Khalifa **04 330 7300**
ramadadowntowndubai.com
Map **2 F6** Metro **Burj Khalifa/Dubai Mall**
For diners looking to escape the shopping frenzy of The Dubai Mall, Orchid offers up international dishes from the hotel's in-room dining menu. Tucked away on the second floor, the restaurant has indoor and outdoor poolside seating – both with ample flat screen TVs. While not a destination in its own right, Orchid does give neighbourhood diners a good meal away from the crowds.

Peppercrab — Asian
Grand Hyatt Umm Hurair 2 **04 317 2222**
restaurants.dubai.hyatt.com
Map **2 L8** Metro **Dubai Healthcare City**
If you're looking for the ultimate Singaporean gastronomic experience, Peppercrab won't disappoint. You can even watch the chef in action in the kitchen. Order a smaller portion for children, who can enjoy

the kids' club during the meal. The restaurant's famous chilli pepper crab remains a must-try and the wine selection is generous.

Ranches Restaurant & Bar   International
Arabian Ranches, Wadi Al Safa 6 **04 360 7935**
arabianranchesgolfdubai.com
Map **1 Q13**
Ranches serves unpretentious fare in comfortable surroundings, with a focus on traditional British dishes. The outdoor terrace offers a more intimate dining experience overlooking the course. Tuesday is a popular quiz night, and there are themed buffets during the week.

Shores   International
Ramada Plaza JBR, Marsa Dubai **04 439 8888**
ramadaplazajbr.com
Map **1 K5** Metro **Jumeirah Lakes Towers**
The restaurant is open for breakfast, lunch and dinner and has a relaxing terrace at plaza level. It's ideally located next to The Walk at JBR if you fancy a stroll after dinner.

Silver Fox   American
City Walk Mall, Al Wasl
04 705 9794
silverfoxcafe.com
Map **2 F5** Metro **Burj Khalifa/Dubai Mall**
High primes steaks are the speciality, and the affordable menu also includes fish and seafood. Part of a well-respected US chain of high-quality restaurants.

Spice Island   Buffet
Al Muteena **04 262 5555**
Map **2 P5** Metro **Abu Baker Al Siddique**
A trip to the Spice Island buffet is suitably informal and really good fun. Be entertained by a singing trio as you agonise over which cuisine you are going to choose. There's a choice of alcoholic and non-alcoholic packages, and the kids can hang out in the play area.

Thyme Restaurant   Mediterranean
JBR, Marsa Dubai **04 315 4200**
thethymerestaurant.com
Map **1 K4** Metro **DAMAC**
Think heavy wood, cast iron fittings, chalk boards, open kitchens and oversized wine glasses. This Mediterranean brasserie plays host to families, couples and groups of friends, all tucking in with gusto. There's even a kids' corner with Wii station and toys.

Hidden Gems

Perhaps not so much 'hidden' as less well-known or talked about on Dubai's dining circuit, these restaurants still deliver some fantastic dining options.

Al Dahleez   Middle Eastern
Umm Hurair 2 **04 324 3000**
alboom.ae
Map **2 L8** Metro **Al Jadaf**
This cavernous shisha cafe with juices and Arabic grills is always packed. Al Dahleez serves some of the best

Peppercrab

shisha in Dubai, and boasts an extensive menu. Its bizarre, faux-cavern interior is a great place to spend a few hours playing cards or backgammon. A great place for a dose of Emirati authenticity.

Amala
Indian

Jumeirah Zabeel Saray Nakhlat Jumeira **04 453 0444**
jumeirah.com
Map **1 L3** Metro **Nakheel**

This elegant restaurant serves authentic north Indian cuisine focusing on contemporary Mughalai curries, tandoori and biryani dishes. The service is attentive and the the a la carte menu is great value for money.

Armani/Amal
Indian

Armani Downtown Dubai, Burj Khalifa **04 888 3888**
dubai.armanihotels.com
Map **2 F6** Metro **Burj Khalifa/Dubai Mall**

With its open kitchen and vaulted framework, this award-winning restaurant evokes a hip nightspot in a converted Indian marketplace. The high-end Indian cuisine is vibrant. Outside, the terrace is a magical spot with views of the Burj Khalifa tower and the perfect spot to watch the Dubai Fountain light show.

Asado
South American

The Palace Downtown Downtown Dubai, Burj Khalifa
04 888 3444
theaddress.com
Map **2 F6** Metro **Burj Khalifa/Dubai Mall**

A combination of moody lighting, passionate music, and a meat lover's dream menu cement Asado's position as a steakhouse to be reckoned with. Excellent meat and an enormous wine selection, with terrace views of Burj Khalifa thrown in, make this Argentinean restaurant something special.

Asha's
Indian

Umm Hurair 2 **04 324 4100**
wafirestaurants.com
Map **2 L7** Metro **Dubai Healthcare City**

This is an atmospheric Indian eatery run by Indian superstar Asha Bhosle, who has clearly put a lot of love into this restaurant. Beautifully decorated, the quality of the atmospheric interior is equalled by the eclectic menu, which includes Indian classics, Asha's signature dishes, and some fusion choices. There are great cocktails too.

Bastakiah Nights
Middle Eastern

Al Fahidi Neighbourhood Al Souk Al Kabeer
04 353 7772
bastakiah.com
Map **2 M4** Metro **Al Fahidi**

This is a magical place celebrating local cuisine and culture, and a good spot to take visitors. The venue offers a perfect amalgamation of great location and delectable food. Choose from the fixed menus or a la carte offerings – there's no alcohol on the menu, but you'd be a fool to let that put you off.

Blue Elephant
Thai

Al Bustan Rotana Al Garhoud **04 282 0000**
blueelephant.com/dubai
Map **2 N7** Metro **GGICO**

This stalwart of Dubai's Thai restaurant scene has changed little in its 15 years. If it isn't broke, why fix it? The food is excellent; Blue Elephant sticks to what it knows – pad thai, curries, and dim sum – plus adds more unusual options such as fresh lime sea bass.

Center Cut
Steakhouse

Ritz-Carlton DIFC Zaa'beel 2 **04 372 2222**
ritzcarlton.com
Map **2 G6** Metro **Financial Centre**

Center Cut's first impression of austerity is offset by friendly staff and an attractive menu. This is a meat-lover's paradise. Appetisers include salmon, scallops, foie gras and oysters but your main is all about meat. Choose from Australian or US cuts, add cocktails, wines, desserts and cheeses, and you're done.

El Malecon
Cuban

Dubai Marine Beach Resort Jumeira 1 **04 346 1111**
dxbmarine.com
Map **2 H4** Metro **World Trade Centre**

Graffiti-covered turquoise walls and low lighting create a sultry Cuban atmosphere that builds up during the evening, helped along by live music and salsa dancers. Big windows overlook the glowing Dubai Marine lagoon. Malecon's doors are constantly swinging; it's a great place to start or end the night with Cuban food and a superb drinks selection.

Fish Market
Seafood

Radisson Blu Deira Creek Al Rigga **04 222 7171**
radissonblu.com
Map **2 M5** Metro **Baniyas Square**

This novel restaurant lets diners pick raw ingredients from a large bank of fresh, raw seafood and vegetables, and then request how they'd like it cooked. The food is not outstanding but the concept is entertaining.

Ginger
Asian

Ramada Jumeirah Hotel, Al Hudaiba **04 702 7000**
ramadajumeirah.ae
Map **2 J4** Metro **ADCB**

Travel through Asia with every bite from this modern Asian kitchen that specialises in fusion dishes. Food is from Thailand, China and Japan, and you can watch it being prepared in the open kitchen. There's a good choice of Bento, sushi, curry and vegetarian dishes. Dine to the soothing sounds of lounge music. Prices are reasonable too.

Center Cut

Manga Sushi
Japanese

Jumeira 2 **04 342 8300**
mangasushi.ae
Map **2 D4** Metro **Business Bay**
As the name suggests, this Japanese eatery is all about Japan's cult comics, from the large screen showing Manga movies to the artworks on the walls. You may feel like you've drifted into Tokyo, where traditional fare has a modern edge.

Nina
Indian

Al Sufouh 2 **04 399 9999**
oneandonlyroyalmirage.com
Map **1 M4** Metro **Nakheel**
The refined menu includes roti and naan with savoury pickles and salads such as seared tuna with mustard cress and lime vinaigrette. The spinach kofta is exquisite, as are the tandoori prawns with lemon rice. Indian sauvignon blanc pairs with lighter dishes, while the shiraz matches meatier options.

Pachanga
Latin American

Hilton Jumeirah Marsa Dubai 04 318 2530
hilton.com
Map **1 K4** Metro **Jumeirah Lakes Towers**
Pachanga's well-rounded Latin-American menu hails from Mexico to Argentina. On Tuesdays, the restaurant celebrates with a Brazilian-style Churrasco barbecue (from Dhs.195) with succulent beef, chicken and lamb carved for you at your table. The peppered rib-eye is particularly tender. Still hungry? The buffet includes chorizo sausage and crispy breaded crab.

Prime 68
Steakhouse

JW Marriott Marquis Business Bay **04 414 3000**
jwmarriottmarquisdubailife.com
Map **2 D6** Metro **Business Bay**
This boutique steakhouse serves up the most succulent steaks with some of the finest cuts you'll find in Dubai, from award-winning Australian full blood Wagyu to prime Black Angus beef. Combine that with breathtaking views from the 68th floor of the world's tallest, polished service and delicious desserts and you have one of the top fine-dining experiences in the city.

Segreto
Italian

Madinat Jumeirah Al Sufouh 1 **04 366 6730**
jumeirah.com
Map **1 R4** Metro **Mall of the Emirates**
Candle-lit lamps lead you through the many walkways of Madinat Jumeirah to this hidden gem. Start with a glass of prosecco on the terrace by the canal, then head into the stylish, modern interior for your meal. The food is aesthetically appealing, despite the fact that the portions seem to be aimed at a catwalk model. However, the traditional Italian flavours shine through in all dishes, from pasta to risotto.

Informal

There are times when all you want is carefree dining without the airs and graces, and where the food needs no dressing up. These restaurants provide just that.

Al Bandar Restaurant
Seafood

Al Shindagha **04 393 9001**
alkoufa.com
Map **2 M4** Metro **Al Ghubaiba**
With an idyllic creekside location and good seafood, Al Bandar is the perfect venue to ease visitors into the Arabian dining experience. The restaurant caters for a dressed down clientele, making a pleasant change from the usual five-star hotels, so there's no need to throw on your coolest threads. The menu is good value, and the nearby resident camels make for excellent photo opportunities.

Almaz By Momo
Moroccan

Mall of the Emirates Al Barsha 1 **04 409 8877**
altayer.com
Map **1 R6** Metro **Mall of the Emirates**
The subdued atmosphere inside this Moroccan restaurant inside Harvey Nichols is a refreshing contrast to the retail buzz outside. Take a break from shopping at the Mall of the Emirates with refreshing mocktails, tasty stews, tender lamb and fluffy couscous, served in generous portions. You won't be going anywhere fast – the service is as laidback as the vibe.

Reem Al Bawadi

If it's Middle Eastern fare that you're craving, head for this Dubai institution. This atmospheric eatery serves traditional dishes at excellent prices as well as shisha. The Jumeira Road branch is by far the best, with its large outdoor garden, but there are also great spots in Downtown, Marsa Dubai and Sheikh Zayed Road. The falafel and hummus are possibly the best in town... and then there's the fluffy Arabic bread!

Apres   International

Mall of the Emirates Al Barsha 1 **04 341 2575**
emiratesleisureretail.com
Map **1 R6** Metro **Mall of the Emirates**
This cosy eatery has a comfortable bar area and an unrivalled view of the Ski Dubai slopes. The menu offers wholesome fare including steaks, fondue and pizzas. During the day, it's great for families and, at night, the laidback vibe and cocktail list encourage chilled socialising.

The Butcher Shop & Grill   Steakhouse

Mall of the Emirates Al Barsha 1 **04 347 1167**
thebutchershop-me.com
Map **1 R6** Metro **Mall of the Emirates**
This restaurant is all about steak, so pick your giant fillet, rump, T-bone, prime rib or rib-eye and tuck in. There's quality as well as quantity and, best of all, you can take home a few cuts from the in-house butcher's counter complete with cooking tips. Also located at The Walk, JBR and Mirdif City Centre.

Carluccio's   Italian

Dubai Mall Downtown Dubai, Burj Khalifa
04 434 1320
carluccios.com
Map **2 F7** Metro **Burj Khalifa/Dubai Mall**
From the hearty dishes to the shelves laden with cookery books and deli produce, Carluccio's is a slice of Italy. The alfresco dining is stylishly modern and the terrace has great views of Dubai Fountain. Serving breakfast, lunch and dinner, outlets are also open at Mirdif City Centre and Dubai Marina Mall.

Claw BBQ   American

Souk Al Bahar Burj Khalifa **04 432 2300**
clawbbq.com
Map **2 F6** Metro **Burj Khalifa/Dubai Mall**
With its very own mechanical rodeo bull, drinks served in jam jars and lively decor, Claw BBQ guarantees an entertaining evening out. A casual bar-cum-diner vibe makes everyone feel comfortable, and the menu serves a gastronomic playground of American South delights. There's a terrace overlooking the Burj Khalifa and Dubai Fountain, so it'll impress visitors too.

Der Keller   German

Jumeirah Beach Umm Suqeim 3 **04 406 8999**
jumeirah.com
Map **1 S4** Metro **First Gulf Bank**
In a cosy pseudo-subterranean setting with brick arches, wine barrels and solid oak furniture, Der Keller delivers fine German cuisine and imported beer. You'll find pretzels, schnitzels, frankfurters and fondue, as well as hearty meat dishes. Try to resist (if you can) as the fresh bread as the starters are as big as mains and the mains are bigger than Austria.

El Chico Cafe   Mexican

The Walk at JBR Marsa Dubai **04 705 9680**
elchico.com
Map **1 K4** Metro **DAMAC**
One of the most popular dining options on The Walk at JBR, this is proper Mexican overindulgence. Nachos dripping with cheese are dunked into the fresh guacamole for starters, while burritos, fajitas and enchiladas filled to bursting point make the best main courses, although spicy chicken and steaks are also on the menu. The restaurant is unlicensed but its location along the buzzing JBR is great for people-watching.

Ewaan   Mediterranean

The Palace Downtown Downtown Dubai, Burj Khalifa
04 888 3444
theaddress.com
2 F6 Metro **Burj Khalifa/Dubai Mall**
Surrounding the palm-lined pool in the Arabian-themed Palace Hotel, the private cabanas at this shisha joint sit directly beneath the towering Burj Khalifa. Customers can stretch out on Arabic seating while a musician plays the oud and attentive staff serve up shisha and tasty mezze.

Gourmet Burger Kitchen   European

Mirdif **04 285 5109**
gbkinfo.com
Map **2 P12** Metro **Rashidiya**
This popular chain serves up a winning formula – good juicy meat, fresh produce, a diverse choice of toppings and sauces, and hearty portions of fries in trendy canteen-style settings. Burgers are made to order, and the delivery service has saved many a hungry couch potato. See the website for other locations around Dubai.

Japengo Cafe   International

Mall of the Emirates Al Barsha 1 **04 341 1671**
binhendi.com
Map **1 R6** Metro **Mall of the Emirates**
An impressive Japanese-western hybrid menu with top-notch food, in a neon bright, minimalist setting. The menu ticks all the boxes, ranging from sushi, rice and noodle classics such as nasi goreng to fish and

Apres

Bamboo Lagoon

Al Hambra

chips, New York strip loin and Mexican taquitos. Other locations include Ibn Battuta, Mall of the Emirates, Palm Strip, Souk Madinat Jumeirah and Dubai Festival City.

Fish & Chips

You may not find a 'chippy' on every street corner in Dubai, but if you're really hankering for some good old fish and chips there are a few choices at your disposal. The Fish & Chips Room at JBR is popular, as is the nearby Bob's Fish & Chips on the other side of the marina. Both stay open until the wee hours of the morning too. Mirdif Fish & Chips, 26C Street, near the mosque on 15 Street is a good option for Mirdif dwellers. The Irish Village, Barasti, Boardwalk, the Dhow & Anchor and Apres all deserve a special mention for the quality of their fish and chips. MORE Cafe (morecafe.biz) also has excellent fish and spicy chunky chips.

Ketchup   American
Boulevard Plaza Burj Khalifa **04 363 8595**
ketchup.ae
Map **2 F6** Metro **Burj Khalifa/Dubai Mall**
The gimmick here is quite literally the ketchup – you are served five kinds to work your way through, ranging from the sweetest, maple, through to BBQ, curry, Louisiana and then the spiciest (and rather tongue-tingling), chipotle. And to help you try these out, there are three kinds of fries: skinny, fat and sweet potato.

Maria Bonita Taco Shop & Grill   Mexican
Nr Spinneys Centre Umm Suqeim 1 **04 395 5576**
mariabonitadubai.com
Map **2 B5** Metro **Noor Bank**
Maria Bonita stands out as a friendly, well-worn neighbourhood eatery serving traditional Mexican and Tex-Mex dishes that include nachos, spicy quesadillas and meaty fajitas, served in a laidback atmosphere. Also at The Green Community (Casa Maria, 04 885 3188).

Shooters   Tex-Mex
Hessyan 1 **04 814 5604**
jaresortshotels.com
Metro **Jebel Ali**
A modern western saloon with denim-clad waiters, and surprisingly quiet despite the gunfire from the five floodlit shooting ranges below. The menu is simple but considered, mainly offering fish and steak dishes. King-sized prawns and lobster tails are firm favourites.

Singapore Deli Restaurant   Asian
Nr BurJuman Centre Al Karama **04 396 6885**
Map **2 L5** Metro **BurJuman**
From bowls of steaming noodles to traditionally cooked nasi goreng, the authentic dishes available at

Singapore Deli Restaurant are consistently excellent. The casual atmosphere and home-style cooking draws a large crowd of regular customers who come for a taste of home.

Sushi Art   Japanese
Marble Walk – Gate 5, DIFC Trade Center 2 **800 220**
sushiart.ae
Map **2 G6** Metro **Financial Centre**
The sushi here is inspired by award-winning chef Thierry Marx. Sushi Art is a lunchtime hub for DIFC workers, but is usually pretty quiet in the evenings. The menu uses sustainably sourced fish, with some inspirational twists, such as the sea bream kiwi tartare.

YO! Sushi   Japanese
Mirdif **04 284 3995**
yosushi.com
Map **2 P12** Metro **Rashidiya**
Friendly staff explain the dishes, which pass by on a conveyor belt. The coloured plates indicate the price. Branches are also in Dubai Festival City, BurJuman, Dubai Marina Mall, The Dubai Mall and DIFC.

Live Music

If you fancy a bit of entertainment while you dine, then check out one of these venues below. There's everything from belly dancing to jazz and pianists.

Al Basha   Middle Eastern
Habtoor Grand Marsa Dubai **04 399 5000**
grandjumeirah.habtoorhotels.com
Map **1 L4** Metro **DAMAC**
Fine Lebanese food, with live music from 9.30pm. The set menus are wide-ranging; wafer-thin pita, cheese rolls and grilled meat start from Dhs.220 per person up to Dhs.350 with prawn and lobster. Dine on the terrace, and watch the belly dancers.

Al Diwan   Middle Eastern
Metropolitan Palace Al Muraqqabat **04 227 0000**
habtoorhotels.com
Map **2 N6** Metro **Al Rigga**
Enjoy traditional Lebanese food and belly dancing from 11pm at this cosy restaurant. The selection of wine, Montecristo cigars and Beluga caviar provide a special treat.

Al Hambra   Spanish
Al Qasr Al Sufouh 1 **04 366 6730**
jumeirah.com
Map **1 R5** Metro **Mall of the Emirates**
A mariachi duo sets the mood at this excellent Spanish venue. The seafood paella is a must, but there are also delicious tapas and tasty vegetarian options.

Al Koufa Restaurant   Middle Eastern
Nr Al Nasr Leisureland Oud Metha **04 335 1511**
alkoufa.com
Map **2 L6** Metro **Oud Metha**
In true Arabic style, Al Koufa comes alive around 11pm. Enjoy a great atmosphere, delicious fruit juices and excellent traditional Arabic food, including some lesser known and Emirati dishes, into the early hours. A charge of Dhs.30 covers the live performances.

Antique Bazaar   Indian
Four Points Bur Dubai Al Hamriya **04 397 7444**
antiquebazaar-dubai.com
Map **2 L5** Metro **BurJuman**
Antique Bazaar offers a full range of curried delights to an ever-present musical accompaniment. When in full swing, the live music show is a memorable cultural experience, but can detract from the great food. Arrive early for conversation, late to party.

Bamboo Lagoon   Asian
JW Marriott Al Muraqqabat **04 607 7977**
marriottdiningatjw.ae
Map **2 P6** Metro **Abu Baker Al Siddique**
Bamboo Lagoon's staggering range of exquisite fusion cuisine is presented in a bottomless buffet with everything from sushi to curries and grills. At 9pm a band takes to the stage and grass-skirted singers serenade diners with Polynesian tunes and fun covers.

Cravin Cajun   American
Novotel Al Barsha Al Barsha 1 **04 304 9000**
Map **1 Q6** Metro **Sharaf DG**
Don't be fooled by the smart but generic decor, the food here has bags of personality. Authentic Cajun cooking is whipped up by a chef from New Orleans, who serves up gumbo, jambalaya and other tasty dishes. A fabulous jazz band plays every night, and the location on Sheikh Zayed Road is very convenient.

Dhow Ka Aangan   Indian
Dhow Palace Al Mankhool **04 359 9992**
dhowplacedubai.com
Map **2 L5** Metro **ADCB**
Traditionally decorated in rich wood with many elaborate ornaments nailed to the walls, the atmosphere and live in-house music mingle well with the authentic food. Savour its range of biryanis, special curries and kebabs from the charcoal-smoked clay oven, plus excellent desserts.

Jazz@Pizza Express   Italian
Nr Movenpick JLT Al Thanyah 5 **04 441 6342**
pizzaexpressuae.com
Map **1 J5** Metro **Jumeirah Lakes Towers**
A pizza chain, but one with dignity, that also taps into the community music scene. The sleek, contemporary setting next to JLT's lake retains a cosy atmosphere, especially on Tuesday's open mic nights. Friday's brunch is also a great deal, with a steady stream of Pizza Express's tasty classics, a low key vibe and sultry jazz.

The Rupee Room   Indian
North Podium, Marina Walk Marsa Dubai
04 390 5755
therupeeroom.com
Map **1 K5** Metro **Jumeirah Lakes Towers**
Offers a wide selection of tasty north Indian dishes in relaxed surroundings. The glass-fronted kitchen allows you to keep an eye on the action and there is often a great trio of live musicians playing. There are a handful of tables outside offering marina views.

Senses   Buffet
Mercure Gold Madinat Dubai Al Melaheyah
04 301 9888
mercure.com
Map **2 J4** Metro **Al Jafiliya**
Senses offers a relaxing contrast to the bustle of nearby 2nd December Street. The a la carte menu offers pizzas and pastas and the modest buffet changes theme each evening, the most popular being the carvery night. Live music is played each evening, yet the restaurant remains family friendly and reasonably priced.

Troyka   Russian
Ascot Al Raffa **04 352 0900**
ascothoteldubai.com
Map **2 L4** Metro **Al Fahidi**
Troyka conjures up a little of Russia's old world charm. The Tuesday night buffet is all-inclusive and comprises time-honoured Russian delicacies such as chicken Kiev and beef stroganoff. A band plays every night from 10.30pm and an extravagant, live Vegas-style cabaret begins at 11.30pm.

Quick Bites

When you don't have time to linger for hours over a meal but still want something tasty and satisfying, these are the places to go.

The Academy   International
Creek Golf Club Port Saeed **04 295 6000**
dubaigolf.com
Map **2 M7** Metro **Deira City Centre**
A wide assortment of international appetisers, sandwiches, salads, main courses and beverages is available in this snack bar overlooking Dubai Creek's golf course; a cheerful colour scheme fits in well with the view of luscious greens and happy golfers.

CafeM
Cafe

Media One Al Sufouh 2 **04 427 1000**
mediaonehotel.com
Map **1 M5** Metro **Nakheel**
Ideal for a business tete-a-tete during the day, CafeM takes on a bar atmosphere when the post-work crowd hits. From 7pm to 11pm on Sundays to Thursdays, enjoy unlimited wine and cheese for a bargain price. Great for a no-fuss night out with friends.

Sushi
Japanese

Grand Hyatt Umm Hurair 2 **04 317 2222**
restaurants.dubai.hyatt.com
Map **2 L8** Metro **Dubai Healthcare City**
Artfully prepared in the open kitchen of this petite venue, sushi and sashimi portions are served up delightfully and your bill is determined by the number of pieces you feel like indulging in. The careful preparation and the melt-in-your-mouth morsels are of high quality. The grill station is a new addition.

Wafi Gourmet
Middle Eastern

Umm Hurair 2 **04 324 4433**
wafigourmet.com
Map **2 L7** Metro **Dubai Healthcare City**
Deliciously prepared traditional Lebanese dishes, along with pastries, sweets, icecreams, exotic juices and hot drinks, make Wafi Gourmet a great sustenance stop when on a shopping spree. Make sure you browse the delicatessen and you're sure to leave with more bags than you arrived with.

Wagamama
Japanese

JBR, Marsa Dubai **04 399 5900**
wagamama.ae
Map **1 K5** Metro **Jumeirah Lakes Towers**
The internationally renowned Wagamama is modelled on a traditional Japanese ramen bar with communal tables. The venue's streamlined design works well for a quick bite. Orders are immediately and freshly prepared and you can choose from tasty Thai, Japanese and other Asian specialities. The edamame beans are among the best in town. Also at Crowne Plaza and The Greens (though the Greens venue is not licensed to serve alcohol). Delivery is available.

Wavebreaker
International

Hilton Jumeirah Marsa Dubai **04 399 1111**
www3.hilton.com
Map **1 K4** Metro **Jumeirah Lakes Towers**
A beach bar that serves snacks, light meals, barbecue grills and a variety of cocktails and mocktails. Enjoy juicy burgers, jumbo prawns or even lobster. Wavebreaker is perfect for a laidback afternoon, while at sunset, it's quiet, cool and the beach view is stunning, making you want to linger for more than just one of their delicious sundowners.

Romantic

If your aim is to sweep your date off his or her feet, these are the restaurants that go the extra mile to provide the perfect heartwarming setting for couples. Service is top-notch, settings are dreamy and the food is really very special.

Amaseena
Middle Eastern

Ritz-Carlton Dubai Marsa Dubai **04 399 4000**
ritzcarlton.com
Map **1 L4** Metro **DAMAC**
With a torch-lit entrance, sounds of the oud, the aroma of shisha, and exotic belly dancing under the stars, a trip to Amaseena is a truly magical Arabian experience. The food – which takes the form of an all-you-can-eat Arabic buffet – is excellent, and you can sit in your own private *majlis* (a traditional cushioned seating area). The perfect setting for an unforgettable and intimate evening.

Armani/Hashi
Japanese

Armani Downtown Dubai, Burj Khalifa **04 888 3888**
dubai.armanihotels.com
Map **2 F6** Metro **Burj Khalifa/Dubai Mall**
What better way to impress than to dine in the Armani Hotel, inside the world's tallest building, the Burj Khalifa? Inside, the restaurant is beautifully elegant, but the prime seats are outside with the Burj Khalifa's sky-piercing spire above you and the romantic Dubai Fountain in front. The service is refreshingly down-to-earth, yet the food is as exquisite and out of the ordinary as the surroundings.

Bateaux Dubai
International

Nr British Embassy Al Hamriya **04 814 5553**
bateauxdubai.com
Map **2 M5** Metro **Baniyas Square**
Take your date on a boat cruise while you dine and watch Dubai's twinkling city lights glide past. This sleek, glass-topped vessel offers four-course fine dining from a varied international menu, with five-star surroundings to match. Intimate lighting, with cosy tables and splendid views of the city, make for a top pick for romance or a special tourist treat. A bubbly Friday brunch is also available.

BiCE Mare
Italian

Downtown Dubai, Burj Khalifa **04 423 0982**
bicemare.com
Map **2 F6** Metro **Burj Khalifa/Dubai Mall**
Sister to BiCE, the 'mare' signifies a seafood-dominated menu of delicious dishes that bring fish lovers back time and time again. Dine inside and be entertained by the sultry jazz hands of the resident pianist or, if the weather allows, take in the splendid Dubai Fountain show from the terrace.

Celebrities
European

Palace At One&Only Royal Mirage Al Sufouh 2
04 399 9999
oneandonlyresorts.com
Map **1 M4** Metro **Nakheel**

Dine under crystal chandeliers at this elegant restaurant, which offers romantic views of softly lit gardens from tables peppered with rose petals and iridescent stones. The well-priced European menu contains dainty but filling dishes such as sea bass and baked rack of lamb, or try the tasting menu for a wider variety of options.

Embassy Dubai
European

Grosvenor House Marsa Dubai **04 317 6000**
embassy-dubai.com
Map **1 L5** Metro **DAMAC**

This is a nightclub, restaurant, and champagne and vodka bar. The decor is opulent, with stunning views of Marsa Dubai. Fine-dining appetisers include oysters, caviar (at Dhs.2,000 for 50g), and foie gras. It's not cheap – dinner is Dhs.500-600 per person without alcohol – but you won't be disappointed.

Fazaris
International

The Address Downtown Downtown Dubai, Burj Khalifa **04 888 3444**
theaddress.com
Map **2 F7** Metro **Burj Khalifa/Dubai Mall**

With 12 pages of mouthwatering dishes from Japan, south-east Asia, India, Arabia and the Mediterranean, this is a menu that tries to cater for everyone. The

inside is cavernous and bright, while outside is more romantic, with views of the Burj Khalifa.

Hong Loong
Chinese

Sofitel The Palm Nakhlat Jumeira **04 455 6600**
sofitel.com
Map **1 P1** Metro **Nakheel**

A delectable dining experience in a beautiful setting that transports you immediately to China. Specialities include traditional clay pot dishes and there's also delicious dim sum, seafood and meat dishes, along with veggie options and thought-provoking desserts. Staff are knowledgeable about the customs behind each dish. There's even a resident Tea Sommelier.

Medzo
Italian

Umm Hurair 2 **04 324 4100**
pyramidsrestaurantsatwafi.com
Map **2 L7** Metro **Dubai Healthcare City**

Back with a new look and a new, longer menu, Medzo still delivers the same splendid gastronomy. Elegant white mixes with chandeliers and dreamy drapes to create a more romantic atmosphere set to a soundtrack of soft piano. When the weather permits, the tree-shaded terrace completes the experience.

Moana
Seafood

Sofitel Dubai Palm Jumeirah **04 455 6677**
sofitel-dubai-thepalm.com
Map **1 P1** Metro **Dubai Internet City**

Moana is a charming Polynesian-themed restaurant located away from the main hotel in a pagoda-style

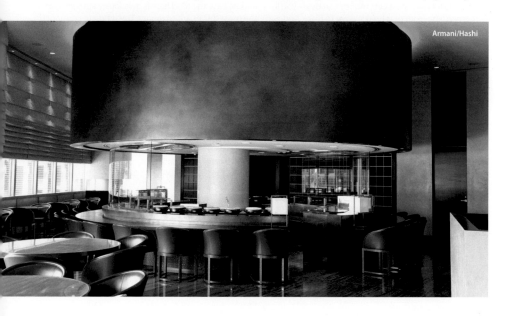
Armani/Hashi

beachside setting. Brunch includes sharing platters of seasonal oysters marinated in apple lime, baked crab legs and salt-crusted sea bass.

Ossigeno   Italian
Le Royal Meridien Marsa Dubai **04 316 5550**
ossigeno-dubai.com
Map **1 L4** Metro **DAMAC**

Traditional Italian ingredients are fused with new flavours to create divine dishes. The emphasis is on sharing and there's a wide selection of antipasti as well as fish and meat dishes. Pizza and pasta lovers won't be disappointed either. A modern, relaxed and stylish vibe and impeccable service complete the package.

Pai Thai   Thai
Al Qasr Al Sufouh 1 **04 366 6730**
madinatjumeirah.com
Map **1 R5** Metro **Mall of the Emirates**

You'll have a night to remember at the stunning Pai Thai, from the abra boat ride to the restaurant to the nouvelle Thai cuisine. The outdoor seating offers delightful views across the canals, and the menu provides some exciting twists on familiar favourites.

Porterhouse   Steakhouse
Sofitel The Palm Nakhlat Jumeira **04 455 6677**
accorhotels.com
Map **1 P1** Metro **Nakheel**

Indisputably romantic with a wonderful outdoor terrace area overlooking Sofitel's pretty pools and palm trees. This is a place for steak aficionados looking to splash out on the best cuts money can buy – you'll find everything from purebred Wagyu to Black Angus, and the highlight is a prime Chateaubriand for two that's carved theatrically at your table.

Rare Restaurant   Steakhouse
Desert Palm Warsan 2 **04 323 8888**
desertpalm.peraquum.com
Metro **Rashidiya**

This tranquil tucked-away haven is a meat-lover's dream. Steaks, mostly 300 or 400 day grain-fed Australian beef, are the headline act, but grilled fish and seafood, and corn-fed chicken will tempt the most ardent carnivores. The atmosphere is relaxed and refined. The wine list is lengthy, but manageable.

Siddharta Lounge   Asian
Grosvenor House Marsa Dubai **04 317 6000**
siddhartalounge.com
Map **1 L5** Metro **DAMAC**

Soak up some rays during the day at this slick white venue with a pool terrace that's home to the glam crowd. In the evening there's a chilled lounge vibe, which ramps up a notch at 9pm when the DJ starts to play. The menu is innovative, as are the cocktails.

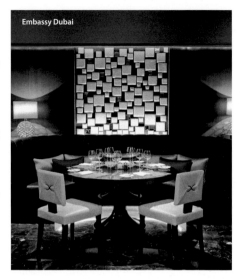

Embassy Dubai

Tagine   Moroccan
The Palace At One&Only Royal Mirage Al Sufouh 2
04 399 999
oneandonlyroyalmirage.com
Map **1 M4** Metro **Nakheel**

Duck down and enter through the tiny carved wooden doorway into a beautiful Moroccan den of embroidered hangings, glowing lanterns and sultry music. Providing a little taste of Marrakesh in the Middle East, the food here is deliciously authentic, and the meat dishes are so tender. The intimate cushioned booths are the best seats in the house for a relaxed and romantic evening.

Showstopper

In this land of make-believe and headline-grabbing mega projects it's only fitting that some of Dubai's restaurants put on a show to remember. We've selected some venues that you won't forget.

Al Mahara   Seafood
Burj Al Arab Umm Suqeim 3 **04 301 7600**
jumeirah.com
Map **1 S4** Metro **First Gulf Bank**

Al Mahara is more than just a restaurant – it's an experience. Your visit starts with a simulated submarine ride 'under the sea', arriving at an elegant restaurant curled around a huge aquarium. The fine-dining menu is predominantly seafood – with gourmet delights such as Alaskan king crab and foie gras ravioli or poached Tsarskaya oysters – with prices to match. Gentlemen are required to wear a jacket.

At.mosphere
International
Downtown Dubai, Burj Khalifa **04 888 3444**
atmosphereburjkhalifa.com
Map **2 F6** Metro **Burj Khalifa/Dubai Mall**
The wow factor at the world's highest restaurant goes beyond the stupendous views; the opulent dishes use premium ingredients and boast exquisite presentation (and prices). The Grill serves lunch and dinner and is the equal of any of the UAE's top restaurants. The Lounge opens from midday to 2am for drinks and snacks; it is also home to the highest high tea in the world.

Hakkasan
Chinese
Emirates Towers Trade Center 2 **04 384 8484**
hakkasan.com
Map **2 H6** Metro **Financial Centre**
Hakkasan shows how well a London restaurant can work in Dubai. Hakkasan favourites are on the menu such as crispy duck salad and stewed Wagyu beef. Mains such as the Pipa duck and sweet and sour pomegranate chicken – are best for sharing. Expensive, but as good as dining gets in Dubai.

Icho Restaurant
Japanese
Radisson Royal Trade Center 1 **04 308 0550**
radissonblu.com
Map **2 H5** Metro **Emirates Towers**
Given the luxury venue on the 49th floor, elevated standing of the chef and the high-end cuisine served here, Icho is surprisingly warm and welcoming. There's a relaxed atmosphere which is complemented by the jolly, yet professional staff, making Icho feel high class without being intimidating. This is a restaurant where even Japanese food aficionados can discover new flavours and textures in dishes that are nothing short of works of art.

Kris With A View
International
Park Regis Kris Kin Al Karama **04 377 1111**
kris.ae
Map **2 L5** Metro **ADCB**
Dining on the top floor of the Park Regis Hotel gives you a unique vantage point over the city without paying the premium usually attached to lofty views. Enjoy dishes from across Asia, each prepared by a regional expert chef. Order dessert to be served at the adjacent wine bar, so you can enjoy live music and a great selection of wine.

Neos
Cafe
The Address Downtown Downtown Dubai, Burj Khalifa **04 436 8888**
Map **2 F7** Metro **Burj Khalifa/Dubai Mall**
Neos is the perfect place for that special occasion. Drag your eyes from the stunning skyline panorama to take in the extensive menu of cocktails and small bites.

Dress smart, sit back and enjoy the pianist in the glamorous bar. Reservations are recommended.

Ossiano > p.275
Seafood
Atlantis Nakhlat Jumeira **04 426 2626**
atlantisthepalm.com
Map **1 N1** Metro **Nakheel**
Famed Spanish chef Santi Santamaria serves up delicate Catalan-inspired seafood dishes at this impeccable eatery. Glistening chandeliers and floor-to-ceiling views of the Ambassador Lagoon aquarium provide a formal but romantic setting to enjoy the incredible and incredibly expensive fare – and you can watch 65,000 marine animals gliding by.

Pierchic
Seafood
Al Qasr Al Sufouh 1 **04 366 6730**
jumeirah.com
Map **1 R5** Metro **Mall of the Emirates**
Situated at the end of a long wooden pier that juts into the Arabian Gulf, Pierchic offers unobstructed views of the Burj Al Arab, which probably reflects in the heftier price tag. The superior seafood is meticulously presented and the wine menu reads like a sommelier's wish list. The sea surrounds on all sides, making this a unique dining location.

Studio Du Chef
French
Sofitel The Palm Nakhlat Jumeira **04 455 6677**
sofitel.com
Map **1 P1** Metro **Nakheel**
At Studio Du Chef, not only can you watch chefs conjure up modern gourmet French cuisine in the open kitchen – either round the table or on the screens dotted around the restaurant – but you can dine on some of the very best food to be served in Dubai. Select the Trust Your Chef menu and you will be served a superior five-course menu of seafood, fish, *amuse bouche* and fine cuts of meat and desserts – each meticulously presented, delicately cooked, and expertly explained personally by the chef himself.

Taste Of Home

Part of being an expat means missing the friends, family and food that you leave behind. These eateries can take you back in a biteful.

Bentoya Kitchen
Japanese
Al Kawakeb Bldg, Shk Zayed Rd Trade Center 2 **04 343 0222**
bentoya.info
Map **2 G6** Metro **Financial Centre**
Bentoya's popularity with Dubai's Japanese expats vouches for the authenticity of its fresh, good-quality maki, sushi and bento boxes. The teriyaki beef is

particularly recommended. The compact, double-storey restaurant is well priced and ideal for a casual bite.

BiCE   Italian
Hilton Jumeirah Marsa Dubai **04 318 2520**
hilton.com
Map **1 K4** Metro **Jumeirah Lakes Towers**
The old European feel of the place is a far cry from the trattoria-style bistro, but Italian is what this restaurant unashamedly is. Pizzas and pastas feature heavily, barely overshadowed by imaginative meat cuts and seafood. Or opt for fish from the trolley – prepared to order. Prices are fairly high but it's full all week.

Brauhaus   German
Jumeira Rotana Al Bada' **04 345 5888**
rotana.com
Map **2 J4** Metro **Al Jafiliya**
Join German expats and those after authentic Bavarian food and beer in this casual spot. The booths are the choice spot to enjoy substantial portions of well-cooked schnitzels, bratwursts and sauerkraut. Top it all off with one of the imported German bottled beers or draft ales.

Cafe Habana   Mexican
Souk Al Bahar Downtown Dubai **04 422 2620**
habana-dubai.com
Map **2 F7** Metro **Burj Khalifa/Dubai Mall**
A menu that's small in size but big on flavour with all the Mexican staples thrown in, from huevos rancheros and nachos to quesadillas and burritos. The talk of the town though is the Mexican-style grilled cobs topped with cheese, lime and chilli powder. The flair bar-tending and upbeat Cuban grooves add to the atmosphere – just how a Mexican joint should be.

The Cheesecake Factory   American
The Dubai Mall Downtown Dubai, Burj Khalifa
04 325 3521
cheesecakefactory.com
Map **2 F7** Metro **Burj Khalifa/Dubai Mall**
Famed for its large portions, this American restaurant chain serves up eye-poppingly large portions of comfort food – from avocado rolls to the indulgent mac and cheese burger. And then there's the cheesecake; more than 40 different types. It's certainly not good for the waistline, but this is the place to come if you want to have your cake and eat it!

Cu-ba   Cuban
Jumeirah Creekside Al Garhoud **04 230 8459**
jumeirah.com
Map **2 M8** Metro **GGICO**
Ride the glass lift to the top floor and see the stunning roof terrace with panoramic city views, and then enjoy a taste of Cuba with infused rum

beverages and an extensive selection of cigars. There's a selection of contemporary tapas to enjoy while seated on a plush couch by the pool, or private cabanas for an intimate escape.

Interactive Eating
If you like your dining interactive, then the stylishly modern Blue Flame restaurant at Jumeirah Creekside (04 230 8459) is the place to connect with. Step inside its 'cooking pod' and watch the chef prepare your meal while teaching you a whole range of tasty tricks, from preparation to plating. Up to five people can be hosted for cooking lessons in the pod too, which could make for a fun alternative for a day or evening out with friends.

Hofbrauhaus   German
JW Marriott Al Muraqqabat **04 607 7977**
marriott.com
Map **2 P6** Metro **Abu Baker Al Siddique**
Modelled on the original Hofbrauhaus in Munich, this is a fun place for a night out. When it's hearty Bavarian food and hops that you're after, and dainty dishes just won't cut the mustard, head for Hofbrauhaus. From the tangy sauerkraut to the white sausage with sweet mustard, all rounded off with tasty strudel, everything on the menu here is top notch. Add in the great German beer, Bavarian garb for the fun-loving staff and accordion music, and you have a fun night out.

The Ivy   British
Trade Center 2 **04 319 8767**
theivy.ae
Map **2 H6** Metro **Emirates Towers**
If you've visited the Ivy's London sibling, you'll know exactly what to expect: ultra-fashionable interiors, impeccable service and, of course, great food. The restaurant serves predominantly British cuisine (think a high-end twist on traditional favourites like liver and crispy bacon and confit pork belly) but also adds in international dishes such as beef tataki and Scandinavian iced berries. Be sure to make a reservation as this is a busy and popular eatery.

The Noodle House   Asian
Trade Center 2 **04 319 8088**
thenoodlehouse.com
Map **2 H6** Metro **Financial Centre**
A refreshingly relaxed affair, where you order by ticking your desired dishes on the notepads. The mouthwatering food is well priced, with big portions of soups, noodles and stir-fries served up in record speed. The modern decor, open kitchen and zingy cocktails add to the vibrant atmosphere. See the website for listings of other branches.

Prego's   Italian

TECOM, Al Thanyah 1 **04 435 0201**
rotana.com
Map **1 P6** Metro **Dubai Internet City**
Prego's takes one cuisine for its buffet – Italian – and
specialises in it. From soups with shavings of parmesan
and an antipasti station laden with marinated
vegetables, to hearty pastas and pizzas for mains, the
authentic dishes are all extremely satisfying.

Ravi Restaurant   Pakistani

Nr Satwa R/A, Al Satwa Rd Al Satwa **04 331 5353**
Map **2 J5** Metro **World Trade Centre**
Ravi's has legendary status among western expats,
and is one of the cheapest eateries in town. This
24 hour diner offers a range of Pakistani curried
favourites and rice dishes. The prices are cheap at
double the price and the dishes keep punters coming
back for more. The venue is basic and dining is
available inside or outside.

The Reform Social & Grill   British

The Lakes Club Al Thanyah 3 **04 454 2638**
reformsocialgrill.ae
Map **1 M6** Metro **DAMAC**
A cosy gastro-pub with top-notch old British
favourites, great service and an alfresco terrace. Divine
offerings include smoked salmon Scotch eggs with
oats, asparagus and Hollandaise sauce; lamb cutlets
with black truffles, wild mushrooms and beetroot; a
selection of salads; catch of the day; and the 'Josper
Charcoal Grill' where several cuts of Angus steak sizzle
away with an optional addition of garlic snails.

Rivington Grill   British

Downtown Dubai, Burj Khalifa **04 423 0903**
rivingtongrill.ae
Map **2 F6** Metro **Burj Khalifa/Dubai Mall**
Straight out of London, this intimate eatery brings
the best in European cuisine. The meat is cooked
to perfection, presented beautifully and served up
with sides good enough to be mains. Watch the
Dubai Fountain shows from the terrace and linger
to enjoy the dessert menu. The Rivington Bar & Grill
is now open at Souk Madinat Jumeirah, including a
standalone bar on the second floor serving British
cocktails and beers on tap with regular promotions.

Tribes   African

Mall of the Emirates Al Barsha 1 **04 395 0663**
tribesrestaurant.com
Map **1 R6** Metro **Mall of the Emirates**
The menu at this African eatery is as vast as the
continent and features dishes from Morocco to South
Africa. The friendly staff know their delicious menu
inside out and they also have some notable musical
talent to really ramp up the atmosphere.

CAFES

Breakfast

These popular cafes shine by providing some of the
best eggs Benedict and continental breakfasts in town
– and a mean cup of coffee too!

The Archive

Al Wasl **04 349 4033**
thearchive.ae
Map **2 D5** Metro **Business Bay**
A library and cafe, The Archive conjures up delicious
and healthy breakfasts. It boasts a beautiful location
next to the lake in Safa Park and has an outdoor
terrace with unbeatable views. The cafe also runs a
packed programme of cultural events and workshops.

Baker & Spice

Downtown Dubai, Burj Khalifa **04 425 2240**
bakerandspiceme.com
Map **2 F6** Metro **Burj Khalifa/Dubai Mall**
The menu here is based on organic ingredients
sourced from local farmers, and changes daily. What
is constant, however, is the carefully prepared 'home-
cooked' flavour of every dish. If you're lucky, Barista
Henji (a visual artist) will be on duty and maybe 'paint'
the Burj Khalifa into the top of your cappuccino – if
not, you can always see the record-breaking building
itself from the terrace.

Cafe Havana

Spinneys Centre Al Safa 2 **04 394 1727**
binhendi.com
Map **2 B5** Metro **Noor Bank**
Dotted all over Dubai, this chain offers consistently
good cafe-style food with a Middle Eastern twist.
Filling breakfasts include French toast, pancakes,
omelettes, fruit, croissants and full English fry-ups.
Quality is high, prices reasonable and the service spot
on. See website for branch listings.

Counter Culture

Marriott Harbour Marsa Dubai **04 319 4793**
counter-culture.dubaimarriottharbourhotel.com
Map **1 L5** Metro **DAMAC**
A tasty hot and cold breakfast buffet, fresh fruit
juices, the sun shining on the terrace and a newspaper
spread across the table… all weekends should start this
way. This little gem is welcoming at any time of the day
or night, and the food is deliciously unfussy. There's a
wealth of choice and the friendliest of service.

Epicure

Desert Palm Warsan 2 **04 323 8888**
desertpalm.peraquum.com
Metro **Rashidiya**
This licensed gourmet deli serves freshly baked bread
and pastries, fruit compotes, and cooked breakfasts
while you gaze over the Desert Palm's swimming pool
and polo fields or devour the day's newspapers. Lunch
options and snacks are also available, along with juices
and hot drinks.

Fraiche

Swiss Tower, Y Cluster, JLT Al Thanyah 5 **04 369 7821**
fraiche.ae
Map **1 L5** Metro **DAMAC**
Set at the foot of one of JLT's many skyscrapers, this
modern, light and airy bistro cafe serves breakfast
through to evening meals. Diners enjoy views over
JLT's lake, and the terrace overlooks a green, leafy
area. There's also a fresh herb garden. Head over in the
morning to try the Dhs.55 'craft your own a la carte
breakfast', which lets you tailor-make your meal –
served with coffee and fresh juice.

Game On!

There's a growing selection of cafes serving up a
cappuccino with helping of board games and books.
You can play chess and Trivial Pursuit on the comfy
leather couches of Bert's Cafe in the Greens Village, or
test your wits and patience in a game of Scrabble or
Jenga at Tea Junction in Oud Metha. Teens will love the
video gaming rooms at The Living Room Cafe at Festival
City, where UNO and billiards are also on the menu.
If you'd prefer to turn the pages of a book while
savouring your morning eggs Benedict, then head to
the reading cafes such as BookMunch in Wasl Square,
The Archive in Safa Park or The Magazine Shop in DIFC –
where there's a great selection of books and journals to
peruse at your leisure.

Maison Bagatelle

Shk Mohd Bin Rashid Blvd Downtown Dubai,
Burj Khalifa **04 420 3442**
Map **2 F7** Metro **Burj Khalifa/Dubai Mall**
In the heart of Downtown Dubai, and next to the
Souk Al Bahar, this fresh, vibrant and sophisticated
cafe with reasonable prices and Parisian vibe, serves
an array of breakfasts, salads, crepes and evening
meals of an exceptional standard. Think classic dishes
with a luxury twist – burgers made with Wagyu beef
and Gruyere cheese and mac and cheese served
with truffles. Be sure to try the French pastries and
specialist coffee menu. Floor-to-ceiling windows look
out to the terrace and the queue of people eager to
gain entry. There's also valet parking.

Coffee Mornings

Dubai hasn't always been known for its cafe culture
but the situation is improving, with more and more
places to go and linger over a cup of coffee.

Armani/Dubai Caffe

The Dubai Mall Downtown Dubai, Burj Khalifa
04 339 8396
thedubaimall.com
Map **2 F7** Metro **Burj Khalifa/Dubai Mall**
Classy Italian dishes are served up with the kind of
flair you'd expect from this cafe's designer namesake,
and the surroundings live up to the label too. It's all
about moody reds and dark wood tones that create an
ambience, which is welcoming and effortlessly stylish.

Circle

Jumeira 2 **04 342 8177**
circle-cafe.com
Map **2 D4** Metro **Business Bay**
Light, bright and gloriously feminine, the decor
at Circle suits its menu of yummy bagels, salads,
smoothies and puddings. Walls are lined with mirrors
and quirky photos, and there's even a resident
goldfish. Also at Dubai Media City (04 391 5170/1).

Gerard's

Jumeira 1 **04 344 3327**
Map **2 H4** Metro **World Trade Centre**
The courtyard setting gives this popular meeting
spot and coffee house traditional French
atmosphere and, there's also a good selection of
croissants, pastries and chocolate covered dates. Ideal
for morning coffee, hot chocolate or afternoon tea.

Madeleine Cafe & Boulangerie

The Dubai Mall Downtown Dubai, Burj Khalifa
04 438 4335
madeleinecafe.com
Map **2 F7** Metro **Burj Khalifa/Dubai Mall**
This spacious, tucked-away cafe resembles a
traditional Parisian restaurant. Wooden tables and
chairs are accompanied by kitsch French ornaments.
The menu offers casual French cuisine; sandwiches,
soups and crepes, in hearty portions; try the freshly
baked fairy cakes too. The pièce de résistance is the
spectacular view of the Dubai Fountain show.

Vienna Cafe

JW Marriott Al Muraqqabat **04 607 7979**
marriottdiningatjw.ae
Map **2 N6** Metro **Al Rigga**
The wood panelling and delicate tablecloths are not
readily associated with Deira, but the decor blends well
with the grandeur of the JW Marriott hotel. There is a
good selection of food, from light salads to steaks, but

the real draw is people-watching while enjoying a good coffee. Order a slice of the home-made Baumkuchen.

Working Lunch

Recommended for their central location, business facilities or quiet environment, these cafes are ideal for meetings, working lunches and personal workspace.

1762

DIFC Zaa'beel 2 **800 1762**
1762.ae
Map **2 G6** Metro **Financial Centre**
1762 has created a pleasant atmosphere to relax and enjoy the taste of artisan sandwiches, soups, salads and cakes. Its imaginative, deli-style menu features bursts of international flavours such as mango chilli chicken and wasabi labneh with salmon. And, as well as a daily changing variety of salads, quiche and soups, there are home-made pies, pastries and desserts.

Bagels & More

Marina Diamond 3 Marsa Dubai **04 430 8790**
bagelsandmore.com
Map **1 L5** Metro **DAMAC**
Take advantage of free wi-fi at this NYC-style deli and linger for ages over your morning bagel and coffee, or enjoy a hearty lunch outside on the terrace. The bagels come in a myriad of flavours and are crammed with a host of delicious fillings from lox to pastrami – pretty close to a genuine New York bagel experience.

Madeleine Cafe & Boulangerie

Balance Cafe

Al Qouz 1 **04 515 4051**
balance-wellness-centre.com
Map **2 C6** Metro **Noor Bank**
The menu features nutritionally balanced and tasty dishes inspired by Mediterranean, Indian and Japanese cooking. Choose between wraps, soups and sushi for light bites or opt for the heartier mains that include pasta, kebabs and barbecue grub. There's an emphasis on vegetarian dishes but meatier options like grilled prawns and lamb biryani are also available. Nutritional information is provided for all dishes and the prices are incredibly reasonable.

MAKE Business Hub

An urban cafe for the mobile worker, MAKE Business Hub (04 392 9216, makebusinesshub.com). offers a cool space where you can concentrate, and serves tasty nosh to keep the brain cells firing. Find it in the Marsa Dubai area in Al Fattan Office Tower – in between JLT and DAMAC Metro stations. It's open from 8am to 8pm (Saturday to Thursday) and 10am to 7pm (on Friday). Also hosts events to promote entrepreneurship, technology and design. Its Facebook page has more information.

Bert's Cafe

The Greens, Al Thanyah 1 **04 361 9292**
bertsdxb.com
Map **1 N5** Metro **Dubai Internet City**
Love board games? Head to this healthy eatery to indulge your inner geek with some chess or Trivial Pursuit. Food-wise, the emphasis is on nutrition and you'll find scrumptious salads, soups and sandwiches alongside heartier dishes. Bright and breezy, this welcoming cafe also makes a perfect lunch-stop for workers in TECOM as well as a cosy breakfast spot to while away your time with coffee and newspapers.

Elements

Umm Hurair 2 **04 324 4252**
Map **2 L7** Metro **Dubai Healthcare City**
Vibrant yet stylish furniture and walls crammed with paintings give Elements the feel of an industrial art warehouse. Lunchtime is always a busy affair thanks to the bargain three-course buffet, while the shisha terrace fills up in the evenings as diners dig into sushi, tapas, pasta and Arabic dishes.

Jones The Grocer

Indigo Central 8 Al Manara **04 346 6886**
jonesthegrocer.com
Map **1 T6** Metro **First Gulf Bank**
This is more than a grocer – it's a Dubai institution: an emporium of home-made pastas, freshly baked breads, gourmet fresh and imported treats such as pestos

and sweets, and a fromagerie of artisan cheeses. And that's just the deli. The urban chic cafe is not to be missed for breakfast or lunch and the bakery section is overflowing with fresh croissants. Unsurprisingly, it's packed on weekend mornings too.

The Lounge
Ramada Plaza JBR Marsa Dubai 04 439 8888
ramadaplazajbr.com
Map **1 K5** Metro **Jumeirah Lake Towers**
A great pit-stop for a light working lunch, The Lounge is located in the Ramada Plaza hotel, and serves hot drinks, pastries and light dishes.

Medley
Pullman Deira City Centre Port Saeed **04 294 1222**
pullmanhotels.com
Map **2 N7** Metro **Deira City Centre**
Warm yellow walls enclose beautifully appointed tables with fresh flowers and low lighting. The 'power lunch' at Medley, Sunday to Thursday, is always a hit with diners, who round off an excellent main with a winning dessert and satisfying beverages.

Panini
Grand Hyatt Umm Hurair 2 **04 317 2222**
restaurants.dubai.hyatt.com
Map **2 L8** Metro **Dubai Healthcare City**
Set among the tropical indoor 'rainforest' in the lobby of the Grand Hyatt, complete with lush greenery and jungle mist, Panini is a good place to meet up with friends or business associates for a lunch on the run. The food is nothing special but it is very convenient.

Tom&Serg
Al-Joud Centre Al Qouz **04 338 8934**
jonesthegrocer.com
Map **1 U6** Metro **Noor Bank**
The newest kid on the breakfast scene, Tom&Serge is causing quite a stir. Popular with the grungy hipster crowd, the utilitarian warehouse setting is softened with quirky touches and a focus on good, tasty food. It's just what Dubai's been missing.

Afternoon Tea

The quintessentially British pastime of afternoon tea – with its quaint scones, finger sandwiches and china teacups – has found a welcome home in Dubai.

Arcadia
H Hotel Trade Center 1 **04 501 8615**
h-hotel.com
Map **2 J5** Metro **World Trade Centre**
The relaxing lobby lounge at the H Hotel is the perfect place to be ensconced with your scones. Start with a

tower of sandwiches and a bottomless teapot, before moving on to scones and finally the patissier's platter.

Hey Sugar
Jumeira 1 **04 344 8204**
Map **2 H4** Metro **Emirates Towers**
Choose from the rainbow of delicious cupcakes, pair with a coffee or shake, and gorge yourself silly. Takeaway and delivery are available too.

Karat
The Address Dubai Mall Downtown Dubai, Burj Khalifa **04 438 8888**
theaddress.com
Map **2 F6** Metro **Burj Khalifa/Dubai Mall**
This is afternoon tea with serious style: settle on an opulent, high-backed leather seat and choose from 26 teas before the four-course feast arrives. Devonshire cream scones are followed by finger sandwiches, miniature cakes, pastries and Arabic sweets. It's vast by any standard and, at Dhs.125, it's one not to be missed.

Lobby Lounge
Ritz-Carlton Dubai Marsa Dubai **04 399 4000**
ritzcarlton.com
Map **1 L4** Metro **DAMAC**
Tea at the Ritz is an exquisite experience. Delicate finger sandwiches and dainty pastries, succulent scones with clotted cream and a selection of jams, a fabulously colonial selection of teas and the fine china are all deliciously regal. It feels exclusive, but everyone is welcome. Also try The Lobby Lounge & Terrace at DIFC – perfect for an informal business meeting.

Lobby Lounge

Lobby Lounge & Terrace
Ritz-Carlton DIFC Zaa'beel 2 **04 372 2323**
ritzcarlton.com
Map **2 G6** Metro **Financial Centre**
Lofty ceilings and comfortable armchairs make for an informal business meeting. The Lobby Lounge & Terrace offers a traditional afternoon tea with raisin scones and English Wilkinson Jams. Try the comforting caffeine-free African amber tea with hibiscus and vanilla. High tea is 2pm to 6pm and costs Dhs.140.

Paul Bakery & Restaurant
BurJuman Al Mankhool
04 351 7009
boulangeries-paris.com
Map **2 L5** Metro **BurJuman**
A pleasant chain of cafes serving French pastries, cakes, desserts and light savoury dishes such as sandwiches, soups and salads. The cafes are modelled on a Parisian tea room and thus make for a relaxing place to stop and enjoy afternoon tea. Branches are throughout Dubai, including Dubai Mall, The Walk at JBR and Mall of the Emirates, to name a few.

Plantation
Sofitel Jumeirah JBR, Marsa Dubai **04 448 4848**
sofitel-dubai-jumeirahbeach.com
Map **1 K5** Metro **Jumeirah Lakes Towers**
A welcome change to stuffy alternatives, Plantation's light and airy surroundings have a 'modern colonial' feel. The conservatory makes a pleasant setting for afternoon tea or a light bite. As the lights of JBR's towers start to glow, it becomes a relaxed lounge bar.

Rhodes In Residence
Grosvenor House Marsa Dubai **04 317 6000**
rhodesinresidence.com
Map **1 L5** Metro **DAMAC**
Formerly a restaurant, the venue has been transformed into a stylish cafe, perfect for taking afternoon tea. Warm reds and browns give a welcoming feel. Afternoon tea includes top-notch delights such as quail's egg cress and mayonnaise sandwiches, duck and cranberry pasties, warm honey Dundee cake and a myriad of different teas.

Sahn Eddar
Burj Al Arab Umm Suqeim 3 **04 301 7600**
jumeirah.com
Map **1 S4** Metro **Mall of the Emirates**
It may be an expensive cuppa, but this is the ultimate afternoon tea experience – as well as being the perfect way to see inside the Burj Al Arab, which otherwise requires a reservation in one of the hotel's restaurants or rooms. Your tea begins with a glass of bubbly and continues with course after course of dainty sandwiches and fine pastries. Sahn Eddar is on

the first floor, but to make it really memorable, also go to the Skyview Bar to enjoy the stunning vistas.

Sultan's Lounge
Jumeirah Zabeel Saray Nakhlat Jumeira **04 453 0444**
jumeirah.com
Map **1 L3** Metro **Nakheel**
The Sultan's Lounge is finely appointed for a Turkish-themed tea and coffee lounge. The English and Ottoman afternoon teas feature all manner of savoury and sweet treats with jam and cream and a wide variety of teas and coffees. Served with views of the beach and Palm Jumeirah.

Tea Junction
Nr Movenpick Hotel Oud Metha **04 357 6677**
teajunction.ae
Map **2 K7** Metro **Oud Metha**
A hip and arty hangout complete with board games and shisha. There are cosy sofas, big windows, free wi-fi and great music too. Diners can choose from a wide range of teas, mocktails and fresh fruit juices, as well as a generous selection of omelettes, crepes and healthy sandwiches.

Family Friendly
For a relaxed place to take the kids where they can run riot, order off a kiddie friendly menu, and be entertained – then look no further.

Arabian Tea House
Al Fahidi Historical Neighbourhood
Al Souk Al Kabeer **04 353 5071**
arabianteahouse.co
Map **2 M4** Metro **Al Fahidi**
Previously known as Basta Art Cafe, this courtyard cafe and gallery offers quiet sanctuary amid busy and atmospheric Al Fahidi Historical Neighbourhood (formerly known as Bastakiya). Visitors get to sit on *majlis*-style cushions or under a canopy while choosing from the menu of hearty breakfasts, healthy salads and tempting paninis. Its sister outlet at Arabian Ranches has a similarly rustic-chic atmosphere. Follow with a wander around the historical neighbourhood.

Cafe Ceramique
Jumeira 1 **04 344 7331**
cafeceramique.ae
Map **2 F4** Metro **Burj Khalifa/Dubai Mall**
Reserve this cafe for when you, or the kids, need to release your creativity. Choose an item and decorate it using paints and stencils – it will then be glazed for collection at a later date. The menu has light snacks, kids' choices and hot and cold drinks. It's also

a popular place for children's parties. There's another branch in Festival Centre.

Le Paradis du Fruit
The Beach, Marsa Dubai
leparadisdufruit.ae **04 425 7749**
Map 1 K4 Metro **DAMAC**
The outdoor terrace looking onto Zen-inspired water feature is a good spot for kids to run around. There are traditional French breakfasts, plus an a la carte menu. Food is tasty, service is attentive and there's free wi-fi.

The Lime Tree Cafe & Kitchen
Nr Jumeirah Mosque Jumeira 1 **04 349 8498**
thelimetreecafe.com
Map 2 H4 Metro **World Trade Centre**
The Lime Tree Cafe & Kitchen is a true Dubai institution, and a great spot for breakfast with friends or a casual lunch. The menu nods towards Mediterranean cuisine, and features plenty of roast vegetables, halloumi cheese and grilled chicken paninis, as well as delicious salads, satay kebabs and quiches. Don't leave without sharing an enormous slice of the superlative carrot cake, which is widely thought to be the best of its kind in Dubai. There are good alfresco dining options too. Also at Al Qouz and Sheikh Zayed Rd.

THE One
Jumeira Rd Jumeira 1 **04 345 6687**
theone.com
Map 2 H4 Metro **World Trade Centre**
Tucked away on the first floor of THE One furniture store, this funky cafe features an extensive and imaginative menu with high-quality food, fresh juices and some astounding cakes. The all-day brunch menu includes creative dishes such as banana French toast (which the kids will love) as well as a zaatar and halloumi omelette. There's a good dedicated kids' menu to peruse too. A good spot for a family-friendly breakfast on the weekend.

Shakespeare and Co. > p.425
Al Saqr Business Tower Trade Center 2 **04 329 1040**
shakespeareandco.ae
Map 2 G6 Metro **Financial Centre**
With chic Victorian flair, an eclectic menu featuring cuisines from the US, Italy and the Middle East, and period-inspired decor, this ubiquitous chain offers more than just exquisite food and a relaxed atmosphere. Try the delicious smoothies, mocktails and hot and cold drinks and tuck into the home-made hand-wrapped chocolates and delicious French pastries. It's also a great option for a casual evening over fresh juices and shisha. Catering services are also available. There are 23 branches across the UAE – most have a dedicated kids' playroom.

BARS, PUBS & CLUBS

Whether you're looking for a quiet night munching on tapas and nursing a glass of red, or are dressed to take on the dancefloor, you'll probably find a suitable venue amongst the ever-growing selection of nightspots on offer.

As with the restaurant scene, dress codes veer towards the smart rather than the casual. Large groups of gentlemen will have problems getting into most venues, so try and break up into mixed gender groups or couples. Some establishments have a shiny 'members only' sign on the door, which is generally ignored, but may be enforced on busy nights.

Although the drinking age is 21, you are well advised to take some form of ID even if you're well above the legal requirement. Arguing with the doorman is pointless and if you are refused entry due to your youthful glow, you will be left to make your way home alone. If you decide to book a table in a nightclub, expect to be subjected to a hefty minimum spend.

Club Rush
Got a 13-going-on-30 year old? Bored teens will love Club Rush at Atlantis – a teenage hang out with a mocktail and snack bar, chill out lounge, internet cafe, games room, dancefloor and big sound system, and you'll love it too because it's supervised and alcohol free. Birthday parties with a DJ are also available (04 426 1365).

Happy Hour
Drinks can be expensive in Dubai, but thanks to the numerous happy hours around the city, you can enjoy a drink without emptying your bank account. It's not just bars desperate for custom that offer happy hour promotions – stylish joints such at The Observatory at the Marriott Harbour Hotel offer a three-hour Happy Hour daily; as does ICON Bar and Lounge, Radisson Blu, Media City. The usual start time is 5pm or 6pm, so don't forget to pencil in dinner to avoid that soul-crushing hangover the next day.

Safer Driver
If you've enjoyed a few drinks with dinner then leave the car and contact Safer Driver. You'll be breaking the law if you drive after even one drink, but this clever service means you avoid that and the hassle of picking up the car in the morning. Simply call 04 299 9544 and a driver will take you and your car home then be on his merry way. Be sure to book in advance.

Beach Bars & Sundowners

If your idea of the perfect night involves sea views with your sundowners, you've come to the right emirate. Take your pick of some of our favourites.

Under Age

The law in Dubai states that drinkers must be 21 or over. If you're lucky enough to look like you barely remember the 80s, make sure you carry some ID such as a passport or driving licence.

Barasti

Mina Seyahi **04 399 3333**
barastibeach.com
Map **1 M5** Metro **Nakheel**
Expats flock to this lively venue in flip-flops or their Friday finery. A tasty menu, combined with a sea view, big screens, live music and a friendly crowd make for a good night out. Entry is free all day, so you can spend the day on the beach and then head to the bar!

BidiBondi

Shoreline Apartments Nakhlat Jumeira **04 427 0515**
emiratesleisureretail.com
Map **1 N4** Metro **Nakheel**
Relaxed and informal, this Aussie bar on Palm Jumeirah has a beach diner feel. The menu offers hefty burgers, salads, bar snacks, breakfast and kids' specials alongside a range of cocktails, beers and wines.

The Jetty Lounge

One&Only Royal Mirage Al Sufouh 2 **04 399 9999**
royalmirage.oneandonlyresorts.com
Map **1 M5** Metro **Nakheel**
With awe-inspiring panoramas and chic beachside lounging, this is the perfect post-work hangout venue. After drinks you can jump aboard a private boat to the sister hotel, One&Only The Palm.

Koubba Bar

Al Qasr Al Sufouh 1 **04 366 6730**
jumeirah.com
Map **1 R5** Metro **Mall of the Emirates**
Stunning views of Dubai await you from the terrace of this sumptuous cocktail bar. Check out the Armoury Lounge, where you can indulge in Cuban cigars.

Meydan Beach

The Walk at JBR Marsa Dubai **04 433 3777**
meydanbeach.com
Map **1 K4** Metro **Jumeirah Lakes Towers**
Perfect beachfront setting boasting pools with floating loungers. Great range of drinks and live DJs from sunset. Also houses a gym, spa and salon.

Nasimi Beach

Atlantis Nakhlat Jumeira **04 426 2626**
atlantisthepalm.com
Map **1 N1** Metro **Nakheel**
Next to Atlantis hotel, Nasimi Beach has a relaxed vibe. The restaurant's menu features expertly prepared seafood and meat dishes and, as evening becomes night, superstar DJs take to the decks and the glamour levels soar. Not cheap, but a great Dubai experience.

Sporting Action

The glitz and glamour of Dubai's bar scene is all very well, but sometimes you just want a joint where you can catch the big match and enjoy a pint with your mates. These venues are recommended for supping and spectating: Barasti, Boston Bar, Champions, Double Decker, Girders, Nezesaussi, and The Underground.

Cocktails

Serving both cocktails and mocktails, this selection of bars really knows how to mix it up – and you'll often enjoy a display of flair bartending too!

Balcony Bar

Shangri-La Dubai Trade Center 1 **04 405 2703**
shangri-la.com
Map **2 G6** Metro **Burj Khalifa/Dubai Mall**
Dark, masculine wooden panelling and black leather armchairs dominate this sophisticated cocktail bar. The drinks list is extensive, and each cocktail is artfully presented. For the extravagant pocket, there are some eye wateringly expensive champagnes and vintage whiskies, while teetotallers can choose from a basic selection of booze-free beverages.

Dress Code

While many bars have a reasonably relaxed attitude towards dress code, some places will not allow you in if you are wearing shorts and sandals, while others require a collared shirt and have a 'no jeans or trainers' policy. In general, nightclubs are more strict, so dress to impress.

Cin Cin

Fairmont Trade Center 1 **04 311 8316**
fairmont.com
Map **2 J5** Metro **World Trade Centre**
With a stylish backdrop of warehouse-high wine shelves, and walls fashioned like falling water, it's easy to get carried away ordering imaginative cocktails and fine wines, but brace yourself for the bill – this is expense account territory.

Crossroads Cocktail Bar

Raffles Umm Hurair 2 **04 314 9888**
raffles.com
Map **2 K7** Metro **Dubai Healthcare City**
Home of the Dubai Sling, an imaginative mix of
coriander, chilli, fig and lemon, and the drink of choice
for surveying the nearby sparkling skyline. With
extremely knowledgeable staff, well-executed bar
snacks and a dizzying choice of drinks, you won't mind
paying above-average prices for the experience.

Left Bank

Downtown Dubai, Burj Khalifa **04 368 4501**
emiratesleisureretail.com
Map **2 F6** Metro **Burj Khalifa/Dubai Mall**
With its black wallpaper, deep red velvet booths and
white leather couches, this bar feels like an exclusive
spot in a cosmopolitan city. The stylish food and
cocktails fit well with the swanky surroundings, and
the 'small plates' menu begs to be explored with a
cocktail in hand. Alternatively, order a sharing platter
to sample as many dishes as possible. There's a more
low-key version at Souk Madinat Jumeirah.

QD's

Creek Golf Club Port Saeed **04 295 6000**
dubaigolf.com
Map **2 M7** Metro **Deira City Centre**
Sitting so close to the water's edge that you can
almost dip your toes into the creek, you can watch the
passing abras as the sun sets over Sheikh Zayed Road
from this charming and atmospheric locale. Elegant
bar snacks accompany an excellent cocktail list and,
as the night wears on, the live band keeps the shisha-
smoking crowd entertained.

Sanctuary Pool Lounge

Sheraton Mall of the Emirates Al Barsha 1
04 377 2000
sheratondubaimalloftheemirates.com
Map **1 R6** Metro **Mall of the Emirates**
Head to Sanctuary's poolside during the day to
soak up some rays and enjoy relaxed light bites and
cocktails with a fabulous view. At night, you can enjoy
the chilled ambience with simple cuisine and cracking
cocktails – or simply sit back and smoke a shisha pipe.

Sho Cho

Dubai Marine Beach Resort Jumeira 1 **04 346 1111**
sho-cho.com
Map **2 H4** Metro **World Trade Centre**
It may be a Japanese restaurant with delicate and
imaginative dishes, but the huge terrace, not to
mention the sunshine holiday vibe, is what attracts the
beautiful clientele. The mix of house and trance music
and a gorgeous view of the shoreline make this a must.
And the cocktails add the perfect finishing touch.

Story Roof Top Lounge

Nr Zayed University Knowledge Village, Al Sufouh 2
04 365 9911
storydubai.com
Map **1 N5** Metro **Dubai Internet City**
An arty urban hangout with two rooftop terraces
offering sweeping views from the Palm across to
Jumeira. The bar is chic, yet bohemian, with funky,
abstract Latin-American murals decorating the walls –
a nod to the venue's passion for art. The varied cocktail
menu will keep you occupied for hours.

Trader Vic's Mai Tai Lounge

Al Fattan Tower JBR Marsa Dubai **04 386 5646**
tradervics.com
Map **1 K4** Metro **DAMAC**
The livelier cousin of the Crowne Plaza and Madinat
Jumeirah eateries (04 366 5646), this Tiki bar is decked
out in Polynesian style. Mai Tai's totally tropical (and
rather potent) cocktail list is accompanied by tasty,
if expensive, bar snacks and the spacious dancefloor
provides a clubby feel.

Voda Bar

Jumeirah Zabeel Saray Nakhlat Jumeira **04 453 0444**
jumeirah.com
Map **1 L3** Metro **Nakheel**
Futuristic and minimalistic, with a spacious floor plan
that includes a handful of attractive white egg-shaped
chairs and white leather sofas. There is a 15 page list of
exotic Japanese inspired cocktails. The food served is
specifically Japanese – beautifully presented and ideal
for sharing. It's pricey, but it is money well spent.

Left Bank

Ladies' Nights

Lucky ladies can go out almost any night of the week and enjoy free drinks. Of course, this isn't a charitable venture by Dubai's bar scene; where ladies are drinking, the men and their wallets inevitably follow. Tuesday is the biggest ladies' night with many bars and pubs offering at least two free drinks. The most legendary venues are Oeno and Healey's Bar & Terrace, while Boudoir and Blends are very lady friendly, with free bubbly or cocktails nearly every night of the week. Icon Bar is perfect for free post-work drinks straight from your office in Media City. In the interests of equality, the Media One Hotel is now hosting Madmen in Z:ONE on Mondays – where the boys get to enjoy two free drinks.

Pubs

These are the bars that do their best to focus more on beer, quiz nights and your favourite pub grub – and are all the more fun for it.

Dhow & Anchor

Jumeirah Beach Umm Suqeim 3 **04 406 8999**
jumeirah.com
Map **1 S4** Metro **Mall of the Emirates**
Dhow & Anchor's bar is a popular spot, particularly during happy hour and sporting events – try the outdoor terrace and enjoy glimpses of the Burj Al Arab. The menu includes terrific curries, pies, and fish and chips. There's a pub quiz on Tuesday night.

Double Decker

Al Murooj Rotana Trade Center 2 **04 321 1111**
rotana.com
Map **2 G6** Metro **Financial Centre**
Double Decker is famed as the venue to go to when you feel like a raucous night out and a king-sized hangover the next day. You won't find Dubai's elite 'It' crowd here. Adorned with London transport memorabilia, this two-storey bar serves upmarket pub grub including plenty of stodgy choices and tasty sharing platters. It is packed on Fridays with revellers attracted by its lively, bargain brunch. Weekly karaoke and ladies' nights plus plenty of big screen sports ensure there is something for everyone.

The Dubliner's

Le Meridien Al Garhoud **04 702 2307**
diningatmeridiendubai.com
Map **2 N8** Metro **Airport Terminal 1**
Cosy and lively, this Irish pub has a weekly quiz, good music and plenty of screens for watching sports. The menu is full of fresh, tasty and reasonably priced dishes. Save room for the Bailey's cheesecake.

Fibber Magee's > *p.431*

Saeed Tower One Trade Center 1 **04 332 2400**
fibbersdubai.com
Map **2 H5** Metro **World Trade Centre**
Succeeding where many fail, Fibber's has the unpolished feel of a true pub. Televised sport, DJs, themed entertainment evenings (including the excellent Easy Tiger quiz on Tuesdays), great value promotions make it perennially popular.

Girders

JA Ocean View JBR, Marsa Dubai **04 814 5590**
jaresortshotels.com
Map **1 K5** Metro **Jumeirah Lakes Towers**
A welcoming, traditional British pub with a Gaelic-themed menu. This is a place to come to enjoy the pub quiz, big-screen sporting action and a daily happy hour between 6pm and 10pm. From the modern steel furnishing to the cosy fireplace, this is the perfect spot to sample the well-stocked bar, hearty dishes such as the full Scottish breakfast and shepherd's pie, and soak up the lively atmosphere.

Quiz Night

If you want to test your brain power and knowledge of useless trivia then grab a group of mates and head to one of Dubai's many pub quiz nights. Try Boston Bar or Player's Lounge on Mondays, or Tuesdays at the Dhow & Anchor, Jumeirah Beach Hotel. If you don't mind fierce competition, give the quiz at the Arabian Ranches Golf Club a go, or enter the Girders quiz and enjoy some Scottish pub grub at the same time.

Harvester's Pub

Crowne Plaza Trade Center 1 **04 331 1111**
szrdining.com
Map **2 H5** Metro **Emirates Towers**
The decor at Harvester's is exactly what you would expect from a themed English pub, as in fact is the drinks menu. What you come here for though is the pub-style menu which is classically hearty and tasty, with a chicken tikka masala that would put many Indian restaurants to shame.

The Irish Village > *p.429*

Aviation Club Al Garhoud **04 282 4750**
irishvillage.ae
Map **2 M8** Metro **GGICO**
This laidback Irish pub offers both indoor and alfresco seating, managing to create an authentic pub experience complete with a sprawling beer garden. There's a good selection of pub grub on offer that comes in generous portions and at a reasonable price, including freshly baked soda bread, Irish stew and Bailey's cheesecake. Also hosts concerts and events.

the only real irish experience
in the heart of dubai!

Whether you decide to sit inside the traditional wooden pub or out on the terrace overlooking the garden and lake,
let the music entertain you while sampling authentic meals served with a warm and friendly Irish smile - what better way of experiencing Ireland in Dubai!

WHAT'S ON BEST PUB FOOD 2002, 2003, 2004, 2005, 2009 & 2012
TIME OUT DUBAI NIGHTLIFE AWARDS - **BEST LIVE MUSIC CONCERT 2011**
TIME OUT NIGHTLIFE AWARDS - **BEST MUSIC VENUE** 2010 & 2011
WHAT'S ON 2012 - **FAVOURITE BAR**
TIME OUT 2012 - **BEST PUB**

The Irish Village Dubai. Al Garhoud next to Dubai Duty Free Tennis Stadium.
P.O. Box 55400. Dubai U.A.E. Tel: +971 4 2824750. www.theirishvillage.com

Visit us at:

McGettigan's Irish Pub
Bonnington JLT, Al Thanyah 5 **04 356 0560**
mcgettigansdubai.com
Map **1 K5** Metro **Jumeirah Lakes Towers**
This fairly cavernous bar is pretty rowdy all week. A far-cry from the old-fashioned 'Oirish t'bae sure' themed bar, there are plenty of stools, tables and nooks for drinkers and diners, with a menu that focuses on inexpensive but hearty fare over haute cuisine. Big matches are shown, the quiz is a hoot and there's regular live entertainment. The Guinness is well kept and well served, the Irish stew comes piping hot with a couple of doorstops of bread, and the singer kicks off with Dirty Old Town… what more could you want?

Nelson's
TECOM, Al Thanyah 1 **04 435 0000**
rotana.com
Map **1 P6** Metro **Dubai Internet City**
Pitch up to this unpretentious bar if you want to watch football, tuck into traditional English dishes and enjoy some British banter. The bar in the centre resembles a typical Victorian pub, and punters can settle into large armchairs, prop themselves up on bar stools, or cluster around wide-screen TVs.

Oak N Barrel
Grand Excelsior Al Barsha 1 **04 444 9999**
grandexcelsior.ae
Map **1 R7** Metro **Mall of the Emirates**
The deep leather chairs, mahogany bar counters and classical taps all add to the character of this traditional English pub. Choose classic pub-style malt beverages

Warehouse

or cocktails, or order a light meal while watching sports events. Regular events include the pub quiz every Sunday, Spare ribs & Steak Night, Friday Roast Lunch, a daily happy hour and promotional nights for ladies and teachers.

Speakeasy Bar & Restaurant
Ramada Plaza JBR Marsa Dubai **04 439 8888**
ramadaplazajbr.com
Map **1 K5** Metro **Jumeirah Lakes Towers**
An American-themed bar reflecting the prohibition era of 1920s in the States. Serves burgers and snacks as well as dishes from an a la carte menu, and also offers cigars and a wide selection of drinks. There's plenty of live musical entertainment, plus themed nights, and a darts area.

Warehouse
Le Meridien Al Garhoud **04 702 2560**
diningdubai.com
Map **2 N8** Metro **Airport Terminal 1**
Warehouse is a stylish and unusual addition to the old-school side of the creek because it houses several different themes: there is a beer bar and garden on the ground floor serving fish and chips and the like, while up the spiral staircase you'll find a dual-personality restaurant – half fine dining and half sushi – where the food is deliciously inventive. There is also an intimate nightclub should you want to continue the night.

The Whistler
JA Ocean View JBR, Marsa Dubai **04 814 5590**
jaresortshotels.com
Map **1 J4** Metro **Jumeirah Lakes Towers**
Wine, cheese and a whole lot of luxury are what you'll find when you walk into The Whistler. Located on the 25th floor, this is the place to admire Dubai's skyline and unwind. Let the sommelier advise you on the perfect pairing of fine cheese and wine, and enjoy a 'wine flight' – tasting a variety of red and white wines served using the popular Enomatic system. Live music from a saxophone player sets the mood perfectly.

Rooftop

Take advantage of balmy evenings with rooftop drinks under the stars. Sundowners overlooking the skyline of Dubai is a tough act to follow.

360 Bar Lounge & Club
Jumeirah Beach Umm Suqeim 3 **04 406 8999**
jumeirah.com
Map **1 S4** Metro **First Gulf Bank**
This two-tiered circular rooftop bar boasts all-round views of the Arabian Gulf and Burj Al Arab. House DJs spin at the weekends, and late afternoon loungers

Enjoy the Craic!

Great Food ☘ Great Drinks ☘ Great Value

Tel: +9714 3322400 • Fax: +9714 3323100 • Email: info@fibbersdubai.com

www.fibbersdubai.com

smoking shisha give way to scruffily chic stylistas sipping cocktails as the tempo rises. The bartenders here make a mean mojito, but for something sweeter, try the vanilla version. Open from 4pm and at weekends, arrive in time to catch the holiday snap-worthy sunset. It's the perfect place to take visitors for drinks but be sure to get your name on the guestlist through platinumlist.ae.

Cabana

The Address Dubai Mall Downtown Dubai, Burj Khalifa **04 888 3444**
theaddress.com
Map **2 F6** Metro **Burj Khalifa/Dubai Mall**
Cabana's Miami-cool pool bar and restaurant sit sweetly beneath the Burj Khalifa. Lounge on sunbeds and beanbags by the pool, or enjoy the privacy of a cabana as you enjoy the eclectic menu and chilled soundtrack. It's the perfect setting for cocktails, and Friday brunch is a lively occasion.

THE DEK On 8

Media One Al Sufouh 2 **04 427 1000**
mediaonehotel.com
Map **1 M5** Metro **Nakheel**
A popular post-work drinks spot, the bar takes on an alfresco club atmosphere at weekends with a resident DJ. Sip champagne and sample cocktails as you laze on white sofa beds and take in the stunning views of Marsa Dubai. The venue now hosts an indie rock night once or twice a month on Thursdays for those in search of something more down-to-earth.

Nawwara

JW Marriott Marquis Business Bay **04 414 3000**
jwmarriottmarquisdubailife.com
Map **2 D6** Metro **Business Bay**
A glow of candlelight greets you when you enter this sublime setting. The feel is palatial without being intimidating – there's a vast lounge where a DJ plays post-dinner, and those not up for dancing can chill on the outdoor terrace with a shisha. The menu features hot and cold mezze and signature main dishes; all delicious and beautifully presented. The food is Middle Eastern and you'll find some items not commonly seen on other Arabic menus, which are unusual and tasty. The waiters can explain all the dishes if required.

Rivington Bar & Grill

Souk Madinat Jumeirah Al Sufouh 1 **04 366 6464**
rivingtongrill.ae
Map **1 R5** Metro **Mall of the Emirates**
With five outdoor terrace areas, and unobstructed views across the Dubai skyline, this is one of the finest spots to enjoy a cosy drink with friends. And with regular wine and cheese nights, happy hour deals, and a classic British menu of nibbles, it's hard to refuse.

The Rooftop Terrace & Sports Lounge

One&Only Royal Mirage Al Sufouh 2 **04 399 9999**
oneandonlyroyalmirage.com
Map **1 M4** Metro **Nakheel**
Rooftop is a hangout for the beautiful people, so expect to pay high prices for your tall drinks. That aside, views of The Palm are superb; cleverly placed Arabic cushioned seats promote interaction between the clientele in one of the most funky and chilled-out bars in Dubai.

Sama Lounge

Ramada Plaza JBR Marsa Dubai
04 439 8888
ramadaplazajbr.com
Map **1 K5** Metro **Jumeirah Lakes Towers**
Ideal if you're looking for a chilled-out vibe, and an Arabian dining experience. Every Thursday and Friday from 8pm until midnight there's live Arabic music and oud performances, while clientele laze in comfortable chairs and gaze over sea views from the 35th floor. They serve hot and cold mezze and many flavours of shisha.

Shades

The Address Dubai Marina Marsa Dubai
04 436 7777 theaddress.com
Map **1 K5** Metro **DAMAC**
For relaxed poolside dining with a delightfully spacious and breezy terrace, Shades manages to come up trumps. Located on the fourth floor of The Address Dubai Marina, Shades is divided into two sections; the first is on a raised-deck platform, equipped with glass tables and wicker chairs. The other is a pristine lounging area with large white comfy sofas, perfect for pre-dinner drinks or shisha. Though it's a little pricey, the courteous service, wonderfully relaxing atmosphere and sublime food make it money well spent.

Tamanya Terrace

Radisson Blu Media City Al Sufouh 2 **04 366 9111**
radissonblu.com
Map **1 M5** Metro **Nakheel**
Tamanya treats its patrons to panoramic views of Media City, including iconic landmarks such as the Burj Al Arab, The World and The Palm islands. The clientele are a good mix of tourists and expats and the resident DJ spins tunes from house and funk to sultry Latin grooves. Unlike some bars, the music is just loud enough to enjoy without having to scream in your mates' ears all night. There are typical bar snacks if you're peckish, while Tamanya boasts a very good selection of tasty cocktails at very reasonable prices. Those not in the mood for cocktails can also choose wines from the Certo menu if the particular wine they want is not on the bar's menu.

The Jetty Lounge

Barasti

BidiBondi

The Terrace
Media Rotana TECOM, Al Thanyah 1 **04 435 0000**
rotana.com
Map **1 P6** Metro **Dubai Internet City**
This rooftop bar is the perfect alfresco drinking spot, with the option of perching at the long bar or relaxing in the garden style furniture. Food is served during the day but after 5pm it is just drinks and shisha and the chill-out tunes of the resident DJ.

Karaoke Bars
Harry Ghatto's in Emirates Towers is a popular haunt, while the post-brunch karaoke sessions at Double Decker range from the sublime to the ridiculous. Also try Checkers Bar at the Majestic Hotel in Bur Dubai. For a unique night, try 'curryoke' at It's Mirchi in the Ramee Royal Hotel, Bur Dubai, which serves up Indian fare. Or sing your heart out at the Hibiki Music Lounge, a cosy karaoke lounge with three private rooms. For something a little more low-key (where you can also grab a tasty bite to eat), check out Kung Korean Restaurant and Karaoke in TECOM's Byblos Hotel.

Uptown Bar
Jumeirah Beach Hotel Umm Suqeim 3 **04 406 8999**
jumeirah.com
Map **1 S4** Metro **First Gulf Bank**
Uptown Bar certainly lives up to its name, offering both a stylish night out and incredible views from its location on the 24th floor of Jumeirah Beach Hotel.

From its terrace you can enjoy stunning vistas of the Burj Al Arab and beyond, and the interior is classy enough – in a James Bond kind of way. An extensive menu of lip-smacking cocktails with price tags to match is complemented by tapas and bar snacks.

Vista Lounge
InterContinental Festival City Al Badia, Al Kheeran **04 701 1127**
diningdfc.com
Map **2 L9** Metro **Emirates**
With fabulous views over the creek from the relaxed terrace, a romantically lit piano bar and a modern cocktail bar, Vista is a welcome addition to the 'other side of the creek'. It serves sandwiches and salads.

Showstopper

Dubai has no shortage of party hotspots, and the following showstopping venues are the best places to throw on your swankiest threads and dress to impress.

Bahri Bar
Madinat Jumeirah Al Sufouh 1 **04 366 6730**
jumeirah.com
Map **1 R5** Metro **Mall of the Emirates**
The spacious terrace has fantastic sea views, and inside, lavish but comfortable furnishings create an intimate atmosphere. A selection of delicious drinks and nibbles, plus live music at the weekends, complete a picture of perfection.

Buddha Bar

Buddha Bar

Grosvenor House Marsa Dubai **04 317 6000**
royaldiningcollection.com
Map **1 L5** Metro **DAMAC**
The domain of the stylish set, this half restaurant,
half bar nightspot never fails to impress with moody
lighting, a huge Buddha statue and marina views.
If the waiter can hear you over the funky Buddha
bar beats, then order a sublime cocktail and ask for
recommendations from the south-east Asian menu.

Skyview Bar

Burj Al Arab Umm Suqeim 3 **04 301 7600**
jumeirah.com
Map **1 S4** Metro **First Gulf Bank**
Located in the iconic Burj Al Arab hotel, this bar has
attitude, and those who enter must be prepared to
spend a fair chunk of cash. A cocktail here can easily
run into triple figures and you have to book well
in advance – there's a minimum spend of Dhs.320
per person just to get in. But it is worth it for special
occasions or to impress out-of-town visitors. The views
are amazing, as you would expect. You can also take
afternoon tea here.

XL Beach Club

Habtoor Grand Marsa Dubai **04 399 5000**
grandjumeirah.habtoorhotels.com
Map **1 L4** Metro **DAMAC**
With ample style and more than a pinch of decadence,
XL Beach Club lives up to its grandiose name.
Energetic beats and shimmering swimming pools
set the scene, superstar DJs regularly spin the decks
here and, once darkness falls, the chic outdoors venue
plays host to some of the best parties in town. If you're
feeling flash, splash out on one of the private cabanas.

Wine Bars & Cigar Lounges

For anyone who enjoys the finer things in life these
stylish bars offer the very best selections of grape,
cheeseboards and cigars.

The Agency

The Boulevard at Jumeirah Emirates Towers
Trade Center 2 **04 319 8088** jumeirah.com
Map **2 H6** Metro **Financial Centre**
At The Agency, the focus is firmly on what this popular
venue does best: wine. There are more than 400
varieties of wine to test the palates of discerning
oenophiles. These include a sommelier's selection and
collection of Mondavi wines from California. Cheese
platters and a selection of light bites are available, and
the adjoining Rib Room has burgers. The Agency also
offers Grape Academy and Blind Tasting events, as well
as a daily happy hour from 5pm to 8pm.

Chinwaggery

CafeM

Media One Al Sufouh 2 **04 427 1000**
mediaonehotel.com
Map **1 M5** Metro **Nakheel**
Ideal for a business tete-a-tete during the day, CafeM
takes on a bar atmosphere when the post-work crowd
hits. From 7pm to 11pm, on Sundays to Thursdays,
enjoy unlimited wine and cheese for a bargain price.
Great for a no-fuss night out with friends.

Chinwaggery

Movenpick Jumeirah Beach JBR, Marsa Dubai
04 449 8888
moevenpick-hotels.com
Map **1 K4** Metro **DAMAC**
Derived from an English phrase to 'have a chin wag',
meaning an informal talk or chat, Chinwaggery is the
perfect venue for a casual get-together or post-work
wind down. Though its name may be British-inspired,
Chinwaggery's decor and ambience takes its cue from
across the Atlantic, New York style. The slick, elegant
indoor lounge provides an intimate setting while an
open air terrace, overlooking JBR, is ideal for group
get-togethers during cooler months.

The Cigar Bar

Fairmont Trade Center 1 **04 311 8316**
fairmont.com
Map **2 H5** Metro **World Trade Centre**
The Cigar Bar boasts its own walk-in humidor in a
swish country house setting. Sit back in soft leather
armchairs and puff away with a glass of your favourite
cognac or whisky. The perfect end to a long day.

The Cigar Lounge
The Address Downtown Downtown Dubai, Burj Khalifa **04 436 8888**
theaddress.com
Map **2 F7** Metro **Burj Khalifa/Dubai Mall**
Whether for post-work cocktails or pre-dinner drinks, this is the spot. Take stunning views of the Burj Khalifa, add an extensive selection of cocktails, delicious cheeses, tapas and sweets, choice cigars and a chic atmosphere and mix with soothing jazz, and you've got a recipe for a venue where you'll want to pass the whole night.

Library Bar
Ritz-Carlton Dubai Marsa Dubai **04 399 4000**
ritzcarlton.com
Map **1 L4** Metro **DAMAC**
With its dark wood, comfy sofas and dimmed lighting, the Library Bar could be mistaken for a study in an English country house. The bar serves light bites, main meals, a good range of cocktails and, of course, top-quality cigars.

No 5 Lounge & Bar
Ritz-Carlton DIFC Zaa'beel 2 **04 372 2323**
ritzcarlton.com
Map **2 G6** Metro **Financial Centre**
Not one for a raucous night out, this is a place to sip a nice malt whisky or expertly prepared Martini while snacking on some of the poshest bar bites you'll find anywhere and listening to the smooth tunes of the resident DJ. Refined and ideal for an after-hours meeting or low-key catch-up.

Oeno Wine Bar
The Westin Marsa Dubai **04 399 4141**
westinminaseyahi.com
Map **1 M4** Metro **Nakheel**
Fine wine, more than 50 types of cheese and excellent service set Oeno apart from other wine bars. The decor is stylish and the wine wall, complete with library-style bookshelf ladder, adds a sense of decadence. Food is served tapas-style, and Tuesday nights bring three free glasses of sparkling wine for ladies from 7pm-11pm.

Oscar's Vine Society
Crowne Plaza Trade Center 1 **04 331 1111**
szrdining.com
Map **2 H5** Metro **Emirates Towers**
Wine cask tables, dim lighting and a warm welcome set the mood at Oscar's for indulging in full-bodied reds and ripe cheeses. Special dining offers throughout the week offer good value for great French dishes such as cassoulet and moules mariniere. Friendly bartenders and a 'cheese master' are happy to explain the selections.

Vantage
Sheraton Mall of the Emirates Al Barsha 1 **04 377 2356**
sheratondubaimalloftheemirates.com
Map **1 R6** Metro **Mall of the Emirates**
The plush, purple interior of this wine bar offers an opulent, but intimate, setting to sample an extensive wine and cocktail list, while the terrace affords sweeping coast views. Arabic snacks dominate the menu, which also features a classic cheese platter.

Vintage Cheese & Wine Bar
Umm Hurair 2 **04 324 4100**
pyramidsrestaurantsatwafi.com
Map **2 L7** Metro **Dubai Healthcare City**
Boasts an exclusive list of cold meat and cheese platters, costly vintages, burgundies and champagnes – but manages to retain the feel of a friendly local. The bar is small, so arrive early or very late to bag a sofa.

The Whistler
JA Ocean View JBR, Marsa Dubai **04 814 5590**
jaresortshotels.com
Map **1 J4** Metro **Jumeirah Lakes Towers**
Wine, cheese and a whole lot of luxury are what you'll find when you walk into The Whistler. Located on the 25th floor, this is the place to admire Dubai's skyline and unwind. Let the sommelier advise you on the perfect pairing of fine cheese and wine, and enjoy a 'wine flight' – tasting a variety of red and white wines served using the popular Enomatic system. Live music from a saxophone player sets the ambient mood perfectly.

Nightlife Options
There is a whole host of clubs to boogie the night away in as well as a few places for impromptu dance routines. Classy venues on the club scene include the Cavalli Club at the Fairmont Dubai and Republique at The Address Dubai Mall. For something a little more down and dirty, check out Rock Bottom at the Regent Palace Hotel, Bur Dubai. For an eclectic music selection try Fridays at 360, which regularly hosts international DJs. For entry before 8pm on Fridays and Saturdays, you will need to get on the guestlist at platinumlist.net.

Nightclubs
Dubai is one of the best (and safest cities) for partying; there are loads of clubs with local and international DJs. The city is famed for its swanky, high-class clubs, but there is also a more authentic side, with venues playing retro, indie rock and 80s and 90s tunes; and you can enter without sporting designer labels.

Amnesia Underground
Grand Excelcelsior Hotel Al Mankhool
050 115 2544
Map **2 L5** Metro **ADCB**
Amnesia has filled a bit of the alternative dance void that exists in the city. It doesn't start to fill up until midnight, and the spaceship-meets-submarine decor might miss the mark, but Amnesia's DJs will quickly remind you how diverse club music can be.

Boudoir
Dubai Marine Beach Resort Jumeira 1 **04 345 5995**
myboudoir.com
Map **2 H4** Metro **World Trade Centre**
This exclusive spot has maintained its edge as the place to see and be seen for more than a decade. While it can be difficult to get into, once inside you'll be treated to a Parisian-style club with opulent fabrics, hypnotic tunes and moody lighting. The music varies through the week and there are drinks deals for ladies.

Cavalli Club
Fairmont Trade Center 1 **04 332 9260**
cavalliclubdubai.com
Map **2 H5** Metro **World Trade Centre**
Roberto Cavalli's leopard print and Swarovski encrusted nightspot is one of the city's places to be seen if you're part of the 'It' crowd. Make sure you dress to impress or you may not even be granted entry. Earlier in the evening, before the dancefloor comes alive, the club serves up some good Mediterranean fare in its Italian restaurant. After that, move to the cocktail and cigar lounge, wine bar, or even the boutique shop.

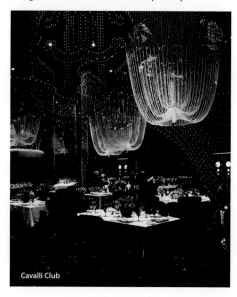
Cavalli Club

Chameleon Club
Byblos TECOM, Al Thanyah 1 **04 448 8000**
chameleonclubdubai.com
Map **1 N6** Metro **Dubai Internet City**
Entry to this flashy and flamboyant club is via a red carpet that delivers you into an elevator to the penthouse level. You are greeted by a spectrum of neon lighting and a giant chameleon positioned over the bar with its tongue protruding across the dancefloor. Although dining is an option, most patrons arrive from 11pm, in time for the techno to be turned up.

Chi@The Lodge
Oud Metha **04 337 9470**
chinightclubdubai.com
Map **2 L6** Metro **Oud Metha**
Best in the winter when the vast garden dancefloor is open, Chi@The Lodge is always busy with its three or four different rooms of contrasting music, lots of seating, large screens and VIP 'cabanas'. The regular fancy dress and themed nights are hugely popular as is the annual Rugby Sevens afterparty that takes place here. It's easy to get taxis outside, there's a shawarma stand in the car park and entrance is free before 10.30pm on most nights.

Kasbar
One&Only Royal Mirage Al Sufouh 2
04 399 9999
royalmirage.oneandonlyresorts.com
Map **1 M4** Metro **Nakheel**
Set over three vibrant floors, Kasbar combines the mystique and luxury of regal Arabia with the feel of an exclusive dance party. In keeping with the Arabian decor of the Royal Mirage, this is a sultry, candlelit nightclub perfect for liaisons, as well as dancing and chilling out.

Magnum
Ramada Jumeirah Al Hudaiba **04 702 7072**
ramadajumeirah.ae
Map **2 J4** Metro **Al Jafiliya**
From Edward Maya and Avicii to Ritchie Hawtin and Sven Vath, Magnum has all your favourite beats covered six days a week. During ladies night on a Tuesday, come in for tasty starters, receive free bubbly till midnight and relax in the trendy chic lounge to ultra-chill tunes. On Fridays, be sure to wear high tops or at least a comfortable pair of kicks, as DJ Nuthiya will have you breakdancing to rhythm and blues all night long. At Magnum they know Saturday usually means 'short changed' but not 'burnt out' so head down and receive 50% off on selected beverages and get footloose to the up-tempo beats pouring out of the speakers. Magnum also has an exclusive FACE card deal, which will knock 50% off your bill every time.

Rare The Place
TECOM, Al Thanyah 1 **04 435 0000**
Map **1 P6** Metro **Dubai Internet City**
One of TECOM's best kept secrets. Reminiscent of a drawing room from the Versailles Palace, Rare The Place is small but elegantly attired in baroque furnishings, and fuses old with new in a way that creates a unique theatrical atmosphere for guests to relax in and enjoy their night. Comprising three areas, Rare's main bar takes centre stage with two surrounding seating sections – a lounge space kitted out in comfy leather furniture, and a casual club area with dancefloor. Operating as a bar/lounge in the evenings before turning into a fully lively nightclub after midnight, the venue offers nights suitable for everyone's taste – from house music to live jazz, and Arabic pop to R&B.

A Class Of Its Own
Cavalli 54, based on the legendary Studio 54, is a regular night at the Cavalli Club featuring classic hits from the 70s and 80s. Over the top details are introduced to the already lavish, crystal-decked club to help recreate the Studio 54 experience, from theatrics and backdrops, to retro-glam performers and dancers.

Rock Bottom
Regent Palace Al Karama **04 396 3888**
rameehotels.com
Map **2 L5** Metro **BurJuman**
Your experience at Rock Bottom, a real Dubai institution, depends on your time – or condition – of arrival. Early on in the evening, it draws a respectable-ish crowd enjoying the reasonably priced diner food or a game of pool, before undergoing a nightly transformation into the sweaty, heaving, hedonistic home of the legendary Bullfrog cocktail and a cracking cover band. So unique is its appeal, it seemed impossible to repeat elsewhere, but the second TECOM venue (04 450 0111) perfectly captured the spirit and the sweat.

Societe
Marina Byblos Hotel Marsa Dubai **050 357 1126**
societe.ae
Map **1 K5** Metro **Jumeirah Lakes Towers**
You may wander into this nightspot and feel like you've crashed a wedding thanks to the unashamedly cheesy music from the 70s, 80s and 90s (as well as current tunes), but you won't feel like you shouldn't be there. Refreshingly unpretentious, this club attracts anyone who wants to have a good, old-fashioned boogie. The venue also hosts live performances and comedy nights. There's a second venue in the Capitol Hotel, called Societe Jumeirah.

White Dubai
Meydan Nadd Al Shiba 1 **050 443 0933**
whitedubai.com
Map **2 D10** Metro **Business Bay**
This achingly cool club is the Dubai version of its immensely popular sister-club in Beirut. It's become the latest place to be seen. It's a must for lovers of electronic and house music thanks to the great guest performers and DJ line-ups, though be prepared to splash some cash as it's not the cheapest night out.

XL Beach Club
Habtoor Grand Marsa Dubai **04 399 5000**
grandjumeirah.habtoorhotels.com
Map **1 L4** Metro **DAMAC**
With ample style and more than a pinch of decadence, XL Beach Club lives up to its grandiose name. Private cabanas and a shimmering pool set the scene, and superstar DJs regularly spin the decks. Stylish crowds, an eye-popping drinks list and lively vibes complete the picture. It doesn't get going till late, but this is partying under the stars at its finest.

Zinc
Crowne Plaza Trade Center 1 **04 331 1111**
szrdining.com
Map **2 H5** Metro **Emirates Towers**
The soundtrack to Zinc is modern, funky R&B, house and hip-hop, with Housexy (Ministry of Sound) and Kinky Malinki ferrying over their rostas of UK DJs. Design-wise, there are shiny flatscreens, lounge areas and glitzy mirrored walls, as well as a big dancefloor sectioned off by a mammoth bar.

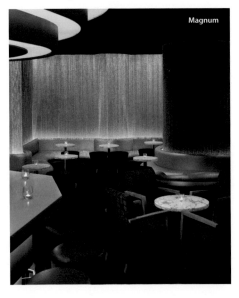
Magnum

ENTERTAINMENT

When you're not eating in fantastic restaurants, enjoying a spa or partaking in the numerous sporting activities around the city, then you may just find time to sample what else Dubai has to offer.

Cabaret

A recent growth in theatre and entertainment venues in Dubai has seen the launch of The Act (04 355 1116) at the Shangri-La Hotel, which aims to be the world's highest theatre on 42nd and 43rd floors. It's a version of venues already popular in Las Vegas and London and boasts international acts flying in from all over the world, as well as a Peruvian dining experience. It's not really theatre, but a hybrid of cabaret and a nightclub, with circus-like acts appearing throughout the night. After dinner, the tables are cleared and the expensively dressed crowd strut their stuff on the dancefloor.

The Lebanese crowd was delighted to welcome a home import in the form of Music Hall at Jumeirah Zabeel Saray on the Palm, a theatre club with varied acts. And Amsterdam's Supperclub is now also open at Jumeirah Zabeel Saray – an innovative, cutting edge venue with art, fine dining and entertainment.

Also new on the scene since the end of 2013 is Cafe de la Danse – an entertainment provider with dancers, musicians and theatrical acrobats (04 331 1543). Performers are available for corporate events, or can be seen at various venues around Dubai – see their website for up-to-date information (lecafedeladanse.com).

Cinema

If you've left the cinema feeling like you've somehow missed something, then it's likely you have. Nevertheless, censorship is less heavy handed than it used to be, when you might have been forgiven for wondering if Harry even met Sally (although gratuitous violence is rarely cut). Freezing air conditioning, mobile phones, babies and general chattering is also likely to interfere with your movie experience. The big cinemas are located in the shopping malls, and most of the Hollywood and Bollywood blockbusters make it to Dubai screens. Also, sound quality can be a little off and Arabic (and often French) subtitles cover the bottom of the screen. That said, it's a great place to cool off during summer. VOX Cinemas rents out screens for private use if you

want it all to yourself; you can even play video games on the big screen.

The IMAX theatre at Meydan in Nadd Al Shiba shows all of the big 3D movies (as does the IMAX at Ibn Battuta Mall) as well as the occasional documentary.

Novo Cinemas Al Badia, Al Kheeran, 04 232 8328, *novocinemas.com*
Novo Megaplex/IMAX Ibn Battuta, Jabal Ali 1, 04 366 9898, *novocinemas.com*
Reel Cinemas Dubai Mall, Downtown Dubai, Burj Khalifa, The Beach 04 449 1988, *reelcinemas.ae*
VOX Cinemas MoE, Al Barsha 1, 04 341 4222, *voxcinemas.com*

Movies Under The Stars

During the temperate winter evenings, you can flop down onto a beanbag or comfy sun lounger and watch a movie under the night sky. Food and drinks are often available too. Try rooftop viewings at Wafi Mall every Sunday from October to the end of May for free; or on Fridays try The Address Montgomerie's Dive In Movies where you can tuck into popcorn, a tasty barbecue and other snacks as you relax on inflatable chairs – in the pool or on the deck. Movies & Munchies at Desert Palm (04 323 8888), or poolside movies at Dubai Polo & Equestrian Club (04 361 8111) are also worth checking out.

Alternative Screenings

While most of the cinema multiplexes only show big Hollywood movies, several bars and clubs put on screenings of older, foreign and independent films, usually early in the week and free of charge. The Scene Club is a monthly film club that screens international independent films, followed by a Q&A with the director or producer. These free screenings are held in Knowledge Village, and simply sign up to register for a seat (thesceneclub.com). It is also worth keeping an eye on the local press for details of one-off screenings at some of the city's more progressive art spaces, such as the jamjar and Shelter (shelter.ae).

Film Festival

Every October the Abu Dhabi Film Festival (ADFF) showcases Arabic and international film making talent. Films are shown in venues across the city, like Marina Mall or Emirates Palace, and film fans even get the chance to vote for their favourites and take part in question and answer sessions with the directors. Worth checking out if your movie appetite stretches beyond Hollywood blockbusters. Then there's the Dubai International Film Festival, held every December, with screenings at cinemas across the emirate as well as outdoors in Burj Park and at Madinat Jumeirah.

Comedy

The comedy scene in Dubai is slowly growing and attracting a regular fanbase. To get involved, your best bet is to keep an eye on the Laughter Factory (thelaughterfactory.com) website for upcoming shows. Acts are imported from the UK and shows are usually held at Zinc at the Crowne Plaza, the Movenpick Hotel at JBR, and the Grand Millennium at TECOM. Also look out for monthly comedy shows staged by Punchline Comedy Club at Jumeirah Creekside Hotel.

There are also several one-off events featuring comedians from around the world, as well as local talent; some of these shows are organised by Dubomedy (dubomedy.com). Remember that a lot of comedy is regional, so unless you're familiar with the comedian's country, you might not get the joke.

The Fourth Dimension

4DX is a new style of movie watching that engages all five senses. Get moved about in seats with motion simulators, experience fog, rain, wind and even thunder and lightning, and sniff out the various scents that waft under your nose. Now showing at VOX cinemas at Mirdif City Centre and Deira City Centre.

Live Music

Dubai hosts a number of concerts each year, and it seems to be attracting bigger and bigger names. Past acts to play here include J-Lo, Kylie, Robbie Williams, Mariah Carey and Muse. These big name acts usually play at outdoor venues such as the Tennis Stadium, Dubai Autodrome, Dubai Festival City, Dubai World Trade Centre Arena, the amphitheatre at Media City or the Sevens Stadium. Smaller gigs with the likes of Bob Geldof, Texas and the Happy Mondays have been held at the Irish Village. Outdoor concerts tend to take place between November and April due to the weather.

Further afield, dance music events such as Creamfields are put on by Flash Entertainment at du Forum, while Beats on the Beach takes place around the Formula 1 weekend; a free concert on Abu Dhabi's Corniche beach that has seen Ludacris, Missy Elliott and Sean Kingston perform.

In terms of local bars that host live bands, Dubai is not as musically progressive as say, London, but there are a few choice venues around. The Fridge is an alcohol-free venue in a converted warehouse in Al Qouz that has performances from local and expat artists; The Music Room in Bur Dubai has live bands and jam sessions; Barasti at Le Meridien Mina Seyahi Beach Resort & Marina has live guitar bands; and there's usually performances at The Irish Village

in Garhoud. Also check out Freshly Ground Sounds, an initiative to create a community of independent acoustic musicians who play live across Dubai.

The Emirates Airline Dubai Jazz Festival

This popular event goes from strength to strength with past performers including The Script, James Morrison, James Blunt, Jools Holland and Macy Gray. The 2014 event attracted more than 60,000 fans over nine days with a mix of jazz, blues, funk, swing, acid, rock, contemporary, modern, and fusion. It takes place at Dubai Media City Amphitheatre.

Sandance

Sandance is a hugely popular music festival held on Nasimi Beach at Atlantis, The Palm. Past acts have included Ellie Goulding, Stereophonics, Dizzee Rascal, Kaiser Chiefs, and The Killers. Early birds can chill out on the beach as the sun goes down, before the party kicks off and hundreds of people are dancing in the sand. There are several live music acts as well as DJs. VIP tickets sell out fast.

Theatre

The First Group Theatre at Madinat Jumeirah and the theatres at DUCTAC are the city's main performance venues and between them offer a range of shows. There's also a good choice of child-friendly shows from The Gruffalo to We're Going On A Bear Hunt.

The Dubai World Trade Centre Arena is adding more acts each year, with previous performances including Michael Jackson THE IMMORTAL World Tour show by Cirque du Soleil and Swan Lake. Keep an eye on small art spaces like Shelter (shelter.ae) and The Fridge (thefridgedubai.com) for one-off performances, as well as the American University in Dubai (AUD) Auditorium staging performances by student and community theatre groups.

Abu Dhabi National Exhibitions Company (adnec. ae) has hosted large-scale productions such as Lord Of The Dance. The Act (theactdubai.com) in the Shangri-La Hotel on Sheikh Zayed Road teams an interesting performance calendar with a top-class Peruvian restaurant. Most tickets can be purchased at ticketmaster.ae or itp.net/tickets.

The Act

Shangri-La Dubai Trade Center 1 **04 355 1116**
theactdubai.com
Map **2 G6** Metro **Burj Khalifa/Dubai Mall**
Prepare to have your senses bombarded with a mix of performers, innovative dining and expertly mixed cocktails. Expect dancers, acrobats and stars from TV talent shows. After the show the DJ takes over.

WHSmith

Dubai Community Theatre & Arts Centre

Mall of the Emirates Al Barsha 1 **04 341 4777**
ductac.org
Map **1 R6** Metro **Mall of the Emirates**
A cultural hub offering art classes for all ages.
Decorative arts, drawing, painting, photography,
sculpture and paper craft are just some of the wide
variety of activities offered to help budding artists
hone their creative talents. A variety of artist-led
classes are held at the centre, and details are listed
online and updated regularly. DUCTAC also has
art galleries and studios for performance, comedy
and dance (the am-dram productions are pretty
good). There's a cafe, art supplies shop and lending
library all clustered around a small open courtyard.
Open daily from 9am to 10pm and 2pm to 10pm on
Fridays.

Play The Part

Fancy getting into character on stage? Based in The
Courtyard in Al Qouz 1, Drama Dubai is a theatre group
with a 60 seat auditorium that offers improv, corporate
training and adult workshops, as well as functioning as
a casting agent (dramaworkshopsdubai.com). There's
also Dubai Drama Group, a non-profit organisation that
welcomes non-members to its workshops for a small
fee. The group has been in existence for more than 25
years (dubaidramagroup.com). See Clubs & Groups for a
list of drama groups across the emirate.

Dubai World Trade Centre

Shk Zayed Rd Trade Center 2 **04 332 1000**
dwtc.com
Map **2 J6** Metro **World Trade Centre**
Home to the enormous Trade Centre Arena and to
smaller arenas inside, this is the go-to venue for large
scale productions. Easily accessed by the metro (or
there's ample parking if you drive), this indoor venue
has an exciting programme of shows, comedy acts,
concerts and events – and there's often a licensed bar
and snacks available once you're inside too.

Madinat Theatre

Souk Madinat Jumeirah Al Sufouh 1 **04 366 6546**
madinattheatre.com
Map **1 R5** Metro **Mall of the Emirates**
The theatre's 442 seat auditorium has witnessed an
impressive list of performances over the years. From
'treading the boards' classics to musicals and innovative
comedy shows, make sure you keep your eyes open
for what's coming into town next, and chances are you
won't be disappointed. Spend time in the Souk Madinat
before a show, or eat in one of the nearby restaurants.

STAYING IN

Fun at home is well catered for in Dubai. No matter
where in the city you are, you'll have access to all kinds
of delivery services and ways to entertain without
having to lift much more than a phone.

Home Delivery

It won't be long before you've assembled an
impressive stash of flyers and delivery menus in a
drawer of your otherwise under-utilised kitchen.
Assuming you can actually convey your location
to the restaurant in question, home delivery is a
cheap and cheerful way to enjoy a night home with
friends or in front of the TV. Fortunately, there are a
number of websites that bring all of your favourite
menus together – you can choose what type of
cuisine you want, find out who delivers locally, make
your order and in, some cases, even pay online.
Try dubai.foodonclick.com, roomservice-uae.com,
casseroleonline.com, thesecretchef.me and 24h.ae.

We love Dinnertime (dinnertime.me) because they
deliver fresh produce and recipe cards, so you can
cook delicious, healthy meals without having to plan
them yourself, or hurry to the supermarket. Simply let
them know what kind of food you like and they'll do
all the planning and shopping for you.

Pretty much all restaurants will deliver, but here are
a few of our favourites to get you started.

Al Reef Lebanese Bakery Nr Union Co-op, Jumeira 3,
04 394 5200
Chez Sushi by Sho Cho Al Safa 1, 800 78744,
chezsushi.com
Dinnertime No physical address, 055 790 8733,
dinnertime.me
KFC Dubai Mall, Downtown Dubai, Burj Khalifa,
04 339 8275, *kfc-arabia.com*
The Noodle House Dubai Mall, Downtown Dubai,
Burj Khalifa, 04 388 4825, *thenoodlehouse.com*
Subway Dubai Mall, Downtown Dubai, Burj Khalifa,
04 339 8808, *subwayarabia.com*

Parties

If you really want to push the boat out when
entertaining at home, the companies listed below
offer a complete party planning service, from event
organisation to hiring performers and equipment

rental. For a novel outdoor party idea, you can get your own shawarma stand set up in the garden, complete with shawarma maker, or hire an icecream van from Desert Chill (desertchill.ae).

Caterers

There are several companies in Dubai that can do all the cooking, decorating and cleaning up, leaving you with more time to concentrate on your witty after-dinner anecdotes. Many restaurants, hotels, and clubs have catering departments, so pick your favourite and ask if they can help out.

Cheeky Little Events
04 388 6114
CheekyLittleEvents.com
Specialises in parties for children, from babies through to teenagers, as well as hen parties or baby showers are just as doable. Not only looks after the catering, but the entertainment and decorations too.

ChoCo'a
Nr Mall of the Emirates Al Barsha 1 **04 340 9092**
chocoa.ae
Map **1 R6** Metro **Mall of the Emirates**
ChoCo'a chefs offer a selection of cakes, pastries, Arabic delicacies and individually-designed speciality cakes and chocolate arrangements for birthdays, graduations, anniversaries and weddings.

Decorative Cakes
050 594 6708
Perfect for kids' parties, weddings or just about any event that requires a cake, this company can create an edible masterpiece in any design you ask of them.

Dish Catering & Events
China Cluster, International City International City 1, Warsan 1 **04 422 1613**
dish.ae
Promises to deliver 'food that steals the show'. Dish caters for functions from 20 to 700 people.

Dubaipartyqueen
HDS Tower JLT, Al Thanyah 5 **04 348 9475**
dpq.ae
Map **1 K5** Metro **Jumeirah Lakes Towers**
From corporate shindigs to money-no-object weddings, this company can arrange parties for all occasions and age groups.

Flying Elephant
Shk Zayed Rd Al Qouz Ind. 1 **04 347 9170**
flyingelephantuae.com
Map **1 U6** Metro **Noor Bank**
This company has existed for more than 16 years and offers everything from theme decorations and

catering to invitations and entertainment. Its Pink Elephant division specialises in organising kids' parties. It also organises corporate events.

Harlequin Marquees & Event Services
Nr Marlin Furniture Al Qouz Ind. 1 **04 347 0110**
harlequinmarquees.com
Map **1 U6** Metro **Noor Bank**
Everything you need for an outdoor event, including marquees, tables, chairs, and even outdoor AC units.

Indigo Entertainment
Grosvenor Business Tower TECOM Al Thanyah 1
04 420 3732 indigouae.com
Map **2 H5** Metro **Dubai Internet City**
Offers an array of solutions for private and corporate events, children's parties, and holiday camps.

Italian Chef At Home
04 444 3627
chefathomedubai.com
Prepares personalised menus for dinners and lunches, prepared and served in your own home – and the kitchen is always left spotless!

The Lime Tree Cafe & Kitchen
Nr Times Square Al Qouz Ind. 1 **04 325 6325**
thelimetreecafe.com
Map **1 U6** Metro **Noor Bank**
Lime Tree prepares customised catering for your event, from canapes to full-on gourmet.

Marta's Kitchen
Swiss Tower Al Thanyah 5 **050 379 8002**
martaskitchen.com
Map **1 L5** Metro **DAMAC**
Specialises in canape-based and buffet menus, from traditional food to more avant-garde gastronomy.

Procat Catering Services
Dubai Investment Park 1 **04 885 9990**
dineout.ae
Map **2 L4** Metro **Jebel Ali**
Large, professional catering outfit that is particularly suited to bigger catering jobs, such as large wedding parties or corporate catering gigs.

Sweet Connection – The Gluten Free Kitchen
Mayfair Bldg Dubai Investment Park 1 **04 880 0656**
sweetconnectiondubai.com
Map **1 G10**
A welcome service for those with special diets, Sweet Connection is dedicated to developing recipes for coeliac disease sufferers and anyone who needs to follow a gluten-free diet: offers tasty breads, pizzas, cupcakes and biscuits.

OUT OF
THE CITY

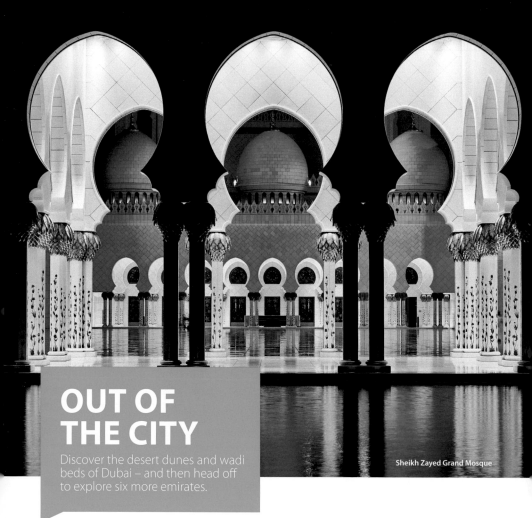

Sheikh Zayed Grand Mosque

OUT OF THE CITY

Discover the desert dunes and wadi beds of Dubai – and then head off to explore six more emirates.

Dubai may have everything from ski slopes and souks to boutiques and beaches, but there are six other emirates in the UAE and five other countries in the GCC, all of which warrant exploration.

All six other emirates – Abu Dhabi, Sharjah, Ras Al Khaimah, Umm Al Quwain, Ajman and Fujairah – are within a two-hour drive of the centre of Dubai (see overview map at rear). From the cultural grandiose of Sharjah to the Garden City of Al Ain in Abu Dhabi, each emirate has something different to offer, and each can be explored, at least in part, over a weekend.

The country's vast deserts and rugged mountains are equally accessible with a copy of the *UAE Off-Road Explorer*, and can be reached within a 45 minute drive of Dubai, if you need to escape civilisation for a while. Amongst these landscapes you'll find historic forts, pretty waterfalls and pools.

The neighbouring GCC countries of Oman, Saudi Arabia, Qatar, Bahrain and Kuwait are all less than 90 minutes' flight away. Oman is considered by many to be one of the most beautiful and culturally interesting countries in the region and it can easily be reached and explored by car – Muscat is just a four-hour drive from Dubai.

Door To Door

Driving from Dubai to Abu Dhabi or Al Ain takes an hour and a half; it's an hour and a quarter to Ras Al Khaimah; 35 minutes to Ajman; 45 minutes to Umm Al Quwain; around two hours to get to Fujairah; and only 20 minutes to Sharjah.

Low-cost carrier flydubai operates cheap flights to nearby countries like Oman, as do regional airlines like Emirates, Oman Air and Qatar Airways.

ABU DHABI

Dubai may be the UAE's brashest member, but Abu Dhabi remains both the nation's capital and the richest of all the emirates, with a blossoming, burgeoning city to prove it. Recently, there has been a greater commitment to tourism, and mega-projects such as Yas Island with its Grand Prix racetrack and the development of the Desert Islands are proof of that.

The city is a series of islands, connected to the mainland by bridges. Each of the main islands is growing into its own destination, and each enjoys stunning views of the Gulf. The islands to the west of the city are popular with boating and watersports enthusiasts, and driving in that direction reveals kilometre upon kilometre of gorgeous open water and beaches. There are also plans to launch a ferry service from Abu Dhabi to Oman.

The city is home to numerous internationally renowned hotels, shopping malls, heritage sites and souks, and is marketed as the cultural capital of the UAE with an annual jazz festival, a film festival, and a music and arts festival. Find out more from the Abu Dhabi Tourism and Culture Authority (adach.ae).

For more information and ideas for exploring Abu Dhabi, check out Explorer's *Abu Dhabi Visitors' Guide*, *Al Gharbia Visitors' Guide* or the *Abu Dhabi Residents' Guide* – order copies at askexplorer.com.

Attractions

Abu Dhabi Corniche
Corniche West St Abu Dhabi
visitabudhabi.ae
No trip to Abu Dhabi would be complete without spending some time on the Corniche, with its golden beaches and pleasant promenade. Of the six kilometres of parks, play areas and cafes, Family Park is a highlight, with leafy gardens, picnic areas and tree-lined walkways. Watch fishermen casting their lines into the Gulf and stop for lunch at Havana Cafe.

Al Forsan International Sports Resort
Khalifa City Abu Dhabi 02 556 8555
alforsan.com
The ultimate multi-sports hub, Al Forsan's superb cable-boarding facilities are well worth checking out. Similar to wakeboarding, you grab a cable instead of being pulled by a boat, and you can even try it on your knees if you're nervous. There is also paintballing, karting, horse riding, clay pigeon shooting and archery.

Emirates Park Zoo
Al Rahba Abu Dhabi 02 501 0000
emiratesparkzoo.com
Both kids and adults are sure to enjoy a trip to this recently renovated zoo which houses more than 2,000 species of animals, including white tigers, blue monkeys and brown bears. The emphasis is on allowing you to get close to your favourite animals through touch and interaction; for example, at the Giraffe Cafe, visitors can feed the giraffes and zebras. Young visitors can even volunteer as a 'zoo keeper'.

Bird Watchers
The Abu Dhabi Falcon Hospital (02 575 5155, falconhospital.com) specialises in treating the region's falcons and various other species of birds. The hospital offers two-hour guided tours on weekdays that must be booked in advance.

Ferrari World Abu Dhabi
Yas Island Abu Dhabi 02 496 8000
ferrariworldabudhabi.com
Ferrari World Abu Dhabi is part F1 amusement park and part museum dedicated to the Italian supercar. There's plenty to keep kids entertained, as well as rides for teen and adult adrenaline junkies. One of the highlights is undoubtedly Formula Rossa – billed as the world's fastest rollercoaster, it reaches such high speeds (up to 240kph) that anyone adventurous enough to give it a go has to wear goggles.

Murjan Splash Park
Khalifa Park Abu Dhabi 050 878 1009
murjansplashpark.weebly.com
Located in the vast Khalifa Park, this attraction is the perfect destination for water babies with plenty of rides and games aimed at children aged three to 12. The highlight is an enormous water play climbing structure with tunnels, water guns and waterslides, and a giant tipping bucket. The Surf Wrangler is a surf board simulator, and for youngsters that don't fancy making a splash, there's the Lily Pad hop, a collection of four trampolines with harnesses.

Sheikh Zayed Grand Mosque
Shk Rashid Bin Saeed Al Maktoum Rd Abu Dhabi
02 419 1919
szgmc.ae
This stunning Abu Dhabi icon is a truly remarkable architectural feat, reminiscent of a sultan's palace from the Arabian Nights. Unlike most mosques in the UAE, it is open to non-Muslims and you can take guided tours throughout the day (except Friday mornings). It has a capacity for an astonishing 40,000 worshippers and the world's largest hand-woven Persian carpet.

The Entertainment Island

A handy guide to making the most of Yas Island's wet, wild and wonderful attractions.

Stay in style

Yas Island's six hotels – five at Yas Plaza and the Yas Viceroy Abu Dhabi – account for 22 of the island's restaurants and 12 of its bars .

Some of the most popular include Angar and Kazu at Yas Viceroy, Barouk at Crowne Plaza, and Fillini at Radisson Blu. Whether you're after fantastic value or something more high-end, every taste is catered for and each hotel has its own standout features; stunning views, brilliant pools or incredible design. And now Yas Mall is also open. It covers three floors and houses a 20-screen cinema and family entertainment zone, as well has hundreds of shops.

Get active

Regarded as one of the best courses in the world, Yas Links Golf course is a beautiful venue that offers serious golfers a real challenge, with a separate course where less confident golfers can hone their skills.

Yas Marina Circuit's driving experiences cater for your inner speed demon with everything from Aston Martin GT4s to Formula Yas 3000 single seaters. If you prefer to shun petrol power, run or cycle around the circuit on Tuesday evenings – for free!

On Yas Beach, Noukhada Adventure Company (noukhada.ae) has your watersports needs covered with windsurfing, sailing and kayaking.

Feel the rush

Ferrari World Abu Dhabi draws crowds from around the world with the lure of the 'world's fastest rollercoaster', the Formula Rossa. Head inside and you'll also have fun driving miniature cars, ogling world famous Ferraris and exploring a mini Italy.

Yas Waterworld makes for a fabulous family day out with kid-focused interactive games and the excellent Marah Fortress splash park. But 'big kids' can have fun too, lounging by the pool, relaxing in a private cabana or enjoying one of the park's adrenaline-pumping slides. Highlights include the heart-thumping Liwa Loop. Wet and wild fun at its best.

Shop 'til you drop

Shopping was limited to theme park stores, hotel shops, a pro shop at Yas Links and big hitters IKEA and ACE Hardware. But Yas Mall, which opened at the end of 2014, is now the second largest mall in the UAE.

Party the night away

For the ultimate nightclub experience, head to either the super exclusive O1NE Yas Island – a purpose-built club from the team that created Beirut's world famous Sky Bar – or Rush, the party spot on Yas Viceroy's impressive circuit-crossing bridge.

FLASH Entertainment regularly brings world famous musical acts to perform at the island's du Arena. Madonna, Muse, Jay Z and a host of other pop, rock and dance talent have performed there. The smaller du Forum has a variety of fascinating entertainment throughout the year such as boxing events, Oktoberfest celebrations and science festivals for kids.

Dock, dine and discover

From US-inspired food at Stars 'n' Bars to funky alfresco tapas at Diabolito and fine dining at Cipriani and Aquarium, Yas Marina is one of the hottest food spots in town. To work up an appetite why not charter a boat for a tour of Abu Dhabi's waters from Azure Charters, or if you want to dock your own boat, berths can be had from Dhs.16,455 – which includes F1 passes, concert tickets and dining discounts. A great, relaxed place to hang out, eat or party.

Formula 1 weekend

Every November Yas Marina Circuit, and the whole of Yas Island, hosts the Abu Dhabi FIA Formula 1 World Championship. Huge yachts pour into the marina and the atmosphere is charged with excitement as helicopters buzz overhead. Even if you're not an F1 fan, the concerts, restaurant and bar events, and boat parties make for four days you don't want to miss. Past performers have included Muse and Depeche Mode.

Yas Express

A free bus, the Yas Express covers two circuits of the island. The Blue Route will ferry you between Yas Waterworld, Yas Plaza, Yas Viceroy, central Yas and Ferrari World Abu Dhabi/Yas Mall; the Red Route goes from Yas Plaza, to Yas Viceroy then on to Yas Marina and Yas Beach followed by Yas Links Golf Club. The free Saadiyat route leaves from St. Regis and Park Hyatt hotels on Saadiyat Island three times every morning with drop-offs at Yas Waterworld and Ferrari World. For timetables, see yasisland.ae.

Explorer's Top 5

If you're visiting Yas Island, this checklist should help you make the most of your stay.

1. Watch the sun go down over Abu Dhabi at Yas Links Golf Club, either from the course or with a chilled drink on the terrace of Hickory's bar
2. Be courageous by braving Yas Waterworld's infamous Dawwama ride
3. Be even more courageous by taking the front seat of the Formula Rossa rollercoaster at Ferrari World Abu Dhabi
4. Take a kayak eco tour from Yas Beach to learn about Abu Dhabi's mangroves and sea life
5. Experience the Yas Marina Circuit with one of their driving experiences then head to Skylite at the top of the Yas Viceroy for an evening under the iconic canopy

Yas Waterworld

Yas Waterworld Abu Dhabi

Yas Island West Abu Dhabi 02 414 2000
yaswaterworld.com

You could easily spend an entire day at this gargantuan water park on Yas Island, trying out the 43 rides, slides and attractions. Each one is handily categorised into one of four groups: Adrenaline Rush, Exciting Adventure, Moving and Grooving, or Young Fun, and there's something for everyone. For thrill seekers, the Liwa Loop – the first and only waterslide of its kind in the Middle East – is a near-vertical drop that shoots you through a winding loop at an incredible speed.

Emirates Palace Events

More than just a grand hotel, Emirates Palace is one of Abu Dhabi's top cultural and entertainment centres. It has staged major international concerts, including world-renowned pop artists like Coldplay and Elton John, and is a venue for the Abu Dhabi Festival, featuring classical orchestras and art installations. The hotel also hosts major art exhibitions, which have featured pieces from the likes of Pablo Picasso, and is part of the yearly Abu Dhabi Art Fair (abudhabiartfair. ae). Keep an eye on the Abu Dhabi Tourism website (abudhabitourism.ae) for details of upcoming events.

Hotels

Crowne Plaza Yas Island

Yas Island West 02 656 3000
ichotelsgroup.com

Sitting right next to Yas Links Abu Dhabi golf course, this hotel has four excellent restaurants and two bars to tempt guests and visitors. For sports and leisure fans, it's just a short walk to both the Yas Marina Circuit and Yas Marina, as well as Yas Beach.

Eastern Mangroves Hotel & Spa By Anantara

Shk Zayed Bin Sultan St Abu Dhabi 02 656 1000
abu-dhabi.anantara.com

This is Anantara's first city-based hotel in the Middle East. The views are lush, green and skyscraper-free, thanks to the resort's enviable location alongside the mangroves. Some of the leisure activities include kayaking and sailing.

Emirates Palace

West Corniche St Abu Dhabi 02 690 9000
kempinski.com

The lavish $3bn Emirates Palace – arguably the world's most costly hotel – boasts 392 opulent rooms and suites, all decked out with the latest technology and sumptuous decor. Several outstanding food outlets offer 'seven-star' service (the afternoon tea is famed) and guests can enjoy the private beach, two amazing pools and indulgent treatments at the exclusive Anantara spa.

Fairmont Bab Al Bahr

Nr Al Maqtaa Bridge Abu Dhabi 02 654 3333
fairmont.com

With its luxurious rooms, outdoor pools overlooking the creek, and stunning views of Sheikh Zayed Grand Mosque, it's no wonder that the Fairmont Bab Al Bahr is a much sought after Abu Dhabi destination. It also has some of the best dining and drinking spots in the city, and there are even more at the nearby Souk at Qaryat Al Beri complex.

St. Regis Saadiyat Island Resort

Saadiyat Beach Saadiyat Island 02 498 8888
stregissaadiyatisland.com

A true beach resort that's quite unlike any other hotel in the UAE, the St. Regis looks more like a California retreat, with stunning colonial style rooms all offering views over the beautiful central pools, restaurants and private sandy beach (and one hole of the neighbouring Saadiyat Beach golf course). The restaurants alone are worth travelling for, and 55 and 5th The Grill is particularly recommended. The perfect place to escape the city, while being just a short drive away.

Westin Abu Dhabi Golf Resort & Spa

Abu Dhabi Golf Club Khalifa City
02 616 9999
westinabudhabigolfresort.com

A smart and peaceful resort located at Abu Dhabi Golf Club, with rooms overlooking the course. Its location on the mainland, away from the city centre, makes it a convenient option from the airport. There are plenty of amenities whether or not you plan to tee off, including two pools and a great spa. It's also home to the outrageous Bubbalicious Brunch at Fairways, a Moroccan restaurant and theme nights.

Yas Viceroy Abu Dhabi

Yas Island West Abu Dhabi 02 656 0000
viceroyhotelsandresorts.com

This extraordinary hotel straddles the Formula 1 racetrack at Yas Marina Circuit and became an instant architectural classic and Abu Dhabi icon when it opened in 2009. The property is at once utterly modern but equally tactile, functional, sumptuous and welcoming. Rooms and suites all enjoy incredible views over the racetrack and surrounding Yas Island, and the restaurants are all individually worth a visit. The two rooftop pool bars are otherworldly locations, and the nightlife scene is renowned.

ROYAL ROSE
ABU DHABI

A CLASS OF ITS OWN

Count on a majestic experience the moment you set foot at Royal Rose Hotel. Feel like going back in time with hotel's classy architecture and interior resembling a 17th century French palace. Located at the heart of Abu Dhabi, Royal Rose Hotel offers the best of what the capital has to offer from cultural landmarks to the bustling commercial complex. Check in into a world of luxury along with modern Arabian hospitality at Royal Rose Hotel.

302 Zayed The First (Electra or 7th) Street, P.O. Box 4708, Abu Dhabi, U.A.E
T +971 2 672 4000 | F +971 2 672 0001 | E info@royalrosehotel.com | www.royalrosehotel.com
A member of City Seasons Group of Hotels

Abu Dhabi Art Scene

An ever-growing arts scene and the imminent arrival of world-class galleries will make Abu Dhabi a cultural hub for the UAE and beyond.

The art of the city

Saadiyat Island is already a special place; golden beaches stretching into the turquoise sea and top class dining venues, all only minutes from downtown Abu Dhabi. However, it's about to get a stroke of added artistic inspiration as it becomes host to the city's Cultural District. Aside from the Zayed National Museum and the Performing Arts Centre, both to be housed within stunning architecture, the globally recognised institutions of the Louvre and the Guggenheim will be represented, making Abu Dhabi, and the UAE, a focal point for the arts across the world.

Louvre Abu Dhabi
(Due to open: 2015)
The Louvre Abu Dhabi will be the first of the new museums to open, and construction is well underway behind its high walls. The building, designed by the legendary Jean Nouvel, will be an impressive landmark boasting a diameter of 180 metres, with a 7,000 tonne dome sat atop four pillars on a man-made platform. The area is dammed off, but before its opening in 2015 water will be flooded back to give it the feel of an island. The large dome will also let natural light through, dappling the public areas with sunshine.

Inside, the museum will present major objects from the fields of archaeology, fine arts and decorative arts, plus all regions, periods (including contemporary art) and the narrative of art history.

Guggenheim Abu Dhabi
(Due to open: 2017)
The fantastic Frank Gehry-designed architecture for the Guggenheim Abu Dhabi will be spectacular and create one of the most unusual buildings in the country. The 137,000 sq m museum will house a huge collection of modern and contemporary art, as well as special exhibitions from the Guggenheim Foundation's extensive collection. It will be built on the corner of the island stretching out to sea and will incorporate many traditional Arabic design cues.

Manarat Al Saadiyat
Home to a fascinating exhibition showing the future development of the island, Manarat Al Saadiyat is also a functioning gallery in its own right. The high ceilings and light, airy feel of this contemporary space create the perfect place to appreciate the sculptures, paintings and other works displayed in ever-changing exhibitions of local and international art.

Next to Manarat Al Saadiyat is the Norman Foster designed UAE Pavilion. The striking structure was first exhibited at the Shanghai World Expo 2010 then shipped to Saadiyat Island and re-erected. It's now a regular space for art and other exhibits.

Elsewhere in the city
There are a number of independent galleries around the city including the Salwa Zeidan Gallery (salwazeidangallery.com), that recently moved to Saadiyat Island, and Ghaf Gallery (ghafartgallery.com). The newly opened Etihad Modern Art Gallery in Al Bateen is an extension of the Etihad Antique Gallery (etihadgallery.com), both of which are now open to visitors. For something different, Abu Dhabi Pottery (abudhabipottery.com) showcases some fine ceramics and also holds classes. To find like-minded people to explore Abu Dhabi's art scene with, try groups like Abu Dhabi Art Squad (theartsquad.com).

Art work can also be found in many of the city's hotels, from classic antiquities at The Barakat Gallery in Emirates Palace, to contemporary work from international artists at places like the Lightbox in the Yas Viceroy. The Souk Qaryat Al Beri also houses Gallery One. Other hotels like the Rosewood, Fairmont Bab Al Bahr and the Jumeirah at Etihad Towers have all hosted one-off exhibitions too, so keep your eyes open for those as they crop up.

Abu Dhabi Art Hub
If you want to get more involved, the Abu Dhabi Art Hub (adah.ae) in Mussafah is the place to go. As well as having a gallery and holding affordable art fairs, it's also a working studio. Most months a small group of artists from a specific county is invited to live and work in the specially designed accommodation for residency artists. Not only do they each produce a series of works inspired by the region, but they also give classes and workshops to UAE residents, helping to spread their knowledge and techniques. ADAH also promotes traditional crafts and tries to help artists find new ways of incorporating them in contemporary pieces.

Super Saadiyat

The UAE is on track for a cultural awakening, the heart of which will undoubtedly be Saadiyat Island's Cultural District. With the Louvre Abu Dhabi, designed by Jean Nouvel, due to open in 2015, and the Frank Gehry-designed Guggenheim to follow, there'll be some seriously impressive exhibitions housed in soon-to-be iconic buildings. Zayed National Museum is another eagerly awaited centre that will soon find a home on Saadiyat. It's a refreshing and admirable investment by the capital, and puts Abu Dhabi firmly on the global map.

Zayed National Museum
(*image: Tourism Development & Investment Company*)

AL AIN

Al Ain is Abu Dhabi emirate's second city and of great historical significance in the UAE. Its location on ancient trading routes between Oman and the Arabian Gulf rendered the oasis strategically important.

Commonly known as 'The Garden City', Al Ain features many oases and lovely patches of greenery for the public to enjoy. After a greening programme instigated by the late Sheikh Zayed, the seven natural oases are now set amid tree-lined streets and beautiful urban parks. Its unique history means that Al Ain is home to interesting sights and attractions, including the Hili Archaeological Garden and the Al Ain Palace Museum, although there are modern amusements too like Hili Fun City.

Just outside the city sits one of the largest mountains in the UAE, Jebel Hafeet, while the sand dunes of Bida Bint Saud are great to explore on camelback (Al Ain Golden Sands Camel Safaris runs tours that include transfers from Al Ain. Call 050 447 7268 for the details). Al Ain's archaeological and historical legacy is of such significance that the city was recently placed on the list of World Heritage Sites by UNESCO.

Al Ain National Museum

Attractions

Al Ain Camel Market
Nr Bawadi Mall, Zayed Bin Sultan St Al Ain
adach.ae
Conditions at the souk have improved dramatically, with spacious pens for the animals and ample parking for visitors. A visit to the market is a fantastic way to mingle with locals and witness camel and goat trading taking place in the same way it has for centuries. Arrive early, preferably before 9am, to soak up the buzzing atmosphere.

Al Ain National Museum
Zayed Bin Sultan St Al Ain **03 764 1595**
abudhabi.ae
The oldest museum in the UAE is divided into three main sections. The ethnography section focuses on traditional life, culture and pastimes and the archaeology section has examples of Stone Age, Bronze Age and Iron Age objects excavated from sites around Al Ain. The 'gifts' section hosts some weird and wonderful items that were presented to Sheikh Zayed by visiting dignitaries, including golden palm trees, ornamental camels and jewel-encrusted daggers.

Al Ain Oasis
Nr Al Ain Museum Al Ain
visitabudhabi.ae
This impressive oasis in the heart of the city is filled with palm plantations, many of which are still working farms. You are welcome to wander through the plantations, but it's best to stick to the paved areas. The farms have plenty of working examples of *falaj*, the traditional irrigation system which has been used for centuries to tap into underground wells. There are eight different entrances, some of which have arched gates, and there is no entry fee.

Al Ain Palace Museum
Central District Al Ain **03 751 7755**
abudhabi.ae
The museum was originally a palace belonging to Sheikh Zayed bin Sultan Al Nahyan, dating back to 1937. Now, it tells the story of its previous owner and his remarkable achievements turning the desert state into a wealthy, popular and thriving country. Guided tours are free and highly recommended, and the Emirati guides are proud and knowledgeable. You'll learn about Emirati traditions and culture in general, and gain a real sense of time and place. The museum is a lovely, quiet place to stroll around and explore.

Al Ain Zoo
Nahyan the First St Al Ain **03 799 2000**
alainzoo.ae
This zoo is not characterised by small cages and meagre wildlife displays. Instead, it feels much more like a safari park, with spacious enclosures spread

across its 365 hectares interspersed with smaller exhibitions. Highlights include watching the hippos splash around in their 10m long ravine, catching a glimpse of the rare white lions in their enclosure, and getting up close to the giraffes at their feeding station. It's also an important conservation centre, with nearly 30% of the 180 species being on the endangered list.

Al Jahili Fort

Nr Central Public Gardens Al Ain **03 784 3996**
abudhabi.ae

Al Jahili Fort is over 100 years old and one of the UAE's largest forts. Celebrated as the birthplace of the late Sheikh Zayed bin Sultan Al Nahyan, it is set in landscaped gardens and has been the stunning venue for a number of concerts during the Abu Dhabi Classics series (abudhabiclassics.com). The distinctive three-tiered fort appears on the UAE's Dhs.50 note.

Hili Archaeological Park

Mohammed Bin Khalifa St Al Ain
abudhabi.ae

These landscaped gardens are home to a Bronze Age settlement (2,500-2,000BC), which was excavated and restored in 1995. Many of the artefacts found are displayed in Al Ain National Museum. Entry is Dhs.1.

Hili Fun City

Mohammed Bin Khalifa St Al Ain **03 784 4481**
hilifuncity.ae

This recently renovated, 22 hectare theme park offers you the best of both worlds: a theme park packed with rides and activities, and a scenic picnic spot for more relaxed get-togethers with friends. It's best to arrive early and make a day of it. There are more than 30 attractions, ranging from gentle rides for the little ones, such as the zebra-striped safari jeeps, to nail-biting, highflying rides for teens and adults, like the terrifying Sky Flyer that spins 360 degrees.

Jebel Hafeet

South of Al Ain

Among the highest peaks in the UAE, Jebel Hafeet towers over the border between Al Ain and Oman at an imposing 1,240 metres. It's an impressive backdrop to the city, and the winding road to the top is considered to be one of the world's best driving roads; head to the summit to be rewarded with fantastic views over Al Ain. Alternatively, if you're feeling active, the road is also a challenging cycle route.

Wadi Adventure

Jebel Hafeet Al Ain **03 781 8422**
wadiadventure.ae

A must for adrenaline junkies, this water park with a difference has white water rafting and kayaking runs, of more than a kilometre in length. A huge wave pool generates three-metre high breaks for surfing, or if water isn't your thing, the air park, zip line, climbing wall and canyon swing should keep your excitement levels high. There's a family swimming pool, man-made beach and a splash pool for little ones, making it a fantastic option for a family outing.

Hotels

Al Ain Rotana

Shk Zayed Rd Al Ain **03 754 5111**
rotana.com

This city centre spot is a nightlife hub, thanks to six popular dining spots which include the lively Trader Vic's and the excellent Lebanese restaurant Min Zamaan. The rooms are attractive and spacious, and the pool and gardens are great for sunbathing.

Danat Al Ain Resort

Al Salam St Al Ain
03 704 6000
alain.danathotels.com

Well known for being one of the UAE's best inland resorts, with its luxurious guestrooms and deluxe villas, landscaped gardens and swimming pools. There are plenty of family friendly facilities, while adults are sure to enjoy the luxury spa and the swim-up pool bar, as well as the Horse and Jockey Pub.

Green Mubazzarah Chalets

Nr Green Mubazzarah Park Al Ain **03 783 9555**
Mubazzarah.150m.com

Situated among the lush and picturesque foothills of Jebel Hafeet, these fully-furnished two and three-bedroom chalets are ideal for enjoying the Green Mubazzarah natural springs and parkland.

Hilton Al Ain

Khatm Al Shikle St Al Ain
03 768 6666
hilton.com

Located near the heart of Al Ain, this ageing hotel is a key landmark and sits in lush, landscaped gardens that contain a nine-hole golf course, tennis and squash courts, a health club and a nice pool area. It is particularly convenient for visiting Al Ain Zoo. The Hiltonia Sports Bar and Paco's Bar are popular haunts.

Mercure Grand Jebel Hafeet

Al Ain **03 783 8888**
mercure.com

This hotel's impressive location near the summit of Jebel Hafeet affords spectacular views of Al Ain. The rooms here are simple and comfortable, and there's plenty of fun to be had with three swimming pools to choose from, a waterslide and a mini-golf course.

AL GHARBIA

Al Gharbia is Abu Dhabi's Western Region – a vast 60,000 square kilometres or 60% of the total area of Abu Dhabi emirate and 51% of the UAE. Al Gharbia's natural resources such as palm trees, pearls, oil, gas and solar energy contribute 45% to the UAE's GDP. The region boasts the highest sand dunes in the world and 350km of coastline with beaches, rare wildlife, and beautiful desert islands such as Delma and Sir Bani Yas fast becoming popular tourist destinations.

Liwa

For most visitors to Al Gharbia, all roads lead to Liwa. On the way, you pass through tumbleweed towns such as Ghayathi (good for stocking up on authentic Bedouin souvenirs) and the regional capital Madinat Zayed. The land in this region holds evidence of life from ancient times; eight-million-year-old fossils have been found at Bu Ghar, while oases and the occasional farmstead are dotted throughout the region. Modern Bedouin criss-cross the interior with entire bungalows on the back of big-wheeled trucks.

Liwa Oasis is one of the largest oases on the Arabian Peninsula. This fertile crescent stretches for more than 150km and is home to the Bani Yas tribe, ancestors of the ruling family of Abu Dhabi. It's a quiet area, dotted with date plantations and small towns. Visitors go to see its ancient forts, traditional falconry, camel racing and trading, and because Liwa is the northern gate to the great desert.

It's at Liwa that you'll find the legendary sand dune known as 'Tel Moreeb', or the Hill of Terror, a 300m high slope which attracts only the most confident off-roaders. Prepare for the most adventurous desert driving – and incredible scenery – the UAE has to offer. For detailed routes and practical information, get a copy of Explorer's *UAE Off-Road*.

The Empty Quarter

The Rub Al Khali – also known as the Empty Quarter – spreads south from Liwa and is the biggest sand desert on the planet. It measures a mind-boggling 650,000 square kilometres and spreads over parts of Oman, Yemen, southern UAE and almost all of southern Saudi Arabia. Its dunes rise as high as 250m. The Rub Al Khali is one of the world's greatest attractions on an unsurpassed scale of majesty. It was historically regarded as the edge of civilisation by people living in the region. But there is an extraordinary beauty to this landscape, despite it being so harsh and inhospitable. Even today man has

been able to make little mark on it. Desert driving in this area is more of an expedition than just a spot of dune bashing, so go prepared for the adventure of a lifetime. The opportunities for camping in the region are endless, and sleeping under the stars is a great way to experience the peace and tranquillity of the desert. Unless of course there's a sand storm.

The Pearl Coast

Drive west from Abu Dhabi and the first stop will be Mirfa, set up in the 1970s as a fishing port and pearling centre. Mirfa is quiet but may change once the Mirfa Corniche is developed under Abu Dhabi's 2030 regional plan. In the meantime the refurbished, 114 room Mirfa Hotel has breathed new life into the area. For now, the biggest draw to Mirfa remains the annual Al Gharbia Watersports Festival (algharbiafestivals.com), opposite the hotel. Crowds flock for a weekend of fireworks, competitive kitesurfing, wakeboarding and kayaking.

A hundred kilometres along the 'pearl coast' is Jebel Dhanna, another historic pearl diving destination. There are two hotels here on a great beach with clear, shallow sea and fantastic facilities that make for a great weekend getaway from Abu Dhabi. Nearby, Ruwais is a town built for ADNOC employees which holds little interest for visitors.

The last stop before the Saudi Arabia border is Sila, a true frontier town. There isn't much happening in Sila today but that may change when it's one of the regular stops of the proposed GCC railway network. Until then, if you're in Sila head down to the harbour for fresh fish from the Abu Dhabi Fishermen's Co-operative Society (02 673 0888). If a beach barbecue is on the menu, pick up extra provisions at Al Rahi Home Grocery next to the co-operative. Drive north, with the quarry-scarred embankment on your left, along the beach track, and find a spot away from the beach houses. This is one of the few spots along the coast where you can camp. Two headlands further west, you'll find an even more pristine spot with white sand, turquoise sea and bobbing pink flamingos.

Kitesurfing Mania

Every year, the world's best kitesurfers gather for the 10 day Al Gharbia Watersports Festival (algharbiafestivals.com) in Mirfa, which takes place in April.

Desert Islands

This eight-island, eco-tourism project involves the larger Sir Bani Yas and Delma islands, and the six uninhabited Discovery Islands.

Sir Bani Yas Island was once Sheikh Zayed's personal retreat and is becoming a noted wildlife reserve. The Desert Islands Resort & Spa By Anantara has received numerous accolades for eco-sensitive luxury, and its even more luxurious sister properties on the island – Al Yamm Villa Resort and Al Sahel Villa Resort – have beautiful self-contained units. Sir Bani Yas Island is 9km off the coast from Jebel Dhanna and offers safaris where you'll see a multitude of animals including giraffes, oryx and maybe even a hyena. There are also a few routes for mountain biking and the clear blue waters and creeks offer peaceful snorkelling and kayaking. Catch the ferry to the island or fly from Al Bateen Executive Airport.

Beyond Sir Bani Yas and 42km off the coast lies Delma Island, a two-hour ferry ride from Jebel Dhanna or a 45 minute flight from Abu Dhabi International Airport. Delma Island is only nine by six kilometres, but until recently it was the most important island in the Gulf. With fertile land and more than 200 wells of fresh water, it was a favourite stopping point for traders, fishermen and pearlers for thousands of years. Evidence of human habitation on the island dates back more than 7,000 years and even today it supports more than 4,000 locals whose livelihood is fishing and farming. The island's rich earth supports the cultivation of more than 20 varieties of African, Asian and European fruits.

The volcanic landscape literally sparkles and ospreys watch over the fields of ostrich, but even with car ferries plying the route from the mainland, the island's attractions are works in progress. The only accommodation is the Delma Motel (02 878 1222), or you can camp.

Hotels

Anantara Sir Bani Yas Island Al Yamm Villa Resort
Sir Bani Yas Island Ruwais 02 801 4200
al-yamm.anantara.com
This special resort offers 30 five-star units in a serene location on the eastern shore of Sir Bani Yas Island, half of which are located on the beach and the other half in the tranquil mangroves. The rooms have beautiful views of the water, either the turquoise sea or the bird-filled lagoon. Two more properties owned by Anantara – Sir Bani Yas Island Al Sahel Villa Resort and Desert Islands Resort & Spa – also offer impeccable luxury and access to the island's wildlife reserve.

Danat Jebel Dhanna Resort
Jebel Dhanna Ruwais 02 801 2222
jebeldhanna.danathotels.com
Sitting on 800 metres of private, picturesque beach, this undiscovered treat of a hotel offers 109 luxurious rooms and suites including six waterfront villas. It has a health club and a spa that includes beach massage huts and a nice pool area with swim-up bar.

Dhafra Beach Hotel
Jebel Dhanna Ruwais 02 801 2000
dhafrabeach.danathotels.com
A very pleasant and reasonably priced hotel with a variety of rooms and suites to choose from, as well as a handful of dining options, a fitness centre with a sauna, and two swimming pools. A good option if heading west – you can even hire the late Sheikh Zayed's presidential suite for Dhs.3,000 per night.

Arabian Nights Under The Stars
An essential part of any Liwa adventure, camping in the desert is a truly unforgettable experience. The expanses of sand rolling into the distance at early dawn is quite magical. You can camp just about anywhere, so take any of the roads and tracks into the desert off the main road, but make sure that you drive far enough to find a peaceful spot. Try to get settled long before the sun goes down, for safety reasons and to allow you to enjoy the sunset. One particularly good area is on the road to Moreeb Hill passing the Liwa Resthouse. This minor, paved road heads into the desert for 11.5km, leading you into some of the best dunes, and crossing plenty of *sabkha* (salt) flats.

Liwa Hotel
Mezaira Liwa 02 882 2000
almarfapearlhotels.com
With its raised location giving spectacular views of the Rub Al Khali (or Empty Quarter) desert, the green oasis and the neighbouring palace on the hilltop opposite, Liwa Hotel is a good option if you're not keen on camping but still want to enjoy the scenery. The hotel has spacious rooms and green, landscaped grounds with an attractive pool. There's also a choice of good dining options and evening venues.

Liwa Resthouse
Mezaira Liwa
A little past its prime, this guesthouse has been eclipsed by the nearby Liwa Hotel and its (mainly Arab) clientele includes visiting business travellers, government officials and families on holiday. Although pretty basic compared to local hotels, it is clean and functional, and the cheapest alternative to camping.

Mirfa Hotel
Sila Highway Mirfa 02 883 3030
almarfapearlhotels.com
Located in the quiet town of Mirfa, 160 kilometres from Abu Dhabi, this hotel is perfect for a weekend break or as a stopover if you're driving to Saudi Arabia. The hotel has been renovated and now features 114 comfortable rooms and suites, and lush gardens as well as leisure facilities including two pools, floodlit tennis courts and a kids' playground.

AJMAN

The smallest of the emirates, Ajman still has lots to offer travellers, including fine dining, luxury hotels and pristine beaches, with a few heritage attractions thrown in for good measure. It's a more relaxed emirate in all senses of the word; life has a slower pace, while dress codes are a bit more lenient and alcohol can be bought without a licence.

The emirate's star attraction, Ajman Museum, houses a variety of interesting displays in a restored fort that is well worth visiting, as much for the building as for its contents. The emirate's main souks are a reminder of days gone by, while the modern Ajman City Centre is home to shops, foodcourts and a cinema. The tiny emirate is known for being one of the largest boat building centres in the region; while mainly modern boats emerge from the yards these days, you may still catch a glimpse of a traditionally built wooden dhow sailing out to sea.

Attractions

Ajman Corniche

Corniche Road Ajman

Life in Ajman revolves around its pleasant seafront corniche, especially during the milder months. It is lined with cafes, shops, stalls, and there's a tidal pool for safe swimming. There are some excellent traditional restaurants, too. Try the seafood at Themar Al Bahar or the Middle Eastern cuisine at Attibrah.

Ajman Museum

Ioarh 1 Ajman **06 711 6642**

No trip to Ajman would be complete without a visit to the Ajman Museum. This attractive building is based inside a fort, thought to have originally been built during the late 18th century. The popular cultural attraction houses an astounding collection of artefacts and archaeological finds, including centuries-old manuscripts, weaponry and pottery.

Al Zorah Nature Reserve

This serene mangrove creek is teeming with wildlife, including a huge flock of flamingos. The area is currently under development but you can get a peek from the viewing deck on Al Zorah Street. The development will add more luxury resorts to the city, a golf course and a marina.

Attibrah

Corniche Road Ajman **06 744 8383**

A good option for sampling some authentic Emirati dishes with traditional local flavours. Go for the *gideesha* (a fragrant spiced fish dish) and some *harris biliyan* (a rich eggplant side dish), along with the usual Middle Eastern mezze spread.

Fish Market

Ajman

One of the best local fish markets in the country, head here early to see the day's catch being offloaded from fishing dhows and choose something fresh to have prepared and cooked onsite.

Hotels

Ajman Palace

Al Nakheel 2 Ajman **06 701 8888**
theajmanpalace.com

This gorgeous hotel may not serve alcohol (unusually for Ajman) but it's a relaxing place to spend time. Leisure facilities include an infinity pool, a private beach and a fully equipped spa and fitness centre.

Ajman Saray

Al Nakheel 2 Ajman **06 714 2222**
starwoodhotels.com

This brand new hotel from the Luxury Collection has its own private beach and brings a splash of glamour to Ajman. There are several restaurants, including a beach bar and grill.

Ajman Corniche

Kempinski Hotel Ajman

Al Nakheel 2 Ajman 06 714 5555
kempinski.com
This beautiful five-star hotel offers the ultimate in luxury and hospitality. There's a stunning stretch of white sand beach overlooking the Arabian Gulf that's perfect for trying out watersports or simply soaking up the sun. You can even request to have a table set up in the surf for a romantic dinner for two. Be sure to sample the renowned Indian cuisine at the excellent Bukhara or the Italian fare at Sabella's.

Ramada Beach Hotel

Shk Humaid Bin Rashid Al Nuami St Ajman
06 742 9999
ramadabeachajman.com
For a cheap and cheerful stay on the water's edge, this four-star hotel has a lot to offer. It has its own private beach where you can get spa treatments, and an enormous five-bedroom penthouse with its own Jacuzzi that can be rented at a very reasonable rate.

Lap of Luxury

Little Ajman is making big strides in the luxury travel stakes. While the Kempinski remains a hugely popular option for a weekend of pampering, the newly opened Ajman Saray brings more choice for a deluxe break, and a new offering from the Fairmont will open on the beachfront in 2014. Further luxury resorts are in development at the Al Zorah Nature Reserve.

FUJAIRAH

Fujairah may be less than a two-hour drive when travelling from Dubai, but the dramatic landscape of the east coast makes it feel like a different world. The journey itself takes you through the spectacular Hajar Mountains before arriving at this picturesque location along the Gulf of Oman. Fujairah city has seen little development compared to cities on the west coast, but the real draw here is the landscape. The mountains and wadis that stretch west of the coast contain some of the country's best and most accessible camping spots, and the beaches, reefs and villages that line the coast attract visitors from every emirate.

Dibba

Located at the northern-most point of the east coast, on the border with Musandam, Dibba is made up of three fishing villages. Unusually, each part comes under a different jurisdiction: Dibba Al Hisn is part of Sharjah, Dibba Al Fujairah is Fujairah and Dibba Bayah is Oman. The three Dibbas share an attractive bay, fishing communities, and excellent diving locations – from here you can arrange dhow trips to take you to unspoilt dive locations in Musandam. The Hajar Mountains, which run parallel to the east coast, provide a dramatic backdrop, rising in places to over 1,800 metres. There are good public beaches too, where your only company will be crabs and seagulls, and where seashell collectors may find a few treasures.

East Coast Made Easy

From Dubai, getting to the UAE's east coast takes anything from 30-90 minutes. For speed alone, take the Sharjah-Kalba Road and then the Sheikh Khalifa Highway. For a more scenic route through the mountains, take the E88 from Sharjah to Masafi, passing fruit sellers and local landmark the Friday Market, and then turn left to Dibba or right to Fujairah. If you're heading to Dibba outside of rush hour, it's usually quicker to head north on Sheikh Mohammed bin Zayed Road and take the truck road (at exit 119) across the country to the E87, which brings you to Dibba.

Fujairah City

A mix of old and new, its hillsides are dotted with ancient forts and watchtowers, which add an air of mystery and charm; most are undergoing restoration work. Fujairah is also a busy trading centre, with its modern container port and a thriving free zone attracting major companies from around the world. Off the coast, the seas and coral reefs are great for fishing, diving and watersports. It is a good place for birdwatching during the spring and autumn migrations as it's on the route from Africa to Central Asia. Since Fujairah is close to the mountains and many areas of natural beauty, it makes an excellent base from which to explore the countryside and discover stunning wadis, forts, waterfalls and even natural hot springs.

Kalba

Just to the south of Fujairah you'll find Kalba, which is renowned for its mangrove forest and golden beaches. Technically the town belongs to Sharjah, but it's a pretty fishing village that still manages to retain much of its historical charm. You can visit Bait Sheikh Saeed bin Hamed Al Qasimi, an old house dating back 100 years that's home to fascinating heritage displays and historical artefacts.

South of the town is the beautiful tidal estuary of Khor Kalba (*khor* is Arabic for creek), one of the oldest mangrove forests in Arabia. It is home to a variety of wildlife not found anywhere else in the UAE. The mangroves in the estuary flourish thanks to a mix of seawater and freshwater from the mountains, but are now receding due to the excessive use of water from inland wells. For birdwatchers, the area is especially good during the spring and autumn migrations when rare species of bird can be spotted, including Sykes's warbler. It is also home to a rare subspecies of white collared kingfisher, which breeds here and in Oman, and nowhere else in the world. Canoe tours have been put on hold while conservation work is carried out, but check with Desert Rangers (04 357 2200) in case the tours have been re-opened to the public.

The road through the mountains linking Kalba to Hatta makes for an interesting alternative for returning towards Dubai or Abu Dhabi.

Attractions

Al Badiyah Mosque
Badiyah Fujairah

The site of the oldest mosque in the UAE, Bidiyah is one of the oldest settlements on the east coast and is believed to have been inhabited since 3,000BC. The mosque is made from gypsum, stone and mud bricks finished off with plaster, and is believed to date back to the middle of the 15th century. It is still used by worshippers for daily prayer, so non-Muslim visitors can't enter. Built next to a low hillside with several watchtowers on the ridge behind, the area is colourfully lit up at night.

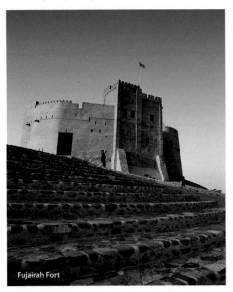
Fujairah Fort

Dibba Castle
Dibba Fujairah

Hidden away in the Omani part of Dibba (aka Daba), next to vast farms and plantations, Dibba Castle is an interesting place to have a walk around. Built over 180 years ago, it has been restored and, while there aren't a lot of artefacts on show, you can access all the rooms and climb up the towers, where you'll get views over the castle and its surroundings. It is signposted off the road past the UAE border check post.

Fujairah Fort
Nr Fujairah Heritage Village Fujairah
fujairahtourism.ae

The majestic Fujairah Fort is one of the oldest and most important in the emirate, as well as being among the most photographed. It's an impressive building located on a raised hilltop overlooking the city and just a few kilometres from the sea. Although you can't enter Fujairah Fort itself, the surrounding heritage buildings are open to the public, and the nearby remains of traditional houses are easily viewed.

Bull Butting

On Friday afternoons at around 4.30pm during winter, crowds gather close to the corniche to watch 'bull butting'. This ancient Portuguese sport consists of two huge bulls going head to head for several rounds, until after a few nudges and a bit of hoof bashing, a winner is determined. It's not as cruel or barbaric as other forms of bullfighting, but animal lovers may still want to avoid.

Fujairah Heritage Village
Nr Fujairah Fort Fujairah
fujairahtourism.ae

Situated just outside of Fujairah city, this purpose-built village takes you back in time to experience traditional life in the emirate. Walk around the village and see first-hand the realities of what traditional Bedouin life was like in the unforgiving desert climate. After a morning of cultural immersion, you can stay and relax in the sun, as there are two spring-fed swimming pools for men and women, and chalets that can be hired for the day.

Snoopy Island
Khor Fakkan

Snoopy Island, so named because of its resemblance to the beloved comic book dog, is a popular snorkelling spot. The Sandy Beach Hotel & Resort's beach is a great launch pad (there's a small fee for non-guests to enter), as it's just a short swim away. Or, you can rent a kayak, as well as snorkelling gear. For the best visibility, go early; expect to be rewarded by an abundance of sea life including turtles and rays.

Hotels

Hilton Fujairah
Al Faseel St Fujairah **09 222 2411**
hilton.com

Set at the north end of Fujairah's corniche, just a stone's throw from the foothills of the Hajar Mountains, this relaxing resort has all the facilities needed for a wonderful weekend away. If you get tired of lounging by the swimming pool, or activities like tennis, snooker, basketball or even watersports on the private beach, you could always explore the rugged splendour of the surrounding mountains. The hotel is great for families, and there is a safe play area to occupy the little ones.

Le Meridien Al Aqah > p.463
Al Aqah Fujairah **09 244 9000**
lemeridien-alaqah.com

All of the rooms at Le Meridien Al Aqah have views over the Indian Ocean, and the grounds are covered by lush foliage. It is particularly geared up for families, with a kids' pool and outdoor and indoor play areas. There's an extensive spa and dive centre on site, as well as daily full or half-day fishing trips leaving from the beach. Entertainment options include a cinema, bars and restaurants serving a range of Thai, Indian and European cuisine.

Fujairah Rotana Resort & Spa – Al Aqah Beach
Al Aqah Beach, Dibba Rd Fujairah **09 244 9888**
rotana.com

This resort puts its beachside location to good use, with each of the 250 guest rooms and suites boasting its own balcony with views over the sea. Some of the highlights of the hotel include its private beach, the swimming pool with pool bar and the indulgent spa offering plenty of pampering treatments. You can even opt to have a massage in a hut on the beach with an ocean view.

Sandy Beach Hotel
Al Aqah Fujairah **09 244 5555**
sandybm.com

Snoopy Island has long been recognised as one of the best diving spots in the United Arab Emirates, with an abundance of fish and even reef sharks. The island is right off the coast from the Sandy Beach Hotel, making it a firm favourite with UAE residents. Day trippers can purchase a day pass to the hotel to access the temperature-controlled pool, watersports and beach bar services. There is also a five-star PADI Dive Centre within the hotel that hires out diving and snorkelling gear for exploring the reefs around Snoopy Island, as well as offering courses for novices or those looking to improve their diving.

RAS AL KHAIMAH

Nature lovers, take note: Ras Al Khaimah boasts the best natural scenery in the UAE. With the stunning Hajar Mountains as its backdrop and the sparkling waters of the Arabian Gulf on its shore, the northernmost emirate is the perfect destination for an outdoor break with plenty of opportunities for camping, hiking and soaking up the sun. Several five-star hotels offer more for your dirham than you could expect to get in the bigger cities.

Ras Al Khaimah contains several archaeological sites, some dating back all the way to 3,000BC. Take the Al Ram road out of Al Nakheel district and towards the Hajar Mountains to discover some of the area's history, including the Dhayah Fort, Shimal Archaeological Site and Sheba's Palace. The bare ruins of the Dhayah Fort can be spotted from the road, but you might need a 4WD to access them.

The town is quiet, relaxing and a good starting point for exploring the surrounding mountains, visiting the ancient sites of Ghalilah and Shimal, the hot springs at Khatt, and the quirky local camel race track at Digdagga. Al Hamra Village, just south of the city, is a gorgeous development with its own mall (with a VOX Cinemas, restaurants, play centre and a supermarket), golf course, marina and five-star hotels.

Attractions

Al Hamra Golf Club
Al Hamra Village Ras Al Khaimah **07 244 7474**
alhamragolf.com

Al Hamra Golf Course meanders around four inter-connected open water lagoons that merge with the water of the Arabian Gulf. The club offers lessons for beginners, golf under the stars and a restaurant, sports bar and cafe, which is open to members and non-members alike.

The Haunted Village

Rumour has it that the residents of Jazirat Al Hamra saw spirits, or *djinn*, coming out of the sea and evacuated overnight in fear. This huge area of houses has been deserted for 40 years, and with hints of a bygone era, it is a fascinating, and somewhat creepy place to explore. Head north from Al Hamra Marina, take a u-turn at the pink pet shop, and turn right at the signpost to the archaeological park. Follow this road to the end.

Al Hamra Marina

Al Hamra Village Ras Al Khaimah
07 243 2274
alhamramarina.com

You can apply for membership to the club online, and daily membership is also available if you just want to visit for a short time. Facilities include a restaurant and there are charter boats.

Al Qawasim Corniche

Ras Al Khaimah

Ras Al Khaimah's Al Qawasim Corniche is a social hub that's lined with cafes. Enjoy the natural beauty of the mangroves and visit the Pearl Museum to learn about the emirate's pearling traditions, followed by a bit of local knowledge at the National Museum of Ras Al Khaimah. You can hire bikes for exploring the area. Round off your evening at Italian restaurant Pesto, followed by shisha on the rooftop terrace overlooking the serene mangroves.

Camel Racing

Around half an hour along Truck Road (turn left past Ras Al Khaimah Airport) is the camel race track at Digdagga, where local folk meet up early in the morning to compare and race their camels as they have done for centuries – albeit with robot jockeys atop the camels and the owners tearing around the course in their battered SUVs with horns blaring in encouragement. It's a brilliantly bonkers, wonderfully unapologetic slice of local life.

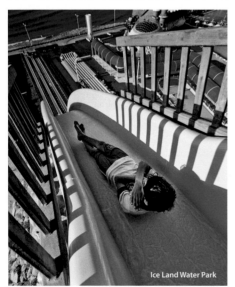

Ice Land Water Park

Bassata Desert Village

Ras Al Khaimah **055 993 8589**

Experience traditional Arabian activities including a belly dancer, Egyptian tanoura, a henna lady, camel riding and dune bashing. The Arabic BBQ dinner at sunset is a great way to end the day.

Bedouin Oasis Desert Camp

Ras Al Khaimah **04 266 6020**
arabianincentive.com

This camp provides visitors with the perfect opportunity to explore desert living. Using only traditional and natural materials the Bedouin Oasis Desert Camp is a step back to the days when tent roofs were originally made from goat hair and there was only fire or an antique gas light to provide heating and lighting.

Catamaran Freedom

Ras Al Khaimah **050 377 6613**
facebook.com/Freedomtobesailing

'Freedom' cruises from Ras Al Khaimah Corniche and takes in the emirate's scenic coast. This is a good trip for group parties, romantic getaways or corporate excursions. Trips are tailored to individual requirements and can include swimming, snorkelling, fishing sunset dinners or champagne packages.

Ice Land Water Park

Al Jazeera Al Hamra Ras Al Khaimah **07 206 7888**
icelandwaterpark.com

With its ice-capped mountains and plastic penguins in the middle of a desert landscape, this polar-themed water park is certainly a sight to behold. Without a doubt, Ice Land is a magnet for tots and toddlers, who can't help but love the quirkiness of it all. There's Penguin Bay, an interactive play area that's home to the world's biggest rain dance pool and also Penguin Falls, the tallest man-made waterfall in the world.

Jazira Aviation Club

Jazirah Airport Ras Al Khaimah **07 244 6416**
jac-uae.net

Enjoy scenic views of the desert, beach, sea and mountains from the air with light aircraft flights from Al Jazirah Aviation Club. There are short piloted flights in a variety of aircraft, or keen enthusiasts can embark on courses to gain their pilot's licence.

Prince of Sea

Al Hamra Marina Ras Al Khaimah **050 372 1772**

Hop aboard this fabulous yacht for a daytime, sunset or dinner cruise. Depending on which excursion you choose, you could enjoy swimming in the Arabian Sea, snorkelling off the coast of Al Marjan Island (look out for the rare green turtles) or simply dining on delicious barbecued seafood as you watch the sun go down.

LE MERIDIEN
AL AQAH BEACH RESORT

T +971 9 244 9000
lemeridien.com/fujairah

Le MERIDIEN

IGNITE
INSPIRATION

Explore the endless opportunities to unwind and relax in style at
Le Méridien Al Aqah Beach Resort. Fujairah offers rich cultural traditions
and contemporary luxury. Just 90 minutes from Dubai, you enjoy all of the
seclusion and privacy your heart desires. The resort is only 50 kilometers from
Fujairah City and within easy reach of the area's unique attractions, including
ancient fjords, palm groves, hot springs, and historical landmarks.

For more information or to make a reservation,
visit lemeridien.com/fujairah or call +971 9 244 9000

N 25° 30' E 56° 21'
DESTINATION UNLOCKED

Luxury hotels in Ras Al Khaimah

The evening trips usually include a welcome drink, DJ music and a buffet dinner, as well as traditional Arabian entertainment such as belly dancing.

RAK Sailing Academy
Al Hamra Marina Ras Al Khaimah 056 352 4659
raksailingacademy.com

Located in Al Hamra Marina, RAK Sailing Academy is a commercial club, open to all. The academy is equipped with dinghies, a catamaran and fixed keel sailing boats for juniors and seniors. Visitors are able to rent different types of boats either for cruising (with or without skipper) or for training courses. RAK Sailing Academy was founded by round-the-world sailor and expert sailing instructor Enrico Malingri. He's sailed through hurricanes, completed numerous ocean passages, and taught some of the world's most accomplished sailors. Instructors at the academy are also all very experienced, and deliver their lessons in a friendly and easy-to-understand manner. A trip here is a perfect family day out.

Ras Al Khaimah Country Club
Ras Al Khaimah 056 706 4774

This newly opened equestrian club is already proving popular with local horse riding enthusiasts and visitors from the UAE and abroad. As well as boasting superb equestrian facilities and expertly trained staff, there's also a restaurant and bar for lingering over a delicious meal or relaxing drink, and a large, scenic swimming pool for cooling off while you soak up some sun. Riding lessons and excursions are available to visitors of all ages and experiences. Contact info@rasalkhaimahtourism.com for more information.

Tower Links Golf Club
Ras Al Khaimah 07 227 8555
towerlinks.com

One of Ras Al Khaimah's two 18 hole championship courses, Tower Links Golf Club is set in a beautiful mangrove reserve with the Hajar Mountains as a majestic backdrop. The club welcomes active and social members.

Hotels

Al Hamra Fort Hotel & Beach Resort
Al Jazeerah St Ras Al Khaimah 07 244 6666
alhamrabeachandgolfresort.hilton.com
With traditional Arabic architecture set among acres of lush gardens and a long strip of sandy beach, this hotel offers a peaceful getaway. A range of watersports and activities, including two floodlit golf courses and an onsite dive centre, will keep you entertained, as will the live entertainment concerts that take place on the beach. The themed eateries also offer a wide variety of international cuisines.

Stellar Cellar
Al Hamra Cellar, although owned by MMI (mmidubai.com), is a tax-free liquor store that is well worth the trip. You can take advantage of RAK's relaxed alcohol laws and browse a wide range of fine wines, spirits and beers at extremely competitive prices. Call 07 244 7403 for more info.

Al Hamra Residence
Vienna St Ras Al Khaimah 07 206 7222
alhamraresorts.com
Located on a private beach in the Arabian Gulf, this five-star resort offers luxurious suites with fully equipped kitchenettes. The Sea Breeze restaurant serves traditional Arabic food, while guests can have a refreshing swim in the outdoor pool or enjoy the tennis court and fitness centre. The resort is just a five-minute drive from Al Hamra Golf Club.

Banyan Tree Ras Al Khaimah Beach
Al Jazirah Al Hamra Ras Al Khaimah 07 206 7777
banyantree.com
The sister property of the gorgeous Banyan Tree Al Wadi (see Desert Resorts for more information), this stunning resort offers 32 beachfront villas built in the style of the Bedouin's tents – but far more luxurious. It's a lovely hideaway for some serious relaxation (each villa has its own plunge pool and comfy cabana), and it's also great for thrill seekers, with snorkelling, sailing and watersports all on offer.

Bin Majid Beach Resort
Shk Mohd Bin Salem Rd Ras Al Khaimah 07 244 6644
binmajid.com
Guests can relax and unwind along an 800m sandy beach at this affordable four-star hotel. As well as plenty of sports facilities for the active, including jet-skiing and parasailing, there is a great selection of licensed bars and restaurants serving Indian and international dishes. There's also a large pool with swim-up bar and a children's play area.

The Cove Rotana Resort
Shk Mohd Bin Salem Rd Ras Al Khaimah 07 206 6000
rotana.com
This sprawling resort, comprising more than 200 rooms and 72 villas, has the feel of an old Mediterranean hill town, thanks to its location built into the hillsides overlooking the Arabian Gulf. The centrepiece is undoubtedly the lagoon that it is built around, which is protected from the sea by 600 metres of pristine beach.

Golden Tulip Khatt Springs Resort & Spa
Khatt Ras Al Khaimah 07 244 8777
goldentulipkhattsprings.com
Simple and subdued, Golden Tulip Khatt Springs Resort & Spa relies on mountain views, uninterrupted tranquillity and incredible spa packages to attract weekend visitors. Next to the hotel, you can take a dip in the public Khatt Hot Springs – piping hot water which, it is claimed, has curative powers. Men and women have separate pools and a variety of massages are also available. It's a good idea to visit the hot springs in the morning and avoid Fridays as it can get very busy with families.

Hilton Ras Al Khaimah Resort & Spa
Al Maareedh St Ras Al Khaimah 07 228 8844
hilton.com
With 1.5km of private, white sandy beach, six swimming pools, five-star service, loads of watersports on offer and some super fine dining options, you won't really need to leave. As well as rooms in the main building, there are 151 quaint villas with direct beach access, and for all that's on offer, it's actually rather good value.

Waldorf Astoria
Vienna St Ras Al Khaimah 07 203 5555
waldorfastoria.com
An enormous hotel styled on an Arabian palace, the Waldorf Astoria is set on 350m of private beach and has various dining options, including the excellent Lexington Grill, as well as a cigar bar, spa, gym, and gorgeous pools. Following in the traditions of Waldorf Astoria hotels around the world, every inch of the place is beautifully designed but favouring elegance over ostentation, and each venue with its own style and story to tell.

New Hotels
RAK's distinguished list of hotels continues to grow, with the 2014 openings of Rixos Bab Al Bahr, DoubleTree by Hilton Resort, and Marjan Island Resort & Spa on the man-made Marjan Island - RAK's answer to the Palm Jumeirah. Still underway is its Santorini Hotel.

Short Breaks From The UAE

As much as we love living in the UAE, there are so many fantastic places to visit just a few hours away by plane. Here are just a few.

Dubai is an ideal base to explore the region. Fly in style with Emirates from Dubai, or Etihad out of Abu Dhabi, or check low-cost carriers. Air Arabia flies from Sharjah Airport and flydubai from Dubai Airport or Al Ain.

Cyprus
Flight time: *Four hours, five minutes (from Dubai) or four hours, 20 minutes (from Abu Dhabi)*
The three main towns, Larnaca, Limassol and Paphos, offer unique accommodation and leisure options, and the capital city Nicosia is great for shopping and nightlife. Drive up the mountains for crisp, cool air and awesome views, and explore the local villages.

India
Flight time: *Three to four hours*
Cruise the serene backwaters of Kerala and witness timeless rural life, or party on the beautiful beaches of Goa. Explore the vibrant city of New Delhi before catching the train around the Golden Triangle, taking in architectural marvel, the Taj Mahal, and the majestic palaces and forts of Rajasthan. And that's barely scratching the surface of this diverse subcontinent.

Jordan
Flight time: *Three hours, 10 minutes*
Jordan's capital, Amman, will keep you busy for a few days, but heading south to Petra, the ancient city carved into solid rock canyons, is an absolute must. Stop at the Dead Sea to bathe in the mineral-rich black mud and test the buoyant waters. Be sure to head to Jerash, which has been continuously inhabited for 6,500 years, and visit holy sites, such as the brook where the baptism of Jesus Christ is said to have taken place.

Azerbaijan
Flight time: *Two hours, 55 minutes*
Azerbaijan is rapidly changing; its capital Baku is fast becoming a rather surprising party town and it's scattered with affordable accommodation. The oil-rich Baku is well poised to become the Middle East's next big luxury travel destination. Culturally, its main claim to fame is the well-preserved Old City, a maze of honey-coloured limestone streets dating back to the Arab conquest that is full of mosques, caravanserais (traditional roadside inns) and madrasas (religious schools), surrounded by 13ft-thick walls.

Sri Lanka
Flight time: *Four hours, 40 minutes*
An easily accessible paradise with rainforests, unspoilt beaches, well-populated game parks, great surf and gorgeous hotels offering exceptional rates. Have we got your attention yet? Add into the mix a charming blend of Buddhist, Hindu, Muslim, Christian and indigenous cultures, along with spicy, traditional curries, rotis and egg hoppers – and you have the ideal Sri Lankan holiday.

Seychelles
Flight time: *Four hours, 40 minutes*
Few travel destinations evoke the image of an island paradise as much as the Seychelles, and with good reason. Lush unexplored jungles, powdery white-sand beaches and an azure ocean teeming with marine life create the overall impression of a modern-day Eden. You can stay on 15 of the 115 islands scattered through the Indian Ocean, 1,600 kilometres east of Africa. The largest is Mahe, but the smaller Praslin and La Digue have much to offer too.

Maldives
Flight time: *Four hours, five minutes*
As one of the world's best destinations, if not the best, for diving and snorkelling, there are few places on earth where you can walk from a stunning beach straight into the ocean and see a lively coral reef a few feet below you. Time seems to slow down in the Maldives and spending a few days in awe of the ocean, relaxing in a hammock over impossibly pristine beaches, or sipping cocktails and dining on all-inclusive seafood buffets can certainly make for a dream holiday.

Kenya
Flight time: *Five hours, five minutes*
Here you'll find one of the highest concentrations of wild animals on the planet, including, of course, the Big Five. Witness an alpha lion stalk across the dusty plains in the dawn light, or a herd of elephants cross a crocodile-infested river under the hot African sun, or simply sip sundowners while the animal kingdom gathers at the watering hole below – head to Masai Mara National Reserve and you can experience all of that in just a few days.

Book It Online
Don't waste hours scouring the internet; whether you want to book an extravagant honeymoon to the Seychelles or a shoestring weekend break to Europe, dnata (dnatatravel.com) is a one-stop shop for hotels, flights and holiday packages. Book online or call 04 316 6666 – and sign up on the website for all the latest travel deals.

Explore Your Options
For more information on these and many more short-haul destinations out of Dubai, pick up a copy of Explorer's *Short Breaks From And Within The UAE*.

The Maldives

SHARJAH

Dubai's neighbouring emirate was named the cultural capital of the Arab world by UNESCO in 1998 and the Capital of Islamic Culture for 2014 by the Organisation of Islamic Conference, due to its well-preserved heritage area, an evolving arts scene, some wonderful museums and a thriving cafe culture. Sharjah Art Foundation (06 568 5050, *sharjahart.org*) organises a programme of cultural events. Regular events, such as the Sharjah Light Festival and Sharjah Biennial, draw visitors from all over the UAE and beyond, and that's just the city – the emirate is home to some fantastic desert, including popular spots Big Red (a 90m high sand dune) and Fossil Rock, and a few enclaves on the east coast.

For a sense of what the city is all about, head to Khalid Lagoon. At Al Majaz Waterfront you can choose from a cluster of restaurants to watch the nightly fountain show on the lagoon, take an abra ride, or check out the kids' play areas.

A wander further north brings you to the city's heritage and arts areas, currently being restored and developed under the Heart of Sharjah project, with one of the most impressive collections of museums and heritage sites in the region. Shoppers will have a blast too, searching for gifts in Sharjah's souks – Souk Al Arsah is a more authentic experience than those in the rest of the country.

Sharjah Museum of Islamic Civilisation

Attractions

Adventureland
Sahara Centre Sharjah **06 531 6363**
adventureland-sharjah.com
Adventureland's recent revamp has made it a popular indoor attraction with a new jungle theme and 25 major thrill rides and attractions including a family fun train and a two-level indoor go-kart track.

Al Mahatta Museum
King Abdul Aziz St Sharjah **06 573 3079**
sharjahmuseums.ae
Home to the first airfield in the Gulf, opened in 1932, Sharjah played an important role as a primary stop-off point for the first commercial flights from Britain to India, and the museum looks at the impact this had on the traditional way of life in Sharjah and beyond. Four of the original propeller planes have been fully restored and are on display. Located behind Al Estiqlal Street, entry is Dhs.5 for adults and Dhs.10 for families.

Al Qasba
Nr Al Khan Lagoon Sharjah **06 556 0777**
alqasba.ae
Canal-side hub Al Qasba is packed with popular cafes and restaurants, and has some interesting attractions, such as Maraya Art Centre and the Eye of the Emirates observation wheel. Al Majaz Park is good for little ones; there are plenty of kids' play areas including a lovely splash park. Restaurants along the waterfront overlook Khalid Lagoon, where Sharjah's nightly answer to the Dubai Fountain is a colourful affair.

Al Tamimi Stables
Al Zubair Sharjah **06 743 1122**
tamimistables.com
This private but friendly farm offers kids the chance to get up close to their favourite animals, from little mice to fluffy rabbits and even a friendly parrot. There's also pony rides, falcon shows, horse displays and guided nature trails, making for the perfect family day out.

Heart of Sharjah
Al Mareija St
heartofsharjah.ae
The region's largest heritage project encompasses the heritage and arts areas and is dedicated to restoration and renovation; some of the traditional coral stone buildings date back more than 200 years. The narrow alleys and shady cobbled courtyards transport you to another era, and there are several fascinating museums. Check out Majlis Al Midfaa, an iconic round wind tower, as well as Sharjah Heritage Museum and Sharjah Art Museum, both of which use the unique and beautiful spaces of the area's traditional buildings. The 150 year-old Souk Al Arsah is located here too.

BEGIN YOUR JOURNEY
OF DISCOVERY

 @sharjahmuseums

 /SharjahMuseumsDept

 @sharjahmuseums

 SharjahMuseums

www.SharjahMuseums.ae

إدارة متـــاحف الشــارقــة
Sharjah Museums Department

Sharjah Art Museum > *p.469*

Shwaihean Sharjah 06 568 8222
sharjahmuseums.ae

Permanent displays here include a personal collection of paintings and maps belonging to the ruler, HH Sheikh Dr Sultan bin Mohammad Al Qasimi, such as the fascinating work of several 18th century Orientalists, with oil paintings and watercolours depicting traditional life in the Arab world. Temporary exhibits include modern works by renowned international artists, especially during Sharjah Biennial, an important event on the international calendar.

Sharjah Classic Car Museum

Al Dhaid Rd Sharjah 06 558 0222
sharjahmuseums.ae

This fantastic and well-curated museum Is definitely worth a visit, whether or not you are 'into' cars. There's a large number of vehicles on display, all dating from 1979 or earlier. Many of the cars are from His Highness Sheikh Dr Sultan bin Mohammad Al Qasimi's personal collection, including a stunning 1934 Rolls Royce. Displays are quirky, fun and well presented – it's a great place to soak up some history and to impress any auto-enthusiasts.

Sharjah Desert Park

Al Dhaid Rd Sharjah 06 531 1501
epaashj.com

Located just off the E611, this complex is worth heading to for its three animal-themed attractions. Arabia's Wildlife Centre is one of the UAE's best in terms of animal care and presentation, and home to a host of fascinating wildlife indigenous to the Arabian region, including the rare Arabian leopard. The Natural History & Botanical Museum features interactive displays on the relationships between man and the natural world in the UAE and beyond, while over at the Children's Farm petting zoo, you can feed some friendly camels, goats and more. The entrance fee, Dhs.15 for adults and Dhs.5 for children, covers all three attractions.

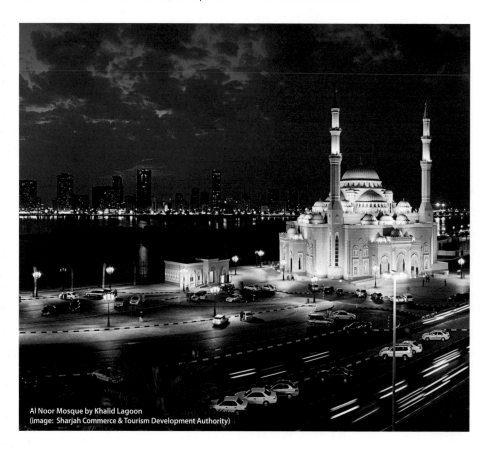

Al Noor Mosque by Khalid Lagoon
(image: Sharjah Commerce & Tourism Development Authority)

DISCOVER CONTEMPORARY ART
WITH SHARJAH ART FOUNDATION

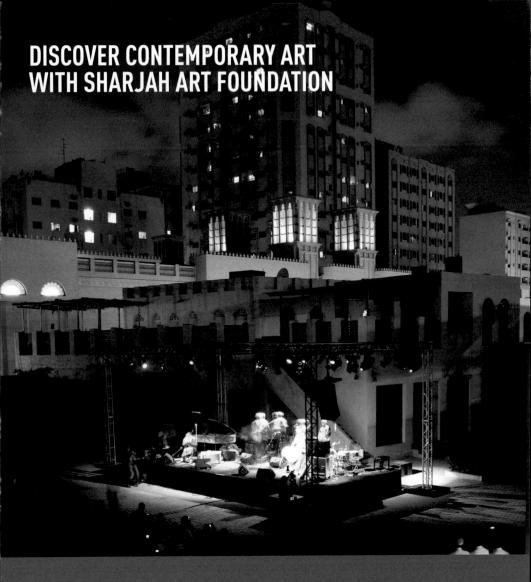

Sharjah Biennial 12, March 5 - June 5, 2015 Don't miss the UAE's own internationally acclaimed Sharjah Biennial. Every two years Sharjah welcomes artists from all over the world for this major exhibition that takes place in the SAF Art Spaces, streets, courtyards and sites across the Emirate of Sharjah.

Year round activities Exhibitions • Performances • Music • Film Screenings • Education Programme (for Children and Adults) • Community Garden. All activities are open to the public and free of charge. **Opening Hours** Saturday - Thursday: 10am - 10pm, Friday: 4pm - 10pm

SHARJAHART.ORG +971 52 695 8517

SHARJAH ART FOUNDATION

Sharjah Discovery Centre

Al Dhaid Rd Sharjah **06 558 6577**
sharjahmuseums.ae

The Discovery Centre is divided into educational zones. The star attraction is Drive Town and its electric cars, where children learn the rules of the road.

Sharjah Golf & Shooting Club > p.vi, vii

Shk Mohammed Bin Zayed Rd Sharjah **06 548 7777**
golfandshootingshj.com

With golf, shooting, archery and paintball on the menu, there's enough to fill a whole weekend at this club. Once you're done with the activities, there's a choice of excellent restaurants.

Sharjah Museum of Islamic Civilization

Corniche St Sharjah **06 565 5455**
sharjahmuseums.ae

More than 5,000 artefacts from across the Arab world, all informatively displayed and housed in a beautiful building that was once a souk.

Hotels

Coral Beach Resort

Al Muntazah St Sharjah
06 522 9999
coral-beachresortsharjah.com

With its own pristine sandy beach and a swimming pool with a waterslide, this is one hotel that's bound to keep the kids (and adults) happy. There's also a host of activities and sports facilities on offer, as well as a spa and hammam where you can wind down after a long day exploring the city. Be sure to try the excellent seafood at the restaurant Casa Samak during your stay, or visit Al Bahar for their Sunday roast.

Hilton Sharjah

Al Majaz 3 Sharjah **06 519 2222**
hilton.com

A beautiful new art deco-styled resort which is located right on Khalid Lagoon and boasts some of the best facilities in the emirate. Enjoy succulent kebabs at the authentic Shiraz restaurant or indulge in a chilled mocktail on the pool terrace.

Radisson Blu Resort

Corniche St Sharjah **06 565 7777**
radissonblu.com

This reliably smart hotel chain has a five-star offering in a great location close to the city's historic centre and with its own beach. Facilities are plentiful and include temperature-controlled swimming pools, watersports, tennis courts, a spa and fitness centre, as well as several great dining options.

UMM AL QUWAIN

A visit to Umm Al Quwain is a great way to see traditional Emirati life; fishing and date farming are still the main industries, as they have been for centuries. It has plenty of modern attractions too – its beach resorts are popular (and extremely affordable) hangout spots among UAE expats, and it was the first place in the country to offer skydiving (visit emiratesdropzone.webs.com for details).

The emirate has six forts, and a few old watchtowers surrounding the town. With plenty of mangroves and birdlife, the emirate's lagoon is a popular weekend spot for boat trips, windsurfing and other watersports. Another popular family activity is crab hunting at Flamingo Beach Resort. At nightfall, groups of hunters set off into the shallow mangrove waters with a guide, where they spear crabs, which are then barbecued and served on return to the resort.

Emirates Motorplex (motorplex.ae) hosts various motorsport events, including the Emirates Motocross Championship, and Dreamland Aqua Park is one of the most popular attractions. Barracuda Beach Resort is a favoured destination for Dubai residents, thanks to its well-stocked, duty-free liquor store.

Attractions

Dreamland Aqua Park > p.xiii

Al Rafaah Umm Al Quwain **06 768 1888**
dreamlanduae.com

This impressive water park is both huge and hugely popular. Perfect for a family day out, there are more than 30 rides, including four 'twisting dragons' that promise white knuckle thrills. There's also a lazy river and a play area if you're looking for something a little more relaxing, as well as a high-salinity floating pool. You can camp overnight, staying in one of the tents or huts provided. However, note that Fridays and public holidays are for families only.

Umm Al Quwain Marine Club

Al Khour 1 Umm Al Quwain **06 766 6644**
uaqmarineclub.com

This watersports centre takes advantage of the calm waters of the placid lagoon, which provides the perfect conditions for wakeboarding, as well as kayaking and stand up paddleboarding through the mangroves. All these and more are offered at competitive prices, and day members can use the pool and kids' play facilities.

Hotels

Barracuda Beach Resort
Nr Dreamland Aqua Park, Khor Al Baida
Umm Al Quwain **06 768 1555**
barracuda.ae

This comfortable, laidback resort is perfect for a short break or even a quick weekend getaway, especially as prices are very reasonable. There's a variety of rooms, but you might prefer one of the lagoon-side one-bedroom chalets, each of which accommodates up to five people. These are fitted out with kitchenettes and barbecues, which make them ideal for private overnight parties, and the hotel boasts a large pool and Jacuzzi too. You can also take advantage of the tax-free booze emporium while you're there, and there's a lovely gourmet shop opposite the liquor store that's worth a look before you head home.

Flamingo Beach Resort
Nr Horsehead R/A Old Umm Al Quwain **06 765 0000**
flamingoresort.ae

This cheap and cheerful hotel is perfect for nature lovers, as it's surrounded by a shallow lagoon and green islands that attract a variety of fauna, including visiting flamingos. The hotel organises a variety of excursions to keep guests entertained, including flamingo tours and deep sea fishing trips. Guests can also go on a night-time crab hunt – not an activity for the faint-hearted, you head out to the shallows with a guide (and a spear), and whatever you catch will be cooked for you back at the resort. There's a beach bar, cafe and dhow restaurant too.

Dreamland Aqua Park

OMAN

The most accessible country in the Gulf for Dubai residents, Oman is a peaceful and breathtaking place, with history, culture and spectacular scenery, from the southernmost city of Salalah to the quaint capital Muscat, and up to the Musandam Peninsula, which is separated from the main body of Oman by the UAE.

A flight from Dubai to Muscat takes about an hour but, when you factor in check-in times and clearing customs, it's not much quicker than driving – and you miss out on some stunning views en route.

Like the UAE, summers in Oman are incredibly hot and winters much milder, although southern Salalah is actually rather cool, wet and green during the summer.

Buraimi

This historical town nudges Al Ain from just over the Oman border; although the only problem getting from Al Ain to Buraimi is finding it, as there are almost no signs. If you're heading there in a UAE taxi, agree a price, as once they've crossed the border their meters may magically stop working. You don't need a visa but you will need your passport.

Find pottery, silver jewellery and woven crafts at Buraimi Souk, and check out the many forts. Al Khandaq Fort is 400 years old; it has been lovingly restored and offers great views from its battlements.

Musandam

The UAE's northern neighbour, Musandam is an isolated enclave belonging to Oman. The region is dominated by the same Hajar Mountains that run through the eastern UAE. As the peninsula juts into the Strait of Hormuz, it splits into a myriad of jagged, picturesque fjords. Spending a day exploring the fjords on a wooden dhow is a must for anyone. Most trips originate from the region's capital, Khasab. The marine life here is some of the best in the region; set off from Dibba with your snorkel and explore the reef of corals around Dibba Island, where you are virtually guaranteed to spot a turtle, or take a dive trip to one of the many dive sites – at the Landing Craft you can explore a well preserved shipwreck – and see if you spot a whale shark.

Alternatively, you can access the famous Wadi Bih off-road route from Dibba and spend a weekend camping. See Explorer's *UAE Off-Road* for more information about the route.

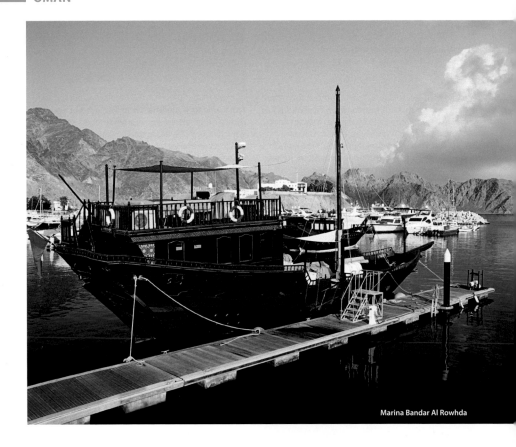

Marina Bandar Al Rowhda

Golden Tulip Resort

Mina Rd Dibba **968 2683 6654**
goldentulipdibba.com

In the foothills of the Hajar Mountains, the Golden Tulip Resort is on a private beach on the east coast of the Musandam Peninsula. It's a great base for snorkelling and diving, with a coral reef located just off the coast, and there's also the chance to go rock climbing and exploring the mountains from the resort. Facilities include a Jacuzzi, swimming pool with temperature control and a children's indoor play area.

Six Senses Zighy Bay

Zighy Bay, Musandam Daba **968 2673 5555**
sixsenses.com

Located in a secluded cove in Musandam, the resort has been designed in a rustic style and is made up of individual pool villas. Like all Six Senses resorts, the focus here is on relaxation. The spa treatments available are of the highest quality, and expertly prepared dinners can be enjoyed from either the comfort of your own villa or from the mountainside restaurant with breathtaking views of the bay.

Muscat

One of the most charismatic and visually striking capitals in the Middle East, once you've visited, you'll understand why many count Muscat as their favourite regional city. With beautiful beaches, lots of green spaces, a collection of great restaurants and cafes, and some fascinating museums, you'll need at least a few days to fully discover this clean and friendly city.

Rather than a bustling CBD characterised by countless skyscrapers, gridlocked traffic and smog, Muscat has many separate areas nestling between the low craggy mountains and the Indian Ocean. Visit the old town of Muscat or Mutrah, charming clusters of pretty whitewashed buildings sandwiched between rocky hills. The warren-like Mutrah Souk is one of the best markets in the region that's jam-packed with

Omani silver, frankincense, perfume oils and spices. The impressive Sultan Qaboos Grand Mosque held the record for the world's largest carpet and the world's largest chandelier, until Abu Dhabi's own Sheikh Zayed Grand Mosque raised the bar.

Exploring the city's majestic coastline is a must, and there are plenty of rocky coves for snorkelling and dive sites a short distance away. At Ras Al Jinz Turtle Reserve in Sur, south of Muscat, you can camp overnight and watch nesting turtles lumber up the beach to lay their eggs, and then, after a few hours' sleep, the mass of tiny hatchlings struggle out of their eggs and make their journey into the sea.

The Chedi Muscat

18th November St Muscat **968 2452 4400**
chedimuscat.com

This beautiful boutique hotel on the shore is famed for its clean lines, five-star luxury and an impressive sense of tranquillity – the stunning spa and outstanding restaurant don't hurt either. With an infinity pool, private beach and library, this is the perfect destination for a break from the city hustle and bustle, but perhaps isn't an ideal choice for families.

Crowne Plaza Muscat

Al Qurm St Muscat **968 2466 0660**
crowneplaza.com

This hotel boasts cliff top views over Al Qurum and the beach below. Many of the 200 guest rooms benefit from the striking vistas and several of the restaurants boast outdoor terraces. There's a large swimming pool, gym, spa and dolphin watching trips available, making it a great choice for those looking for relaxation and for visitors who want an action-packed break.

Oman Dive Center

Nr Qantab R/A, Al Jissah St Muscat
968 2482 4240

Just south of Muscat, a stay here is a welcome remote break whether you're a diver or not. You can book a barasti hut (they are actually made of stone, with barasti covering) for an average of RO.66 (around Dhs.600) for two people, including breakfast and dinner. Accommodation is a little worn around the edges, but is a pleasant departure from the glitz of Dubai.

Shangri-La's Barr Al Jissah Resort & Spa

Al Jissah St Muscat **968 2477 6666**
shangri-la.com

With three hotels catering for families and luxury seekers, this is one of the most gorgeous resorts in the region. The hotels have several swimming pools and enough play areas to keep children occupied for days. The exclusive, six-star Al Husn is incredibly luxurious and perfect for a weekend of out-of-town pampering.

Salalah

Home to several museums and souks, Salalah – in the south of Oman on the Arabian Sea coast – is best known for its lush landscape and is especially attractive over the summer when it is cooled by the monsoon rains sweeping across the Indian Ocean. From June to September, when Dubai is hitting 50°C, Salalah is enjoying temperatures in the 20s. This climatic quirk has given the region an important place in the history books – it is one of the few places in the world that grows frankincense, and has been exporting it to kings and pharaohs for millennia. It's a fascinating, not to mention fragrant, place to visit – head to the Museum of the Frankincense Land to learn more, and then to Souk Al Hafah to pick up some quality samples. The climate also enables banana plantations and coconut groves to thrive, and fruit stalls line the roadsides giving the place a tropical feel far removed from the desert landscape of the UAE.

Salalah's wild and truly magnificent coastline ranges from wide, untouched beaches to towering jagged cliffs, and is home to the famous blowholes at Al Mughsayl. Thundering waves have eroded caverns underfoot and explode through openings in the rock, drenching the more adventurous visitors.

Taking an impossibly windy road that zigzags its way up a mountain ascent, while minding out for charging camels and wandering donkeys, brings you to the incredible picnic spot of Shaat. At 1,000m above sea level, it's a stomach-turning cliff top that drops straight down to the ocean. Salalah is a 1.5 hour flight from Dubai.

Hilton Salalah Resort

Sultan Qaboos St Salalah **968 2321 1234**
salalah.hilton.com

This attractive resort is set on the beach by the Arabian Sea, and has beachfront pools (with a waterslide and kids' area), a sea-view restaurant, a lively bar, tennis courts and a gym, and a dive centre. The rooms have balconies overlooking the water or the gardens. The Hilton is about 12 kilometres from the city centre, so it's as easy to explore Salalah as it is to escape the crowds.

Juweira Boutique Hotel

Salalah Beach Marina, Salalah **968 2323 9600**
juweirahotel.com

This relatively new hotel is on an inlet used by local fishermen. Each room has a terrace and overlooks the waterfront promenade, the fluffy cloud-capped mountains, the sea or the plentiful coconut trees that Salalah is famous for. Suites are spacious and light, a heavenly pool area has a bar and comfy sun loungers, and the seafood restaurant serves deliciously fresh Omani lobster.

Western Hajar

The Hajar Mountains stretch all the way down the east coast of Oman, right from the Musandam Peninsula. The most spectacular section is that of the Western Hajar, southwest and inland from Muscat, and is a must for outdoorsy weekend breakers.

Jebel Shams, the 'Mountain of the Sun', has a rugged terrain that is actually a fairly easy trek with several good camping locations. Below the summit, Wadi An Nakhur has some of the most stupendous views in the country as you drive through the 'Grand Canyon of Oman'. Sayq Plateau on top of Jebel Akhdar has beautiful mountain villages.

More popular spots for hiking include the amazing rock formations of Al Hoota Cave, the challenging but spectacular Snake Canyon (which involves some daring jumps into rock pools and a fair bit of swimming through ravines) and the pools of Wadi Al Abyad, just over an hour west of Muscat.

Nizwa

After driving deep into the Hajar Mountains, you'll find Nizwa, the largest city in Oman's interior. This oasis city offers fascinating sights and heritage, including the impressive 17th century Nizwa Fort, set amid a verdant spread of date palms. This fine citadel features a maze of rooms, doorways, terraces, narrow stairways and corridors; its most striking feature is its colossal central tower, soaring 35m above the fort. Nearby Jabrin Fort, notable for its ceiling decorations and secret passageways, is also worth a visit. Be sure to pick up some freshly made local *halwa* (a sweet dessert) at Nizwa Souk, and it's also a hotspot for souvenir shopping. From Nizwa you can also explore the mountains and hill towns that surround the city.

Sahab Hotel
Jabal Al Akhdar Nizwa **968 2542 9288**
sahab-hotel.com
On the Sayq Plateau, 2,004m above sea level, this boutique hotel overlooks an incredible canyon and a village perched precariously on a cliff face. The surrounding gardens contain marine fossils dating back 270 million years. There are stunning sunrise and sunset views from the infinity pool, and from the hotel you can trek the mountains, have a go at goat herding with the locals, or stay up late to watch the stars.

Visas On Arrival

Most travellers for Oman will be issued a single entry visa on arrival for Dhs.50. Women may require a letter of no objection from their employer (if single) or husband (if married), while visitors to Dibba must pre-arrange their visa with their accommodation.

QATAR

Qatar once had a sleepy reputation, but things are changing fast. Development and investment in the country means it is becoming increasingly popular with visitors, especially UAE residents, as it is less than an hour's flight from Dubai.

With an attractive corniche, world-class museums and bustling cultural centres, the capital Doha makes a perfect weekend retreat, with the focus firmly on luxury travel and tourism. Away from the city, the Inland Sea (Khor Al Adaid) in the south of the country makes for a great day trip.

Qatar has a very hot summer and the best time to go is usually over the winter, between October and April. Explorer's *Qatar Visitors' Guide* has more details and includes a pull-out map.

FIFA 2022 World Cup

The choice of Qatar as host of the FIFA 2022 World Cup has been a controversial one, largely due to the intense heat of the Qatari summer and the reported deaths of migrant workers who died whilst constructing the various stadiums around the country. FIFA still intends to go ahead with plans in Qatar, with the possibility of moving the tournament to the winter.

Attractions

Bir Zekreet
70km west of Doha
The beach destination of Bir Zekreet is one of Qatar's most popular spots for weekend warriors, and the desert landscape surrounding the city is a great place to spot the picturesque natural formations known as 'desert mushrooms'.

Katara Cultural Village
Lusail St Doha **974 4408 0000**
katara.net
This is a unique development, bringing together all the artistic elements in Qatar including music, dance, theatre, photography, painting and sculpture. The site, which looks like a large village, allows artists to meet and collaborate on different projects. It is also open to the public with two concert halls designed for opera, ballet and large theatrical productions, an outdoor amphitheatre which holds 5,000 people, as well as galleries, workshops, cafes, restaurants and souks.

Salalah

Ruwi neighbourhood of Muscat

The Chedi Muscat

Khor Al Adaid

80km south of Doha Doha
qatartourism.gov.qa

A popular day trip destination also known as the Inland Sea, Khor Al Adaid is a wide inlet which narrows in the centre and widens out to a large, seawater lake. It's surrounded by crescent-shaped dunes, and the border between Qatar and Saudi Arabia runs down the middle. Although strong currents make the narrows too dangerous for swimming, taking a dip around the shore is popular and safe. A number of tour companies organise trips to this spectacular landscape, either for a few hours or a full overnight camping stay. Other popular activities in the area include dune bashing, camel riding and sand skiing.

Mathaf – Arab Museum of Modern Art

Education City Doha **974 4402 8855**
mathaf.org.qa

Housed in a former school, redesigned by the French architect Jean-François Bodin, Mathaf holds its own impressive permanent collection and regularly welcomes other exhibitions. Education is central to the museum, and there's a great library full of resources, as well as a museum shop and relaxed, contemporary cafe space.

Museum of Islamic Art

Doha Port Doha **974 4422 4444**
mia.org.qa

Culture vultures should not miss a trip to this iconic attraction on an island of reclaimed land just off the corniche. The masterful Islamic-influenced architecture is the work of IM Pei, the legendary architect responsible for the iconic pyramid of the Louvre in Paris. The museum houses a marvellous collection of temporary and permanent exhibitions showcased as a journey through time, countries and cultures, and the oldest pieces date from the ninth century. There's also a cafe and a 200 seat auditorium.

The Pearl Qatar

Al Gassar Doha
thepearlqatar.com

Doha's beloved Pearl is a stunning series of interconnected man-made islands that are perfect for a leisurely stroll, so much so that the area has been nicknamed the Arabian Riviera. One of the most popular areas is the island Porto Arabia, which boasts everything a visitor could possibly desire, from high-end shopping options to fine restaurants and cafes serving up international cuisine. Indeed, The Pearl Qatar is the perfect destination for foodies (alcohol is prohibited), who can indulge in everything from nouveau Mexican at Pampano to modern Japanese dishes at Megu. Perhaps best of all are the decadent treats on offer at Alison Nelson's Chocolate Bar.

Souk Waqif

Abdullah Bin Jassim St Doha

The city's oldest market, Souk Waqif was renovated in 2004 using traditional building methods and materials. The resulting warren-like complex is now one of the most beautiful and authentic modern souks in the Gulf. The most refreshing aspect of the souk area is its dual purpose – tourists can easily stroll the narrow alleys in search of exotic wares and souvenirs while locals can purchase everything from fishing nets to pots and pans. Aside from the shops and restaurants, there is the Waqif Art Centre, which houses several small galleries and craft shops. Alternatively, simply find a cafe, order a Turkish coffee or sweet mint tea and some apple-scented shisha, and watch the world go by.

Hotels

Four Seasons

Diplomatic St Doha **974 4494 8888**
fourseasons.com

One of the finest hotels in the city, the Four Seasons has an exclusive beach and marina, first-class service and excellent restaurants, including the classy Italian eatery Il Teatro.

Grand Hyatt Doha

Al Gassar Doha **974 4448 1234**
doha.grand.hyatt.com

The majority of rooms at this Doha institution enjoy stunning views of the Arabian Gulf, and guests can relax on an expansive 400m private beach or at the outdoor swimming pool. Be sure to indulge in a pampering treatment at the luxurious Jaula Spa.

La Cigale

60 Suhaim Bin Hamad St Doha **974 4428 8888**
lacigalehotel.com

A short drive from the airport, La Cigale has a reputation for first-class hospitality and is an exclusive nightlife destination. It has five restaurants ranging from sushi to Mediterranean, a sleek gym and spa, city views from the Sky View Lounge on the 15th floor, and 225 rooms and suites from which to choose.

Movenpick Doha

Corniche St Doha **974 4429 1111**
moevenpick-hotels.com

This modern hotel boasts breathtaking views of the corniche, where guests can enjoy a morning jog or afternoon stroll. Popular with business travellers, this boutique-style hotel also attracts tourists with its excellent restaurants and leisure facilities which include a swimming pool, whirlpool and steam bath. The hotel's location is convenient for the airport.

Museum of Islamic Art

Radisson Blu Doha
C Ring Rd Doha
974 4428 1428
radissonblu.com
With plenty of restaurants, bars and lounges to enjoy, this is a staple of Doha's nightlife. Renovated in 2012, the hotel's draws include a large swimming pool and a wide variety of fitness facilities. There is a champagne bar, and an excellent seafood restaurant, Pier 12.

Ritz-Carlton Doha
Al Gassar Doha 974 4484 8000
ritzcarlton.com
The opulent Ritz-Carlton is a perfect stop-off if you're sailing in the region, with its 235 berth marina and clubhouse. All of the 374 rooms and suites have breathtaking views over the sea or marina. The beach club has a great selection of watersports and there's a lavish spa, plus a whopping nine restaurants – the delicious French-inspired seafood served at La Mer is particularly recommended.

Sharq Village & Spa
Ras Abu Abboud St Doha 974 4425 6666
sharqvillage.com
Reminiscent of a traditional Qatari town, Sharq Village & Spa is another example of Qatar's insistence on spectacular architecture. The Six Senses Spa was constructed using traditional building techniques and the resort's restaurants are some of the finest in Doha. With pool or sea views from the 174 luxury suites and villas, this Ritz-Carlton managed resort makes for a perfect Qatari getaway.

W Doha
Diplomatic St Doha 974 4453 5000
whoteldoha.com
Adding a touch of fun to Doha's rather conservative luxury hotel scene, the W hotel chain is known for its funky design and fabulous level and quality of individualised service. Every inch of the hotel is an exercise in architectural minimalism, and its central location makes exploring Doha easy.

Desert Resorts

Within a 45 minute drive of Dubai – and with a copy of Explorer's *UAE Off-Road* – the UAE's vast deserts can be easily accessed, should you need to escape civilisation for a while. A range of hotel accommodation options exist, from five-star luxury resorts, like Al Maha Desert Resort & Spa and the Banyan Tree, to less expensive resorts for those on a tighter budget.

Out in the desert, you can ride camels, dune buggies and horses. Many resorts have excellent spas, which are perfect for unwinding in these exotic, tranquil surroundings; some also have kids' clubs to keep the little ones equally as happy.

Arabian Nights

For a more authentic experience, check out Arabian Nights Village in Abu Dhabi. They run all sorts of unique desert activities for intrepid explorers, from camping under the stars to dune bashing. Plus, the delicious food, awesome entertainment and pristine pools provide plenty of luxury in the midst of your adventure.

Al Maha Desert Resort & Spa

Dubai – Al Ain Rd **04 832 9900**
al-maha.com

Set within the 225 sq km Dubai Desert Conservation Reserve, with breathtaking views of picturesque dunes and rare wildlife, this luxury getaway was named as one of the best ecotourism models by National Geographic in 2008. Al Maha is designed to resemble a typical Bedouin camp, but conditions are anything but basic – each suite is beautifully crafted and has its own private pool and butler service. Activities include horse riding, camel trekking and falconry. There is also a superb spa.

Bab Al Shams Desert Resort & Spa

Nr Endurance Village Mugatrah
04 809 6100
meydanhotels.com/babalshams

This is a beautiful desert resort built in the style of a traditional Arabic fort.

Each of its 115 rooms is decorated with subtle yet stunning Arabian touches, and pristine desert dunes form the backdrop. The authentic, open-air, Arabic desert restaurant Al Hadheerah is highly recommended; during dinner, guests are treated to an incredible heritage show.

There is also a kids' club, two large swimming pools (complete with swim-up bar), desert activities, falconry shows and lawn games on offer, as well as the luxurious and indulgent Satori Spa.

Banyan Tree Al Wadi

Al Mazraa Ras Al Khaimah
07 206 7777
banyantree.com

Built in traditional Arabian style and set within a wildlife conservation area in the impressive desert landscape of Wadi Khadeja, this stunning resort combines the wild beauty of its surroundings with exclusive luxury. Villas and luxury 'tents' each have a private pool and sundeck, and views of the desert, where oryx trip skittishly by.

Qasr Al Sarab Desert Resort By Anantara

Al Wathba South **02 886 2088**
qasralsarab.anantara.com

This hotel has a stunning location amid the giant dunes outside Liwa. Designed as an Arabic fort, the resort features enormous villas, each with its own private pool. Guests can enjoy a wide range of desert activities before relaxing in oversized bathtubs, dining on gourmet dishes and being pampered in the spa. Around three hours from Dubai, it's a truly peaceful escape from life.

Tilal Liwa

Liwa **02 894 6111**
tilalliwadanathotels.com

This affordable, four-star desert hideaway has a charming pool area and a range of rooms and suites which blend old and new design elements, and provide gorgeous views over the endless sands. Desert safaris in the dunes should be at the top of every visitor's itinerary.

Life is **a safari,**
let's conquer it **together**

nettours
L e a d i n g   t h e   w a y . . .

Head Office – Dubai
Al Barsha Boutique Bldg., Office# 105
P.O.Box: 50777
T: +971 04 425 4450
F: +971 04 427 0411

Abu Dhabi Branch:
Khalifa Street, Opp. Sheraton Hotel
P.O.Box: 37907
T: +971 02 679 4656
F: +971 02 671 1232

INDEX

INDEX

Explorer Products

Residents' Guides

Visitors' Guides

Photography Books & Calendars

Check out ask**explorer**.com/shop

Maps & Street Atlases

Adventure & Lifestyle Guides

Apps & eBooks

+ Also available as applications. Visit askexplorer.com/apps.

* Now available in eBook format.

Visit askexplorer.com/shop

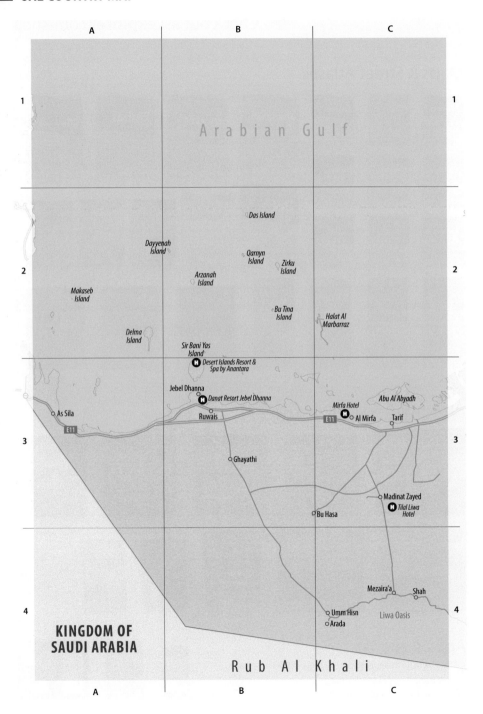

Arabian Gulf

Das Island

Dayyenah
Island

Qarnyn
Island

Zirku
Island

Makaseb
Island

Arzanah
Island

Bu Tina
Island

Halat Al
Marbarraz

Delma
Island

Sir Bani Yas
Island

Desert Islands Resort &
Spa by Anantara

Jebel Dhanna

Danat Resort Jebel Dhanna

Mirfa Hotel

Abu Al Abyadh

As Sila

Ruwais

E11

Al Mirfa

Tarif

E11

Ghayathi

Madinat Zayed

Tilal Liwa
Hotel

Bu Hasa

Mezaira'a

Shah

KINGDOM OF
SAUDI ARABIA

Umm Hisn

Arada

Liwa Oasis

Rub Al Khali

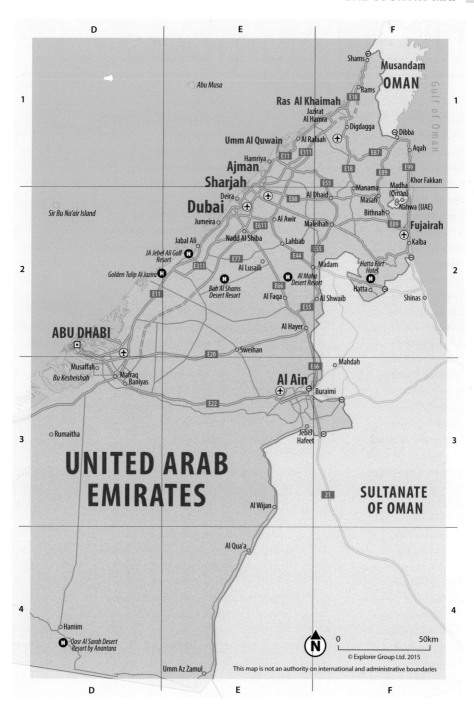

Useful Numbers

Embassies & Consulates

Australian Consulate	04 508 7100
Bahrain Embassy	02 665 7500
British Embassy	04 309 4444
Canadian Consulate	04 404 8444
Chinese Consulate	04 394 4733
Czech Embassy	02 678 2800
Danish Consulate	04 348 0877
Egyptian Consulate	04 397 1122
French Consulate	04 408 4900
German Consulate	04 349 8888
Indian Consulate	04 397 1222
Iranian Consulate	04 344 4717
Irish Embassy	02 495 8200
Italian Consulate	04 331 4167
Japanese Consulate	04 331 9191
Jordanian Consulate	04 397 0500
Kuwaiti Consulate	04 397 8000
Lebanese Consulate	04 397 7450
Malaysian Consulate	04 398 5843
Netherlands Consulate	04 440 7600
New Zealand Consulate	04 331 7500
Norwegian Consulate	04 382 3880
Omani Consulate	04 397 1000
Pakistani Consulate	04 397 0412
Philippine Consulate	04 220 7100
Qatar Consulate	04 396 0444
Russian Consulate	04 328 5347
Saudi Arabian Consulate	04 397 9777
Spanish Embassy	02 626 9544
South African Consulate	04 397 5222
Sri Lankan Consulate	04 398 6535
Swedish Embassy	02 417 8800
Swiss Consulate	04 329 0999
Thai Consulate	04 348 9550
US Consulate General	04 309 4000

Emergency Services

Ambulance	998/999
DEWA Emergency	991
Dubai Police Emergency	999
Fire Department	997

Police Services

Al Ameen (for neighbourhood problems)	800 4888
Department for Tourist Security	800 423
Dubai Police	04 609 9999
Dubai Police Information Line	800 7777

Directory

Dubai International Airport Help Desk	04 224 5555
Flight Information	04 216 6666
Baggage Services	04 224 5383
Directory Enquiries (du)	199
Directory Enquiries (Etisalat)	181
du Contact Centre (mobile enquiries)	
From mobile	155
From any phone	055 567 8155
du Contact Centre (home enquiries)	04 390 5555
Dubai Consumer Protection	600 54 5555
Dubai Municipality	800 900
Dubai Rent Committee	04 206 3456
Etisalat Customer Care	101
Etisalat Information	144
International Operator Assistance	100
Mobile Phone Code (du)	052/055
Mobile Phone Code (Etisalat)	050/056
Ministry Of Labour Hotline	800 665
National Center Of Meteorology & Seismology	02 222 7777
RTA Complaints Line	800 90 90
Salik	800 72545
Speaking Clock	141

Airlines

Aeroflot	04 222 2245
Air Arabia	06 508 8888
Air France	800 23823
Air India	04 227 6787
Air Mauritius	04 221 4455
Air New Zealand	04 335 9126
Air Seychelles	04 286 8008
Alitalia	04 282 6113
American Airlines	04 316 6116
Austrian Airlines	04 211 2538
Biman Bangladesh Airlines	04 2203 2029
British Airways	800 0441 3322
Cathay Pacific	04 204 2888
China Airlines	04 271 8555
CSA Czech Airlines	04 294 5666
Cyprus Airways	04 221 4455
Delta Airlines	04 397 0118
Egypt Air	04 230 6666
Emirates	600 555 555
Etihad Airways	04 407 2200
flydubai	04 231 1000
Gulf Air	04 271 6207
Iran Air	04 224 0200
Japan Airlines	04 217 7501
KLM Royal Dutch Airlines	800 556
Kuwait Airways	04 228 5896
Lufthansa	04 373 9100
Malaysia Airlines	04 325 4411
Middle East Airlines	04 223 7080
Oman Air	04 351 8080
Pakistan International Airlines	04 223 4888
Qantas	04 316 6652
Qatar Airways	04 231 9999
RAK Airways	04 294 5666
Royal Brunei Airlines	04 334 4884
Royal Jet Group	02 575 1777
Royal Jordanian	04 294 4288
Saudi Arabian Airlines	04 229 6227
Singapore Airlines	04 316 6888
Swiss Air	04 381 6100

Hospitals

American Hospital	04 377 6644
Cedars Jebel Ali Int'l Hospital	04 881 4000
Dubai Hospital	04 219 5000
Iranian Hospital	04 344 0250
Latifa Hospital	04 219 3000
Medcare Hospital	04 407 9111
Mediclinic City Hospital	04 435 9999
Mediclinic Welcare Hospital	04 282 7788
Neuro Spinal Hospital	04 342 0000
Rashid Hospital	04 219 2000

24 Hour Pharmacy

Life Pharmacy	04 344 1122
IBN Sina Pharmacy	04 355 6909
Yara Pharmacy	04 222 5503

Taxi Service

Al Arabia Taxi	04 285 5566
Cars Taxi	800 227 789
Dubai Taxis	04 208 0808
Metro Taxi	600 566000
National Taxi	600 543322

Car Rental

Autolease Rent-A-Car	04 282 6565
Avis	04 295 9899
Budget Car & Van Rental	800 2722
Diamondlease	04 885 2677
Dubai Exotic Limo	800 5466
EuroStar Rent-A-Car	04 266 1117
Hertz	800 437 89
Icon Car Rental	04 257 8228
National Car Rental	04 283 2020
Payless Car Rental	04 384 5526
Thrifty Car Rental	800 4694
United Car Rentals	04 285 7777

Road Service

Arabian Automobile Association (AAA)	800 4900
MESAR Roadside Assistance	050 204 5208

NOTES